# *A fine day in Hurstpierpoint*

# *—*

# *the diary of Thomas Marchant 1714 — 1728*

Transcribed and researched by
Hurst History Study Group

Edited by Anthony Bower

Published 2005

Copyright ©Hurst History Study Group

All rights reserved

Typographical Design by Alan Roberts
Typeset in Garamond, 10pt

The Hurst History Study Group
wishes to dedicate this book to its ex-chairman

***Ian Nelson***

and thank him for his keen support and
years of work on the history of Hurstpierpoint

## CONTENTS

Foreword                    Page v

The Diary                   Page 1

Glossary                    Page 308

# Foreword

The Marchant diary has ruled my life for many years. Originally I only knew that it had still existed in Victorian times when Edward Turner, a first cousin to Thomas three times removed, transcribed 5% of the document. Then some 10 years ago I was told that the original had found its way into the Yale University library. This proved to be a red herring and I had almost given up the quest when Ian Nelson (then chairman of the Hurst History Study Group) provided me with the address of Mr R H M Kelsey who is the present owner.

I contacted Mr Kelsey and we are indebted to him that he generously made the diary available to the West Sussex Record Office in Chichester for a number of weeks. There two independent copies were made – one by the Record Office and one by me.

My copy was farmed out to Rose Cottis, June Kentsley and Bunty Parkinson and, over many months, the four of us prepared the transcript, which was faithfully typed up by my wife, Renate – all of us members of the Study Group. In the background my cousin, Diana Mitchell, like me a 7th great-grandchild of Thomas, continued work on the family tree and produced transcripts of many documents which have helped us greatly with the analysis of the diary. A further member of the Study Group, David Blake, brought the diary to life for us with his deep knowledge of local farming.

In an effort to fund the printing of the finished document we decided to issue a CD Rom of the diary. Originally intended as a means to an end the disk proved to be extremely popular in its own right and is sold worldwide to people interested in the Marchant family in particular or Sussex in general. The disk contains both the transcript and the digital copy of the original diary as well as a vast database of the Marchants and many related families spread over some 500 years. This data is backed up by a large collection of wills and other documents. The beauty of the electronic version is that it is so easy for serious family history researchers to analyse.

Through worldwide distribution a User Group has sprung up and homes in on our website at: http://www.hurst-hsg.net/ where we gather vast amounts of new information provided by individual Users and eventually feed it back to the whole group. Only two years ago the original family tree, produced by Diana and me over 30 years, contained some 1,800 entries. Since we released the disk in December 2003 the database has blossomed and in August 2005 contained over 9,400 entries. Thanks are here due to the tireless efforts put in by certain members of our User Group who help in many ways – some financially, some with contributions of information.

Thanks go also to my son Simon in Hamburg for the work he does in running our website which has been the medium for marketing both the Marchant CD and this book and which produces valuable funding for this and other Study Group projects.

Lastly I am indebted to my friend of over 60 years, Alan Roberts, who took one horrified look at my amateur attempts at artwork and went on to redesign the cover and repaginate the whole book to produce what you now have in front of you. Any shortcomings are not his but due to the flawed material with which I provided him.

If you have any comments or information to add to our database I would be grateful if you would contact me at the following address:

Ruselerweg 2, 21033 Hamburg, Germany

or email: abbo700@hotmail.com

Anthony Bower
Hamburg, September 2005

## THOMAS MARCHANT'S DIARY

### 1714

The 29th September 1714 Wednesday, Michaelmas. John Shelly went away. Set 4 pigs to fatting yesterday. Lent Ja Reed 4 oxen. Paid John Gun a guinea. Went by Henfield to Stenning Fair and receiv'd 31s-6d of John Goffe part of three guineas I had lent him. I bought 5 runts of Thomas Joanes at £16. I drank with Thomas Vinall of Cowfold at John Beard's. Met with John Gold of Brighthelmstone at Bramber as we were comeing home and concluded as he should have a load of wheat at £7-10s deliver'd a Fryday senight next at the Rock but we agreed for no barly because somebody had told him 'twas mow burn'd. Ned Grey kept holy day. A dry day. Took 22 pidgeons.

The 30th September 1714 Thursday. Part of the day wet, we plough'd in the forenoon. After dinner plated the plough, then _____ sifted a load of malt for my Father Stone and as much for our selves. Ned May ground it half. Took 9 pidgeons.

October the first 1714 Fryday. A dry day, only a short showr about 3 aclock. I was at Danny with Mr John Cheal, Mr Philip Shave, John Hill of Nut Knowle and a Frenchman. Staid 'till twelve at night. Appointed to go to Nut Knowle a Saturday next with Mr Henry Campion *(Ed: born about 1680)*.

The 2nd October 1714 Saturday. Showry towards night. Begun work upon Tully's fallow haveing finisht the Rookwood yesterday. Supt at Mrs Catherine Beard's.

The 3rd October 1714 Sunday. A fine forenoon, showry afternoon and very wet evning. Mr Jeremiah Dodson preacht. My Cousin John Lindfield *(Ed: born 1674 in Hurstpierpoint)* and his wife Elizabeth *(Ed: née Dumbrell born 1677 in Cuckfield)* din'd with me. Mr John Hart receiv'd the sacrament to qualify himself for a certificate from the Sessions.
We had a parish meeting at Church. I saw Mrs Susan Courthope at Mrs Catherine Beard's. She promis'd to take care to prevent the above mentioned journey to Nut Knowle. The cooper show'd his burrough book at Church but nothing was resolved on it. William Roach's burrough charge was order'd to be paid by the overseers.

The 4th October 1714 Munday. John Paine and John Gun rung hops in the morning. Tom Tully went to mill with 2½ bushels of barly for the pigs. Ned Grey went to Brighthelmstone with 3 bushels of pares. John Paine and Ned May workt on the fallow in the afternoon. My Wife and I went to Wanbarrow and when I came home I reckon'd with John Gun for all his work before Michaelmas except wheat thrashing. A very fine day. In the morning win'd 28 bushels of Jack Bartlet's head wheat by _____ and 2 bushels tail.

The 5th October 1714 Tuesday. A wet forenoon and a showr or two in the afternoon. Win'd 4 quarters head wheat _____ and 3 bushels tail of John Gun's. Mrs Catherine Beard and her mother set out for London. Reckon'd with Old William Brand. Robert Pierce and William Muddle were here and Muddle promis'd to come about Xmas to make some hoops. Lent Michael Stacey a long yoak. Sent home Mr Jeremiah Dodson's saw.

The 6th October 1714 Wednesday. A dry day. Fetcht 6 bushels of seed wheat from my Cousin John Lindfield and Young White came to plough about ten aclock. Nick Marchant din'd with me. Begun sow Tully's fallow under furrough. Mr Richard Whitpaine and his wife Mary and daughter supt here.

The 7th October 1714 Thursday. A dry day only a showr about 4 aclock. We carry'd a load of wheat to the Rock in the morning for John Gold. I went from thence to Brighthelmstone and there sold him an other load at eight pounds to be deliver'd at Brighton. Receiv'd £4-5s of John Bull. Merchant Cook bid 19s per quarter for barly but 'twas affirm'd in the company that one Hayler had given 20s per quarter. We went through Mr Burry's ground with the wheat. Win'd 13 bushels of tick beans and 6 quarters of Jack Bartlet's barly and a bushel head and a bushel tail of the field by Wickham's. The pigs have eat 4 bushels of oates and the horses 2 and the pigs have 5 bushels of barly to eat that was skatter'd in the great barne's floor reckoning the 2½ bushels above written.

The 8th October 1714 Fryday. A dry day. I went to the sessions at Lewis where we had a tryal with the parish of Cuckfield about the settlement of Thomas Mitchell and we cast them. Din'd at the Crown. Mr John Hart was sworn and had a certificate. Mr Norden, Mr Richard Whitpaine, John Lindfield, Mr Hart and I came home together and drank 14 pints of wine at John Smith's. I sold my Cousin John Lindfield two oxen at £28. Receiv'd two guineas in hand. Spent 2s-6d. Paid 4s at Lewis for ¼lb tea ----- 9d for a quire of paper and 6d for two mouse traps.

The 9th October 1714 Saturday. A dry day. Mr John Bateman din'd with me. *(Ed: JB was clerk and curate of Hurstpierpoint)* White had a bushel but half win'd. Paid Jack Bartlet 14s-9d. Chang'd the fatting oxen. John Paine fetcht 3 bushels of wheat from my Cousin John Lindfield's.

The 10th October 1714 Sunday. A very fine day. Mr John Bateman preacht and read prayrs in the afternoon. After evning prayr Mr Henry Campion, Mr Hay, Mr John Bateman, a Frenchman, Mr John Hart and I went to Mr Richard Whitpaine's at Westtowne. Drank 3 bottles of beer and a small bowl of punch and came home at 7.

The 11th October 1714 Munday. A fine day. We made an end of sowing Tully's wheat. I had the seed of John Lindfield. Sow'd 9 bushels but the south headland was sow'd with my own wheat. The field was all sow'd under furrough except 4 ridges and the headland, the 4 ridges beginning at a ridge the middle of which lyes straight between two oaks on a large spire tree in the north hedge and the other a small pollard in the south hedge and so counting westward, Memdum all the furrows to the east of those ridges were sprinkled with wheat after they were plough'd but those to the west were not. Win'd 14½ bushels Jack Bartlet's head barly and ½ a bushel tail of the Homefield. Receiv'd 2s-4d of Stephen Bine for 14 foot of Jack board. Paid the Widdow Tully 2s for her son's feeding hogs, given the pigs half a bushel of tail barly boyld. Nick Marchant din'd here and my Wife and he and Bett went to Brighthelmstone.

The 12th October 1714 Tuesday. A fine day. Begun sow the field by Wickham's. Henry Ford cut the boares and spaid 4 pigs. Jack Lindfield cleft staves for a bucken tub and some cross slits for gates. Ned Grey and Young White struck the furrows in Tully's field. Mrs Shaw, widow of Mr Shaw formerly Rector of Hurstpierpoint parish was buried here. *(Ed: Elizabeth Shaw according to Hurst Parish Register)* Mrs Susan Courthope was here in the forenoon. White had 6½ bushels of Jack Bartlet's barly. Henry Ford had 1s for spaying.

The 13th October 1714 Wednesday. A fine day. Jack Lindfield saw'd down some trees. Cleft some posts etc. We sow'd in the field by Wickham's. Paid Jack Lindfield 3s for 2 day's work. White drove plough.

The 14th October 1714 Thursday. A fine day. Henry Ford cut my bull for which I paid him 2s and 3s for ensuring him at £3. I went to Brighton and there agreed with John Gold for a load of Mrs Catherine Beard's wheat to be made fit for seed and he to fetch it at Hurst. He promis'd to be here a Wednesday next. Borrow'd Old Thomas Farncombe's coat at Patcham. Spent at Brighton 14d. Receiv'd £3-17s of Harry Scrase for Stephen Bine and paid it him as I came home. Win'd 14 bushels of John Gun's head wheat by Burt's.

The 15th October 1714 Fryday. A fine day. Sent home Thomas Farncombe's coat. Plough'd with two teems after eleven aclock, took 4 pidgeons. Lent Mr Richard Whitpaine my fore harness to the chaese to go to Arundell. Receiv'd 3 bushels of oates of Mr Richard Whitpaine. Mr John Hart, my Wife and I, my Sons William and John supt at Mr Richard Whitpaine's. Yesterday I sent half a bushel of cooking pease to John Stone's to be carry'd to Merchant Cook's.

The 16th October 1714 Saturday. A fine day. Made an end of wheat sowing. Sent a bushel and a half of oates and half a bushel of tick beans to mill for the pigs. Receiv'd a letter from Mrs Catherine Beard and Mrs Kettilby. Paid J Prince 12s-6d for work and half a day. My Wife paid a bill at Mrs Courthope's of 10s-1d sow'd 20 bushels in the field by Wickham's.

The 17th October 1714 Sunday. A fine day. Mr Jeremiah Dodson preacht. I din'd at Dean House. Mrs Courthope din'd here. My Sisters Ann and Betty were here in the afternoon.

The 18th October 1714 Munday. Dry 'till towards night. Sent a bushel and a half of oates and half a bushel of beans to mill for the pigs. Receiv'd a bible from Mr

Wilkin at 15s and some cuts (?). Let the grubbing of the hedge between the Hovelfield to John Terry at 4s-5d per cord and 2s-6d per cord for the slub wood when cleft. Also put the ditch at the lower side of the Shaw by the lower Hovelfield at 2d per rod and a new ditch on the outside of the Shaw at 4d per rod. Also sold him a quarter of barly at 20s. Henry Ford's boy was here to look after the bull. Ned Grey kept holy day. Receiv'd a hundred weight of malago rasins from Tourl at Lewis at 32s. Receiv'd 6lbs of hops of Dick Wood at 2s per lb *(Ed: Dick Wood was a blacksmith)*. Brew'd a quarter of malt, half for Mr John Hart and half for my self at 2s-6d per quarter.

The 19th October 1714 Tuesday. A showry day. Went to Mr Richard Whitpaine's but did not stay at all. As I came home talkt with Stephen Bine. Ellis Geer came just before noon. I sold him 14 bushels of barly at £14 to be deliver'd at Hyder's. I went with him to Mr Richard Whitpaine's to sell him clover seed and from thence to Henry Wickham's to desire Ellis Geer might have a load of the barly I had sold to Wickham which he consented to and accordingly I appointed to meet him a Wednesday sennight at Hyder's with seaven quarters and a half at ten aclock. We fetcht a load of posts etc for Stephen Bine from Thomas Norton which I promis'd to give him for the use of his pully's in the Sumer. Carry'd a quarter of barly to Towner at 30s. Receiv'd 5s in hand of Ellis Geer.

The 20th October 1714 Wednesday. A fine day. Sent the post woman 6½ bushels of apples at 2s per bushel and 8lbs of lard at 4d per lb and a bushel to an other woman. King George's coronation day *(Ed: George I, first King of the House of Hanover 1660-1727)*. Here was a gentleman from Lewis, William Hasloup to see Mr John Hart. In the evning went to the bonfire and from thence to Danny. Staid late with Mr Dunstall, Mr Hay, Mr Hart, Thomas Norton. Thomas Norton, John Stone call'd at the old butchers as we came home but did not stay.

The 21st October 1714 Thursday. A very wet day. I had my head shav'd. Win'd five quarters of Jack Bartlet's head barly of the field by Wickham's and 2 bushels tail. Carry'd home Mr Scutt's ladder. Jack Bartlet had a bushel of malt at 3s-6d. Robert Pierce plough'd.

The 22nd October 1714 Fryday. A very stormy wet day. Carry'd 3 quarters and 5 bushels and a half of barly to Harry Wickham's at 18s per bushel. Sent the rim of a sieve to Sanders at Whitmans Green by Ned May. Appointed Harry Peckham to go to Homewood Gate a Fryday morning next early to buy a pond of fish of Mrs Dabson of Lewis.

The 23rd October 1714 Saturday. A fine day. Deliver'd 7½ quarters of Ellis Geer's barly. It weigh'd 231lbs per sack. We pitch't it in Young Harry Gates's house because he can not come to day to meet us. Receiv'd 19s of John Towner for a quarter of barly. Paid him 6d for sawing. Brought home Willy's press. My Brother Will was here in the afternoon. I call'd at White's and he promis'd to lend me his horse a journey or two for which I am to plough one of his fields, he to find a driver.

The 24th October 1714 Sunday. A dry day. Mr Jeremiah Dodson preacht. My Cousin John Lindfield sent me his mails by Old Richard Banks. I receiv'd ten pounds at night of my Cousin John Bodle *(Ed: This relationship seems to be through Elizabeth Marchant – a second cousin once removed)*.

The 25th October 1714 Munday. A fine day. Sent £5 to my Mother by John Paine. Sent a bushel of beans and five bushels of oates to mill for the pigs. Receiv'd 3 bushels of oates of Mr Richard Whitpaine. My Wife and I went to Nunnery. I rode my Cousin John Lindfield's bay mare. My waggon also went thither and in their way carry'd the tub staves to Grey the cooper at Hand Cross which I ow'd him for those of which my brew fat was made. Carry'd also a load of malt to Nunnery etc and 6 cheeses. Receiv'd a letter from Mr [....... d].

The 26th October 1714 Tuesday. A fine day. We return'd from the Nunnery. The teem brought home a couch, two barrels and some other things. I came by Hand Cross and paid Grey 3s-6d which with a guinea he had before was 25s for makeing the above written fat. I paid him also 10s for the hoops to the fat. Mr Scutt was with Mr John Hart when we came home but stay'd not long after. Win'd 4 quarters, 9 bushels of John Gun's head wheat and 2 bushels tail. Receiv'd 26s of my Father Stone for the aforesaid malt.

The 27th October 1714 Wednesday. A fine day. Win'd 20 bushels of Jack Bartlet's barly that is 4 bushels of the field by Wickham's and 15 bushels head of the Homefield and 1 bushel tail. Mrs Catherine Beard's people win'd 29 bushels head and a bushel tail of their wheat. Yesterday Hollingall and Jack Smith haveing been 8 days and a half thrashing it, so I turn'd Hollingall of this morning and agreed with John Terry and his brother to come to thrashing there tomorrow morning at 2s per quarter. John Gold was here and I concluded to carry him a load of wheat to morrow and half a load more to Richard Divall at Bird's Hole at £8 per load. Receiv'd £7-10s of John Gold. Appointed to go to Dean House a Saturday in the afternoon. John Terry had a sack of barly. Sent a bushel of beans and 2 bushels of oates to mill for the pigs. Receiv'd the oates of Mr Richard Whitpaine.

The 28th October 1714 Thursday. A fine day. Carry'd 40 bushels of wheat to John Gold's at £8. I went to Brighton with it and there receiv'd 2s of John Gold for half a bushel breaking pease and the same of Merchant Cook and promis'd to send half a bushel to Goodman Ladger by Mr Richard Whitpaine at the same price that wheat yields when they are deliver'd. I sold ten quarters of barly to John Gold at £10 to be deliver'd in a month. I went to John Gold with Daniel Beard, Thomas Beard, Mr Roots and his wife, Mr Richard Whitpaine and Michael Stacey and there was John Greenyer. We stay'd 'till about 7 aclock.

The 29th October 1714 Fryday. A very fine day. I went to North Barnes ~~to see~~ near Homewood Gate to see the pond fysht. I bought all the fish of a foot long and upwards at 50s per 100 and appointed to fetch them a Munday morning early. Dick Vinall kill'd one of our porkers, he weigh'd 8 nail and 5 lbs. Win'd 2 quarters head and 2½ bushels tail of Jack Bartlet's oates. I am to give Mrs Dabson 200 store fish over and above the aforesaid bargain but she is to send to me for them. John Westover and Nick Marchant went with me.

The 30th October 1714 Saturday. A very fine day. We fetcht 244 carp in 3 dung courts from ~~the pond~~ a stew of Parson Cityeon's at Street being brought thither last night out of the above written pond. I paid Mrs Dabson £6 for them. We put them all into my new pond except 5 which we put into the marl fish stew. I borrow'd Mrs Dabson's court and dill harness and one horse of my Brother Peter Marchant's and also Mrs Catherine Beard's court and 2 horses and Jack Smith. I gave him 6d. Paid John Paine 6s for a week's work. My Wife, Mrs Hart, my Sons and I supt at Dean House and my Cousin John Lindfield gave me a hare to bring home and one we had for supper.

The 31st October 1714 Sunday. A very fine day. Mr Beaumont preacht. I couldn't go to Church being forced to stay at home to look after and let down fresh water to the fish mentioned yesterday they being as I suppos'd sick because they lay on the surface of the water and were easily taken out but towards evning they sank. Mr John Bateman, my Cousin John Lindfield and Thomas Butcher din'd here. We had a hare for dinner etc. They went away about 4 aclock. Yesterday Richard Smith of Brighton fetcht five quarters of Mrs Catherine Beard's wheat which I sold to John Gold. He brought a note from John Gold wherein he promis'd to see it paid for (*Ed: xxx text deleted xxx*) 17 bushels head and 2 tail. Paid to John Picknall of Arundell for Mrs Catherine Beard £3 and £2 for my self.

November the first 1714 Munday. A very fine day. Shut up 4 hogs. Gave them a bushel of oates. Took 8 pidgeons and sent them to Nunnery with a gallon of breaking pease by R Chapman. Ned Grey and Ned May kept holy day. I wrote to Mr Edmead the fishmonger. Sent John Westover my young horse to ride to Lewis. White and his two boys cut the weeds in the new pond for which I paid them 1s. Sold him a quarter of barly at 20s to be deliver'd by Xmas. Set the hogs out 3 bushels of oates more. John Westover brought me a payr of brass spurs at 16d and a paper book from Norman's. Reckon'd with White and outset 6s-6d for his own work in harvest and 6s-8d for the boys ploughing with 4s-10d he paid me. Made 18s for a quarter of barly he had. Ned Grey and John Paine carry'd dung.

The 2nd November 1714 Tuesday. A very fine day. Ned Grey and John Paine carry'd dung. Mr Beaumont din'd here. Jack Bartlet and Ned May cut some stuff for hoops. My Wife went to Wanbarrow in the afternoon. I went to meet her. Sold John Smith a steer at £6 certain and if he proves worth it I am to have a noble more. Paid John Westover 16d for my spurs and 2d for colouring a payr of shooes.

The 3rd November 1714 Wednesday. A very fine day. Clean'd the pidgeon house. There was one good load of dung which with about half a load which was laid in a heap in the New Orchard was spread in the Edgly Mead on this side the great ditch beginning about 4 rod from the upper end and goeing almost to the bottom and almost half the breadth. John Paine and Ned Grey carry'd dung. Borrow'd Mr Richard Whitpaine's syder mill. John Smith fetcht the steer. Chang'd the calves. Jack Bartlet thrasht barly. Mrs Barbara Campion, Mrs Courthope, Mrs Ann Dodson, Mrs Mary Whitpaine, my Sister Nanny and Nanny Faulkoner was here in the afternoon.

The 4th November 1714 Thursday. A very fine day. Stephen Bine's man came to set up a syder press. Borrow'd a 5 foot post of him. John Paine and Ned Grey carry'd dung. Ellis Geer of Cuckfield was here at dinner and paid me £7. I sold him a sack of beans at 13s and a bushel of breaking pease and am to carry both with the rest of his barly about Wednesday sennight the pease are to be at the price that wheat yields at that time. I wrote to Mrs Catherine Beard and Jude Storer. I also sent a note by John Stone to John Gates of Brighton to pay John Stone £8 for Mrs Catherine Beard's wheat. Receiv'd 2 of my sacks of Ellis Geer and there is 13 behind. Receiv'd also 13 of Ellis Geer's sacks to put the rest of his barly in. Chang'd the runts. Begun to serve the lean oxen and the 2 yearlings a mornings. Receiv'd £7-19s-6d of John Gold by John Stone for Mrs Catherine Beard's wheat, likewise £5 of John Stone for Mrs Catherine Beard's use.

The 5th November 1714 Fryday. A fine day. Win'd 20 bushels of John Gun's head wheat by Burt's and carry'd 15 of it to Richard Divall's of Bird's Hole for John Gold, brought the steer John Smith had. He weigh'd something above 19 stone. I had a stone of it at 18d per stone. John Paine and I made syder. Mr Beaumont and his wife and Mrs Scutt and her sister were here towards night. E Chapman brought us a piece of sturgeon yesterday from Nunnery. Jack Bartlet had a bushel of wheat to day at 4s. I sent a bushel of beans and 2 bushels of oates to mill for the hogs.

The 6th November 1714 Saturday. A very fine day. I set out the hogs a bushel of oates and boyld a bushel of tail barly for the pigs. Kill'd one pig. He weigh'd 9 nail 2 pounds. My Wife and Kitt Ede went to Lewis. They brought me a hat from David Douglas in the Cliffe at 9s. Mr Healy was here towards evning *(Ed: Reverend Ralph Healy of Twineham)*. Nick Plaw came to see me. John Paine and Ned May made syder. Paid John Paine 5 shillings for 5 day's work. Nunnery Dick came for Kitt Ede. Lent John Westover 20s.

The 7th November 1714 Sunday. A very fine day. Mr Jeremiah Dodson preacht. Kitt Ede went home. I receiv'd a letter from John Gold by Thomas Norton of Edgly dated the first of this month. Mr Sixsmith was here towards night and staid supper. I promis'd him half a bushel or a bushel of breaking pease. Set out the fatting hogs an other bushel of oates.

The 8th November 1714 Munday. A fine day. Made an end of makeing syder. Lent Thomas Norton of Edgly 6 sacks. Begun fallow in the field by Burt's. I wrote to John Gold to let him know that I could not dele over the barly so soon as he desires. Fisht the hole in the further Marldfield. Young Nye drove plough. Paid John Parsons 2s-6d for new mounting my wig and 1s to John Paine for a day's work.

The 9th November 1714 Tuesday. A very misty day. Win'd 10 bushels of John Gun's wheat by Burt's. Note all the wheat in that field is 24 quarters, 1 bushel. Ned Grey and Nye plough'd, Mr Richard Whitpaine, J Chainey, a butcher at Arundell were here a little before noon and Michael Stacey. I sold Stacey 20 quarters of barly to be deliver'd as soon as I can conveniently at £20. I paid John Snashall 30s for setting Ned Grey's leg. Ned May and Jack Bartlet carry'd home Mr Richard Whitpaine's syder mill. Lent Michael Stacey two iron rakes. Richard Balchild of Wonersh near Guildford servant to Mr Edmead of Mill Brook in Hersel about 8 miles beyond Guildford came hither at night to buy my fish. Deliver'd 4 bushels of wheat more to Richard Divall by Ned May. He left the sack there. Stacey brought home my long yoak.

The 10th November 1714 Wednesday. A dry day. I took out the fish that I bought of Mrs Dabson and sold 239 to Richard Balchild for his master and 4 or more I expect to be in the stew all at £10. He is to fetch them a Munday next. Receiv'd the 6 sacks of Thomas Norton. Receiv'd £12 of John Gold and he paid £8 to Thomas Field (they being both) here for John Lindfield. John Gold gave me the liberty 'till to morrow sennight to tell him whether I will deliver the 10 quarters of barly that I sold him or no. Put 57 carp and 10 tench into the

Marldfield stew and 3 large fish into the flat stew. Ned Grey and Nye plough'd by Hyder's.

The 11th November 1714 Thursday. A fine day. Balchild went home. I gave Stephen Bine the note I had of John Goffe for 33s, he being goeing to Henfield and said he would get the mony for me if possible. Ned Grey and Nye plough'd by Hyder's. Ned May carry'd a bushel of beans and 2 bushels of oates to mill for the hogs. He also carry'd 4 bushels of barly to John Terry. I went to William Balcomb and to Osbourne at St John's Comon to see after fish but to no purpose. Receiv'd 13s yesterday of Richard Christopher for a sack of beans and deliver'd the beans by Ned Grey. I promis'd them an other sack if I have them to spare and to day Nick Plaw desir'd a sack if I can spare any more. Paid Abel Muzzall 8s for mending a court wheel.

The 12th November 1714 Fryday. A fine day. Win'd 20 bushels of Jack Bartlet's Churchfield barly and 3 quarters head and 3½ bushels tail of the field by Wickham's. Ned Grey and Nye made an end of the field by Hyder's. Win'd 4½ bushels of Jack Bartlet's pease. Stephen Bine brought me the 33s from John Goffe. Mr Henry Campion, Mrs Courthope's brother and the French man were here. Gave the pigs a bushel of tail barly. Receiv'd 4lbs of bohea tea from Mr Tourl. Took 6 pidgeons.

The 13th November 1714 Saturday. A dry day. Paid Dick Wood 12s for 6lbs of hops. Fetcht 500 tiles and 12 ridge tiles from Marten's at the Comon and half a load of wheat from Broad Street and some hop poles wood for Old William Brand. The whole journey I value at 6s. Michael Stacey was here towards night to desire the half score of barly that I sold to John Gold saying that he had his consent. I told him I would take some time to consider of it. Mr John Hart and I went to Stephen Bine's in the evning. Mr Scutt came to us late.

The 14th November 1714 Sunday. A dry day. Mr Beaumont preacht. My Cousin John Lindfield din'd with me. There was no prayrs at Church in the afternoon. Thomas Packham brought a letter from my Mother Stone with the news of my Brother James Ede haveing the smallpox. John Westover and Ned May watch the stew.

The 15th November 1714 Munday. A misty day. Win'd 3 quarters and 2 bushels of John Gun's and Jack Bartlet's barly by Wickham's. Ned Grey and Nye plough'd by Burt's. Sent 2 bushels of oates and a bushel of beans to mill for the hogs and boyld a bushel of barly for the pigs. Mr Webb's teem came about one aclock for the above mentioned fish. They came from home as they said about one in the morning. Thomas Field and Downer the miller were here to talk with Balchild. They then told me the pond of Lye would be fisht a Wednesday. Mr Webb's teem had 2 bushels of oates for their 6 horses. The two Terry's shovel'd the towne.

The 16th November 1714 Tuesday. A dry day. Sent £5 to my Mother by my Sister Ann. We took 242 fish out of the stew for Mr Edmead and loaded them about two aclock in the morning. Receiv'd £10 of Richard Balchild for them. They were about 13 inches one with an other. Deliver'd 6½ quarters of Ellis Geer's barly by John Paine and Ned Grey also 3½ of beans and 2 bushels of breaking pease and I sent a sack of pease to Henry Gates for the trouble of his horse, it being ditcht there. Win'd 11 bushels of Jack Bartlet's head oates and 1 bushel tail. I went to Henry Wickham and promis'd him his barly a Munday next. Call'd at Mr Richard Whitpaine's as I came home. Mr Healy was there. I staid about an hour.

The 17th November 1714 Wednesday. A fine day. Yesterday in the evning I deliver'd a bag of mony to Stephen Bine of £40 seal'd with two seals thus **TM** desiring him to lay it up 'till I call'd for it. Deliver'd 4 bushels of wheat to Stephen Bine's Grey to day. My Wife and I went to Nunnery with Jacky and Ned Grey. Win'd 4½ of beans. John Paine begun thrash barly. I overtook a drover that liv'd about Hand Cross and gave him a quart of beer to do Ellis Geer word that his barly goeing at Hyder's.

The 18th November 1714 Thursday. A dry day. My Wife and I and my Mother Stone went to Newdigate in Surrey to see my Sister Mary Ede. We met her at Mr Wood's. John Paine thrasht barly at home.

The 19th November 1714 Fryday. A dry day. Mrs Pryaulx and her daughter din'd at Nunnery. John Paine thrasht barly at home. We were at Deers Wood in the morning at Mr Gales.

The 20th November 1714 Saturday. A dry day. I went up to Rusper parsonage in the morning to view the building. Gave Smith the carpenter 1s for goeing with me. In the afternoon my Wife, Kitty Stone and I went to Horsham. I bought Ned Grey a hat at 2s-6d.

The 21st November 1714 Sunday. I were at Rusper church in the morning. Mr Woodhouse preacht there. Mr Roberds din'd at Nunnery. Mr Beaumont preacht at Hurst. A dry day.

The 22nd November 1714 Munday. A wet forenoon especially towards noon. We set out for home about 11 aclock. I came by Thomas Field's and Mr Edmead's man was just come for some fish. Balchild promis'd to leave me a brace with Thomas Field. Win'd 3 quarters 1½ bushels of John Gun's wheat by Tully's coppice head and 1½ bushels tail. Paid John Paine 6s for last week's work. Sent 2 bushels of oates and of beans a bushel to mill since I have been from home for the hogs and the pigs. Have had a bushel of barly and about a bushel of the screenings barly and the hogs have eat 3 bushels of oates _____ . Memdum I am to give Balchild a brace of fish for those above mentioned if ever he buys any more fish of me.

The 23rd November 1714 Tuesday. A misty morning but dry afternoon. Win'd 5 quarters and 6 bushels of John Paine's head barly by Wickham's and 1½ bushels tail being the last of that field, in all 24 quarters and 5 bushels. Nye and Ned Grey plough'd by Burt's. John Paine and I put up my turning lath poles and then John Paine went to puging of clover. Sent 2 bushels of oates and a bushel of beans to mill for the hogs. Sent Ned May to Ellis Geer's with 1½ bushels of tick beans. Order'd Richard White to begin mole catching in the wheat and meads. Jack Bartlet mended the hedge against Tully's wheat. Paid Mr Jeremiah Dodson half a year's tythe. Ned May brought my 13 sacks from Ellis Geer. He said he never had any word before that the barly was at Hyder's. The drover's name was John Harden. Receiv'd my bag of mony again of Stephen Bine's wife.

The 24th November 1714 Wednesday. A misty forenoon and dry afternoon, John Gun and John Paine pug'd clover. Ned Grey and Nye plough'd by Burt's. Ned May and I fetcht 190 store carp from Thomas Field's about 4 inches long and 75 about 6 inches at 2s-6d per hundred one with an other. Paid him 2s which with 3s I paid to Terry at Lewis for him was in full for the aforesaid fish because he gave me all that was above 200. I sent Ned May to Henry Packham to do Mrs Dabson or Mr Cittizen word to fetch them to morrow. We brought also the brace of large fish for Stephen Bine. They were 13 inches but lean and old. I went part of the way to Wanbarrow with my Wife. Ned May brought word that they could not fetch them yet. Mrs Catherine Beard came home from London this evning. I went up to her and paid her £4-19-6d being all the mony I had of hers. Mr Richard Whitpaine was here in the evning and order'd me to give John Gold what answer I pleas'd about the barly. John Bodle kill'd one of my pigs in the morning of which he is to have but half. The pig weigh'd 79¼ lbs.

The 25th November 1714 Thursday. A very fine day. Henry Packham came in the morning and told out 200 fish for Mrs Dabson and his man fetcht them. John Paine and Ned May screen'd 8 quarters 1½ bushels of barly and 4 bushels of the screenings which was screen'd twice over and made pretty good. Ned Grey, Jack Bartlet and Nye carry'd Towne dirt with 2 horses. And haveing one horse and court of Michael Stacey and White's horse they lam'd the ball mare and carry'd but 20 loads. John Bodle brought the side of my pig which weigh'd 38½lbs and the other side weigh'd 40½ lbs. He bought the half at 22d per nail. I went to Brighton and there sold to Richard Lagate, William Goring, John Beard, John Gold, Richard Ladger, Thomas Walls and James Friend each a bushel of breaking pease at 4s to be deliver'd in a week or two. I promis'd Henry Ford also a bushel. Mr Jeremiah Dodson's tythe feast was to day. Paid Mrs Catherine Beard 4d for 6 cuts and 3s for 5 quires of paper. My dinner and expences at Brighton 15½d.

The 26th November 1714 Fryday. A misty forenoon and very fine afternoon. Nye, Jack Bartlet and Ned Grey carry'd 19 loads of Towne dirt. Sent home Michael Stacey's horse and court. John Gun begun thrash barly. Deliver'd 8 quarters 1½ bushels of barly to Harry Wickham by John Paine, Ned May and my self. Sold him 10 quarters more at £10 to be deliver'd about Xmas. Michael Stacey was here in the morning and we concluded that he should have the barly I sold to John Gold and 20 besides, in all 30 lbs. At night I went to Mr Jeremiah Dodson. There was Mr Bullins, Mr Scutt and Mr Richard Whitpaine. We supt and staid 'till 11 aclock.

Mr Dodson said John Norton had sworn that his land in Hurst was but 19 _____ and askt me what I thought of it. I told him I know no more than Mr Bullins. Sent a bushel of beans and 2 bushels of oates to mill.

The 27th November 1714 Saturday. A dry day. Kill'd the 4th pig. He weigh'd 10½ nail. Nye and Ned Grey made an end of fallowing the fields by Burt's about noon. They carry'd the beans into Tully's barn. Ned May put the tags into the Homefield. Paid John Paine 6s for a week's work. Sent White's heifer home. Mr John Hart and I went to Westtowne in the evning and supt there. Staid 'till near 11 aclock. Sold Towner 4 bushels of course barly at 8s and promis'd to furnish him with 3 or four bushels more at 2s-6d per bushel.

The 28th November 1714 Sunday. A dry day. Mr Healy preacht in the forenoon. We had no prayrs in the afternoon. After dinner Stephen Bine and his hog man Mr Robert Chapman was here and staid 'till near sun set. Jack Westover supt here. My Wife supt at Mrs Catherine Beard's and I fetcht her home. Promis'd my Cousin John Lindfield 10 quarters of barly at £10.

The 29th November 1714 Munday. A dry day. Win'd 11 bushels of head beans and a bushel tail. 2 of Stephen Bine's men cut down 7 trees. Sanders of Whiteman's Green brought my barly ridder which he had new bottomed and prov'd the rim for which I paid him 2s-6d and 1s for mending 2 other sieves. He also brought a new wheat ridder for Mrs Catherine Beard for which she paid him 5s. He carry'd home an other wheat ridder of mine to mend. Ned Grey and Ned May went to Thomas Peckham's and brought 12 bags of Stephen Bine's tan up to my house to be carry'd to the Rock. Mr John Hart din'd here and staid 'till about 3 aclock. Paid Nye 5s-6d for his boy's ploughing. Sold Mr Healy a paper book at 16d. The hogs had a bushel of whole oates.

The 30th November 1714 Tuesday. A gloomy day but very little rain. Two of Stephen Bine's men cut down 4 trees in the forenoon. Win'd 7 bushels of oates. Sent 2 bushels of oates and a bushel of beans to mill for the hogs and 2 bushels of oates for the stack sow. She farrow'd 9 pigs a Sunday night. My Cousin Nick Marchant and Peter Marchant of Lewis din'd here and so did Betty Homan's father. Ned Grey went to Bolny Fair. Mr John Hart went to Mr Osbourne's with Mr Scutt and his wife came home about 11 aclock. Sent a pattern of cloath to Thomas Friend to get 5 yards of the best narrow cloath for me _____ .

The 1st December 1714 Wednesday. A fine day. Carry'd the load of tan we fetcht from Thomas Peckham's to the Rock for which I am to have 15d. Receiv'd the sack from Richard Divall. Stephen Bine and I went to Shoreham. My dinner there and expences 19½d. I there agreed with James Haslegrove for the tomb stone for my Father at 3s per foot and 7s-6d for squaring him and working the edges and a penny a letter for the inscription. John Paine workt a cleaning the Hovelfield stew. Mrs Stone and Mrs Catherine Beard supt here. I came home about 9 aclock.

The 2nd December 1714 Thursday. A showry day. Win'd 9 bushels of Jack Bartlet's pease. Paid Widdow Tully 2s for several jobbs of work of her self and boy. Win'd 3 quarters 7 bushels of John Gun's head barly of the Hovelfield. Sent 2 bushels of oates and a bushel of beans to mill for the hogs. John Paine workt on the new pond. Ground 3 bushels of barly malt and as much oaten malt. Michael Stacey sent home my rakes. Abraham Muzzall workt here. Shut up the fatting oxen. Chang'd the sowes and lean oxen.

The 3rd December 1714 Fryday. A fine day. Win'd 4 bushels head and a bushel tail of John Gun's Homefield barly. Went to the Rock with 5 bags of Stephen Bine's bark haveing 2 of Edgly horses on Stephen Bine's account and he got leave to go through Mr Burry's ground. Sent home White's horses. Sent a bushel of oates and a bushel of beans to mill and order'd the boy to borrow a bushel of oates of his master Plaw. Mr Richard Whitpaine and his wife Mary supt here and he promis'd to send me 2 bushels of oates to morrow morning. He also spoke for ½ bushel of breaking pease. John Paine workt on the new pond.

The 4th December 1714 Saturday. A showry day. Receiv'd a guinea of Stephen Bine for the tan carriage to the Rock. Sent 8 bushels of breaking pease to John Gold and a bushel to Mr Goring. Receiv'd 4s for the last 3 sacks at John Gold's. Paid John Paine 4s. Deliver'd 5 quarters 1 bushel of the Homefield barly to Mr Stacey's by Ned Grey and Ned May. Mr Scutt and his wife supt here. Receiv'd 2 bushels of oates of Mr Richard Whitpaine.

The 5th December 1714 Sunday. A stormy day but little rain. Mr Jeremiah Dodson preacht. We had a meeting in the afternoon. The Widdow Parsons was there and desir'd the parish to assist her against her son in law, but nothing was concluded in that affair. Dr Lintott was at Church in the afternoon. I went home with Mr Scutt and staid there with Weeks the miller 'till eight aclock. The charges of Frank Osbourne's illness was allow'd all but the doctor's bill which she is to pay her self. My Wife was at Mrs Ann Dodson's *(Ed: Ann née Todd was the wife of the Hurstpierpoint rector Jeremiah).*

The 6th December 1714 Munday. A stormy day. Win'd 13 bushels of Jack Bartlet's pease. Mrs Catherine Beard had a gallon of pease. Receiv'd 1s of the Widdow Herriot's girl for 2 gallons. Sent a bushel to Nunnery by Ned May. Jack Bartlet, Ned Grey and I draw'd home 3 trees. I wrote a coppy of a letter to Mr White of Shipley for Stephen Bine. My Wife, Mrs Stone and Mrs Catherine Beard went to Danny in the afternoon. Mr Peter Courthope and Mr Henry Campion rode through my ground in the morning.

The 7th December 1714 Tuesday. A fine day. John Gun and Ned Grey draw'd home 6 trees. Receiv'd 6 bushels of Jack Bartlet's oates. Mr Jeremiah Dodson came to bring Mr John Hart some mony from Danny. He stay'd 'till 11 aclock. Paid a bill of 8s to my Lord Treep.

The 8th December 1714 Wednesday. A fine day. Sent 2 bushels of oates and a bushel of beans to the mill for the hogs and a bushel of oates for the sows. Ned Grey spread dung in the Edgly Mead. Mrs Catherine Beard, my Wife and I went to John Norton's in the afternoon. Staid 'till about 6 aclock. Put the 2 yearlings into the lower ground. The runts into the way mead and the calves into Tully's Mead. Dick Wood shooed the colts hind feet.

The 9th December 1714 Thursday. A fine day. Win'd 3 quarters 6 bushels of John Gun's Homefield barly. I went to Brighton and settled my account with Mr Long for 7 years wool. Paid him 6d for my self and 6d for Mr Richard Whitpaine and had a Let Pass for both. He gave me a bottle of wine. Receiv'd 4s of John Beard for a bushel of pease. Dinner and expences 11d. Dick Wood mov'd all my old horse shooes in the morning. Ned Grey spread dung part of the day. I came home about 7 aclock. Nick Plaw supt at my house. Paid James Pierce 1s in the morning.

The 10th December 1714 Fryday. A showry day. My Brother Will brought me a hare. Win'd 19 bushels head and 2 bushels tail of Jack Bartlet's oates. Paid him 20s and 6d to John Parsons for shaveing my head. Sent 2 bushels of oates and a bushel of beans to mill for the hogs. Receiv'd 4s of Mr Gatland's son Harry and 2s of Robert Chatfield of Bently for a bushel and ½ of breaking pease. Met Ellis Geer at Mr Richard Whitpaine's and receiv'd £6-15s of him which with 5s-9d receiv'd in hand is for the last 7 quarters of barly. Also 13s for a sack of beans and 4s for a bushel of pease. Mr John Hart call'd me there and we with Mr Richard Whitpaine went to Mr Healy's. Staid 'till 11 aclock. I desir'd Ellis Geer to buy me 1½ bushel of Nonsuch seed. Brother Peter sent home the blind mare.

The 11th December 1714 Saturday. A fine day 'till towards night and then a showr of sleet and some snow. We went to Wanbarrow and din'd there. Paid my Brother Will £4-10s for my Brother Henry Faulkoner. Win'd 10 bushels of John Gun's Homefield barly and John Gun and I carry'd 5 quarters of that barly to Michael Stacey's and a single yoak of his. My Wife, Ned Grey, Willy and Ned May went to Lewis. May came home at 9 aclock. My Wife carry'd £5-3s. Willy carry'd a quire of paper to Norman's to be bound. My Wife, Willy and Ned Grey stay'd at Lewis all night because Will's little horse was taken with the gripes. Last night a frost.

The 12th December 1714 Sunday. A dry day. Mr William Martin preacht here and read prayrs in the afternoon. My Sister Nanny din'd here. My Wife and my Cousin Peter Marchant walkt from Lewis and came home about 2 aclock. My Cousin Peter ~~went~~ rode home again at night. Ned Grey and Ned Salter brought the bald mare and little horse home. Stephen Bine was here in the afternoon. John Westover paid me the 20s I lent him November the 6th. Last night a frost.

The 13th December 1714 Munday. A fine day. Stephen Bine's man and boy workt here. John Box sr was here in the morning. Jack Bartlet had a bushel of wheat and a peck of pease. Sent 2 bushels of oates and a bushel of beans to mill for the hogs and a bushel of oates that I borrow'd of Nick Plaw some time ago. Deliver'd 20 bushels of wheat to Stephen Bine by Ned Grey and John Gun. Paid Old John Smith 20s for my Window Tax at Lady Day 1714. Receiv'd £11 of Harry Wickham of Albourne for barly. My Wife was at Mr Scutt's 'till near 9 aclock. Stephen Bine was here in the evning and complained that the aforesaid was smutty. I promis'd to take it again at any time if he persisted in the complaint. Receiv'd 5½ yards of narrow cloath at 6s per yard of Mr Thomas Friend of Lewis and 33 buttons with mohair and canvas and silk.

The 14th December 1714 Tuesday. A fine day. Last night a frost. Ned Grey and Ned May fetcht wood out of Tully's ground. Stephen Bine's man and boy workt here as did J Norris and Old William Brand's boy forenoon. Sent a bushel of oates and a bushel of beans to mill for the hogs. Mr John Hart and I begun to make a fire in our stoves. Stephen Bine came in the morning to set a shore to the granary but we found it needless.

The 15th December 1714 Wednesday. A very misty day. A frost last night. Stephen Bine's man and boy workt here and J Norris and William Jarvice 'till noon. William Nicholas dug a sawpit for which I paid work 1s. Ned Grey fetcht home rubbish wood and carry'd the grit that was dug out of the sawpit which was 11 load it being 12 foot long 3 foot 2 inches wide and 5 foot 9 inches deep. Mr John Hart and I supt at Mrs Catherine Beard's and Mrs Ann Dodson. My Wife was at Westtowne with Mrs Scutt in the afternoon. Ned May went to Horsham with 5½ yards of cloath to Robert Hurst's to make me a great coat and my old coat for a pattern. Paid Bonny 5d toward making the goods.

The 16th December 1714 Thursday. A very thick mist all day. It thaw'd all day and last night. John Towner and Ja Reed begun sawing. I was at Westtowne in the morning. Mr Richard Whitpaine wrote a letter of advice to Mr Nicholas Knapp in Wallbrook in London a woolstapler to pay me or my order £18 on a bill he had given me a Wednesday payable at sight on the aforesaid Mr Knapp it being my wool which Mr Richard Whitpaine had sold him and was weigh'd last Saturday at Pangdean by John Alcock. It weigh'd 22 todd 16 lbs. Sold at 16s per todd. Win'd 8 bushels of John Gun's Churchfield barly. Chang'd the runts. Ned May came home from Nunnery about sun set. He brought a letter from my Mother. The Gooders were here to day. Borrow'd a thing of the cooper to shave the inside of my scooper. Paid John Gatland of Cuckfield 5s for mending my clock. Receiv'd 10d of Michael Stacey. Ned May brought word that Robert Hurst could not make my coat before the Saturday after Xmas and that then it should be ready.

The 17th December 1714 Fryday. A fine day. Stephen Bine's man workt here. Sent 2 bushels of oates and a bushel of beans to mill for the hogs and a bushel of oates for the sow. Harry Morley sweept the kitchin and hall chimneys. He had 1s for one and 4d for t'other,

The 18th December 1714 Saturday. A dry day, only a very small showr about noon. Stephen Bine's men John Stammer and Tom Vinall workt here. Sent a pig to Mr Scutt's and one to Mrs Catherine Beard and to Wanbarrow 2 or 3 days ago. Ned Grey carry'd 4 loads of dung in Tully's Mead and 2 loads of flints to make a way to the school. Receiv'd 3½d of the Widdow Herriot's boy for a gallon of barly.

The 19th December 1714 Sunday. A dry day. Mr Healy preacht. My Cousin John Lindfield and his wife Elizabeth din'd here. Receiv'd 9s-6d of him to lay out for sugar etc at Lewis. He appointed to be here again a Wednesday. Willy went home with them and to return the morning. Receiv'd 2s for half a bushel of breaking pease he had about a month ago.

The 20th December 1714 Munday. A very fine day. Stephen Bine's men Tom Stammer and John Vinall workt here. Receiv'd 6s for a bushel and a half of breaking pease of John Peckham for Mr Barham of Lindfield. Mr Healy din'd here to day. He staid 'till ten in the evning. Nick Plaw came for him and supt here. Sent a grist to mill for the hogs. Win'd 5 quarters 2 bushels of the Churchfield barly, John Gun's head and *(Ed: text ends here)*.

The 21st December 1714 Tuesday. A fine day. Stephen Bine's men workt here. I shot a pheasant in the lower side of the ponds. Win'd 2 quarters of John Gun's Homefield barly head and 3 bushels tail and 1 bushel tail of the Churchfield. Carry'd 5 quarters of the Churchfield barly to Tott for my Cousin John Lindfield and 2 quarters for Michael Stacey. Ned Grey spread dung half the day. Nunnery boy was here and brought Bett a large silver spoon. He carry'd home a pig. I was at Mrs Catherine Beard's in the evning 'till near 7 aclock.

The 22nd December 1714 Wednesday. A dry day. Stephen Bine's men workt here. My Cousin John Lindfield did not come as was expected. John Pickstone din'd here. I deliver'd the note on Mr Knapp to him mention'd in the 16th of this month and he promis'd to take the mony of him and to pay Mr Barrwick in Fryday Street for the use of Mr Thomas Friend of Lewis and to send me the bill. He offer'd £29-1-6d for the oxen I sold to my Cousin John Lindfield and take them to morrow. My Cousin Lindfield paid £5 to Henry Lintott of Walshurst for me which was offset for the 5 quarters of barly mention'd a Tuesday last.

The 23rd December 1714 Thursday. A fine day. Ned Grey spread dirt. Stephen Bine's man workt here and the boy in the afternoon. My Cousin John Lindfield came in the morning and paid me 21 guineas and 1s which with 2 guineas I had in hand is in full for my oxen. He sold them again to day to John Pickstone at a guinea proffit and took a guinea in hand. Harry Morley being here thatching was immediately sent away with them to Hand Cross for which John Pickstone paid him 18d. John Towner and Ja Reed made an end of sawing and I paid them 11s which with 15s outset for 7½ bushels of course barly to be deliver'd to Towner to morrow, is 26s being all their sawing came to. I also paid Reed for work he did long ago. Stephen Bine supt here. Receiv'd 4s of Mr Friend's boy of Sadlescombe for a bushel of pease.

The 24th December 1714 Fryday. A gloomy morning but fine afternoon. Win'd 10 bushels head and 1 bushel tail of John Gun's Tully's wheat. Sent £25 to my Brother Will by Ned May. He brought back the note I had given for it. Win'd 4 quarters 5 bushels head and about 3 pecks tail of John Gun's Churchfield barly. Deliver'd Towner's barly by Ned Grey. Stephen Bine's man John Stammer workt here. I went to Clayton Woods but shot nothing. Reckon'd with John Gun and paid him £4-2s in full for all sorts of work to this evning. I gave him 6d for jobbs. Memdum I accounted with him for thrashing 3 bushels of pease which is not set down anywhere. Sent home the gallon of oates I borrowed of Mrs Catherine Beard by Ned May. Paid my Lord Treep 1s for work about Willy's gun.

The 25th December 1714 Saturday. Xmas Day. A wet day. Mr William Martin preacht. Jack Bartlet and his 2 boys din'd here. I offer'd Jack Bartlet a hog at 2s per nail. After evning prayr Thomas Norton of Edgly, Michael Stacey and I spent £3 a piece at John Smith. My Wife and I supt at Mrs Catherine Beard's. William Balcomb's wife died to day.

The 26th December 1714 Sunday. A fine day. Mr William Martin preacht. Thomas Jacket and his wife and Jack Gun and his mother din'd here. Mr Letchford's mony was given in the afternoon. Mr William Martin and Mr Richard Whitpaine supt here. My Sisters Nanny and Bett was here after evning prayr. I begun ¼lb tea in the morning. Receiv'd it of Tourl about 10 days ago.

The 27th December 1714 Munday. A very fine day. Call'd Mr Richard Whitpaine very early to go to shooting. We return'd about noon haveing lookt all Wick Woods and Albourne Woods and shott nothing but one rook Mr Richard Whitpaine's man shot. Mrs Stone was here in the afternoon. Abraham Muzzall workt here. My Lord Treep clean'd a gun and carry'd an other to clean.

The 28th December 1714 Tuesday. A fine day. Mr Scutt and Thomas Butcher were here and Thomas Butcher had his sack again. Nick Marchant din'd here. My Brother Peter was here towards night. I paid him my Poor Tax being 1s-9d per £ for the whole year. I paid him £4-5-6d which with £1-10-9d outset for my expences when Churchwarden for the year 1713 is the sum aforesaid. I also paid him 4s-6d for duty and making 6 bushels of oaten malt I had of him for oats some time ago. Mrs Ann Dodson supt here. Borrow'd £3 of Mr John Hart. Deliver'd 3 bushels of barly to White per Ned Grey. Sent a grist to mill for the hogs.

The 29th December 1714 Wednesday. A fine day. My Cousin John Lindfield and the Pickstones were here in the morning. Mr Healy and Mr Richard Whitpaine just call'd here. My Wife and I went to my Cousin Ann Balcomb's funeral. She was buried at Henfield. Win'd 4 quarters 3 bushels of Jack Bartlet's tick beans being the last of them and makes in all 8 quarters 1 bushel. Spent 6d at the George at Henfield.

The 30th December 1714 Thursday. A fine day. Sent home my Cousin John Lindfield's coat per Goodman Terry. Laid up 18 three inch plank in the fatting hovel and there was 9 ashen inch board there before 12 oaken inch board and 1 two inch plank per Ned Grey, John Gun and Ned May. They also carry'd some slabs into the stall. Mrs Catherine Beard, Mrs Stone, Mrs Mary Whitpaine and Mrs Polly Whitpaine supt here. Paid Mr Peter Courthope 3s-8d for ¼ lb 3 ___ sizd shot.

The 31st December 1714 Fryday. A dry day. Win'd 12 bushels of Jack Bartlet's oates. Jack Bartlet and I agreed that he should have a hog of me evry year (for as long as he works for me) at 2s per nail indifferently fat. Deliver'd 5 quarters of the Churchfield barly to Michael Stacey per Ned Grey and Ned May. Mrs Catherine Beard sent for me to let part of her great Towne field to the Hubbards for flax. They bid her £3 per acre, she to plough and harrow, but they did not fully agree whilst I were with them. My Wife and I and Mr John Hart supt at Mr Scutt's with Mr Jeremiah Dodson and his wife and Mrs Mary Whitpaine, Mr Richard Whitpaine and Bett was there, Mr William Martin was there but did not stay to supper. Mr Dodson went away about an hour after supper. We staid 'till after 12 aclock. Receiv'd 2s of Sarah Hallet's brother for half a bushel of pease. Mrs Beard let part of her field aforesaid came away 5 acres at £3 per acre, she to plough and harrow. The hogs have had 2 bushels of whole oates lately. About this time Stephen Bine's men finisht my calf house the material of which came to about 4 guineas and the carpenter's work about 1 guinea. Note: the sawing is reckon'd amongst the material and I think the carpenter did not earn his wages.

The 1st January 1714 Saturday. A windy very cold day and a little snow towards night. Ned May carry'd a grist to the mill for the hogs and also a peck of barly, a peck of oates and half a gallon of beans for cramming meal for the ducks. Ned Grey kept this and all the preceding holy days of Christmas. Reckon'd with John Bodle and there is due to me £10-17s for which he gave me a note of his hand. I also reckon'd with Dick Wood and paid him 29s in full of all accounts. My Mother Marchant sent me a pig which we had for dinner. Mr Jeremiah Dodson sent me a coppy of the Register per Mr John Hart relating to my Father's buriall which was the 17th August 1706.

The 2nd January 1714 Sunday. A dry very cold day. A frost last night. Mr Jeremiah Dodson preacht. We had a meeting in the afternoon but passt no accounts Thomas Field not being at Church. I went into Mrs Catherine Beard's after evning prayr. There was Mr Peter Courthope and Mrs Whitfield. I staid 'till about 7 aclock. John Terry,
Thomas Terry and William Terry's boy din'd here. So did my Cousin John Lindfield.

The 3rd January 1714 Munday. A windy day and snow'd hard towards night. Deliver'd 4 bushels barly to Whiteman's Green. My Wife and I and Mr John Hart and Willy din'd at Danny with Mr Healy. Mr Richard Whitpaine and his wife Mary, Mr Bill and Mrs Whitfield and the French man. Mr Whitpaine came not 'till towards night. We staid late and drank too much. I shot a rook in Tully's coppice in the morning. Mr Beaumont came in the afternoon but went away before supper. He wore my hat home instead of his own and I sent for him the next morning. Gave my gardener a shilling.

The 4th January 1714 Tuesday. A cold windy day, the frost continuing. We were invited to sup at Mr Jeremiah Dodson's which Mr John Hart and I, my Son John and Daughter Bett did. There was Mrs Catherine Beard and her mother, Mrs Scutt, Mr Richard Whitpaine and his wife Mary but my Wife was out of order and could not go. We came away before the rest of the company.

The 5th January 1714 Wednesday. A windy, cold day the frost continuing. The hogs had a bushel and a half of oates and ½ a bushel of beans. Receiv'd 2s of Jack Bartlet for ½ a bushel of pease for John Wickens, William Beard's boy had ½ a bushel of pease for Tully of Bolny but did not pay for them. My Cousin John Bodle kill'd one of my hogs this afternoon. He weigh'd 24 nail. Jack Bartlet had a bushel of wheat to day and so had John Standbridge at 4s. The fleath weigh'd 11½ lbs.

The 6th January 1714 Thursday. A dry day, the frost continuing. Receiv'd the 3 sacks from John Gold's. Mr Healy din'd here. Jack Bartlet kill'd his hog mention'd the 31st of last month. He weigh'd 21½ nail. The fleath weigh'd 11 lbs. The hogs had 2 bushels of whole beans.

The 7th January 1714 Fryday. A fine day, the frost but little. My Wife, Mr John Hart and I and Jacky supt at Mr Richard Whitpaine's with Mrs Catherine Beard and her mother, Mr Jeremiah Dodson and his wife and Mr Scutt and his wife. We came away about half an hour past eleven aclock.

The 8th January 1714 Saturday. A fine day, thaw'd a little. Receiv'd 18d of Harry Morley's wife for 3 gallons of pease. Win'd 3 quarters of Jack Bartlet's pease. Ned May went to Lewis and brought me a paper book from Norman's and a note from Thomas Friend for £18 on demand. Reckon'd with Stephen Bine and receiv'd £7-13-6d in full of all accounts. Reckon'd also with Mr John Hart and clear'd all accounts with him to Christmas Day last. Receiv'd £10 for half a year and half a quarter's board, 2s-6d for a quarter of malt and 10s for hops and paid him £3-15s for 3 quarters schooling. I also paid him the £3 borrow'd of him the 28th of December last. John Channel brought my new great coat from Robert Hurst's at Horsham. My Wife and Bett was at Wanbarrow.

The 9th January 1714 Sunday. A fine day, continued thawing. Mr Jeremiah Dodson preacht and begun to mention the King's titles in his prayr before sermon. He read a brief for the repair of a church to which I gave nothing. After evning prayr Mr Henry Campion went into Stephen Bine's and the French man. I just went home and went up to them. They staid 'till about 7 aclock. I staid about an hour after them. Lent Mr Campion a pamphlet.

The 10th January 1714 Munday. A very misty morning but fine afternoon, continued thawing. Kill'd the 2 great hogs, one weigh'd 36 nail, his fleath 20½ lbs, the other 30 nail his fleath 17½ lbs. All 4 of them have eaten 44 bushels of oates and 18 bushels of tick beans and they all together weigh 111 nail 4lbs. Stephen Bine's man John Stammer workt here. Receiv'd 2s of a woman from Ditcheling for half a bushel of pease. Deliver'd 3 bushels of pease to Harry Morley at 3s-6d per bushel per Ned May. One Rapley's boy from Board Hill in Cuckfield was here for a service. I promis'd to send for him (when I begun fallow) for a tryall if I did not bargain with an other boy before that time. Michael Stacey sent my wantys again. Paid Mr Scrase of Pangdean £15-15s for 42 ewes and spent 6d at the same time at the Swan. My Wife and I, Mr John Hart and Bett supt at Mrs Catherine Beard's with Mr Jeremiah Dodson and his wife, Mr Scutt and his wife, Mr Richard Whitpaine and his wife Mary. We staid 'till 12 aclock. Paid 5s-6d to Brand's girl for picking 5½ loads of flints and 2s for 4 day's work. Also 11 or 10d to Jane Brand for work in the Sumer. I gave her 6d instead of a harvest supper. Note reckoning a very moderate price for the fatting the aforesaid hogs can't be valued, lean, at more than £4-14s unless more than 2s per nail.

The 11th January 1714 Tuesday. A windy, cloudy day continuing to thaw. Michael Stacey sent his malter to tell me the last barly I deliver'd him was mow burn'd. He brought some of it begun workt *(sic)* and it appeared to be a little damaged so I bid him tell his master I would make a reasonable allowance especially if he took more. He had 5 quarters of that sort and no more. The malter own'd that which I deliver'd for my Cousin John Lindfield workt very well. Ned Grey and I fetcht a load of sand out of the Sandfield for Old William Brand. Deliver'd a bushel of tick beans to Harry Courtness. I went up to Mrs Catherine Beard's and staid about an hour. John Gun, Ned Grey and Ned May cut the hop poles wood and put it into the wood house.

The 12th January 1714 Wednesday. A windy forenoon and wet towards night. Deliver'd 7 quarters 6 bushels of the Churchfield barly to Harry Wickham the same that was last deliver'd to Michael Stacey. I told him the complaint that Stacey made and promis'd if it had any damage to make it good. Win'd 10 quarters 6 bushels of John Gun's Churchfield head barly and 2½ bushels tail. Shut up 3 of the black pigs and the boar a fatting. Mr Jeremiah Dodson and his wife, my Grandmother and Mrs Catherine Beard, Mr Richard Whitpaine and his wife Mary and daughter, Mrs Scutt and Mr Healy supt here. Mr Scutt came after supper. I gave Mr Dodson 1s for which he is to give me 10s if both the Tory candidates are chosen at the ensuing election. Mr Healy took a shilling of Mr Richard Whitpaine upon the same terms.

The 13th January 1714 Thursday. A wet stormy day. Deliver'd a cord of wood to Mr Jeremiah Dodson at 14s. Deliver'd 30 quarters 2½ bushels of barly to Harry Wickham and 6 bushels I order'd to be taken out of that I deliver'd yesterday, in all 4 quarters half a bushel to be malted for my self. Michael Stacey was here in the evning and we talkt about the aforesaid barly but agreed very well. However I promis'd to fling him 9 bushel of barly or some thing of like value. He also own'd my Cousin John Lindfield workt very well. The above mentioned wood and barly was deliver'd per Ned Grey.

The 14th January 1714 Fryday. A dry forenoon but very wet afternoon and evening. Deliver'd a bushel of beans to Harry Courtness. Dick Wood shooed my old horse's two fore feet. Shut up the other two fatting oxen. Win'd 2 quarters 3 bushels of Jack Bartlet's oates.

The 15th January 1714 Saturday. A wet day. Gave the hogs 3 bushels of oates. Paid William Roach 18d for mending windows at Tully's and my Thomas and his boys work. Harry Morley made an end of thatching the hovel. Reckon'd with John Smith and there is due to me £3-19-4½d. Order'd the old horse a gallon of oates by M_____ every morning.

The 16th January 1714 Sunday. A very wet day. Mr Jeremiah Dodson preacht. I was not at Church in the forenoon because my head acht very much. We had a meeting in the afternoon and order'd a bon fire and 5s for the ringers a Thursday. Edgly and I went into the Swan to read the news but did not stay. I went from thence to Mrs Catherine Beard's. She spoak for 2 bushels of tick beans. I staid 'till 6 aclock. Receiv'd a letter from my Cousin Peter Marchant at Lewis about his mare per Henry Wickham's man *(Ed: Peter, a periwig maker in Lewes, was born 1679, the son of Peter Marchant of Ditchling and was thus a second cousin to Thomas)*.

The 17th January 1714 Munday. A stormy showry day. Ned Grey carry'd up 2 quarters of tick beans into Tully's garret. Ned May went to John Paine to desire him to come to work but he could not. Ned Grey spread the flints at the school. Jack Bartlet had a bushel of wheat at 4s. I was at Stephen Bine's a little while in the afternoon. There was my Cousin Harry Goffe of Henfield. I sent the blind folds that I ow'd to Mrs Catherine Beard per Ned May. Receiv'd 14s of Mr Jeremiah Dodson for a cord of wood.

The 18th January 1714 Tuesday. A dry day. John Westover brought me a new payr of slippers. We mov'd the calf house and took up the working oxen into the close. Mr Richard Whitpaine was here in the evning and told me of a letter he had receiv'd from Knapp the woolstapler wherein he complain'd the wool was damaged and expected an allowance. He staid 'till about 7 aclock. Paid Thomas Parker 2s-8d for 4 hundred of quicksets. Paid Harry Morley 7s-6d towards his thatching.

The 19th January 1714 Wednesday. The morning and evning dry, the rest wet. Bony, John Gun, Jack Bartlet and Ned Grey begun thrash clover. I saw Mr Richard Whitpaine in the morning and he told me Mr Penny would give me 17s-6d per bushel for what I could get ready in time but I desir'd him to get 18s for me if he could. I sent Young Stoneham for the mare to Lewis but he came not home. My Cousin William Wood and his wife *(Ed: née Elizabeth Marchant of Ditchling, born 1673, a second cousin to Thomas)* and my Cousin Peter Marchant's wife *(Ed: née Sarah Walter)* din'd here. The women staid all night but he went home about 6 aclock and then Willy and I went to see my Brother Peter. There was John Snashall, William Borrer, Abraham Muzzall. My Cousin John Lindfield's boy was here and had a few turnips _____ half a bushel of pease for which he paid my Wife.

The 20th January 1714 Thursday. A dry forenoon but wet afternoon. My Cousin William Wood and his wife Elizabeth and my Cousin Marchant din'd here again and went home about 4 aclock. Sent 2 bushels of oates and a bushel of tick beans to mill for the horse. Mr Jeremiah Dodson preacht. I was at Church but none of my servants or workmen because Jack Bartlet was fetcht to thrash for straw for the oxen and the rest to thrash clover that I might deliver it in time. Mr John Hart and I went up to Mr Dodson's and from thence to the bon fire in Mrs Catherine Beard's great Townfield, being the Thanksgiving Day for a deliverance from           . From thence we return'd to Mr Dodson's again but Mr Hart and I staid not long but left the company there. Paid 6d to Ned Burt for tacking the vines. One of my ewes cast a lamb last night.

The 21st January 1714 Fryday. A very fine day. William Stoneham return'd with the mare from Mr Mall of Kingston near Lewis. If I keep her he is to have the first colt when weanable and if she will not have a colt I am to have her for nothing. She is       years old next Spring. I made 4 boxen wheels to the pullys to the harness tack. Paid Parker 3½d for a jobb of litter carrying. Nick Marchant and Ned Harraden of Ditcheling was here towards night. Receiv'd 1s of Harraden for a peck of pease. Jack Westover seal'd my thick shooes and brought them down in the evning. Let Bony the ditch in the Little Meads at 2½d per rod.

The 22nd January 1714 Saturday. Most part of the day a wet mist. Stephen Bine's Tom Mall and Robert Gatland workt here. Paid Roach 18d for the window to the calf house, 10d for his boys fetching the above mentioned mare and 4½d for haveing her home again to day because thought her too slight to breed by. Mr Gold was here and paid me 28s for 7 bushels of pease left at his house the 9th of November last. The hogs had 1 bushel of oates. My Cousin John Lindfield sent me a pig _____ to go kill on a Fryday next. Mr Healy was here and we appointed to go to him a Munday next _____ . Mr Gold show'd me an account (in a letter from Mr Page near London) of the late fire that it begun last Thursday was sennight and had burnt 100 houses or more haveing consumed Bare Key and very narrowly sear'd the custom house. I saw in the same letter that one Thomsen a great corne merchant in London allow'd Young Hayler of Stenning 9d per quarter for buying wheat for him in this country and Mr Page offer'd Mr Gold the same. John Gold acknowledged that he ow'd my Cousin Lindfield for a load of wheat but did not pay him. My Cousin Lindfield told me that the bayliff had seized all Mr John Warden's effects.

The 23rd January 1714 Sunday. A very fine day. Mr Healy preacht here in the forenoon. We had no prayrs in the afternoon. Mr Healy, my Wife and Jacky went to Albourne church and call'd me at Wanbarrow. Got home about 7 aclock and the bells were ringing for Frank Dodson's wedding who was marry'd this morning at Poynings. I had an other lambe dead this morning. Tom Knapp was here this evning and promis'd to come to work as soon as he could.

The 24th January 1714 Munday. A fine day. John Standbridge and Stephen Bine's boy workt here. I saw Ned Pickstone in the morning at the Swan and went down to Edgly with him but my Cousin Thomas Norton not being within I did not stay. My Wife and I went to Mr Wood's at Broad street. I and Ned Grey went from there to one Edmund King's to buy Nonsuch seed but he was not at home. His wife promis'd he should bring me a sample to morrow morning. Paid Old Bonny 5s. Sent 2 bushels of oates and 1 bushel of beans to mill for the hogs.

The 25th January 1714 Tuesday. A dry day. King did not come with a sample of seed as was expected. John Standbridge and Robert Gatland workt here. Sent 2 bushels of pease to Rusper per Ned May. Receiv'd 4s of Count Tully of Bolny for half a bushel of pease he had to day and half a bushel he had some time ago per Beard's boy. Paid Parker 1s for picking 2 bushels of pease. Mr John Hart, Mr Scutt, Mr Richard Whitpaine and I supt at Mr Healy's. We had a trout for supper 2 foot 2 inches long from eye to fork and 6 inches broad weigh'd 30½ lbs. He was caught in Albourne Brook nere Trussell House. Mr Scutt said it was properly call'd a salmon pool. We staid very late and drank enough. Receiv'd £5 of Michael Stacey.

The 26th January 1714 Wednesday. A dry day. Old William Brand set up a thing in the sink to wash on. John Standbridge and Robert Gatland workt here. I went to Wanbarrow in the evning. Young Stoneham fetcht home the founder'd mare yesterday and to day I had her shooed. My Cousin Bodle of Hailsham came at night being on his way to Horsham with a man that had stol'n a mare.

The 27th January 1714 Thursday. A dry day 'till towards night. John Standbridge and Robert Gatland workt here. I had 2 lambs fell to day. Deliver'd a bushel of barly to White. Sent a hog grist to mill. Lent Michael Stacey 2 oxen. Stephen Bine was here in the evning. My Cousin Bodle went away before we were up. Paid Stephen Bine 2s-6d for 10 very mean five foot posts yesterday or t'other day.

The 28th January 1714 Fryday. A very wet day. Tom Knapp begun work here. Mr Healy din'd here. My Sister Mary Ede and Molly Ede came just before noon. Stephen Bine mended the great oval table. Mr Healy, Mr Scutt, Mr John Hart, Mr Richard Whitpaine and I went to Dean House towards night. We supt there. We staid 'till about midnight and drank moderately. I had one lamb last night.

The 29th January 1714 Saturday. A dry day 'till towards night. My Unkle Courtness had 2 bushels of barly for which I receiv'd 5s. I sold him 8 bushels of oates at 12s to be deliver'd in a few days. I had my head shav'd. In the afternoon Ned May and I draw'd the trees for Mrs Catherine Beard.
My clover trashers rough clean'd their seed and there was 6 bushels which stood me in £1-1-10d after 'twas pug'd. Mrs Beard did not pay me for drawing the trees. Shut up Jack Bartlet's young beasts and put 2 of the heifers in the Marldfield.

The 30th January 1714 Sunday. A fine day. Mr Jeremiah Dodson preacht and gave notice of to morrow to be observ'd instead of to day. I went to Wanbarrow in the evning and my Brother Peter desir'd me to go to Lewis for him in a day or two. I told him I would. I had 2 lambs last night.

The 31st January 1714 Munday. A dry windy day. I was at Church. We had no sermon. Paid Jack Bartlet 10s and he had a bushel of wheat. Win'd 2 quarters 1 bushel head and 1½ bushel tail of John Gun's Tully's wheat being the last of that field in which was 7 quarters and half a bushel. John Gun, Ned Grey and Ned May mov'd the wheat mow. Old William Brand lay'd a ridge tile over the hall chimney to prevent it smoaking. Stephen Bine's man John Stammer and Robert Gatland workt here this afternoon and finish the double work at the end of the great barne. The workmanship of which comes to about 8s the rack staves being cleft to their hands and shav'd so that I don't think they earn'd their wages. Mr Richard Whitpaine was here in the evning. Receiv'd £3 of John Smith and Thomas Smith.

The 1st February 1714 Tuesday. A wet stormy forenoon but dry afternoon. We clean'd 4½ bushels of clover seed for market. It weigh'd but 67½ lbs. Win'd 3½ bushels of the wheat at Hyder's head and half a bushel tail all shatter'd out in moveing the mowe but shall be reckon'd as John Gun's thrashing. Sent a bushel of tail pease and 2 bushels of oates to mill for the hogs. Mr Healy had a bushel of beans at 3s-3d. Receiv'd 3d of my Unkle Courtness for half a gallon of pease. I had one lamb to day.

The 2nd February 1714 Wednesday. A very stormy day, most part wet. I had one lamb last night and one to day. Receiv'd 6d of Old Hyder for a gallon of pease. Reckon'd with Jack Bartlet for his Michaelmas rent and bullock serving and all manner of work to this day and there is due to me £3-2-3¼d. Mrs Catherine Beard and her mother was here all the afternoon and staid 'till about 10 aclock. Mr Richard Whitpaine came about sun set and staid 'till 9 or quarter past.

The 3rd February 1714 Thursday. A fine day only a storm about 5 aclock. Nick Plaw came to look on an ox that was grip't but it was over before he came. Abraham Muzzall had half a bushel of wheat and a gallon of pease. Deliver'd 4 bushels of oates and as many pease to my Unkle Courtness, the oates at 12s per quarter, the pease at 28s per quarter. Mr John Hart and I went to Brighton after dinner. There I bought 1½ of Nonsuch seed of Edmund King at 13s-6d. I sold 20 bushels of my best pease to John Reedford of Famer at 4s per bushel, 2 bushels to John Gold, a bushel to Mr Long, an other to Rogers and one to the Garners that keep a shop all to be deliver'd in a fortnight. Mr Hart bought a hat of Mr Roland at 9s and a whip at 5s. Three lambs to day and last night. Win'd 10 quarters 7 bushels of Jack Bartlet's Churchfield barly head. Sent a hog grist to mill.

The 4th February 1714 Fryday. A fine day. I went to Michael Stacey's to see my oxen and from thence to Wanbarrow, from thence to Harry William's, from thence to Westtowne and so home to dinner. My Wife and Sister Mary Ede went to Westtowne and staid 'till about 6 aclock. Receiv'd 1s of Ned Stanmer of Cuckfield and 18d of Thomas Haslegrove for 5 gallons of pease. Deliver'd 10 quarters and 5 bushels of barly to Harry Wickham per Ned Grey and Ned May. 2 lambs to day.

The 5th February 1714 Saturday. A fine day. Win'd 12 bushels of John Gun's pease. Deliver'd a bushel of pease to Edmund King per Ned May and receiv'd 1½ bushels of Nonsuch seed of him. Mr Beaumont din'd here. Markt 10 ewes red on the right side of the neck, the most being first clip't and then 10 lambs with a fork on the right ear. Note the black ewe is one of them. Mr Hasloup was here in the afternoon to see Mr John Hart. I had 2 lambs to day. King's Nonsuch is at 9s per bushel.

The 6th February 1714 Sunday. A very cold day with snow and hail and towards night much rain. Mr Jeremiah Dodson preacht. I did not go to Church in the afternoon because my Wife was not well and besides the weather was bad. 2 lambs last night.

The 7th February 1714 Munday. A very wet day. Deliver'd 4½ bushels of clover seed at the Rock on Mr Richard Whitpaine's account per Ned May. Lent to my Brother Peter the blind mare. Lost 1 lamb last night. We try'd to sow the pond by Tully's but the water came in so fast we could not do it. Paid Parker 6d for helping. Receiv'd 16s of Robert Chatfield of Bentley for 4 bushels of pease for himself and Mr Gatland of Pilsty. Watt Carpenter of Ditcheling was here and agreed for 10 bushels of pease at 4s per bushel deliver'd at Ditcheling. Receiv'd 2s-6d in hand. 2 lambs last night. Mr Courtness spoke for last mow of the course pease at 3s-6d per bushel.

The 8th February 1714 Tuesday. A fine morning but very wet the rest of the day. 4 lambs to day and last night. Michael Stacey had a peck of pease. Mr Richard Whitpaine had half a bushel. Fisht the Marldfield stew. My Brother James Ede came about 2 aclock. Mrs Catherine Beard and my Grandmother spent the afternoon and evning here. Stephen Bine was here in the evning to desire me to fetch a load of deal from the Rock which I agreed to do as soon as I could at 15s.

The 9th February 1714 Wednesday. A dry forenoon but showry afternoon. My Cousin John Lindfield had 4 bushels of beans at 3s-3d per bushel. Parker had half a bushel of wheat at 4s per bushel. Mr Healy paid me £2-15-6d for 12 bushels of malt, a bushel of beans, a watch chain and a paper book. He left an old watch chain with me to be chang'd for him for which he is to have all the mony. Paid Richard Patching 1s for bleeding me. Win'd 3 quarters half a bushel of John Gun's head pease and half a bushel tail. Paid my Brother James Ede a bill of 28s which he had paid for me to Mr Roberds. Paid him also 27s-6d for a calf which I veryly thought I had paid before and so I think still. Young Stoneham workt here and went to Mr Beaumont's. Mr Richard Whitpaine came towards night and staid 'till 9 aclock. I gave Mr Ede Mr Healy's old watch chain to get it chang'd. Two lambs fell this evning. Set the hogs out a bushel of oates.

The 10th February 1714 Thursday. A fine day. One lamb towards night. Jack Bartlet had a bushel of wheat at 4s. Receiv'd 4s of Mr Rogers and 4s of Mr Long for each a bushel of pease. Deliver'd 2 bushels of pease to Mr Gold. Ned May brought the mony for a crock of lard he carry'd to Henfield. Sent a grist to mill for the hogs. Dinner and expences at Brighton 2s-6d with R Norris, John Chatfield, William Jeffery. Paid John Chatfield 2s for a lease on Diftcheling Comon last year.

The 11th February 1714 Fryday. A fine day. 3 lambs to day, 2 of them being twins. One of them put to the sheep which lost her lamb. Deliver'd 20 bushels of pease to John Bradford per Ned Grey and Ned May. Win'd 6½ bushels of John Gun's pease being the last of the field, in all 12 quarters one bushel. Sent a hog grist to mill. Nick Marchant din'd here. William Muddle begun make hoops. Win'd 14 bushels of Jack Bartlet's oates. Mr John Hart, Mr Edward, his wife and I supt at Mrs Catherine Beard's. Receiv'd 20s of Mr Courtness for 4 bushels of course pease and as many oates.

The 12th February 1714 Saturday. A fine day. My Cousin John Lindfield sent home two red yearling steers he bought for me at Stephen Hill's sale of Bolny. They cost £3-10s. The twin lamb dyed that was put to the other ewe. Deliver'd 10 bushels of pease to Watt Carpenter per Ned Grey and Ned May. My Brother James Ede and I went Lewis. Paid Mr Tourl the grocer a bill of £1-17-2d. Paid Thomas Friend a bill of £1-18-5d. Receiv'd of Thomas Friend £18 being mony paid to his use in London. Paid a bill to Mr Fissenden £2-12-4d. dinner and expences 4s. Paid a bill to Mr Court 15s -8½d. It all that was due to Norman. Paid to Mr Short a bill of 6 or 7s all that was due. I forgot to pay my Cousin Peter what he paid to John Sayers.

The 13th February 1714 Sunday. A fine day. Mr Jeremiah Dodson preacht. My Cousin John Lindfield and Thomas Butcher din'd here. We went into Mrs Catherine Beard's after evning prayr but did not stay the evning.

The 14th February 1714 Munday. A fine day. My Son John begun his accadence. John Gun and Ned Grey fisht Tully's middle pond and stored him again with 2 old carp 9 inches long and 10 carp 7 inches and 1 tench. My Sister Mary Ede and my Wife went to Danny in the afternoon. Receiv'd 2s of William Nicholas for an ashen stem at Holden's.

The 15th February 1714 Tuesday. A fine day. Begun fallow the Homefield. Yoakt the stag. Receiv'd 4s of Edward Burry for store fish. He staid 'till night. I was at Wanbarrow in the morning. One lamb fell last night.

The 16th February 1714 Wednesday. A very fine day. Sent a hog grist to mill. I sent William Roach's boy with a letter to Ned Stammer. I had 5 hoops made to put a lilt on to a waggon to go to Chichester with free holders. Markt ten sheep on the left side of the neck and 10 lambs on the left ear some time ago. Henry Sharp, John Galliard, William Buckwell, Goodman Sanders and John Smith the sadler all of Cuckfield call'd here and drank. I had them all to the Swan.

The 17th February 1714 Thursday. A showry day. We set out for Chichester about 110 _____ . Joined Mr Beaumont and Mr Cheal and others and made a very considerable body, suppos'd to be 300 or 400 men by the time they came to Chichester. Mr Bourne, Mr Beaumont, Thomas Norton of Egly, one Mr Davis, John Pickstone, Dick Marshall and I went by Arundell and lay there. I lay at Mr Picknall's a talow chandler. Œ waggon carry'd 8 men vizt Jacob Hubbard of Ditcheling and all those 5 from Cuckfield except William Buckwell mentioned yesterday, also James Haslegrove and John Haslegrove of Bolny and Harry Burtenshaw of Cuckfield. Œ lamb fell tonight.

The 18th February 1714 Fryday. A fine day. 2 lambs fell to night. I went to Chichester with the 4 Mr Leave's with some people from Arundell, in all about 40 men to the election of the knights of the shire begun yesterday and ended to day. The candidates were Mr Bertram Ashburnham, Mr Ferffield, Mr Butler and Mr Spencer Compton. The two latter carry'd it by a vast majority but as was suppos'd by all manner of indirect practices particularly by the Erl of Cl--------e their great patron. I din'd to day with my Cousin Libbard and return'd to Arundell with Mr Richard Whitpaine etc.

The 19th February 1714 Saturday. A dry day. Œ lamb to day. Sent a hog grist to mill yesterday. I return'd from Arundell to day with Mr Jeremiah Dodson, Mr Bourne, Mr Beaumont, Mr   Richard Whitpaine and William Roach. Markt 10 lambs on both ears and markt the sheep in the forhead with red. Turn'd all the sheep and lambs into the Rookwood wheat. My Brother James and Sister Mary Œe *(Ed: née Stone)* went home yesterday. I lent John Westover my young horse a Thursday to go to the election and he run a nail in his foot and brought him home lame. Œ cow calf to day.

The 20th February 1714 Sunday. A dry, windy day, the wind very high last night. Mr Jeremiah Dodson preacht. I was at Mrs Catherine Beard's in the afternoon, Mrs Courthope with us.

The 21st February 1714 Munday. A dry, cold day. Sent a hog grist to mill. Molly Œe went home. John Snashall was to see my young horse and said she was like to do well. Richard White brought 24 douzen of mole tails for which I paid him 4s and outset 20s for a quarter of barly he had at several times, in all 1s per douzen for catching the moles. I also paid him 9s-6d for weaving. There were 2 lambs some days ago that were not set down.

The 22nd February 1714 Tuesday. A fine day but very cold. Œ lamb to day. Paid William Muddle 16s for makeing of hoops at 4s per hundred, reckoning 120 to the 100 of the usual size from 10 to 5 foot and some few shorter. They are such as are comonly call'd flitch and rend worth about 7s-6d per _____ . I had 300 and ¾ _____ 14 hoops. Paid Harry Morley 12s and 7s-6d paid him before and 10s-6d outset for 3 bushels of course pease, in all 30s for 7½ squares of thatch on the yoaking hovel and 4½ squares on the great barne. Paid him also 2s for mending and spars and for lathing etc. I was at Wanbarrow all the afternoon and evning.

The 23rd February 1714 Wednesday. A fine day but cold. Paid Bony 3s-6d for clover thrashing and 3d more towards his ditch of which he says there is 30½ rod. Dick Wood cut the young horse of the Lampas. My Wife was at Danny in the afternoon.

The 24th February 1714 Thursday. A showry day. Œ bull calf to day. John Standbridge, Ned May and I cut down 3 trees and begun the work about Tully's close. Jack Bartlet had a bushel of wheat at 4s. My Cousin Peter Marchant's man Tester came this evning. Ned Grey plough'd Richard White's field. Bottl'd out the last of the stale beer and set it at the south end of the bottle hole. There was 43 bottles.

The 25th February 1714 Fryday. A showry day. Kll'd 2 pigs, one weigh'd 10 nail, the other 12 nail. Ned Tester carry'd his master 2 very good fish. John Standbridge and Tom Mall workt here. Win'd 25 bushels of Jack Bartlet's oates. Chang'd runts and sheep. Lent John Towner my stilliards.

The 26th February 1714 Saturday. A showry day. John Standbridge and Thomas Mall workt here and finish'd the crib in Tully's close and stable. My Cousin John Bodle cut out the pigs and supt with us. Towner brought home the stilliards. Left the hedges and wedges in Tully's hovel per the spitter.

The 27th February 1714 Sunday. A dry day. I went to Wanbarrow in the morning. Mr Jeremiah Dodson preacht and went to Twineham in the afternoon. Mrs

Catherine Beard and my Grandmother were here in the afternoon.

The 28th February 1714 Munday. A fine day. My Unkle Courtness had a bushel of course pease. Sent a hog grist to the mill. Ned May and Ned Grey made an end of the Homefield and begun Tully's wheat earsh. Mov'd the calf house into the orchard. Abraham Muzzall workt here.

The 1st March 1714 Tuesday. A little rain, the rest of the day dry. Shrove Tuesday. I measur'd Bony's ditch and found it but 29 rod and ½ and in the afternoon paid him all that was due to him.

The 2nd March 1714 Wednesday. A dry day. Chang'd the young beasts. Borrow'd a chit of Stephen Bine. My Wife and I were at Church in the forenoon and she was at Wanbarrow in the afternoon. My Cousin John Lindfield and John Stone were here towards night. Parker had half a bushel of wheat at 2s. William Greenaway jr and Jonas Stoneham helpt Jack Bartlet winnow oates. Abraham Muzzall workt here to day and yesterday.

The 3rd March 1714 Thursday. A fine day. Ned May and Ned Grey made an end of ploughing Tully's wheat earsh. Yesterday and to day win'd 8 quarters 3½ bushels of Jack Bartlet's oates being the last of the field, in all 24 quarters. Sent my leather bags to my Cousin John Lindfield per the fuller. Reckon'd with my Unkle Courtness and clear'd all accounts. Put the ewes and lambs into the turnips. Sent the founder'd mare to Ditcheling Comon per Stoneham.

The 4th March 1714 Fryday. A fine day only a showr in the forenoon. Deliver'd 6 quarters of barly to Lo Wickham per Ned Grey and James win'd 13 quarters 2 bushels of Jack Bartlet's Churchfield head barly. Chang'd the tags and misst one of them. Carry'd 7½ quarters oates up into Tully's millhouse chamber. Receiv'd my malt again being 4 quarters 2 bushels of 4 quarters of barly. Nick Plaw's ba_____ cow calved a bull calf this morning. John Standbridge workt here to day.

The 5th March 1714 Saturday. A fine day. Win'd 9 bushels tail of Jack Bartlet's Churchfield barly. Deliver'd 6 quarters 2 bushels of barly to Harry Wickham per Ned Grey and Stoneham. Deliver'd 12 bushels of beans to Mr Henry Campion per Ned Grey and Stoneham at 3s-3d per bushel. Paid William Greenaway 2s-9d for work. Ned May set some beans in the orchard. Sent a hog grist to mill. Mr John Hart had a new payr of boots from Morfee of Brighton. Young Jarvice went to Nunnery on foot.

The 6th March 1714 Sunday. A wet day especially afternoon. Mr Jeremiah Dodson preacht. My Cousin John Lindfield din'd here and wore my great coat home. My Wife and I were at Mrs Catherine Beard's after evning prayr and she was let blood for which I paid Richard Patching 1s. Joseph Muzzall gave notice of a Court Baron next Tuesday sennight.

The 7th March 1714 Munday. A fine day. Lent Mr Richard Whitpaine 12 sacks per Bony. I went to Wanbarrow in the morning. In the afternoon I went to Mrs Catherine Beard's and measur'd 3 acres at the west side of the great Townefield and 2 acres on the east side both for Goodman Hubbard. Also 3 acres next to Hubbard's on the west side for Richard Herriot and one acre between them for her self. I staid the evning there and Mr Henry Campion supt there. Sold my Brother Peter 100 hoops at 7s-6d.

The 8th March 1714 Tuesday. A very windy day and wet towards night. I measur'd the little field by Tully's orchard and he is 3 roods 4 rods. Mrs Catherine Beard had 3 bushels of pease at 4s per bushel and 2 bushels of beans at 3s-3d per bushel per Phillips and John Smith. Ned Grey and Ned May begun plough the little field aforesaid this afternoon. Dick Wood sharp'd my horse harrows yesterday. Mr Richard Whitpaine sent home my sacks to night. My Wife supt at Mrs Catherine Beard's and I fetcht her home.

The 9th March 1714 Wednesday. A fine day. Lost a barren ewe in the Churchfield. Jack Bartlet had a bushel of wheat at 4s. Ned Grey and Ned May ended the little field and begun the other. Nick Plaw came to see the calves, they being a little sick but we suppos'd it to be occasion'd by the closeness of the room as much as any thing.

The 10th March 1714 Thursday. A very fine day. Jack Bartlet had half a bushel malt. Nan West begun set the little field with beans and William Greenaway came to help her about 9 aclock. Nunnery boy was here and brought mony for two bushels of pease. Ned Grey and

Ned May plough'd in Tully's first field in the afternoon. Sent half a bushel of pease to Nunnery per Dick. My Wife and I were at Mr Burry's in the afternoon. Lent my Cousin Thomas Norton of Edgly the shed chain per William Norton. Mr John Hart was at Mr Scutt's all the evning.

The 11th March 1714 Fryday. A wet forenoon, the afternoon dry. Mrs Catherine Beard sent us a yew tree per Goodman Philips which he set in the middle of the garden. Grey made a cart whip, the bone cost 20d. Very dear. Goodman Marten of Cuckfield was here and clip't the sheep for which I paid him 14d. Nan West and Greenaway set beans again to day.

The 12th March 1714 Saturday. A very wet forenoon and last night but dry afternoon. One sheep had two lambs this afternoon. Ned Grey and Ned May plough'd half the day. No beans set to day. Mrs Catherine Beard and my Grandmother spent the afternoon and evning here. John Bodle's wife was brought to bed of a son this afternoon. *(Ed: John Bodle was married to Elizabeth Tidey, third cousin to Thomas Marchant)*

The 13th March 1714 Sunday. A fine day. Mr Jeremiah Dodson preacht. I sent Ned May to the Ewans's in the morning about pease. Mr John Hart and I went to Wanbarrow after evning prayr. There was Dr Tabor. We stay'd 'till about 8.

The 14th March 1714 Munday. A fine day. Nan West and Greenaway set beans to day. Ned Grey and Ned May plough'd to day. Thomas Ewans's brother was here to tell me I might have what grey pease I would. I bargain'd for 8 bushels at 4s per bushel. Mr Healy din'd here. Shut up 3 sheep in Tully's close and brought 2 steers from thence into the home close. Mr Healy, Mr John Hart and I went to Mr Richard Whitpaine's in the evning, we supt there, staid late and drank enough.

The 15th March 1714 Tuesday. A very fine day. Took the sheep out of the Rookwood wheat. Nan West and Greenaway made an end of setting beans in the little field. They set a bushel and seaven gallons of beans, the rows 2 foot 3 inches asunder and the east half of the field. They set double rows and the other half single rows. They have been 3 days and a half setting all the fields which is 3 roods and 4 rod. Paid Nan West 2s for 4 day's work. Sent 2 bushels of barly to mill for the hogs.

I went up to the Royall Oak after dinner to the court according to notice there was Mr John Norton, John Stone and my self which was all the tenants that were there and no business appearing. Mr Warden did not keep a court. We spent 3d a piece. Mr Warden demanded a herriot of Old Harry Wickham heir for Crouch House and Young Harry Wickham was there to treat with him. He alleged that no herriot was due because none had been paid, time out of mind, but the other insisted on it and offer'd to take 50s. Paid Greenaway 3s-6d for 3 days and a half. Receiv'd 8 bushels of grey pease of the Ewans of Cuckfield at 32s. Sent the founder'd mare to Ditcheling Comon per Stoneham.

The 16th March 1714 Wednesday. A fine day. Ned Grey begun sow pease in Tully's first field being the first course he ever sow'd. I was at Wanbarrow in the morning. Mr Richard Whitpaine was here towards night and staid supper. I call'd at Stephen Bine's and desir'd him to pay Mr Wilkin for my bible. I call'd also at Mr Jeremiah Dodson's and desir'd him to buy me a pocket book, he being just setting out for London with Mr Henry Campion and Stephen Bine. Mrs Catherine Beard was here in the evning but did not stay. Nan West and William Greenaway workt here and Ned Burt measur'd Tully's first field and he is 2 acres 3 roods and 14 rods.

The 17th March 1714 Thursday. A very wet day after the morning. I went to Wanbarrow in the morning and measur'd 2 acres of ground for John Haslegrove at the east side of my Brother Peter's north west part of the Marldfield for flax. I came away a little before noon Dr Tabor being just come thither. I call'd at Mr Richard Whitpaine and took my slideing rule and Everard's gauging which I had lent him. Mr Scutt and Mr Marston came here with Mr John Hart about half an hour past 2 aclock and staid 'till 8. Win'd 2 quarters 6 bushels of John Gun's head wheat at Hyder's.

The 18th March 1714 Fryday. A very fine day. We made an end of sowing Tully's pea field. There was 8 bushels of grey pease sow'd and almost 2 bushels of white. The grey pease are parted from the white in the middle of a land and a stake being driven exactly between them and the white pease being at the west side of the field and there is also a knotch cut in the body of an ash in the south hedge that points exactly to the middle of the warp whereat my pease part. John Gold's man fecht away 23 tags there being 2 _____ . They were in very good condition. I had 25 at first. My Cousin Nick Goffe's Widdow, my Cousin Bab Goffe *(Ed: Probably referring to Susan née Boniface, widow of Nicholas of Henfield born 1682 and his sister Barbara born 1695 – third cousins to Thomas)* and my Cousin Plump were here in the afternoon and my Sister Nanny but my Wife and Mrs Catherine Beard were gone to Danny. Ned Burt workt here and Greenaway 'till noon and then to begin dig in the pare orchard. Ned Grey and Ned May measur'd 2 _____ of oates to sow.

The 19th March 1714 Saturday. A very fine day. Ned Grey sow'd the little field by Tully's coppice with oates. He sow'd 12 bushels and the field was counted 3 acres but I measur'd him and found him but 2 acres and 28 rod. Stephen Bine's Tom Vinall workt here. I had a bull calf this morning of the hip fallen cow. Paid Terry 30s for work and outset 20s for a quarter of barly.

The 20th March 1714 Sunday. A fine day. Mr Beaumont preacht. I went to Dean House after dinner and staid 'till about 7 aclock. Nick Plaw was here this afternoon and draw'd away the clean from the hip fallen cow. My Daughter Bett and Betty Homan went to Dean House afternoon.

The 21st March 1714 Munday. A gloomy windy day. Win'd 9 quarters 1 bushel of John Gun's homefield head barly and 4 bushel tail. Paid William Greenaway 3s-2d for digging 19 rod of ground at 2d per rod. Paid him also for all the rest of his _____ 2s and outset 6d for a pound of butter and clear'd all accounts. Paid my Sister Nanny £6-5s for a year's intrest. She return'd 5s. Sent my Cousin John Lindfield a sample of barly. My Wife went to Westtowne in the morning and Mr Richard Whitpaine, my Cousin Nick Goffe's Widdow and my Cousin Bab Goffe spent the afternoon and evning here. Here was a very poor looking fellow this afternoon that pretended to be a dancing master.

The 22nd March 1714 Tuesday. A gloomy day, but very little rain. We went into the field by Hyder's intending to sow barly but found it too wet to set them to stirring. I measur'd the field and found it but 2 acres 2 roods and seavan rods measuring only so far as 'tis plough'd and mow'd but hedge rows and all it may be 3 acres. Paid Hollingall 6d for half a day's work. I went to Wanbarrow in the afternoon, Mr John Hart came after school time. We staid 'till about 7 aclock. There was Nick Marchant, John Stone, John Snashall and my Brother William.

The 23rd March 1714 Wednesday. A dry day. My birthday, being 38 years old. Borrow'd £4 of Stephen Bine for a note of my hand. Reckon'd with Terrys and clear'd all accounts. Paid them 6s for Mrs Catherine Beard and 32s-3d for my own work. I receiv'd a receit from Mr Wilkin of Stephen Bine but forgot to pay him the mony. Put two runts to pasture in the Churchfield Nonsuch. Paid Nan West 6d for setting beans to day. Jack Bartlet had a bushel of wheat. Bottled part of one tub of elder wine and markt the corks (EL).

The 24th March 1714 Thursday. A fine day but very windy. Yesterday Ned Grey and Ned May made an end of stirring the wheat earsh by Hyder's and in the night Ned Grey run away. Mr Jeremiah Dodson's man Thomas King went to London with his master's horse to day and I am apt to think Ned Grey met him on the road and went with him. Receiv'd 7 pounds of John Bodle. Paid Stephen Bine the £4 borrow'd and also 15s he paid to Mr Wilkin. Stephen's man John and Robert Gatland workt here in the afternoon. Mrs Catherine Beard and her mother were here in the afternoon but were sent for by their tennant Mr Hill. After supper I went to Stephen Bine's. There was Mr Hill. I told him what he had reported of Mr Henry Campion but he positively deny'd it. Sent a bushel of oates and half as many pease to mill for the hogs.

## 1715

The 25th March 1715 Fryday. Lady Day. A showry day especially the afternoon. Agreed with Thomas Scrase to be here 'till Maytide at 2s per week. Reckon'd with John Gun and paid him £2-19-1½d. Betty Homan went away to day and Sarah Hallet yesterday. Sarah Morley came to day at 10s per annum. My Wife and I were at Mrs Catherine Beard's this afternoon and evning. Ned May kept holy day in the afternoon. Receiv'd 27s of Mrs Beard in full of all accounts.

The 26th March 1715 Saturday. A showry day. Thomas Scrase came this morning. Thomas Vinall and John Standbridge workt here. Bargain'd with William Charman 'till Michaelmas at £4 to come Tuesday. Mr Healy was here towards night but would not stay supper.

My Wife was at Mr Jeremiah Dodson's this afternoon. Tom Scrase and Ned May litter'd both the closes to day. Receiv'd. Watt Carpenter's mony for pease per Stephen Bine

The 27th March 1715 Sunday. Wet towards night. Mr Jeremiah Dodson preacht. My Cousin John Lindfield din'd here. Paid Mr Jeremiah Dodson 4s for ¼lb tea and 2s-6d for a pocket book, Nick Plaw's great cow calved a bull calf with a star in the forehead and white spot on the tip of the tail.

The 28th March 1715 Munday A dry day. Sarah Sargeant came to day at 45s per annum. Hollingall begun plough in the field by Burt's. Took the sheep and lambs out of the wheat by Wickham's. Mr Marston din'd here and staid 'till about 2 aclock. John Snashall fix'd my young horse's pole to prevent the poll evil which was coming apace being much swol'n. William Charman came at night. Thomas Scrase ground 5 bushels of barly malt.

The 29th March 1715 Tuesday A fine day. Begun sow barly. Hollingall plough'd. I sow'd 8 bushels of barly in the field by Burt's. William Charman thrasht barly. Set Ned May out 4 bushels of oates for the horse. Ned Penfold went to Lewis with butter. He brought me ¼lb tea from Mr Tourl. My Wife went to Dean House in the afternoon.

The 30th March 1715 Wednesday A fine day. Hollingall plough'd. Sow'd about 7 bushels barly. Put an other runt into the hop garden. Nick Marchant was here and had 20s of me. He left some goods. Mrs Catherine Beard and her mother were here in the afternoon. William Charman thrasht barly all day.

The 31st March 1715 Thursday A fine day. Hollingall plough'd. Lent Mr Richard Whitpaine 3 wantys per King. William Charman thrasht 'till 10 aclock. Win'd his barly and there was 2 quarters 3 bushels of the Homefield. Sow'd 6 bushels to day. Stacey sent home my oxen per George West. Plough'd with the 6 oxen to day haveing plough'd single before. My Cousin John Lindfield fetch 8 sacks of barly, sacks and all.

The 1st April 1715 Fryday A fine day, very windy. Hollingall plough'd. William Charman thrasht half a day. Mr Richard Whitpaine sent home the wantys. Mr Cousin John Lindfield had 2 sacks of barly, sacks and all. Sow'd 7 bushels of barly. Receiv'd 4 payr of sheets and 4 silver spoons of my Cousin Nick Marchant, as a paun for £4 which I lent him. Mr John Hart and I went to Mr Jeremiah Dodson's about 6 aclock and staid 'till 11. My Cousin John Bodle sold a calf for me to a Brighton butcher at 12s. Kill'd the boar hog. He weigh'd 184 lbs, his fleath but 11 lbs. John Gun had the pig. He weigh'd 16 nail 2lbs alltogether, his fleath 8 lbs. The hogs had a bushel of whole oates at severall times.

The 2nd April 1715 Saturday A dry forenoon, the wind very high. William Charman thrasht. Hollingall plough'd. Mr Jeremiah Dodson had 4 bushels of oates. Reckon'd with my Cousin John Bodle and clear'd all accounts. Reckon'd with Dick Wood and clear'd all accounts. My Cousin John Lindfield had a sack of barly, sack and all. Receiv'd £2-18-3d of John Bodle and paid Dick Wood £1-2s. Dick Wood speak for 2 loads of wood and faggots. Sow'd 5 bushels of barly to day being the last of the field, in all 4 quarters 1 bushel and is just 6 bushels per acre. I went to Wanbarrow towards night and there was Jude Storer of Guildford. I staid 'till near 10 aclock. There was also John Cunningham. He paid my Brother for his clover seed and wool. There was my Brother William.

The 3rd April 1715 Sunday. A dry windy day. Mr Jeremiah Dodson preacht. We had a parish meeting in the afternoon. The Widdow Cecilia Marks was allow'd cloaths. John Lindfield agreed to keep his sister 'till about Xmas next, the parish to find her cloaths. Jude Storer din'd with me and went away about 3 aclock. My Sister Nanny and Bett were here after evning prayr.

The 4th April 1715 Munday A gloomy forenoon and windy, the afternoon very fine. William Michell sow'd the field by Burt's with Nonsuch. I did not pay him because he was to come again to sow more. William Charman thrasht in the afternoon. Mr Marston din'd here. Mr John Hart and he went to Mr Healy's in the afternoon. Hollingham helpt Jack Bartlet winnow 7 quarters 1 bushel head and 4 bushel tail of the Homefield barly. My Cousin John Lindfield had a quarter of barly and the 2 sacks. My Wife and I were at Philips's and afterwards I went to Mrs Catherine Beard's and from thence to the Swan. Spent 6d alone. Lent Old William Brand 6s.

The 5th April 1715 Tuesday. A very fine forenoon but gloomy afternoon with some rain. Hollingall helpt screen barly and helpt William Charman winnow 2 quarters of his Churchfield barly. In the afternoon Hollingham and William Charman begun thrash clover. Hollingham is to have half three shillings per bushel and his boy 4d per day to help. The boy is to begin to morrow morning. My Cousin John Lindfield had 8 bushels of barly and 2 of my sack per William Haslegrove. I went to Wanbarrow towards night. Staid 'till about 7 aclock. Nunnery Boy came about 2 aclock. Staid all night. Ned Penfold went to Lewis with butter.

The 6th April 1715 Wednesday. A wet day. Return'd my Father Stone's beech oyl _____ . Ned Penfold went home with Dick Purvey. Mr Jeremiah Dodson had a cord of wood deliver'd per Ned May and G Scrase. Sold Anthony Heal of Lindfield a runt at 6s to be kill'd before May Day. Receiv'd in hand 5s. Hollingall and William Charman thrasht clover. Tom Scrase and Ned May washt the 5 rams and 6 dry sheep in a tub. Half the load of wood carry'd to Mr Jeremiah Dodson was of John Gun's cutting.

The 7th April 1715 Thursday A very showry day. Ball workt half the day. Hollingham and William Charman made an end of thrashing clover. There was a bushel and three pecks. Paid Hollingham 2s-7½d for his share and 8d for his boy. Paid him also 7s-2½d for 7½ day's work so that there is 3½d due to him. Begun plough the Homefield to day but the rain beat us off about nine aclock. Stephen Bine's men John Stammer and Robert Gatland workt here. They cut down an elm in Tully's orchard and we brought him home and hew'd it. The little brown nos'd cow went to John Snashall's bull to day. I went to John Snashall's in the morning to see 2 bargans. We did not deal but he promis'd not to sell them 'till we had talkt again. I let the 2 yearling heifer bleed she being broak out all about the neck and throat and her eyes sore.

The 8th April 1715 Fryday A showry day, towards night very wet. Hollingham and his boy plough'd. Paid Ball 1s-6d for his work to day and before. Sow'd 2 quarters of barly in the Homefield. I borrow'd Goodman White's horse to day. My Cousin John Lindfield had 12 bushels of barly to day and three of my sacks. He sent home all my sacks he had before. My Cousin John Lindfield, Thomas Butcher and John Row were here a little before noon to buy my young horse but because of his poll we did not try to deal. William Charman thrasht barly.

The 9th April 1715 Saturday. A wet day. William Charman begun serve the 3 heifers. Win'd 9 bushels of William Charman's Churchfield barly being the last of the fields, in all 53 quarters 3 bushels. Carry'd 2 quarters, 3 bushels of wheat into Tully's garret. Nick Plaw was here and drenched the 2 yearling heifer. Paid him 2s that he had. Paid Young Gillham for mending my Grandfather's grave rail in Albourne churchyard. Mr Jeremiah Dodson came hither towards night. He supt and staid 'till 12.

The 10th April 1715 Sunday. A fine day. Mr Jeremiah Dodson preacht. My Cousin Peter Marchant of Lewis and his son din'd here. I outset 2s-6d which he paid John Sayers and 6d he paid me, in all 3s for a brace of fish he had of me per Ned Tester. Tom Scrase begun serve the cows to day. Jack Bartlet din'd here. Paid Henry Hooker £5-10-5d for half a year's Land Tax yesterday. Joseph Muzzall was here with him.

The 11th April 1715 Munday. A very fine day, only a short showr about 3 aclock. Hollingham and his boy plough'd. Sow'd 15 bushels of barly. Receiv'd a letter from Jude Storer and sent one to my Brother James Ede. I was at Mrs Catherine Beard's towards night. My Wife was at Wanbarrow.

The 12th April 1715 Tuesday. A very fine day. Hollingham and his boy plough'd. Paid Hollingham 4s-6d for his own and his boy's work 3 days. Sow'd 9½ bushels of barly in the Homefield, in all 5 quarters half a bushel. John Standbridge and Thomas Vinall workt here mending wattle etc. Mr Hasloup was here in the afternoon and my Sister Nanny. John Snashall was here towards night to dress the young horse. Ned May had 4 bushels of oates to night from Tully's for his horses.

The 13th April 1715 Wednesday. A fine day. William Michell sow'd 2 bushels and a gallon of course clover seed on the Homefield and we finish him. Receiv'd 2 barren heifers of John Snashall at £5. Paid William Michell 2s-6d for sowing seeds to day and before. Jack Bartlet had a bushel of wheat and 10s in mony. Mr John Hart and I din'd at Mr Jeremiah Dodson's with Mr

Healy and Mr Scutt. The calf of Nick Plaw's least cow dy'd this evning.

The 14th April 1715 Thursday. A showry day. Mr Healy din'd here. Jack Bartlet sow'd the field by Hyder's with 15½ bushels of barly and I _____ to sow it on the fallow because it plough'd very badly and I thought it the best season to, the fallow haveing been stirr'd just before Lady Tide. Mrs Catherine Beard, her mother and Mrs Mary Whitpaine were here in the afternoon. Paid Goodman Marten 8d for sheering 6 dry sheep and 5 rams. One of the rams is Mr Scrase's and I have markt him with 2 half moons on the rump.

The 15th April 1715 Good Fryday. A gloomy forenoon but very fine afternoon. Mr Jeremiah Dodson preacht. I were at Church in the forenoon. We finisht the barly field in the morning being the last of our season. The short tetted cow went to John Snashall's bull. Mrs Catherine Beard and her mother were here towards night. John Gun begun pole the hop garden. Turn'd my old heifer into the Nonsuch. Paid my Unkle Courtness 15d for a small bottle of Daffy's elixir.

The 16th April 1715 Saturday. A showry day. Sent a calves skin to John Hart per Ned May. Win'd 3 quarters of Jack Bartlet's homefield barly being the last of the field and makes in all 38 quarters 5 bushels on 7 acres. Note, half an acre of the field was sow'd with turnips. Deliver'd 4 quarters of it to Harry Wickham per William Charman and Tom Tully. Also they carry'd 4 quarters and a bushel of course barly thither to be malted for my self. Turn'd the 2 heifers from John Snashall's into the Nine Acres. The long tetted cow calv'd a bull calf to day.

The 17th April 1715 Sunday. A fine day. Easter Sunday. Mr Jeremiah Dodson preacht. I did not go to Church because not well, nor my Wife because the least child was ill. Mrs Catherine Beard, Mrs Mary Whitpaine, my Sister Nanny and Bett was here.

The 18th April 1715 Munday. A fine day. My Brother Peter and Thomas Field overseers and John Marchant and Mr Richard Whitpaine Church wardens past there accounts and all continu'd in their offices again. I were at Wanbarrow in the morning to finish my Brother Peter's accounts and carry'd them to Church because he could not go. My Cousin John Lindfield din'd here and he and I reckon'd. Receiv'd of him £3-5s in full of all accounts. Memorandum, he paid me £1-5s for half a year's intrest and also we did not reckon for 4 bushels of beans which I find on my book. Whether it had been paid before I know not. John Marchant was here and I paid him his Church land charges being 8s-6d which I am to have again of the parish. My Cousin John Lindfield, Mr John Hart and I went to Mr Jeremiah Dodson in the evning. Drank 3 bottles of clarret. Took 22 pidgeons at _____ about this time.

The 19th April 1715 Tuesday. A fine day, the wind very high. Turn'd the 7 twelve monthlings into the Churchfield Nonsuch. Receiv'd 4s-9d of Stephen Bine for 9½ foot of small knees. John Snashall dress'd the young horse's poll in the morning. Mr Healy was here in the morning but did not stay at all. Took 2 pidgeons to day. I sent my Brother Peter's accounts per John Snashall. Receiv'd £20 of Henry Wickham and £2-2-9d of Michael Stacey. I allow'd Michael Stacey 2s-6d for the damage of the barly. Mr John Hart was at Danny with Mr Jeremiah Dodson. My Sister Nanny came a little before noon. Mrs Catherine Beard, Mrs Scutt were here towards night. Ned Penfold went part of the way to Lewis with butter but the wind blew him off his horse so he came back again.

The 20th April 1715 Wednesday. The wind high. Ned May, 4 bushels of oates. My Wife, William Charman and Ned May went to Lewis. Tom Scrase and I took 8 carp out of the Hovelfield stew and put them into the flat stew and left the other stew dry. Mrs Catherine Beard, Mrs Stone and Mrs Scutt were here in the afternoon. My Sister Nanny came about noon. Mr John Hart went to Mr Watson's with Mr Jeremiah Dodson.

The 21st April 1715 Thursday. A dry windy day. Sent 2 bushels of oates to mill for the sow and 10 pigs. Deliver'd 2 quarters 3 bushels of barly to Henry Wickham per William Charman and Tully. I had a severe fitt of an ague to day. John Turner's wife, her sister, my Aunt Courtness and Mrs Susan Courthope were here in the afternoon. My Sister Nanny was here most part of the day and Bett in the afternoon. Captain Whitpaine's wife was buried this evning.
*(Ed: shown as Elizabeth Whitpaine in Hurst Parish Register)*

The 22nd April 1715 Fryday. A fine day but about ten aclock there was a total eclipse of the sun so that it was more dark than a moonlight night and continu'd so about the space of a minute and a half during which time it was likewise very cold and several stars were plain to be seen. Note, the eclipse was very visible for more a quarter of an hour. Before and after it was so dark. I were at Wanbarrow in the forenoon and were between Joseph Muzzall and John West's when it was so dark a goeing thither. Receiv'd a load of lime of Mr Burry. John Standbridge workt here. Fetcht 2 loads of sand from Michael Stacey's pitt. Last night the long tetted heifer calv'd a cow calf. Paid John Snashall £5 for his two barrens.

The 23rd April 1715 Saturday. A fine day. Brand's man made out my mortar yesterday. Thomas ____ man summon'd me for the sessions as Churchwarden for the year 1713 about the charitable use mony. I had a severe fit of an ague again to day. Receiv'd a letter from my Brother James Ede. Mrs Catherine Beard, her mother and Mrs Scutt were here this afternoon.

The 24th April 1715 Sunday. A very fine day. Mr Jeremiah Dodson preacht twice. My Cousin John Lindfield din'd here and paid me 13s for the beans that were forgot when we reckon'd. I were at Church in the afternoon. We had a parish meeting.

The 25th April 1715 Munday. A fine day. I had my ague more moderately. My Cousin Thomas Turner din'd here and my Sister Betty *(Ed: Thomas of Ditchling born 1693 was a first cousin to Thomas through the Chatfield family).*
She was here all day and staid all night.
Towards night Mr Scutt, Mr Richard Whitpaine and my Cousin John Lindfield came and staid 'till past 10. Mr John Hart treat'd them with punch. I gave my Cousin John Lindfield 4 guineas and 3 broad pieces to lay out for me at Crawley Fair. Agreed with Mr Scutt to keep his mare in the Nonsuch at 2s per week. The brown nosed heifer calv'd to day a cow calf. John Gun and George West drove the long tetted cow to John Snashall's bull but she was so little bulling that 'tis a question whether she will stand by it.

The 26th April 1715 Tuesday. A showry day. I cut the oldest bull calf. Anthony Neal fetcht the runt and paid me £5-15s in full. I was at Wanbarrow towards night. My Sister Betty went home. William Charman begun how beans about 3 aclock. Lent Mr Richard Whitpaine my great chain yesterday.

The 27th April 1715 Wednesday. A showry forenoon, the afternoon very wet. Ned May went to Crawley Fair after my Cousin John Lindfield. Nunnery boy was here and brought 2 large baskets at 3s-6d. He also brought a douzen of syder, a present from my Mother with the liberty to keep the bottles at 22d per douzen which we did. Mr Jeremiah Dodson and Mr Richard Whitpaine were here in the evning and staid late. Ned Penfold went to Lewis with butter and staid all night, being wet. Turn'd the three two yearlings steers into the Nonsuch yesterday and the two three yearlings into Tully's close in their room.

The 28th April 1715 Thursday. A very wet day. Ground 3½ bushels of oaten malt and 2½ of barly. Reckon'd with Stephen Bine and paid him £2-10-6d for work and all accounts. Receiv'd 4s of him for John Standbridge's bushel of wheat. Win'd 6 bushels of John Gun's head wheat at Hyder's and 1½ bushels tail. Jack Bartlet had a bushel of wheat at 3s-9d and bargain'd for 8 bushels more at 30s. I went to Mrs Catherine Beard's in the afternoon and staid about 2 hours.

The 29th April 1715 Fryday. A fine day only a short showr or two. I went to Thomas Harrison's to buy 2 calves but we did not deal. Paid Mr Jeremiah Dodson half a year's tythe but did not outset the wood 24s and a sack of oates at 7s which is to stand 'till Michaelmas. Mr Jeremiah Dodson spoke for 2 cord of wood and 100 faggots more. He supt here and staid 'till 10 aclock. Mrs Catherine Beard, my Grandmother and my Sister Nanny were here this afternoon. I bought a cow calf of Mrs Catherine Beard at a guinea to suck about a fortnight longer. Also agreed to keep her horse in the Nonsuch at 2s per week.

The 30th April 1715 Saturday. A showry day. Mrs Catherine Beard put her horse in the Nonsuch. Tom Scrase went away, I paid him 10s for his time. I bought 3 barrens of Mr Scrase at Pangdean at £8-5s and brought them home. I promis'd to pay for 'em in a week. William Charman how'd beans. My Sister Nanny was here in the afternoon. I was at Wanbarrow in the afternoon. I call'd at Mr Richard Whitpaine's as I came home and he assured me he had discharged the indictment about the charitable use mony for the year 1713.

The 1st May 1715 Sunday. A very wet morning and showry all day. Mr Jeremiah Dodson preacht. My Wife and I receiv'd the sacrament. There was no parish meeting for Mr Dodson was to go Twineham but the water was up so he came back again and we had prayrs. I went to Westtowne but Mr Richard Whitpaine was gone to Albourne. The biggest three yearling heifer calv'd a bull calf to day.

The 2nd May 1715 Munday. A gloomy morning but fine afternoon. Paid Roach 2s for his boy's work. We fetch a load of trundle pins out of Thomas Norton's wood for Stephen Bine and draw'd them up to the top of the hill by Mr Scrase's Nore in order to go to the Rock and when I have carry'd them thither I am to have 20s. To day or yesterday a ewe was lost in the ditch, markt the left side. Mr Hasloup din'd here but came just as we had din'd. Ned Penfold went to Lewis with butter, but they will take no more at 6d per lb. Receiv'd ¼lb of bohea tea of Mr Tourl per Ned Penfold. Ned May fetch my Brother Peter's two horses to help us to morrow.

The 3rd May 1715 Tuesday. A very fine day, the wind pretty high. We went to the Rock with the pins. I paid Mr Scrase £4-5s and order'd him to take £4 of John Bradford being in full for the barrens. My Cousin John Lindfield brought me two barrens at Lindfield Fair at £4-17-6d which I fetch to day from Thomas D_____. He gave me £2-19s again which makes up the mony I sent by him.

The 4th May 1715 Wednesday. A dry windy day. Sent 2 bushels of oates to mill for the sows. Sold my Cousin John Bodle Mr Scrase's ram at 14s. Sold him also 5 barren ewes at 10s per ewe. John Snashall was here and dresst the young horse. Jack Bartlet and William Charman workt half a day on the middle pond bay.

The 5th May 1715 Thursday. A showry day towards night very wet. Receiv'd 3s-8d of Young Tully of Bolny for ½ bushel of pease and as many beans. Jack Bartlet, John Gun, William Charman and Ned May workt on the pond bay. I went to John Snashall to see a calf for my Brother Peter but they had agreed for him before. Tom Tully fetch a peck of barly from Nick Plaw's. Mr Jeremiah Dodson's tythe feast was to day, I was not there. John Standbridge workt here half a day.

The 6th May 1715 Fryday. A dry day. My Cousin John Lindfield sent for the cow at £4. Jack Bartlet, John Gun, William Charman and Ned May workt on the pond bay.

Mr Burry and his sister were here in the afternoon. John Snashall was here to dress the young horse. Paid Mr Burry 11s for a load of lime.

The 7th May 1715 Saturday. A very fine day, a brisk wind. John Gun, Jack Bartlet and William Charman workt on the pond bay. Put Mr Scrase's 7 barrens and one of them my Cousin John Lindfield brought into the Nine Acres. Put two 4 yearlings into the Nonsuch and took the Duke horse out. Put the sheep and lambs into Tully's farther field. I let the cart horse and my old horse blood. I went to Wanbarrow in the afternoon. My Brother Will was here about 5 aclock. Paid William Nicholas 2s-6d for his clerk's wages £10 for Little Park and West Edgerly. Ned May and Tom Tully fetch my malt from Harry Wickham's. There was bushels of 4 quarters and a bushel of barly. Paid the Widdow Tully 6s-6d that is 5s for Tom's work and 18d for hers. Ned Penfold was at Lewis with butter, it yielded but 5d per lb. Mrs Catherine Beard fetch her horse out of the Nonsuch.

The 8th May 1715 Sunday. A gloomy dry day. Mr William Martin preacht in the forenoon. Turn'd the cows to pasture in the Hovelfield. Mr John Hart and I went to Westtowne towards evning. We supt there and staid 'till almost 10 aclock. Mr William Martin preacht at Albourne in the afternoon.

The 9th May 1715 Munday. A dry windy day. The least of Nick Plaw's cows went to my Brother Peter's bull. Bignall begun work on the new pond about 8 aclock at 14d per day. John Standbridge and Robert Gatland workt at the lower end of Tully's ground. Ned May parted the sheep in 4 parcels and rol'd the oates. Ned May had 2 bushels of oates yesterday. Sold my Cousin John Bodle 2 runts at £11-5s and their tongues, one to be kill'd before Whitsun Tide and the other in a fortnight after. My Wife and I, Bett and Jacky went to _____ in the afternoon and Mr John Hart, but my Cousin Thomas Turner and my Cousin _____ were gone from home.

The 10th May 1715 Tuesday. A fine day. Bignall workt on the new pond to day an yesterday. John Standbridge and Robert Gatland workt here. Ned May sold the oates. My Sister Nanny was here towards night. Jack Bartlet had 5s to day. He and William Charman mended hedges.

The 11th May 1715 Wednesday. A wet morning, the rest of the day dry. Ned May drove Plaw's great cow to the bull but she would stand. Put all the beasts out of the Nonsuch except the horse. Receiv'd a heifer calf of Mrs Catherine Beard at a guinea. John Bodle kill'd the brown nosed heifer's calf at 2d per lb and I am to have a qarter (or half)a guinea at ____ price and the bell for nothing. My Brother Peter's sheep that I saw weigh'd at John Smith's weigh'd 11 nail 3 pound, alive, hard weight. Deliver'd half a cord of wood and 50 faggots to Mr Jeremiah Dodson. Dick Wood set a new payr of shooes on my old horse's forefeet.

The 12th May 1715 Thursday. A dry windy day. Bignall and John Gun workt on the new pond. Weigh'd the calf at John Bodle's and he weigh'd jst 14½lbs per qarter. I had a side again and the bell and runnet. Turn'd the working oxen to pasture. Borrow'd 3 mud casters of Mr Peter Courthope. Jack Bartlet and William Charman mended hedges. I was at Wanbarrow towards night.

The 13th May 1715 Fryday. A dry windy day, only a showr or two afternoon. John Gun, Jack Bartlet, William Charman, Ned May, my Cousin John Lindfield, Haslegrove the flax dresser, Tully, Bonner, Ball, Bignall, Coates and John Standbridge workt on the new pond. Paid Ball 14d for his day's work. Mrs Catherine Beard and her mother were here in the afternoon. Paid Mrs Catherine Beard a guinea for her calf and receiv'd 2s for her horse. John Snashall dresst the young horse.

The 14th May 1715 Saturday. A fine day. Turn'd Plaw's great cow to pasture. John Standbridge, Bignall, Haslegrove, Bonner, Coates, John Gun, William Charman, Ned May and Tom Tully workt on the new pond. Paid Bignall 5s-8d, Coates 2s-4d, Bonner 2s, left 4d due to him. I gave Haslegrove 1s. Paid Mr Courtness 5d for 25 doubletons. Mr Peter Courthope's man fetcht 2 of his mud casters again. Dr White call'd here in the afternoon and upon my reqest went to see Jack Bartlet's boy that was ill. Jack Bartlet workt but little above half a day on the pond. Stephen Reeve fetcht a piece weigh'd 10lbs net and all.

The 15th May 1715 Sunday. A fine forenoon, gloomy after with little or no rain. Mr William Martin preacht twice. I supt at Mrs Catherine Beard's. My Wife call'd me as she came from Wanbarrow. Mr Henry Campion was jst gone and had sent me 5 pamphlets per Mr John Hart.

The 16th May 1715 Munday. A dry forenoon but wet afternoon. John Standbridge, Robert Gatland, John Gun, William Charman and Bonner workt on the new pond 'till 4 aclock. Paid Bonner 16d which is all was due to him. Sold Henry Dubbins of Brighton a runt at £5-2-6d. He is to fetch him this day fortnight. Mr John Hart and my Wife reckon'd and clear'd all accounts for board and schooling to Lady Day last. Nunnery boy came a Saturday night and went home yesterday morning. He carry'd home a pig. Mr Beaumont din'd here but did not stay long after. Ysterday I lent my old dog Porter to my Cousin Turner of Old Land *(Ed: this is probably 1st cousin Richard born 1689)*. Turn'd the 4 fatting oxen to pasture in the Nonsuch. My Cousin Bull Widdow of Albourne Street dyed this evning. Reckon'd with Thomas Westover about this time and clear'd all accounts, only he left 14s in my hands for a load of wood and faggots to be deliver'd this Sumer.

The 17th May 1715 Tuesday. A fine day. Roach's boy fetch home the founder'd mare. John Gun, Robert Gatland, Ned May and Tom Tully workt on the new pond. My Aunt Turner *(Ed: Sarah née Chatfield of Old Land)*, my Cousin Dungate, my Cousin Plump and my Cousin Thomas Turner *(Ed: son of Richard and Sarah, born 1693)* were here this afternoon. Jack Bartlet had a bushel of wheat at 2s-9d. The biggest of Mr Scrase's barrens went to bull. Westtowne.

The 18th May 1715 Wednesday. A fine day. Cropt 10 sheep of both ears. John Gun, Robert Gatland and Tully workt on the new pond and also Jack Bartlet. Ned May went to Brighton to have the great saddle mended. My Wife and I was at Goodman Hooker's and call'd Westtowne and supt here. William Charman and I took 46 store carp out of the hole in the Middle Piece and 7 tench and put them in the Marldfield stew.

The 19th May 1715 Thursday. A fine day. Jack Bartlet had half a bushel of malt. Turn'd the fatting oxen into the field by Hyder's. Turn'd Jack Bartlet's steers into the Churchfield. William Lashmer and Anne Taylor marry'd. Lent Mrs Catherine Beard a key to the gates through the ground. John Gun, Jack Bartlet and Tully workt on the new pond. John Bodle kill'd Mr Scrase's ram at 14s. My

Wife and I, my Sons William and John set out for Nunnery about 11 aclock.

The 20th May 1715 Fryday. A fine day. My Wife and I and the boy went to Horsham. Paid Robert Hurst 6s for making my great coat and for buckeram, silk etc. Mrs Pryaulx and her daughter were at Nunnery towards night. Reckon'd with my Mother Stone and there remains due to me £1-2-6d which she did not pay. John Gun, Jack Bartlet and Tully workt on the new pond.

The 21st May 1715 Saturday. A fine day. We return'd from Nunnery late. John Gun, Jack Bartlet and Tully workt on the new pond. Mrs Kettilby and Mrs Bell's sister came to Mrs Catherine Beard to day.

The 22nd May 1715 Sunday. A fine day. Mr William Martin preacht twice. I went to Wanbarrow after evning prayr and call'd at Mrs Catherine Beard's as I came home. Staid 'till 10 aclock.

The 23rd May 1715 Munday. A very fine day. John Snashall dresst the young horse. John Gun, Jack Bartlet and Tully workt on the new pond. John Gold was here and paid me 46s for keeping his tags and 5s for 2 bushels of pease being in full of all accounts. I agreed with him to keep 25 tags next winter. John Standbridge and Robert Gatland workt here setting up posts and rails all day a Fryday last and half Saturday. _____
Bonner workt carrying dung with William Charman and Ned May out of the home close, 36 loads. The founder'd mare went to John Hart's horse this evning. I went to see my Brother Peter's court bushes. My Wife was at Wanbarrow and my Sister Nanny came home with her. Receiv'd 18d of R Kester towards ½ bushel of course pease at 21d.

The 24th May 1715 Tuesday. A gloomy windy day, some rain after noon. John Gun, Jack Bartlet and Tully workt on the new pond. Bonner, William Charman and Ned May carry'd dung, 30 loads. Sold Old John Smith 36 lambs and 3 rams at £19-10s all to be gone by Midsumer. Receiv'd a guinea in hand. Mr John Hart went to Mr Burry. I was invited but could not go. John Bodle kill'd the great heifer's calf. He weigh'd 71lbs at 2d per lb. Mr Richard Whitpaine was here towards night.

The 25th May 1715 Wednesday. A very fine day. Laid out 8s at Mr Court's. My Wife and I and my Sister Betty went to Lewis. Paid a bill at Mr Tourl's of 26s. John Gun, Jack Bartlet and Tully workt on the new pond. The two yearling heifers went to Whitpaine's bull. The runt cow calved a bull calf to day. My Wife had £15 of me to day.

The 26th May 1715 Holy Thursday. A very fine day. I took a purge to day. William Charman and Ned May kept holy day. I was at Wanbarrow in the afternoon. Mr John Hart rode the ball mare to Lewis. Nick Goffe's Widdow and Nick Plaw's wife were at Wanbarrow.

The 27th May 1715 Fryday. A very fine day. Dick Wood shooe'd the young horse. John Gun, Jack Bartlet and Betty workt on the new pond. Bonner, William Charman and Ned May carry'd dung, 40 loads. I went to Counsellor Burrell's for my Brother Peter and paid him 10s for my Brother. Call'd at Dean House as I return'd and staid 'till near 9 aclock.

The 28th May 1715 Saturday. A very fine day. William Charman washt the sheep. Bonner, William Charman and Ned May carry'd dung half the day and finisht the upper close. They carry'd 28 loads. All the dung in the upper close is 142 loads without the stable dung. Bonner and Ned May helpt wash the sheep. John Gun and Tully workt on the new pond. Jack Bartlet workt on the flat stew. Mr Henry Campion and Mr Beaumont came to see me this afternoon and Mr William Martin came to see Mr John Hart. Mr Jeremiah Dodson came in about 5 aclock to speak with Mr Henry Campion and staid about an hour. Mr Healy came about the same time and they went also away about 9 aclock. Mr Richard Whitpaine was here towards noon and desir'd me to accompany my Cousin John Lindfield to his house in the afternoon but he did not call me.

The 29th May 1715 Sunday. Mr William Martin preacht twice. A fine day. I went to Wanbarrow in the afternoon and call'd at Mrs Catherine Beard's as I went. My Brother Peter paid me the 10d I gave Mr Burrel 10s. I call'd at Westtowne as I came home and supt there with Mr Healy, Mr John Hart and Mr Scutt and Nick Plaw. John Bodle fetcht a runt this evning. Receiv'd the 2 guineas of Mr John Hart that I lent him.

The 30th May 1715 Munday. A fine day. Mr John Hart set out for London and thence to Cambridge. John Gun, John Haslegrove and Tully workt on the new pond.

Turn'd the 2 four yearlings to the fatting oxen at Hyder's. Also Plaw's great cow to the fatting cows. Bonner, William Charman and Ned May carry'd dung out of the fatting close, 39 loads. Paid Bonner 5s-10d being all that is due to him.

The 31st May 1715 Tuesday. A very fine day. Henry Dubbins fetcht the runt I sold him and paid for him. Sold him and John Bull an other runt at £5-15s to be kill'd in a fortnight at farthest. John Gun, Haslegrove and Tully workt on the new pond. Jack Bartlet and Ned May carry'd dung out of the fatting close half the day, 12 loads, in all 51 loads. John Bodle brought the runt again from Horsham Fair. Agreed with Jack Bartlet to carry the dung out of Tully's close for 5s and to lay it behind the stable. John Snashall was here in the morning to dress the young horse but did not dress him because he thought it grow'd up but it run again a little in the afternoon and it is the seaventh journey he has had to him. John Gun and Haslegrove stak't faggots against the middle pond bay.

The 1st June 1715 Wednesday. A very fine day. John Snashall dresst the young horse. Sold John Snashall the hip fall'n cow at £4-10s to have her next Munday. I sold her at Wanbarrow in the morning. William Charman begun thrash wheat at noon. Ned May and I carry'd a load of Kester's flints into the highway. John Gun and Jack Haslegrove workt on the lower pond bay after they had done winnowing. Win'd 17 bushels of John Gun's wheat per Hyder's. Jack Bartlet begun carry the dung out of Tully's close. Mrs Kettilby, Mrs Betty Lister, Mrs Catherine Beard and her mother were here in the afternoon. Turn'd the 3 yearling steers into Tully's cow field. Jack Bartlet had 4 bushels of wheat at 3s-9d a bushel. The long tetted cow went to bull again to Edgly bull but she is not likely to stand by it. Paid Jack Haslegrove 3s-6d for 3 day's work. Mr Povey came at night to Mrs Catherine Beard etc and went home with them.

The 2nd June 1715 Thursday. A gloomy forenoon, fine afternoon. Paid Jack Haslegrove 7d for half a day's work. John Bodle fetcht the runt again last night haveing sold him to the Brighthelmstone butchers. William Charman thrasht wheat and Jack Bartlet carry'd dung. Put the yearlings into the Churchfield. Receiv'd a letter from Mr John Hart from London. Paid Goodman Marten 21d for shearing 35 sheep. Also sent 32s by him to Mr Ewins for 8 bushels of seed pease. I went to Mr Richard Whitpaine's towards night and reckon'd with him and there was due to me £5-13-9d which he paid me. We did not reckon for the hops nor the things my Wife bought for Mrs Mary Whitpaine. Ned May fetcht a bushel of oates from Tully's.

The 3rd June 1715 Fryday. A very fine day, only a short showr in the morning. Lent my Brother Peter the blind mare. My Father Stone sent for a payr of 3 yearlings that I lent him. I sent the two steers I bought of my Brother Will. Ned May and I took 45 carp and 6 tench out of the Marldfield stew and put them in the new pond. Put 2 large carp, one large tench, 3 carp 10 inches and one small tench into the Marldfield stew again. Jack Bartlet carry'd dung and William Charman thrasht wheat. Put 3 three yearling steers to the working oxen. Mrs Mary Whitpaine paid my Wife the mony she laid out for her. Jack Bartlet made an end of the dung in Tully's close, in all 70 loads. My Wife went to Wanbarrow towards night. John Bodle turn'd a horse into the Nonsuch to night at 1s per week.

The 4th June 1715 Saturday. A showry day. William Charman thrasht wheat. Ned May and I carry'd 2 loads more of Kester's flints into the highway. Paid Kester 3s for picking up 3 loads of flints. Sent home John Bodle's horse at night per Ned May. May ground 3 bushels of barly malt. Jack Bartlet cast the dung at John Bodle's. Reckon'd with Jack Bartlet and clear'd the account this morning. Dick Wood dock't the sorrel colt. Bodle's horse was a rig and cover'd the little mare which was the reason I sent him home.

The 5th June 1715 Whit Sunday. A very fine day. Mr William Martin preacht twice. We had no meeting in the afternoon. I went to Westtowne towards night. There was Mr Henry Campion and Mr Scutt. We staid 'till 9 aclock. Ned May brought me a book from Mr Osbourne's, of fish etc to be return'd in a fortnight.

The 6th June 1715 Munday. A very fine day, only a showr about 3 aclock. John Snashall sent for per William Borer and J Guildford. Soon after he came to dress the young horse and paid me 30s and order'd me to take £3 of my Brother Peter. In the morning I let bleed three of the fatting oxen vizt Star and Peert and Broad. Bet and I rode to Wanbarrow. My Cousin Bodle of Hailsham and his wife din'd here and went towards night for Henfield. John Bodle turn'd an other horse into the Nonsuch. When I was at Wanbarrow they told me my Cousin John Goffe of Henfield was broak and run away.

The 7th June 1715 Tuesday. A very fine day. Sent 3 bushels of oaten malt to mill. Weigh'd one of the ewes John Bodle bought. She weigh'd 11lbs per quarter. Agreed with him to keep his horse in the hop garden at 2s per week. John Bodle fetcht the other runt haveing sold him to an other of the Brighton butchers. I was at Wanbarrow in the afternoon. There was John Wood of Yewhurst and my Brother William.

The 8th June 1715 Wednesday. A very fine day. William Charman thrasht wheat. I went to Wanbarrow in the morning. There was Ed Parr. He had bought my Brother's lambs, 40 at 9s-6d per lamb and 9 at 9s per lamb. Ned May and I carry'd a load of flints into the highway. Dr Woodward was here in the afternoon. My Sisters Nanny and Bett were here this afternoon. Tom Tully return'd from Nunnery and brought a letter from my Father wherein he appointed to meet me at Handcross a Tuesday next with his team for half a load of malt.

The 9th June 1715 Thursday. A very fine day. William Charman thrasht wheat. Mr Richard Whitpaine call'd me in the morning to go to Cuckfield Fair but I did not go with him. Ned May and I fetcht a load of great chalk. Paid Goodman Jordan and Wood 1s for digging it. Mrs Woodward, Mrs Gratwick, Mrs Stone, Mrs Catherine Beard, Mrs Kettilby and Mrs Lister came hither in the afternoon and Mr Henry Campion and his lady and Mrs Courthope (finding them from home) came after them. I sent for Dr Woodward to Mr Jeremiah Dodson's and Mr William Martin came with them. They all staid here 'till night. We went all to Mrs Catherine Beard's (except Mr William Martin). We supt there and staid late. Drank moderately. Tom Tully carry'd a bushel of oates to mill for the sow.

The 10th June 1715 Fryday. A showry day, last night very wet. The Pretender's birthday. Lent my Cousin Thomas Norton of Edgly 4 sacks per William Norton. Last night they sent a very mean pig from Wanbarrow. I was at Wanbarrow in the afternoon as I return'd from Harry Wickham's with whom I agreed for 5 quarters of malt for my Father Stone at 27s per quarter. I went to Danny about 5 aclock. There was Mrs Catherine Beard's family and Dr Woodward's. We staid 'till 11 aclock. Receiv'd 39s of Mr Henry Campion for 12 bushels of beans. Win'd 3 quarters 1½ bushels of William Charman's wheat per Hyder's which he had been 6½ thrashing.

The 11th June 1715 Saturday. A very fine day. Bett went to Greatham with Mrs Scutt. Paid Tom Howell 2s for this day's work. William Charman brought up 3 bushels of oates from Tully's. Receiv'd 10d of John Stone for 4 ox bowes. Receiv'd the sacks again.

The 12th June 1715 Sunday. A very fine day. Mr William Martin preacht twice. My Cousin John Lindfield din'd here.

The 13th June 1715 Munday. A fine day. Cut the least bull calf. Deliver'd 100 faggots to Thomas Westover at 13s paid for. Deliver'd 100 faggots to Dick Wood at 13s. Fetcht 5 quarters of malt from Harry Wickham's at £6-15s. Win'd 2½ bushels of the wheat per Hyder's being the last of the field, in all 9 quarters 6½ bushels. Carry'd 35 bushels of wheat into Tully's garret and 19 bushels before, in all 54 bushels. My Wife and I and Jack supt at Westtowne. Paid Thomas Roberds of Brighton 14d for leather and mending a saddle.

The 14th June 1715 Tuesday. A fine day. Borrow'd a horse of my Brother Peter. Carry'd the half load of malt to Handcross for my Father Stone whose team met us there. He brought a half tun to carry fish in and gave it me. Lent him one sack to carry half a bushel of pease in. About Fryday or Saturday last the old white sowe farrow'd 11 pigs. The young sowe farrow'd within this day or two but we cant find her pigs.

The 15th June 1715 Wednesday. A very fine day. Jack Bartlet a bushel of malt. Ned May and I fetcht 812 tiles from Marten's kiln for my self. In the afternoon we fetcht a load of small chalk. Mr Richard Whitpaine supt here. The young sowe's pigs were found to day, 3 of 'em.

The 16th June 1715 Thursday. A very fine day. Jack Bartlet begun mow. Ned May and I fetcht 2 loads of small chalk. Old William Brand his man and 3 boys workt on the pidgeon house. Robert Gatland workt here half the day. Paid William 8d that he spent at Lewis. I made a leather halter for the young horse. We lost our cart whip last night and Thomas Butcher found it.

Mr John Hart return'd from London. Paid Jack Bartlet 9½d due by mistake in the last reck'ning.

The 17th June 1715 Fryday. A very fine day. Brand, his man and 3 boys workt on the pidgeon house. Ned May and I fetcht 2 loads of small chalk. The Widdow Tully begun hay. Tom Tully went to Nunnery. Receiv'd a bushel of hair of John Hart per Tom Tully.

The 18th June 1715 Saturday. A very fine day. Fetch a load of small chalk. John Gun and Brand's daughter begun haying. I went to Bolny and agreed with Edward Jenner to dig sand stones for setting up my Father's tomb stones at 5s. I gave him 6d to drink that he might be the more carefull. He promis'd to get 'em ready in 10 days and to give me notice. I gave John Bodle leave to put a sheep in the Churchfield. My Wife went to Danny at night with a small basket of cherrys.

The 19th June 1715 Sunday. A very fine day. Mr William Martin preacht twice. My Cousin Bodle of Hailsham, his wife and daughter din'd here. I did not go to Church in the afternoon. Ned May rode the young horse to Henfield at night in an errand for my Cousin Bodle. Ned May fetcht 3 bushel of oates from Tully's 3 or 4 days ago and 2 bushels to day.

The 20th June 1715 Munday. A fine forenoon, a showr at noon, fine after. John Gun, Ned May and Tom Tully carry'd Tully's clover, 6 small load. Widdow Tully and Sarah Brand workt here, haying. I was at Wanbarrow in the forenoon and at Mrs Catherine Beard's in the afternoon. My Brother Peter was here in the afternoon but I (not being at home) did not see him. My Cousin Bodle, his wife and daughter went home this morning. Jack Bartlet and William Charman begun the Edgly Mead this morning.

The 21st June 1715 Tuesday. A very wet morning, the rest of the day dry. Jack Bartlet and William Charman did not mow to day. Mrs Stone, Mrs Catherine Beard, Mrs Kettilby and Mrs Lister were here to day. Dick Wood mov'd one of the young horse's fore shooes. Paid Marten 13s a Sunday last for the tiles.

The 22nd June 1715 Wednesday. A very wet forenoon, dry 'till near night. John Bull and Henry Dubbins sent for the runt per 3 boys. William Charman and Ned May begun fallow Tully's clover at 3 aclock. Jack Bartlet workt the afternoon turning the lower pond water. Will carry'd a basket of cherrys to Wanbarrow. Mrs Mary Whitpaine was here in the afternoon 'till 8 aclock. Young Stoneham had the founder'd mare to Ditcheling Comon.

The 23rd June 1715 Thursday. A showry day. William Charman and Ned May plough'd. Tom Tully carry'd 2 bushels of oates to mill. Jack Bartlet workt on the lower pond watering. Tully and I had a fatting heifer to Edgly bull. John Standbridge made a ladder. Old John Smith draw'd 36 lambs. Receiv'd of him £18-8-6d. Sold young John Smith the biggest of John Snashall's heifers at £5-10s to be kill'd in a fortnight and if she stay 3 weeks I am to have her tongue. Mr William Martin was to see Mr John Hart towards night. Paid Thomas Westover 9d for leather. Tully workt to day.

The 24th June 1715 Fryday. Midsumer, a wet forenoon, showry after. William Charman and Ned May plough'd 'till noon, kept holy day after. Borrow'd my Cousin John Lindfield's bull per Will and Tom Tully. Paid the Widdow Tully 6s-2d for Tom's work to Saturday last. I went to Wanbarrow towards night and paid my Mother half a year's thirds due at Lady Day last. Paid my Sister Sarah a year's intrest, she gave me 5s. Receiv'd 2s-10d of my Mother for half a pound of coffee.

The 25th June 1715 Saturday. A showry day. I bad Mrs Storer £150 for her house. William Charman and Ned May plough'd part of the day. Reckon'd with Harry Wickham and clear'd all accounts. The Widdow Tully, Tom Tully and Sarah Brand hay'd about 3 hours.

The 26th June 1715 Sunday. A dry day, only a short showr towards night. Mr William Martin preacht twice. Mrs Courthope was here in the afternoon. My Cousin John Lindfield and his wife Elizabeth and Mr Healy supt here. Joseph Muzzall gave notice of a Court Baron a Tuesday next.

The 27th June 1715 Munday. A fine day, only flying showrs but miss'd us. William Charman and Ned May made an end of Tully's fallow by 2 aclock. The Widdow Tully, her son and Sarah Brand and John Gun hay'd. Jack Bartlet mow'd thistles 'till 2 aclock, hay'd afterwards. My Wife went to Westtowne towards night.

The 28th June 1715 Tuesday. A very fine day. Jack Bartlet and William Charman mow'd. John Gun and Ned May carry'd 2 small load of hay out of the hop garden. Widdow Tully, her son and Sarah Brand hay'd. Mrs Scutt was here in the afternoon. Sent home Mr Osbourne's book per Mr Scutt. Tom Hart put a horse in the Churchfield at 1s per week.

The 29th June 1715 Wednesday. A very windy day with flying showrs. Widdow Tully, Sarah Brand and Parker's wife hay'd half a day. John Gun and Ned May fetch a load of great chalk of that we brought down in the dray. Paid Wood 1s for it. Turn'd the cows into the hop garden. Tom Tully workt all day. Paid Mr Courtness 4d for a rake yesterday and 1½ for a rubber (?) to day. I saw my Cousin John Lindfield's cow weigh'd at John Smith's. She weigh'd 12 stone 3 quarter and a pound over in the whole bullock. John Bodle took the horse out of the Churchfield and put an other into the hop garden at 2s per week. Brew'd 2 bushels of barly malt.

The 30th June 1715 Thursday. A very wet day. Bottled most part of the last tub of elder wine. Jack Bartlet and William Charman mow'd about half an acre. John Gun workt part of the day, Tom Tully also. Sent 2 bushels of oates to mill and brought up a bushel whole.

The 1st July 1715 Fryday. A very wet day. Tom Tully workt all day. William Charman and Jack Bartlet mow'd but little. Receiv'd 7 lambs my Cousin John Lindfield bought for me at Midsumer Fair at 3s-10d per lamb. Will had one of 'em. Nick Plaw was here in the afternoon. I sold him 40 bushels of wheat at £5-15s to be deliver'd at his house. John Gun workt half the day mowing the court etc.

The 2nd July 1715 Saturday. A gloomy day, wet towards night. Widdow Tully, Sarah Brand and Parker's wife hay'd from 10 aclock to 5. Tom Tully workt all day. Reckon'd with John Gun and clear'd all accounts to Midsumer. Paid John Gun £3-6-6d. He workt all day. Jack Bartlet and William Charman mow'd.

The 3rd July 1715 Sunday. A showry day. Mr William Martin preacht twice. My Cousin John Lindfield was here after evning prayr. Mr John Hart, my Wife and I supt at Mr Scutt's.

The 4th July 1715 Munday. A dry forenoon, very wet towards night. Receiv'd ¼lb of tea of Mr Tourl per Nick Marchant. Receiv'd 4s of Old Hyder for 8lbs of wool.

Sent 6lbs of wool to Widdow Webb for the parish at 6d per lb. Marten at Cuckfield shore the above written lambs and 2 of my own. Paid him 7d for it. Jack Bartlet and William Charman made an end of mowing the Edgly Mead at noon and begun the lower pond. Widdow Tully, her son, Parker and Brand workt 'till 4. John Gun and Ned May hay'd and at night screen'd a load of wheat. My Brother James Ede came hither toward night haveing brought his unkle Thomas Ede's wife to Mrs Catherine Beard's.

The 5th July 1715 Tuesday. A dry day 'till towards night and then very wet. Widdow Tully, Parker and Brand made yesterday a whole day and workt 'till about 4 aclock in the afternoon. Deliver'd the load of wheat to Nick Plaw per John Gun and Ned May. I paid Mr Warden 2s for entring and my licence to bring of my wheat and 1s for 3 loads at a groat per load. Jack Bartlet and William Charman ended the pond.

The 6th July 1715 Wednesday. Very wet last night and this morning, the afternoon fine. Reckon'd with Dick Wood and clear'd all accounts. Agreed with Jack Bartlet to mow the hither Marldfield thistles at 1s. My Brother James Ede went home about 4 aclock. Mr Colebrand of Brighton call'd here and went with him in his way to London. Widdow Tully and Sarah Brand workt this afternoon. Jack Bartlet and William Charman hay'd from 5 aclock. John Gun sick. Lent Brother Peter the blind mare to go to Handcross to morrow. Mr William Martin came hither with Mr Colebrand.

The 7th July 1715 Thursday. A wet day. Lent Old William Brand's wife 12s-3d. Paid Old John Smith 3s-4d for 2lbs of hops. Bought Mrs Storer's house of her at £150 to enter at Michaelmas next. Also brought a large peese for cloaths of her for 100 faggots and half a cord of roots. Mr John Hart went to Fiseek(?). Agreed with Jack Bartlet to mow the thistles in the field below Tully's fallow for 18d. I went to Wanbarrow towards night.

The 8th July 1715 Fryday. A fine forenoon, a very great showr about 3 aclock. Widdow Tully, Parker, Brand workt half a day. Tom Tully also deliver'd a cord of roots to Mrs Storer per William Charman and Ned May. James Storer was here towards night and confirmed the bargain I had made with his mother. Sent home my Cousin John Lindfield's bull per Tom Tully. Brought home one cord of roots to day and one cord before. Jack Bartlet workt half a day mowing the New Orchard.

The 9th July 1715 Saturday. A dry forenoon, the afternoon very wet. Dick Wood shooed the stag. Brought home 2½ cord of roots. I was at Mrs Catherine Beard's towards night. Staid about an hour.

The 10th July 1715 Sunday. A fine day only a showr about noon. Mr Jeremiah Dodson preacht twice. My Cousin Thomas Norton of Edgly was here after evning prayr. Ned May went to Nunnery in the morning, Return'd late and brought me 6 guineas from my Father in part for the malt.

The 11th July 1715 Munday. A very fine morning and all day dry. John Bodle paid me £11-5s. He also kill'd the black runt's calf. I was at Wanbarrow in the morning. Jack Bartlet and William Charman begun the Little Mead by the middle piece and hay'd the afternoon. Paid Parker's wife 2s. Lent John Bodle my Murrols and Martingale. Mr Henry Campion went through the ground in his way to Horsham. John Gun, Parker's wife, Sarah Brand, Widdow Tully and Tom Tully hay'd all day. William Stephens a journey man shoomaker and Thomas Challoner workt from half an hour after 3 aclock.

The 12th July 1715 Tuesday. A very fine hot day, only a showr about 6 aclock. Carry'd 9 loads of hay out of the Edgly Mead into Tully's rick. John Gun, Kneller, Stephens, Thomas Challoner, Mr Holden, Parker, Brand, Widdow Tully, her son, Hollingham's boy, Ned May and one Richard Brand that came from about Chichester hay'd all day 'till it rain'd and workt (most of 'em) afterwards. Paid Richard Brand 1s. Thomas Hart took his horse out of the Nonsuch. Weigh'd the runt's calf and he weigh'd 23½lbs per quarter only wanted half a pound in one quarter at 4d per pound. We weigh'd him yesterday with the skin gambrel backset and foot just as he hung drest. He weigh'd 15 nail ½ pound. Jack Bartlet and William Charman mow'd. Brand mow'd for Jack Bartlet in the morning.

The 13th July 1715 Wednesday. A very fine day. Jack Bartlet and William Charman mow'd. John Smith kill'd the biggest of John Snashall's heifers yesterday. He told me she weigh'd just 16 stone per quarter. All those that hay'd yesterday hay'd to day. Carry'd ten loads of hay to the rick in the southeast corner of the Fifteen Acres out of the Edgly Mead. I was at Wanbarrow in the forenoon. Receiv'd a tongue of John Smith.

The 14th July 1715 Thursday. A very fine hot day. The same work'd to day as yesterday and Goody Hollingam Carry'd 8 loads of hay out of the Edgly Mead, 4 to the rick in the Fifteen Acres and 4 to that in Tully's rick steddle. I went to Lewis to the sessions and got off my self and my Cousin John Lindfield for 2s-6d a piece. dinner and expences 26d. Paid Mr Tourl 10s-10d in full of all accounts, 4s being for ¼lb tea for my Brother Peter. Receiv'd Jude Storer's purchase deed for the Black Lyon of Mrs Swaine of Lewis for which I gave a note of my hand. I spoke with Mr Lindfield of Horsham for my Brother Peter and left the depositions of Richard Heath etc with him.

The 15th July 1715 Fryday. A very fine hot day. Stephen Bine's maid workt to day. Widdow Tully, her son, Hollingham and her son, Parker, Sarah Brand, Richard Brand, Thomas Smith and Holden and John Gun workt all day. Kneller, Stephens, Jack Bartlet and William Charman carry'd hay half the day. Carry'd one load of hay out of Edgly Mead to the fatting rick, 7 loads thither out of the way mead and 2 loads out of the Little Mead by the Middle Piece only there was about 2 lain brought out of the way mead and made up in the Little Mead the last load set in the barne to be unloaded to morrow.

The 16th July 1715 Saturday. A fine day. Stephens workt the afternoon. John Gun, Sarah Brand, Richard Brand, Widdow Tully, Tom Tully, Parker and Young Hollingham workt all day. Carry'd 5 loads out of the Little Mead below the way mead to the fatting rick and set a small load in the barne out of the dry pond. Mr Hasloup was to see Mr John Hart. My Wife was at Danny towards night. Paid Richard Brand 5s-8d in full at 16d per day and agreed for next week at 15d per day. Jack Bartlet and William Charman mow'd 'till 6 aclock, then helpt cart hay.

The 17th July 1715 Sunday. A fine day. Mr William Martin preacht twice. Receiv'd 2s-6d of my Cousin John Lindfield that I paid for him at Lewis. My Brother Peter was here after evning prayr.

The 18th July 1715 Munday. A dry day. Widdow Tully, Tom Tully, Young Hollingham, Sarah Brand, Richard Brand, John Gun and Thomas Challoner workt to day.

Carry'd 3 loads of hay out of the dry pond and unloaded that was set in the barne, also 2 loads out of the Little Mead by the Middle Piece and 2 loads out of the Edgly Mead all to the lean oxen's rick by the home close. Jack Bartlet and William Charman mow'd. Ned May and I fetcht 750 bricks from Marten's at the Comon for Thomas Westover at 7s per thousand to the house by Barestake that was Thomas Reeves. The biggest 3 yearling heifers went to Edgly great bull. Paid my Lord Treep 3s-6d for cleaning guns, pistols etc.

The 19th July 1715 Tuesday. A dry day. Widdow Tully, her son, Hollingham and her son, Sarah Brand, Richard Brand and John Gun workt to day. Carry'd 2 loads to the fatting rick out of the Little Mead, one load to Stephen Bine's Cobbs Croft and one load to John Bodle at 20s per load both out of the Little Mead. Receiv'd 20s of Stephen Bine for his load. Jack Bartlet and William Charman made an end of the Little Mead. Dick Wood shoo'd the young horse, round.

The 20th July 1715 Wednesday. A gloomy, windy day. Henfield Fair day. John Gun and Richard Brand workt 'till noon. They cut the rick by Tully's house and that at the lower end of the Mead. Paid Robert Pierce 3s for putting a new bottom in the rain water tub and 1s for hooping it. Mr John Hart and I was at Mr Richard Whitpaine's. He was from home. Jack Bartlet and William Charman mow'd in the Bankfield 'till 4 aclock. Widdow Tully and her son and cut White's pease. I carry'd home Mr Richard Whitpaine's rick prong.

The 21st July 1715 Thursday. A fine day. Jack Bartlet and William Charman made an end of Bankfield. John Gun and Widdow Tully, Tom Tully, Sarah Brand, Young Hollingham hay'd. John Norton, his wife and her mother were here towards night and staid about an hour. Thomas Norton's wife and her mother were here in the afternoon and he came for them at night. Mr Henry Campion, Mrs Catherine Beard, Mrs Kettilby and Mrs Lister was angling in my pond. I went to Mrs Catherine Beard with them in the evning. Staid 'till 11 aclock.

The 22nd July 1715 Fryday. A gloomy day, windy but no rain. John Gun, Kneller, Stephens, Thomas Challoner, Richard Brand, Sarah Brand, Parker's wife, Widdow Tully, her son, Hollingham and her son hay'd all day. Carry'd 4 loads out of the Little Meads and 2 loads out of the Bankfield all to the rick by the home close. Jack Bartlet and William Charman begun mow Tully's Mead. Mr Ede of Aldhurst was here towards night. Mrs Scutt was here towards night. Mr Henry Campion and Mrs Catherine Beard's family and Mr Osbourne went to Brighton all day. They staid late but did not go a strugging because the sea was rough.

The 23rd July 1715 Saturday. A dry day. Deliver'd a load of roots to Jack Bartlet per Ned May. I was at Wanbarrow in the morning. John Gun, Richard Brand, Sarah Brand, Widdow Tully, her son, young Hollingham workt all day, only Widdow Tully and Hollingham begun at 10 aclock. I sent a letter to my Brother James Ede. John Bodle and Mary Dean's man of Brighton was here to buy my sheep but we did not deal. Ned May and Richard Brand brought home about 50 faggots. Jude Storer of Guildford came hither at night. He consented to the bargain I had made with his mother.

The 24th July 1715 Sunday. A fine day. Mr Denham preacht twice. My Cousin John Lindfield and Jude Storer din'd here. I did not go to Church in the afternoon. After evning prayr Mr Burry and my Brother Peter were here. Paid Richard Brand 5s-7½d in full for work done last week. Mr Henry Campion was at Church forenoon and afternoon.

The 25th July 1715 Munday. St James's Day. The forenoon gloomy, fine afternoon. Paid Mr Holden 4s for 4 day's work. John Gun, Stephens, Sarah Brand, Widdow Tully and her son, Hollingham and her son and Ned May workt all day. Jack Bartlet and William Charman mow'd 'till 8 aclock then carry'd hay. They carry'd 2 loads out of the Little Meads and 3 out of the Bankfield 1½ to the rick by the home close and 3½ to the rick behind the yearling hovel in the hop garden. John Gun and Stephens carry'd 3 loads out of the Little Meads and three loads out of the Bankfield. 2½ they unloaded at the rick by the home close and 3½ at the aforesaid rick behind the hovel. John Gun and Stephens also carry'd a load of white pease which they set in Tully's barne. Jack Bartlet and William Charman set near half a load of the same in the wheat barne. Mrs Scutt and my Wife went after dinner to Thomas Norton in the North End and about 4 aclock Mr Scutt and I went to fetch them home. We got home about 9. Mr John Hart went to Lewis and about 9 came home. He brought me ¼lb of tea from Mr Tourl.

The 26th July 1715 Tuesday. A fine day. Jack Bartlet and William Charman mow'd. John Gun, Stephens, Ned May, S Hollingham and her son, the Widdow Tully and her son workt all day. Carry'd 2 small loads out of the Bankfield and 4 out of the Little Meads all to the rick behind the hovel. John Gun and Stephens unloaded the load of pease in Tully's stable. Paid William Stephens 11s for all his work at 18d per day. About this time there was a great talk that the Duke of Ormond went off at Shoreham with Sir Harry Goring, Mr Midleton and one or two more who went of a Saturday as 'tis said, 'twas also reported Mr Henry Campion went with them but that is false whatever the rest be. *(Ed: Colonel Sir Harry Goring was suspected of Jacobite sympathies. In June 171, as a result of political pressure, he lost his seat in the House of Commons and three months later was obliged to sell his commission. On his retirement Sir Harry, then 36, returned to Sussex. When he died at Horsham on 12th November 1731 at the age of 52, he was the father of nine sons. Lady Goring survived him by another 37 years, and died at the age of 100.)*

The 27th July 1715 Wednesday. A fine day 'till five aclock then a showr. John Gun, Richard White, Ned May, Parker, Sarah Brand, Richard Brand, Widdow Tully, Tom Tully, Hollingham and her son workt all day. Widdow Tully and her son, Sarah Brand and Young Hollingham begun cut the grey pease, the women at 8d per day and the boys at 6d per day. Carry'd 6 loads of hay to the rick by the quince tree in Tully's rick steddle and one load to the rick lower side Tully's Mead, all out of Tully's Mead. Paid Richard Brand 1s for this day's work, he begun late. Jack Bartlet and William Charman made an end of Tully's Mead. Jack Bartlet was sick and Richard Brand mow'd after 5 aclock. Tom Picknall's boy begun tend hogs to day at 3d per day. I went to Stephen Bine in the evning, there was Mr Burry. Ground 6 bushels of barly malt. Paid Stephen Bine 6d for his maid's haying. Dick Wood let the young horse bleed.

The 28th July 1715 Thursday. A dry day. Chang'd the fatting beasts. John Gun, Richard Brand, Sarah Brand, Parker, Widdow Tully and her son, Hollingham and her son and William Charman and Ned May workt all day. Carry'd 3 loads out of Tully's Mead, one to the lower rick and 2 to the rick by the quince tree. Paid Richard White 1s for his work part of this day but forgot to pay for yesterday. Widdow Tully, her son, Sarah Brand, Hollingham and her son cut pease in the morning.

Picknall tended the hogs. Jack Bartlet gave me notice to night that he intended to leave my house and work at Lady Day next. I let my reaping to Jack Bartlet and John Gun (William Charman to go a share) at 4s-6d per acre for Tully's field, the field by Wickham's and 2 acres of the Rookwood and 3 acres of the Rookwood at 6s per acre, they to pitch all and if any want turning I am to do it half. John Standbridge workt here on the back dore. My Aunt Holden of Henfield was here in the afternoon.

The 29th July 1715 Fryday. A gloomy day. A showr in the afternoon. Jack Bartlet, John Gun and William Charman cut the fatting rick in the forenoon and in the afternoon begun reaping. I was at Wanbarrow in the forenoon. Receiv'd a small lot of bief of John Smith (I think 11 lbs) at 20d per nail and sold him a little brown runt heifer at £3-5s to be kill'd against Hurst Fair. I went to Westtowne in the afternoon after my Wife and met John Bodle and James Langford and sold the best score of my ewes to Langford for his Mrs Mary Dean of Brighton at £11 all to be gone by St Bartholomew's Day. Picknall tended the hogs. Receiv'd in hand 2s-6d. I supt at Mrs Catherine Beard's and stay'd 'till 11. James Langford drove 5 ewes home with him. Widdow Tully, her son and Sarah Brand cut pease for half a day. Paid Parker's wife 4s.

The 30th July 1715 Saturday. A fine day. The reapers workt all day. Widdow Tully, her son and Sarah Brand cut pease 'till 11 aclock. Afterwards hay'd and Ned May hay'd also. I was at Mrs Catherine Beard's in the morning and also in the evning. My Wife and Mrs Scutt went to Danny after my Sister Nanny went home. Ed Penfold went to Nunnery this afternoon. Parker's wife hay'd this afternoon and Elizabeth Tully.

The 31st July 1715 Sunday. A dry day. Mr William Martin preacht twice. My Mother and Sister Betty din'd here. Paid Richard Brand 15d for Thursday's work. Ed Penfold return'd from Nunnery. My Brother and I and my Wife were at Mrs Catherine Beard's after evning prayr.

The 1st August 1715 Munday. A wet day. King George's accession to the Crowne. My servants and workmen were at Church but I was not. John Gun, Jack Bartlet, William Charman, Ned May, Tom Tully workt allmost all day. Carry'd one load of hay of Tully's Mead to the rick southeast in Tully's rick steddle. Mrs Catherine

Beard and her family and Mrs Susan Courthope were here in the afternoon. John Edwards was here towards night. I let him my Tully's house where Jack Bartlet lives to enter at Lady Day next at 20s per annum and he is to serve out all the straw and hay that I set on that ground into the bargain. When I employ him by the day between Michaelmas and Lady Day 1 a.m. to give him 12d per day from Lady Day to Midsumer 14d, and in haying 16d per day, 18d an acre for mowing grass and 14d for clover. He is to live in part of Mrs Storer's house from Michaelmas to Lady Day next at 15s. I gave him one of the great sow's pigs. Deliver'd 50 faggots to John Gun per Ned May and himself.

The 2nd August 1715 Tuesday. A dry day, only a very great showr about 5 aclock afternoon. Paid John Gatland 1s for mending the clock and 1s for a new line. The reapers reap't 'till noon then John Gun fell sick. Jack Bartlet and William Charman reapt part of the afternoon. Paid John Kneller 5s-6d for 4 days and a piece at 16d per day haying. Paid Thomas Westover 7s for 5 days and a piece for Thomas Challoner at 16d per day. Thomas Tully went to Cuckfield and to Poynings. Widdow Tully workt about half the day. Mr Holden hay'd about 2 hours.

The 3rd August 1715 Wednesday. A showry day, last night very wet. Lent my Cousin John Lindfield the Duke horse to go to Darkin for _____ Receiv'd 5s of young Thomas Surgeant for 2 pigs. My Wife and I went to Warninglid and met my Father Stone and Mother at William Procter's. John Smith fetcht the little runt cow. She weigh'd 10 stone per quarter. Receiv'd 6s of my Father Stone in full for the malt.

The 4th August 1715 Thursday. A wet day. Fetcht the pease from Mrs Storer. Frank Marshall rowel'd the sorrel colt in the stifle joynt for which I paid him 2s-6d. Paid John Paine 2s for 8lbs of eels, put 22 into the new pond. Carry'd 300 faggots to the Widdow Tully on the parish's account, also 100 faggots to Jack Bartlet per Ned May and William Charman.
I order'd the postwoman to bring £5-15s from John Bull and Henry Dubbins. Paid the Widdow Tully 10s. I receiv'd all the writings of Mrs Storer concerning her house and deliver'd them to Mr Scutt and gave him orders to make the writeings between us.

The 5th August 1715 Fryday. A wet day. We went to Stephen Bine's b____ in Mrs Mary Whitpaine's ground in Slaugham for laths. We brought 5400, a set load is 6000. Stephen Bine and I din'd at Warninlid at Mr Lound's. Dinner and expences 2s. Paid her 3d for a pot of beer. John Harden, a drover to Mrs Mary Whitpaine and Bab Goffe was here, staid supper. Mr William Martin supt here. Dick Purvey was here yesterday and carry'd home 12 bottles of stale beer and a quire of paper. Jack Picknall ended tending hogs to day.

The 6th August 1715 Saturday. A dry forenoon, and all day. Jack Bartlet had a bushel of wheat at 3s-9d. My Cousin John Lindfield's teem came home with a load of crocks. Paid my Lord Treep 2s for 4 casements springs. Spent 2s with Mr Pointin the exciseman at John Smith's and made an entry of my hop ground. Widdow Tully and her son cut and turn'd pease from 10 aclock. Hollingham and her son turn'd pease about 2 hours. Mr Richard Whitpaine and spent the evning here. The reapers reapt all day. Paid Richard White 18d for one day's work being all that is due to him.

The 7th August 1715 Sunday. A fine day. Mr William Martin preacht twice. I was not at Church because my head ach'd much.

The 8th August 1715 Munday. A fine day. William Balcomb of Albourne dy'd in the morning. John Box and one of William Balcomb's men call'd me in the morning to go to Albourne Place because the aforesaid William Balcomb had made John Box and I trustee to his will. I went with them but refus'd to act in anything 'till I had further consider'd of it. Mr Healy broak up the will. Nick Plaw was here in the evning to persuade me to act. He was also at Albourne Place in the morning.
*(Ed: William who was only 40 when he died left a will providing for his three children, confirming his ill-health and mentioning his friends Thomas Marchant and John Box sr of Clayton)*
John Gun, Jack Bartlet and William Charman mow'd the oates in the forenoon and hay'd and turn'd and bound some wheat in the afternoon. Widdow Tully and her son cut pease in the morning, workt all day. Receiv'd £5-15s of Thomas Stone of Brighton in full of all accounts from him, John Bull and Henry Dubbins.

The 9th August 1715 Tuesday. A very fine day 'till in the afternoon, then wet. John Box and I went to Albourne

Place, we found £60-10s in William Balcomb's chest, left 10s with his mother and the £60 with Nick Plaw with orders to get evrything ready for his funeral and to help look after all the business. I brought home his will. My Aunt Holden was here to persuade me to undertake the trust____ . Turn overleaf for the rest of the day. Carry'd 5 loads of hay to the southeast rick one to the southwest rick and one to the rick by the qincy tree in Tully's rick steddle and set one load in the barne, all out of Tully's Mead, being the last of the mead. John Gun, Jack Bartlet, William Charman, Ned May, Widdow Tully and her son workt all day and Thomas Challoner 'till 4 aclock. I saw John Bodle open a sheep about 14lbs per qarter, he had 8lbs of fat in the caul.

The 10th August 1715 Wednesday. A very wet forenoon, dry after. Hurst Fair. Paid the Widdow Tully 20s in full to this day. Paid my Cousin Peter Marchant £1-7-6d for a wig. He and his son Harry *( born 1708 in Lewes)* were all that din'd with us. James Langford was here and markt 7 sheep to be fetcht to morrow. My Brother Peter, Nick Marchant, Mr Healy, Mr Mitchell, Nick Plaw and Yung Thomas Norton was here in the evning *(Ed: Thomas Norton born 1691, son of Thomas and Frances née Whitpaine).*

The 11th August 1715 Thursday. A fine day. William Balcomb buried at Henfield. John Box and I agreed with one Richard Greenfield for a month's work in William Balcomb's harvest at 55s, he to board himself and with Cooper at 30s to be in the house. James Langford sent for the 7 sheep aforesaid. I was at William Balcomb's funeral and my Wife but neither of us went to Henfield. I was at Mrs Catherine Beard's after. I came home to see Mr Ralph Beard who came from London to day.

The 12th August 1715 Fryday. A very fine day. Carry'd 6 loads of the Rookwood wheat, laid in the bottom of the great bay of the wheat barne. John Gun, Jack Bartlet and William Charman workt from 10 aclock opening sheavs, turning it and carrying, all day after. Thomas Challoner workt the afternoon and Jack Smith from 2 aclock. John Gun had a bushel of malt. Paid Mr Healy 1s-9d for his old watch and chain.

The 13th August 1715 Saturday. A fine day. I was at Mrs Catherine Beard's in the morning. Tom Challoner and Ned May carry'd 5 loads of the grey pease and laid them in the south end of Tully's barne. They begun at 11 aclock. Tom Tully workt all day. Paid Parker's wife 3d¼

in full. Ned Penfold went to Lewis for Mr John Hart. Old John Westover died this morning.
*(Ed: Hurst Parish Record shows burial on 16 August)*

The 14th August 1715 Sunday. A fine day. Mr William Martin preacht twice. Mrs Courthope, my Cousin John Lindfield and my Brother Peter were here after evning prayr. My Cousin John Lindfield staid supper. Nick Plaw was here in the morning.

The 15th August 1715 Munday. A dry, gloomy forenoon, a small showr at noon, dry after. The least 3 yearling heifer went to Edgly bull. Lent Mr Richard Whitpaine my old waggon. The reapers made an end of the Rookwood. Carry'd one great load of wheat and 2 small ones to the aforesaid mow. My Wife was at Danny this afternoon. John Westover was here with his father's will. I hurt Molly's arme in the morning playing with her and in the evning sent for John Snashall. He said the lesser bone was broaken below the elbow. Mrs Catherine Beard and Ralph was here.

The 16th August 1715 Tuesday. A wet forenoon, last night very wet, showry afternoon. Frank Marshall was here and had away the young horse to cure his poll. He demanded 2s-6d per week for keeping. Sarah Surgeant was taken sick last night. The reapers rung the hogs and pigs. Receiv'd 12s-6d of Stephen Bine for a journey to Slaugham. Henry Osbourne (now a servant to the Duke of Newcastle)was here with a young horse (late William Balcomb's) Sold to Mr Goldham of Seaford at £15-1s to be kept 'till Michaelmas. Receiv'd £15-1s of Harry Osbourne for him. Paid him a guinea for rideing and selling him. The great 3 yearling heifer went to Edgly great bull.

The 17th August 1715 Wednesday. A showry day. John Westover lay here last night. Mrs Scutt, her mother and sisters were here in the afternoon. Stephen Bine's man Joseph Wood workt here makeing shutters to the window by the great chest.

The 18th August 1715 Thursday. A fine day. Widdow Tully and her son workt from ten aclock at harvest. William Charman and Ned May carry'd 2 small loads of pease, two small load of oates and one load of Tully's wheat. Paid 10s to Counsellor Burrell for his opinion on William Balcomb's will.

The 19th August 1715 Fryday. A fine day. I saw my Cousin John Lindfield's bullock weigh'd. I was at Albourne Place in the morning and sold the Burgaines, Katherns and Sugar Pares to George Wickham at 18d per bushel in the place. My Cousin Whitpaine was here in the morning. I lent him 5 guineas for a note of his hand. Paid Sarah Brand's mother 18s-6d in full for all her work. Widdow Tully and her son workt the afternoon. William Charman and Ned May carry'd 3 small loads of oates and 2 jobbs which was a load of Tully's wheat, all the oates lye on the grey pease. Mrs Catherine Beard and her family supt here.

The 20th August 1715 Saturday. A fine day. The mowers made an end of the barly field by Burt's in the morning by 10 aclock. William Charman helpt Old Bartlet and John Gun afterwards. Widdow Tully and her boy workt from 11 aclock turning hay. Ed Burt and Ned May carry'd a load of Tully's wheat and laid about a third part of it on the South Mow, the rest they pitch on end in the other bay as they did half a load before. Paid a bill of 2s at Frank Holden's. George Wickham had 3 bushels of pares at 18d per bushel. Paid John Westover 4s for ¼lb of tea for my Brother Peter. Tom Tully went to Nunnery towards night.

The 21st August 1715 Sunday. A fine day. Mr William Martin preacht twice. I was at Mrs Catherine Beard's after evning prayr but did not stay long. Mr Richard Whitpaine was there. I offer'd my Brother the tea John Westover brought but he said he had sent for more so did not take it. Tom Tully came home late and brought me a coat from Mr Ede.

The 22nd August 1715 Munday. A very fine day. Receiv'd a new pocket book from London. Sold John Smith a cow of William Balcomb's at 2d per lb. John Snashall had the tea for my Brother and paid for it. Carried 3 small load of barly out of the field by Burt to West Mow in the Barly Barne. Carry'd also a very small load of barly out of Tully's wheat and set it in the barne. Laid one load of the wheat carry'd before in the little stable. Turn'd the fatting oxen in to the Edgly Mead. Widdow Tully and her boy workt half a day. John Standbridge workt here, he set up the bars between the Fifteen Acres and Edgly Mead and afterwards helpt harvest.

The 23rd August 1715 Tuesday. A fine day only a slight showr about one aclock. John Standbridge workt here. Widdow Tully and her boy workt as much as half a day. Paid William Shepard 6d for reaping 'till it rain'd. Thomas Challoner workt above half a day. Carry'd 3 small load of barly to the West Mow. Carry'd also a great load of the wheat by Wickham's and laid it in the North Mow of the wheat barne. Nick Plaw was here and brought 2lbs of bisket at 8d per lb. He was here again at night about goeing to Wiston. Jack Bartlet had a bushel of wheat at 3s-9d.

The 24th August 1715 Wednesday. A very fine day. St Bartholomew. Agdean Fair and Brighton Fair. Paid 14d for an apron and makeing for Molly Balcomb. The black sow went to hog by our white boar. Paid a journeyman shoemaker 1s for part of a day's work. Paid Thomas Challoner 18d for this day's work. Paid Thomas Howell 2s for this day's work mending the chaese in the morning and harvest in the afternoon. Stephen Bine's man Thomas Vinall workt here. Widdow Tully and her boy workt from 10 aclock. William Jarvice workt here. He made an end of grinding 14 bushels of malt to be brew'd to morrow. Trod the mow. Carry'd 10 small loads of barly cut of the field by Burt's to the West Mow, the last __ of the field. Gather'd the apples off the tree in Tully's first field, 8 bushels. John Smith's maid ET workt part of the day. William Balcomb's children were here and Goode Parsons

The 25th August 1715 Thursday. A showry forenoon, dry after. John Box was here in the morning. I went to Wiston with Nick Plaw to make up William Balcomb's accounts which we did to Lady Day 1715 and there was due for rent £236-14-10d. Ned May and Willy carry'd about 2 lain of the wheat by Wickham's. Brew'd 14 bushels of malt, one third of it for Mr John Hart. Receiv'd 12lbs of hops of Mr Richard Whitpaine a third of them for Mr John Hart.

The 26th August 1715 Fryday. A dry forenoon, the afternoon showry. The young white sow went to hog by Edgly black boar. Sold John Smith jr 3 cows at £13-10d, one to be kill'd next week, one the week after and the other before Michaelmas next, two of Mr Scrase's and one I had of John Snashall. Sold Harry Dubbins and

Thomas Stone 16 ewes at 9s per ewe. If any die after Michaelmas they are to bear the loss. Carry'd a small load of wheat to the North Mow. Ed Burt went to Shoreham with 3 bushels of pares.

The 27th August 1715 Saturday. A wet forenoon, dry after. My Cousin John Lindfield call'd me about noon. We went to Albourne Place. John Box came to us. We took an inventory of all the goods within doors. I paid the mony I receiv'd for William Balcomb's horse to Nick Plaw and brought home all the writeings I could find and the leg of one payr of drawers. We went from thence to Mr Healy's. Supt and staid late. Jude Storer was here about noon with a new merchant. He promis'd to come in a little time to seal the writeings between us.

The 28th August 1715 Sunday. A fine day. Mr Healy preacht here twice. Mr William Martin rode the ball mare to Twineham but 'twas on Mr Healy's account. I was not at Church in the afternoon because my head ach'd. I borrow'd Nick Plaw's coat last night. Sent him home to day per _____ .

The 29th August 1715 Munday. A dry day. Crawley Fair. Tom Challoner turn'd barly from 5 aclock. I wrote to my Brother James Ede for a hundredweight of raisins. Sold my Cousin John Bodle the brown heifer that was Mr Scrase's at 4d under their selling price per stone whenever she's kill'd. Sent 45 fleeces of wool weighing 106½lbs to Pangdean per Ned May. I was at Mrs Catherine Beard's a while in the afternoon. Carry'd a very small load of wheat. Mr John Picknall of Arundell was here in the evning. Tom Tully went to Nunnery in the afternoon.

The 30th August 1715 Tuesday. A dry day. I was at Mrs Catherine Beard's in the morning. Paid Henry Ford 1s for spaying 6 pigs and 4d for cutting the boar. Widdow Tully workt half the day, her boy return'd from Nunnery _____ . Tom Challoner workt from half an hour after 10. Carry'd a load and 2 lain of wheat. Carry'd 3 small load of the Homefield barly to the East Mow. Lent Stephen Bine 2 oxen to carry his oates and as he came to me they carry'd one load of the aforesaid barly. Paid John Marchant £4 for the Widdow Weller of Henfield.

The 31st August 1715 Wednesday. A showry forenoon, the afternoon also. Tom Tully workt half the day. Deliver'd a cord of wood and 100 faggots to

Mr Jeremiah Dodson per William Charman and Ned May. I din'd at Mr Dodson's. Carry'd half a load of wheat. Dick Vinall fetcht the brandled heifer and the little red one they fetch yesterday or t'other day.

The 1st September 1715 Thursday A dry day 'till near sun sett then very wet. Widdow Tully and her boy workt half the day. I was at Westtowne in the forenoon with Mr Duke and his wife. There was Mr Penderhill and Bab Goffe. Ned Burt workt the afternoon at harvest. Thomas Westover helpt me harvest part of the afternoon. Thomas Challoner workt from 9 aclock. James Langford was here and markt his 8 sheep. Carry'd 3 small load of the Homefield barly to the East Mow. Carry'd a small load of the wheat by Wickham's being the last of the field (except a very few sheavs) and all laid in the North Mow of the wheat barne. My Wife was at Danny. I sent the chaese for her.

The 2nd September 1715 Fryday A dry day. Made an end of reaping. Widdow Tully and her boy workt all day. I saw my Cousin John Lindfield's cow weigh'd at John Smith's. Mr Jeremiah Dodson, Mr Duke, Mr William Martin and Mr Beard were here in the afternoon and staid the evning.

The 3rd September 1715 Saturday. A fine day. I was at Pangdean in the morning to see ewes but we did not deal. Carry'd 5 small load of barly of the little field by Hyder's _____ field and laid it on the top of the West Mow, being all this field, also 3 loads of the Homefield to the East Mow. Thomas Challoner, Jack Bartlet and Ned Burt and Thomas Vinall workt half the day, John Gun, Widdow Tully and her boy all day.

The 4th September 1715 Sunday. A fine day. Mr William Martin preacht twice. My Wife receiv'd the sacrament. My Wife and I were at Mr Scutt's after evning prayr.

The 5th September 1715 Munday. A very fine day. Made an end of harvest. Carry'd 10 loads being the last of the Homefield barly, all on the East Mow being 18 loads on the field and the mow is full to the top but it was not horse trod, only 4 or 6 loads at first. Thomas Challoner, Widdow Tully and her boy, William Nicholas, Thomas Picknall and John Maynard workt the afternoon. John Gun, Jack Bartlet, William Charman and Ned May cut ricks in the morning and harvested the afternoon. Paid William Nicholas 1s for this afternoon's work and 16d for railing the graves of my 4 children. Paid Ned Burt 2s for this day's work and 2 half days before. Paid Thomas Picknall 2s-6d for his boy's tending hogs and I gave him 2s-6d. I also gave Thomas Challoner 1s. My Son William went to Patcham with his ñkle Peter. Jack Bartlet had a bushel of wheat at 3s-9d the last of his bargain. The Widdow Tully had half a bushel of wheat at the same price. Brought 4 bushels of wheat home out of Tully's Garret.

The 6th September 1715 Tuesday. A very fine day. Paid 20d for a ribband and slouch for Molly Balcomb. Paid Henry Ford 3d for spaying a young black sow. She was gone to hog a week or more. Receiv'd 25 tags from John Gold of Brighton to keep 'till Lady Day next at 2s per tag. Receiv'd also 2 black ewe lambs which I intend to keep some years for the sale of their wool. Receiv'd ¼lb of tea and several other goods from Mr Tourl. Receiv'd a book call'd Lex Testementaria of Mr Norman per Ned May, also a paper of 3 inch nails and some courtain rod of Mr _____, also 4lbs of powder of my Cousin Peter Marchant. My Wife was at Westtowne. I went to fetch her home. My Cousin Matt Pryaulx was here about noon *(Matthew born 1693 was a 2nd cousin to Thomas's wife)*. Did not stay. Tom Tully, John Gun and William Charman tipt ricks. Stephen Bine's mare went to Albourne at 1s per week.

The 7th September 1715 Wednesday. A fine day. Mrs Ann Dodson brought to bed of a son William Charman and John Gun tipt a rick in the morning 'till near 8 aclock. Afterwards John Gun shovel'd the towne and William Charman begun reap Tully's beans at 9 aclock. Jack Bartlet mow'd grass in the Nine Acres. Tom Tully went to St Leonard's. Afterwards hay'd. I was at Wanbarrow in the afternoon. My Wife supt at Mrs Ann Dodson's.

The 8th September 1715 Thursday. A dry day. Cuckfield Fair Day and Stenning also. Jack Bartlet and Ned May begun stir Tully's fallow. Chang'd the 6 working oxen into the Marldfield and turn'd Benbow into the fatting oxen. Turn'd 5 of the calves into the wheat earsh by Wickham's. William Charman reapt beans. Nick Plaw was here in the evning. Mr Wilkin of London and Mrs Catherine Beard call'd here in their way to Cuckfield. Mr Jeremiah Dodson was here to see Mr John Hart in the afternoon. Tom Tully workt here all day. Ned Burt was here in the evning and bought 4 hives of William Balcomb's bees at 20s and also 3 of Nick Plaw's at 18s. Lent Michael Stacey 10 wattles.

The 9th September 1715 Fryday. A dry day, only a small showr about 3 aclock. Jack Bartlet and Ned May plough'd on the fallow. William Charman made an end of reaping the beans about 2 aclock. Tom Tully workt all day. I went to Albourne and made an end of takeing William Balcomb's inventory with John Lindfield and John Box. It came to near £1200 without the hops. We also let the Eastout land to Goodman Champion 'till the heir shall come of age at £30 per annum. I saw Mrs Catherine Beard's cow weigh'd 17 stone per qarter wanting 1lb in the whole. Memorandum; the sugar that was us'd for the strong elder wine came to 4s-8d. Ned Burt and Ned May brought home the 2 hives of bees.

The 10th September 1715 Saturday. A fine day. My wedding day, 15 years. William Charman and Ned May plough'd on Tully's fallow. Thomas Challoner workt from 10 aclock. Jack Bartlet and John Gun workt the forenoon on the ricks. In the afternoon Jack Bartlet went to work at Wanbarrow. John Gun and Thomas Challoner workt on the ricks in the afternoon. I went to Albourne Place in the afternoon and reckon'd with all William Balcomb's hayers and harvesters and Nick Plaw paid them all out of the mony in his hands. I gave William Balcomb's mother *(Ed: Bridget née Norman)* part of his cloaths for her son Norman. I also helpt the Widdow Parsons to 2 caps and 2 aprons and a handcerchief and 2 of William Balcomb's shirts and 2 old crevats for the children and some other small things.

The 11th September 1715 Sunday. A fine day. Mr Scott preacht in the forenoon and Mr William Martin in the afternoon. Dick Purvey brought Mrs Howard from Horsham about noon to stay here 'till my Wife is brought to bed. Mr Willard of Bourne and his family were at Church as also Mrs Anne White and her niece.

The 12th September 1715 Munday. A fine forenoon, towards night showry. John Gun workt in William Charman's stead. Ned May and Jack Bartlet plough'd 'till about 3 aclock and afterwards carry'd a small load of beans. I went to Frank Marshall's to see my young horse. Mr John Hart and I spent the evning at Mrs Catherine Beard's. Tom Tully tended the beans all day.

The 13th September 1715 Tuesday. A showry day afternoon. Tully workt all day. Jack Bartlet and Ned May made an end of Tully's fallow and begun the pease earsh. Abraham Muzzall had 5½ yards of cloath at 3s and a yard of linsey at 2s-3d per yard for G Burt. Mrs Mary Whitpaine, my Brother Peter, Goode Parsons and the children were here in the afternoon. My Grandmother Stone was here also. Carry'd 100 faggots to Mrs Storer's that was due for her cloath press and brought as many home. I measur'd some ground for Mrs Catherine Beard and carry'd home her chain. Paid Jack Bartlet half a guinea.

The 14th September 1715 Wednesday. A dry day. Jack Bartlet and Ned May plough'd. Tom Tully workt all day. John Gun and William Charman brought home 200 faggots and carry'd a load of Tully's beans. Paid Joseph Muzzall half a year's Land Tax and lent him a ram lamb to go with his ewes. Receiv'd the 5 guineas I lent to Mr Richard Whitpaine. Nick Plaw din'd here. I sent a letter to Mr Vinall. Abraham Muzzall workt here. John Gun and William Charman loaded 50 faggots for John Gun and 22 that were due to him to be carry'd in to morrow. Jack Bartlet and Ned May gather'd part of a tree of pig pares. Mr Jeremiah Dodson's teem came through the ground to day and three times before.

The 15th September 1715 Thursday. A fine day. St. John's Comon Fair. Jack Bartlet and Ned May plough'd 'till 10 aclock then broak their plough. I went to the Fair and there bought 47 ewes, that is, my 24 of Mr Hamshire at £9-10s which I paid for and 23 of Mr Gold at £8 which I also pay'd for. Receiv'd £4 of John Lindfield for the cow I sold him in the Spring and paid him for 7 lambs £1-7s and 3s-9d for 3 sacks of coals and 8s which he paid for me to Stephen Carter for 2 payr of blindfolds. I came home by John Lindfield and din'd there. My Brother James Ede and his wife came hither towards night. John Gun and William Charman brought home         faggots.

The 16th September 1715 Fryday. A fine day. Stephen Bine's man Joseph Wood workt here. Paid Tom Howell 6d for work about a plough and spoke for a _____ . William Charman and Tully fetch home my ewes from my Cousin John Lindfield. Jack Bartlet and Ned May plough'd the afternoon. We were at Mr Beard's in the evning. My Brother James Ede and I were at John Snashall's. Paid John Parsons 1s for shaveing my head and face.

The 17th September 1715 Saturday. A fine day. Jack Bartlet and Ned May made an end of ploughing Tully's pease earsh at noon. They brought home half a cord of wood. My Brother James Ede and Sister Ede went home about 3 aclock. Ned May went with them. My Sister Nanny was here towards night. John Gun and William Charman made an end of cutting the wheat mow and thrashing it. They had 5 bushels of wheat. Paid my Brother James Ede 4s-6d for 2 payr of shooes, £2-15s for a coat and 8d for sending it to the burrough, 9s-4d for coffee and tea and 2s-8d for blew. Mr Healy was here for William Balcomb's bitch but I had lent her my Cousin John Lindfield. Stephen Bine's man Joseph Wood workt here. John Snashall was here in the morning. William Shepeard carry'd home a piece for ticking 5 ¼lbs net in all. Tully workt all day. We gather'd some apples vizt loggerheads etc.

The 18th September 1715 Sunday. A very thick mist 'till 9 aclock, the rest of the day fine. Mr William Martin preacht twice. My Cousin John Lindfield din'd here. My Sister Nanny din'd here. Ned May brought home 112lbs of rasins of the son. Mr Henry Campion, Mrs Anne White and her niece Molly and Mrs Courthope was here after evning prayr.

The 19th September 1715 Munday. A fine day. Begun work on Tully's fallow. Receiv'd £11 of James Langford for 20 sheep. Harry Dubbins was here and draw'd 10 sheep. Stephen Bine's man Joseph Wood workt here. He finisht my draws by eight aclock and begun the bee bench at 12. John Gun begun thrash seed wheat. Tully workt all day. Carry'd a small load being the last of Tully's beans. Ground 6 bushels by strike of barly malt. Ned May brought home yesterday about noon 112lbs of raisons of the son for elder wine at 37s. I was at Mr Scutt's in the evning with Mrs Catherine Beard and Mr John Hart and Mrs Hart lay there to make room for Mrs Howard.

The 20th September 1715 Tuesday. A fine day. Stephen Bine's man Joseph Wood workt the afternoon. Jack Bartlet and William Charman begun plough in Tully's fallow about 10 aclock being the 2nd stirring after the fallow. Ned May workt with the horses harrowing and rowling. John Gun gather'd apples in the afternoon, thrasht the morning. I was at Mrs Catherine Beard's a little while in the evning. Willy went to Dean House in the evning. Receiv'd 10s-10d of Thomas Field for cloath and linsy for G Burt.

The 21st September 1715 Wednesday. A fine day. Jack Bartlet and William Charman plough'd. Nick Plaw brought William Balcomb's mare for Ned May to ride to Rusper. I also sent for Mr Richard Whitpaine's black horse for the Widd mare to come on and Ned May went about 4 aclock haveing harrow'd and rowl'd 'till then. John Gun gather'd apples the afternoon, thrasht the forenoon and brought up 3 bushels of wheat from Tully's. John Smith fetcht the last of his 3 cows. Frank Marshall brought home my young horse but I bid him have him home again for an other week. Tom Tully workt all day and half yesterday.

The 22nd September 1715 Thursday. A very fine day Tully workt all day. Paid Hollingham's wife 9s-8d for her self and her boy's haying. Jack Bartlet and William Charman plough'd. Sent home Mr Richard Whitpaine's horse. My Mother Stone came and nurse mare towards night. John Gun rowl'd and harrow'd in the forenoon, gather'd apples the afternoon. My Mother Stone brought us a hare and Mr Scutt gave us one about 3 days ago. Mr Beaumont, Mr Scutt, Mr Beard, Mrs Woodward, Mrs Kettilby, my Grandmother and John Snashall's wife were here in the afternoon. Mr Beaumont invited Mr Scutt, Mrs Catherine Beard, Mr John Hart and I to dinner with him a Saturday.

The 23rd September 1715 Fryday. A very fine day. Tully workt all day. Eliz Cheal, Widdow Nicholas, Sarah Nicholas, Widdow Herriot, Webb, Sarah Wood, Widdow Parsons, Heath and her daughter, 2 of Sargeant's girls, Widdow Tully and her girl, Parker's wife, Elizabeth Alcock, K Courtness, E Westover, Widdows Leach, John Gun and Hambledean pickt my hops by noon. Paid them all (but Widdow Gun and Eliz Cheal) 3d a piece. Stephen Bine's man Joseph Wood workt the afternoon on the bee bench. I sent my hops to Westtowne to be dry'd and a tub to put 'em in which weigh'd 59½ lbs. Ned Burt workt to day. I also sent a sack of cole per Ned May. Receiv'd 6 bushels of seed wheat from Albourne Place per Ned May and 2 of their sacks and left 2 of my sacks there for more. Sent home William Balcomb's mare. Henry Wood of Highhatch was here for leave to come through the ground with his teem. I lent him a boy. John Gun pull'd poles, carry'd the hops etc. Ned May harrow'd and rowl'd. Jack Bartlet and William Charman made an end of ploughing Tully's fallow.

The 24th September 1715 Saturday. A gloomy day. My Wife was brought to bed of a girl about a quarter past eleven aclock in the forenoon. We begun sow in Tully's fallow about 10 aclock. Sow'd about 2 bushels and a half. Jack Bartlet sow'd and knockt clods. John Gun knockt clods, so did Tully. Ned May went to Cuckfield mill with Mrs Howard. I gave her 5s. My Wife gave her a guinea. Ned Burt workt to day. Stephen Bine's man workt to day on the bee bench. Mrs Stone, Mrs Catherine Beard and Mrs Kettilby din'd here. So did my Sister Nanny. My Cousin Thomas Norton of Edgly sent us a very good pig. I gave the maid 6d. Mrs Ann Dodson and Mrs Duke went through my ground in their way to London. Receiv'd 1½lbs of hops from Albourne Place yesterday that were good for little or nothing.

The 25th September 1715 Sunday. A wet forenoon, the afternoon showry. Mr William Martin preacht twice. I was at Church in the afternoon but not in the forenoon because of bad _____ . My Cousin John Lindfield and Mrs Mary Whitpaine were here afternoon.

The 26th September 1715 Munday. A showry day and towards night very stormy. William Charman and Ned May plough'd in Tully's wheat field. John Gun knockt clods and Jack Bartlet sow'd and knockt clods. Stephen Bine's man Joseph Wood finisht the bee bench. Tully workt all day. He fetcht 3 bushels of wheat from Albourne Place. Stephen Bine was here at night. John Gun and William Charman fetcht my tub of hops from Westtowne after they left work. Mrs Catherine Beard and her family spent the afternoon here but Mr Ralph went away about 5 aclock and Mr John Hart and he went to Mr Courtness's. Sow'd 3½ bushels to day and a little over. I told Widdow Tully I would give her but 3d per day for barly from this time.

The 27th September 1715 Tuesday. A very wet day after a very wet night. Paid William Roach 1s for mending the pumps to day and 2s-2d for his boy's work etc before. John Gun mended the horse collers and thrasht wheat. Jack Bartlet and William Charman cut the East Mow in the barly barne. Receiv'd £10 of John Smith jr. Receiv'd

£6 of Nick Plaw in sale for a load of wheat seed _____ . Receiv'd 5 bushels more of William Balcomb's seed wheat. Tully workt all day.

The 28th September 1715 Wednesday. A stormy day. Win'd 5 bushels of barly scatter'd in the floor. Win'd 4½ bushels of beans. Jack Bartlet had a bushel of wheat at 4s per bushel _____ and ½ a bushel at £1-9-d. Paid Widdow Tully 11s and outset for the wheat she had and clear'd all to Saturday night last. Deliver'd Jack Bartlet's 19 faggots per Ned May and William Charman and 25 faggots to John Edward's. Paid William Charman 4d and clear'd all accounts with him. I was at Wanbarrow and at Mrs Catherine Beard's in the afternoon. Mrs Mary Whitpaine and Mrs Scutt were here in the afternoon and my Sister Nanny all day. Frank Marshall brought home my young horse. I paid him 15s for his keeping.

The 29th September 1715 Thursday. A very wet morning and evning, the rest of the day dry. I was at Stenning Fair and bought 5 runts of David Williams at £3-7-6d per runt. I call'd at Albourne Place and rode William Balcomb's mare. Nick Plaw went with me. Nick Plaw paid William Balcomb's man E Bine all that was due to him and took a receit of him. I din'd at John Box's at Stenning with John Box of Albourne. Nick Plaw, John Stone and Thomas Marten the thatcher, Nat Hobbes went in with us but did not stay. Dinner and expence 9d. Nick Plaw paid for my horse. Mr Scutt and Mr Ralph Beard was here when I came home. They staid 'till about 8 aclock. I left my old horse at Nick Plaw's.

The 30th September 1715 Fryday. A dry day. Tully workt all day. James Storer, Andrew and Betty Storer came to seal the writeings to me and they and their mother did seal but Jude did not come 'till after they were gone home. We had a dish of pease to day for dinner. Paid Mrs Storer 20d for some small things I bought at the sale. I spent 2s and they 1s at the sealing the writeings. I sent home William Balcomb's mare per Tully. He brought Nunnery _____ .

The 1st October 1715 Saturday. A dry day 'till evning, then wet. Tully workt to day. Jude Storer seal'd the above written writeings at my house. He din'd with me. Ned May fetch home a new turnrist plough from Tom Howell's. Paid Mr Scutt a guinea for makeing the writeings. Paid John Edwards 6d for 2 lemons he brought from Lewis. Mr Sixsmith came in the evning, supt with us and went to Mr Jeremiah Dodson's. Stephen Bine's man Tom Mall workt part of the afternoon for me at Mrs Storer's. Ned May carry'd 150 bricks up thither. Mrs Barbara Campion, Mrs Anne White and both her nieces were here in the afternoon *(Ed: Barbara Campion née Courthope was born in Hurst in 1675 and went on, as sole surviving child of Peter Courthope, to inherit much property in Sussex and Kent in 1725)*. Tom Tully went to Nunnery about 3 aclock.

The 2nd October 1715 Sunday. A wet showry stormy day. John Edwards and Elizabeth Alcock _____ . Mr Sixsmith preacht in the forenoon, no service in the afternoon. My Mother Stone din'd at Mrs Catherine Beard's. Frank Marshall was here and drest the young horse yesterday. Tom Tully came home from Nunnery before noon.

The 3rd October 1715 Munday. A very wet stormy day, some thunder in the afternoon. Win'd 20 bushels of Jack Bartlet's head oates and 2 bushels tail. Tom Tully workt all day. Receiv'd a bushel of hayslenutts of Mr Richard Whitpaine that came from Wayhills at 2s-8d and a payr of sizzors at 11d. William King, a mason, workt a laying Mr Storer's room and some other jobbs about that house from 9 aclock. I took 2 large carp and 3 small ones out of the Marldfield stew and left 2 tench in. Sold John Smith Nick Plaw's great cow at £6 but if she went above £4 per quarter of 18 I am to abate 5s, to be kill'd this week. John Bodle promis'd to kill the brown heifer next week at _____ . Receiv'd a letter from my Brother James Ede per Harry Wickham. Nick Plaw sent his boy with William Balcomb's bitch. I gave the boy 2d. He had been at Albourne Place.

The 4th October 1715 Tuesday. A wet day. Tully workt all day. My Daughter Anne christen'd, Mr John Hart godfather. Mrs Anne White and my Sister Nanny godmothers. Mr Sixsmith christen'd her at home because of the weather and went to christen a child at Richard Banks. W King workt the forenoon on Mrs Storer's house. Paid Jack Bartlet 10s. Ned May fetch my Sister Nanny. Paid Mr Courtness 6d for 100 walnuts per Tully. Sent home Mr Scutt's ladder per Bartlet.

The 5th October 1715 Wednesday. A dry windy day. John Paine came at noon at 5s per week, meat and drink he begun make syder. My Sister Nanny went home in the afternoon. Tully workt all day. Edgly bull broak into

the yearlings and I doubt put the little heifer to bull that came from Nunnery. Shut up 3 of the black sow's pigs and 3 other hogs a fatting. They had 4 bushels of oates. My Cousin's wife of Old Land was brought to bed of her first son a Saturday last *(Ed: Jane née Gratwick gave birth to a son Richard who however died just over 12 months later)* and his brother John Turner's wife at Kymer Street of her first son yesterday or this morning.
*(Ed: Mary née Bray gave birth to John).*

The 6th October 1715 Thursday. A dry forenoon, the afternoon wet. John Edwards helpt John Gun winnow wheat and thrasht a bushel of beans that grew in the orchards. Win'd 20 bushels head and 2 bushels tail of John Gun's wheat and of Tully's field. Borrow'd Mr Richard Whitpaine's screen. John Paine made syder and perry. Mr Scutt and his wife, Mr C Minshall and his wife, Mrs Minshall, Mrs Catherine Beard and Mr Richard Whitpaine were here towards night and spent the evning. Frank Marshall was here and drest the young horse. Tully workt all day. Paid Mr Courtness for 100 walnuts per Sarah Morley, 6d.

The 7th October 1715 Fryday. A dry day, wet evning. Tully workt to day. Paid Frank Holden 6d for a quart of tar and 3s on his books. I colour'd the bee bench with the tar, had just enough. John Paine made an end of the perry and Ned May and he draw'd some trees. Sent home Mr Richard Whitpaine's screen per Ned May. I was at Wanbarrow towards night. Mr Burry and his sister were there. John Edwards workt to day, stript the hop poles and set 'em up. Nick Plaw was here in the evning to desire me to fetch Mrs Storer.

The 8th October 1715 Saturday. A wet day. Tully workt all day. Reckon'd with John Bodle and clear'd all accounts to that day. Receiv'd £2-11s of him, his bill was £3-9-4d. Reckon'd with Dick Wood and clear'd all accounts. Paid him 13s-6d. Frank Marshall was here and drest the young horse. Paid John Paine 3s for his work this piece of a week. The hogs had 4 bushels of oates.

The 9th October 1715 Sunday. A stormy day but little rain. Mr Beaumont preacht in the forenoon. Mr Jeremiah Dodson was at Church but I was not because not well. Mr Ralph Beard was to see me in the evning.

The 10th October 1715 Munday. A wet forenoon, the afternoon stormy. My Mother Stone went home after dinner. John Gun and Ned May went with her. Tully workt to day. John Paine had home 2 of the old sow's pigs at 14____ . Paid John Edwards 2s-6d for 2 day's work and 6d that he laid out for me at Lewis for 2 lemons. Nick Plaw was here again to day.

The 11th October 1715 Tuesday. A wet stormy day. Tully workt to day. Stephen Bine's man Joseph Wood workt here but lost 2 or 3 hours. Paid Frank Marshall a bill of 10s for William Balcomb. Carpenter, a mill right was here to fitt up the carriage to fetch Nick Plaw's mill stone to morrow. Paid John Gun 20s. Ned May and he came from Nunnery about noon. Mrs Catherine Beard, her son and family were here in the evning. Mr Richard Whitpaine was here with them. He wrote the Chuchwardens presentiment and I set Jo Marchant's name to them. Receiv'd my chain from Mr Richard Whitpaine per Tully.

The 12th October 1715 Wednesday. A fine day. Tully workt all day. 3 of my horses, 2 of Mr Richard Whitpaine's, Albourne Place mare and a horse of John Box fetcht a mill stone on my carriage for Nick Plaw. They brought me 2 new swads, half a paper of 6d nails and a payr of bellows. Paid Robert Pierce 5d for setting 5 hoops and sold him 100 of my hoops at 7s-6d if we can agree about dividing them. I sent a letter to Mrs Swaine wherein I appointed to be at Lewis in a fortnight at farthest. John Towner and Ja Reed begun sawing.

The 13th October 1715 Thursday. A fine day 'till 3 aclock then wet. Tully workt. Robert Pierce hew'd the tub staves. He was just half a day. Win'd 8 quarters and 2 bushels of Jack Bartlet's oates being the last of the field, in all 11 quarters. Reckon'd with Jack Bartlet to this day and there was due to him £3-0 -1½d but I did not pay him. Paid Mr Courtness 3s-8d for fustian and thread. Paid £5-10s to Thomas Muzzall of Henfield for my Aunt Holden being what was due to her from Molly Balcomb for half a year at Michaelmas last for Eastout. Abraham Muzzall workt all day.

The 14th October 1715 Fryday. A showry day. Tully and Abraham Muzzall workt all day. Mrs Dean's brother fetcht her 8 sheep. My Brother Peter's horses and mine fetcht stones from Bolny and carry'd home Count Tully's Jack per Ned May. I lamed my old horse goeing after the teem. Paid 4d to J Simons for setting a shooe on my Brother Peter's horse. Mr John Hart and I were at

Mrs Catherine Beard's. There was Mr Richard Whitpaine. Paid 2s for muslin for John Balcomb.

The 15th October 1715 Saturday. A fine forenoon, the afternoon showry. Bine and Ned May rak't stubble. Tully workt all day. I went to Albourne Place to meet Sir Robert Fagg and staid there all day but he did not come. *(Ed: Sir Robert Fagg 1673 – 1736, owner of Wiston House which his family acquired at the time of the Civil War).* Receiv'd the £5-10s of Nick Plaw that I paid my Aunt Holden. Paid Nick Plaw what he laid out for me at Lewis. Mrs Catherine Beard, her son and family supt here. Mrs Mary Whitpaine and Mrs Ann Dodson were here in the afternoon. My Sister Nanny went home to night haveing been here above a week. I din'd at Nick Plaw's. John Box and I appointed to go to Lewis Tuesday next.

The 16th October 1715 Sunday. A wet forenoon, the afternoon dry. Mr Jeremiah Dodson preacht. I was not at Church in the forenoon. Harry Wickham brought me 7 knives and as many forks from Horsham in exchange for some sent by Mr Ede. Paid Harry Wickham 10s-9d which he paid for the knives. Nick Plaw was here in the evning and brought me William Balcomb's book. John Box gave me a letter which he receiv'd from Mr Langford about William Balcomb's land in Lindfield.

The 17th October 1715 Munday. A wet day. Tom Tully workt all day. Paid Edward Jenner of Bolny 5s for sand stones for my Father's tomb. Begun plough the Churchfield towards night. Mr Ralph Beard call'd for the key and he went to London. Mr Gold was here about noon to see his tags. Tom Tully fetcht William Balcomb's mare.

The 18th October 1715 Tuesday. A gloomy misty day. Tully workt all day. Begun sow the Churchfield, sow'd 3 bushels. Jack Bartlet and Ned May plough'd and John Paine sow'd and harrow'd. John Box and I went to Lewis to prove William Balcomb's will. I paid all the charges vizt 2s-2½d for our dinner and beer, 4s to Mr Pierce the surrogate and £1-14s to Mr Ben Handshaw a proctor and 4d for our horses, in all £2-0-6½d. Paid £4-13-6d to Mrs Swaine being the intrest due on Mrs Storer's mortgage to Michaelmas last. I took in Mrs Storer's mortgage and gave Mrs Swaine a bond for £60 from Michaelmas last at £5 per cent. Paid Mr Handshaw 2s-6d for making the bond. I left William Balcomb's will and inventory with Mr Handshaw. The inventory came to £1338-10-7d. Paid a bill at Mr Tourl's £2-19-3d from Midsumer last. Paid a bill of 5s at Mr Sled's. Paid Mr Norman 6s for a book for my self and 2s-6d for a book to keep William Balcomb's accounts. Paid Mr Thomas Friend a guinea for 3½ yards of cloath, 4s-6d for 3 yards of shalloon, 2s for 30 buttons and 6d for mohair. Paid 5s at Mr Court's for drops, a snaffell and knives.

The 19th October 1715 Wednesday. A dry day. Robert Gatland workt 'till 3 aclock. John Gun and Jack Bartlet plough'd. John Paine sow'd and harrow'd, 3½ bushels. Nick Plaw din'd here and carry'd home William Balcomb's book. Nurse Mare went home. Ned May carry'd her on John Smith's mare for which I am to lend him a horse and boy at Xmas. I sent to John Bartholomew to make me a coat but he could not. Mrs Scutt was here in the afternoon. Tully workt all day.

The 20th October 1715 Thursday. A dry day. King George's Coronation Day. Jack Bartlet and Ned May plough'd. John Paine harrow'd and sow'd, 3 bushels. John Gun mended hedges and carry'd dung into the hop garden. Thomas Whiteing a taylor at Blackstone and his boy came to make me a coat but he cut it out and carry'd it home and he is to make it by Munday next at 5s. I was at Wanbarrow in the afternoon, call'd at Mrs Catherine Beard's in the evning as I came home. I saw James Wood's ox weigh'd at John Smith's. Her 4 quarters weigh'd 106 stone and 2 lbs. Tully workt to day. Receiv'd 30s of John Smith for a lean hog, sold to him today. Dick Steer sent the hare he promis'd me per William Lindfield.

The 21st October 1715 Fryday. A fine day. Tom Tully workt to day. Jack Bartlet and Ned May plough'd. John Paine sow'd and harrow'd, 4 bushels. John Towner and Ja Reed sow'd. Sold Towner a hog at 25s to be fetcht by Thursday next. John Gun mended hedge again and carry'd more dung into the hop garden. John Box and I went to the Byshop's Court at New Hall to meet about our admission to Eastout land but we were not admitted because they askt £40 fine. Paid £7 for the herriot, seiz'd on William Balcomb's death. Receiv'd £4-10s of Nick Plaw and 40s of Mr Norton of Chestham for 2½ bushels of William Balcomb's clover seed. We appointed Thomas Champion to meet him at Eastout Fryday. I rode William Balcomb's mare. One of Mr Gold's tags dy'd last night. John Gun flaid it. Frank Marshall was here to dress the young horse. John Bull and Henry Dubbins sent for all their sheep.

The 22nd October 1715 Saturday. A fine day. Tully workt to day. Jack Bartlet and Ned May plough'd. John Paine sow'd and harrow'd, 4 bushels. John Smith fetcht his hog towards night. My Sister Nanny went home towards night. Shut the boar up to the fatting hogs. Mr Hasloup was here. Jack Bartlet had a bushel of malt at 3s-6d and 10s in mony. Paid Thomas Baker 8d for a new payr of gloves. I wrote to Mr Gold, Mr Langford and James Wood.

The 23rd October 1715 Sunday. A dry day, only a showr towards night. My Wife was Church in the forenoon. Mr Jeremiah Dodson preacht. I was not at Church in the afternoon because my head acht.

The 24th October 1715 Munday. A showry day. Tully workt all day. Old William Brand did a little jobb in the morning. John Parsons _____ my wig. Jack Bartlet and Ned May plough'd. John Paine sow'd and harrow'd, 3½ bushels. Jack Whiteing brought home my coat afternoon. Paid him 5s for makeing and 16d for material he bought and 4d for mending other cloaths. Win'd 13 bushels of John Gun's Tully's wheat. Borrow'd Mr Richard Whitpaine's server. Mr Richard Whitpaine spent the evning here.

The 25th October 1715 Tuesday. A dry forenoon, the afternoon stormy with snow and rain. Jack Bartlet and Ned May plough'd. John Paine sow'd and harrow'd, 3½ bushels. Paid William Roach 20d for work here and at Mrs Storer's. John Bodle fetcht the brown heifer was Mr Scrase's. Mrs Barbara Campion, Mrs White, her niece, Mrs Mary Whitpaine and Mrs Ann Dodson supt here and Mrs Mary Whitpaine. Old William Brand did a jobb on the outside of my closet.

The 26th October 1715 Wednesday. A windy cold day. Tully workt all day. Weigh'd the brown heifer at John Bodle. Her 4 quarters weigh'd 50 stone 2lbs at 2d per lb. I had half the hind quarters. Put the fatting oxen in Tully's Mead, the young beasts in the Marldfield, the working oxen in the Edgly Mead and the cows into the Little Meads. Thomas Avery went through my ground with his teem with a load of pease to his house at Danworth. John Towner fetcht his hog at 25s, did not pay for him. Mrs Mary Burry was here in the afternoon.

Jack Bartlet and Ned May plough'd. John Paine sow'd and harrow'd, 4 bushels. Made an end of the Churchfield haveing sow'd in all on him 29 bushels of my own wheat that grew in Tully's 3 acre field. An extraordinary good season not Sumer fallow'd but 'twas sow'd with Nonsuch with _____ to follow it. Mr Osbourne of Poynings buried to day. I was at Mrs Catherine Beard a while in the evning. There was Mr Leonard Gale. I did not stay supper.

The 27th October 1715 Thursday. A showry day, afternoon especially. Tully workt. John Paine made an end of harrowing the Churchfield. Stephen Bine's man Tom Vinall workt here. We cut down 5 trees and draw'd them home. Carry'd half a load of flints and a good half load of mortar to the Church Green for my Father's tomb stone. My Wife din'd at Danny. Ned May and Tully fetcht her home. Mr Gale went through my ground in his way home. Lent Mr Richard Whitpaine 4 sack per Henry Emery.

The 28th October 1715 Fryday. A gloomy day. Some small rain. Tully workt. John Paine and Ned May plough'd and sow'd in Tully's 2nd field below the mead. There was 2 day's work sow'd before the rain and this is the 3rd but the season is now extreamly wet and bad but this is sow'd under furrough as well as the rest cheifly to try how 'twill prove. Sold Dick Wood 2 flitches of old bakon at 3s-4d per nail. John Box and I went to Eastout to agree with Goodman Champion about the repairs etc but we agreed for nothing only we sold him the barly at the price that we have for the comon barly at Albourne Place. He offer'd to do all the out doore repairs for 40s we allowing rough timber but then he offer'd but £6 for all the hay being full 20 loads (but half very mow burn'd hay) and 7s-6d for 4 acres of ruin, 17s-6d for 5½ acres of good clover on the ground and was unwilling to thrash the barly for the straw. I spent the evning at Wanbarrow. We din'd at Thomas Champion's. Nick Plaw was with us. Nick Marchant was here to day. Paid 4d for removing William Balcomb's mare's shooes, that is, I must pay it. Stephen Bine's man Tom Vinall workt part of the day, hewing timber.

The 29th October 1715 Saturday. A very fine day. John Paine and Ned May plough'd in Tully's first field, begun at 10. Receiv'd 45s-3d of Dick Wood for 2 flitches of bakon at 3s-4d per nail. Paid John Gun 28s-9d in all for all work to Michaelmas last. Gave him 1s for a harvest supper and 2s -6d to make his haying the better. I was at Mrs Catherine Beard in the forenoon. I shot a cock in Tully's coppice. Sent home William Balcomb's mare per Tully. I was at Westtowne in the evning. Mr John Hart came to me from Wanbarrow. John Box left a letter here which he receiv'd from James Day as a sumons to _____ Court Baron on William Balcomb's account.

The 30th October 1715 Sunday. A wet day. Mr Jeremiah Dodson preacht. I was at Mrs Catherine Beard's after evning prayr and at Mr Scutt's. My Cousin Nick Marchant came in the evning. Receiv'd a book from Norman's per Mr Henry Campion's man.

The 31st October 1715 Munday. A very fine day. Tully went home sick at 10 aclock. Jack at 10 acres. Win'd 7½ bushels of John Gun's Tully's head wheat and 2 bushels tail being the last of the field, in all 5 quarters 4½ bushels. John Towner and Ja Reed saw'd harrow ledges. Tom Whiteing and his man came to work this morning. Frank Marshall was here to dress the young horse. Mrs Mary Whitpaine was here in the morning. My Wife, Nick Marchant and Ned May went to Lewis. Paid Thomas Friend £1-4-7¼d for cloaths for John Balcomb, also 14s-8d for Molly Balcomb as appears by the bill.

The 1st November 1715 Tuesday. A fine day. John Paine and Jack Bartlet plough'd. Tom Whiteing went home this morning, left his man. John Towner and Ja Reed saw'd. Jack Standbridge workt 2 hours. Jack Smith fetcht the Plaw's cow per Richard Vinall and Ned May. Mr Jeremiah Dodson was here to see Mr John Hart. John Box and Nick Plaw supt here. Nick Marchant went from home to Balcombe.

The 2nd November 1715 Wednesday. A dry day. John Towner and Ja Reed saw'd. Last night Tom Whiteing came again this morning. John Gun, John Paine and Ned May begun dung about 2 aclock in the Bankfield, carry'd 10 loads. My Wife went to Mrs Ann Dodson's in the evning, Staid late.

The 3rd November 1715 Thursday. A showry forenoon, the afternoon wet. John Gun, John Paine and Ned May, carry'd 40 loads of dung. John Towner and Ja Reed saw'd part of the day. Thomas Champion jr and Nick Plaw din'd here, Thomas Champion paid Nick Plaw £7 for the hay at Eastout, the clover on the ground and a parcell of clover hay he bought of William Balcomb in his life time and he is to do all the repairs (except the house) into the bargain at his own charge, we to allow him rough timber. Mr Scutt and his brother Mr Frank Minshall came home with Mr John Hart, staid 'till 3. Whiteing and his man workt to day. Receiv'd 10s of the Widdow Balcomb per Nick Plaw towards buying cloaths for John Balcomb.

The 4th November 1715 Fryday. A wet driveing rainy day. Whiteing and his man workt. John Gun, John Paine and Ned May carry'd 42 loads of dung. Reckon'd with John Towner and Ja Reed and clear'd all accounts. Paid them 11d and outset Towner's hog. Nick Plaw's cow weigh'd about 18½ stone per quarter. The perticulers of John Towner and Ja Reed's work was 723 foot of timber and ashen board's sawing at 3s per hundred £1-1-7½d, 106 foot of oaken board at 2s-6d per cord 2s-7½d and 56 foot of wallnut trees plank a 3s per cord 1s-8d, in all £1-5 -11d.

The 5th November 1715 Saturday. A stormy, showry day. Mr Jeremiah Dodson preacht. Paid Tom Whiteing 6s-8d in full of all accounts. Paid Jack Bartlet a guinea. I was not at Church. About this time 'twas reported the Duke of Ormond landed at Liverpool in Lancashire, but false. My Cousin John Lindfield sent me 2 horses and a court. John Gun, John Paine and Ned May carry'd dung 'till noon. They carry'd 6 loads out of the dung mixen, in all 90 loads which was 192 loads out of the close, so that 2 loads out of the close makes one when well rotten. They also carry'd 9 loads out of the close to day into the Bankfield. Ned May went to Nunnery at in the afternoon with 2 crocks of butter and some candles and some flattice. Ned May had the boy dog to John Snashall's to be bleeded but he would not do it. Dick Wood try'd but made him bleed but little.

The 6th November 1715 Sunday. A showry day, wet towards night. Mr Jeremiah Dodson preacht in the morning and went to Albourne in the afternoon. My Cousin John Lindfield din'd here, staid 'till night. Mrs Ann Dodson, Mrs Courthope, Mrs Catherine Beard and her family were here in the afternoon, the latter spent the evning here. Ned May return'd from Rusper towards night.

The 7th November 1715 Munday. A stormy showry day. St Leonard's Fair. John Paine, Ned May and William Haslegrove carry'd dung, 12 loads (left at John Bodle's by John Smith) into the Bankfield. I bought John Bodle's dung that he left at John Smith's for 2 loads of wheat straw to be deliver'd at his request. Stephen Bine supt here. Tully workt again to day. Mr John Hart reckon'd for board and schooling with my Wife, half a year.

The 8th November 1715 Tuesday. A dry day, John Paine, William Haslegrove and Ned May carry'd eight loads more of John Smith's dung left at John Bodle's and afterwards 15 loads of the dung I bought of John Bodle. Memorandum there was 2 or 3 loads of John Bodle's dung among John Smith's for which I am to give him 2 bundles of straw. My Wife and I were at Wanbarrow in the afternoon. Mr John Hart and I supt at Mr Jeremiah Dodson's with Mr Sixsmith. Mr Dodson promis'd to take 500 faggots of me next Sumer. I offer'd to exchange as much of the Churchfield with Mr Dodson for his plott call'd the reeves but he refused it, supposing that he ought not to alienate any part of the Gleab tho he had what was better. I laid 2 bottles of wine with Mr Dodson that he not so old as Sir George Parker
*(Ed: Sir George of Ratton, Willingdon, born 1677, died 1726, the son of Robert Parker and Sarah Chute).*
I desir'd Harry Wickham to call on Harry Dubbins for £7-4s due to me. Tully workt to day. John Edwards begun rake the wheat stubble at Wickham's at 1s per acre. He is to cart it. John Gun spread dung 'till noon at 10d per score, afterwards mended hedge.

The 9th November 1715 Wednesday. A dry day 'till mist at night. Tully workt to day. Jack Bartlet had half a bushel of course wheat at 1s-6d. Mr Jeremiah Dodson and Mr Sixsmith breakfasted here. Reckon'd with Mr Dodson and clear'd all accounts. John Paine, Ned May and Mr Haslegrove carry'd the rest of the dung at John Smith's, 15 loads in all, 30 loads at that place. They also carry'd 3 loads of Towne dirt. Widdow Tully had half a bushel of malt at 1s-9d. Win'd 20 bushels head and 2 bushels tail of Jack Bartlet's grey pease, being all that was in that part of the field. I gave William Haslegrove 1s.

The 10th November 1715 Thursday. A fine day. Tully workt. John Paine and Ned May carry'd 13 loads of Towne dirt. Stephen Bine's man Thomas Mall workt here setting up rick steddle. Dick Wood shoo'd the old horse round. Turn'd the 5 runts into the Nine Acres. My Wife went to Danny in the afternoon.

The 11th November 1715 Fryday. A cold day, a small showr of snow and hail about noon. John Paine and Ned May carry'd 10 loads of Towne dirt and 5 loads of Thomas Westover's dung into the Bankfield so that there is 162 loads of dung and 26 loads of Towne dirt in the Bankfield. Thomas Mall workt on the rick steddle. Tully workt to day. I was at Mr Jeremiah Dodson's in the morning. I saw a cow of my Cousin John Lindfield's weigh'd at John Smith. The 4 quarters weigh'd 63 nail 1 lb. Mr Marshall and his wife, Mrs Scutt, her mother and Mrs Wood were here in the afternoon. Memorandum I am to give Thomas Westover some straw for his dog He also promis'd to take 2 or 300 faggots next year.

The 12th November 1715 Saturday. A fine day. Tully workt. Jack Bartlet and Ned May begun plough the Bankfield. John Paine sow'd and harrow'd. Thomas Mall workt on the rick steddle. Turn'd the fatting oxen into the Fifteen Acres. I was at Mr Jeremiah Dodson's in the evning a little while. Ned May and Jack Bartlet drove the oxen down through the lane and way to West Edgly, that is, the way _____ Latchets and East Edgly ground and so in of the gate at the upper corner of Tully's Mead which is the only highway to West Edgly alias Tully's ground. They brought the fatting oxen up the same way
_____ .

The 13th November 1715 Sunday. Mr Jeremiah Dodson preacht and went to Woodmancote in the afternoon. *(Ed: xxx text deleted xxx)* Paid Thomas Norton jr 2s-8d for 1lb of tea be brought from Lewis. Mr John Hart took physick and did not go to Church. My Cousin Bodle of Hailsham came in the evning. Mrs Catherine Beard and her family, Mrs Ann Dodson, Mrs Scutt, Mrs Courthope, my Sisters Nanny and Betty were here in the afternoon.

The 14th November 1715 Munday. A dry cold day. Tully workt. My Cousin Bodle went away before I were up. Jack Bartlet and Ned May plough'd. John Paine sow'd and harrow'd. Thomas Mall finisht the rick steddle about 10 aclock. Workt the rest of the day on the little stable. Deliver'd 3 bushels of pease to John Paine per Tully. Receiv'd 3 bushels of wheat from Albourne Place per Tully. Mr Richard Whitpaine's man fetch my court and my Cousin John Lindfield's and a chaine to each court. Mr William Dumsday sr a stay maker at Horsham was here this morning. William Balcomb's bull was weigh'd at John Smith's.

The 15th November 1715 Tuesday. A dry cold day. Tully carry'd 3 bushels more of pease to John Paine and brought home 2 bushels of wheat from Albourne Place. Jack Bartlet and Ned May plough'd, John Paine sow'd. John Gun made an end of spreading dung by 10 aclock. Thomas Mall workt on the   little stable etc. William Balcomb's man E Paine was here but I did not see him. My Brother Will was here towards night. Paid him £4-10s for a year's intrest due to my Brother Henry Faulkoner.

The 16th November 1715 Wednesday. A fine day. Tully fetcht 6½ of wheat from Albourne Place. Jack Bartlet and Ned May plough'd. John Paine sow'd and harrow'd. Harry Morley came to thatching. Nick Plaw was here in the afternoon. Mr Richard Whitpaine spent the evning here. My Wife was at Westtowne. John Gun begun dig the hop garden.

The 17th November 1715 Thursday. A fine day. Tully, John Lindfield and I cut 8 trees in Tully's ground and one in the Nine Acres for laths. Jack Bartlet and Ned May plough'd. John Paine sow'd. Paid John Edwards 5s. Put the calves in the Edgly Mead. Receiv'd £8 of John Smith and sold him a steer at 2d per lb only I am to abate 5s but I am to have the tongue. I was at Mr Jeremiah Dodson's in the afternoon. Supt at Mrs Catherine Beard's.

The 18th November 1715 Fryday. A dry day. Tully workt. Jack Bartlet and Ned May plough'd. John Paine sow'd and harrow'd. They made an end of ploughing the Bankfield by noon and afterwards draw'd home the top ends of the trees cleft for laths. John Paine finisht the field. Harry Morley workt a thatching to day and yesterday. Harry Emre had home my Cousin John Lindfield's court and _____ Mr Richard Whitpaine was here in the afternoon. Jack Bartlet and Thomas Tully brought the oxen every morning (through the way before mentioned to West Edgly) to plough which I order'd purposely that it may be remember'd where the way is. Sow'd 17½ bushels of Albourne Place wheat in the Bankfield. My Sisters Nanny and Betty supt here.

Mrs Storer told me the tythe of her house was 2s-6d per acre.

The 19th November 1715 Saturday. A fine day. Tully workt. Harry Morley thatcht. Jack Bartlet and John Paine thrasht half a bushel of the beans that grew in the orchard and 12 bushels 3 gallons of Tully's beans. My Cousin Hayne of Henfield was here and 2 of her daughters about her husband's inventory. Mr Woodcock went through the ground in his way to London.
*(Ed: xxx text deleted xxx)*
Paid John Smith sr 2s for a quart of white wine.

The 20th November 1715 Sunday. A fine day. Mr Jeremiah Dodson preacht. I was at Mrs Catherine Beard's a little while just after dinner. At Stephen Bine's after evning prayr. Call'd my Wife at Mrs Beard's but did not stay there the evning. Receiv'd ℔ of tea from Mr Tourl and a paper of large 3d nailes from Mr Court per Richard Wood.

The 21st November 1715 Munday. A fine day, a hard frost last night. Jack Bartlet and Ned May made an end of stirring Tully's pease earsh. John Paine heald the asparagus and artichoak bed. Harry Morley and his girls thatched. John Lindfield cleft laths 'till noon. Mr Richard Whitpaine sent home my court and harness per Phillps. I wrote to J Chainey of Arundell for William Balcomb's mony. Robert Pierce had half a hundred of hoops and 6 to set on the bucken tub. Receiv'd 2 bushels of oates from Albourne Place. Paid Thomas Baker 1s for a payr of gloves for my self and my son John.

The 22nd November 1715 Tuesday. A dry cold day. Jack Bartlet and Ned May plough'd. Tully workt, Harry Morley had a paper of nailes and 2 half papers before. Thomas Mall, John Paine and I workt on the rack in the fatting close. I gave John Westover 5s to buy his man tools. Paid my Lord Treep 6d for grinding and riveting my garden sheers. Receiv'd 2 bushels of oates from Albourne Place.

The 23rd November 1715 Wednesday. A dry day 'till towards night, then raine. Tom Mall, John Paine and I workt on the rack in the fatting close. Jack Bartlet and Ned May plough'd. Tom Tully peakt plough. Mr Richard Whitpaine and his wife Mary and Nick Goffe's widdow were here in the afternoon. Mr Scrase of Pangdean was here and paid me £3-3-6d for my wool, being 3 todd

6lbs at 20s per todd. Paid him 6d for the Let Pass. Receiv'd a paper of the largest of 3d nailes per John Westover for Mr Courtness and a table of the acts of this session from Norman. Ed Pickstone and John came in the evning to buy my oxen. They staid all night. Drank too much.

The 24th November 1715 Thursday. A stormy day, some rain in the forenoon. Sold 4 oxen to Ed and John Pickstone at 40 guineas to be gone before Xmas. John Lindfield cleft laths yesterday. Tully ground 6 bushels of _____ to day. John Paine and Ned May fetcht a load of furze out of the lower field into the fatting close, also 2 loads of stubble out of the field at Wickham's. John Gun fetcht his hog to kill him. Jack Bartlet thrasht beans. Richard Patching let my Wife bleed. Sent my Brother Peter 100 coaping brick and my horse court. I borrow'd Mr Jeremiah Dodson's dill harness for him. Shutt the 4 fatting oxen into the close. My Cousin John Lindfield supt here. Staid 'till 9 aclock.

The 25th November 1715 Fryday. A dry day. John Paine, Ned May and Tully carry'd 3 loads of stubble out of the field at Wickham's into the fatting close and brought one load to be laid on the lean oxen. Jack Bartlet and John Lindfield cut a tree in Tully's Mead and John Lindfield cleft laths afterwards. Paid Jack Bartlet a guinea. I saw a cow of my Cousin John Lindfield weigh'd at John Smith's. Receiv'd 2 bushels of oates from Albourne Place. John Gun's hog weigh'd 20 nail 5lbs at 2s per nail. I had half a quarter of bief of John Smith at 17d per nail. Harry Morley and his children thatcht. Paid Thomas Howell 9s for a plough and 5s-11d for the Smith's bill for a new share and other ironwork. Lent John Westover 40s. My Lord Treep clean'd a gun. My Son John had a new payr of shooes and so had William within this day or two last. Thomas Howell hew'd the 2 forebody crooks for my new waggon. Mrs Minshall, Mrs Woodcock and Mrs Scutt were here in the evning.

The 26th November 1715 Saturday. A wet forenoon, dry after. Tully and Ned May and Jack Bartlet made an end of Tully's lower field. Jack Bartlet open'd furroughs after. Ned May and Tully carry'd 10 bushels of pease to John Paine. Receiv'd 4 bushels more of oates from Albourne Place. Jack Bartlet had a bushel of wheat at 4s. I was at Wanbarrow in the afternoon. There was Harry Wickham and my Cousin Dick Bull of Ketches. Harry Morley swept my kitchen and hall chimneys, Mrs Storer's, the Widdow Brooks's and the school chimney and also the Widdow Tully's and Jack Bartlet's. Jack begun serve 4 beasts once a day. Robert Pierce brought home the new bucken tub. He is to have 6s for makeing it of my timber and hoops. My Wife supt at Mrs Catherine Beard's.

The 27th November 1715 Sunday. A fine day. Mr Jeremiah Dodson preacht. I was at Church forenoon and afternoon. I was at Mrs Catherine Beard's just before dinner to take leave of Mrs Kettilby. Nick Plaw was here in the evning. Paid him £5-4s for all the wheat I had from Albourne Place. Receiv'd 50s of him which makes (with the £4-10s I borrow'd) £7 that I paid for the herriot seiz'd at William Balcomb's death. Note; He takes the 40s I then receiv'd of Mr Norton on himself. Bartlet. Din'd here. Lent Nick Plaw £3-5s for a note of his hand.

The 28th November 1715 Munday. A fine day 'till 3 aclock then stormy, some snow. Bartlet, Ned May and Tully begun ridge Tully's first field. John Paine dug some ground and set beans. I was a shooting in Clayton Woods, shot 3 kocks and a pheasant. Mr John Picknall of Arundell was here and Mr J Chainey the butcher. J Chainey was gone before I came home but Mr Picknall staid all night. Paid Mr Picknall's bill, £3-5-4d. Receiv'd 2 bushels of oates from Albourne Place. Mr Picknall made me a present of wash balls.

The 29th November 1715 Tuesday. A fine day, a sharp frost last night. Pain, Ned May and Tully plough'd half a day in Tully's field. Ned May and Tully drove the black runt cow to bull. Mrs Kettilby, Mrs Minshall, Mrs Woodcock, Mr C Minshall and his wife and Mr T Minshall went through my ground with waggon in their way to London. Jack Bartlet's hog weigh'd 23½ nail at 2s per nail. John Smith weigh'd him. Mr Picknall din'd here, went home about 3 aclock. Jack Bartlet and John Gun begun the hedge against Edgly mead. Paid John Lindfield 6s for cleaving laths; the comon laths at 5d per hundred and stone laths at 6d per hundred and cut down the timber into the bargain. Mrs Stone and Mrs Catherine Beard were here in the afternoon. My Sister Nanny din'd here.

The 30th November 1715 Wednesday. A fine day, last night wet. St Andrew's Bolny Fair. John Edwards begun thrash barly. Ned May kept holy day. Tully workt half the day. A Fair at East Grinstead. Receiv'd 2 bushels of oates from Albourne Place. I was a shooting but shot nothing. Mr John Hart was at Lewis. Mrs Scutt and my Sister Nanny were here. My Lord Treep clean'd a gun and there was one done before.

The 1st December 1715 Thursday. A dry day. My Cousin John Lindfield's son Thomas christen'd, Mr Jeremiah Dodson, Mr John Hart, my Wife and I and Son William went to the christ'ning. There was only Mr Norden and his daughter. Mr Norden and my Wife were gossips and my Cousin John Lindfield himself stood for his kinsman, Thomas Butcher. We staid 'till 10 aclock. Drank moderately. John Paine clipt the furze hedges. Jack Bartlet and John Gun hedg'd. Tully begun serve the yearlings. Tom Whiteing the taylor was here in the evning and carry'd home the materials for John Balcomb's cloath. John Paine and Ned May tipt the lean oxen's rick in the morning.

The 2nd December 1715 Fryday. A dry day 'till towards night, then wet. John Paine, Ned May and Tully plough'd in Tully's first field. John Gun and Jack Bartlet hedg'd. John Edwards rak't stubble. Paid John Edwards 7s- 6d. Paid all the intrest due from Mrs Storer to James Wood on bond, being £3-3s to Michaelmas last.
I likewise gave a bond for the principal to Thomas Ilman, servant to James Wood, £30 from Michaelmas last past. James Wood din'd here. Mr Scutt and his wife supt here. Sold him a payr of stockens for 1s. Jack Bartlet had a bushel of wheat at 4s. I used a sheet of stampt paper that was William Balcomb's.

The 3rd December 1715 Saturday. The forenoon wet. John Gun thrasht wheat, Jack Bartlet beans, John Edwards barly. John Paine shav'd rack staves. Ned May mended the cart whip and Tully pickt up chucks etc. I went to Westtowne after dinner. Mr John Hart came in the evning. We supt there. Staid 'till 10. I made 4 ox bows there. My Wife was at Mr Jeremiah Dodson's in the afternoon. Receiv'd 2 bushels of oates from Albourne Place.

The 4th December 1715 Sunday. A gloomy, cold day. Mr Jeremiah Dodson preacht. There was a parish meeting. Mr Litchford's charity was paid to Michaelmas last.

Thomas Field was not at Church. I was at Mr Dodson's after evning prayr with Mr Richard Whitpaine. I agreed with Mr Dodson for his oat straw to thatch my stables at Mrs Storer's at 18d per square, he to deliver.

The 5th December 1715 Munday. A fine day. John Paine and Ned May made an end of Tully's field. Tully fetcht William Balcomb's bay mare. John Gun and Jack Bartlet made an end of the hedge against the Edgly Sandfield. John Edwards thrasht barly. Mr Richard Whitpaine and I were a shooting in Albourne Woods but shot nothing but a snipe. A hard frost. I wrote to Mr Pickstone and Jude Storer. My Wife and Mrs Scutt were at Westtowne. Paid Frank Holden 6d for ¼lb of gunpowder per W_____ .

The 6th December 1715 Tuesday. A gloomy day, a hard frost last night. John Paine and Ned May carry'd a load of roots to John Gun at _____ and brought home 2 loads more and a jobb of Wood. John Gun and Jack Bartlet begun the hedge on the north of Tully's farther field. John Edwards thrasht barly. Mr Richard Whitpaine and I and Tully went to shooting at Albourne and Wick Wood but shot nothing.

The 7th December 1715 Wednesday. A fine day, a hard frost last night. John Paine and Ned May carry'd 4 loads of stubble out of the Rookwood. John Gun and Jack Bartlet mov'd the white pease and some straw. Win'd 4 bushels of John Gun's head wheat of the Rookwood. Shut the 2 old oxen into Tully's close and begun house the cattle. Mr Pickstone's drover came this afternoon, went to William Balcomb's. My Wife was at Wanbarrow in the afternoon. Tully workt. My Brother Peter sent home my dune cow. John Edwards workt on the Rookwood stubble.

The 8th December 1715 Thursday. A fine day, a hard frost last night. John Paine and Ned May carry'd a load of stubble out of the Rookwood and fetcht home the wood about the ground. Tully and I drove the 4 fatting oxen to my Brother Peter's Westtowne barne and there deliver'd 'em to Mr Pickstone's man. Win'd 4 quarters a bushel and 3 pecks head and 1½ bushel tail of John Edwards's Homefield barly. John Gun and John Edwards begun thrash barly together at noon. Shut the 3 fatting steers into the fatting close. My Wife, Mr John Hart, Jacky and I supt at Mrs Catherine Beard's. Jack Bartlet fagotted several parcels of spray about the ground. Mrs Beard's man had Mr Jeremiah Dodson's dill harness here that I borrow'd all but the coller.

The 9th December 1715 Fryday. A fine day, a hard frost last night. Receiv'd 2 bushel of oates from Albourne Place. John Paine and Ned May fetcht home the rest of the wood and faggots. John Gun and John Edwards thrasht barly. Jack Bartlet thrasht beans. Dick Wood clouted the horse dung court wheels with my old clouts. He found nothing but brods. Tully workt.
Receiv'd £7-4s of Henry Dubbins and John Bull per Harry Wickham in full for the 16 sheep. Spent 9d with him at John Smith's. Mrs Catherine Beard's man brought home my fore harness to the chaese. Nick Plaw's boy had home William Balcomb's mare. Paid 10d for shooeing her. Lent Thomas Norton an iron rake per William Norton.

The 10th December 1715 Saturday. A gloomy cold day, a small frost last night. John Paine and Ned May carry'd dung in Tully's Mead with the horse court in the forenoon and Jack Bartlet came to them in the afternoon with the ox court, they carry'd in all 25 loads. John Gun and John Edwards thrasht barly. Tully pil'd wood etc. My Wife, Jacky and Molly din'd at Danny. Ned May carry'd home Mr Jeremiah Dodson's coller yesterday. I was at Stephen Bine's in the evning.

The 11th December 1715 Sunday. A dry, very cold day. A small frost last night. Mr Jeremiah Dodson preacht. Mr Burry was here in the evning. My Cousin John Lindfield's child Thomas bury'd.
(Ed: Hurst Parish Register records "Thos son of John Lindfield) I was at Church forenoon and afternoon.

The 12th December 1715 Munday. A fine day, very little frost last night. John Paine, Ned May and Jack Bartlet carry'd 16 loads of Tully's dung, the last of the mixen, in all 41 loads laid at the northwest corner of Tully's Mead as far as the hedgerow that was grub'd. They also carry'd 2 small loads of stubble out of Tully's wheat earsh up into the rick steddle by the barne. John Gun and John Edwards kockt the stubble and thrasht barly the rest of the day. I was to see Harry Wickham's oxen in the evning. Mr John Hart, my Wife and I supt at Mr Scutt's. I shot a partridge and left it at Mr Richard Whitpaine's. I laid a bottle of wine with Mr Scutt some time ago that Dick Buckwell would not be indighted next assizes or before for poaching. So, to night at Mr Scutt's, we paid back 1s and had the wine and whoever looses to pay the other 1s again.

The 13th December 1715 Tuesday. A gloomy day, a very small frost last night. Win'd 21½ of Tully's beans of Jack Bartlet's thrashing, the last of that plot, in all 37½ bushels. Tom Vinall and Robert Gatland cut down 11 pollards in Tully's ground and one in the Nine Acres. John Paine and Ned May draw'd home 6 of them. John Gun and John Edwards thrasht barly. Tully pil'd wood etc. Harry Wickham was here and I agreed for his oxen for 22 quarters. Mr John Hart set out on foot for London with Christian Sixsmith about 7 in the morning. My Wife, Will, Jacky and Goode Shave was at Dean House.

The 14th December 1715 Wednesday. A fine day, a small frost at night. John Paine and Ned May draw'd home 6 trees. Tom Vinall and Robert Gatland cut 4 trees in Tully's ground, that is 2 pollards and 2 spire trees. Receiv'd 2 bushels of oates from Albourne Place. John Gun and John Edwards thrasht barly. Jack Bartlet faggoted. The young white sow farrow'd to day.

The 15th December 1715 Thursday. A dry day, a small frost at night. Tom Vinall and Robert Gatland cut 1 pollard and 1 spire tree in Tully's ground and 2 pollards in the barly earsh by Hyder's. John Paine and Ned May draw'd home trees. John Gun and John Edwards thrasht barly. Mr Richard Whitpaine, Jack Bartlet and I went to John Lindfield's at Sayer's Comon. Jack Bartlet went to buy his house of him and after Mr Richard Whitpaine and I came away they agreed for £30 only. Jack Bartlet was to have something (such as shelves, hog trows etc) into the bargain. Mr Richard Whitpaine and his wife Mary, Mrs Goffe, my Sister Nanny and Betty supt here. My Brother Peter was here in the afternoon. Jack Bartlet had half a bushel of malt at 3s-4d per bushel.

The 16th December 1715 Fryday. A dry day, a very small frost last night. John Paine and Ned May draw'd home all the rest of the trees. John Gun and John Edwards thrasht barly. Tully walkt to Nunnery. Jack Bartlet fagotted. I was at Stephen Bine's in the evning. Receiv'd 2 fatting oxen of Harry Wickham for which I am to give him 22 quarters of barly. John Towner and Ja Reed begun sawing. Tom Vinall and Robert Gatland workt hewing timber. Paid a bill of 9s to Mary Rust for Molly Balcomb.

The 17th December 1715 Saturday. A dry, cold day, a small frost last night. Receiv'd 4 bushels of oats from Albourne Place. Paid 7s-10d to Thomas Whiteing for making John Balcomb's cloaths as appears by his bill. Clear'd all accounts with John Paine, only he is to have 4 bushels of pease more. John Towner and Ja Reed saw'd. John Gun and John Edwards cleft crown wood. Tom Vinall and Robert Gatland hew'd timber. Jack Bartlet fagotted. John Paine and Ned May brought up faggots. My Cousin John Lindfield supt here.

The 18th December 1715 Sunday. A dry, very cold day, a smart frost last night. Mr Jeremiah Dodson preacht. My Cousin John Lindfield din'd here. We appointed to go thither a Thursday next. We had a parish meeting about John Lindfield's house. I was at Mr Scutt's and Mrs Catherine Beard's after evning prayr. Tully return'd from Nunnery with Dick Purvey and Rachell Potter. They brought a letter from my Father etc.

The 19th December 1715 Munday. A dry, cold day, a hard frost last night. Reckon'd with Old William Brand and clear'd all accounts. Receiv'd £1-5s of him for a hog of William Balcomb's. Paid him £2-3s for setting up my Father's tomb stone. John Gun and John Edwards win'd. Tom Tully workt. John Towner and Ja Reed _____ Robert Gatland workt hewing timber. John Smith kill'd my black steer. Dick Vinall and R Ister kill'd my two piggs. John Box, Nick Plaw and I met at Old John Smith's and reckon'd with Yung John for all his accounts with William Balcomb and there was due to William Balcomb £9-13-6d. We spent 1s. Receiv'd 2 ounces of bohea from Mr Tourl and the hoops from Thomas Friend which I sent to be sold.

The 20th December 1715 Tuesday. A dry, windy, very cold day, a hard frost last night. Win'd 11 quarters 6 bushels head and 5 bushels tail of John Gun's and John Edwards's Homefield barly to day and yesterday. Jack Bartlet and Ned May deliver'd 8 quarters of barly to Harry Wickham. John Gun and John Edwards screen this barly and the 4 quarters that was win'd before. John Towner and Ja Reed saw'd. John Box and I went to a Court Barron at Wiston and John Balcomb was admitted to the reversion of Little Hever by me as his attorney and afterwards John Box and I were both admitted as his guardians. Paid a guinea for the fees of the Court. Paid 6d to Mr Day's man to carry a letter and 11 guineas to Mr Sixsmith the same that was brought to me from Rusper. The fine that was set was £20-6-8d for which we gave a note of our hands but Mr Langford the steward promis'd to get some abatem't if he could. My black steer weigh'd 70 nail 6lbs the four quarters. Receiv'd the tongue and a buttock half weigh'd (I think)10 nail. Receiv'd 2 bushels of oates from Albourne Place.

The 21st December 1715 Wednesday. A very cold day, towards night wet. Snow last night, the wind being high. Deliver'd 6 quarters 1 bushel of barly to Harry Wickham per Ned May and Tully. John Gun and John Edwards finisht the barly in the morning, thrasht afterwards. Jack Bartlet fagotted. Nick Plaw was here to see the bull calf. John Towner and Ja Reed saw'd part of the day. Paid my Lord Treep 6d in full of all accounts. Paid John Edwards 10s.

The 22nd December 1715 Thursday. A cold, rainy day, thawing but little. Deliver'd 12½ bushels of barly to Harry Wickham per Ned May and Tully. Deliver'd the 4 bushels of pease due to John Paine per Tully. John Towner and Ja Reed saw'd a little while. John Gun and John Edwards thrasht barly. Jack Bartlet begun spread dung about 10 aclock. John Paine din'd here. My Cousin John Lindfield was here in the afternoon. I was at Mrs Catherine Beard's in the evning. Mr Scutt was here in the evning and gave me a note from J Balldy (alias Baldy) my Cousin John Lindfield for 23s-6d.

The 23rd December 1715 Fryday. A gloomy day, some snow, continu'd thawing. John Gun and John Edwards hedg'd against the Churchfield. Ned May and Tully fetch some faggots out of Tully's ground. Two of Stephen Bine's men cut down a pollard at the side of the new pond.

The 24th December 1715 Saturday. A fine day, a smart frost last night. Joseph Muzzall sent home my ram per Boniface. Ned May and Tully fetch up a small pbb of furze. Paid John Snashall sr 5s for what he did to the young horse, 2s-6d for Molly's arm and 1s-6d for physick and brandy, in full of all accounts. One of Mr Gold's tegs died. Mr John Hart return'd from London this evning. I was at Mrs Catherine Beard's a little while forenoon and afternoon. Jack Bartlet begun thrash wheat. John Gun and John Edwards thrasht barly the afternoon.

The 25th December 1715 Sunday. A fine day, a smart frost last night. Christmas Day. Mr Jeremiah Dodson preacht. I was at Mrs Catherine Beard's afternoon. Jack Bartlet and his wife and son, John Gun and his mother, John Edwards and his wife and Tom Tully and his mother din'd here. My Wife and I supt at Mr Scutt's.

The 26th December 1715 Munday. A fine day, a smart frost last night. We had a meeting at Church but no surveyors were chosen. We agreed to deliver John Lindfield his bond for his mother's thirds for 50s in hand when he sold his house. Paid R Burt 20s for my Window Tax for 1714. He din'd here. Mr Jeremiah Dodson, Mr Bland, Mr Baldy, Mr Scutt and Mr Richard Whitpaine were here in the afternoon and Mr Sixsmith. Mr Richard Whitpaine and Mr Scutt supt here. Receiv'd half a pound of bohea from Mrs Wolfe and a pint of ink from Mr Beard. Mrs Catherine Beard and her mother and Mrs Courthope were here in the afternoon.

The 27th December 1715 Tuesday. A dry, windy, cold day, a smart frost last night. Paid Joseph Muzzall 18s-4d for a year's Lord's rent to Michaelmas last for West Edgly for which I took a receit. Mr John Hart and I din'd and supt at Mr Jeremiah Dodson's with Mr Sixsmith, Mr Price, Mr Baldy, Mr Bland, Captain Whitpaine, Mr Richard Whitpaine. Mr Scutt came in the evning. Mr Price invited us all to dinner with him to morrow. Paid Mr Baldy 2s for which he is to get me 1 pound of gunpowder of Mr Mathew in the Cliffe.

The 28th December 1715 Wednesday. A fine day but cold and the wind very high. Dick Vinall kill'd my 2 hogs. A smart frost last night. Mr Jeremiah Dodson, Mr Sixsmith, Mr Bland and Mr Baldy came to breakfast with Mr John Hart. Mr Hart went to Mr Price's with Mr Dodson etc but I did not go. Receiv'd 4 bushels of oates from Albourne Place yesterday. My Brother Peter and Nick Marchant supt here. Reckon'd with my Brother Peter and clear'd all accounts including Tully's rent to Lady Day 1716 and this year's Poor Tax and 100 hoops not yet deliver'd.

The 29th December 1715 Thursday. A fine day, very windy, a great frost last night. Mr Healy din'd here and staid 'till about 4 aclock. Ned May hung the Martinsmas bief up in the chimney. Reckon'd with Stephen Bine and clear'd all accounts. His bill of work came to £4 and a few shillings over. Mr John Hart, my Wife and I supt at Mrs Catherine Beard's.

The 30th December 1715 Fryday. A fine day, a hard frost last night. John Towner and Ja Reed saw'd. Sold Mrs Catherine Beard 200 faggots and 1½ cord of wood at 48s, her boy to help carry it. Deliver'd the wood and 30 faggots per Ned May and John Smith. Reckon'd with John Gun to Xmas. Clear'd all accounts but his hog and I am to pay John Smith for the half quarter of bief he had against Xmas. John Gun and John Edwards cleft crown and faggoted. Jack Bartlet thrasht wheat. My Wife and the boys supt at Danny. Paid Shepeard 2d for carrying up the school wood.

The 31st December 1715 Saturday. A fine day, a hard frost last night. John Standbridge and Robert Gatland cut down a tree by the Hovelfield stew and an other at the lower side of the middle piece. John Towner and Ja Reed saw'd. Jack Bartlet thrasht wheat. Deliver'd 170 faggots to Mrs Catherine Beard per Ned May and John Smith. Paid R Lindfield 2d yesterday for fetching William Balcomb's _____ . John Buckwell was buried at our Church to day. John Edwards fagotted. Ned May draw'd home the trees from the stew in the afternoon. I sent a letter to Mr Picknall and my Brother James Ede.

The 1st January 1715 Sunday. A wet forenoon, the afternoon dry. Mr Jeremiah Dodson preacht. Mr John Hart and I receiv'd the sacrament. Abraham Muzzall, his wife and boy din'd here and William Shepeard. Receiv'd the pound of gunpowder from Mr Baldy per Shepeard.

The 2nd January 1715 Munday. A fine forenoon, snow towards night, a frost last night. Receiv'd 4 bushels of oates from Albourne Place and brought home the mare per Tully. My Cousin John Lindfield din'd here. Ned May ground 6 bushels of barly malt. John Towner and Ja Reed saw'd part of the day. Mr John Hart, my Wife and I and the 2 boys supt at Westtowne with Mrs Catherine Beard and her mother, Mr Scutt and his wife and Mrs Margaret Minshall staid late and drank enough. My Cousin John Lindfield's man carry'd home a pig.

The 3rd January 1715 Tuesday. A fine day, a frost last night. Tully workt. John Towner and Ja Reed saw'd Jack Bartlet thrasht wheat. Robert Gatland hew'd timber. John Gun and John Edwards cleft crowns. Mr Scutt, Mr

John Hart and I supt at Stephen Bine's. John Box and I were at John Smith's sr and sold 20 quarters of William Balcomb's barly to John Channel at £14-6d per quarter certain and if the price of barly mend he is to give 6d per quarter more. He is to have half prab and half comon barly.

The 4th January 1715 Wednesday. A very fine day, a frost last night. Jo Wood workt here. We cut down 2 pollards in Tully's coppice. Robert Gatland came to work in the morning but squah *(sic)* his thumb and went home again presently. Jack Bartlet and Ned May draw'd home the trees. John Towner and Ja Reed saw'd. John Gun and John Edwards thrasht barly. Mrs Scutt and Mrs Minshall was here in the afternoon. John Nye's wife that was Nell Marks buried yesterday.
*(Ed: Recorded in the Hurst Parish Register as "Goodwife Nye")*
Tom Tully carry'd a pig to Nick Marchant's. Receiv'd half a rheam of paper that Mr Burry bought at London but he is to have half of it. Clear'd all accounts with Dick Wood yesterday, his bill was 17s.

The 5th January 1715 Thursday. A very wet day. John Gun and John Edwards thrasht barly. Jack Bartlet thrasht wheat the forenoon. Jo Wood workt altring a table, putting up shelves for Mr John Hart. Nurse Holden dy'd last night. Receiv'd 25 guineas of Mr Pickstone per Frank Harden and sent an order by him for the payment of the remainder in London. Mr John Hart, my Wife and I supt at Mr Scutt's with Mr Richard Whitpaine and his wife Mary. Staid late and drank very moderately. Tom Tully went to Ditcheling Comon for the founder'd mare. My Aunt Courtness sent home my stockens per George. I gave him 1s.

The 6th January 1715 Fryday. A dry forenoon, some snow towards night. Tully workt part of the day and serv'd his beasts. Ned May kept holy day. Mr John Hart and I and Mr Scutt din'd at Dean House. Staid 'till 8 and drank moderately. Mr Stacey call'd there and came home with us. Receiv'd a letter from Henry Lintott. Reckon'd with Thomas Westover and clear'd all accounts except Thomas Challoner's harvest and the carriage of his brick. His bill for shoes was 23s-9d since the 11th of June last.

The 7th January 1715 Saturday. A dry, very cold day, a hard frost last night. John Gun and John Edwards fagotted in the morning, corded crown. Jack Bartlet thrasht wheat in the morning, cut part of the pare tree.

Ned May serv'd his beasts in the morning, then was took sick. Mr John Hart and I supt at Wanbarrow. Staid late. Paid my Mother 6 guineas. Nurse Holden buried. *(Ed: Recorded in the Hurst Parish Register as "Goodwife Holden")* Gave my likle Courtness a pig and Mrs Catherine Beard an other. Sent an other pig to Edgly. Tully workt. Turn'd the runts into Tully's teary field.

The 8th January 1715 Sunday. A great snow, a smart frost last night. Mr Jeremiah Dodson read prayrs but had such a cold he could not preach. I was not at Church afternoon. Dick Purvey came in the evning with a letter etc. I begun the half pound of tea I had from London.

The 9th January 1715 Munday. A dry, very cold day, the frost continuing. Receiv'd ½ of sea bisket from London. Ned May workt. Jack Bartlet thrasht wheat. John Gun and John Edwards thrasht barly 'till noon then John Gun fell sick and John Edwards thrasht alone. Mr Richard Whitpaine and his wife Mary and my Cousin Goffe, Mr Sixsmith his wife and sister supt here. Tully workt. Dick Purvey carry'd home a pig and 2 bottles of elder wine. Receiv'd a guinea of Ed Burt for William Balcomb's long gun. Receiv'd 4 bushels of oates from Albourne Place. Put the runts into the Nine Acres again.

The 10th January 1715 Tuesday. A very cold day, a very hard frost last night. Win'd 12 bushels head and 2 bushels tail of Jack Bartlet's Rookwood wheat. John Edwards flung over the stubble and begun litter the home close. He had half a bushel of malt at 1s-8d. Mrs Catherine Beard and her mother supt here. Receiv'd 48s of her in full for wood and faggots. Tully workt. Mr John Hart and my Wife reckon'd for board and school to Christmas Day last. John Towner and Ja Reed saw'd part of the day.

The 11th January 1715 Wednesday. A very cold day, a hard frost and some snow last night. John Edwards thrasht barly alone. Jack Bartlet thrasht pease. John Towner and Ja Reed saw'd half the day. Tully workt. John Edwards begun serve the cows in the Fifteen Acres with hay. Took the lean oxen into the close. Jo Wood workt here in the afternoon.

The 12th January 1715 Thursday. A dry, cold day, some little snow last night. Tully workt. Reckon'd with Mrs Storer and clear'd all accounts to Christmas last. There was £50 due to her for which I gave her a note of my hand on demand with intrest at £5 per hundred. I allow'd her 2s-6d for her part of the well bucket and also moveables (such as etc)except the dresser and the rest of the household goods. Deliver'd 59 faggots to to William Brand at 14s per _per Ned May. John Edwards thrasht barly alone. Gave the lean oxen hay tonight. I sent a pig to Mr Hayne of Clayton for the liberty of hunting his ground after woodcocks, pheasants and coney. Sent a pig to Mr Scutt's per Sarah Surgeant. William Lashmer at Danworth died a Tuesday night last. *(Ed: Burial recorded in Hurst Parish Register on 13 January as "Goodman William Lashmer)* Mr Jeremiah Dodson was here in the afternoon. My Wife spent the evning at Mr Scutt's. Sent 5 faggots up to the school. John Edwards had half a bushel of wheat at 2s.

The 13th January 1715 Fryday. A dry, cold day with a small scattering snow. The mountebank was here to day. John Edwards thrasht barly alone a little while in the morning and then begun winnow. Tully workt. I was at Mr Scutt's a little while in the afternoon. Paid Mrs Margaret Minshall 1s-6d for 14lbs of brown sea bisquetts, 3s-9d for 14lbs white, 2s-6d for a box Porter. Receiv'd 4d, 18d for dying Bett's scarlet stockens, 6d for dying my Sister Nanny's green and 4d for an apron. Receiv'd all my sacks from Mr Richard Whitpaine per Ned May and sent home what we had of his. Ned Penfold workt mending sacks.

The 14th January 1715 Saturday. A dry, windy day, very cold, the frost moderate. Ned Penfold mended sacks. Tully workt. Jack Bartlet mov'd to his purchase per Mr Richard Whitpaine's teem. John Edwards win'd 90 bushels head of the Homefield barly, thrasht between John Gun and he. Stephen Bine's man Joseph Wood workt the forenoon mending the barne's doores. Paid Mr Burry 18d for 1⁄8 of a rheam of paper. He carry'd home ¼ and Mr John Hart had 1⁄8. We are to pay our part of the carryage when he knows what it is. Nick Plaw was here to see a bullock. Shutt up the 2 old sows to fatting. ~~gave them~~.

The 15th January 1715 Sunday. A fine day, the frost continuing but moderately. Mr Jeremiah Dodson preacht. My Cousin John Lindfield din'd here and staid 'till night. We were to blame for not goeing to Church in the afternoon. Joseph Muzzall forbad the Court Baron that was to be held a Fryday next because Sir John Shaw was ill, if not dead.

The 16th January 1715 Munday. A pretty big snow last night and this morning *(Ed: xx text deleted xx)*. My Cousin John Lindfield sent us a hare. Win'd 6½ bushels of John Gun's and John Edwards's tail barly Homefield. Deliver'd 6 quarters 3 bushels of barly to Harry Wickham, the last for the oxen. John Edwards workt the afternoon for me. John Gun thrasht alone. A very smart showr of snow towards night. Tully workt. John Gun begun serve the oxen again and John Edwards the cows. The old sows have had about 2 bushels of good tail barly. Receiv'd 4 bushels of oates from Albourne Place.

The 17th January 1715 Tuesday. A fine day, a smart frost last night. Tully workt. Deliver'd 5 quarters 3 bushels of barly to Harry Wickham to be malted. Paid him 5d for a bushel of charl coal. Edward workt the forenoon for me and in the afternoon we mov'd his goods. John Gun thrasht barly alone. The Widdow Tully had half a bushel of malt at 1s-8d and 5s in mony. Ned Penfold workt mending sacks. Left 11 sacks at Harry Wickham's. Mrs Scutt and Mrs Margaret Minshall was here in the afternoon. Paid Thomas Baker 16d in full of all accounts.

The 18th January 1715 Wednesday. A cold day, a little snow towards night. Frost last night. Ned Penfold workt mending sacks. Tully workt. Paid Thomas Marshall a guinea for cureing the young horse's poll. Win'd 10½f Jack Bartlet's white pease. John Gun and John Edwards thrasht barly. John Standbridge and Thomas Mall workt the afternoon on the hog sty. My Cousin John Lindfield was here in the afternoon. My Wife and I supt at Wanbarrow. Jack Bartlet had half a bushel malt at 1s-8d.

The 19th January 1715 Thursday. Rain and snow most part of the day, thawing. John Standbridge and Tom Mall workt the forenoon on the hog styes. The short tetted cow calv'd a cow calf last night. Ned May carry'd some faggots for Jack Bartlet and Jack Bartlet workt afterwards about 2½ hours for me. John Gun and John Edwards thrasht barly. Tully workt. Mr John Hart and I din'd at Nick Plaw's with Mr Healy.

The 20th January 1715 Fryday. A very cold day, snow at night. A frost last night. John Gun and John Edwards thrash't barly. John Towner and Ja Reed saw'd. John Standbridge workt on the hogsties. Tully workt. John Edwards begun serve the 2 yearlings a Tuesday. Receiv'd a letter from my Brother James Ede yesterday. Receiv'd a letter from Mr Jeremiah Dodson about my Father's tomb. There was the mountebank again at Towne, he calls himself Richard Harness. Mr John Hart and I supt at Mr Richard Whitpaine with Mrs Catherine Beard and her mother and Nick Plaw and his wife.

The 21st January 1715 Saturday. A wet day, a great snow last night. John Standbridge workt the forenoon and finisht the hogsties. Win'd 6 quarters 2 bushels head and 3 bushels tail of John Gun and John Edwards's Homefield barly, the last of the field, in all 35 quarters 6 bushels. Tully workt. Receiv'd 4 bushels of oates from Albourne Place. Paid John Edwards 10d for all bullock serving to Tuesday last. John Gun and John Edwards din'd here as they did for one winnowing day before.

The 22nd January 1715 Sunday. A dry day but continu'd thawing again. Mr Jeremiah Dodson preacht. Tully serv'd his beasts. I was at Stephen Bine's after evning prayr. Supt at Mrs Catherine Beard's.

The 23rd January 1715 Munday. A dry day, a smart frost last night. Tully workt. Deliver'd 6 quarters 5 bushels of barly to Harry Wickham to be malted. Left 9 sacks there. Ned Penfold workt mending sacks. John Towner and Ja Reed saw'd. John Gun litter'd the close etc. Ned May brought up a parcel of corne for Stephen Bine. Turn'd the 5 runts into the field by Hyder's. John Edwards begun thrash wheat. Paid Mr Jeremiah Dodson 2s-6d for the load of straw deliver'd to John Bodle and John Stone. He gave me the rest for goeing through my ground in the Sumer with his teem. Michael Stacey went through my ground with his teem. I was at Mr Richard Whitpaine's as I came from Albourne. Mrs Barbara Campion and Mrs Courthope here in the afternoon with Mrs Catherine Beard and her mother. The 2 last supt here.

The 24th January 1715 Tuesday. Some showrs, thawing apace. Tully workt. I was at Mr Richard Whitpaine's in the forenoon. There was John Box sr, Mr Pointin and John Snashall jr. John Gun begun thrash the barly by Hyder's. John Edwards thrasht wheat. Harry Wickham was here towards night. I sold him my barne at Shermanbury at £7. Tully went to Nunnery in the afternoon. My Wife went to Westtowne in the afternoon with the boys. I went to fetch her home. John Towner and Ja Reed saw'd part of the day.

The 25th January 1715 Wednesday. A wet day. John Gun thrasht barly. John Edwards wheat. Jack Bartlet went about 11 aclock to meet Tom Tully. Ned May and I mended the doore of Tully's calf house. Stephen Bine carry'd home stuff for a table frame. I was at Mr Jeremiah Dodson's with Mr Richard Whitpaine, Mr Scutt and Stephen Bine where we adjusted all accounts about our school. We paid Stephen Bine's bills for the desks etc and Mrs Storer's rent and a quarter's rent to me to Christmas last. Mr Scutt, Mr Whitpaine and I paid 24s a piece and Mr Dodson 48s and Stephen Bine 5s and 38s-6d paid to Mr Whitpaine for wood. Abraham Muzzall workt here.

The 26th January 1715 Thursday. A showry morn, the rest dry, thawing. John Edwards thrasht wheat, John Gun barly half the day and the other half he helpt me about the calf stalls etc. Tom Tully return'd from Nunnery. Jack Bartlet went to meet him. He brought 2s-6d for the goose. John Edwards had half a bushel of wheat, 12 lbs of cheese. John Gun had 10 lbs at 18d per nail. Sent a letter to Mr Colebrand per Harry Wickham. Abraham Muzzall workt. Turn'd the ewes into the wheat earsh. Mr Richard Whitpaine, his wife, Nick Goffe's widdow, Mrs Scutt, Mrs Margaret Minshall came to see Mr John Hart. Supt here. Lent Mr Richard my two sheep racks about ten days ago. John Gun's bore was shut up with the fatting sows.

The 27th January 1715 Fryday. A gloomy day, wet towards night. Tully workt. John Gun thrasht barly. Jack Bartlet spread dung. John Edwards rak'd stubble in the Rookwood. Abraham Muzzall workt. I made a tan'd leather halter for the young horse. The mountebank was here again to day. Nick Plaw came towards night to look on an ox in Tully's close. He thought he ail'd nothing. I gave him a pig which he carry'd home alive. Ground 2 bushels of tail barly and a bushel of beans for the fatting sows.

The 28th January 1715 Saturday. A dry day 'till towards night. Tully was sick and did not work. John Gun thrasht barly. John Edwards workt for him self. Jack Bartlet workt for me 2 hours, spread dung, the rest of the day. My Cousin John Lindfield came in the afternoon. Staid supper. He brought me a receit from Mr Lintott for a year's intrest paid to him, due to Mrs Gratwick which I paid him again. He also paid me a year's intrest due at Christmas last. He staid late. Receiv'd letter from Mr John Picknall of Arundell. Begun the rick the backside of Tully's Hovel for the two oxen there. Turn'd the young beasts into the cow field. Receiv'd 4 bushels of oates from Albourne Place. Paid my Cousin John Lindfield 2s for tires for William Balcomb's people.

The 29th January 1715 Sunday. A wet morning, the wind very high all day. Mr Jeremiah Dodson preacht. I was at Mrs Catherine Beard's before evning prayr and afterwards a little while at Stephen Bine's.

The 30th January 1715 Munday. A very cold day, the wind very high, a frost. I was at Church in the forenoon. Mr Jeremiah Dodson did not preach. John Standbridge workt putting up a frame for the vine to run on the brew house. Paid John Towner and Ja Reed 48s for sawing 1280 foot of board at 2s-6d per hundred and 539 foot of timber at 3s per cord. John Edwards thrasht wheat. John Gun did not work. Paid William Roach 3s-9d for sodering the pipes from the pump to the furnace. Paid my Unkle Courtness 9d for 100 of 10 inch nails. Mr Richard Whitpaine, Mrs Goffe, my Sisters Nanny and Bett were here before Church time and my Sisters came after evning prayr and staid supper.

The 31st January 1715 Tuesday. A dry, cold day, a smart frost last night. Paid Mrs Catherine Beard 1s for Mr Leslie's picture. Portsmouth Carrier sent an old man from Brighton with a whelp which Mr John Picknall of Arundell sent me. I gave the old man 6d, the carriage being paid by _____ . John Standbridge workt 'till noon on the vine frame. After cut down 4 pollards in Tully's ground. Jack Bartlet helpt half a day. John Gun and John Edwards cleft crowns. I was at Mr Jeremiah Dodson in the morning before he set out for London. He went through my ground. My Wife and I was at Mrs Catherine Beard's all the evning. Paid Ned Burt 1s for this day's work tacking the vines.

The 1st February 1715 Wednesday. A gloomy day, thawing. John Edwards rak'd stubble. John Gun thrasht barly. Jack Bartlet and Ned May draw'd home the trees. My Cousin John Wood of Ewhurst was here afternoon to buy my barne that I sold to Harry Wickham. Mrs Ann Dodson and Mr Orton's daughter supt here. I was at John Smith's sr with John Box, Nick Plaw and John Channel about William Balcomb's barly but we did not fully agree while I was with them.

The 2nd February 1715 Thursday. A gloomy day. John Gun thrasht barly. R Jeoffery of Ditcheling Comon was here. Paid him 1s for looking after my mare 2 years. Paid Mary and John Balcomb 1s for pocket mony. Paid John Edwards 10s. Wean'd the black sow's pig. Dick Wood shooed the young horse round. Sent 1½ bushels of tail barly and half a bushel of beans to mill for the sows. Thomas Champion jr din'd here. We talkt of severall matters but came to no solutions. The lowest price I mentioned for the Eastout barly was 14s-6d per quarter. I was at Stephen Bine's towards night. There was Mr Bird of Bolny, my Cousin Harry Goffe of Henfield, Mr John Hart and Mr Richard Whitpaine.

The 3rd February 1715 Fryday. A dry day. John Gun thrasht barly. The mountebank was here again. Lent Mrs Catherine Beard my waggon. John Edwards workt for himself. Ingram was here (as he said) from my Aunt Holden for 10s but I lent none. Turn'd the founder'd mare into the horse pond. Mr Richard Whitpaine was here in the evning but did not stay supper. I wrote 2 letters for him, he haveing hurt his hand. Set out 3 bushels of pease to the Widdow Tully to pick. One lamb of John Gold's sheep last night.

The 4th February 1715 Saturday. A dry day. John Gun dug in the hop garden. John Edwards thrasht wheat. Ground 6 bushels of malt. Dick Wood made me a horse chape for a turnrist plough for which he is to have 4s. My Wife and I and the boys were at Wanbarrow in the afternoon. I let Mrs Storer the room she lives in and part of the shop (when parted) at 30s per annum to begin at Lady Day next. She is to pay the tythes and to have the use of the brewhouse and as much of the celler as can be spared from my other tennants. Paid my Unkle Courtness 15d for 3 payr of joynts, 2 of which Stephen Bine had for my table he is makeing. Receiv'd 2 bushels of Albourne oates.

The 5th February 1715 Sunday. A gloomy, cold day. Mr Bird of Bolny preacht in the forenoon; no prayrs afternoon. My Mother din'd here.

The 6th February 1715 Munday. A gloomy day with some small rain. John Edwards and Ned May begun plough the Rookwood and brought a load of stubble home with them. John Gun dug in the hop garden. Tully workt again. My Brother Peter was here in the afternoon. I was at William Lashmer's at High Fields. John Edwards and Tully brought the 3 yearling heifers to the cows. Lent Mr Richard Whitpaine two iron rakes per Harland.

The 7th February 1715 Tuesday. A gloomy day. George West and Tully begun plough the field by Wickham's about 9 aclock and at noon. Jack Bignall came to help Tully drive. Ned May and John Edwards plough'd in the Rookwood after John Edwards had helpt John Gun ring the hogs. John Gun made water furroughs and mended some gaps etc all day. 2 lambs of Mr Gold's sheep one of which the young white sows kill'd and eat part of it. 1 lamb of William Hamshurst sheep. Paid John Edwards 2s-2d for serving the cowes. John Gun begun serve them this morning. George West begun serve the working oxen and fatting oxen. My Wife and Willy was at Dean House afternoon. William Norton brought home my iron rakes. John Shave workt a gardning, set pease etc. Ned Penfold went to Nunnery. I wrote to my Father per Mr Ede.

The 8th February 1715 Wednesday. A gloomy day. Tully, George West and Bignall plough'd. Ned May and John Edwards plough'd. Harry Morley and John Reed thatcht. John Gun dug in the hop garden. Put the three 3 yearling steers into the home close. Reckon'd with John Smith and there is due to me £7-8-3d. His bill of meat was £8-7-4d since January the 15th 1714. Sold him my hous'd calf at 3d per lb when he's fitt to kill. Ed Penfold return'd from Nunnery, brought a letter from my Father in which he said he would have my steers. Sold a heap of barly to Harry Wickham at 15s per quarter. Lent Mr Richard Whitpaine an other iron rake per R Lindfield. George West begun this morning at 2s-6s per week to Lady Day and he is to have 3s per week after to May Day, meat and drink.

The 9th February 1715 Thursday. A gloomy day. George West and the boys plough'd. Ned May and John Edwards plough'd. Harry Morley thatcht. Receiv'd 4 bushels of whole oates from Albourne. Jack Howard fetcht the bay mare from thence. John Gun set out 4 bushels of pease to Widdow Tully to [pay] and measur'd half a bushel of wheat for John Edwards. Mr Healy din'd here. Yak'd 2 three yearlings. I was at Mrs Catherine Beard's in the afternoon. Nick Plaw supt here. Receiv'd a letter from Hugh Douglas per Thomas Norton of Edgly concerning Albourne Place hops. John Gun workt makeing water furroughs and fetcht my Father Stone's herrings from Danny.

The 10th February 1715 Fryday. A dry day. The mountebank here again. Mrs Mary Whitpaine lay here last night as she came from William Lashmer's wive's labour *(Ed: Ann Taylor)*; so did Mrs Woolgar the midwife. George Hill of Rigate was here to buy my oxen but we did not deal. They bid me £34 for all or £15-10s for the _____ . Receiv'd 2 bushels of ground oates from Albourne. George West and the boys plough'd, so did Ned May and John Edwards. I was at John Smith's jr a little while in the afternoon. There was George Hill and Robert Skinner, Michael Stacey, Thomas Norton and Edward Burry and E Dennet of Bolny and Mr Bird, the 2 latter were here. My Grandmother and Mrs Catherine Beard supt here. John Gun workt a while for me in the forenoon. Harry Morley workt a thatching. John Hart was here with George Hill. My Brother Peter here towards night. Paid John Gatland 1s for cleaning the clock etc.

The 11th February 1715 Saturday. A wet morning, the rest of the day fine. George West and the boys plough'd. John Gun and John Edwards plough'd in the Rookwood. Ned May carry'd home Rachell Potter. Dick Wood shoo'd my old horse's fore feet. I went to Albourne Place with George Hill and Robert Skinner and sold them the 10 oxen and a steer at £110. Afterwards sold them my own 4 at £34-10s. John Bodle and Thomas Hart was there with them. John Bodle bid £19 for 4 barrens fat. Mr Healy was there.

The 12th February 1715 Sunday. Mr Bird preacht, no afternoon service. My Cousin John Lindfield and his wife Elizabeth din'd here. My Wife and I supt at Mrs Catherine Beard's. Mr Jeremiah Dodson and Mr Scutt return'd from London this evning.

The 13th February 1715 Munday. A fine day only windy, a showr afternoon. The boys and George West plough'd. Ned May and John Edwards stirred the bean plot. Harry Morley thatcht and helpt fetch part of a load of straw from Mr Jeremiah Dodson's. Mr John Hart and I supt at Mr Richard Whitpaine's with Mr Dodson and his wife.

Divided Dog Smith's mony. I measur'd a piece of Mrs Catherine Beard's great Townfield for Richard Herriot to sow with flax being 5 ch 64 links broad and 7 ch 54 links long; 4 acres 1 rood; the rood was allow'd for wet ground. John Standbridge workt half a day hewing timber.

The 14th February 1715 Tuesday. A gloomy day, the wind very high, some rain forenoon. Receiv'd the rest of the load of straw from Mr Jeremiah Dodson. Ned May and George West ridg'd Tully's bean plot that was stir'd yesterday. John Edwards and the boys made an end of fallowing the field by Wickham's about noon, rakt stubble afterwards. I bargain'd with Joseph Clifford from 3 days after Lady Day to Michaelmas at £3-10s but if I like him and he stay the whole year, he is to have £5-5s; he lives now at Thomas Marten's of Fragbarrow. John Standbridge workt half a day sawing etc. John Towner and Ja Reed saw'd. Harry Morley thatcht the hogsties and some mending. My Brother Peter was here in the afternoon. 2 lambs fell to day of Gold's sheep.

The 15th February 1715 Wednesday. A gloomy day, some raine. John Standbridge workt. George West and Ned May begun plough the field by Tully's coppice. John Edwards and the boys rak't stubble in Tully's wheat earsh. John Towner and Ja Reed saw'd. Harry Morley thatcht. Sold Towner the young white sow at 15s. Receiv'd 2 bushels of Albourne Place oates. 3 lambs of John Gold's sheep fell to day and last night. Lent Mr Jeremiah Dodson the lugs and hames of my dill harness. Paid Mr Friend of Lewis a bill of £4-12s in full of all accounts: he was here in the forenoon. Mr Richard Whitpaine, his wife, my Cousin Goffe and my Brother Will was here in the afternoon. I was at Mr Dodson's in the evning, supt there. Desir'd Mr Friend to buy 2 hats for my boys, he being to go to London next week. Receiv'd £16-2-6d of Mr Thomas Friend the same which Mr Pickstone paid for his use in London and in full for the 4 oxen sold to him before Christmas. John Gun and Jack Bartlet made an end Tully's farther hedge.

The 16th February 1715 Thursday. A wet day being small driving rain, the wind light. Towner fetcht the young sow at 15s. Harry Morley thatcht. John Edwards and the boys made an end of the Rookwood at the north headland. John Gun thrasht barly. Paid Bignall's wife 1s for part of her boy's work. George West and Ned May plough'd in Tully's field. Receiv'd an other load of straw of Mr Jeremiah Dodson. Receiv'd £2-1-10d of Mr John Hart a Munday last for sugar _____ carriage, carpenter's work, malt and hops. Paid Richard King 1s for digging 6 rods of bean ground.

The 17th February 1715 Fryday. A wet day, that is with small driving rain. Ned May and George West made an end of the field by Tully's coppice and carry'd a load of stubble out of Tully's wheat earsh. Receiv'd 4 bushels of Albourne Place oates whole. Deliver'd 2 bushels of barly at 15s per quarter to Towner. I din'd at Michael Stacey's with Mr Thomas Butcher and Mr Edward Burry and as soon as we had din'd my Cousin John Lindfield came and towards night John Box sr and John Smith jr. I sold John Smith the 4 fatting cows at Albourne Place at £20. Receiv'd a guinea in hand. Lost a lamb of John Gold's sheep last night. John Gun thrasht barly, John Edwards wheat; Harry Morley thatcht. John Towner and Ja Reed saw'd. Tully workt. Skreen'd 11 bushels of John Gun's barly by Hyder's. Receiv'd 2 bushels of Albourne oates for the lean hogs.

The 18th February 1715 Saturday. A fine day. John Towner and Ja Reed saw'd. Tully workt. John Gun thrasht barly half the day, John Edwards wheat all day. George West and Ned May begun Tully's wheat earsh. Harry Morley thatcht. Sold Morley 2 quarters and Towner 12 bushels of my best barly at 16s-6d per quarter. My Wife and I and my Sister Nanny were at Albourne Place and brought home some cloaths that wanted washing. John and Molly Balcomb went with us to Wanbarrow and John Balcomb went to the Place. John Box, Nick Plaw, John Stubbs, Stephen Pryor and I met at John Smith's in the evning. John Stubbs paid the £53-16s due to William Balcomb on bond _____ and we paid £52-17s to Stephen Pryor being due from William Balcomb on a note of his hand and Stephen Pryor paid Nick Plaw for roots etc £5-4s.

The 19th February 1715 Sunday. A very fine day. Mr Jeremiah Dodson preacht. Nick Plaw's cow calv'd a cow calf this morning. My Sister Nanny din'd here. I was at Stephen Bine's after evning prayr with Mr Scutt.

The 20th February 1715 Munday. A fine day. John Towner and Ja Reed saw'd. Tully workt, Harry Morley made an end of thatching the great barne about noon and afterwards begun John Lag's shop. John Standbridge workt hewing timber 'till noon and then workt mending the roof of Lag's shop. 2 lambs of John Gold's sheep and one of Mr Hamshire's. George West sow'd 2 6⁄8 bushels of white peas on Tully's little field. Ned May workt at Albourne Place with the ball mare and left 9 sacks at Harry Wickham's. John Edwards thrasht wheat and helpt winnow barly ‗ Win'd 19 bushels of John Gun's barly by Burt's. Gun cut down ash at the corner of the Bankfield and fagotted it the rest of the day. William Jarvice helpt us winnow etc 'till noon. My Brother Peter was here towards night. Jake Harden a drover, came at night for the oxen I sold George Hill and Robert Skinner but I would not give him quarters because on the 17th of November 1714 I hir'd him to do an errand for Ellis Geer which he never did. Receiv'd 2 new books from London from Mr Cooper. Paid Ball 2s for a bottle of brandy. Brew'd 9 bushels of old malt, put in near 8lbs of hops for keeping beer.

The 21st February 1715 Tuesday. A dry day only a very small showr afternoon. Harry Morley thatcht on John Lag's shop. John Towner and Ja Reed made an end. Deliver'd the 4 fatting oxen to John Harden per George West. Ned May and my self, George West went as far as Greenaway's. John Standbridge and Thomas Mall workt on the chaff house. West and May plough'd in Tully's wheat earsh. John Gun thrasht barly, best part of the day, John Edwards wheat. Win'd 3½ bushels of Gun's tail barly by Burt's in the morning. Edwards helpt. Sent the barly to mill for the fatting sows. John Gold's sheperd was here. Tully workt. One lamb of John Gold's sheep.

The 22nd February 1715 Wednesday. A dry day. Harry Morley thatcht. Tully workt. George West and Ned May made an end of Tully's wheat earsh. John Gun thrasht barly, put the 2 old oxen into the fatting close. *(Ed: xxx text deleted xxx)* One lamb of Mr Hamshire's sheep. Lost one lamb of John Gold's sheep. Deliver'd 8 bushels of my best barly to Towner, 4 to Harry Morley per Tully. Widdow Tully had ½ bushel of malt at 1s-8d and 5s in mony. John Standbridge and Thomas Mall made an end of the chaff house. Paid my Lord Treep 3s in full of all accounts.

The 23rd February 1715 Thursday. A fine day. Deliver'd 4 bushels of barly to Harry Morley per Tully. Morley made an end of thatching the chaff house and hogstie and begun at Tully's rick etc. George West and Ned May did severall jobbs in the forenoon and begun plough the barly earsh by Hyder at 3 aclock. 2 lambs of Mr Hamshire's sheep. Lent Michael Stacey my stilliard. John Gun thrasht barly. John Edwards workt for himself to day and yesterday. John Smith sent for the hous'd calf per Dick Mall.

The 24th February 1715 Fryday. A fine day. The mountebank here again. George West and Ned May plough'd. John Gun and Tully win'd part of the day ‗ 2 lambs of Mr Hamshire sheep dy'd and 2 more lambs ‗ Mr Price, John Hill of Nut Knowle, Thomas Champion and his wife din'd here. Mr Jeremiah Dodson came towards night. Mr Price and he staid late. Harry Morley thatcht ‗ Paid Mr Dodson 11s-6p for 2 loads of oat straw and a pound of tobacco. Lent Mr Dodson Mioros Paral. Proph.

The 25th February 1715 Saturday. A fine day. John Gun made a ditch west end of Tully's orchard. John Edwards thrasht wheat. Paid Stephen Bine 2s-9d for 2 bushel of oates. Receiv'd 1 bushel. One lamb of William Hamshire's sheep. Receiv'd a letter from Mr George Hill of Rigate concerning Old Mr Luxford's will of Southampton. George West and Ned May plough'd by Hyder's. Old William Brand workt the forenoon, underpinning the chaff house and hogsty. John Edwards had a bushel of wheat at 4s. *(Ed: xxx text deleted xxx)*. Paid John Parsons 6d for shaveing my head.

The 26th February 1715 Sunday. A dry cold day. Mr Jeremiah Dodson preacht. Lost one lamb of William Hamshire's sheep. Mr John Hart and I supt at Mr Richard Whitpaine's with Mr Dodson and his wife. Receiv'd     lb of tea of Mrs Mary Whitpaine.

The 27th February 1715 Munday. A dry day only a showr before noon. Tully workt. Reckon'd with Harry Morley and clear'd all accounts, his work came to £3. He had a quarter of barly to day per Ned May and a quarter before at £1-13s and I paid him £1-7s. George West and Ned May made an end of the field by Hyder's about 2 aclock. Tom Mall workt here making a trough for the calves. Win'd 6 ½ bushels head and 5 ½ bushels tail of the barly by Hyders, last of the field, in all 8 quarters 3½ bushels. Win'd also a bushel of that by Burt's. Sent an answer to

Mr Hill's letter by the post. John Edwards helpt winnow part of the day.

The 28th February 1715 Tuesday. A dry day. Tully set beans where King dug. John Gun thrasht barly. John Edwards wheat. Deliver'd 7 quarters of barly to Harry Wickham per George West and Ned May. Receiv'd some of my malt. Deliver'd a sack of barly to Towner per George West and Ned May. Nick Plaw was here in the afternoon. Spent 2s with Mr Pointin at the Swan in the evning. 3 lambs of William Hamshire's sheep. I was at Westtowne about noon. Let William King the east part of the stables at Mrs Storer's a Saturday last for a year from Lady Day next at 5s. Abraham Muzzall workt here to day and yesterday. He made me a payr of breeches and did some work besides. The fatting sow had 2 bushels of tail barly and a bushel of beans.

The 29th February 1715 Wednesday. A wet stormy day. Tully workt. John Gun thrasht barly, John Edwards wheat. Bargain'd with George West for a year from May Day next at £5-10s. Receiv'd the rest of my malt from Harry Wickham's per George West and Ned May. There was 12 quarters 6 bushels of 12 quarters of barly. Reckon'd with John Towner and Ja Reed and clear'd all accounts. Their sawing was 530 foot of timber at 3s per cord and 273 foot of board at 2s-6d per cord. Allow'd 6d for drawing. One lamb of John Gold's sheep and one lamb dy'd. Deliver'd a load of straw to William Beard by John Bodle's order. Sent home Albourne Place mare per Ned May. My Wife was at Danny in the afternoon.

The 1st March 1715 Thursday. A fine day, only some small showrs of hail. John Gun and John Edwards made the hedge westend of Tully's orchard and begun that on the north side of the pease earsh. George West and Ned May win'd 2 quarters 5 bushels of oates for seed and brought them up into the wheat garret and 6 bushels of tail into the chaff hole. Put 6 oxen into Tully's close. John Edwards serv'd them. I was at Wanbarrow in the afternoon but my Brother was not at home. I call'd my Wife at Westtowne but did not stay at all. Tully workt. Lent Mrs Catherine Beard 8 bushels of mortar per John Smith.

The 2nd March 1715 Fryday. A dry day, a pretty big frost last night. Tully workt. George West and Ned May begun sow Tully's first field with 3 bushels beans, under furrough. John Gun and John Edwards hedg'd. Receiv'd £5 of John Smith jr. The mountebank here. One lamb of William Hamshire's sheep. Lent Mr Richard Whitpaine my long yoak per Philipps.

The 3rd March 1715 Saturday. A fine day, a frost last night. Tully workt. Ned May and George West plough'd and sow'd 4 bushels of beans. John Gun dug for him self and John Edwards. Sent 2 bushels of tail barly and a bushel of beans to mill for the fatting sows. I was at Albourne Place and put the linnen etc in order in Molly Balcomb's chest of drawers and they brought them hither with a payr of sheets and 12 napkins and 2 pillow coates for each boy. I call'd at Wanbarrow as I came home and reckon'd and clear'd all accounts with my Mother to Michaelmas last.

The 4th March 1715 Sunday. A gloomy, windy day. Mr Jeremiah Dodson preacht. One lamb of William Hamshire's sheep. My Wife and I were at Wanbarrow after evning prayr. Ned May fetcht William Balcomb's bay mare.

The 5th March 1715 Munday. A fine day. John Gun and Tully carry'd in timber etc. John Gun and John Edwards plough'd. They made an end of Tully's first field haveing sow'd just 12 bushels of beans in him. Receiv'd £34-10s of George Hill and Robert Skinner in full for my 4 oxen per John Harden for which I gave a receit. Mr John Hart went to dine at Mr Price's according to our invitation, but I could not go. Paid William Bull 2s-6d for dressing my hop garden to day being 10d per cord, which he says is the comon price. My Wife, Willy and Ned May went to Lewis and she and I went to Mrs Catherine Beard's after she came home.

The 6th March 1715 Tuesday. A fine day. George West sow'd 2 quarters of my Cousin John Lindfield's white oates on Tully's field below the mead. Ned May harrow'd. Receiv'd 4 quarters of oates of my Cousin John Lindfield at 12s per quarter per Tom Tully. John Edwards fagotted. Win'd 4 quarters 2 bushels head and 2 bushels tail of John Gun's barly per Burt's. Eliz Cheal and Widdow Tully helpt 'till noon. Will Jarvice workt all day. Stephen Bine's man Joseph Wood workt 'till 4 aclock on the oat hatch and then begun the slide. The 3 yearling heifer calv'd a bull calf. John Harden had away all William Balcomb's oxen for George Hill etc. Abraham Muzzall workt here.

The 7th March 1715 Wednesday. A fine day. Stephen Bine's man Joseph Wood finisht the slide. John Gun and John Edwards hedg'd. Tully workt. Paid George West 10s. George West sow'd pease on the west part of the 2nd field below Tully's Mead but did not make an end of it. Ned May harrow'd, they finish the oat field that they begun yesterday. Mr Pointin the excise man supt here and staid late. Last night there were very strange appearances in the air sometimes resembling fire, sometimes smoak and most part of the night much lighter than usual.

The 8th March 1715 Thursday. A fine day. John Gun and John Edwards hedg'd. Tully workt. Paid Mr Jeremiah Dodson 6s-3d for the straw to thatch Lag's shopp being most oat straw at 18d per square. Receiv'd the book again which I lent Mr Dodson. George West sow'd more pease in the field as above and afterwards sow'd 12 bushels of oates on the little field east of Tully's coppice. Ned May harrow'd. Stephen Bine's man Joseph Wood workt on the little door of the wheat barne and afterwards mended 2 harrows. I went to Nick Plaw to meet Sir Robert Fagg and he say'd he would be there again at the sale. Paid Nick Plaw 3s-10d for my hop duty which he is to carry to the sitting for me with that for Albourne Place. Mrs Barbara Campion and Mrs Courthope, Mrs Catherine Beard and her family were here in the afternoon. My Cousin Peter Marchant of Lewis was here in the morning. Sent 2 bushels of tail barly and a bushel of beans to mill. Paid Harry Wickham's man 1s for his care in makeing my _____ . I was at John Snashall's yesterday to see his calves and he came hither afternoon and promis'd me I should have the 2 red calves at a moderate price about fortnight in May.

The 9th March 1715 Fryday. A fine day but windy. John Gun set beans for him self etc. George West and May finisht the field east of Tully's coppice and William Michell sow'd about 3 pecks of my own old clover seed on him. The mountebank here again. They also finish the west part of the 2nd field below Tully's Mead haveing sow'd about 6 bushels of pease on him. Paid John Edwards 10s. He thrasht wheat. Ed Burt workt here. Spent 2s with my Cousin Peter Marchant. My Unkle Richard Turner and Mr Scutt the full day here at the Swan. The long tetted cow calv'd a bull calf yesterday. Receiv'd 3 pecks of Albourne Place seed per Tully.

The 10th March 1715 Saturday. A windy day with some skattering of snow and hail. My Cousin Marchant went home this morning, lay here. George West sow'd 14½ bushels of red oates on the field by the lane to Hyder's. May harrow'd. I was at Mr Jeremiah Dodson's in the morning before he set out for Broadwater. Tully workt. One lamb of William Hamshire's sheep. Ed Burt workt. John Gun and John Edwards hedg'd against Tully's coppice. William Michell came about 4 aclock and sow'd 3 pecks of Albourne Place seed and they finisht the field above mentioned being the last of my oat season for this year. I went to Wanbarrow and supt there. My Wife was at Westtowne. Paid my Brother Peter 15d for 3 quires of writeing paper.

The 11th March 1715 Sunday. A dry, cold day. Mr William Martin preacht. My Cousin John Lindfield and my Sister Nanny din'd here, I was not at Church afternoon. Paid my Cousin Lindfield 48s for 4 quarters of oates. Mr John Hart and I supt at Westtowne with Mr Jeremiah Dodson.

The 12th March 1715 Munday. A fine day. George West mended gaps and put all the ewes and lambs in the Churchfield. Sent 2 bushels of tail barly and a bushel of beans to mill. There was a Court Baron at the Royall Oak. My Wife, Jack and Nanny, May, Sarah Morley, Tully and I set out for Nunnery afternoon. John Gun and John Edwards hedg'd upper side Tully's Mead. I mett George Hill of Rigate as I went to Nunnery and order'd him to pay the mony for Albourne oxen to Nick Plaw which he did. £110.

The 13th March 1715 Tuesday. Dry 'till towards night then a showr. Tully came home on foot. George West thrasht barly. My Wife, May and I went to Horsham. Paid 18d for a purse for my Cousin John Lindfield. Paid 5s for a straw hat for Molly Balcomb and 6d for mending my old saddle for the little horse. Paid also 6d for shaveing me. John Gun and John Edwards hedg'd.

The 14th March 1715 Wednesday. A wet morning, fine after. Tully workt. Mrs Pryaulx din'd at Nunnery. May went to Horsham to have the saddle mended _____ . Paid 1s for mending it again. Paid also 9d for 3 quires of tobacco paper. John Gun and John Edwards hedg'd. George West thrasht barly.

The 15th March 1715 Thursday. A gloomy day, some small rain. Tully workt. Reckon'd with my Father Stone and clear'd all accounts except the oxen sold to him at £10. There was due to me £10. Mr John Hart and Willy came to us night. George West thrasht barly, John Edwards wheat.

The 16th March 1715 Fryday. A fine day. Tully came to Nunnery on foot. We were to see Mrs Pryaulx afternoon. May went to Horsham to have the chaese saddle mended. Paid 18d for mending it. George West thrasht *(Ed: xxx text deleted xxx)* barly. John Gun cut coppice, John Edwards thrasht wheat. The mountebank here again.

The 17th March 1715 Saturday. A fine day, only a showr towards night. We came home from Nunnery afternoon and my Sister Nanny went home at night haveing been here ever since we went from home. John Gun poll'd trees cut spires, John Edwards thrasht wheat, George West barly. I set a young tree yew tree at the south west corner of the grass plot in the garden, which Mr John Hart took up as he came home, in a coppice in Bolny.

The 18th March 1715 Sunday. A showry day. Mr William Martin preacht. Paid 2d for crying William Balcomb's sale. Nick Plaw told me he had receiv'd the mony for Albourne oxen and half the hops and that he had paid the fine for Little Hever being £20 to John Box. Mr Richard Whitpaine was here a little while after evning prayr. Mr Scutt and his wife was here in the evning.

The 19th March 1715 Munday. A fine day. Dick Vinall kill'd the 2 old sows. Paid Marten the sheep sheerer 14d for clipping my sheep. Receiv'd my 10 wattles again of Michael Stacey. Paid Robert Pierce 6s for makeing the bucken tub and receiv'd 7s-6d of him for 100 hoops, ½ not deliver'd. George West and May begun stir the lower part of the Rookwood. John Gun did severall jobbs, John Edwards cut coppice. Tully workt. Nick Plaw was here to see an ox that was out of order. Put a bushel and a half of oates into the oat chest at night.

The 20th March 1715 Tuesday. A fine day. John Gun workt for me half the day. John Edwards helpt winnow barly about 3 hours. Tully workt. Put 10 sheep and 10 lambs (of the left ear) into Tully's Mead, also 9 sheep and 9 lambs (of the right ear) into the Little Mead. George West and May made an end of stirring the lower part of the Rookwood and George West helpt Ed Burt afterwards. Paid Jack Bignall 1s for his ploughing, all that is due. Paid Frank Holden 2s-4½d for half a bushel of salt. Dick Vinall cutt out the old sowes. The white sow weigh'd 20 nail, the other 2lbs more. I gave Dick Vinall 1s. May begun harrow the Rookwood after. George West and Tully brought up the 5 young oxen out of Tully's close.

The 21st March 1715 Wednesday. A showry day. Ed Burt workt a gardning. George West, May, Tully and Tom Tipping begun sow the Rookwood with barly. John Gun helpt about 2 hours. Ed Penfold went to Nunnery. Nan West weeded the garden. Gun and John Edwards cut coppice. John Edwards had ½ bushel of wheat.

The 22nd March 1715 Thursday. A fine day. Ed Burt workt a gardning. George West, May and Tully plough'd and sow'd in the Rookwood. John Gun and John Edwards cut coppice. Nan West weeded. Mr John Picknall of Arundell was here in the morning. Mary Balcomb came to board here this evning. Nick Plaw din'd here haveing brought Willy Balcomb to board with Widdow Parsons at the same price she had for the other. Deliver'd the other 60 hoops to Robert Pierce. I was a little while at the German's helpale, gave him _. Ed Parson's widdow buried to day. *(Ed: Recorded in the Hurst Register as Ann Parsons)* Put 4 bushels of head oates into the oat chest this evning.

The 23rd March 1715 Fryday. A fine day. My birthday, 39 years. Mr John Picknall lay here last night, went away this morning. George West, May and Tully plough'd and sow'd in the Rookwood. Ed Burt workt. Nan West weeded. John Gun cut coppice, John Edwards also. My ükle Richard Turner *(Ed: Richard was nicknamed "Box" – was there a connection to the Box family)* and John Box sr were here in the morning *(Ed: John was married to Charity Norton whose distant relation Sarah Norton later married Thomas's son William)*. William Balcomb's sale. I staid late. There was a very great company, the goods sold very well. One payr of Nick Marchant's sheets (that I had on pawn) were sold there with pillow coats to Anne Whiteing for £1-4-0d and two other payr of 'em to Mrs Anne Lancaster at £1-5-8d. The mountebank here.

Paid £100 to Sir Robert Fagg for William Balcomb's arrears of rent. I have the receit but Nick Plaw paid the mony. John Gold sent for his tags, 23, two more dead.

The 24th March 1715 Saturday. A fine day. George West, May, Tully and Tippins plough'd and sow'd in the Rookwood 'till noon. George West and May thwartled in the afternoon and the boys roll'd. They have sow'd 3½ quarters. I were at Albourne Place in the morning. Ed Burt workt a gardning. Nan West weeded. Mr John Hart and Bett went to Mr Beaumont. Goode Shave was here making sausages. Paid Ed Burt 7s-6d for 7½ days work and 6d for parsnips. Paid Nan West 18d for 3 day's work weeding.

## 1716

The 25th March 1716 Sunday. Lady Day. A dry, cold day. Mr Orton preacht. I din'd at Dean House and my son William. After evning prayr here was Mr Orton, Mr Scutt and Mr Richard Whitpaine to see Mrs Hart and Mrs Catherine Beard and her family. Mrs Scutt and Mrs Courthope to see my Wife and Mr William Courthope came for his sister. Receiv'd half a pound of bohea tea from Mr Roberds per Mr Richard Whitpaine.

The 26th March 1716 Munday. A fine day. John Gun ground 6 bushels of malt and workt 'till noon. May and Sarah Surgeant went away. Clear'd all accounts with both. George West went to the Fair, I lent him 2 horses to carry his flax seed. Win'd 23 bushels of the barly by Burt's per Snashall. Paid Jack Gun 5s. My Cousin Peter Marchant din'd here. Reckon'd with the Widdow Tully and clear'd all accounts. E Tasker brought a horse from my Cousin Marchant for me to see, I gave him 1s for his pains. One of William Hamshire's sheep had 2 lambs to day. My Sister Nanny and Brother Peter were here afternoon. Bett went to the Fair, carry'd my Cousin Nick Marchant a ribspare. Goode Shave went with her. Paid my Cousin Marchant 1s for a bottle of Stoughton Drops which Ned Tasker brought. Receiv'd 18s-2d of my Cousin Marchant for the sheep my Wife bought at the sale for him. Paid Ned Burt 1s for the day's work.

The 27th March 1716 Tuesday. A fine day, a smart frost last night. George West, John Gun and my Son Willy plough'd and sow'd 'till Joseph Clifford came, John Gun mended hedges afterwards. Paid Sarah Morley 10s in full, she went away. Susan Vinall came yesterday at          per annum. Paid Joseph Muzzall £5-10-5d being the half year's Land Tax due at St Michael's last past. He gather'd it for Henry Hooker. My Wife was at Mr Jeremiah Dodson's. Nick Plaw was here about the sheep. Thomas Vinall workt at Tully's house part of the afternoon. Receiv'd my 2 iron rakes from Mr Richard Whitpaine and a chain from Mrs Catherine Beard. Dick Steer came at night for the young horse.

The 28th March 1716 Wednesday. A fine day. George West and Jo plough'd in the Rookwood 'till noon. Afterwards sow'd and harrow'd. They finisht the field haveing sow'd 4 quarters 6½ bushels in it. Ed Burt and Willy went to Horsham and brought Mary Mills. Ed Burt rode John Smith's mare. I was at Mr Richard Whitpaine's, supt there. Bargain'd with Edward Morley at 35s 'till Michaelmas next and if his vailes be not 5s I promis'd to make it so. He is Robert Morley's son at Cuckold's Green, who (when a boy) lived with my Father. I was at St John's Comon to see a steer but did not deal, also lookt on George Buckwell calves. He was not at home. John Gun thrasht barly.

The 29th March 1716 Thursday. A fine day. Edward Morley came this morning. George West, John Edwards and he win'd 3 quarters 6 bushels head and 2 bushels tail of John Edwards's wheat in the Rookwood. John Edwards had a bushel at 4s. Receiv'd 4 bushels of oates and 8 bushels of Nonsuch in the husk from Albourne Place per Joseph Clifford. John Gun thrasht barly, Joseph helpt him afternoon. Willy went to Lewis to have the cart whip mended, which cost 10d and the leather bags 6d and a douzen of pint bottles at 20d. He brought home 6. Paid for it all. I was at a sale at Little Ease and brought a dripping pan at 6s-8d and a chair at 1s, left the chair with Thomas Field and brought the other home. Joseph Clifford begun serve John Gun's cows to night. Put a bushel of oates into the oat chest. Lent Dick Vinall a wanty yesterday.

The 30th March 1716 Fryday. A fine day. Good Fryday. Mr William Martin preacht. One lamb of Mr Hamshire's and one of Mr Gold's _____ . Win'd 2 quarters 6 bushels of John Gun's barly by Burt's. My men were all at Church, did severall jobbs. I was at Mrs Catherine Beard's in the evning, did not stay supper. Dick Steer came in the evning. Willy and Dicky Whitpaine went to Nunnery afternoon. Lent my Brother Peter 30s.

The 31st March 1716 Saturday. A fine day. George West and Ned carry'd chucks from the sawpit into the orchard. Joseph Clifford workt in the garden etc. John Gun cut coppice. John Edwards workt for himself. I promis'd Thomas Westover to see him paid for Abraham Muzzall's girl's shooes, as far as 8 or 10s. George West and I cut the hedge goeing to Church. I saw a ship of William Balcomb's weigh'd at John Bodle's. Weigh'd just £12 per quarter, sold to him at 3d per lb.

The 1st April 1716 Easter Sunday. A fine day. Mr William Martin preacht. Mr Richard Whitpaine was here after evning prayr. John Godly spoke for 8 bushels of barly. I promis'd it should be ready a Thursday night. Thomas Howell was here in the morning and appointed to come to morrow morning to begin my waggon. Paid Mr Richard Whitpaine a guinea that he paid for me in London.

The 2nd April 1716 Easter Munday. A very fine day. Ed Morley's mother Joan was here and made some scruples about her son's service and so away they went together. George West kept holy day. Joseph Clifford harrow'd on the fallow by Wickham's. Receiv'd the 30s of my Brother Peter which I lent him. Receiv'd 6s of E Chapman towards her rent for part of Mrs Storer's house. I had a boy came from Wivelsfield but I thought him a great deal too small. So did not bargain. She that was Elizabeth Midhurst was here. We had a meeting at Church, as usual. Paid George West 5s. I gave Joseph Clifford 1s for harrowing to day. Reckon'd with John Westover and clear'd all accounts, his bill was 26s-3d. he spoke for 100 faggots for his mother. Mrs Stuart and my Sister Mary Ede came at night. They brought Molly Ede. Dicky Whitpaine and Willy came home.

The 3rd April 1716 Tuesday. A fine day 'till towards sun set then raine. Hollingham did not come to plough as he promis'd. I went to Albourne Street and agreed with James Banks's son to come to plough to morrow at 9d per day. George West and Joseph Clifford plough'd in the field by Wickham's, did not sow. Mrs Catherine Beard and her family were here in the afternoon and Mrs Scutt. Dick Purvey went home this morning, Ed Penfold went afternoon to Nunnery. Nick Marchant was here in the afternoon. John Gun begun serve the cows again last night.

The 4th April 1716 Wednesday. A wet morning, showry after. George West, Joseph Clifford and James Banks clear'd Nonsuch. Ed Penfold return'd from Nunnery. Paid Dick Wood's bill £1-4s. The weather of Mr Gold's sheep dy'd. 2 lambs of Mr Gold's sheep. John Gun and John Edwards workt for themselves. Mrs Stuart, my Sister Mary Ede and I supt at Mrs Catherine Beard's per Bett.

The 5th April 1716 Thursday. A gloomy morning, dry all day after. George West, Joseph Clifford and Banks plough'd and sow'd by Wickham's. Thomas Howell came about 10 aclock and lookt out the stuff for a new waggon, pull'd the old to pieces etc. Mrs Stuart, Mrs Ede and my Wife were at Mrs Scutt's. Put 2 runts into the hop garden. John Gun and John Edwards poll'd trees.

The 6th April 1716 Fry day. A fine day. George West, Joseph Clifford and Banks plough'd and sow'd. Receiv'd 16s-6d of John Godly for a quarter of barly. Thomas Howell and his man workt on the waggon. Ed Penfold went to Nunnery with Mrs Katherine's horse. Mr Healy din'd here. Mrs Mary Whitpaine and Mrs Goffe came in the afternoon. John Gun and John Edwards thrasht barly. Mrs Stuart, Mrs Ede, my Wife and I rode up the hill. Took 4 carp out of the Hovelfield stew for dinner and left 4 in.

The 7th April 1716 Saturday. A fine day. George West, Joseph Clifford and Banks plough'd and sow'd. Thomas Howell and his man workt on the waggon. Win'd 14 bushels head of John Gun's and John Edwards's barly by Bank_____ . Mr Gold sent me 2 thrashers. I agreed with them to thrash barly at 1s per quarter and wheat at 2s per quarter. Mrs Stuart and my Sister Mary Ede went away after dinner. Mr John Hart, my Wife and I went with them to Westtowne. We staid all there 'till 4 aclock. Reckon'd with Mrs Ede and clear'd all accounts. I agreed with Edwards to find the thrashers lodging and small beer at 1s per week each.

The 8th April 1716 Sunday. A fine day. Mr William Martin preacht in the forenoon, Mr Healy afternoon. Mrs Susan Courthope din'd here. Mr John Hart and I were at Westtowne after evning prayr. Paid Mr Richard Whitpaine 4s for ¼lb of tea he brought 26th February. Paid Robert Pierce 3s for making a small tubb, out of the old bucken tubb, about a week ago. A brown ram lamb of Mr Gold's sheep to day. There is as many hoops due to Robert Pierce as is on the tub.

The 9th April 1716 Munday. A very fine day. George West, Joseph Clifford and Banks, plough'd and sow'd. Stephen Bine's man Joseph Wood made 2 hen coops for me. Thomas Howell and his man workt on the waggon. Paid Isaac Muzzall a bill of 2s-8d for William Balcomb before he died, one of 2s-5d for Molly Balcomb and one of 10d for John Balcomb, took receits. One lamb of Mr Hamshire's sheep. Old William Brand did a jobb at Tully's. Lent Mrs Catherine Beard a horse harness per James Holden. John Gun and John Edwards fagotted. Abraham Muzzall had half a bushel of wheat at 2s. Lent Mr Richard Whitpaine 6 sacks per J Davey.

The 10th April 1716 Tuesday. A very fine day. George West, Joseph Clifford and Banks made an end of ploughing and sowing the field by Wickham's, haveing sow'd 4 quarters 7¼ bushels of barly. John Gun and John Edwards thrasht 3½ bushels of the barly by Burt's and finisht the Nonsuch thrashing, there was about 2 bushels of good seed and one half a bushel tail. Thomas Howell and his man finisht the waggon for which I paid him 18s, that is, 12s for making the waggon, 1s more above because all was larger than usuall and the rest for boarding at the sides, hurting (?), plateing and singing the stuff and geteing it cut etc. Sent the founder'd mare to Ditcheling Comon per Ned Penfold. One lamb of Mr Hamshire's sheep. My Wife and Bett was at Danny afternoon. Paid John Edwards 5s. Ed Burt workt here.

The 11th April 1716 Wednesday. A fine day. George West mended gaps 'till noon and afterwards. He, Joseph Clifford and William Michell sow'd the field by Wickham's with a bushel and 5 gallons of Nonsuch. Joseph Clifford roll'd in the morning. Paid Ed Burt 2s for this day's work and yesterday. I went to Brighthelmstone afternoon and there paid 8d for stuffing and mending my saddle, 6d for a horne main comb and spunge and 2d for a boxen one. I was at John Gold's a little while. My Wife was at Wanbarrow afternoon. John Gun and Banks thrasht barly. Banks went to Dean House at noon. John Edwards faggotted. Ed Penfold carry'd a peck of barly to Nunnery, he went by Horsham. Nick Plaw was here in the morning. Benjamin Shave begun clean shooes at 3d per week.

The 12th April 1716 Thursday. A fine day, George West and Joseph Clifford mended gaps all the forenoon and in the afternoon washt the dry sheep and tags. John Gun and Banks thrasht barly. Turn'd the 3 other runts to pasture yesterday. Receiv'd a pint of ink of Mr Scutt which he had from Petworth, for which we outset 1s due to me on a waggon about Dick Buckwell and Mr Osbourne. Joseph Clifford was took sick this evning. Mr Richard Whitpaine and I went to his ground at Slaugham. I bought 800 of his scrub faggots at 3s-6d per hundred. He is to stack them out of the coppice by the sawpit. Stephen Bine came home with me, I supt at Westtowne. One of the tags had a lamb, but we found it dead.

The 13th April 1716 Fryday. A gloomy day, a little rain towards night. Mr Richard Whitpaine was here in the morning. Lent him 12 guineas. Win'd 3 quarters 3 bushels head of John Gun's and Banks's barly by Burt's. Deliver'd 2 quarters of it to my Brother Peter per Bignall, at 16s per quarter, for seed, not screen'd. Thomas Parker begun look after the young horse at 18d per week. He also undertook to ride him and gentle him, which if he effect I am to pay him according to the trouble he has in doeing it. Receiv'd 5 douzen of soap at 4s-4d per douzen, 1lb of pepper 3s and 2lb of wash balls at 7d per lb from Mr John Picknall at Arundell by his man, to whom I deliver'd my Cousin John Lindfield's bushel of cow grass. Mr Norden and his wife and my Cousin John Lindfield's wife Elizabeth din'd here and my Cousin John Lindfield came about 3 aclock. John Edwards faggotted. Receiv'd 48s of my Cousin John Lindfield for 3 quarters of Albourne barly. Receiv'd £6-10s of the Widdow Alcock for the bed she bought at William Balcomb's sale. Took half a douzen of pidgeons. John Snashall was twice here to see Joseph Clifford. Richard Patching came in the evning about 10 aclock and let him bleed for which my Wife paid him 6d. George West roll'd the Rookwood barly. I helpt with Richard Burtenshaw and he agreed to pay me 2s-6d per load for half the flints I shall lay in the lane between his ground and mine. Receiv'd 2s of Thomas Bignall for half a bushel of wheat. My Sister Nanny was here in the afternoon.

The 14th April 1716 Saturday. A gloomy day. George West helpt Marten sheer the 14 dry sheep and 9 tags. Paid Marten 14d for sheering them. Sent Ed Penfold to Ditcheling Comon for Jo's father. Parker and I and Ed Penfold fetcht William Balcomb's bull and put him among my cows. My Cousins Mr William Olchin and Mr Phillip Cheal din'd here in their way to Henfield. Mr Beaumont, Mr William Martin, Mr Burry and my Brother Peter were here in the afternoon. John Gun, had 15lb of cheese at 18d per nail. Mrs Catherine Beard and her mother and Mrs Kettilby were here afternoon. Deliver'd 4 bushels of barly to my Brother Peter per Parker. John Gun and Banks thrasht barly. John Edwards poll'd and faggotted.

The 15th April 1716 Sunday. A fine day. Mr William Martin preacht. I was not at Church, not being well. Joseph Clifford's friends was here to see him. John Snashall was here in the evning. John Box sr was here after evning prayr. My Wife and Willy went to Mrs Catherine Beard's after supper.

The 16th April 1716 Munday. A very fine day. Win'd 3 quarters 2 bushels head and 3 bushels tail of John Gun's and Banks's barly by Burt's and 2 bushels tail of John Gun's and Edward's being the last of the field, in all 23 quarters 5½ bushels is to be paid for, 3 quarters 6 bushels of what was between Banks and he. Paid Banks 8s-1d in full for all to this night. Elizabeth Boyce came towards night at 50s per annum. George West helpt winnow, change sheep etc. My Sister Nanny was here towards night. Paid her £6-5s, being a years intrest. She gave me 5s. Mr William Martin was here to pray with Joseph Clifford. John Snashall sr was to see Joseph in the morning and young John, twice towards night.

The 17th April 1716 Tuesday. A very fine day. Banks begun thrash wheat 'till noon. Afterwards George West and he carry'd 50 of Edward's hedg faggots to Mr Jeremiah Dodson and they brought home. They also brought home 150 of Jack Bartlet's hop poles. Harry Wickham was here afternoon. I sold him all the barly I have left at 15s per quarter. Deliver'd 12 bushels of barly to Bignall for my Brother Peter. He has 2 of my sacks and a wanty. Young John Snashall was here in the morning, towards night his father. Sent a 3 yearling steer to my Brother Peter per John Gun and George West. John Gun and John Edwards fagoted. Lent Mrs Catherine Beard my fore harness to the chaese. Put the 2 yearlings in to Tully's close. Draw'd off the stale beer and put 1lb of hops in each barrel. Mr William Martin was here to see Joseph Clifford. Nick Plaw was here in the evning.

The 18th April 1716 Wednesday. A gloomy day, some rain. John Box sr and I went to a Court at Balneath and there was admitted John Balcomb, by me as his attorney, paid the fine £7 and the fees of the Court 10s-8d. Parker rode the young horse with us. Mr Virgoe of Cuckfield was steward, there was Mr Langford, Mr Astie, Mr Barham, Walter Vinall and his son, Peter Marten, Old Sawyer and his son, Walter Burt, William Holman, John Attree, etc. George West roll'd all the oates, John Gun and John Edwards fagoted. Mr Richard Whitpaine, his wife and Mrs Goffe were here. Took 11 pidgeons, sent 6 to Wanbarrow per William. Deliver'd 4 bushels of barly to Bignall for my Brother Peter per Willy. John Gun begun serve Jo's cows this morning. Receiv'd 6 guineas of Mr Richard Whitpaine.

The 19th April 1716 Thursday. A fine day. George West went to Stanmer to see how Su Vinall was and whether she design'd to come again, She sent word she would come as soon as she was able (haveing been sick) to do anything. John Gun begun pole the hop garden. John Edwards fagotted. I was at John Snashall's in the forenoon. I wrote to Mr Hill, for my Brother Peter. Mr Scutt gave me some oyl for my wig. Mr Healy was here just at noon, did not stay dinner.

The 20th April 1716 Fryday. A cold windy day. John Box and I went to a Court at New Hall and were admitted guardian to William Balcomb and William was admitted to Eastout by me as his attorny. The fine £40, paid £20 in part of the fine and gave a note for £20. Paid £1-2s-4d being the steward's fees and 3s to the cryer, as will appear by their receits. One Mr Towner who lives somewhere in or near Broadwater was deputy steward, Mr Williams being indisposed. Receiv'd 20 guineas of Nick Plaw as we went to the Court. Paid 12s to Thomas Broomham for one years Quit Rent for Eastout due at Michaelmas last. George West rol'd the barly by Wickham's and mended gaps. John Gun poled the hop garden, John Edwards fagoted. Thomas Parker went with us to the Court. Mrs Margaret Minshall came to Mr Scutt's to day, my Wife went up to her in the evning. My Wife and I was at Wanbarrow and Molly Balcomb yesterday in the afternoon to see my Sister Mary Faulkoner. My Brother Peter sent my steer home and his with him which I am to have at £5 any time before May Day, or return him them.

The 21st April 1716 Saturday. A fine day. Mr Richard Whitpaine came to breakfast with me, he also din'd here, I gave him 5 of my best barren sheep for his young, stoned colt. He is to have 4 of the sheep next week and the other by Horsham First Fair, to mark them all now and if the last dies before the Fair he is to have the next best. I am to have the colt in a few days, he being allmost a year old. Lent him my roller. Receiv'd 4 bushels of Albourne oates per Parker. Carry'd 4 loads of Abraham Muall's flints into the lane between Richard Burtenshaw and I per George West. Jo Wood workt 'till noon lengthening a trough for the flat stew. John Gun fagoted in the coppice, John Edwards in the Edgly Mead. 7 sheep and 6 lambs stray'd into the hop garden yesterday. William Dumsday of Horsham brought my Wife a new payr of pumps, instead of stays. She paid him 36s-6d for them. Smith jr came to tell me of a calf at Richard Burtenshaw's. My Sisters Faulkoner, Nanny and Betty, were here in the afternoon and towards night, my Brothers William and Peter *(Ed: xxx text deleted xxx)*.

The 22nd April 1716 Sunday. A fine day. Mr Healy preacht forenoon and afternoon. My Cousin John Lindfield din'd here. Mr Healy supt here. Nick Plaw was here after evning service. I had the 7 sheep and 6 lambs cod. Joseph Clifford went home to his brother's, to stay there 'till he was able to work. Paid Nick Plaw 20s and settl'd the account about the fines and Widdow Alcock's bed as may be seen in his book of my own writeing.

The 23rd April 1716 Munday. A fine day. Henfield Fair. Nutley Fair, for barrens. Bought a bull calf of Richard Burtenshaw at 25s certain and 2s-6d more if he demand it, to be wean'd about a week or 10 days in May. George West carry'd 3 loads of Abraham Muall's flints into the highways. Mr Richard Whitpaine fetch the 5 sheep he is to have for the colt, in the morning and in the afternoon. Sent the colt per R Harland and             Prat. My Wife and I and Willy went to Ed Steel's at Cuckfield where we bought, materials for cloathing for which I paid him £4-4-11d and took a receit on the bill. John Snashall spoke for 2 cord of Wood.

The 24th April 1716 Tuesday. A fine day. Sold John Smith jr 2 rams and 3 ewes at 55s to be kill'd in 2 weeks. One of Mr Richard Whitpaine's ewes came back again. Put 9 ewes and 9 lambs into Tully's farther, teary field. Paid Michael Stacey £3-7-6d for a barren cow which he is to send home to morrow morning. Nick Marchant was here to day. He brought some stuff his wife had spun, for which my Wife paid him. Parker had half a bushel of oates for the young horse. Mr Whitpaine was here in the afternoon. Put the cows into the plot on th'other side the pond. George West fetcht home Su Mall. John Gun fagotted in the coppice, John Edwards in the Edgly Mead. Paid Michael Stacey 1s for 12 broomes. Receiv'd 18d of the Widdow Tully for ½ bushel of malt.

The 25th April 1716 Wednesday. A cold dry day. Cliffe Fair. Deliver'd 2 cord of wood to John Snashall per George West. George also brought out of the coppice 100 hop poles. My Cousin Nan Marchant, Bett, Parker and I went to the Fair. Bett and I din'd at my Cousin Peter's. Paid a bill of £2-2-5d¼at James Tourl's. Took 10 pidgeons yesterday. Mr Andrew Laurence the taylor took measure of me for a coat. He promis'd to make it by Thursday sennight. [........w'd]the cow from Michael Stacey.

The 26th April 1716 Thursday. A very fine day. Deliver'd 3 qarters 6 bushels of barly to Harry Wickham per George West and my self. The long tetted heifer calv'd a bull calf. Mr Picknall was here this morning. Receiv'd a letter from my Brother James Ede. Nan Marchant went home this morning. Deliver'd 25 ashen faggots to Edwards per George West. [...... d]the sheep and every thing out of the Homefield clover. [. ks]fetch William Balcomb's mare for 2d and afternoon George West fetcht the 15 Acre hay into the barne. Reckon'd with Jack Bartlet and clear'd all accounts with him, 9s. My Brother Peter was here afternoon. Receiv'd 1℔ of bohea and 1lb of coffee per Mr Healy's man.

The 27th April 1716 Fryday. A fine day. Crawley Fair. Sent 15 guineas to my Cousin John Lindfield to buy me oxen per JL yesterday. George West and I fetch 140 faggots from Slaugham at 2s-6d per cord. John Gun and John Edwards fagotted. Banks thrasht wheat. Paid Mrs Waller 2s-6d for a payr of gloves she sent which Mr John Hart had and an other payr she is to send me. I saw her at a house by Sprenket as I went to Slaugham. Picknall's boy begun tend hogs out of the clover. Mr Burry and Kight of Stenning were here in the afternoon. Receiv'd 15d of Mr John Hart for the afore mentioned gloves.

The 28th April 1716 Saturday. A gloomy morning, a dry day after. John Gun mended some gaps in Tully's lower field, fagoted. Picknall tended hogs. John Edwards fagotted. George West and I fetcht 110 scrub faggots and 20 birchen faggots from Slaugham. My Cousin John Lindfield sent home a payr of oxen and a cow that he bought for me at Crawley Fair, the oxen at £13-15s, the cow at £3-13s. Paid him the rest of the mony besides the 15 guineas. Paid all accounts at my ükle Courtness's, 15s-6d. Mr Healy, Mr William Martin, Mr John Hart and I were at Edgly towards night. Banks helpt George West unload the faggots.

The 29th April 1716 Sunday. A fine day. Mr William Martin preacht. I was at Albourne Church in the afternoon. Call'd at Nick Plaw's and at Westtowne and agreed with Mr Richard Whitpaine not to have the 800 of scrub faggots, that I bargain'd for, but to have what I could fetch of the old faggots, at 2s-6d per hundred. Turn'd Mr Stacey's cow and the cow my Cousin John Lindfield bought for me into the dry pond. James Burt was here in the evning to desire me to meet his ükle and others at Tott to morrow.

The 30th April 1716 Munday. A gloomy morning, dry after. George West and I fetcht 125 scrub faggots from Slaugham. Banks helpt unload. Bought Mr Richard Whitpaine's mare colt, a year old, at 20s. Sent materials for a coat to Andrew Laurence at Lewis, per Mr Jeremiah Dodson. John Smith kill'd one of my sheep. My Cousin John Lindfield, William Jup, James Burt and I met at Tott and let the house and land there to James Burt reserving the tan yard and 2 fields to John Burt with other conditions for which Mr Scutt is to make articles of agreement, he came at Michaelmas.

The 1st May 1716 Tuesday. A very fine day. Fair at Lindfield. Paid George West 12s. Picknall tended the hogs to day and yesterday. Parker, Jack Bartlet and John Davy fisht Mr Richard Whitpaine's pond at Wickham, but the fish were not good. Put 8 of them into the Marldfield stew about 9 inches. The Widdow Alcock buried. *(Ed: Recorded in the Hurst Parish Register as "Jane Alcock")* John Gun fagoted. George West went to the Fair. Lent Mr Richard Whitpaine a colour'd handcerchief and swad basket. Sold John Smith jr the red ox my Cousin John Lindfield bought at 18d per nail after the usual way of reckoning 5 qarters.

The 2nd May 1716 Wednesday. A very fine day. George West and I fetcht 115 faggots from Slaugham, in all 510. Joseph Clifford came again, ground 6 bushels of malt. John Gun and John Edwards fagoted. Paid Mr Jeremiah Dodson £5-5s for half a years tythe, by a bill I drue on Mr Richard Whitpaine. Mr Whitpaine supt there with me.

The 3rd May 1716 Thursday. A fine day. Arundell Fair. Mr Jeremiah Dodson's tythe feast to day. Deliver'd 25 ashen faggots and 75 coppice faggots to Thomas Westover, 50 ashen faggots to John Smith jr and 225 coppice faggots to Frank Holden per G and Joseph Clifford. My Cousin John Lindfield was here, I sold him a four yearling cow at £5 if she calves before Saturday sennight at night, else but £4-15s. Abraham Muall workt ½ day. Paid Ned Burt 2s for this day's work and yesterday's. John Smith jr put his horse in the Bowling Ally at per week for the 2 first weeks and 18d per week afterwards. John Gun and John Edwards fagotted. John Gun mended the gap upper side Edgly Mead. Parker rode the young horse to Arundell Fair to show him to a Gentleman that was to meet there from Chichester but did not see him.

The 4th May 1716 Fryday. A fine day. Deliver'd 75 faggots to Frank Holden, 300 to Mr Jeremiah Dodson per George West and Joseph Clifford. Reckon'd with John Edwards for all his work to this day except his coppice fagotting and there is due to me 9s-2d½ Borrow'd Mr Richard Whitpaine's old gig mare per Banks. I saw one of William Balcomb's sheep weigh'd at John Bodle's. Nick Plaw was here towards night. 2 of William Hamshire's sheep lamb'd about 4 days ago. Picknall tended hogs to day and yesterday.

The 5th May 1716 Saturday. A gloomy day, a short showr about 11 aclock. Deliver'd 75 coppice faggots and 25 to Mrs Storer and 200 to Mr Jeremiah Dodson per George

West and Joseph Clifford. I was at John Snashall's and agreed with him for two calves at £3. Mrs Catherine Beard and her family were here towards night. My Cousin Thomas Norton of Edgly, Mr Beaumont and Mr Scutt were her in the afternoon. I were at Wickham Street to speak with John Box sr. Young Picknall tended hogs to day. Receiv'd my coat from Mr Andrew Laurence per John Maynard and a bill for makeing and some material 9s-8d. He charged 6s-6d for makeing. John Gun and John Edwards fagotted.

The 6th May 1716 Sunday. A cold, dry, windy day. Mr William Martin preacht. We had a meeting at Church. Mr Richard Whitpaine and his wife Mary, my Sisters Nanny and Betty supt here. Dick Purvey came at night. I gave Mr Whitpaine a note under my hand that I had and paid for a Let Pass for severall years wool of his, on or about the 9th of December 1714. Picknall tended hogs part of this day. Mrs Susan Courthope was here after evning prayr.

---

**(Ed: Gap in diary from 7th May until 26th September 1716)**

The 26th September 1716 Wednesday. Dry 'till towards night then wet. Willy, John Gun, George West and Joseph Clifford mov'd the wheat and other jobbs. John Edwards fagotted 'till noon, thrasht wheat after. Brand's man and William Jarvice workt here. R Chatfield of Handly din'd here. He came to look on the young horse, for Mr Gratwick of Jarvice. Receiv'd 21d for half a bushel of wheat of E Lashmer. Willy fetch a horse coller from Nick Marchant's and a book. He brought both from Lewis.

The 27th September 1716 Thursday. A wet forenoon, showry after. John Standbridge workt all day, Brand's man and William Jarvice the afternoon. Willy, John Gun, George West and Joseph Clifford mov'd the clover and other jobbs. John Edwards thrasht 'till noon afterwards. He, Stacey's man and John Gun win'd 13 bushels and a peck of Edward's Bankfield wheat. Borrow'd 2 wheelbarrows full of mortar at Edgly per Joseph Clifford.

The 28th September 1716 Fryday. A dry day. George West, Joseph Clifford and John Gun carry'd dung, 28 loads. James Holden helpt part of the day, broak pares the rest. John Standbridge, Old William Brand's man and William Jarvice workt. Harry Morley thatcht the little house in the afternoon. Paid Joseph Clifford £1-19-6d and 1s for working a holy day. Outset 10s 6d for the time he lost when sick, being a month and 2 days and 20s paid before, in full. Michael Stacey fetcht 12 bushels of seed wheat per 2 of his people at 4s-6d per bushel. Willy was at Ed Steel's. Harry Morley bargain'd for 4 bushels of old wheat at 3s-6d per bushel.

The 29th September 1716 Saturday. Michaelmas. A very wet day. A Fair at Stenning. George West kept holy day. John Gun did not work. Paid George West 6s and 10s to John Gun and 10s to John Edwards. Receiv'd £18 of John Smith jr. Receiv'd 12s-6d of Thomas Surgeant for half a year's rent for Mrs Storer's orchard due this day and let it him for an other year at the same rent only he is to pay 18d tythe which Mr Jeremiah Dodson has rais'd. Receiv'd also 3s-6d of him for a bushel of old wheat. John Edwards went to Mr Steel's and brought severall goods.

The 30th September 1716 Sunday. A fine day. Mr William Martin preacht. I was not at Church in the forenoon. Mrs Courthope was here in the afternoon. Ned May came yesterday in the afternoon at 5.

The first October 1716 Munday. A dry day. Dick Lashmer begun work here. He and George West mov'd Edward's faggot stack and the Widdow Tully's. Fisht the orchard pond and threw out some of the mud. John Gun and James Holden prest the perry in the morning, after John Gun, Ned May and Dick Lashmer had ring'd the hogs. Then Ned May fetcht 16 bushels of run lime from Mr Richard Whitpaine. Afterwards John Gun and he fetcht 2 loads of sand from Danny. John Standbridge and Brand's man and Samuel Jarvice workt here. My Cousin Plump and Nanny Norton were here at breakfast. The smallpox came out on Nan Silsby a Fryday last. John Edwards thrasht wheat.

The 2nd October 1716 Tuesday. A showry day. A Fair at Ditcheling Comon. I was at the Fair and bought 8 runts of John Jones at £25-4s, paid him for them. John Edwards thrasht wheat. Dick Lashmer workt part of the day scouring the orchard pond. John Gun and George West thrasht red oates part of the day, 7 bushels. Took 18 pidgeons and some other small rooks. Ned May went to Cuckfield, carry'd home the callicoes to Mr Steel's and brought some black and white stuff. I was at Edgly in the evning. Sent a letter to Mr Gold by John Farncombe. Paid the turner at Wivelsfield 3s-6d for 12 trenchers. Brand's man and boy were here a little while in the morning.

The 3rd October 1716 Wednesday. A showry day. Willy, John Gun, Ned May and George West carry'd dung 18 loads the last of the mixen, in all 114 loads. Brand's man and Sam Jarvice workt here. Lent N Morley 39s per his wife. Reckon'd with William Roach and clear'd all accounts. Paid him 6s-6d, his bill of work was 19s-6d. Nunnery boy was here. My Wife was at Westtowne. George West, John Gun and Ned May tipt the 2 ricks at the upper close. I wrote to Mr John Picknall of Arundell.

The 4th October 1716 Thursday. A wet forenoon dry after. John Gun and George West mended gaps etc. John Edwards thrasht. My Wife and I and Ned May went to Rusper, met with _____ at Mathew's and my Cousin Bodle. My Mother gave my Wife Kitty Stone's cloathes. Willy went to coursing with his Unkle John Box. The smallpox came out on Master Jervis and Sarah Grey to day or yesterday.

The 5th October 1716 Fryday. A dry day. John Gun and Ned May carry'd ____ dung, 12 loads and 8 loads out of Mrs Storer's close. George West helpt Ned May shelve and spread dung between whiles. Willy helpt spread dung. John Box sr was here in the evning, brought me a couple of coneys.

The 6th October 1716 Saturday. A dry day. John Gun and Ned May carry'd 12 loads of dung out of Mrs Storer's close. John Standbridge workt here, cut down 3 spire trees. John Gun helpt him. They cleft the trees to posts and rails and pole lengths and one length for laths. Sent a letter to John Gold per the post for which I am to pay her 1d. Put the fatting oxen into the meads, the lean oxen into the Nine Acres, the runts and yearlings into the Churchfield and the calves into the bean earsh.

The 7th October 1716 Sunday. A very wet day. Mr William Martin preacht. I was not at Church. John Westover was here afternoon to tell us that he went to London a Tuesday next.

The 8th October 1716 Munday. A very wet day. Brand's man and Samuel Jarvice workt. John Standbridge workt, so did Richard Lashmer. He had half bushel old wheat. Receiv'd 10s of Thomas Surgeant for 2 pigs and 14d of Widdow Westover for faggots. Harry Morley mended a hole or 2 on the hovel. John Gun thrasht some oates and other jobbs, so did George West. Ned May had the young horse to Mr Gold's.

The 9th October 1716 Tuesday. A showry day. Brand's man and Samuel Jarvice workt. John Standbridge workt, so did Richard Lashmer. John Gun and George West thrasht oates part of the day and other jobbs. Win'd 3 quarters 5½ bushels of Tully's field of wheat, all that was of the first sowing. John Edwards thrasht. Receiv'd a mourning ring from my Brother James Ede per the carrier. Mr Richard Whitpaine, his wife and 2 sons supt with us at Little Park.

The 10th October 1716 Wednesday. A wet forenoon, dry after. Win'd 13½ bushels of red oates, per John Gun, George West and Ned May. John Gun and George West tipt up the straw rick which fell down last night. Mended gaps etc. John Standbridge workt all day. John Edwards thrasht wheat. Dick Lashmer and he cutt down 2 spire trees in Tully's ground in the afternoon. Deliver'd 3 bushels of old wheat to Richard Lashmer, 3 bushels to Dick Wood and 4 bushels to N Morley. Reckon'd with Dick Wood and clear'd all accounts. His bill of work was £1-11-11d. Paid Wood and Jordan 6s in full for chalk vizt 3s for 3 loads they dug and 3s for 6 loads we dug our selves. Paid 2s-6d to Mr John Hart yesterday. He is to pay it to Mr William Martin for breaking the ground in the churchyard for James Ede.
*(Ed: Hurst Parish Register shows burial 1st September 1716 of James Ede son of Mr James Ede of Cudworth)*

The 11th October 1716 Thursday. A dry day. I was at Westtowne in the morning. George West and Ned May carry'd 4 loads of dung from Old William Brand and 4 loads from the wheat barne's doores into the orchard. John Gun spread dung at 10d per score. John Edwards thrasht wheat. John Standbridge cleft laths in the forenoon and Richard Lashmer thrasht beans and in the afternoon they workt on the stew. Stephen Bine came to us at the stew. Willy and William Norton went a coursing. Kill'd 1 hare. Nick Plaw cut the white bore. Receiv'd a letter from my Cousin Hayne of Henfield to let me know the Court for the Mannor of Streatham to be the 23rd of this month.

The 12th October 1716 Fryday. A fine day. John Standbridge workt 'till noon. Dick Lashmer helpt winnow beans etc, 13 bushels. George West dryd beans and other jobbs, Ned May did severall jobbs. John Gun spread dung, John Edwards thrasht wheat. Nunnery boy came at night. Mr John Hart supt here.

The 13th October 1716 Saturday. A gloomy day. Dick Lashmer workt. John Gun spread dung. George West did severall jobbs. My Wife and I and Jacky went to my Brother John Box's. Call'd at Westtowne and Mr Richard Whitpaine and his wife Mary went with us. We did not see my Brother. Staid 'till after sun set, came back to Westtowne and supt there. John Edwards thrasht wheat. Nunnery boy went home about noon. Paid John Parsons 1s for shaveing my head and face. Receiv'd a black wig of him for which I am to give him 100 good house faggots. Turn'd the working oxen into the Little Mead and the fatting oxen into the Edgly Mead.

The 14th October 1716 Sunday. A dry day. Mr William Martin preacht. I was not at Church.

The 15th October 1716 Munday. A fine day. Begun soweing in the field by Burt's. George West, Willy, Ned May and Richard Lashmer helpt. Paid John Reed 8s-6d in full of all accounts. Sold John Gillian the old runt cow and calf at £3-5s. He paid me for 'em and had them away with him. Receiv'd 20s of John Standbridge towards his faggots. Sold W Berrick a lean hog at 25s to fetch him the 1st of November. Receiv'd a letter from my Cousin Bodle per Mr Ede. I was at Westtowne in the afternoon. Nunnery boy came this evning. John Gun made an end of spreading dung and helpt gather a few apples.

The 16th October 1716 Tuesday. A fine day. Mr Richard Whitpaine lent me his teem and Jack Smith to plough. He, Lashmer, Willy and Ned May plough'd. George West sow'd and he and John Gun mended gaps etc. They hedg'd up the gap at the corner of the homefield and Bowling Ally. Pull'd up some hop poles and stript 'em. I gave Jack Smith 1s. John Edwards thrasht. John Smith jr fetcht Stacey's cow and I show'd him the 30 ewes sold to Ed Parr and William Tourl. The young red sow farrow'd 8 pigs.

The 17th October 1716 Wednesday. A dry day. Willy, George West, Lashmer, etc plough'd and sow'd in the field by Burt's. John Gun and John Edwards carry'd 3 half loads of straw to John Hart. Deliver'd a cow to Samuel Hart per George West and Ned May. Mr Sergeson's gardiner was here with him. Gave Dick Lashmer 2 or 3 of the young sows pigs, drown'd one and the rest were dead before.

The 18th October 1716 Thursday. A showry day, George West, Willy, Ned May and Lashmer made an end of ploughing and sowing the field by Burt's about noon and Ned May and Lashmer harrow'd about half in the afternoon, 'till rain beat 'em off. John Edwards thrasht wheat. John Gun did not work, his mother being sick. Paid my Unkle Courtness 2s-6d for 2½ ells of canvas for a round frock for Willy. Mr Richard Whitpaine and his wife Mary, Mrs Stone and Mr Beard and Mrs Scutt supt at Little Park with Mr John Hart, so did my Wife and I. Stay'd late. Mr Tatersell and Mr Nordon were there in the evning. They came to speak to Mr Richard Whitpaine. Sow'd 18 bushels of wheat wanting a gallon in the field by Burt's.

The 19th October 1716 Fryday. A fine day. Return'd to Little Park from Tully's. George West and Ned May mov'd the goods. John Gun did not work. John Edwards thrasht wheat 'till noon. Workt for himself. Mr Beard was here a while in the evning. Paid John Westover 5s-6d for a payr of stockins he bought at London. Paid Thomas Baker 2s yesterday for 2 payr of breeches for Tom Picknall. Outset 1s for mud he threw out of the Bowling Ally pond, up against his pales. Mr Stacey's cow was weigh'd at John Smith's.

The 20th October 1716 Saturday. A very wet day. George West, Ned May, John Edwards and Willy win'd wheat. John Edwards din'd here. Ned May carry'd the Widdow Gun to Charles Smith's in the chaese, the smallpox being come out on her. William Nicholas was here in the evning to set up a bed and he helpt us the afternoon yesterday.

The 21st October 1716 Sunday. A fine day. Mr William Martin preacht. I was not at Church. A meeting in the afternoon about the smallpox. Mr Richard Whitpaine and his wife Mary here towards night.

The 22nd October 1716 Munday. A dry day. Clear'd all accounts to this day with John Edwards. [Win'd] 4 qarters 5 bushels head and 4 bushels tail of his Bankfield wheat, the last of the field, in all 14 qarters 7℔ reckon'd for. Thrasht oates. George West helpt winnow etc. So did Ned May. Mended 6 of Edgly sacks a Saturday. George West and Ned May made an end of harrowing the field by Burt's. Turn'd the working oxen into Tully's Mead towards night. Shut the bore and an other hog up a fatting.

The 23rd October 1716 Tuesday. A great showr in the forenoon, dry after. Begun sow the Rookwood. John Gun thrasht oates. John Edwards fagotted, or thrasht beans. I was at a court at New Hall and paid 2s for the stewards fees and 11s to the Lord for a Licence to let Eastout for 11 years. Call'd at my Aunt Holden's and J Norman's.

The 24th October 1716 Wednesday. A fine day. John Gun thrasht oates till noon and afterwards mended the thatch on Mrs Storer's stable. John Edwards workt about 2 hours, trying to winnow the oates, fagoted the rest of the day. George West, Ned May and Willy plough'd and sow'd in the Rookwood. Dick Purvey brought my Cousin Bodle from Nunnery towards night. Turn'd the cowes into the Little Meads. George West fetcht my long yoak from Mr Richard Whitpaine yesterday.

The 25th October 1716 Thursday. A wet morning, dry after. My Cousin Bodle went home. Lashmer, John Gun and George West win'd 3 qarters 1½ bushels of John Gun's red oates by Hyder's. Willy and Ned May plough'd one warp in the Rookwood. Lashmer and John Gun and George West workt the afternoon on the flat stew. John Edwards thrasht beans and fagoted.

The 26th October 1716 Fryday. A fine day. John Gun thatcht on Mrs Storer's stable. Paid my Brother William 4 guineas for my Mother. Willy, Ned May, Lashmer and my Brother Peter's man plough'd in the Rookwood. George West sow'd. I had my Brother's horses. John Edwards fagoted etc. My Brother James Ede came at night. Receiv'd 3s of Thomas Surgeant jr for a bushel of course _____ . Sold C White 4 bushels of wheat at 19s to be deliver'd a Munday. Dick Purvey came back from Hailsham towards night.

The 27th October 1716 Saturday. A fine day. Willy, George West, Ned May, Lashmer and my Brother Peter's man Mathew plough'd and sow'd in the Rookwood. John Edwards fagoted. John Gun mended thatch on Mrs Storer's stables. Scour'd the Marldfield stew. Dick Purvey went home and carry'd Bett with him. _____ had my Brother's horses, the man had 'em home.

The 28th October 1716 Sunday. A fine day, Mr William Martin preacht. I was not at Church. My Cousin Plump din'd here. My Brother James Ede went home after dinner. Mrs Scutt and Mrs Courthope was here after evning prayr. Peckham marry'd. Thomas Peckham's son. *(Ed: Hurstpierpoint Parish Register shows marriage of John Peckham to Susannah Vinall)*

The 29th October 1716 Munday. A fine day, finisht the Rookwood, haveing sow'd _____ bushels. Willy, George West and Ned May plough'd and sow'd. John Edwards workt on the flat stew. John Edwards ridded the hedge and ditch on the south side of Tully's coppice. Paid James Holden 18d for syder making. Paid Mr Holden 1s for hedging. Receiv'd 54s of John Hart for 12 bushels of wheat, 15s for 1½ bushels of wheat straw and 2s-6d for the founder'd mare's skin. Promis'd Ester 4 bushels of beans at 10s. William Fowle came at night for his sheep and his drover.

The 30th October 1716 Tuesday. A fine day. John Gun and George West carry'd dung from the mixen 10 loads into the little field by the orchard and 12 loads into the first field and some other jobbs. Paid Sam Hart 3 guineas and half a crown and outset £5-10s for the last cow, in all £8-17s, for 20 ewes at Dean House. Ned May and I went to Nunnery with Bett's cloaths. John Edwards ridded the hedge etc as yesterday. John Standbridge workt on the Marldfield stew and Fifteen Acres rick steddle. Receiv'd 11 guineas of William Fowle and one I had in hand being 2s short for 30 ewes he had away to day. Clear'd all accounts with John Bodle, his bill of meat from October last was £4-3s _____ d. Clear'd all accounts with Frank Holden. Paid him 11s-8¾d for goods for Molly Balcomb. Sent Mrs Ann Dodson £1-8-6d per John Westover, which with 500 faggots at 14s and 50 faggots at 13s per cord makes £5-5s being my half years tythe due at Michaelmas last. I have no receit, Mr Jeremiah Dodson being at London. Paid John Westover 5s for a payr of high topt shooes for Willy which he had new this evning. Richard White had 4 bushels of seed wheat to day or yesterday.

The 31st October 1716 Wednesday. A very gloomy morning, fine afternoon. George West, Ned May and John Gun carry'd 14 loads of dung into Tully's first field, the last of the mixen, in all 36 loads. They also carry'd 7 loads from Tully's Slutt's hill and 3 out of the close, so there is 36 loads in the first field. John Standbridge finisht the Marldfield stew and hew'd tree posts etc. John Edwards scour'd the stew, begun at 9 aclock. Willy went a courseing with his Unkle William, brought home a hare. The Rookwood sow'd after the following manner. Plough'd plaine next the lane. Sow'd under furrough, the next eastward 16 ridges above furrough. Next 6 ridges under furrough. Next 23 ridges above furrough. Next 3 rods broad, plaine above furrough. All the rest plaine under furrough.

The first November 1716 Thursday. A dry day. George West and Ned May begun sow Tully's first field with wheat. John Gun spread dung. Receiv'd 25s of William Berwick for a hog. Receiv'd 54s of Michael Stacey for 12 bushels of seed wheat. John Edwards ditcht against Tully's coppice. My Cousin John Lindfield supt and spent the evening here. Receiv'd a letter from Mr Picknall to day or a Munday. John Hart had a bushel of wheat at 4s-6d per Tom Picknall's son.

The 2nd November 1716 Fryday. A dry day. George West and Ned May plough'd and sow'd in Tully's first field. They had one of Mr Richard Whitpaine's horses. Sent him home per Tom Picknall's son. Paid the £50 and £6-5s for intrest, due to Mr Draper, deceas'd, to Richard Weeden for the use of Mr Holmes of Burpham and took in the bond. I was at Westtowne in the morning. Mr Richard Whitpaine and his wife Mary and my Sister Ann Box supt and spent the evning here. Willy and young Tippens fetcht my 20 ewes from Dean House. John Gun spread a load of pidgeon dung on the sow'd field which is to be plough'd in and afterwards pull'd hop poles and stript 'em. John Edwards ditcht.

The 3rd November 1716 Saturday. A fine day. Ned May and George West plough'd and sow'd. John Gun made water furroughs in the Rookwood and spread pidgeon dung on Tully's sow field. John Edwards ditcht. Reckon'd with John Gun for all his work to this day and there is due to him (his Michaelmas rent outset) £3-10-9d. Mr John Hart went to Nunnery this afternoon. I was at Stephen Bine's towards night.

The 4th November 1716 Sunday. A fine day. Mr William Martin preacht. I was at Church in the afternoon, a parish meeting. I was at Westtowne after evning prayr. Supt there.

The 5th November 1716 Munday. A fine day. Ned May and George West kept holy day.
Paid John Gun £3-10-9d in full of all accounts and gave him 1s for a harvest supper. I was at Wanbarrow in the afternoon. Paid my Sister Sarah a year's intrest, she gave me 5s. Mr John Hart return'd from Nunnery and my Brother James Ede and Jacky Ede with him.

The 6th November 1716 Tuesday. A dry day. George West and Ned May finisht Tully's field haveing sow'd 8½ bushels. John Gun did not work, John Edwards thrasht wheat. Dick Vinall kill'd the 2 black hogs, John Edwards helpt from 4 aclock. My Brother James Ede and I went to Basedean to see the young horse. Mr William Martin supt here.

The 7th November 1716 Wednesday. A very gloomy day, small rain. I cut out the hogs, shut up 2 more. Paid Ed Burt 21s for tending Jacky Ede. He had half a bushel of beans at 15s, did not [pay]. John Gun and George West made water furroughs. My Brother James Ede went away after dinner. Mr Richard Whitpaine supt and spent the evning here. Paid Brand's wife 18d and 10d (I think) was paid before for her work and her daughter's this Sumer.

The 8th November 1716 Thursday. A dry day. John Gun and George West made an end of water furroughing in the Rookwood before noon and afterwards. John Gun workt on the flat stew. George West and Willy helpt John Edwards winnow 5½ bushels being all the latter. Sow'd wheat in Tully's field. Deliver'd 4 bushels of old course wheat to Thomas Surgeant jr _____ 12s per Ned May. He went afterwards to Nunnery. The Widdow Hollobone died to day or yesterday.

The 9th November 1716 Fryday. A dry day. Bett return'd from Nunnery and Jane Brooks. John Edwards ditch in

the forenoon. Willy and George West litter'd the fatting close. Jo Wood, John Standbridge and John Gun workt on the flat stew all day and John Edwards the afternoon. Jo Wood came at 9 aclock. Robert Gatland workt there also all day. The Widdow Hollobone buried to day.
*(Ed: Recorded in the Hurst Parish Register as Ann Hollowbone)*

The 10th November 1716 Saturday. A dry day. John Standbridge, Robert Gatland, John Gun, John Edwards, George West and Ned May workt on the flat stew. Paid John Parsons 6d for shaveing my head. Mrs Mary Gratwick of Jarvice was here in her way to Lewis. Turn'd the 6 runts into the Marldfield. Paid 3d for a letter from my Brother Peter to my Mother. Received a letter from Mrs Swaine of Lewis wherein she demanded her mony, principall and intrest, Lady Day next.

The 11th November 1716 Sunday. A dry day. Mr Price preacht in the forenoon *(Ed: Rector of Clayton)*. There was no evning service, I was not at Church. Cousin John Lindfield jr din'd here. Aunt Courtness and Sister Bett here in the afternoon.

The 12th November 1716 Munday. A gloomy day. John Gun, George West and John Edwards workt on the flat stew. Ned May did severall jobbs. Receiv'd 12s of Thomas Surgeant for old wheat. John Hubbard of Ditcheling was here to take a field for flax but we did not deal. Willy went a coursing with William Norton. My Sister Ann Box din'd here.

The 13th November 1716 Tuesday. A gloomy day. My Wife, Jacky, Ned May and I set out for Nunnery after noon. Mr Healy marry'd. *(Ed: Reverend Ralph Healy of Twineham married the widow Mrs Susan Goffe née Boniface of Henfield)* George West and John Gun mow'd the clover and finisht the flat stew. John Edwards corded his wood being half a cord and ⅙ of a cord.

The 14th November 1716 Wednesday. A dry day 'till towards night. John Edwards thrasht. Mr Sixsmith, Mr Harvey of Slinfold and Mr Woodhams were at Nunnery last night when we came in. George West shovel'd the home close. John Gun rakt stubble.

The 15th November 1716 Thursday. A gloomy day and some small raine. My Father and I went to Darkin to meet Mr Potting, but he did not meet us. George West shovel'd the close, John Gun rakt stubble and John Edwards thrasht beans. I left my Father at Darkin and return'd to Nunnery.

The 16th November 1716 Fryday. A Fair at Horsham. A gloomy forenoon, wet after. John Edwards thrasht. My Brother James Ede came from Darkin with my Father. Ned May carry'd home Bett's cloaths yesterday and went to Horsham to day and had the great saddle mended. John Gun rakt stubble. George West shovel'd the close and thrasht some oates.

The 17th November 1716 Saturday. A dry day, only a small showr. John Edwards thrasht. Richard Collens jr was at Nunnery in the morning and agreed to take a lease of all the land my Father has in his hands at £54 per annum, to enter at Lady Day next etc. My Brother James Ede and I agreed also with my Father to take all his concerns (except the Horsham estate) out of his hands and to pay him £15 per annum, between us 'till we could sell the estate and then the £15 to fall and to pay him intrest for all the mony that is left when debts etc are paid but all this is only by word of mouth and we are to consider it for some time. John Edwards had a bushel of course wheat at 3s. Return'd from Nunnery late.

The 18th November 1716 Sunday. A gloomy day, wet towards night. Mr William Martin preacht. I was at Church forenoon and afternoon. We had a parish meeting.

The 19th November 1716 Munday. A showry day. George West, Willy and Ned May fetcht the Widdow Tully's goods. John Edwards thrasht. Receiv'd a payr of boots for Willy from London. rakt stubble in the forenoon and in the afternoon scour'd ditches etc in order for fishing. Mr Richard Whitpaine and Nick Plaw spent the evning here. Receiv'd 4s of Nick Plaw for Willy's old boots. Ed Penfold workt here. Paid Thomas Baker 10d for a payr of new gloves.

The 20th November 1716 Tuesday. A stormy day some rain. John Gun helpt fish. Fisht the new pond, put 41 the largest carp into the Hovelfield stew and 511 store carp into the flat stew. Win'd 7 quarters 6 bushels of Edward's beans, the last of the field, in all 9 quarters 3 bushels. Receiv'd 2 bushels of oates from Albourne Place. Mr Pointin spent the evning here. The Widdow Tully helpt winnow.

The 21st November 1716 Wednesday. A dry windy day. John Gun rakt stubble. John Edwards cut the bushes against the ditch in Tully's Mead. Deliver'd 4 bushels of beans to Kester per Ned May and brought home 8 bushels. George West thrasht oates in the forenoon and in the afternoon carry'd 6 quarters 2 bushels of beans into Tully's garret. Reckon'd with John Smith jr and there is due to me £9-9-6d. His bill of meat from the 8th of February last was £12-8-4d. Willy and I was at Osbourne's at St John's Comon to see a pond of fish, but it was not out. The Widdow Tully had half a bushel of malt.

The 22nd November 1716 Thursday. A dry day. George West thrasht oates. John Gun rakt stubble 'till noon then helpt fish. John Edwards cut bushes 'till noon, helpt fish after. Brew'd 8 bushels of malt for keeping beer, half for Mr John Hart and put 2 bushels to it for mild beer. My Cousin John Lindfield here in the morning, fisht the great pond. Put 220 of the biggest carp into the new pond and 18 the biggest tench. Put also 258 store carp into the flat stew and 36 tench. Put also 550 very small carp into a hole in the cow field. Mr Richard Whitpaine was here in the forenoon.

The 23rd November 1716 Fryday. A dry day. John Gun helpt about the middle pond in the forenoon and in the afternoon helpt George West thrash. John Edwards thrasht barly out of Tully's stable. John Harland came to help fish the middle pond but the water was not out. Gave him 1s. Stephen Carter of Rigate din'd here. I went with him to John Smith's. There was Harry Wickham and John Channel. Staid late and drank too much. I paid 30d. Sold Harry Wickham my little colt for a sack of malt.

The 24th November 1716 Saturday. A fine day. Fisht the middle pond. Put 66 large carp into the new pond, 380 store tench into the flat stew and 12 large carp, 10 large tench and 57 middle siz'd tench into the Hovelfield stew. John Gun rakt stubble 'till noon then helpt fish. John Edwards helpt fish in the afternoon and George West. My Wife carry'd Mrs Catherine Beard, Mrs Scutt and Mr Courtness each of them a few eels. Mr William Martin and my Sister Bett spent the evning here.

The 25th November 1716 Sunday. A dry forenoon, wet after. Mr Price preacht and din'd here. Thomas Challoner watcht the new pond last night. Receiv'd 2 bushels of oates from Albourne Place yesterday.

The 26th November 1716 Munday. A dry day. John Gun, Willy, Ned May and I went to fish Richard Burtenshaw's ponds, but that at the Green had no fish of any value in it and the other we could not get the water above half out. George West and James Holden mov'd the clover that was fall'n down on the oates and afterwards win'd 13½ bushels of red oates. George West thrasht after that. John Westover watcht the new pond last night. John Edwards thrasht barly. I din'd at Nick Plaw's. Paid Robert Pierce's man 5d for setting hoops on a half tub. Turn'd 5 cows and the bull into the cow field.

The 27th November 1716 Tuesday. A dry day. John Harland and John Gun fisht the upper pond. John Edwards helpt about 2 hours, thrasht later. Put 55 sale fish into the new pond and 25 store carp, put 56 carp about 10 inches into the Hovelfield stew and 12 tench about 8 inches. Jo Wood and Robert Gatland mended the grates of the upper pond in the afternoon. My Cousin John Lindfield din'd here. I let him the Nine Acres to sow with flax at £3 per acre. I am to take a small piece of the upper side (formerly a shaw) to my self and to abate for so much as that comes to. He is to find a plough holder for which I am to allow him 12s-6d. Receiv'd in hand a guinea. Receiv'd (I think) 2 bushels of oates from Albourne.

The 28th November 1716 Wednesday. A gloomy day. John Gun mended hedges round the cow field. John Edwards thrasht barly, George West oates. They both watcht the new pond last night. Ned May went to Rigate yesterday, return'd to night. Sold Ed Pickstone my 4 oxen at £39-1-6d to be deliver'd at Wineham a Munday next. Receiv'd in hand a guinea. Sent 2 carp, one tench and some eels to Nunnery per Ed Penfold. Receiv'd 10s-9d of Mr John Hart for malt. He also paid my Wife for his board to Michaelmas last.

The 29th November 1716 Thursday. A gloomy, cold day. George West thrasht oates. John Gun and Ned May carry'd the mud and dung out of the watering place in the upper close, 1 load and in the afternoon they and John Edwards mov'd the fish out of the new pond into the upper pond, 358. Put, (I think) 8 carp and 2 tench into the Marldfield stew, for a sample. Ed Penfold return'd from Nunnery. Put 9 tench into the Hovelfield stew. Receiv'd a parcell of flannel from my Cousin John Lindfield per Isaac Muzzall.

The 30th November 1716 Fryday. A dry, cold day. A Fair at Bolny and East Grinstead. James Holden workt making syder. George West and Ned May kept holy day. John Gun did not work. Mr John Hart, Bett and I spent the evning at Westtowne, there was Mr Shave and Mr Harry Goffe. Nick Plaw was here to see a calf. Paid George West 14s and he told me I should pay John Smith jr 10s on his account.

The first December 1716 Saturday. A fine day, a sharp frost last night. George West thrasht oates, John Gun and James Holden made syder. Win'd 3 quarters 4 bushels head and 2½ bushels tail of Edward's barly by Wickham's. Widdow Tully helpt. Willy and I went to Horsham and thence to Nunnery. Sold Stephen Carter 300 fish, one half to hold 13 inches one with an other and the other half a foot. Receiv'd in hand a guinea. I offer'd him 50 more under size fish at 30s if he liked them when he saw them. Expences 3s-6d.

The 2nd December 1716 Sunday. A dry, cold day, the frost continuing.            preacht at Hurst. Willy was at Rusper Church in the afternoon.

The 3rd December 1716 Munday. A fine day, thawing, but a frost last night. George West drove my fatting oxen to Wineham. John Gun and James Holden made syder. John Edwards thrasht. Ned May came to Nunnery last night on foot and I gave Dick Purvey 1s to go to Hurst in the night to order the oxen for London. Willy, Ned May and I return'd from Nunnery by Hand Cross where I met Ed Pickstone, he paid me £38 in full for my oxen and all accounts. There was William Ball of Albourne. Expences 3s-4d. My Brother came to Hurst a Saturday and return'd to day, but I did not see him. Receiv'd 10s for R Kester for a sack of beans and clear'd all accounts.

The 4th December 1716 Tuesday. A fine day. Win'd 5 quarters 2 bushels of the red oates to day and yesterday, the last of the field, in all 14 quarters 1½ bushels. Lent Mr Richard Whitpaine 40 wattles per R Steel and himself. John Gun and James Holden made syder 'till noon. John Gun rakt stubble afterwards 'till he finisht the field and then went to fetch his mother home. Paid James Holden 21d and he had half a bushel of wheat, in full for all his work. My Wife, Willy and Ned May went to Lewis afternoon. They carry'd 2 carp about a foot and 3 tench to my Cousin Peter Marchant. John Edwards thrasht pease. Widdow Tully had a bushel of oates.

The 5th December 1716 Wednesday. A stormy forenoon with snow, fine after. John Gun begun thrash barly, George West wheat. John Edwards workt on the ditch against Tully's coppice. Dick Wood dress't the old Duke horse's foot (being stub'd) yesterday morning. Shutt Tail and Lively into the fatting close. My Wife, Ned May and Willy return'd from Lewis.

The 6th December 1716 Thursday. A dry, very cold day, a hard frost last night. John Standbridge, George West and I cut down 3 oaken pollards and 2 ashen in the Edgly Mead and 3 spire oakes in Tully's first, 3 corner'd field. Paid my Mother 5 guineas, I sent per my Sister Betty. John Gun thrasht barly, John Edwards ditcht against the coppice. Mrs Catherine Beard and her family, Mrs Scutt, Mrs Courthope, Mr Richard Whitpaine and his wife Mary supt and spent the evning here. They came on Mr John Hart's account. John Edwards had a bushel of course wheat at 3s.

The 7th December 1716 Fryday. A dry, cold day, the frost continuing. Return'd what was left of the black and white crape to Mr Steel, 32½ yards, per J Muzzall, last night. Paid Old William Brand 10s. John Edwards had an other bushel of course wheat, 3s. John Gun thrasht barly, John Edwards pease. John Standbridge, George West and I cut down 3 spire trees and a pollard in Tully's ground. Ned May and Willy drew them home.

The 8th December 1716 Saturday. A cold day and some snow. John Gun, George West, Ned May and Willy and I broak the ice and took the fish out of the upper pond and put them into the fatting close pond. John Edwards helpt us in the afternoon, thrasht before. Receiv'd £6 of John Smith jr. Sent William Smith, the German's son to tell Mr Healy we could not come to day, but a Munday. John Box sr was here and spoak (I think) for 60 store carp and 20 tench. Paid the half bushel of oates borrow'd of Mrs _____ per John Smith, her man.

The 9th December 1716 Sunday. A fine day, the frost continuing. Mr Jeremiah Dodson preacht. We had a parish meeting and took John Haslegrove's accounts.

Thomas Surgeant was there with William Haslegrove. I supt and spent the evning at Mrs Catherine Beard's.

The 10th December 1716 Munday. A fine day, the frost continuing. John Gun and George West thrasht, so did John Edwards. Ned May went to Lewis and brought a Cheshire cheese and 1000 of large 6d, 1000 of short 6d, 1000 of 3d and 500, 4d nailes from Mr Court's. Mr Scutt and his wife and my Wife and I din'd at Mr Healy's and supt at Mr Scutt's.

The 11th December 1716 Tuesday. A gloomy day, thaw'd a little. John Gun and George West thrasht, so did John Edwards. Ned May drew home trees out of the Edgly Mead and John Edwards had 3 pecks of the course wheat 2s-9d.

The 12th December 1716 Wednesday. A gloomy day, thawing, rain towards night Win'd 2 quarters 3½ bushels of Edward's pease, Widdow Tully and Richard Tully helpt. John Gun thrasht barly. Dick Vinall kill'd a porker in the afternoon. One of the ewes I bought of Samuel Hart was kill'd by a dog this afternoon. George West did severall jobbs. Ned May drew home wood and faggots. My Brother James Ede came at night and Nunnery boy.

The 13th December 1716 Thursday. A gloomy day. John Gun thrasht barly, George West wheat. My Brother James Ede and Willy went a shooting. John Edwards thrasht. Ned May did several jobbs. The Gooders were here.

The 14th December 1716 Fryday. A very wet day. John Gun thrasht barly, George West wheat. Ned May did severall jobbs. I mended the Hovelfield gate. Mr Richard Whitpaine supt and spent the evning here.

The 15th December 1716 Saturday. A gloomy day, small driving rain. John Bodle turn'd a horse into the Churchfield last night. Ned May fetcht the young black horse from Mr Gold's. John Gun thrasht barly. John Edwards oates. George West mended a hole in the thatch of Tully's barne (John Edwards helpt him) thrasht wheat the rest of the day. Paid John Parsons 1s for shaveing my head and tying my wig 2 or 3 times. Mr James Ede, Mr John Hart, my Wife and I supt and spent the evning at Westtowne and the 2 boys. Mr Richard Whitpaine's pump was set up to day.

The 16th December 1716 Sunday. A gloomy day. Mr Jeremiah Dodson preacht. Mr James Ede and I were at Stephen Bine's after evning prayr.

The 17th December 1716 Munday. A gloomy day, with some raine. John Standbridge workt hewing timber. George West and Ned May carry'd 17 loads of dung out of the home close to the other side of the pond. John Gun thrasht barly, John Edwards oates. Mr James Ede, Mr Richard Whitpaine and Willy went to shooting in Clayton Woods. They shot 3 woodcocks. I went to Cuckfield and return'd 15 yards of blue and white stuff and 2 yards of shalloon to Mr Steel, receiv'd and enter'd per John Steel. I was also at Mr Burrell's and gave him 10s for his opinion in my Father Stone's business. Widdow Tully had half a bushel of malt at 16d.

The 18th December 1716 Tuesday. A fine day. George West thrasht wheat. John Gun barly. Turn'd 5 runts into the field by Hyder's. John Edwards thrasht. Put 3 runts into Tully's Close. Mr James Ede, my Wife, Willy and I din'd at Dean House. There was Mr Warden of Butler's Green. My Cousin John Lindfield paid him £20 for a year's rent of Floods Farme due (I think) at Michaelmas last. He paid him £15-12-6d in mony or thereabouts, the rest of the £20 was outset for repairs and taxes. The perticulers of the mony was 4 guineas, 1 half guinea, a half broad piece at 11s-9d and £10-4s in silver. Settled all accounts (except Jacky Ede's and his own board) with Mr James Ede and there is due to me 14s-9½d. I allowed him 40s in exchange for his horse.

The 19th December 1716 Wednesday. A gloomy day, a very hard frost last night. Willy, George West and Ned May carry'd a load of stubble into the fatting close and 3 loads into the home close out of the Bankfield. John Gun thrasht barly, John Edwards oates. My Brother James Ede went away after dinner. John Box and I went to Albourne Place and to Nick Plaw's. I brought home a great hammer at 1s.

The 20th December 1716 Thursday. A dry day. George West, Ned May and Willy carry'd a load of stubble, the last of the Bankfield, in all 5 loads. Shutt up the lean oxen. John Gun thrasht barly, John Edwards oates. Mr Healy din'd here, Mr Scutt and his wife supt here. Nick Plaw was here in the evning.

The 21st December 1716 Fryday. A dry day. George West thrasht wheat, John Gun barly. John Edwards thrasht oates. Ned May did severall jobbs. Willy, Jacky Ede and I went to Nunnery afternoon. Edwards had half a bushel of malt at 1s-4d.

The 22nd December 1716 Saturday. A dry cold day. George West thrasht wheat, John Gun thrasht barly, John Edwards oates, Ned May did jobbs. I was at Horsham, Stephen Carter promis'd to send for my fish the Fryday after Xmas week. I spent 1s with my Cousin John Lindfield and M Storer.

The 23rd December 1716 Sunday. A dry cold day. Willy was at Rusper Church. He and I came home afternoon and brought home the sacks that were at Darkin with wheat. We carry'd 100 oisters to Nunnery, cost 18d.

The 24th December 1716 Munday. A stormy day, the wind very high at night.
George West thrasht wheat till noon, did jobbs after. Ned May carry'd home the mortar borrow'd at Edgly and brought the rest home.
Annointed the sheep. John Gun thrasht barly, John Edwards oates.
I cut a gap into the Bowling Ally for John Smith to wash his horse at the pond till ~~Lady Day~~ this Winter and at Lady Day he is to enter on the field and pond together at £1-2s-6d per annum. No body to wash himself and to pay me 5s for this Winter's wash. I gave my Cousin John Marchant of Lox an old payr of _____
(Ed: John, born 1657, was 2nd cousin once removed to Thomas).

The 25th December 1716 Tuesday. Xmas day. A very fine day. Mr Jeremiah Dodson preacht. John Edwards and his wife, John Gun and Widdow Tully and Eliz Cheal din'd here. I was at Wanbarrow after evening prayr, supt there, call'd at _____ and wrote a note to Mr Saxby _____ Mr Richard Whitpaine's wood.

The 26th December 1716 Wednesday. A showry day. George West and Ned May kept holy day. I was at Church to choose new surveyors. Mrs Catherine Beard and her family, Mr Scutt and his wife supt here. Paid Mr Scutt 3s for making an order from Mrs Margret Fagg to John Box and I to pay William Balcomb's rent to the present Sir Robert Fagg.

The 27th December 1716 Thursday. A dry very cold day, the wind high, a storm of hail. I was at Brighton. Sent a letter etc to Mrs Fagg and my Brother James Ede per the post. Expences 18d. I was at Old John Mockford's and he agreed to give me 8s-6d per nail for old bakon if I sent it. Receiv'd 50s for the tags sold to Henry Dubbins the 4th of June. Paid George West 6s.

The 28th December 1716 Fryday. A showry stormy day. The men kept holy day to day and yesterday. Paid John Edwards 10s. My Wife, Mr John Hart and I supt at Mrs Catherine Beard's with Danny family and Mr Jeremiah Dodson.

The 29th December 1716 Saturday. A fine day, a frost last night. John Towner and Ja Reed begun sawing. George West thrasht wheat, John Gun barly, John Edwards oates. Paid Joseph Muall 18s-4d for a year's Lord's rent and 6d for 2 Amercements for not appearing at the Court. My Cousin John Lindfield was here towards night. Lent Old William Brand 8 sacks per William Jarvice.

The 30th December 1716 Sunday. A gloomy day, with rain towards night, a hard frost last night. Mr Jeremiah Dodson preacht. My Wife supt at Mrs Catherine Beard's. Lent Old William Brand 6 sacks more per Sam Jarvice. I had one lamb of Mr John Hart's sheep a Saturday.

The 31st December 1716 Munday. A wet day, small driveing raine. John Towner and Ja Reed saw'd a little while. George West did severall jobbs. John Gun thrasht barly. My Wife, Mr John Hart, Jacky and Ned May went to Nunnery.
I went to Cuckfield, saw Mr Steel and T Warden. Appointed to meet Mr Steel at his brother Lintott's a Tuesday next. John Edwards thrasht. I was also at Mr Burrell's. My Brother William was here and stay'd the evning. Paid him £4-10s for a year's intrest due to my Brother Henry Faulkoner. Paid 3d for a letter from Mrs Margret Fagg on William Balcomb's account. John Parsons cutt off Willy's hair.

The first January 1716 Tuesday. A very wet forenoon, dry after. John Edwards thrasht. John Gun went to Nunnery with my own 3 horses, one of my Cousin John Lindfield's and his waggon. George West kept holy day. Paid Dick Tully 3s-2d for faggoting etc. Paid      Ilman 30s for a year's intrest due at Michaelmas.

Paid Nan Kester 3s-9d in full of all. Paid John Parsons 2s-6d for new mounting an old wig for Willy and cutting off his hair. I was invited to dinner at Danny but could not go. Receiv'd 2 sacks of Old William Brand.

The 2nd January 1716 Wednesday. A very wet, stormy day. George West thrasht barly, John Edwards oates. John Gun returned from Nunnery, brought my Sister Katherine's saddle and whip, her chest of draws, a cooler and some other things, 5 sacks cloaths. I went to meet them as far as Collwood on John Smith's horse. Dick Purvey came with John Gun and 3 of my Father's horses.

The 3rd January 1716 Thursday. A wet forenoon, dry after. Paid Dick Wood 13s-1d in full of all accounts. Reckon'd with Stephen Bine and clear'd all accounts, his bill of work for me was £8-1s-5d and 11s for Jemmy Ede's coffinn.
*(Ed: Under 1st September 1716 Hurst Parish Register shows the burial of "James Ede son of Mr James Ede)*
Receiv'd 11s-6d of him for carrying Mrs Catherine Beard's plank and timber to the Rock at 10s per load, and 8s for 2 pieces of my own timber 17 foot. Paid Molly Balcomb 1s for pocket mony. Dick Purvey went home on the grey horse, left the ball horse with me and the mare at Mrs Catherine Beard's He carry'd home 6lb of candles, half a bushel of salt, and a linnen mop from Frank Holden's. Paid George Wickham 6d for 3 brooms. Paid John Parsons 6d for shaveing Willy's head. The Albourne cow calv'd a bull calf. John Gun thrasht barly afternoon, John Edwards oates all day. George West carry'd home Wanbarrow apple crackers etc. Harry Morley thatcht in the afternoon. Ned May return'd from Nunnery at night.

The 4th January 1716 Fryday. A gloomy forenoon, fine after. John Gun thrasht barly. George West and Ned May took the fish out of the great pond and put them in the Marldfield stew, 283. Stephen Carter and my Cousin John Lindfield and Ed Older a butcher were here. Receiv'd £10-15s of Stephen Carter and guinea I had in hand in full for the fish above. Put 41 culling fish into the flat stew. John Edwards helpt afternoon. My Father, Mr John Hart, my Wife, and the boys return'd from Nunnery at night, John Dale and Dick Purvey came with them. One Michell's teem of Buckswood came for the fish.

The 5th January 1716 Saturday. A dry day. John Gun thrasht barly, John Edwards oates. George West and Ned May took the rest of the fish, 34, out of the great pond that could not be found last night (it being dark.) Ned May had my Cousin John Lindfield's waggon home. John Towner and Ja Reed saw'd to day and yesterday. I sent 4 carp to Mr Jeremiah Dodson, per Ned May. The fish tun went away this morning. They had a half tun of me, which Richard Michell promis'd to deliver again at Hand Cross next week. My Father, Mr John Hart, my Wife, Willy and I supt at Mr Jeremiah Dodson's. Receiv'd a letter from my Brother James Ede.

The 6th January 1716 Sunday. A very wet day. I went to Hicksted to meet Ed Steel of Cuckfield and settled all accounts with him.

The 7th January 1716 Munday. A dry day. John Towner and Ja Reed saw'd. George West rakt stubble in the Churchfield. John Gun thrasht barly, John Edwards oates, Ned May ground malt. My Father, Mr John Hart, my Wife and I supt at Mr Scutt's. Willy was at Cuckfield with a letter to Ed Steel.

The 8th January 1716 Tuesday. A fine day. George West and Ned May begun fallow the _____ field. John Gun thrasht barly, John Edwards oates. Towner, Reed, Tom King, and William Jarvice rakt stubble in the Churchfield. I was at Wanbarrow towards night. Paid my Cousin John Marchant of Lox £11-9-8d for half a year's Land Tax, he din'd here. I was at Mr Jeremiah Dodson's in the morning. Receiv'd £13 of my Father. Gave him my best bridle.

The 9th January 1716 Wednesday. A wet forenoon, dry after. George West and Ned May plough'd. John Gun thrasht barly, John Edwards oates. Dick Purvey went home afternoon. Paid Towner, and Reed 11s-4d for sawing, 2s-8d for stubble raking, and 2s to Reed for goeing to the Rock with my teem in the Summer. Paid John Smith jr 20s for a year's Window Tax. Old King and his boy begun rake stubble.

The 10th January 1716 Thursday. A gloomy day with small driving rain some times. Willy and I went to Lewis. We were at Dr White's, gave him half a guinea for his advice for Willy. He order'd phisick from Fifendeans, cost 3s-6d. Paid Mr Court 19s-11d in full of all accounts. Clear'd all accounts with my Cousin Peter Marchant.

John Ledgeter at the Starr told me he would give me 6d per lb for carp a foot long and upwards and that it was the comon price. I agreed with Mrs Atkinson to board and teach Bett at the rate of £13 per annum. Clear'd all accounts at T Norman's. John Gun thrasht barly and kill'd his hog, John Edwards thrasht oates. George West, and Ned May plough'd. Dick return'd from Nunnery. Mrs Catherine Beard and her family supt here. I call'd at Mr Jeremiah Dodson's as I came from Lewis.

The 11th January 1716 Fryday. A gloomy day, with small raine. My Father went home. I was at Cuckfield before the Commission in a Commission of Bankrupt awarded against Ed Steel were sworne and examin'd. Due to him £19-8-9½ d. Win'd 7 quarters 4 bushels 5 bushels tail of John Edwards's white oates, carry'd into Tully's chamber. Dick Tully helpt winnow. John Gun thrasht barly. John Edwards din'd here. Abraham Muzzall here.

The 12th January 1716 Saturday. A fine day. John Gun and Dick Vinal kill'd 2 hogs, John Gun thrasht barly after. George West and Ned May plough'd. John Edwards thrasht pease. Paid John Gun 25s for his days' works and rakeing stubble to Xmas last. I gave Mrs Catherine Beard 3 carp and 2 tench per John Smith. I weigh'd a carp about 12½ inches long yesterday, indifferently good, it weigh'd 2lb hard weight. My Wife, Mr John Hart, and Jacky were at Danny. Jacky Ede scalded his leg yesterday. Dick Wood shooe'd the bay horses fore feet. I wrote to John Gold by post.

The 13th January 1716 Sunday. A fine day. Mr Jeremiah Dodson preacht. Thomas Howell was here in the morning. Mrs Catherine Beard and Mrs Kettilby was here in the evning to see Willy take a vomit. Paid John Smith sr 1s for a pint of white wine. Two lambs of the Westcountry sheep last night.

The 14th January 1716 Munday. A dry day. John Gun thrasht barly, John Edwards pease. Shut up two pigs a fatting. George West, Ned May, and Willy carry'd 3 loads of stubble of the Churchfield into the home close etc. One lamb of the Westcountry sheep. Mr John Hart and I supt at Westtowne. Fetcht 4 bushels of oates from Tully's chamber. Receiv'd ½lb of bohea and a whip lash from Mr Ede per Dick Purvey a Fryday last.

The 15th January 1716 Tuesday. A dry cold day, after a gloomy morning. John Gun thrasht barly, John Edwards pease. George West and Ned May plough'd in the Bankfield. John Gold sent for the blind mare. Jo Wood and Robert Gatland workt here. They mended the penstock of the middle pond and cut 3 ashes, and a pollard oak. My Brother James Ede came at night. Harry Morley swept the kitchen chimney and the hall and 4 chimneys at Tully's. Borrow'd a payr of paniers of Thomas Surgeant jr per Ned May. Abraham Muzzall workt here the afternoon.

The 16th January 1716 Wednesday. A dry cold day. Fisht the flat stew, put 34 carp about 10 inches into the new pond, 105 carp into the Upper Pond about 6 inches, 210 carp about 5 or 6 inches into the great pond, and 105 into the ditch in the Homefield for the middle pond. I broak the screw of the tomkin. Sent 32 carp to Lewis per Ned May which he sold for 19s. My Cousin Peter Marchant left 3s to pay for what he bought. Jo Wood workt here setting up the cooler afternoon. John Gun and George West workt at fishing. John Edwards thrasht. Mr Peter Courthope had 100 store tench about 7 inches for which I intend to have 7s-6d per John Grey and the coachman.

The 17th January 1716 Thursday. A dry cold day, a frost last night. John Edwards workt for George West. Win'd 2 quarters head 2½ bushels tail of George West's wheat in Churchfield. Carry'd the head into Tully's garret. Widdow Tully helpt winnow. Young Thomas Norton marry'd to Nancy Byshe yesterday or a Tuesday. *(Ed: 16 January at Slaugham, she was the daughter of the Rector of Pyecombe).* My Brother James Ede made an oak chest in the little stable and has had 2 bushels of oates put in it this evening. Mr Jeremiah Dodson's tythe feast. Mr Dodson supt and spent the evning here last night. One lamb of the Westcountry sheep.

The 18th January 1716 Fryday. A fine day, but cold: a frost last night. George West thrasht wheat, John Gun barly, John Edwards pease. Stephen Bine and his man Jo drew the tomkin of the flat stew. Paid my Lord Treep 6d for new brazeing the screw.
Ned May, and Willy drew home 2 ashes etc. Chang'd [sheep]. I was at Westtowne afternoon to help Mr Richard Whitpaine contrive his shop. Mr James Ede was a shooting. Mrs Ann Dodson and Miss Jenny supt here. One lamb of the Downish sheep.

The 19th January 1716 Saturday. A gloomy day, thawing. John Gun and John Edwards thrasht. George West and Ned May made an end of the Bankfield. I gave Richard Burtenshaw 70 store carp and 30 tench per ____ Pierce and J Burtenshaw. Put 52 carp and 52 tench into the Edgly Mead pond. Put 100 tench into the Churchfield pond. Put 4 carp 5 inches and 2 tench 6 inches into the pond in Tully's orchard. Those above (all but a few) were of the same size. Paid William Nicholas 14d in full of all accounts.

The 20th January 1716 Sunday. A gloomy day Mr Jeremiah Dodson preacht. He read a brief for Relief of the Episcopal Churches in Poland. I was not at Church, nor Mr John Hart. Mr Richard Whitpaine and my Sister Bett was here after evning prayr.

The 21st January 1716 Munday. A gloomy showry day. John Gun thrasht barly, John Edwards, George West, Ned May and Willy carry'd 2 loads of stubble into the fatting close. Robert Gatland workt here hewing, and cut and ash in the Fifteen Acres. Mrs Catherine Beard etc were here, about the evning with my Wife, she being very ill with the toothache. Nick Plaw was here and let the 2 fatting oxen bleed. John Towner and Ja Reed saw'd.

The 22nd January 1716 Tuesday. A fine day. Win'd 4 quarters 1 bushel head, and 4 bushels tail of John Edwards's white pease, being the last, in all 7 quarters 3½ bushels. John Edwards din'd here. Receiv'd 3s-6d of John Box sr for 30 carp about 5 inches and as many tench about 7 inches long. Robert Gatland workt here. John Towner and Ja Reed saw'd. John Gun begun rid the Nine Acres hedge. Mr Sixsmith and Mr Scutt supt here and Mr Sixsmith lay here. Receiv'd 3s of Thomas Surgeant for 1 1/3 bushel of apples.

The 23rd January 1716 Wednesday. A very wet day. Mr Sixsmith went away in the morning to Mr Jeremiah Dodson's. Put 10 very small tench, 5 about 7½ inches, and 5 carp about 5 inches into the Bowling Ally pond and put 60 carp 5½ inches into a hole at the lower side of the middle piece. Put 108 such carp into the middle pond. Put 110 of the same carp and 5 tench 7½ inches, and some small tench into the hole in the farther Marldfield. George West, Willy, John Gun, and Picknall win'd barly. Paid Dick Tully 19d for severall jobbs. John Gun din'd here. Mrs Catherine Beard etc were here to see my Wife.

The 24th January 1716 Thursday. A fine day. John Gun thrasht barly, John Edwards oates. George West, Ned May, and Picknall carry'd 3 loads of stubble, the last of the Churchfield, in all 8 loads. Paid Richard King 3s yesterday towards stubble rakeing. John Towner and Ja Reed saw'd. Paid Frank Marshall 18d for annoynting the sorrel colt's leg. John Snashall sr was here in the morning to see my Wife. Paid John Parsons 6d for shaveing my head. Put the 6 yearlings into Tully's cow field.

The 25th January 1716 Fryday. A very fine day. John Gun thrasht barly, John Edwards oates. Nick Plaw was here in the morning and drew away a lamb from one of the Downish ewes, he left £12 of William Balcomb's mony with me and sent me £65-10s more per Willy. I had 11 nail 6lbs of bief of John Smith at 18d per nail. George West and Ned May begun fallow the Churchfield. Paid Towner per Reed 4s for sawing ashen board at 3s per cord and clear'd all accounts.

The 26th January 1716 Saturday. A very fine day. George West and Ned May plough'd. John Gun thrasht barly, John Edwards oates. The ewe aborted. Paid Old William Brand 19s and clear'd all accounts, his bill of work was 37s-2d. He offer'd to nail my stone healing for 3s-6d per square, I to find all. Mrs Scutt was here in the morning to bake for my Wife. Paid John Smith sr 1s for a pint of white wine. My Brother James Ede and Willy were a shooting towards Broad Street. They shot 4 cocks and a partridge.

The 27th January 1716 Sunday. A wet day. Mr Jeremiah Dodson preacht. A meeting at Church about Snatt in the forenoon because no service afternoon. One lamb of each sort of sheep.

The 28th January 1716 Munday. A dry day. John Gun thrasht barly, John Edwards oates, George West wheat. Paid John Edwards 10s, he had half a bushel of malt at 16d. Ned May and Willy mended gaps etc. I were at Mr Richard Whitpaine's pond afternoon. Thomas Howell and William Sheperd were here to set out the plough. John Gun had the ball mare to ride to his cousin _____.

The 29th January 1716 Tuesday. A dry, cold day. George West and Young Prat plough'd in the Churchfield with the oxen. Willy and Ned May begun the field below Tully's Mead. Receiv'd half a bushel of breaking pease from Wanbarrow per Jack Picknall. John Gun thrasht barly, John Edwards wheat, he had a bushel wheat at 5s. Mrs Barbara Campion and Mrs Phill Dyke was here afternoon and Mrs Scutt and Mrs Kettilby and Mrs Catherine Beard at night. 2 lambs of the Downish sheep and one of t'other.

The 30th January 1716 Wednesday. A dry, cold day, a smart frost last night. Ned May and Willy plough'd. J Prat peekt plough. Young Picknall pickt chucks etc. John Gun thrasht barly, John Edwards oates, George West wheat. I was at Mrs Catherine Beard's in the evning. She had £3-10s certain for my Father's mare at 10s, more if she have _____.

The 31st January 1716 Thursday. A gloomy day, some small rain, a smart frost last night. George West and Prat plough'd, so did Ned May and Willy. Picknall peekt. John Gun thrasht barly, John Edwards oates. I wrote to my Father by the post. Paid Mrs Swaine of Lewis £64 per Stephen Bine in full for principal and intrest of £63 due to her on bond. Mrs Catherine Beard and her family, Mrs Ann Dodson and Mrs Scutt were here this afternoon. John Gun swept my chamber chimney. Paid 11s for 6 yards of Irish cloath at 22d per yard for Molly Balcomb for shift and aprons paid to a Scotchman.

The 1st February 1716 Fryday. A dry, cold day, the frost continuing. Dr White came to my Wife. Jack Howard went for him. George West and Prat plough'd, so did Will, Ned May and Picknall. Mrs Catherine Beard, my Cousin Plump and Sister Ann Box here afternoon. John Gun thrasht barly, John Edwards oates. Mr John Hart, my Brother James Ede and I supt at Mr Scutt's.

The 2nd February 1716 Saturday. A very fine day. George West and Ned May kept holy day. Reckon'd and clear'd all accounts with Harry Morley. Stephen Ridge din'd here. I gave him 1s which I got of Mr James Ede for him. My Sister Bett lay here last night. One lamb of the Westcountry sheep.

The 3rd February 1716 Sunday. A fine day, the frost continuing. Mr Jeremiah Dodson preacht. Mr James Ede went away afternoon. Ned May went with him and had home Nunnery horse. Dick Purvey came at night. Mrs Catherine Beard and her family supt here.

The 4th February 1716 Munday. A fine day, the frost continuing. Ned May return'd from Nunnery. John Gun thrasht barly, George West wheat. Paid John Bodle 9s-6d for 6 nail 2lbs of bief. Young Picknall workt here in the afternoon. Edwards went from home. Dick Tully mov'd the oat heap in Tully's barne. Dick Purvey went home a yesterday. One lamb of the Downish sheep. Paid my Unkle Courtness 10s-3d for 6½ yards of fustian at and ½ _____ a Saturday last. Paid Frank Holden 14d for a brush. Paid Kester's wife 4d for Jack Howard's journey to Lewis.

The 5th February 1716 Tuesday. A very fine day, the frost continuing. Stephen Bine's man John Stammer and Robert Gatland workt here, cut down 2 pollard oaks in the Nine Acres, one in the dry pond, an ash in the cow field, an other in Tully's coppice and 2 pollard oaks, one spire tree in Tully's lower field and 2 pollards in the oat earshes. Ned May and Willy drew home the trees. John Gun made an end of thrashing barly about 10 aclock and workt ridding the Nine Acres hedges after. I paid Frank Holden 2s for 4lbs of candles per Willy. Paid John Smith snr 1s for a pint of white wine per Willy.

The 6th February 1716 Wednesday. A very fine day, the frost but small. Stephen Bine's man John Stammer and Robert Gatland hew'd timber. John Gun ditcht against the Nine Acres. George West thrasht wheat. Ned May drew home wood etc. Picknall pickt chucks and helpt Willy put 3 runts into Tully's teary field. Markt 10 lambs of the Westcountry sheep on the right ear and burnt a cross on the right horne of 8 of the sheep, cut the right ear of the other 2 sheep, they haveing no horns. Put them into the upper wheat again. They have been there 4 or 5 days. Receiv'd £17 of John Smith jr in part for cows of William Balcomb's. One lamb of the Downish sheep and 1 of the other.

The 7th February 1716 Thursday. A very fine day, the frost continuing. John Edwards ditcht. Win'd 12 quarters head and three bushel tail of John Gun's barly by Wickham's. Ned May drew home wood and faggots etc. Picknall helpt winnow. Mr Healy and his wife, Mr Richard Whitpaine and his wife Mary and Mrs Scutt supt here. Stephen Bine's man John Stammer workt howing. Abraham Muzzall had a bushel of tail wheat at 4s.

The 8th February 1716 Fryday. A very fine day, the frost continuing. Deliver'd 15½ quarters barly to Harry Wickham to be malted for my self per George West and Ned May. Went through John Stone's ground and Westtowne. John Gun ditcht, so did John Edwards. My Cousin Nick Marchant here afternoon. My Cousin John Lindfield and his wife Elizabeth supt here. She was churcht to day after lying in of her daughter Mary.
*(Ed: Mary was baptised at Hurst on 15 January 1716 as daughter of John and Elizabeth).*

The 9th February 1716 Saturday. A wet morning, dry after. John Gun ditcht. Carry'd 6 quarters 4 bushels of pease into Edwards's chamber. Win'd 6 quarters 7 bushels head and 6 bushels tail of John Edwards's oates. Carry'd the head into the milkhouse chamber there and brought the tail home. Widdow Tully helpt. Paid John Parsons 10s-9d for making Willy's wig and some ____ . 4 bushels of the barly above, is not to be malted. I was at Old Hobbes's to look on some barly for seed but did not like it. Old William Brand and William Jarvice swept the stoves.

The 10th February 1716 Sunday. A gloomy day. Mr Jeremiah Dodson preacht. We had a meeting afternoon about Snatt. I supt and spent the evning at Mrs Catherine Beard's. Mr James Ede came the evning.

The 11th February 1716 Munday. A stormy day. John Towner and Ja Reed came to saw. Win'd 11 quarters head and 8 quarters tail of John Edwards's white oates. Ned May and Prat plough'd in the Churchfield, Picknall win'd. Jo Wood workt here. Abraham Muzzall workt here. Paid Mr Courtness 17s-9d in full of all accounts except _____ . Mr Ede had 2 bushels of oates.

The 12th February 1716 Tuesday. A gloomy day, some raine. John Towner and Ja Reed saw'd. George West, Prat, Ned May, Willy and Picknall plough'd. John Gun ditcht. John Edwards workt for himself. Jo Wood workt 'till noon. Abraham Muzzall workt. Mr Ede and I were at Pangdean to see seed barly. Agreed for 15 quarters at 13s-4d per quarter if I sent word in 2 or 3 days. We went to Wanbarrow after my Wife. Dick Wood mov'd my old horse's fore shoes. Paid Old King 3s-2d in full of all.

The 13th February 1716 Wednesday. A gloomy, stormy day. John Towner and Ja Reed saw'd. George West and Prat plough'd afternoon, thrasht etc in the morning.

John Gun ditcht. John Edwards workt for himself. Paid Roach 4s-4d in full of all accounts. Mrs Catherine Beard and her family, Mr Scutt and his wife and my Sister Bett supt and spent the evning here. Deliver'd 50 faggots to Old William Brand per Ned May and Picknall.

The 14th February 1716 Thursday. A gloomy morning, fine after. George West and Ned May begun plough the field below Tully's Mead. John Gun and Tully, Prat and Picknall win'd barly out of the chaff only. Paid John Towner and Ja Reed 16s in full of all accounts. Towner had 2 bushels of barly at 3s-4d. John Edwards etc win'd 10 bushels of his white oates, in all 29 quarters 7lbs a Wednesday. John Standbridge workt here about half the day, cut his leg.

The 15th February 1716 Fryday. A gloomy day. John Gun and John Edwards cut bushes in the Nine Acres. George West and Prat plough'd in the Churchfield. Ned May and Picknall carry'd in Beard's etc. Fisht the Hovelfield stew afternoon. Tom Picknall helpt. Put 28 carp about 11 inches and 10 tench into the new pond. Put 20 tench about 9 inches into the great pond. Put 15 tench into the middle pond. Put 15 tench into the upper pond. Put 4 large carp and 4 about 11 inches, 2 large tench and 4 less tench into the Hovelfield stew. Put 3 large carp, 3 less, 3 large tench, 4 less into the Marldfield stew. Put 2 large carp, 4 less, 1 large tench, 3 less into the flat stew. Receiv'd 10s of Mrs Catherine Beard for 26 carp about 10 inches and 8 tench about 8 or 9 inches long. Abraham Muzzall workt here.

The 16th February 1716 Saturday. Wet day. John Gun, Willy etc heav'd barly. George West and Prat made an end of the Churchfield before noon. Helpt winnow etc afterwards. Mr Richard Whitpaine rode my bay horse to Dean House with Ned May. Paid Young Prat 5s for 10 day's work. Picknall workt. Paid Mr Burry 56s and outset 15s for Widdow Tully's half year's rent due at Lady Day next being the 2nd, 12d books for the year. Sent Old William Brand 20s and took a note of his hand for 27s including 50 faggots deliver'd to him a Wednesday last at 7s. John Edwards kill'd his hog after John Gun and he had workt about 2 hours in the _____ . Abraham Muzzall workt here part of the day.

The 17th February 1716 Sunday. A wet forenoon. Mr Jeremiah Dodson preacht. 2 lambs of the Westcountry sheep, one of the other. I were not at Church.

No service afternoon. Receiv'd a horse coller from Stephen Carter of Brother Peter's man.

The 18th February 1716 Munday. A fine day. George West and Ned May plough'd at Tully's. Weigh'd John Edwards's hog, 22 nail 3lbs at 2s per nail. Grey and John Edwards begun a ditch in the Nine Acres at 2d per rod. John Standbridge cleft laths. Mr James Ede and I were at Cuckfield at Mr Steel's sale, spent 1s. Sent Willy to Mr Scrase's to tell him I would have 15 quarters of his Dungton barly at 13s-4d per quarter but Mr Scrase was not at home. Mrs Ann Dodson, Mrs Scutt and my Cousin Plump supt here on Mr John Hart's account.

The 19th February 1716 Tuesday. A very fine day. George West and Willy plough'd. John Gun and John Edwards plough'd, hedg'd. Picknall workt. John Standbridge cleft laths. I was at Wanbarrow in the afternoon. Abraham Muzzall workt here (I think) but part of the day.

The 20th February 1716 Wednesday. A dry day only a short shower afternoon. My Wife, Mr James Ede, my Cousin Bodle of Hailsham, Ned May and Young Prat set out for Lewis afternoon with Bett to Mrs Atkinson's. John Gun and John Edwards workt in the Nine Acres. George West and I carry'd up posts and rails to Mrs Storer's etc. I was at Mrs Catherine Beard's in the morning and she here towards night about Robert Cowdry's house. John Standbridge workt clearing laths and mended the Churchfield gate.

The 21st February 1716 Thursday. A very fine day 'till towards night, then wet. Receiv'd 7s-6d of Mr Peter Courthope for tench some days ago per my Wife. Ned May and Prat return'd last night from Lewis and went again to day. They carry'd the pillion to _____ Avery's to be mended. John Gun had a bushel and a half of malt at 2s-6d per bushel. John Gun and John Edwards workt in the Nine Acres. Widdow Tully had half a bushel of malt at 2s-6d per bushel. One lamb of the Downish sheep last night. John Standbridge cleft laths. Lent my Brother Peter my clover sieve per Thomas Bignall sr. Lent Old King an iron rake. Old Surgeant begun grub the west side of the Nine Acres to clear it for the plough at 4s per cord.

The 22nd February 1716 Fryday. A gloomy day. Surgeant and John Gun grub'd. George West and Ned May made an end of Tully's field about 2 aclock. Stephen Bine's man John Stammer and Robert Gatland workt in the Nine Acres. Put 6 young bullocks comeing 2 years old to keeping to my Lord Burt's at 4s per week per Willy and Picknall. Reckon'd with my Brother James Ede and he paid Jacky Ede's bond to Christmas last and we clear'd all other accounts. He went away afternoon. Paid my Lord Treep 17d in full of all accounts. Mr Scrase of Pangdean was here and we agreed for 15 quarters of his barly at 13s-6d per quarter and I am to see it win'd and to order it my self. Agreed with John Gun to live in part of my Tully's _____ at Michaelmas next at 40s per annum and I am to pay him _____d per bullock for all the bullocks he serves. John Edwards workt for himself.

The 23rd February 1716 Saturday. A fine day. John Gun and John Edwards hedg'd. Surgeant grub'd. John Stammer and Robert Gatland workt here. George West and Ned May drew bushes out of the Nine Acres. Turn'd 8 cows, the bull and 2 runts into the cowfield. Ned Burt and Young Picknall workt here. I was at Mrs Catherine Beard's in the evning. I sent a letter to Mrs Mary Gratwick per Edgly people.

The 24th February 1716 Sunday. A fine day. Mr Jeremiah Dodson preacht. My Cousin John Lindfield din'd with us. Mr John Hart and I supt at Mr Scutt's.

The 25th February 1716 Munday. A dry day. John Gun and John Edwards hedg'd. Surgeant grub'd. Surgeant had a bushel of barly at 14s per quarter and half a bushel of beans at 30d per bushel. John Stammer and Robert Gatland workt here, so did Picknall. Ed Burt workt here. Paid 8s to Thomas Friend at Lewis for 3 yards of callimanco at 2s-2d per yard and ¾ foot of silk at 2s per foot for Molly Balcomb, also 4d to Mr Court for a knife for her a Wednesday last. Receiv'd my clover sieve again from Brother Peter. Mr Richard Whitpaine din'd here. He came for the brief for the Episcopal Churches in Poland. Lent Mr Jeremiah Dodson 2 chains per Jo Wood. John Gun had half a bushel of oates and a gallon before.

The 26th February 1716 Tuesday. A dry, cold day. John Gun and John Edwards hedg'd. Ned May and George West plough'd Tully's little field. Ned Burt workt here. Jo Wood, John Stammer and Robert Gatland workt at Mrs Storer's orchard. King brought home my iron rake.

The 27th February 1716 Wednesday. A dry, cold day. John Gun and John Edwards hedg'd round Tully's orchard. John Gun grub'd, so did Surgeant. John Edwards had half a bushel of malt. My Cousin John Lindfield begun plough the Nine Acres. Ned Burt workt here. Ned May did severall jobbs. Mrs Catherine Beard gave my Wife two trees viz a box and_____ . Jo Wood, John Stammer and Robert Gatland workt at Mrs Storer's.

The 28th February 1716 Thursday. A dry, cold day. John Edwards and George West hedg'd and cut the bushes in Tully's field below the mead. My Cousin John Lindfield and Willy plough'd. Ned May did jobbs. Jo Wood, John Stammer and Robert Gatland workt at Mrs Storer's. John Gun and Surgeant grub'd in the Nine Acres. My Cousin Hayne, Thomas Whiteing's sister, Thomas Champion and his son din'd here. My Cousin Hayne promis'd me that my Aunt Holden's annuity of £12 per annum should be forborn towards the payment of the mortgage and intrest on her mill on William Balcomb's account. Receiv'd £16-1s-7½d in mony of Thomas Champion to outset a bill of 18s-4½d for glazeing and repairing the glass windows at Eastout in full for half a year's rent for Eastout due also at Michaelmas last, £15 outset nothing for taxes. We met John Box at the Swan and seal'd Thomas Champion's leases of Eastout. Paid 20s for William Balcomb's half part of the leases as by agreement and spent 2s-11d. Receiv'd 10s of Thomas Champion for his part of the lease not to be accounted for. Receiv'd 7s-6d of him for an old rowber winnower and _____ William Balcomb's at Eastout by which is to be accounted for. Paid 2d for carrying a note to John Box sr to come to Mr Thomas Champion.

The 1st March 1716 Fryday. A showry day. My Cousin John Lindfield plough'd. John Gun, Surgeant and George West grub'd. John Edwards did not work. Stephen Bine's 3 men workt 'till 9 aclock at Mrs Storer's, and afterwards John and Robert Gatland cut down and cleft a spire tree in one of Tully's little fields and left off soon after noon. John Standbridge cleft some laths. My Wife went to Westtowne afternoon, I went towards night for her, we did not stay the evning. My Cousin John Lindfield sent home my dung court, and a horse to help plough. 2 lambs of the Westcountry sheep. George West and John Gun clean'd the pidgeon house in the morning.

The 2nd March 1716 Saturday. A dry day. My Cousin John Lindfield and Willy plough'd. Surgeant, John Gun, George West, John Edwards, and Ned May grub'd. John Stammer, and Robert Gatland workt at Mrs Storer's and cut and cleft a tree in the Nine Acres. John Standbridge mended wattles and cleft one length of pales. Surgeant had a bushel of barly and half a bushel of beans. Tom Picknall pickt up chucks at Mrs Storer's.

The 3rd March 1716 Sunday. A showry forenoon, dry after. Mr Jeremiah Dodson preacht. Mr Scutt and his Wife supt here. A parish meeting at Church.

The 4th March 1716 Munday. A dry day. My Cousin John Lindfield and Ned May plough'd. John Gun, George West, John Edwards, and Surgeant grub'd. Win'd 3 quarters 6 bushels of John Gun's barly, Rookwood towards night. I were at Wanbarrow in the morning, din'd at Westtowne and were at Mr Scutt's in the evning. Thomas Godly of Balcombe was with me at Westtowne to take thrashing or other work. Agreed to dig hop garden at 1d per _____ .

The 5th March 1716 Shrove Tuesday. A showry day. Last night very wet. Win'd 12 quarters 7 bushels of John Gun's Rookwood barly. Ned May, and my Cousin John Lindfield's man R Butcher plough'd. Surgeant grub'd. John Standbridge mended some wattles. Paid George West 12s. John Edwards workt for himself. Mrs Scutt, and my Wife were to see my Sister Ann Box. Receiv'd a letter from Mr Virgoe of Cuckfield, and sent an answer per John Burt. Nunnery boy came last night and went home this morning.

The 6th March 1716 Wednesday. A fine day, last night wet. Ned May and R Butcher plough'd. George West carry'd roots etc. John Gun was sick. Surgeant and John Edwards grub'd. John Standbridge workt part of the day mending wattles etc. Jo Wood and Robert Gatland workt at Mrs Storer's. My Cousin John Lindfield was here towards night. Mr Richard Whitpaine call'd here goeing home from Edgly. A red 3 yearling steer broak of one horne in Tully's close. One lamb of the Downish sheep and one of the other.

The 7th March 1716 Thursday. A fine day. John Gun poll'd trees, John Edwards grub'd. Jo Wood, John Stammer, and Robert Gatland finisht the new fence at east side of Mrs Storer's orchard. John Standbridge hung up the house gate in the Bowling Ally. Deliver'd 15 quarters of barly to Harry Wickham per George West and Ned May brought home 16 quarters 3 bushels of my malt, of 15 quarters of barly. Left part of his sacks, and one of my own. Greenaway, and Ned Burt workt at Mrs Storer's orchard and Old Lag begun dig there at 2d per rod. My Wife bargain'd with Sarah Surgeant to come at Lady Day. Deliver'd 40 bushels of pease to my Cousin John Lindfield at 12s a Munday.

The 8th March 1716 Fryday. A fine day. John Gun, Banks, John Edwards, and George West grub'd. Surgeant grub'd part of the afternoon per the day. Greenaway and Ned Burt workt on Mrs Storer's garden. Old Lag dug there, by the end he dug 6 rods to day and yesterday. Ned May drew Surgeant's roots etc. John Standbridge begun set up the fence at the north side of Mrs Storer's orchard at 18d per rod. I was at Church to consult with Mr Richard Whitpaine about mending a bell, went from thence to the Swan. Staid late and drank too much. There was Mr Chantler of Chittingly and a butcher that came with him and Stephen Bine.

The 9th March 1716 Saturday. A fine day. Ned May and R Butcher plough'd. Nick Plaw's cow calv'd a bull calf, this morning. John Gun, Surgeant, Banks, John Edwards, and George West grub'd. Ned Burt and Greenaway workt in the garden. John Standbridge workt on the fence. Paid Greenaway 4s-6d in full for his work. Receiv'd a letter from my Brother James Ede. Sent an other to Mr Orlton.

The 10th March 1716 Sunday. A fine forenoon, wet towards night. Mr Jeremiah Dodson preacht. Nunnery boy was here.

The 11th March 1716 Munday. A very wet day, George West thrasht wheat. John Edwards did not work. John Gun, Old Lag, Willy, and Ned May win'd 11 quarters 6 bushels of John Gun's barly. John Box and I went to Albourne, sold Richard Wood some old iron at 32s-6d and a parcell of plough wings etc to Abel Muzzall at a guinea. We din'd at Nick Plaw's, call'd at John Channel's, was at the place, supt at Westtowne. Paid Nick Plaw £5-16-10½d for all the oates I had of William Balcomb's being 11 quarters 5½ bushels at 10d per quarter. Outset the £3-5s I lent on a note of his hand.

The 12th March 1716 Tuesday. A stormy day. George West thrasht wheat. John Gun, Ned May, and Willy win'd 7 bushels of John Gun's barly by Wickham's, the last of the field, in all 16 quarters 1½ bushels. Deliver'd 6 quarters to Harry Wickham per Willy and Ned May. John Gun, and John Edwards litter'd Tully's close afternoon and hedg'd a little while in the Nine Acres. Nicholas Heaver at St John's Comon was here and agreed for 4 bushels of seed pease at 3s per bushel. The long thin sided heifer calv'd a bull calf.

The 13th March 1716 Wednesday. A fine day. John Gun and John Edwards hedg'd. George West and Surgeant grub'd. Deliver'd 7½ quarters of barly to Harry Wickham per Ned May and Tippins. Willy, and I went to Nunnery afternoon.

The 14th March 1716 Thursday. A fine day. George West thrasht wheat. John Gun and John Edwards hedg'd. Ned May, did severall jobbs. My Brother James Ede and I went to Darkin. Din'd at Dr John Budgen's, supt at Mr Edward Budgen's.
*(Ed: Dr Budgen married Mary Ede 25 Feb 1718 – she was sister to "Brother" James Ede who was married to Thomas's sister-in-law Mary Stone)*

The 15th March 1716 Fryday. A wet day. George West thrasht wheat, Ned May did jobbs. John Gun and John Edwards did not work. Willy, and I return'd from Nunnery. The long tetted cow, calv'd a cow calf.

The 16th March 1716 Saturday. A showry day. John Gun and George West thrasht wheat. John Edwards ditch in Tully's Mead. Receiv'd 12s of Nick Heaver for 4 bushels of pease. Clear'd all accounts with the Widdow Tully. Mr Richard Whitpaine supt and spent the evning here. Receiv'd a letter from Mr Orlton, and one from Bridgen _____.

The 17th March 1716 Sunday. A gloomy day. Mr Jeremiah Dodson preacht. Nick Marchant din'd here and after dinner set out for Nunnery on the ball mare and from thence he is to go to London with a letter to Mr Ralph Beard. Paid him 5s towards his expences and journey. I was at Wanbarrow in the afternoon, wrote to Mr Pike of Stenning and Mr Hill at Woodhatch, in my Brother Peter's name.

The 18th March 1716 Munday. A dry day. Win'd 39 quarters 5 bushels head and 2 bushels tail of George West's Churchfield wheat. Carry'd 3 quarters into Tully's garret. George West did jobbs. Dick Tully begun serve the calves yesterday morning. John Gun helpt winnow 'till 10 aclock, faggotted afterwards. Ned May carry'd 2 dung court loads of shingles to the Churchyard for Stephen Bine. John Edwards poll'd trees. I was at John Snashall's in the morning. Willy fetch all my sacks from Harry Wickham's, but 2. Sent an answer to Mr Brigden's letter, per the post afternoon.

The 19th March 1716 Tuesday. A very wet day, afternoon. John Gun fagotted, John Edwards poll'd trees. John Gun, Ned May, and I cut a young spire tree in Tully's orchard and cleft him to railes, and other jobbs. Ned May ground 5 bushels of malt. Mrs Mary Whitpaine was here in the afternoon.

The 20th March 1716 Wednesday. A wet morning, dry afternoon. Banks begun thrash wheat. George West and Ned May did severall jobbs. John Gun faggotted. John Edwards poll'd trees. Jo Wood workt in the granery. Thomas Allence lath'd the afternoon there. My Cousin Nick Marchant return'd from London. Brought a letter from Mr Ralph Beard, and some roll tobacco. Willy was to see Thomas Mathew's calves at Albourne. He promis'd to keep them a fortnight 'till saw them *(sic)*. Ned May had 8 bushels of oates a Munday last. Paid Nick Marchant 3s-6d more for his journey and expences.

The 21st March 1716 Thursday. A dry morning, very wet afternoon. Willy, George West, and Ned May begun plough and sow the Homefield. John Gun fagotted, John Edwards poll'd trees, Banks thrasht. I went to Lewes to Dr White for his assistance in getting an excuse from goeing to London. We were with Mr Lilly. Staid late at Dr White's. Mr Scutt came home with me. One of the Downish sheep had 2 lambs.

The 22nd March 1716 Fryday. A fine morning. Paid Goode Shave 1s for making linnen for Molly Balcomb. Paid Thomas Surgeant 5s towards his grubbing. Paid Thomas Picknall 10s towards his boy's work. George West, Willy, and Ned May plough'd and sow'd. John Gun, and John Edwards hedg'd. Banks thrasht wheat. Picknall's two boys set pease this afternoon. Mr Jeremiah Dodson supt here. My Brother James Ede came this evning. My Brother Peter was here in the afternoon, I wrote an other letter for him to Thomas Pyke. I saw Thomas Mathew of Albourne, he promis'd to keep his calves 'till Munday senight for me to see them.

The 23rd March 1716 Saturday. A gloomy day, some rain. My birthday, 40 years. Ned May, and R Butcher plough'd. The 2 Picknalls set peas. John Gun, George West, and John Edwards grubb'd. Banks thrasht wheat. My Brother James Ede went home afternoon.
Paid Thomas Surgeant 17s in full for all his grubbing, four cord _____ . Receiv'd 5s of him for a bushel of wheat he is to have on demand. I was at Pangdean to know the price of Mr Scrase's horse. My Wife and I sign'd the petition to the House of Commons for the sale of Nunnery etc. Jane Brooks went away this afternoon. I supt at Mrs Catherine Beard's.

The 24th March 1716 Sunday. A dry day. No service in the forenoon. Mr Price preacht afternoon.

## 1717

The 25th March 1717 Munday. Lady day. A wet day. Ditchling Fair. Paid Mrs Courthope 10d for a payr of gloves she bought at Lewis for Molly Balcomb, some time ago. Paid George Wickham 2s for carrying Molly Balcomb's trunck to Lewis a Saturday last. Paid Jack Gun 5s. Paid Mr Ivgoe of Cuckfield £19-8-9d being all the mony due to Ed Steel of Cuckfield on my Father Stone's account. Mr John Hart went away and clear'd all accounts for board and school to this day. George West and Ned May kept holy day. My Wife and I supt at Mrs Catherine Beard's. Susan Nall went away. Elizabeth Towner came in her roome.

The 26th March 1717 Tuesday. A fine morning, afterwards showry. John Gun, George West, and John Edwards grubb'd. Banks thrasht wheat. Ned May, and Willy brought almost a cord of John Gun's wood and 150 faggots out of the Churchfield. I was at Lewis at Dr White's about the Act of Parliament. Sent John Smith (late Mrs Catherine Beard's man) with a letter to my Father Stone, and orders to go to London if he pleas'd to send him. Paid Stephen Avery the sadler 4s for mending my pillion. Paid Mr Wheatly 9d for 3 ounces of syrup of backthorn for Mrs Susan Courthope. Banks had bushel of wheat at 5s. Receiv'd 3s of Goodman Clifford for a bushel of pease.

The 27th March 1717 Wednesday. A very fine day, only a showr in the morning. Ned May carry'd Mrs Scutt to Hand Cross on the ball'd mare. Receiv'd 3s- 6d of Mrs Catherine Beard for a back band and _____ . John Gun, John Edwards, and George West grubb'd in the Nine Acres. Banks thrasht. Thomas Surgeant had the bushel of wheat, paid for some time ago. Abraham Muzzall had half a bushel of wheat at 2s-8d. Mrs Catherine Beard, etc spent the afternoon here. Mr John Hart din'd here. Jo Wood did a jobb, about an hour on my bed. John Edwards is to give 40s per annum for his part of the house, for this ensueing year, and to be paid for what bullock he serves, at the usual rates. Old William Brand's wife had 6lb of crock butter at 6d per lb.

The 28th March 1717 Thursday. A very wet day. Banks thrasht wheat. The young sow farrow'd 7 piggs last night. George West pugg'd clover all day. John Gun and John Edwards half the day. Ned May, did severall jobbs. Dick Wood mov'd all the ball mare's shooes and 2 on the Duke horse.

The 29th March 1717 Fryday. A very fine day. John Gun and John Edwards hedg'd. George West, and Banks hedg'd against the old orchard. Ned May swept the Fifteen Acres in the forenoon, and in the afternoon he and John Standbridge cut a spire tree in Tully's further field, cleft it, and brought it home. Mr Roots and Mrs Beard of Rottingdean, and Mr _____ of Brighton were here to buy my bay horse. Mr Roots bid me £10 for him. Molly Balcomb went to Mr Russell's at Lewis to board at 13d per week. Paid her 5s for pocket mony. Nick Marchant carry'd her.

The 30th March 1717 Saturday. A wet forenoon, dry after. John Gun, and John Edwards hedg'd etc. Ned May did jobbs. Banks thrasht 'till near 2 aclock, George West and he hedg'd afterwards. George West pug'd clover in the forenoon. I was at Mr Jeremiah Dodson's in the morning. Paid him 20s being what he paid to Mr William's steward of Tarring Mannor for searching the Court rolls and the coppys of 3 Admittances.
Receiv'd 2 letters from my Brother James Ede, one by the post, the other by Jack Smith. I was at my Lord Burt's to see my young beasts, agreed with him to keep 4 more at 8d per week per bullock. Supt at Westtowne as I came home.

The 31st March 1717 Sunday. A very fine day. Mr Jeremiah Dodson preacht. My Cousin John Lindfield and Nick Plaw din'd here. Ned Penfold went to Lewis with a letter to Dr White. I supt at Mr Scutt's. Last night there were unusual lights in the air after the same manner as on the night after the 7th of March last was a year ago, but not so great as then. One of the young tags had a black lamb.

The first April 1717 Munday. A very fine day. George West and Banks hedg'd. John Gun went to Mr Scrase's to winnow barly for me. Willy and Young King drove 4 runts to my Lord Burt's. Ned May, and Young King fetcht 4½ quarters of barly from Mr Scrase's in the afternoon. I was at Thomas Mathew's of Albourne in the morning to buy 3 calves, I bid him £4. He askt £4-5s. In the afternoon I grafted some trees in the Hovelfield Orchard, and in the nursery. John Standbridge put up a post and rail by the little house. Reckon'd with John Edwards and clear'd all accounts to this day except bullock serving from Lady Day, and I lent him 10s-6d. Paid Dick Lashmer 6d and clear'd all accounts. I wrote to my Brother James Ede by the post. My Wife went to Danny to dinner with Mrs Ann Dodson. Paid Mrs Mary Whitpaine 18d a Saturday last for a bottle of brandy.

The 2nd April 1717 Tuesday. A dry day. Banks and George West hedg'd. Ned May and Samuel Jarvice fetcht 7½ quarters of barly from Pangdean. John Gun made an end of winnowing Mr Scrase's barly. John Edwards workt in the dry pond, poll'd trees after. I was at Mr Burrell's afternoon, gave him 10s. The Cuckfield Fair cow, calv'd a cow calf. Paid John Smith 6d for his journey to Nunnery and Darkin. Left my watch with John Gatland of Cuckfield to be clean'd.

The 3rd April 1717 Wednesday. A dry day, but wet towards night. King workt. John Gun and John Edwards hedg'd after 2 hours work in the morning. George West and Banks hedg'd. John Standbridge workt from 11 aclock. Nick Plaw cut my lambs, and drew away the clean from the cow, and cut the Albourne cow's calf. Ned May and my Cousin John Lindfield's man made an end of ploughing the Nine Acres _____ _____ had home my Cousin John Lindfield's horse.

The 4th April 1717 Thursday. A very wet day. John Gun and John Edwards ditcht in the forenoon. George West and Banks ditcht in the forenoon, and in the afternoon. Win'd 21 bushels of Banks's Churchfield wheat, John Edwards helpt. Ned May and Young King fetcht 3 quarters of barly from Pangdean, in all 15 quarters at 13-6d per quarter. John Gun did not work afternoon. Paid Mr Jeremiah Dodson £5-5s for half a year's tythe due at Lady Day last. Last one of the Westcountry lambs cut yesterday. Mr Dodson wrote to Mr Stacey, Citty comptroller at Guildhall, King Street, for me. Receiv'd a letter from Mr Ede, sent 2 to him. Paid Dick £1-5-6d in full of all accounts, Dick Wood paid Frank Holden 1s for a deel box.

The 5th April 1717 Fryday. A showry day. John Standbridge workt here. John Gun and John Edwards hedg'd, so did Banks and George West. Deliver'd 20 bushels of wheat to Nick Plaw at £5 per Ned May. I grafted 2 pare trees in Tully's orchard, one a chissel pare, the other a large pare from Steels at Westtowne. I also grafted severall apples in the Hovelfield Orchard.

The 6th April 1717 Saturday. A showry day, after a very wet night. George West and Banks hedg'd, so did John Gun and John Edwards. Ned May did severall jobbs. John Edwards had half a bushel of malt, 15d. Kill'd the Cuckfield cow's calf, it would not suck. Receiv'd a letter from Mr Ede, sent an answer. I was at Mr Jeremiah Dodson's towards night, supt there and spent the evning. Paid Mr Dodson 6s-8d for an other fee to Mr Williams. The Albourne went to bull to day.

The 7th April 1717 Sunday. A dry day. Mr Jeremiah Dodson preacht. I was not at Church. My Cousin John Lindfield and Nick Plaw here towards night, the first supt here. Nunnery boy was here with a letter, I sent an answer.

The 8th April 1717 Munday. A very wet day. Banks thrasht wheat. George West pugg'd clover. John Gun, nor John Edwards did not work. Ned May pugg'd clover before noon, went to meet Ed Penfold after. Paid Dick Tully 7s-9d for work. Mr John Hart, Mr Scutt, and Stephen Bine supt here. Sold Stephen Bine 4 bushels of wheat at 20s to be deliver'd at his request. John Standbridge had half a bushel of wheat at 2s-6d, and half a bushel of barly at 1s.

The 9th April 1717 Tuesday. A very wet day. John Gun and John Edwards ditcht a while. George West and Willy pugg'd clover, Ned May did jobbs. Reckon'd with Thomas Westover. His bill was 17s-3d paid him 2s-4d for a payr of shooes for Jacky Ede, he left 6s in my hands for 2 bushels of malt. My Cousin Hayne of Henfield din'd here. Mr Richard Whitpaine was here in the afternoon.

The 10th April 1717 Wednesday. A showry day. George West and Ned May plough'd, sow'd peas 'till noon. Ned May went to Nunnery afternoon with Old Bean's mare and the Duke horse. George West pugg'd clover afternoon. John Gun, and John Edwards hedg'd and ditcht. Banks thrasht wheat. Paid Frank Holden 10d for 3 douzen of buttons. Abraham Muzzall workt here. Ned Penfold return'd from Nunnery at noon.

The 11th April 1717 Thursday. A fine day. George West and Willy plough'd and sow'd. John Gun harrow'd part of the day. John Edwards workt for himself. Ned May return'd from Nunnery with 4 box trees from Nunnery. Banks thrasht wheat. I receiv'd a letter by the post from Mr Ede.

The 12th April 1717 Fryday. A fine day. George West and Willy plough'd. John Gun harrow'd. John Gun and John Edwards hedg'd in the morning, Banks thrasht wheat. I went to Cuckfield to Mr Burrell's, from thence to Warninglid and met Mr Ede. We din'd there. We went from thence to Nunnery. Paid Mr Burrell 10s for his advice on the bill for the sale of Nunnery etc. Spent 10¾d at Warninglid. Ned May went to Nunnery in the morning and return'd at night. John Edwards had a bushel of wheat per Willy at 5s per bushel.

The 13th April 1717 Saturday. A fine day. John Gun and Willy plough'd. Ned May harrow'd. John Gun workt part of the day in the garden, John Edwards faggoted. My Cousin Peter Marchant came yesterday morning. I return'd from Nunnery towards night. John Gun had half a bushel of malt yesterday. Mrs Catherine Beard and her family were here in the afternoon, and my Sister Ann Box. Goodman Marten of Cuckfield was here yesterday and clipt the ewes.

The 14th April 1717 Sunday. A very fine day. Mr Jeremiah Dodson preacht. I was not at Church. My Cousin Peter Marchant din'd here, went to Cowfold and left his mare here. Mr Richard Whitpaine, Mr John Hart, and Thomas Norton of Edgly here afternoon.

Paid Mr Dodson 10s for Mr Stracey of London. Nick Marchant came again at night.

The 15th April 1717 Munday. A very fine day, Ned May, and George West sow'd Tully's little field next the orchard with flax, and in the afternoon begun harrow the Nine Acres. My Cousin Nick Marchant went for London. Paid him 10s. Benjamin Shave went with him about 10 miles. Receiv'd £4 of Richard Goddard of Henfield for the cow I bought at William Balcomb's sale. Mr Wade of Henfield was here a very little while about noon. Banks thrasht wheat. Mr Scutt and Mr *(Ed: xxx text deleted xxx)* one of Mr Lindfield's clerks were here to execute a fine, for my Wife and I, but I did not like the uses to which the deeds directed, therefore refus'd to sign it. They din'd here. John Gun, begun shovel the Towne. John Edwards faggoted. Turn'd 5 calves, into yearlings, into Tully's teary field. Jack Terry came last night, William Terry's son of Balcombe. Betty Towner (being seiz'd with convulsion fitts) came home (I think) a Fryday last.

The 16th April 1717 Tuesday. A very fine day. George West, and Ned May harrow'd in the Nine Acres. John Edwards faggoted. John Gun made an end of shoveling the Towne, and poll'd trees afternoon. My Cousin Peter Marchant return'd from Cowfold, din'd here and went home, Harry *(Ed: Peter and Sarah's 9 year old son)* with him. My Cousin Wood of Broad Street brought her daughter for a tryall *(Ed: Cousin Elizabeth née Marchant, born 1673 in Ditchling, was the wife of William Wood and Thomas's 2nd cousin).* Banks thrasht wheat. Richard Goddard fetcht his cow, Tom Picknall went with him. Old Picknall had a sack of pidgeons dung for John Hart the tanner. Paid John Westover 3s for 2 sheets of stampt paper, left _____ .Willy went to Lewis afternoon for a pipe to an iron which cost 10d, but it was too small.

The 17th April 1717 Wednesday. A very fine day. George West, and Jack Terry plough'd. Banks, John Edwards and Willy win'd 4 quarters 2 bushels head and 4 bushels tail of Banks's Churchfield wheat. John Gun mended gaps from 8 aclock. Ned May, harrow'd in the Nine Acres. William Jarvice set out for Nunnery at noon. Mr Jeremiah Dodson supt and spent the evning here.

The 18th April 1717 Thursday. A gloomy day, some raine. My Cousin John Lindfield's flax sow'd. George West and Jack Terry made an end of ploughing the Homefield. Banks and John Edwards begun thrash clover. Ned May, harrow'd in the Nine Acres. John Gun workt in the garden a little while towards night. William Jarvice brought home a horse from Nunnery. Benjamin Shave brought a leather pipe from Thomas Robert's. He was at John Gold's for the blind mare, but he would not lend her. Stephen Bine's man Joseph Wood made a gate, here. Mrs Ann Dodson spent the afternoon here.

The 19th April 1717 Good Fryday. A fine day. George West, Ned May, and Jack Terry finisht the Homefield howeing, sow'd 25 bushels of peas in him. John Gun workt in the garden before noon, fetcht Bett home from Lewis afternoon. Banks and John Edwards thrasht clover. Paid Thomas Roberds 2s-6d for a pipe for horse harness. Nick Plaw was here in the evening. Ned May had 8 bushels of oates at night.

The 20th April 1717 Saturday. A showry day. George West, Ned May, and Jack Terry begun the Bankfield about noon. John Gun workt the afternoon in the garden. Bob Burt workt part of the day. John Edwards and Banks thrasht clover, Willy helpt. Dick Wood dockt the 3 calves. Paid John Standbridge 15s. Nick Marchant came home about noon. Paid 3d for a letter from Mrs Margret Fagg, on William Balcomb's account. Deliver'd a sack of wheat to Nick Plaw's boy.

The 21st April 1717 Easter Sunday. A dry day. Mr Jeremiah Dodson preacht. My Cousin at I was at Mr Scutt's before evning prayr and at Westtowne afterwards with Mr John Hart and Mr Scutt.

The 22nd April 1717 Munday. A dry day. Reckon'd and clear'd all accounts with John Gun to this day, and his rent to Lady Day. Paid him £2-12-2d. John Edwards, George West, Ned May, Jack Terry, and Willy plough'd and sow'd in the Bankfield. My Cousin John Lindfield din'd here, and afterwards came Mr John Hart, Mr Richard Whitpaine, and Mr Scutt, and John Oliver. We settled the parish accounts as usual, at Church.

The 23rd April 1717 Tuesday. A gloomy day. A Fair at Henfield, at Nutley a great fair for barrens. A Fair also at Jolsfield. George West, John Edwards, Ned May, Jack Terry, and Willy plough'd and sow'd in the Bankfield. Banks pugg'd clover. John Gun did not work. Nick Marchant brought me ℔ rol'd tobacco from London a

Saturday last. Mr Beard bought it. Paid William Nicholas 2-6d for his clerk's wages for Little Park and West Edgly.

The 24th April 1717 Wednesday. A dry windy day. John Edwards, Ned May, George West, Willy and Jack Terry plough'd and sow'd in the Bankfield. Banks pugg'd clover, had half a bushel of wheat at 3 _____ . John Gun workt in the hop garden. Mrs Stonestreet of Lewis and one Mrs Anne Gratwick din'd here, they came from Old Land hither. Mrs Catherine Beard and her family supt here.

The 25th April 1717 Thursday. A fine day. John Edwards, Ned May, George West, Willy, and Jack Terry finisht the Bankfield, sow'd 31 bushels. John Gun poled the hop garden. Banks pugg'd clover. Receiv'd 7s-6d of my Cousin John Marchant of Lox for a bushel and a half of wheat, he din'd here. The pooking cow calv'd a bull calf. Paid Nan West 1s for weeding, this day and one before. Thursday last I measur'd the Nine Acres, at six times, the contents whereof are as follows.

|  | Acres | Roods | Rods |
|---|---|---|---|
| My Cousin John Lindfield | 4 | 3 | 26.24000 |
| William Michell | 2 | 0 | 02.54400 |
| John Haslegrove | 1 | 2 | 01.12240 |
|  | 0 | 0 | 20.83200 |
|  | 0 | 1 | 00.06080 |
|  | 3 | 0 | 20.87200 |
|  | 8 | 3 | 29 |

The 26th April 1717 Fryday. A fine day. George West, Ned May, and Jack Terry harrow'd and rol'd on the Churchfield fallow, John Edwards helpt 'till ten aclock, afterwards faggotted. John Gun workt in the hop garden, and faggotted. Banks pugg'd clover. Fetcht home the 4 runts per Willy and William Smith. Paid Thomas Roberds 1s for a payr of hamwoods and 4s-6d for a hat for Jacky. I was at Westtowne in the evning.

The 27th April 1717 Saturday. A fine day. George West, Ned May, and Jack Terry harrow'd and roll'd in the Churchfield. Willy fetcht the bay horse's coller from Brighton, and a hat for himself. John Gun shovel'd the Towne before noon, and workt in the garden after. John Edwards faggotted. Banks pugg'd clover. I was at the Swan with Mr Richard Whitpaine and his wife Mary and a kinsman and woman of his. Receiv'd a letter from Mr Ede by the post.

The 28th April 1717 Sunday. A stormy day. Mr Jeremiah Dodson preacht. My Cousin John Lindfield and his wife Elizabeth, Mrs Stapely, Biggs's, and John Bodle's Elizabeth wife supt here.

The 29th April 1717 Munday. A fine day. George West, Ned May, Willy, Jack Terry, John Edwards plough'd and sow'd in the Churchfield. Borrow'd a payr of oxen of Mr Richard Whitpaine. John Smith kill'd one of my Westcountry Ewes, weigh'd 9lb per quarter, for which I am to have 3½d per -------. Sold Harry Wickham of Albourne, the cow I had of Nick Plaw, at £5. Receiv'd 1s in hand. The long tetted cow was bulling to day. John Gun faggott'd.

The 30th April 1717 Tuesday. A dry day. George West, Ned May, John Edwards, Jack Terry, and Willy plough'd, and sow'd in the Churchfield. Banks pugg'd clover, John Gun faggotted. I was at Mrs Catherine Beard's in the evning. Ball lent me his horse to harrow. Paid 2s-2d to Jane Burtenshaw for schooling and altring some caps for Molly Balcomb.

The 1st May 1717 Wednesday. A gloomy day. A Fair at Lindfield. George West, Ned May, Willy, John Edwards, and Jack Terry plough'd and sow'd in the Churchfield. Banks helpt and mended some gaps. Nick Plaw had 2 bushels of wheat per his son. Abraham Muzzall had half a bushel of wheat, 2s-6d. Paid George West 10s. John Gun did not work. Receiv'd 5s of Mr John Hart for an Old Cupboard of William Balcomb.

The 2nd May 1717 Thursday. A gloomy day, with a showr or two. Mr Jeremiah Dodson's tythe feast. George West, Ned May, John Edwards, Jack Terry, and Willy plough'd and sow'd. Banks pugg'd clover 'till noon, helpt harrow etc after. John Gun did not work, being sick. My Cousin John Lindfield was here towards night. Receiv'd a letter from my Brother James Ede. Paid John Parsons 18d for shaveing my head to day and Willy's twice before. Turn'd the 2 cows to pasture in the Fifteen Acres.

The 3rd May 1717 Fryday. A wet day after 10 aclock 'till 4. Deliver'd 14 bushels of wheat to Nick Plaw per Ned May, which makes an even load, at £10. Deliver'd four bushels to Stephen Bine at 20s per George West. Paid my Sister Sarah a years intrest per Willy. Paid my Lord Burt two guineas per Willy towards the keeping of my cattle, and he fetcht home the six two yearlings to day. John Haslegrove came to board here to day at 5s per month, from the Widdow Bide's. Sent home my Father Stone's horse per William Jarvice, he carry'd 6lb of candles, half a bushel of salt, and half a bushel of barly and a payr of loafes. George West, John Edwards, Ned May, and Jack Terry plough'd and sow'd a little while in the Churchfield, afterwards John Edwards helpt Banks pugg clover and Jack Terry ground malt. Paid William Gorman and Thomas King 6d for fetching the blind mare from John Gold's. Mr Jeremiah Dodson spent the afternoon here, Mr John Hart too.

The 4th May 1717 Saturday. A gloomy morning, fine after, last night wet. George West, Ned May, and John Edwards finisht the Churchfield haveing sow'd about 58 bushels of barly. William Michell sow'd clover on it, about 2¾ bushels. I was at Mr Jeremiah Dodson's in the morning, afterwards at Lox. My Cousin Marchant was here afternoon. Richard Lashmer of Daps buried this afternoon. *(Ed: Recorded in the Hurst Parish Register as "Goodman Richard Lashmer")* Jack Terry went home to his father's. Receiv'd half a Cheshire cheese of Mr Scutt weigh'd 27 lb.

The 5th May 1717 Sunday. A dry day. Mr Jeremiah Dodson preacht in the forenoon. No service afternoon. My Mother din'd here. My Wife and I receiv'd the sacrament. I was at Mrs Catherine Beard's in the evning to see a cow.

The 6th May 1717 Munday. A fine day. George West, Willy, and Ned May sow'd the field below Tully's Mead with 18 bushels of oates. Banks and John Edwards thrasht clover. Cowdry's old house was pull'd down, I was there, supt at Mrs Catherine Beard's. Sold Goodman Flint the 3 yearling heifer that I bought at William Balcomb's sale, at £4. I am to keep her 'till she has calv'd, and run all hazards. Le nt the long legg'd heifer to John Gillham 'till Michaelmas next for which he is to give me 10s, he to fetch her a Wednesday sennight.

The 7th May 1717 Tuesday. A gloomy day, some rain towards night. William Michell sow'd Tully's field with almost a bushel of clover. Paid William Michell 2s for sowing this field and the Churchfield. Ned May harrow'd with the ox harrow in the field below, so did George West afternoon. Willy harrow'd etc. John Gun and John Edwards faggoted, Banks pugg'd clover. Banks had a bushel of malt at 3s. Paid Nick Marchant 1s for carrying Molly Balcomb to Mrs Russells. Paid Mr Courtness 6s for a hat for Willy.

The 8th May 1717 Wednesday. A gloomy morning, fine after. Banks pugg'd clover. Mrs Catherine Beard's Family, Dr Woodward and his wife, and Mr Smith of Ashurst breakfasted here. George West, Ned May, and Willy plough'd and sow'd oates in the second field below Tully's Mead. John Gun and John Edwards faggoted. Thomas Champion sr here. The Albourne heifer, sold to Flint calv'd a bull calf last night. Receiv'd £4-19s of Harry Wickham for Plaw's cow. Mr Jeremiah Dodson and my Cousin John Marchant of Lox were here in the afternoon. I went home with Mr Dodson, from thence to Mrs Catherine Beard's and put the frameing of Cowdry's old house to Thomas Hamper at 3s per sqare, out of the old timber and 3s per sqare for laying the floors, and to fell, hew, and saw what new timber is wanting into the bargain, and to cleave, hew, and put up the stantions or studs for the raddle walls, Mrs Catherine Beard is to pay for sawing the boards and he is to be paid for making the doors, and putting up the partitions by the day.

The 9th May 1717 Thursday. A fine day. George West, Ned May, and Willy plough'd and sow'd. John Gun, and John Edwards faggoted. Banks pugg'd clover. My Wife and I were at Westtowne afternoon, and there receiv'd £4 of Goodman Flint for his cow. I were at Mrs Catherine Beard's in the evning and set out some timber for the building. Receiv'd a letter from Mr Ede telling me he had paid £50 to Mrs Margret Fagg, which he receiv'd of Robert Skinner. Receiv'd a guinea of John Westover which I lent him some time ago.

The 10th May 1717 Fryday. A fine day. Ned May, George West, and Willy, plough'd and sow'd. John Gun and John Edwards faggoted. Banks did not work. John Snashall had a sack of oates, per R Butcher. Sold John Smith sr 30 lambs at £16, 20 to be gone 2 weeks before mid Summer, the rest at mid Summer. Receiv'd in hand a guinea. Paid Thomas Baker 2s-10d in full of all accounts. Paid Thomas Roberds 1s for mending a coller, and 6d for 2 throat hasps. Mrs Mary Whitpaine supt here. Stephen Bine here in the morning. Dick Wood mov'd the horse's fore shoes.

The 11th May 1717 Saturday. A very fine, hot, day. George West, Ned May, and Willy finisht Tully's lower oat field. Sow'd 27½ bushels. John Gun clean'd the headland furrow of the other field and helpt harrow between whiles. John Edwards faggoted. Banks thrasht wheat. Banks had half a bushel of wheat per Ned May. Paid Nick Marchant 10s to bear his charges to London, he set out afternoon. I was at Henfield afternoon. Mr Phillip Cheal was not at home, John Box sr was at Henfield, also we agreed with the Widdow Balcomb, we to let the rents of her Albourne land, 'till it came to £20 clear, to lessen Norman's mortgage.

The 12th May 1717 Sunday. A fine day. Mr William Martin preacht. Goodman White was here in the morning. We reckon'd and clear'd all accounts. I supt at Mrs Catherine Beards. We had a parish meeting.

The 13th May 1717 Munday. A fine day. Ned May, and Willy finisht Tully's field. George West, and Banks mended hedges afternoon. Ned May drew Mrs Catherine Beard's trees afternoon. I was at Mr Jeremiah Dodson's with Mr Tattersall, Mr Dunstall, and Mr Richard Whitpaine, Mr Tattersall bought Mr Richard Whitpaine's hops that grow at Cuckfield this year at £80 and the buyer to pick, dry, and pay the duty etc as the bargain is exprest in a note left in Mr Jeremiah Dodson's hands to which Mr Jeremiah Dodson and I are witnesses. Mr Tattersall paid a guinea, in part.

The 14th May 1717 Tuesday. A dry forenoon, wet after. A new Fair at Howard Heath, at the Muster Oak. George West, Ned May, and Willy fetch 63 wattles from Mr Richard Whitpaine's, set up the carriage, etc afternoon. Mrs Kettilby gave me a pruining knife yesterday. Paid John Bodle 18s for a cow calf which he bought of Harry Emore at Albourne. Paid John Edwards 5s, his bullock serving since Lady day, comes to 4s-8½d he had also a bushel of wheat at 5s, and half a bushel of malt at 10d. Dick Wood set 4 new shoos on the sorrel horse yesterday. I begun ride him again to day.

The 15th May 1717 Wednesday. A dry day, George West pitcht the wattles cross the Nonsuch, set off just 3 acres, Ned May and Willy fetch wattles together about the ground, in the forenoon. Banks thrasht forenoon. George West, John Edwards, and John Gun, washt the sheep afternoon. Ned May and Banks harrow'd and rol'd Tully's field afternoon. Willy went to Cuckfield for Mr Virgoe, he came in the evning. Nick Marchant came home at noon. They are to go to London together to morrow. The singing master was here in the evning.

The 16th May 1717 Thursday. A very wet forenoon, showry after. George West, and Ned May went to the Rock with a load plank for Stephen Bine. Willy went to bring back the oxen. Nick Marchant set out for his 4th journy to London. He rode Nick Plaw's mare. Paid him 10s. John Gun, and John Edwards faggoted. Banks thrasht wheat.

The 17th May 1717 Fryday. A wet day. John Gun made shackles etc. Banks, George West, and Ned May mov'd their beds into the wheat and fetcht faggots out of the Fifteen Acres. Turn'd the fatting oxen to pasture in the field by Hyder's. Stephen Bine's man Edward workt above half the day, putting up a window shutter etc in the wheat barne. I know not what John Edwards did. Receiv'd ¼lb of bohea per Nick Marchant a Wednesday. John Norton of Stuckles mov'd to Wellingham near Lewis, yesterday.

The 18th May 1717 Saturday. A showry day. John Gun, and John Edwards faggoted. Banks did not work. Willy and Jack Haslegrove went to Horsham, and Nunnery. Ned May, and I went to the Rock with a load of planks for Stephen Bine, George West went to the top of the hill. Mr John Hart and Mr Scutt were here in the evning.

The 19th May 1717 Sunday. A gloomy day. Mr William Martin preacht. I was at Mr Scutt's before evning prayr, he set out for London, I was there also after evning prayr. The 2 yearling heifer from Albourne Place calv'd a bull calf. Receiv'd a ¼lb of bohea of Mr Richard Whitpaine.

The 20th May 1717 Munday. A fine day only a little showr afternoon. A Fair at Mayfield. Paid Marten 2s for sheering 42 sheep to day and 1s for clipping them some time ago. Ned May and Bignall fetch 2 loads of hop poles from Thomas Norton's coppices for my Unkle

Courtness with my Brother Peter's horse and mine. George West helpt Marten sheer sheep. Win'd 2 quarters 6½ head and 1½ bushel tail of Banks's Churchfield wheat. John Edwards helpt about half the day, faggoted the rest of the day. John Gun workt about the garden etc. Widdow Tully had half a bushel of malt at 10d, Banks half a bushel of wheat at 2s-6d. Paid Frank Holden 5s-10d for severall goods at the shop and 4s-4d for 4 ells of canvas I am to have. Paid John Gatland of Cuckfield 1s for cleaning the clock.

The 21st May 1717 Tuesday. A fine day. Banks did jobbs. John Gun cutt hedges etc. John Edwards begun clean Tully's close. Deliver'd 2 loads of wheat straw to Richard White at 12s per load per Ned May and Willy. White helpt load the last load. Sold 6 young rams, 8 barren sheep and one ewe tag to John Smith jr at 13s a piece all to be gone by Midsumer. George West weeded his flax. Deliver'd 12 faggots to John Gun per Ned May. Nick Plaw sent home the bay horse which he rode to Mayfield Fair yesterday, he is a little lame. Thomas Hamper and I went to Holmbush to set out timber for laths, rails etc for Mrs Catherine Beard.

The 22nd May 1717 Wednesday. A fine day. John Gun workt clipping hedges etc. John Edwards dung'd in Tully's close. Banks thrasht wheat. Ned May fetch home wood etc. George West did severall jobbs. Willy fetch Mrs Howard from Cuckfield Mill. Mrs Barbara Campion and Mrs Catherine Beard's family here afternoon. Sold Samuel Hart 2 runts at £10-15s certain and 5s only if they prove worth it to be gone by Whitsuntide.

The 23rd May 1717 Thursday. A fine day. George West, Ned May and Willy begun clean the home close, carry'd 28 load. John Edwards workt in Tully's close. Banks thrasht wheat. John Gun did severall jobbs about the house. Old William Brand and William Jarvice workt in the pantry chamber. Robert Gatland workt 'till 10 aclock, Abraham Muzzall also to day and yesterday. Mrs Mary Whitpaine here afternoon. Nunnery boy came towards night. Receiv'd 3 bushels of hair of John Hart per Jack Haslegrove. John Gun had a bushel of malt at 3s. Sent an entry of my wool per the post from Mrs Catherine Beard's. Mr Todd came to Mr Jeremiah Dodson's this evning.

The 24th May 1717 Fryday. A fine day. George West, Ned May and Willy dung'd 30 loads. John Gun workt about the gardens etc. Banks mended gaps. John Edwards finisht Tully's close, in all 59 loads. Abraham Muzzall workt here. I was at Westtowne in the forenoon and at Mr Jeremiah Dodson's in the evning. Mrs Catherine Beard's family here in the evning. Paid Mr Courtness 10½d for buttons and mokair. Paid H Hoad 1s per Willy for cutting the boar, 4d for spaying sow and 4d for spaying 2 piggs.

The 25th May 1717 Saturday. A dry day. George West, Ned May and John Edwards and Willy dung'd in the home close, carry'd 42 loads. John Gun faggoted and dug in the hop garden. Banks mended hedges. I was at St Leonard's ponds to meet my Father Stone. Abraham Muzzall workt here.

The 26th May 1717 Sunday. A fine day. Mr William Martin preacht. I was not at Church in the forenoon. We had a parish meeting in the afternoon. I was at Mr Scutt's afterwards, he came home from London to day. He told me he had bought me a galon of train oyl at 2s. Ned May and Ben Shave, went to Nunnery with the chaese for my Mother.

The 27th May 1717 Munday. A dry day. John Edwards, Willy and George West clear'd the home close, 38 loads, in all 138 loads. John Gun dug in the hop garden. Banks thrasht wheat. Richard White had an other load of straw. I am to allow him 1s for helping carry it so there is due to me 35s. Abraham Muzzall workt here 'till noon. Mr John Hart spent the evning and din'd here.

The 28th May 1717 Tuesday. A dry day. George West and Bignall went to Shoreham with a load of treenailes for Stephen Bine at 12s. Receiv'd the 12s of Stephen Bine being 11s-3d outset for cheese for me at 3d per lb and 9d in mony. John Edwards and John Gun dug in the hop garden. Banks thrasht wheat. My Mother Stone came afternoon.

The 29th May 1717 Wednesday. A gloomy day small rain towards night. Fair at Stenning _____ . John Edwards pugg'd clover. John Gun workt in the hop garden. Banks thrasht wheat. George West did severall jobbs. Ned May fetch a load of lime from Marten's for my self, an other Richard Wood for the carriage whereof Marten is to pay me 8s. Samuel Hart fetch a runt. Matt Turner was here at same time. Paid Mrs Scutt 7s-10½d for the half cheese we had some time ago. Willy was at Lewis in the afternoon.

The 30th May 1717 Holy Thursday. A fine day. A Fair at Brighton, at Findon and at the Dicker and at Darkin again. John Edwards pugg'd clover 'till noon, clear'd Tully's rick steddles after. Nick Marchant return'd from London. Paid him 2s-6d more towards the expence of this journey. John Gun faggoted. George West kept holy day. Ned May fetch 2 loads of sand, kept holy day after. Nick Plaw was here to look on the boar.

The 31st May 1717 Fryday. A very fine day. Banks thrasht wheat. John Gun and William Jarvice made mortar in the forenoon. Neither of them workt for me in the afternoon. George West, Willy and John Edwards and Ned May clear'd the home rick steddles of dung in the forenoon, 17 loads. They carry'd dung out of the fatting close afternoon, 10 loads. Willy went to see a cricket match. The Cuckfield Fair cow went to bull.

The 1st June 1717 Saturday. A very fine day. Banks ended wheat thrashing. George West, John Edwards and Ned May carry'd dung out of the fatting close, 28 loads. Willy helpt part of the day, carry'd a letter to Mr V____. John Gun did a jobb in the Nonsuch, faggoted the rest of the day. Paid Mrs Mary Whitpaine 5s for a cheese, being 2½d too much.

The 2nd June 1717 Sunday. A very fine day. Mr William Martin preacht. Nunnery boy came hither at noon. Mrs Howard went away afternoon. Nick Marchant came at night. Mr Richard Whitpaine here. Paid Nick Marchant 10s towards his journey to London tomorrow.

The 3rd June 1717 Munday. A dry forenoon, wet after. Horsham Fair. My Daughter Katherine christen'd. Win'd 3 quarters 5 bushels head and 2 bushels tail of Banks's Churchfield wheat being the last of the field, in all 26 quarters 6 bushels. John Edwards helpt 'till noon, Banks and he begun thrash clover afterwards at 3s per bushel. Ned May deliver'd 12 faggots to Old William Brand. George West and he carry'd 10 loads of dung out of the fatting close. Willy went to Horsham Fair. He brought home 2 barrens at £5-12s which my Cousin John Lindfield bought. I gave him 7 guineas yesterday for that purpose. Mrs Catherine Beard and her family din'd here and Mr William Martin, Mrs Hart and Mrs Scutt were here in the afternoon. My Mother Stone and Mrs Catherine Beard were godmothers and my Brother James Ede (for whom I stood) godfather to my Daughter Katherine. George West begun grubb oaken stone at 5s per cord and to fill the ground in and levell it in the places.

The 4th June 1717 Tuesday. A fine day. John Edwards and Banks begun thrash clover at 3s per bushel. John Gun grubb'd. Ned May fetcht wheat from Hangleton for Old William Brand and roll'd the lower oates in the afternoon. George West trim'd up the dung mixen and other jobbs. John Box sr here in the forenoon. Paid John Gun 5s. Bett was at Danny afternoon. Paid my Lord Treep 20d in full of all accounts. John Marchant of Lox here afternoon. Mrs Mary Whitpaine here towards night.

The 5th June 1717 Wednesday. A fine day. Banks and John Edwards thrasht clover. George West and Ned May carry'd faggots. Nick Marchant return'd from London. Receiv'd 2s (of the 10s I paid him) again and ¼lb of sealing wax at 7½d. I was at Henfield and settl'd the accounts between Mr Norton of Chestham and my Cousin Hayne and as far as we could percieve (Mr Phillip Cheal being there to assist me) there was in Mr Norton's hands £1-11-11¼d which belong'd to the creditors of John Hayne deceas'd which Mr Norton paid to the Widdow Hayne, and she gave him a receit. He likewise paid her £2-4-2d or thereabouts which was due to her on the balance of the account between him and her for which she gave him a receit in full of all accounts, but that is to be understood only of all accounts between him and her self at all relating to her husband's creditors. I was at Petworth, Mrs Mary Whitpaine came home with me.

The 6th June 1717 Thursday. A fine day. Banks and John Edwards thrasht clover. George West, Ned May and Willy carry'd faggots and roots. John Gun grubb'd, he made a cowcumber bed yesterday. Paid Richard Patching 1s for bleeding me. Paid the fuller 9d for dying a payr of stockins. My Father Stone came in the forenoon and Mr Lindfield's man of Horsham and we exemted the fine and deeds (Mr Scutt being here). Mrs Barbara Campion and Mrs White were here afternoon. Receiv'd ¼lb of sealing wax from Mrs Courthope. Stephen Bine and Young Thomas Norton here towards night. Paid my Mother seaven guineas per Nick Marchant. Mr Richard

Whitpaine had 2 qarts of the gallon of train oyl which Mr Scutt brought for me, for which he is to pay me 18d.

The 7th June 1717 Fryday. A fine day. John Edwards and Banks thrasht clover. George West, Ned May and Willy carry'd Towne dirt, 19 loads. John Gun grubb'd. Mr Richard Whitpaine and Mr Burry here in the forenoon and Thomas Norton sr of Edgly about a woman that had a child borne in our parish. Her name is Mary Davis, alias Kg. Mrs Catherine Beard and Mrs Stone here towards night, my Cousin John Lindfield's wife Elizabeth afternoon. Banks had half a bushel of wheat at 2s-6d. Thomas Hart bad me 16s for the heifer's calf at 5 weeks old. Borrow'd Mrs Catherine Beard's dung court.

The 8th June 1717 Saturday. A very fine day. John Edwards and Banks thrasht clover. George West, Ned May and Willy carry'd Towne dirt, 9 loads before noon. George West made 13 faggots in the afternoon like an jole dog. Mary went home with my Father and Mother Stone. John Gun grubb'd. Mr John Hart was here a while afternoon. Mrs Catherine Beard's house was raised. I was there a little while in the forenoon and at Mr Scutt's with my Father.

The 9th June 1717 Whitsunday. A gloomy day, a smart showr afternoon. Mr William Martin preacht. The new singers begun sing in the Church. I was at Mr Scutt's after morning prayr. My Brother John Box and Sister *(Ed: Ann née Marchant)* here. Paid Marten the brick maker 12s in full of all accounts. Mr Cope, an acqaintance and country man of Mr John Hart's was at Mr Scutt's. Ned May return'd from Nunnery, receiv'd a letter from Mr Ede.

The 10th June 1717 Whitmunday. A fine day. George West and Ned May kept holy day. Clear'd all accounts with George West to May Day last and then his second year begun at £-10s. Paid Frank Holden 20s for a year's Window Tax I was at Westto wne in the afternoon, supt there and staid late. There was Mr Cope, Mr Scutt, Mr John Hart, Mr Harry Goffe and Mrs Scutt.
Mr R Qnnol came in after supper. Sold Mr Scutt 2 loads of hay at 2 guineas. Receiv'd 30s-6d of my Cousin John Lindfield being the remainder of the mony I sent by him to Horsham. Receiv'd it yesterday.

The 11th June 1717 Tuesday. A fine day. A Fair at Lewis and Broadwater. John Westover rode the sorrel horse to Lewis Fair. George West and Ned May kept holy day. Mr Cope, Mr Scutt, Mr John Hart and Mr Richard Whitpaine here afternoon, Mrs Catherine Beard and her family also. William Bartlet here in the morning about the 50s due to the parish. Paid Mr Scutt 3s for the oyl and 6d for the bottle.

The 12th June 1717 Wednesday. A very fine day. George West did not work nor come home 'till night. John Edwards and Banks thrasht clover. Ned May and Willy fetcht a load of lime and 425 bricks from Marten's for my self in the forenoon. Ned May and I fetcht a load of lime and 400 bricks thence for Mrs Catherine Beard in the afternoon. George West, Old William Brand, 2 men and a boy workt at Mr Stone's house in the forenoon and in the afternoon John Gun, Old William Brand and William Jarvice, as I think. I was up at the cricket match at Dungton Gate towards night. There I saw Old Thomas Champion and promis'd to allow him 18s towards moveing the hovel at Eastout.

The 13th June 1717 Thursday. A very fine day. Cuckfield Fair. John Edwards and Banks thrasht clover. John Gun went to Nunnery for bees. Ned May and George West unloaded Mrs Catherine Beard's lime and bricks and fetcht 2 loads of sand to Mrs Storer's house and one load home. Stephen Bine workt at Mrs Storer's and a boy he had on tryal. His name is David Marchant from Beeding. Robert Gatland workt there the afternoon. Old William Brand and William Jarvice were there, I think, 'till about noon, but not by the day. Mrs Mary Whitpaine and my Cousin Thomas Norton's wife at Edgly here. Willy went to Cuckfield Fair.

The 14th June 1717 Fryday. A very fine day, exeeding hot. Banks and John Edwards thrasht clover. George West and William Jarvice made mortar. Ned May and Willy fetcht 543 bricks and 406 tiles to Mrs Storer. Paid Marten 6s so that I owe him for 1000 of bricks and a load of lime. I fetcht the bull from John Snashall's and the Nunnery heifer went to bull. Stephen Bine's man Jo Wood, Robert Gatland, Ned Marchant workt at Mrs Storer's and Stephen Bine part of the afternoon. John Gun and R Deerling brought a hive of bees from Nunnery this morning. John Gun grubb'd part of the day. Paid Deerling 10d for his journey per my Wife. Carry'd a load of Abraham Muall's flints into the high ways.

The 15th June 1717 Saturday. A fine day, very hot. Banks and John Edwards thrasht clover. John Gun workt for John Smith. George West and Ned May fetcht a load of sand stone from Peter Hill's pit to Mrs Storer's. Stephen Bine, his man Jo, Standbridge, Robert Gatland and Ned Marchant workt at Mrs Storer's. John Edwards had half a bushel of malt at 1s-6d. John Bodle put his great horse in the hop garden yesterday at 2s per week.

The 16th June 1717 Sunday. A fine day, but a thunder showr at night. Mr William Martin preacht. I was not at Church not being well. The singers went to Ditcheling in the afternoon.

The 17th June 1717 Munday. A fine day. John Gun mow'd clover by Hyder's. Banks and John Edwards thrasht clover. George West mow'd the court and grass plotts. Ned May and I fetcht 750 bricks from Taylor's kiln for Mrs Catherine Beard at 7s-6d per 1000 carriage. Willy went to Lewis for nailes and brought a bill of the portion here from Mrs Court. Mr William Martin put his mare in the Marldfield at 18d per week.

The 18th June 1717 Tuesday. A fine day. John Edwards and Banks thrasht clover. Paid Taylor at the Comon 13s-4d for 500 bricks and 114 ill burnt paveing tile. Ned May fetcht them and carry'd 5 loads of dung out of Mrs Storer's close into the Nonsuch. Willy helpt. Old William Brand and his man workt stone healing. George West faggoted and other jobbs. Lost the strodd and short chain a Sunday night or Saturday. John Smith kill'd the Albourne heifer's calf.

The 19th June 1717 Wednesday. A gloomy morning, fine after. Banks and John Edwards thrasht. ~~George and~~ Ned May did severall jobbs. Willy and George West turn'd clover. I found the strodd and short chain. John Standbridge workt at Mrs Storer's 'till noon. Old William Brand, Thomas Vallence, William and Samuel Jarvice, John Sanders, an old man of Brand's workt stone healing and so paid Old William Brand 5s. John Gun mow'd clover, Tully's. Brother Peter and Cousin Plump here towards night. Receiv'd a bushel of hair from John Hart's per Jack Haslegrove. George West and Willy begun plough in the field by Wickham's _____ .

The 20th June 1717 Thursday. A gloomy day. Banks and John Edwards thrasht. George West mow'd thistles in the middle piece. Ned May went with my teem and Bignall and William Hubbard with my Brother Peter's to Balcombe for sand stones to Mrs Storer's. I am to work a day for my Brother with my teem for it. Jack Haslegrove ground 6 bushels of malt. Old William Brand, John Sanders, Thomas Vallence, William and Samuel Jarvice workt stone healing. Reckon'd with Banks for his day's work to this day and agreed with him to work 'till harvest at 16d per day.

The 21st June 1717 Fryday. A showry day. Banks and John Edwards thrasht clover. John Gun did not work. George West and Willy plough'd up the field by Wickham's. My Cousin John Lindfield was here in the forenoon. We reckon'd and he paid me all the intrest due to Lady Day last and for grease and pease and I paid him 6s-3d for flannel which he bought for me. Nick Plaw din'd here and begun settle the accounts relating to William Balcomb's business. Ned May had the waggon to Thomas Howell's but he was not at leisure to mend her and afterwards carry'd roots and chucks. Paid 3s for 200 of slats which Samuel Jarvice fetcht from Brighton to be used in the stone healing. Old William Brand, John Sanders, Thomas Vallence, Samuel Jarvice workt part of the day stone healing and Old William Brand did small jobb over my wive's closset. Mrs Catherine Beard and her family, Mrs Scutt and Mr John Hart supt here.

The 22nd June 1717 Saturday. A fine day. Banks and John Edwards made an end of thrashing clover. John Gun mow'd in the hop garden. Ned May went with the horses for my Brother Peter. George West and Willy plough'd by Wickham's in the forenoon and in the afternoon they, Jack and Sarah Tully hay'd by Hyder's. Paid John Edwards 10s. He had half a bushel of wheat. Banks had half a bushel of wheat also. Old William Brand, John Sanders, Thomas Vallence and Samuel Jarvice workt stone healing. Natt Hobbes's daughter and one of Thomas Marshall's was here in the afternoon.

The 23rd June 1717 Sunday. A gloomy day. Mr Price preacht. I din'd and supt at Dean House.

The 24th June 1717 Munday. A fine day only a showr in the morning. Ned May and I fetcht 500 bricks for Dick Wood and a load of lime for my self from Marten's. George West kept holy day. Ned May rode to the Fair afternoon. I went to the Fair again afternoon. John Smith fetcht away 27 lambs yesterday.
Paid George West 3s.

The 25th June 1717 Tuesday. A dry day. John Gun and John Edwards mow'd to day and yesterday. Banks and Ned May fetch a load of sand and 5 quarters of malt from Tott for Old William Brand. Hay'd afterwards. George West and Willy plough'd in the morning, hay'd afterwards. Receiv'd £14-18-6d of John Smith for my lambs. Mr Sixsmith din'd here. Mr John Hart supt here. My Cousin John Lindfield came here in the forenoon.

The 26th June 1717 Wednesday. A gloomy forenoon and after too. Paid 5d for thread to mend William Balcomb's sacks. My Cousin John Lindfield's wife Elizabeth rode my old horse to Lewis. Su Waterman din'd here. Banks and George West plough'd in the forenoon, hay'd after. Widdow Tully, Sarah Tully hay'd all day. Ned May and Willy carry'd in the morning, hay'd after. Old William Brand, Thomas Vallence, John Sanders, William Jarvice, Samuel Jarvice workt stone healing and making mortar.

The 27th June 1717 Thursday. A gloomy morning, fine after. Ned May fetch a load of plank from Pickwell for my Cousin John Lindfield to go to the Rock to morrow. Banks and George West and Willy carry'd 3 loads of clover, all that was in the field by Tully's coppice and one load out of the field by Hyder's to the rick behind the hovel. John Gun and John Edwards mow'd in the Edgly Mead. Widdow Tully and Sarah Tully hay'd. Nick Marchant and Mrs Virgoe set out for London about noon. Paid Nick Marchant 10s, he rode Mr William Martin's mare. I was at Mr Price's. Staid late.

The 28th June 1717 Fryday. A showry day. John Gun and John Edwards mow'd. My Wife went to Church. Ned May went to the Rock with my Cousin John Lindfield's plank. Banks went to the top of Sadlescombe Hill. Afterwards George West and he carry'd 2 loads of clover per Hyder's. Willy helpt. Old William Brand, Thomas Vallence, William and Samuel Jarvice workt stone healing. Widdow Tully and Sarah Tully hay'd half the day. Nick Plaw was to see one of the fatting oxen, he being swol'n. Robert Gatland workt a while putting up end board. Paid Mr Scrase £10-2-6d in full for 15 quarters of seed barly. My Wife paid him eight guineas and I paid him the rest, met him as I came back with my Cousin John Lindfield.

The 29th June 1717 Saturday. A showry day. John Gun and John Edwards mow'd. Paid Taylor at the Comon 11s for bricks, tiles etc. Ned May fetch them and hay'd afterwards. Widdow Tully and Sarah Tully hay'd. George West and Banks and Willy carry'd 3 loads to the fatting rick. Set one in the barne, one of them was out of the clover by Hyder's, one out of the way mead and one out of the fields below. Nick Marchant return'd from London. Mr Richard Whitpaine and his wife Mary supt here and my Sister Bett. Old William Brand, Thomas Vallence, William and Samuel Jarvice workt and John Sanders helpt in the afternoon.

The 30th June 1717 Sunday. A gloomy day. Mr William Martin preacht. The singers went to Stenning. We had a meeting about King the travelling woman. I supt at Westtowne.

The 1st July 1717 Munday. A showry day. Banks and John Edwards win'd their clover in the forenoon, 10 bushels head, 3 tail. They workt at Mrs Storer's in the afternoon. John Standbridge and Aldridge set up the gate at the upper side of the Fifteen Acres. Turn'd the runts in there. John Gun and George West workt at Mrs Storer's celler. Old William Brand, Thomas Vallence, John Sanders and William Jarvice made an end of the healing, workt only the afternoon. Receiv'd a letter from Mr Ede per post. Spent the evning at Mr Scutt's, Mr John Hart's birthday. Lent John Westover a guinea. Banks had half a bushel of wheat. John Gun had 11 faggots.

The 2nd July 1717 Tuesday. A very wet day. Banks and George West plough'd 'till noon, made an end of the fallow. George West workt at Mrs Storer's celler afternoon. John Gun and John Edwards mow'd in the morning. John Edwards did not work afternoon. John Gun helpt about the celler. Old William Brand, Thomas Vallence and William Jarvice begun sink the celler at Mrs Storer's. John Edwards had half a bushel of wheat at 2s-3d. John Gun had half a bushel of malt at 2s-8d. Paid Franc Neld 7s-3d for Molly Balcomb. Paid him also £4-12-8d in full of all accounts for my self. Receiv'd 2s of William Lashmer for a bushel of barly.

The 3rd July 1717 Wednesday. A dry, windy day. John Gun and John Edwards mow'd 'till noon. John Gun gather'd cherrys after. John Edwards hay'd. George West, Banks and Ned May fetcht home roots 'till noon, hay'd afterwards. Willy helpt them and gather'd cherrys after. Old William Brand, Thomas Vallence and William Jarvice workt at the celler. John Sanders helpt part of the afternoon or all. Sold John Smith jr the py'd runt at £6-15s to be kill'd next week. I am to have the tongue if worth it. Dick Vinall and he drew out and markt a score of my best ewes. He bid me £11 for them. Frank Cox mended my Cousin John Lindfield's waggon yesterday. William Holford fetcht Sam Hart's last runt. John Smith put his mare in the hop garden to continue there a week at 2s.

The 4th July 1717 Thursday. A dry forenoon, showry after. Banks, George West and Willy carry'd 2 loads of hay out of the Edgly Mead and one of the Little Mead below the way mead to the rick in the Fifteen Acres. In the afternoon Banks and Ned May fetcht a load of great chalk. George West clean'd bricks etc. Widdow Tully, Sarah Tully hay'd. John Gun and John Edwards made an end of mowing the Edgly Mead by noon, hay'd little while. John Gun helpt about a ditch in the Bowling Ally etc. John Edwards did not work for me afterwards. Old William Brand, Thomas Vallence, William Jarvice and John Sanders workt at the celler. I spent the evning at Westtowne. Paid Dick Wood's bill of £1-13s in full of all accounts. Old Box was here to see my Nonsuch.

The 5th July 1717 Fryday. A gloomy forenoon, wet after. Banks and Ned May fetcht 2 loads of great chalk. George West, Willy, Widdow Tully and Sarah Tully hay'd a little while. George West workt in the celler afternoon. Old William Brand, Thomas Vallence, John Sanders, William and Samuel Jarvice workt in the celler and sunk the shop floor to day and an other man of Brand's helpt but workt part of the day (over half) pointing the stone – his name is John. John Standbridge workt at the celler. Goodman Tully of Bolny din'd here. We agreed for a cord of wood and 100 faggots at 10s per load. My Wife was at Wanbarrow, I fetcht her home. Ben Shave was at Nunnery yesterday.

The 6th July 1717 Saturday. A dry morning, wet after. George West workt at the house. Ned May and Banks fetcht 2 loads of great chalk. John Gun and John Edwards mow'd in the dry pond 'till noon and John Gun mow'd in the New Orchard part of the afternoon and John Edwards in the Towne Orchard. Old William Brand, Thomas Vallence, John Weanright, John Sanders and William Jarvice workt at Mrs Storer's. John Standbridge workt there also. Paid Old William Brand 12s. Paid Richard Worsfeld 6s in full of a bill of 6s-3d due to his mother in law Alcock for carriage, took receit. My Wife, Nick Marchant, Jacky Ede, Jack Marchant went to Lewis. Reckon'd with John Edwards and clear'd all accounts. Paid him £2-6s, remains due to me 2d and to him 17 faggots. Paid Molly Balcomb 1s for pocket money and 2s she had of Bett when she was at Lewis.

The 7th July 1717 Sunday. A gloomy day. Mr William Martin preacht. We had a parish meeting. My Wife and I supt at Mr Scutt's.

The 8th July 1717 Munday. A dry day. John Gun and John Edwards mow'd in Tully's Mead 'till 3 aclock, after hay'd afterwards. Abraham Muzzall hay'd. George West, Ned May, Banks and Willy hay'd. So did Widdow Tully and Sarah Tully. Stephen Bine and John Standbridge shor'd the wall and made the parlour window. Old William Brand, Thomas Vallence, John Weanright, William and Samuel Jarvice workt and made an end of sinking the celler. Weanright cut the wall to the street. Paid Old William Brand 10s. Banks had half a bushel of wheat 2s-3d.

The 9th July 1717 Tuesday. A showry forenoon, dry after. Lent Mr Richard Whitpaine 5 guineas for a note of his hand. Banks did not work. John Gun and John Edwards workt in the hop garden afternoon, howing. Old William Brand and his man workt a little while in the forenoon, I don't justly know how much, but he, Thomas Vallence and William Jarvice workt all the afternoon. John Standbridge workt about 2 hours in the forenoon and, I think, all the afternoon. George West workt emptying the celler. Ned May did severall jobbs in the forenoon and in the afternoon fetcht a load of lime from Marten's and 29 watertable bricks from Taylor's. My Wife and I was at Westtowne, supt there. There was Mr Phillip Cheal of Henfield. Mrs Mary Whitpaine was gone to the visitation. Receiv'd 40s of J Norman of Henfield for a year's intrest of William Balcomb's mortgage on his house.

The 10th July 1717 Wednesday. A fine day. Mr Jeremiah Dodson din'd here. Old William Brand, Thomas Vallence, John Sanders and William Jarvice workt. Ned May and Banks fetcht a load of sand. They, George West, John Gun, John Edwards, Abraham Muzzall, Widdow and Sarah Tully hay'd and carry'd out of the Edgly Mead to the Fifteen Acres rick, 7 loads and left 2 on the waggons. John Gun and John Edwards begun 11 aclock, Abraham at 9. Paid T Cox 4s in full for mending my wheels. Mr Richard Whitpaine sent for me to the Swan to treat with Thomas Matton about his bastard child. There was Mr Tydy and Thomas Matton's brother. The least of the 2 yearling heifers went to bull per Mr Richard Whitpaine's bull and I believe an other of them did about a week ago. I was to see the house Edwards had bought. Receiv'd ten guineas of Harry Wickham.

The 11th July 1717 Thursday. A fine day. Old William Brand, Thomas Vallence, John Sanders and William Jarvice workt at Towne 'till noon. George West, Banks and Willy cut the clover rick. Unloaded the 2 loads there, loaded last night. Brought 4 more thither out of the Edgly Mead and left 1 on the waggon. John Gun and John Edwards mow'd 'till 11 aclock. Afterwards they and Ned May carr'd 4 loads out of the Edgly Mead and 1 out of the way mead to the rick next the flax plot in Tully's rick steddle. Abraham Muzzall, Widdow Tully and Sarah Tully hay'd all day. Paid          Wood the chalk digger 5s for 5 loads of great chalk. Lent Mr Richard Whitpaine the chaese and both harnesses to go to Chichester. He supt here. Turn'd the 2 great colts into Tully's teary field.

The 12th July 1717 Fryday. A very fine day. John Gun and John Edwards mow'd. Widdow Tully and Sarah Tully hay'd. Banks, George West and Willy carry'd 3 loads out of Edgly Mead, 1 out of the way mead and unloaded that last on the waggon all at Tully's rick steddle. Ned May and I fetcht 1500 bricks from Marten's to Dick Wood. Paid Taylor 6d for the 29 watertable bricks. Mr John Hart supt here, he pay'd me the douzen of strong beer.

The 13th July 1717 Saturday. A fine day. John Gun and John Edwards mow'd. Jack Smith kill'd the py'd runt this week. Banks, George West and Willy carry'd          load out of Tully's Mead to the fatting rick and 1 thither out of the dry pond. Ned May and I fetcht 750 bricks from Marten's for Dick Wood. Receiv'd 13s of Mrs Catherine Beard for carriage. Clear'd accounts. I was at Mr Norden's, agreed for a stack of faggots, about 500. I am to lay down a load of chalk at his lime kill for every 100 of faggots. Richard White fetcht the peecking cow for 2 or 3 day's tryall. If he likes her he is to give me £5-10s and a day's work or 2 in harvest. Ned Penfold went to Nunnery, carry'd 2 puppies. John Bodle took his horse out of the hop garden.

The 14th July 1717 Sunday. A fine day. Mr William Martin preacht. I was not at Church in the afternoon. My Wife and Willy went to Nunnery in the afternoon. Ned May went with them part of the way. Paid John Gun a guinea in the morning.

The 15th July 1717 Munday. A very fine day. John Gun and John Edwards mow'd. Banks, George West and Ned May carry'd 2 loads of hay out of the dry pond to the rick in Tully's Mead and 3 of Tully's Mead thither, left an other on the waggon, hay'd a while. Widdow Tully and Sarah Tully hay'd all day. John Kneller and Tom King hay'd in the afternoon. My Wife return'd from Nunnery, brought Old William Brand's mony £4-19-6d. Paid Dick Tully 1s for mending William Balcomb's sacks and 5s-2d in full of all other accounts.

The 16th July 1717 Tuesday. A very fine day. John Gun and John Edwards mow'd. Banks and George West carry'd 2 loads of hay to Mr Scutt's, 1 load to the fatting rick all out of Tully's Mead etc. Ned May and I carry'd a load of chalk to Mr Norden's and brought 107 faggots to Tully's. Ned May hay'd after. I was at Wanbarrow in the afternoon. Paid my Mother the remainder of her thirds due at Lady Day last. Widdow Tully and Sarah Tully hay'd all day, Jack Picknall the afternoon.

The 17th July 1717 Wednesday. A very fine day. John Gun and John Edwards mow'd. Paid Old William Brand the £4-19-6d receiv'd of Mrs Ede and 8s-6d on my own account. Receiv'd the guinea I lent John Westover some time ago. Paid Taylor 8s for 500 bricks Ned May fetcht to day. He had the waggon to Thomas Howell's. He fetcht a load of sand from Michael Stacey's pitt. Banks and George West stackt Widdow Tully's faggots. Carry'd 2 loads of Tully's mead to the rick in the Mead and 2 small loads to the rick in the steddle. Widdow Tully, Sarah Tully and Jack Picknall workt all day. Sold a runt to John Smith at 18d per nail and his tongue. He fetcht to day. Paid Abraham Muzzall 8d for mending Molly Balcomb's pettycoat. He had half a bushel of wheat at 2s-3d. Clear'd all accounts with him except the P wheat, his flints and some linsey woolsey. Paid T Cox 2s for a plough he mended to day and 2s for mending a wheel before.

The 18th July 1717 Thursday. A very fine day. John Gun and John Edwards mow'd. Abraham Muzzall workt within doors 'till 10, hay'd after. Moll King hay'd in the afternoon. Ned May, Banks and Picknall fetcht 1½ loads of chalk from the hill. Paid Wood the chalk digger 18d for it. Ned May and Picknall carry'd a load to Mr Norden's and brought home 110 faggots to the Widdow Tully. I din'd at Mr Norden's and staid there 'till towards night. Ben Shave went to Nunnery. George West mow'd 'till noon, in the Nonsuch afterwards. George West, Banks and Moll King carry'd 1 load out of the little Mead by the middle pond to the fatting rick and 2 out of the little Mead by the Rookwood to the fatting rick. Sarah Tully hay'd all day. Eliz Cheal workt the afternoon.

The 19th July 1717 Fryday. A very fine day. John Gun mow'd Nonsuch and hay'd by the day. John Edwards made an end of mowing grass and helpt carry hay about 3 hours. Banks and George West carry'd hay, 1½ loads to the rick in the Fifteen Acres, 1 to the fatting rick and 2 to the oxen's rick. Jack Picknall helpt. Sarah Tully, Eliz Cheal, Abraham Muzzall and Tom King and Willy hay'd all day, Abraham Muzzall all the afternoon. Ned May and I carry'd a load of chalk to Mr Norden's and brought home 115 faggots to Jack Gun. Paid Thomas Howell 2 guineas towards the wheels and tires. Sold the peeking cow to Richard White at £5. Receiv'd 36s of him for straw. Paid him 1s for helping me. Sold the blind mare to          Leary at Broad Street for 20s to have her next Wednesday morning. John Standbridge set up a new stile between the Bowling Ally and hop garden.

The 20th July 1717 Saturday. A very fine day, extream hot. John Gun and John Edwards made an end of mowing the Nonsuch by noon. Helpt hay etc afterwards. Ned May and I carry'd a load of chalk to Marten's at 6s. Brought home 750 bricks for Dick Wood afterwards. Ned May, John Edwards and I fetch a load of William Balcomb's wheat from his Dean's barne in order to carry it for Darkin. Clear'd all accounts with Thomas Howell and John Clark as appear'd by their bills. Brought home my waggon with us and left order for a new payr of fore wheels. Weigh'd the brandl'd runt at John Smith's yesterday. His 4 quarters weigh'd 58 nails 7lbs at 10d per nail, 5 quarters as usual. George West, Banks and Jack Picknall carry'd 1 load out of the dry pond and 5 out of the Little Meads to the oxen's rick. Sarah Tully, Jone and Mary King, Sarah Surgeant and Willy hay'd. Tom Howell was here in the evning for payr bonds for a new payr of fore wheels. Dick Wood and I agreed for the ground to set his little house on. He is to have an old tire that I have and make holes according to my order and to give me nailes to set it on and I am to give him the fetching of 700 bricks. Molly Balcomb came hither last night and went to Henfield Fair. Paid her 1s for pocket mony per my Wife.

The 21st July 1717 Sunday. A very fine, hot day. Mr Healy preacht twice. Nick Plaw brought Molly Balcomb home from Henfield Fair. Stephen Bine and my Sister Betty here also in the evning. Receiv'd a letter from Mr Tattersall per Thomas Marten the thatcher.

The 22nd July 1717 Munday. A very fine day. A thunder showr last night. John Gun, George West, John Edwards, Picknall and Willy carry'd 2 loads out of the little Meads to the oxen's ricks and 3 loads (being all the Nonsuch) into the barne. Tom and Moll King helpt about 3 hours and Sarah Tully and Sarah Surgeant all the afternoon. Banks and Ned May went with a load of William Balcomb's wheat to Nunnery (paid for carrying the wheat to Rusper 12s) to be carry'd to Darkin and 4 bushels of my own wheat for my Father. I was at Church in the morning with Stephen Bine. I went to Nunnery after the teem. Receiv'd 2 guineas of Mr Scutt for his hay.

The 23rd July 1717 Tuesday. A gloomy day but little rain. John Gun did not work. George West, John Edwards, Picknall thrasht and shook Nonsuch. Sarah Tully and Sarah Surgeant weeded the afternoon. Our teem return'd. My Father's came with it, they brought each a load of slabs, planks, timber.

The 24th July 1717 Wednesday. A gloomy day. Banks, John Gun, George West and John Edwards carry'd 2 loads, the last of the little Meads and the Nonsuch to the oxen's rick and begun cut the rick by Tully's hovel. Ned May and Jack Picknall fetch 700 plain bricks and 200 coaping brick from Marten's for Dick Wood. Afterwards they fetcht a load of great chalk from the hill. Paid Wood 1s for it. Paid Thomas Howell 6s for the 4 cast boxes which he bought for my new wheels. Receiv'd the strakes, nailes for the wheels of Dick Wood, which he is to give me by agreem't. Left 10 old strakes with John Clark at the Comon, weigh'd 61lbs for which he is to allow me 2¼d per lb and to make me new strakes at 3½d per lb. My Father's teem went home, carry'd 8 bushels of malt. Receiv'd 20s of R Leary for the blind mare and 2s for her coller.

The 25th July 1717 Thursday. A fine day. A Fair at Lindfield, Shoreham and Charlwood. Neither George West, Ned May, Banks, John Gun or John Edwards workt but in the afternoon John Gun clean'd the garret at Towne for which I am to give him 6d. Paid Robert Pierce 3s-2d in full of all accounts. Stephen Bine and John Standbridge workt on the stairs, John and Robert Gatland making windows. Paid John Parsons 6d for shaveing my head. My Grandmother and Mrs Catherine Beard here in the afternoon. Lent Mr John Hart the sorrel horse to go to Sounting. I wrote to Mr Jeremiah Dodson by him.

The 26th July 1717 Fryday. A fine day. John Gun and John Edwards cut pease etc. George West pull'd flax he is to pay John Edwards for this day. Paid George West 4s. John Edwards had half a bushel of wheat 2s-3d. Banks had half a bushel of wheat. Paid my Cousin John Marchant of Lox £11-9-8d for the last half year of the 4s tax. Borrow'd a payr of oxen of my Cousin John Lindfield also a payr of Mr Richard Whitpaine and a waggon. Ned May carry'd a load of great chalk to Marten's and brought 800 bricks for Dick Wood. Picknall helpt with the teems. Banks carry'd half a load of chalk to Taylor's and brought 750 bricks for my self. Afterwards they fetcht 2 loads of chalk from the hill. Paid Wood 2s for it. Stephen Bine workt 'till noon, Jo Standbridge, Robert Gatland all day. Jo and Robert Gatland workt half the day a Wednesday. Old William Brand and William Jarvice workt setting up windows. Receiv'd a letter from Mr Todd and Mr Jeremiah Dodson and a pot of electuary from Mr Barrow for the head ach.

The 27th July 1717 Saturday. A fine day. John Gun, George West and John Edwards cut rick. Ned May and Banks carry'd 2 loads of chalk to Mr Norton and brought home 100 faggots to John Edwards, 28 for the Widdow Tully and 50 from the stack by his house to Old William Brand's and 75 from the stack in the lane. We brought home a new payr of fore wheels. Paid Thomas Howell 18s for the bare wheels, 2 shillings for shooeing, 2s for boxing, 8d for patching, £2-6s for a new axle and 6d for a new bridge bat. Did not reckon with John Clark but the new strakes weigh'd 13 nail 5lbs at 3½d per lb. Mr Richard Whitpaine and Mr Burry spent the evning here. Paid Mr Burry £1-11-9d and outset 12s for E Chaynie's rent to Lady Day last, 15s for Widdow Tully's rent to Michaelmas next, 30s for 250 faggots for the Widdow Tully which makes in all £4-8-9d in full for my Poor Tax being the first book and at 15d in the pound. Old William Brand and William Jarvice workt at Towne. Jo Wood workt making windows. Jack Picknall helpt serve Old William Brand. Sent home Mr Richard Whitpaine's oxen and waggon per Ned May.

The 28th July 1717 Sunday. A fine day. Mr William Martin preacht. My Cousin John Lindfield din'd here. My Brother John Box and his wife Ann *(Ed: née Marchant)* were here after evning prayr. So was Mrs Susan Courthope.

The 29th July 1717 Munday. A gloomy, dry day. Sarah Tully and Willy cut pease all day, the Widdow Tully the afternoon. John Gun and George West begun reap but *(sic)* Burt's.
John Edwards did not work. Old William Brand, Samuel Jarvice and Jack Haslegrove and John Sanders workt at Towne. Banks and Ned May carry'd 56 foot of 3 inch planck, 95 of 1½ inch, 235 of 2 inch and 58½ foot of timber from Old Land to the Rock for Stephen Bine. Jo Wood made windows etc

The 30th July 1717 Tuesday. A wet day. John Gun workt a while at Towne, afterwards went with Banks to Old Land for a load of boards etc for Stephen Bine. John Edwards did not work. Old William Brand workt about half the forenoon. Samuel Jarvice workt 'till noon. Jo Wood workt making a window. John Towner and Ja Reed saw'd a while, door posts etc. Ned May and I carry'd a load of chalk to Taylor's and brought home 500 brick for my self and a load of lime. Reckon'd with him and I ow him for 1250 bricks. Receiv'd    sacks from my Cousin John Lindfield. Willy and George West screen'd 5 quarters of wheat.

The 31st July 1717 Wednesday. A gloomy day, dry afternoon. Samuel Jarvice and George West workt at Towne making mortar etc. Ned May, Banks and Willy fetcht a cord of wood and 100 faggots for my Father Stone. Paid Goodman Tully's son 20s for it. Paid Widdow 10s in full of all accounts. Mr Ede and Bett Ede came to day. Mr John Hart, my Sister Betty and Bett rode to Ditcheling in the evning.

The 1st August 1717 Thursday. A wet day. John Smith took his mare out of the hop garden. John Gun and Willy win'd the Nonsuch and afterwards John Gun workt at Towne. George West and Ned May fetcht a load of chalk, carry'd it to Taylor's and brought home 750 bricks for my self. Receiv'd the 5 guineas I lent to Mr Richard Whitpaine _____ . John Edwards did not work. Banks went off yesterday. Mrs Scutt, her mother, Mrs Woodcock and Mrs Pelham were here in the afternoon. Willy carry'd a letter to Mr Sixsmith.

The 2nd August 1717 Fryday. A gloomy morning, fine after. John Gun and John Edwards did jobbs in the forenoon, reapt after. John Edwards begun reap round the Rookwood. John Gun and George West reapt by Burt's. Ned May and George West fetcht a load of chalk in the morning from the hill. Ned May went with it to Taylor's and brought 1000 of bricks for Dick Wood at 6s-6d per 1000, carriage. My Brother and Bett Ede went away after dinner. Turn'd the fatting oxen into the way mead. Widdow Tully and Sarah Tully cut pease. My Wife and I were at Wanbarrow towards night. Borrow'd a payr of oxen of Mr Richard Whitpaine.

The 3rd August 1717 Saturday. A fine day. John Gun and George West reapt by Burt's. Ned May and I fetcht a load of chalk and carry'd it to Taylor's and brought home 1000 bricks for Dick Wood. Paid Wood 3s for ½ load of chalk.
John Edwards reapt in the Rookwood. Widdow Tully and Sarah Tully cut pease. Ned May and Willy carry'd a load of the wheat by Burt's in the evning. Lent Eliz Cheal a peashook.

The 4th August 1717 Sunday. A fine day. Mr William Martin preacht. We had a parish meeting. The Widdow Lindfield was took down from 14s per month to 8s and E Ball to nothing. Mr Richard Whitpaine and his wife Mary supt here. Mr Beard came home from London this afternoon.

The 5th August 1717 Munday. A gloomy day. John Gun, George West and John Edwards reapt. Widdow Tully and Sarah Tully cut pease. Ned May, Willy and Tom King carry'd 3½ load of the Homefield pease into Tully's barne, south bay. Borrow'd a payr of hind wheels of my Cousin Thomas Norton Edgly. My Cousin Nick Marchant and his wife were here in the afternoon. He carry'd her home and came again in order to go with the teem to morrow. Banks had half a bushel of wheat per his girl.

The 6th August 1717 Tuesday. A dry day. Widdow Tully and Sarah Tully, Allexander Snatt and Willy cut pease towards night. Snatt and Willy fetcht water. John Gun, George West and ~~Willy~~ John Edwards reapt. Ned May and Nick Marchant went to Nunnery with the teem and a load of my wheat. I was at Nick Plaw's in the morning, brought home 12½lbs of William Balcomb's old iron. Mr Jeremiah Dodson and Mr Sixsmith din'd here. Mr Tattersall came in the afternoon to buy the Rusper liveing but we did not fully agree.

The 7th August 1717 Wednesday. A fine day. Mr Jeremiah Dodson breakfasted here. Willy and Allexander Snatt carry'd 4 loads of the wheat by Burt's and one load of pease etc. John Gun, George West and John Edwards reapt. Widdow Tully cut pease all day. ST helpt. Nick Marchant and Ned May return'd from Nunnery. They brought a table, a trunk of linnen and slabs. Paid Nick Marchant 2s for his journey. Receiv'd 20 guineas of my Cousin John Lindfield towards his flax rent.

The 8th August 1717 Thursday. A gloomy morning, fine after. John Gun, George West and John Edwards reapt. Ned May and I fetcht a load of chalk from the hill, carry'd to Taylor's and brought home 1000 bricks for Dick Wood. Paid Wood 1s for the chalk. I had my Cousin Thomas Norton's wheels. [........xt] at Thomas Howell. Willy and Allexander Snatt carry'd 5 loads of pease to Tully's. Widdow Tully cut pease. Sarah Tully helpt carry. Nick Plaw was here in the evning. Receiv'd £12-17-6d of him in full for all my own wheat. Abraham Muzzall workt here. Paid John Clark at the Comon 23s-6d. Clear'd all accounts.

The 9th August 1717 Fryday. A very fine day. John Gun, George West and John Edwards reapt etc in the afternoon. George West and John Gun carry'd the flax and one load of the wheat by Burt's. George West is to pay John Gun. Ned May and I fetcht a load of chalk and carry'd a load of pease in the afternoon into the great barne. Willy and Allexander Snatt and Sarah Tully carry'd 6 loads of pease all day. Sarah Tully workt only the afternoon. Paid Wood 1s for the chalk. My Cousin Libbard of Chichester and his son call'd here. My Grandmother and Mrs Catherine Beard were here. Thomas Picknall sons fetch Mr Richard Whitpaine's oxen. Ned May gather'd the chissel pares. Old John Holden died suddenly as he was reaping at Mrs Hart.

The 10th August 1717 Saturday. A very fine day. Hurst Fair. Widdow Tully and Sarah Tully and Allexander Snatt made an end of pea cutting by noon. Afterwards Willy and Ned May and Snatt carry'd 2 loads of wheat per Burt's, 2 out of the Rookwood and one small load out of Tully's first field. That of the Rookwood was laid in the North Mow of the wheat barne, that out of Tully's field pitch in Tully's barne to be mov'd again. They carry'd one load of pease into the great barne. My Wife and I supt at Mrs Catherine Beard's. John Gun, George West and John Edwards reapt. Paid Allexander Snatt 10s for his 5 days week. Widdow Tully had half a bushel of malt.

The 11th August 1717 Sunday. A dry day. Mr William Martin preacht, no service afternoon. Old John Holden buried this evning. *(Ed: Recorded in Hurstpierpoint Parish Register. ESRO hold a copy of his will under Ref: 1717 A49 p285 64 where he is described as a tailor)*

The 12th August 1717 Munday. A dry day. John Gun, George West and John Edwards reapt. Ned May and Willy carry'd 2 loads of pease and fetch a load of chalk. John Standbridge put in a window board in the great chamber [at Towne]. Old William Brand, William and Samuel Jarvice mended the pavement in the kitchen at Little Park. Mr Picknall at Arundell supt here. We reckon'd and clear'd all accounts. Paid £1-6-8d for my Father Stone, £3-1-2d for my self. Receiv'd £6-10s of him on John Cherry's account, part of the debt due to William Balcomb. Paid Mr John Hart 25s for a qarter's schooling due at Midsumer last.

The 13th August 1717 Tuesday. A dry day. John Gun, George West and John Edwards reapt. Ned May and Willy carry'd a load of chalk to Taylor's and brought home a load of lime for me, half a load for Dick Wood and 215 watertable brick. Mr John Hart, my Wife and I went to Broadwater to Mr Jeremiah Dodson's.

The 14th August 1717 Wednesday. A fine day. John Gun, George West and John Edwards reapt. Banks and John Edwards had each half a bushel of wheat yesterday. Ned May, Willy and I loaded at Old Land for Stephen Bine of 4 inch plank 36.36. Timber 57.1.1½.2½.1.1½. Stephen Bine helpt load it for which, and a small jobb to the well cirb, he is to have 1s. Mrs Minshall, Mrs Woodcock, Mrs Pickham, Mrs Hart, Mr John Hart supt here. Ned May and Willy carry'd 2 small loads of pease into the great barne, the last of field, in all        loads.

The 15th August 1717 Thursday. A fine day. John Gun, George West and John Edwards reapt from 4 aclock. John Gun and George West carry'd 2 small loads of wheat by Burt's, the last of the field, in all loads on the South Mow and loads on the North Mow. Carry'd also 1 load of Tully's field to the North Mow. Ned May and Willy went to the Rock with the load above. My Father Stone and Kt Ede went home. I supt at Mrs Catherine Beard's with Mr Price, Mr John Hart and Mr Richard Whitpaine.

The 16th August 1717 Fryday. A wet day. John Gun and John Edwards mow'd a little while in the Bankfield and afternoon John Gun cut hedges etc. Ned May &George West fetcht 2 loads of sand and loaded Mr Richard Whitpaine's wattles. Turn'd the fatting oxen into the Edgly Mead. John Gun had half a bushel of malt at 1s-4d. Weigh'd the brown cow that was bought at Horsham Fair, 47 nails 5lb to John Smith at 18d per nail.

The 17th August 1717 Saturday. A showry day. John Gun and George West made mortar 'till allmost night then mended gaps. John Edwards mow'd thistles part of the day, I think, little above half. Ned May and Willy new markt the sheep for John Smith, took 48 tench and 14 carp out of the Edgly Mead pond to put them in the tomkin penstock hole of the new pond. In the afternoon Ned May, Stephen Bine and I went to Old Land and loaded of 4 inch plank 24 foot, 2 inch 27, 22, 20, of 1½ inch 21, 20. Timber 29. 37 and 2. Brought to the hop garden gate. Stephen Bine tore his thumb. Ned May and Willy had home Mr Richard Whitpaine's wattles. My Wife and Willy were at my Brother John Box's. I were at Westtowne in the morning.

The 18th August 1717 Sunday. A gloomy day, some rain. Mr William Martin preacht. Mrs Susan Courthope, her brother William, Mr Richard Whitpaine were here after evning prayr. My Wife and I were at Mrs Catherine Beard's a little while in the evening.

The 19th August 1717 Munday. A fine day. John Gun and George West mow'd barly the forenoon, reapt after. John Edwards mow'd oates the forenoon, reapt after. Allexander Snatt mow'd thistles etc in the Nine Acres at 16d per day. Willy and Ned May went to the Rock with the load above. Receiv'd £9-17-6d from Richard Collens for my load of wheat. It was sold for £10 but 2s-6d was kept back for selling. Nunnery boy was here with a letter. Sent the great porrige by him. I rode about the Ham farm with Mr Beard, staid a while at Mrs Catherine Beard's with Mr Beaumont and Mr Osbourne. Mr Osbourne promis'd to send for my young tench in a few days. My Wife and I supt at Mr Scutt's. Mr _____ and Mr Woodcock and Mr John Hart were gone to Mr Richard Whitpaine.

The 20th August 1717 Tuesday. A dry day 'till towards night. John Edwards reapt and mow'd oates. John Gun and George West reapt and mow'd barly. Ned May and I loaded a load of Cooper's timber at Old Land to go to Shoreham for Stephen Bine. Robert Gatland helpt load. We brought it to our Towne. Allexander Snatt mow'd thistles. Thomas Barker was here to desire me to take some Westcountry sheep of him. I promis'd to see them. John Smith sr and his son John were here in the evning. Sold the black horn'd runt to the young man at £5-10s. Dick Wood had 200 coaping brick of me for which I had as many other brick

The 21st August 1717 Wednesday. A very wet day. John Gun and John Edwards did not work. George West, Ned May and Willy cut the pea mows etc. Paid Banks £4-1s-6d and clear'd all accounts. Mrs Catherine Beard, her mother and Mr Beard supt here.

The 22nd August 1717 Thursday. A dry day, only a short showr afternoon. Ned May and Willy carry'd the load of Cooper's stuff to Shoreham. John Gun and George West mow'd barly and reapt. John Edwards reapt and mow'd oates. Allexander Snatt mow'd thistles, turn'd wheat and towards night John Edwards and he carry'd a good half load of Tully's wheat. Paid Mr Barrow of London 6s-8d at Mr Jeremiah Dodson's yesterday in full of all accounts. Took a receit on the bill.

The 23rd August 1717 Fryday. A fine day. John Gun and George West made an end of mowing the Bankfield, reapt after. Allexander Snatt mow'd thistles etc. Ned May and Snatt carry'd a small jobb of Tully's field and 2 jobbs of the Rookwood. John Edwards made an end of reaping his field and mow'd oates. I were at Cuckfield. Talkt with Mr Carlton about Rusper liveing _____ . Willy went to Cuckfield with many others of our parish to be confirm'd. Receiv'd 15s of Mr Jeremiah Dodson's at Mr Richard Whitpaine's towards the rent of school. Old William Brand and William Jarvice workt at Towne.

The 24th August 1717 Saturday. A fine day. A Fair at Brighton. I were at my Brother John Box's in the morning, my Sister Ann Box went with me to Wanbarrow. Allexander Snatt, Ned May and Willy carry'd boards up to the Towne house in the morning. Afterwards Snatt mow'd thistles etc. Willy and Ned May carry'd 2 good half loads of the Rookwood [wheat]. John Gun, George West and John Edwards mow'd in the Churchfield in the morning and reapt in the Rookwood afterwards. Paid Snatt 5s. Ned Penfold workt here. Old William Brand and William Jarvice workt at Towne. T Cox put a payr of boxes in my old forewheels.

The 25th August 1717 Sunday. A dry day. Mr William Martin preacht. I was not at Church in the forenoon. I was at Mrs Catherine Beard's after evning prayr and at Westtowne.

The 26th August 1717 Munday. A fine day. John Gun, George West and John Edwards mow'd in the morning and reapt after. Thomas Muzzall reapt in the afternoon. Allexander Snatt reapt in the forenoon and helpt carry barly afternoon. Ned May, Willy, Snatt, Abraham Muzzall, John Parsons and Thomas Westover carry'd 4 loads of the Bankfield barly into the East Mow of the great barne. Also a load of the Rookwood wheat to Tully's barne. Old William Brand, Thomas Vallence, John Sanders, William and Samuel Jarvice workt at Towne, also Standbridge and Robert Gatland and at home. John Edwards had half a bushel of wheat at 2s-3d. Nick alias Dr Nick Plaw was here to cure a young bullock's eye. Receiv'd by him 2 [r.......] of William Balcomb's, weigh'd 20½lbs as he say'd. Sold John Bodle the black Horsham Fair cow at £4-5s to be kill'd this week. Sold John Smith a runt at £5-10s (if worth it) to be kill'd this week.

The 27th August 1717 Tuesday. A very fine day. John Gun, George West and John Edwards mow'd in the forenoon and they and Thomas Muzzall made an end of reaping the Rookwood afternoon. Allexander Snatt reapt in the Rookwood 'till noon, carry'd barly afternoon. Ned May, Willy, Allexander Snatt, William Nicholas, Widdow Tully and Sarah Tully carry'd 4 loads of the Bankfield barly and one load of the Rookwood wheat. Receiv'd 12s of Old Kester yesterday for hay. Paid George West 12s today. Old William Brand, Thomas Vallence, John Sanders, William and Samuel Jarvice workt at Towne, so did John Standbridge. Robert Gatland workt setting up the gate by the grindstone. Stephen Bine's man Peter workt on the new school window. My Wife and Mrs Pickham went to Lewis.

The 28th August 1717 Wednesday. A very fine day. John Gun, George West and John Edwards reap'd. Allexander Snatt, Willy and Ned May unloaded the wheat at Tully's the morning and afterwards carry'd barly 3 loads out of the Bankfield, in all 11 loads. They carry'd also 2 loads out of the Churchfield. Widdow Tully and Sarah Tully, Thomas Vallence, William Jarvice and Robert Gatland helpt in the afternoon. Old William Brand, John Sanders workt at Towne all day and Samuel Jarvice, Vallence and William Jarvice the forenoon. Stephen Bine's man Peter workt in the new school all day and Robert Gatland the forenoon. Standbridge workt all day at Towne for ___ . Paid Allexander Snatt 5s.
Ned May and Willy carry'd about a lain, the last of the Rookwood wheat, in all __ loads. Paid Thomas Muzzall 2s-6d for reaping and John Parsons 1s for barly harvest.

The 29th August 1717 Thursday. A very fine day. John Gun, George West and John Edwards made an end of mowing the Churchfield in the morning. John Gun and John Edwards mow'd in Tully's lower oat field 'till 4 aclock, helpt carry barly after. George West mended gaps 'till noon, helpt carry barly after. Widdow Tully and Sarah Tully turn'd oates in the morning, helpt carry barly after. Ned May and Willy carry'd some wheat to Tully's in the forenoon etc. Carry'd barly after, 3 loads. Old William Brand, Thomas Vallence, John Sanders, William Jarvice and Samuel workt at Towne. Stephen Bine's man Peter workt on the school all day. Standbridge and Robert Gatland workt for me the forenoon. Afterwards they workt on the school etc. The 2 one yearling heifers bulling about this time but I hope they did not go to the bull. Receiv'd 15s of Mr Scutt for rent of the school. My Wife bought 20lbs of malago refin'd (when at Lewis) at 26s per lb.

The 30th August 1717 Fryday. A very fine day. John Gun and John Edwards mow'd oates 'till noon, helpt carry barly after. Allexander Snatt helpt the afternoon. Widdow Tully and Sarah Tully turn'd oates and helpt carry barly. Willy and Ned May and George West unloaded in the morning etc and in the afternoon helpt carry 6 loads of barly. Old William Brand T Vallence and William Jarvice workt at Towne all day. Thomas Vallence, John Sanders and Jarvice ¾ of the day, they helpt about Old William Brand's hay. John Standbridge workt all day at Towne for me, Robert Gatland and Peter about the school. Stephen Bine was there himself. Mr Michelbourne servant to Thomas Friend of Lewis din'd here. Agreed with John Parsons the barber he is to have the west end of my Towne house this winter half year at £1-7-6d.

The 31st August 1717 Saturday. A very fine day. John Gun and John Edwards made an end of mowing oates, helpt carry barly and oates. George West and Ned May unloaded after in the morning, helpt carry barly and oates. Sarah Tully workt all day. Goodman White and his son helpt in the afternoon, carry'd 4 loads of barly, the last of the Churchfield, in all 17 loads. Carry'd also 2 loads of Tully's oates next the Mead. Paid John Smith 2s-6d for a new coller for the ball mare. Thomas Vallence, William and Samuel Jarvice and John Sanders workt all day, Old William Brand only the afternoon. John Standbridge workt all day, William Nicholas helpt him saw a piece of timber of Stephen Bine's for a post in the shopp. Peter and Robert Gatland workt on the school.

The 1st September 1717 Sunday. A fine day. Mr William Martin preacht. Horsted Fair, allways this day except it be Sunday. My Sister Betty here after evning prayr. Receiv'd 6s of the Widdow Leach for half a year's rent. Paid my Cousin John Marchant of Lox £4 for a year's intrest which he is to pay to the Widdow Weller of Horsted for me.

The 2nd September 1717 Munday. A wet day. John Gun and Ned May carry'd a load of chalk to Taylor's and brought home 750 bricks for me etc. George West and John Edwards workt at Towne. Standbridge and Robert Gatland workt there also, so did Jo Wood 'till about 4 aclock, then we fell out and he went off. Thomas Vallence, William Jarvice and Samuel workt there also. Stephen Bine here in the evning.

The 3rd September 1717 Tuesday. A showry forenoon, fine after. George West and John Edwards, Ned May and Willy plough'd in the Nine Acres.
John Gun rak'd up weeds there and _____ .
Paid Allexander Snatt 3s-8d in full for all his work. Standbridge and Robert Gatland workt at Towne, so did Stephen Bine in the afternoon.

The 4th September 1717 Wednesday. A gloomy morning, dry after. Allexander Snatt, George West, Ned May and Willy plough'd in the Nine Acres. John Gun and John Edwards rak'd weeds, turn'd oates towards night. Stephen Bine, Standbridge and Robert Gatland workt at Towne. My Wife and I were to see my Sister Ann Box, my Brother not willing. Begun work the mare colt I had of Mr Richard Whitpaine. Allexander Snatt to have 1s per day for driving plough, but if he help harvest any afternoon, he is to have 18d for that day.

The 5th September 1717 Thursday. A showry forenoon, dry after. Allexander Snatt, George West, Ned May, and Willy plough'd in the Nine Acres. John Gun and John Edwards cut the wheat mow etc. Standbridge and Robert Gatland workt at Towne. Paid T Cox 2s for making a wheel to the wheelbarrow and 1s for putting 2 boxes etc to my wheels some time ago. Receiv'd 14 nail 1lb of cheese from Mrs Catherine Beard at
per nail.

The 6th September 1717 Fryday. A gloomy forenoon, dry after. Allexander Snatt, George West, Ned May and Willy plough'd 'till noon, carry'd oates after. John Gun and John Edwards did jobbs 'till 10 aclock, carry'd oates after. John Westover and Robert Gatland helpt carry oates in the afternoon. They carry'd 7 loads out of Tully's lower field. Stephen Bine, Standbridge and Robert Gatland workt at Towne.
J Chainey of Arundell was here. John Box and I sign'd his composition at 5s per £ for the £6-10s due to William Balcomb.

The 7th September 1717 Saturday. A gloomy day. Made an end of harvest. Allexander Snatt, George West, Ned May and John Gun finish'd the Nine Acres by noon, carry'd oates afterwards. Willy went to Brighton in the morning to have 2 horse collars alter'd, helpt carry oates after. John Edwards rakt weeds 'till 11 aclock, carry'd oates. Old Thomas Picknall helpt a while in the afternoon. Carry'd 2 loads out of the field next the mead, in all 4, also 1 load out of the lower field, in all 8, being the last of my harvest. Paid Tom Picknall 5s for his boy's work in the Sumer. Standbridge workt at Towne all day. Stephen Bine helpt. Willy brought 2 throat hasps and 3 whiplashes from Brighton.

The 8th September 1717 Sunday. A dry day. Mr William Martin preacht. I was not at Church in the forenoon. My Cousin John Lindfield din'd here. I was at Mrs Catherine Beard after evning prayr.

The 9th September 1717 Munday. A gloomy, windy day. Pickt my hops. We had three bins. John Edwards had half a bushel of malt. Paid the hop pickers and John Edwards workt for me in the forenoon and afternoon corded his wood etc. Paid the Widdow Tully 12s-2d in full of all accounts. Paid Allexander Snatt 5s in full. John Gun pull'd poles. My Brother James Ede, Kitt Ede and Molly came at night. Standbridge workt at Towne all day. Robert Gatland half. Paid my Brother Peter 20s and clear'd all accounts. George West helpt him harvest this afternoon. Lent him 3 iron rakes per Abraham Muzzall.

The 10th September 1717 Tuesday. A fine day. My wedding day, 17 years. Allexander Snatt, John Gun and Willy cut and tipt the 15 Acre rick and gather'd the Towne apples about 10 bushels. George West, Ned May and John Edwards cut and tipt the lean oxen's rick and begun tip the horse's rick behind the hovel. Paid Old William Brand 2 guineas. Standbridge and Robert Gatland workt at Towne. I were at Westtowne and at Albourne Green before noon. I gave Mr Pointin notice at the Swan that I intended to bag my hops a Thursday morning and that William Bull intended to bag his a Fryday morning.

The 11th September 1717 Wednesday. A dry day. John Gun, George West and John Edwards gather'd apples. Allexander Snatt and Ned May fetch'd 2 loads of wood and faggots from Broad Street for Old William Brand. Receiv'd £10-8s of Thomas Champion sr and outset

£4-12s for two half year's Land Tax, due in all £15 for half a year's rent for Eastout, due at Lady Day last. Mr John Hart supt and spent the evning here. Standbridge and Robert Gatland workt at Towne. I sent Mr Richard Whitpaine an account when I took out the Let Pass for his wool.

The 12th September 1717 Thursday. A dry day. Allexander Snatt, John Gun, John Edwards and Willy gather'd apples. Ned May and George West plough'd for Mrs Catherine Beard. John Towner and Ja Reed saw'd ashen board etc. Standbridge and Robert Gatland workt at Towne. John Edwards had half a bushel of wheat. Will Bull bagg'd my hops. Receiv'd 1½ ell of bagging of Mr Richard Whitpaine and charcoal to dry my hops.

The 13th September 1717 Fryday. A dry day. John Edwards begun thrash wheat. John Gun and Allexander Snatt carry'd 75 faggots to John Edwards's and 17 also 100 for J____ ohn Gun and brought home 2 loads. They win'd the cuttings of the mows, 1½ bushels. George West and Ned May plough'd for Mrs Catherine Beard. Standbridge workt at Towne. Robert Gatland helpt me mend the chaese half the day but Mr Richard Whitpaine is to pay for it. Paid Allexander Snatt 3s for 3 day's work. Paid Mr Courtness 16d for a payr of stirrup leathers very _. Paid my Sister Betty 18d for an ounce of bohea. Robert Whitpaine of Edgly died yesterday being in his 89th year *(Ed: Robert's burial recorded in the Hurst Parish Register on 14 September)* and James Banks died yesterday, also being near as old as the other. My Brother James Ede went home this afternoon. Paid John Parsons 1s for shaveing my head and Willy's.

The 14th September 1717 Saturday. A fine day. John Edwards thrasht wheat. John Gun and Willy fetcht a load of laths for Stephen Bine from _George West workt on his flax half the day. My Wife and I, Jacky, Molly, Kitty, Nan Wood, Ned May and Jack Haslegrove set out for Nunnery afternoon.

The 15th September 1717 Sunday. A fine day. Mr William Martin preacht.

The 16th September 1717 Munday. A fine day. John Edwards thrasht wheat. John Gun and Willy fetcht a load of timber from Old Land for Stephen Bine and afternoon fetcht the hops from Westtowne. George West workt on his flax.

The 17th September 1717 Tuesday. A fine day. John Edwards thrasht wheat. John Gun and Willy fetcht a load of treenails from Old Land for Stephen Bine and went and loaded a load of knees there and brought it to the Stone Pound to go for the Rock. George West workt on his flax. Mrs Pryaulx din'd at Nunnery.

The 18th September 1717 Wednesday. A fine day. John Edwards thrasht wheat. John Gun and Willy went to the Rock. George West went up the hill with them, brought 2 oxen back and workt on his flax afternoon, in all 3 days. My Father Stone and I were at Mr Lindfield's at Horsham. Mr Woodham din'd at Nunnery. Reckon'd with my Father and clear'd all accounts with him, except what relates to the Act of Parliament, Lackroace's]Bill, Greenaway's digging and writeing Widdow Storer's leases. Receiv'd of him £3-16-4½d.

The 19th September 1717 Thursday. A fine day. Win'd John Edwards wheat of Tully's little field 12½ bushels. George West and Willy helpt. John Gun and Allexander Snatt fetcht a load of sand stone for Old William Brand from High Bridge. We return'd from Nunnery, my Brother James Ede with us, call'd at Dean House. My Cousin John Lindfield gave me a hare. Receiv'd of him 3 guineas. Paid my Father 8s-6d yesterday for carrying William Balcomb's wheat, from thence to Darkin.

The 20th September 1717 Fryday. A fine day. John Edwards thrasht wheat. John Gun and Ned May went to Old Land to load for the Rock. George West and Allexander Snatt carry'd grit to fill up holes in the Nine Acres. Old William Brand and Samuel Jarvice workt at Towne. Robert Gatland workt there the afternoon. Willy fetcht 4000 of 3d, 1000 of 6d and some _ from Mr Court's of Lewis. Mr Picknall of Arundell and his wife, Mr Richard Whitpaine and his wife Mary supt here.

The 21st September 1717 Saturday. A very wet forenoon, dry after. John Edwards thrasht. John Gun and Ned May and Willy went with yesterday's load as far as Old Hobbes's and the rain drove them back. Afterwards they fetcht a load of wood and faggots from Broad Street for Old William Brand.
Willy went to Balcombe to see my Brother William. Paid Allexander Snatt 2s for 2 day's work. Receiv'd £3-6s of Harry Wickham and clear'd all

accounts. Sold him my old barly at 13s-6d per quarter. Receiv'd 7s-6d of Widdow Radok in full for her rent, also 3s of Widdow Chapman which with 12s outset with Mr Burry is in full for her rent. Sold John Smith jr 12 ewes at 9s per ewe and 2s-6d over. Receiv'd the 2s-6d in hand. Sold them yesterday.

The 22nd September 1717 Sunday. A fine day. Mr William Martin preacht. I was not at Church in the forenoon. My Wife and I supt at Mr Scutt's.

The 23rd September 1717 Munday. A wet day. George West and Willy and John Gun win'd oates in Tully's chamber, 6 quarters to go to Lewis. Widdow Tully had a bushel. They brought home fleeces of wool. John Edwards thrasht. Ned May carry'd half a load of loam earth to Mrs Storer's. Borrow'd 500 thatching rods of Harry Morley. Old William Brand, Thomas Vallence, John Sanders, Samuel and Will Jarvice workt at Towne, Standbridge and Robert Gatland also. I spent the evning at Mr William Martin's with Mr Price, Mr John Hart and Mr Richard Whitpaine and Mr Scutt was there a little while.

The 24th September 1717 Tuesday. A small showr in the morning, dry after. John Edwards thrasht. Ned May and George West ridg'd in the Nine Acres. Willy harrow'd. John Gun did severall jobbs in the morning, mov'd to Tully's after. Old William Brand and Samuel Jarvice workt at Towne. Standbridge, Robert Gatland and a new man of Stephen Bine's, his name is Moses, workt there also. My Wife was at Danny afternoon. I was at Westtowne at night but Mr Richard Whitpaine was from home. Lent Mr Whitpaine my fish net and spoon net per J Prat.

The 25th September 1717 Wednesday. A gloomy day, some rain. John Edwards thrasht. George West and Allexander Snatt carry'd earth in the Nine Acres. Mrs Catherine Beard's dung court and my own carry'd 5 loads of Old William Brand's slut's hill, 4 of his stable dung hill and 1 of the Towne dirt, all into the Nine Acres. Old William Brand, Vallence, John Sanders, Samuel and William Jarvice workt half the day. Moses, Standbridge and Robert Gatland workt all day. Dick Wood shoo'd the browne colt round. John Gun carry'd 3 bushels of pares to Brighton on the bay horse.

The 26th September 1717 Thursday. A showry day. John Edwards did not work. John Gun mov'd the rest of his goods. George West and Allexander Snatt carry'd grit in the Nine Acres. Coattes harrow'd with Mrs Catherine Beard's horses. Ned May harrow'd with my oxen. Pay'd my Cousin John Lindfield £5-0-9d for 10 weathers. Old William Brand, Vallence, John Sanders, Samuel and William Jarvice, Moses, Standbridge and Robert Gatland workt also.

The 27th September 1717 Fryday. A dry day. Win'd 12 bushels head and 1½ tail of John Edwards's Tully's wheat. John Gun, Allexander Snatt and ~~Edwards~~ Willy helpt and workt the rest of the day at Towne and so did John Edwards near half the day. Ned May and George West plough'd so did Mrs Catherine Beard's teem in the Nine Acres. Receiv'd £5 of Richard White for the peecking cow. Paid George West 2s-6d. Old John Lag mov'd his things out of his shopp. Old William Brand, Vallence, John Sanders, Sam and William Jarvice workt, Moses, Standbride and Robert Gatland also. Bett went to Broadwater in Mr Jeremiah Dodson's waggon. Mr Ede sent a messenger from Horsham with a letter.

The 28th September 1717 Saturday. A dry day. John Gun screen'd wheat and sow'd. Ned May and George West plough'd, so did Mrs Catherine Beard's teem. Willy and John Edwards harrow'd in the afternoon. Stephen Bine, Standbridge, Moses and Robert Gatland workt at Towne. Old William Brand and John Parsons mov'd to my house. Brand is to give me 40s 'till Lady Day next and Parsons 27s-6d. Receiv'd 2s-6d of William King for rent of his part of the stable. Paid him 8d for a jobb about the old school. Receiv'd £12 of John Smith jr. Paid Ned May 45s and 5s he had before in full of his last year's wages.

The 29th September 1717 Sunday. Michaelmas. A gloomy day. Mr Price preacht. Mrs Catherine Beard and my Grandmother supt here.

The 30th September 1717 Munday. A gloomy day. A Fair at Stenning. John Edwards thrasht and George West carry'd a load of loam earth to Towne and afterwards harrow'd in the Nine Acres. Mrs Catherine Beard's teem harrow'd also. Willy and I and Jack Haslegrove went to the Fair. Bought 10 runts for Mrs Beard and 8 of David

Williams at £3-9s per runt. John Smith jr went with me. We call'd at Thomas Walter's of Bramber. Staid late and drank too much. Stephen Bine came to us there. I lost my whip coming home. Sold John Smith 2 runts whilst we were there at £10-10s to be kill'd in a month. Receiv'd 10s in hand. Standbridge workt at Towne. John Norrice, A Lawson, John Sanders, Samuel and William Jarvice workt at Towne.

The 1st October 1717 Tuesday. A fine day. John Edwards thrasht. Mrs Catherine Beard's teem and my own plough'd. John Gun sow'd. Receiv'd 6 bushels of wheat of Richard White at 4s-6d per bushel. Willy went after my whip but could not find it. Moses workt at Towne. Ned May begun his next year at £4.

The 2nd October 1717 Wednesday. A wet morning, dry after. John Edwards thrasht wheat. John Gun, George West and Ned May workt in Tully's barne. Moses workt at Towne, so did John Norrice and William Jarvice. Paid Thomas Barker 15s-8d for 22 ewes. Nick Plaw and Willy went thither with me. Mr William Martin, Mr Scutt and his wife and Mr John Hart supt here.

The 3rd October 1717 Thursday. A very wet forenoon, dry after. John Edwards thrasht. John Gun and George West workt in Tully's barne 'till 3 afternoon then they and Ned May gather'd apples. John Norrice and William Jarvice workt at Towne. Moses workt there also. R Balchild the fishmonger din'd here. John Edwards had a bushel of apples at 18d. John Pierce the taylor workt here.

The 4th October 1717 Fryday. A fine day. John Edwards thrasht and had an other bushel of apples. Mrs Catherine Beard's teem and mine plough'd and sow'd and made an end of the Nine Acres haveing sow'd 15 bushels of my own wheat that grew in Tully's field and 11½ bushels of Richard White's wheat, in all 26½ bushels. Willy and Jack Haslegrove fetcht the ewes from Nick Plaw. John Pierce workt here. Moses workt at Towne, so did John Norrice and William Jarvice. Mrs Beard's teem has workt 7 days for me so that I owe her 5 days.

The 5th October 1717 Saturday. A fine day 'till towards night. John Edwards thrasht, only helpt water furrough about 3 hours. John Gun did severall jobbs makeing water furroughs etc. Ned May and George West workt plough'd for Mrs Catherine Beard. Willy harrow'd with the Duke horse and Old William Brand's mare. John Norrice and William Jarvice workt at Towne. John Standbridge workt there also. John Pierce workt here.

The 6th October 1717 Sunday. A wet morn, dry after. Mr William Martin preacht. We had a meeting in the afternoon. My Sister Bett din'd here. Jos Dale was here in the morning.

The 7th October 1717 Munday. A stormy day. John Edwards begun ditching in the Churchfield. Ned May and George West plough'd for Mrs Catherine Beard. John Gun and Willy went to have the load that was left at Old Hobbes's to the Rock but could go no farther than Warncomb Bottom. I went to Henfield to meet Mr Cheal and Mr Wade to treat about the repairs of my Cousin Haynes's house but came to no conclusion. I din'd at Mr Cheal's.

The 8th October 1717 Tuesday. A fine day. John Edwards ditcht in the Churchfield. Paid him a guinea. Paid Richard White 5s for 12 bushels of seed wheat. Paid Mr Jeremiah Dodson £5-5s for half a year's tythe due at Michaelmas last past. He breakfast'd here. I din'd at Westtowne, parted 100 sheep there. Receiv'd 6 douzen of [soap] from Mr Picknall some time ago at 4s-4d per douzen, 6½ douzen of candles to day at 6s per douzen, 4 quires of tobacco paper at 3d per quire and 5 quires of writing paper at 5d per quire, in all £3-5-1d. Ned May and George West plough'd for Mrs Catherine Beard. John Gun and Willy went with the timber to the Rock, a load and ¾. Deliver'd a sack of oates some time ago to my Unkle Courtness at 6s per George West.

The 9th October 1717 Wednesday. A wet, stormy day. John Edwards workt for himself. John Gun and Willy carry'd half a load of chalk to Taylor's. Brought home 400 of brick for Old William Brand and a load of lime for my self. Afterwards Willy went to Balcombe and John Gun had home my Cousin Thomas Norton's dung court and his hind wheels from under the carriage. Ned May and George West plough'd for Mrs Catherine Beard. Paid John Gun a guinea. Jack Norrice and William Jarvice workt at Towne.

The 10th October 1717 Thursday. A wet forenoon. John Edwards ditcht part of the day. John Gun made water furrows etc. Ned May and George West plough'd for Mrs Catherine Beard. My Wife and I supt at Mrs Scutt's with my Grandmother and Mrs Beard. Paid Mr John Hart 25s for a quarter's schooling due at Michaelmas last.

The 11th October 1717 Fryday. A dry day 'till towards night, a smart thunder in the evning. John Edwards and Davey plough'd 'till noon then went to Dick Tully's funerall.
*(Ed: Recorded in the Hurst Parish Register as "Richard Tully")*
John Gun made water furroughs and gather'd apples 'till noon. Went to the funerall. Allexander Snatt came about 9 aclock, helpt gather apples etc and in the afternoon Ned May and he carry'd a load of Abraham Muzzall's flints and George West's flax. George West workt on his flax all day. Ned May and John Edwards plough'd in Mrs Catherine Beard field 'till noon. Mr William Martin, Mr John Hart and I supt at Westtowne. Paid Marten the brickmaker 1s-9d in full of all accounts. Nick Plaw was witness to it, paid him in the Edgly Mead. My Cousin Hayne of Henfield din'd here.

The 12th October 1717 Saturday. A dry day. John Edwards ditcht. John Gun and Allexander Snatt made an end of water furroughing. Allexander Snatt workt for George West in the afternoon. John Gun made mortar. George West helpt fetch sand 'till noon, workt on his flax after. Ned May fetcht 3 small loads of sand. I measur'd Mrs Catherine Beard's new house that was built out of Cowdry's old one with Thomas Hamper. There was 15 squares at 2s per square and the partitions, doors and stairs were done by the day, which with cleaveing laths etc came to about £5 more, the paleing against the lane being included and the masons work came to nere £3. Thomas Hamper askt to finish my house and to work for me.

The 13th October 1717 Sunday. A fine day. Mr William Martin preacht. I was not at Church in the forenoon. Paid my Sister Ann Box 16s-6d for butter per Willy. I was at Westtowne after evning prayr with Mr John Hart. Receiv'd ¼lb of bohea from Mrs Tourl per John Bodle's man.

The 14th October 1717 Munday. A fine day. John Edwards ditcht 'till noon, mow'd clover after. John Gun made an end of the mortar. Dug up carrots etc. Allexander Snatt, George West, Ned May and Willy plough'd, stirring the fallow by Wickham's.

The 15th October 1717 Tuesday. A fine day. John Edwards and John Gun mow'd clover. Allexander Snatt and Willy plough'd by Wickham's. Paid Snatt 4s for all his work. Paid John Westover £2-8-4d in full of all accounts. Mrs Catherine Beard's teem and mine carry'd John Smith's dung into the field by Wickham's, loads. Molly Balcomb came here from Lewis per Nick Plaw. Ned Burt workt in the garden.

The 16th October 1717 Wednesday. A fine day. John Edwards helpt winnow oates, 2½ quarters 'till noon, mow'd clover after. John Gun helpt winnow, mow'd clover 'till 3 aclock then helpt carry. Allexander Snatt and George West cut the barly mows and helpt carry clover. Widdow Tully and Sarah Tully helpt about the clover afternoon. Carry'd a load out of the field by Hyder's and half a load out of Tully's field into the great barne. Ned Burt workt in the garden. Receiv'd and clear'd all accounts with Dick Wood. Paid him 16s-6d. Mrs Catherine Beard's teem workt for me to day, made an end of John Smith's dung, 20 loads and carry'd the dung to the wheat barne, 15. Receiv'd 10 nails 2lbs of cheese of Mrs Beard per Allan Savage and James Holden.

The 17th October 1717 Thursday. A dry day. John Gun, John Edwards and Willy win'd 1½ bushels head and 2 tail of John Edwards's Tully's wheat, the last of the field, in all 5 quarters 3 bushels. Paid Mrs Waterman 14s-3d for Molly Balcomb. Receiv'd £8 of John Smith jr. He kill'd the Cuckfield Fair cow to day at 16d per nail. John Edwards made an end of mowing clover after he had done winnowing and ditcht. John Gun did severall jobbs. George West, Allexander Snatt and Ned May carry'd 26 loads of dung and helpt carry half a load of Tully's clover into the wheat barne. Old William Brand and William Jarvice did a jobb in the apple garret. Ned Burt workt in the garden. Widdow Tully and Sarah Tully helpt an hour about the clover.

The 18th October 1717 Fryday. A very fine day. John Edwards ditcht. John Gun did severall jobbs and helpt about the clover. Ned May, Allexander Snatt and George West carry'd 29 loads of dung. Paid George West 6s and John Gun 5s. Paid T Ilman 30s for a year's intrest due at Michaelmas. Carry'd a load of clover, the last of it, in all 3 good loads. Ned Burt workt in the garden. Weigh'd the Cuckfield cow, 56 nail 3 lbs, the 4 quarters at 16d, 5 quarters as usual. Mr Richard Whitpaine and his wife Mary and Stephen Bine supt here. Brew'd a sack of straw dried malt for my Father Stone yesterday and 2 bushels for my self.

The 19th October 1717 Saturday. A very fine day. John Edwards ditch. John Gun did not work Allexander Snatt, George West, Ned May and Willy carry'd 32 loads of dung. Paid Allexander Snatt 4s in full. Mr John Hart and I went to Nunnery.

The 20th October 1717 Sunday. A fine day. Din'd at Nunnery and came home in the evning. My Cousin Bodle of Hailsham and his wife were here when we came home.

The 21st October 1717 Munday. A very fine day. John Edwards ditch'd in the dry pond. John Gun cutt hedges. George West, Allexander Snatt, Ned May and Willy carry'd 39 loads of dung. William Roach had a sack of malt. John Gun had half a bushel of malt. Paid a woman from Brighton 9s-4d for ½lb of bohea and the kanester. She said her name was Greenyer. My Cousin Bodle and his wife went home this morning. Paid my Mother 2 guineas. I was at Wanbarrow. I was to see Mr Todd towards night, he was very ill.

The 22nd October 1717 Tuesday. A fine day. John Edwards ditch in the dry pond. John Gun cutt hedges etc. Ned May, Allexander Snatt, George West and Willy carry'd the last of the dung, 37 loads, in all 198 loads into the field by Wickham's. I was at Westtowne in the afternoon. Supt there with Mr William Martin.

The 23rd October 1717 Wednesday. A gloomy day. John Edwards spread dung afternoon. George West and Ned May spread dung till noon. Flung straw out of the hop garden. Stephen Bine, John Shave to the granery in the morning. Allexander Snatt and Willy spread dung all day. Frank Cox begun make a dung cart with dwares and lades at 20d per day. Paid Sarah Surgeant 23s-6d being her half year's wages per my Wife.
Mr Richard Whitpaine came here towards night. Supt here. John Gun made syder. John Edwards had half a bushel of malt at 18d.

The 24th October 1717 Thursday. A very wet day after the morning. Cox workt the 2nd day. John Edwards and Allexander Snatt carry'd faggots. John Gun made syder.

Ned May and Willy plough'd a while in the morning. Afterwards they and George West unloaded and mov'd the clover in the wheat barne and begun screen wheat. Receiv'd 27s of Mr William Martin for keeping his mare. John Edwards had an other bushel of apples at 18d. Receiv'd 18d of Widdow Tully for a bushel of oates, clear'd account.

The 25th October 1717 Fryday. A dry forenoon, very wet after, Cox workt 3rd day. George West, Allexander Snatt, John Edwards, Ned May, Willy and *(Ed: xxx text deleted xxx)* Picknall plough'd and sow'd by Wickham's part of the day, pbb'd the rest. John Gun could not work haveing hurt his rist yesterday pressing syder. My Cousin Peter Marchant of Lewis din'd here. Borrow'd a horse of Mrs Catherine Beard to harrow. Mrs Todd was here in the afternoon.

The 26th October 1717 Saturday. A stormy day with some rain. Cox's 4th day. Allexander Snatt, Picknall, John Edwards, George West, Ned May, Willy plough'd, sow'd and spread dung by Wickham's. John Gun did not work. Reckon'd with John Gun, clear'd all accounts except the _ Paid J ohn Gun £1-5-6d and Snatt 5s-6d in full of all. Bett came home from Broadwater.

The 27th October 1717 Sunday. A dry day. Mr Jeremiah Dodson preacht. My Wife and I were a while with Mr John Hart after evning prayr and he came home and supt with us.

The 28th October 1717 Munday. A fine day. Cox workt the 5th day. Ned May and Willy, Allexander Snatt and Picknall, George West and John Edwards plough'd, sow'd and spread dung.
Receiv'd 2s-6d of A Burt for 2 sacks of pidgeon dung. John Gun harrow'd about 2 hours, thrasht oates the rest. Mrs Mary Whitpaine, Mrs Howard, Old John Box's wife and my Sister Betty were here in the afternoon. Mr Price, Mr John Hart and my Cousin William Wood spent the afternoon and supt here.

The 29th October 1717 Tuesday. A fine day. John Gun thrasht oates. Cox's 6th day. John Edwards spread dung etc till noon and ditcht after. Allexander Snatt, Picknall, Ned May, Willy and George West made an end of ploughing the field by Wickham's haveing sow'd on him 2½ bushels. Set up 4 hogs to fatting a Thursday last.

The 30th October 1717 Wednesday. A dry day. John Edwards ditch, John Gun thrasht. Allexander Snatt and Ned May fetcht a load for Stephen Bine from Old Land. Paid Allexander Snatt 3s in full of all. Paid Cox half a guinea, he finish'd the cart and dills the 7th day. I was at Dean House in the morning, bought 22 ewes of Samuel Hart at 9s-6d per ewe. Willy and Jack Haslegrove fetcht them home. George West and Willy made an end of harrowing by Wickham's. Mr Sixsmith and Mr Henry Johnson of Lingfield supt here.

The 31st October 1717 Thursday. A dry day. John Edwards ditch. Ned May and George West carry'd dung for Mrs Catherine Beard. Win'd 2 quarters 4 bushels head and 2 bushels tail of John Gun's oates. Mr Sixsmith lay over last night, went away this morning. Paid my Lord Treep £3-0-4d in full of all accounts. My Wife and I supt at Mrs Beard's with Mr Johnson and his wife and Mr John Hart. Mrs Beard was at Westtowne.

The 1st November 1717 Fryday. A dry forenoon, showry after. John Edwards ditch. Ned May and George West kept holy day. John Gun did not work. Old William Brand, Vallence and William Jarvice workt at Towne. Stephen Bine did half an hour's work there. I saw Mrs Catherine Beard's cow weigh'd at John Smith's, her four quarters weigh'd 68 nail 3 lbs. I went to Henfield and mett Mr Wade and agreed on a lease of eleven years for £15 per annum for my Cousin Hayne's house. John Haslegrove return'd from Nunnery.

The 2nd November 1717 Saturday. A dry day. John Edwards ditch. John Gun mow'd the grass plots etc. Ned May and Willy carry'd 4 bushels of oates to my Cousin Peter Marchant's and 12 to Mr Lane's. I was at Lewis, sold my wool to Thomas Friend at 20s per todd and 2s-6d over in all. Took up 4½ yards of cloath at 5s per yard with buttons etc for a great coat for Willy. Old William Brand, Vallence and William Jarvice workt at Towne. Stephen Bine and Standbridge workt there. George West workt at Towne in the afternoon. Paid Mr Court 24s for payr of coal grates and a poker for Mr Scutt.

The 3rd November 1717 Sunday. A gloomy day with some rain. Mr William Martin preacht. We had a parish meeting. Receiv'd the mony of Mr Scutt a Saturday for the grates etc.

The 4th November 1717 Munday. A wet day. John Gun helpt in the garden etc. Ned May fetcht home some wood in the morning. Stephen Bine, Standbridge and Gatland workt at Towne. George West begun on his flax. He is to give me 4s per week for his board while he works on it and to outset his wages.
I din'd at Westtowne with Thomas Barber and Nick Plaw. Ned Burt workt in the garden part of the day.

The 5th November 1717 Tuesday. A dry day. John Gun did not work. John Edwards ditch. Paid Mr Brigden of Brighton 6d for a Let Pass for two year's wool, being all I had by me, sold to Thomas Friend. I was at Stephen Bine's towards night. My Brother John Box and his wife and my Sister Betty supt here.

The 6th November 1717 Wednesday. A stormy day with rain. St Leonard's Fair. Thomas Vallence and William Jarvice workt at Towne. Stephen Bine workt part of the day, Robert Gatland all. John Edwards ditch. John Gun and Ned Burt workt in the garden. Deliver'd 2 quarters old barly to Harry Wickham per Ned May and Jack Haslegrove. Paid Michael Stacey 8s for 16 loads of sand. Willy went to the Fair, bought 2 payr of stockens for himself and a payr for Jacky, all for 2s-6d. Receiv'd 8 of William Balcomb's sacks from my Brother John Box and 2 of his own.

The 7th November 1717 Thursday. A stormy day, some rain. John Edwards ditch and hedg'd. John Gun and John Edwards made a piece of hedge against the Rookwood and afterwards John Gun helpt in the garden etc. Ned May and Willy carry'd 3 quarters and 1 bushel of oates to Lewis and the wool. Borrow'd a horse of Mr Richard Whitpaine. Receiv'd £2-5-4½d of Mr Lane for 4 quarters and a bushel of the oates and 11s of my Cousin Marchant for one quarter. Receiv'd £4-15s of Thomas Friend for 4 todd and 20lbs of wool. Paid £7 to Mrs Russell for half a year and 2 week's board for Molly Balcomb. Paid £3-2s to Mrs Atkinson for 8 weeks board and school for Betty. Paid for nails etc at Mr Court's, 13s for a horse whip 2s-8d. Paid for an iron back for Mr Scutt 4s-8d. Paid at Mr Fissenden's 2s and 2s at Norman's. Paid £1-13-6d for goods at Samuel Tourl's. Paid          Laurence 4s for making Willy's great coat. Paid a bill at Thomas Friend's 18s-9d for Molly Balcomb. Mrs Ann Dodson and her daughter went to Lewis with my Wife and I. Paid a small bill of my own

3s-2d at Thomas Friend's and 1s-6d for materials for Willy's great coat. My Unkle Courtness made a feast for his hop pole _____ . Paid my Cousin Peter Marchant 10s which he paid for quilting a red quilt and 1s for 2lbs of hair powder. Jack Haslegrove went to Nunnery in the morning.

The 8th November 1717 Fryday. A gloomy day, much rain last night. John Gun thrasht. John Edwards made an end of ditching in the dry pond. Ned May deliver'd 5½ bushels of old barly to Harry Wickham and fetcht half a load of sand from Michael Stacey's pitt. Sent home Mr Richard Whitpaine's horse and hop bag per Ned May. Borrow'd Nick Plaw's winshook yesterday. Paid George West 2s some days ago. Jack Haslegrove return'd from the Nunnery. John Edwards went to Thomas Fields to meet him, the water being very high.

The 9th November 1717 Saturday. A very wet forenoon, dry after. John Gun thrasht. Reckon'd with John Edwards, and outset his rent to Michaelmas last. Paid him 15s-3d. Win'd 6½ bushels of John Gun's wheat by Burt's, Ned May and Willy helpt. Receiv'd a fore quarter of poark of Mrs Catherine Beard. Weigh'd 11½ lbs. Paid 9s-5d for sugar for Mrs Beard when at Lewis.

The 10th November 1717 Sunday. A gloomy day. Mr Beaumont preacht, no service afternoon. My Wife and I were at Mrs Catherine Beard's afternoon. Sent the draught of Mr Wade's lease to my Cousin Hayne per John Stubbs.

The 11th November 1717 Munday. A gloomy day, some rain. John Edwards begun rake stubble at _____ .
John Gun begun thrash pease and ditch against Tully's Mead. Ned May fetcht 2 half loads of sand from Michael Stacey's pitt.
Bett, Jack Haslegrove and I went to Nunnery.
Paid Taylor the brickmaker £1-10-5d and clear'd all accounts.

The 12th November 1717 Tuesday. A very fine day. John Gun thrasht. John Edwards rakt stubble. Ned May did severall jobbs. My Cousin John Lindfield's teem mett my Father's at Hand Cross with 500 of paveing tiles, lime etc for me. I brought home Bett Ede behind me. Jack Haslegrove brought 4 large fish from Nunnery. Bett Ede and I din'd at Dean House.

The 13th November 1717 Wednesday. A fine day. John Edwards rakt stubble. John Gun thrasht etc. Ned May fetcht half a load of great chalk for Mrs Catherine Beard and as much small chalk to Nick Plaw's with my three horses and Mrs Beard's. My Cousin John Lindfield's teem brought the aforesaid load home. He din'd here, his wife and daughter came towards night. I gave his man 1s and his boy 8d. Mr Picknall of Arundell came in the evning, staid all night.

The 14th November 1717 Thursday. A fine day. John Gun thrasht and ditch. John Edwards rakt stubble. Ned May and Mrs Catherine Beard's man carry'd chalk as yesterday. Thomas Vallence, an other man, John Sanders and William Jarvice workt. My Wife and I supt at Mr Scutt's with Mr Price and his wife. Receiv'd 4s-8d of Mrs Scutt, which I paid for an iron back.

The 15th November 1717 Fryday. A fine day. John Gun and John Edwards as yesterday. The masons workt at Towne as yesterday. Ned May fetcht 2 half loads of sand from Michael Stacey's pitt. Jack Haslegrove went to Nunnery yesterday, return'd to day. Mr John Hart and I supt at Westtowne. I had a lott of bief of John Smith at the same price as if I had a half quarter. He kill'd my last runt.

The 16th November 1717 Saturday. A gloomy day. John Gun and John Edwards as yesterday. Vallence, Thomas Collingham, John Sanders and William Jarvice workt afternoon. Paid Allexander Snatt 1s for this day's work at Towne. Lent him 2s [more]. Willy and Ned May carry'd 6 cart loads of stubble out of the field by Burt's into the fatting close, 2 cart loads being a good waggon load. Mrs Catherine Beard had a load of flints at 2s about ¾ of them were of Abraham Muzzall's girl's picking in Rookfield. If I had carry'd them my self I allways have 3s-6d. Paid Dick Wood 22 bushels of mortar, borrow'd some time ago, but I owe him 200 bricks.

The 17th November 1717 Sunday. A wet day.
Mr Beaumont preacht. No service afternoon. I were not at Church.

The 18th November 1717 Munday. A showry day. Win'd 9 bushels of head and half a bushel tail of John Gun's pease. John Edwards rakt stubble. Ned May and Willy shutt up the fatting oxen, carry'd a cart load of stubble, helpt winnow and put the 2 old oxen into Tully's Mead. I were at Mr Jeremiah Dodson's in the evning with Mr John Hart. Supt at Mr Scutt's with Mr Price. Vallence and William Jarvice workt at Towne.

*(Ed: xxx text deleted xxx)*

The 19th November 1717 Tuesday. A dry forenoon, wet after. John Gun thrasht oates. John Edwards begun thrash of the Rookwood wheat, part of the day. Carry'd 33 faggots to the school per Willy and Ned May. Afterwards they brought home some faggots etc. Mr Sixsmith was here, he din'd at Mr Jeremiah Dodson's and I went to him afternoon. Mr Peter Courthope and Mrs Susan Courthope were there. Allexander Snatt workt at Towne. Old William Brand had a parcell of land a small piece of timber.

The 20th November 1717 Wednesday. A dry day. John Edwards thrasht wheat, John Gun oates. Vallence and William Jarvice workt at Towne yesterday and Munday but not to day. Allexander Snatt workt there to day. Old William Brand workt half the day a Tuesday putting in the celler windows. Paid John Towner and Ja Reed 10s for sawing. Ned May and Willy did severall jobbs. Thomas Baker and I put the pitching of the Ally between our houses to Old William Brand at 5s. Thomas Baker is to pay the workmanship and I to find the materials. The Pickstones of Rigate supt and lay here. John Stone came with them. They bought 3 oxen of him at £29 to be gone before Christmas.

The 21st November 1717 Thursday. A fine day. Mr Jeremiah Dodson's tythe feast. Sold my 4 fatting oxen to the Pickstones at £47 to be gone before Christmas. I order'd them to pay £50 to Mr Roberds by the 20th of December next. John Edwards thrasht wheat and rakt stubble. John Gun thrasht. Paid Allexander Snatt 1s for this day's work at Towne. Vallence and William Jarvice workt at Towne. I gave the masons and carpenters 2 bushels of malt yesterday. My Cousin John Marchant of Lox gave me a fat pig some days ago.

The 22nd November 1717 Fryday. A very wet to day. Win'd 3 quarters 3 bushels of John Gun's oates. John Edwards thrasht. Vallence and Sam Jarvice workt at Towne 'till noon. Receiv'd £15 of John Smith jr. Ned May, Willy and Jack helpt winnow. John Gun and they did a jobb afternoon at Tully's. John Gun din'd here. Paid Samuel Hart £9-9s and outset 20s being £10-9s in full for all 22 ewes.

The 23rd November 1717 Saturday. A dry forenoon, very wet after. John Gun thrasht pease. John Edwards ditcht and rakt stubble. Ned May and Willy did some jobbs and thrasht pease. My Wife was at Wanbarrow towards night. I went to Lewis, Jack Haslegrove with me. Paid Mrs Gratwick £5 in full for all the intrest due to her to the beginning of August last. Paid Mr Court £3-1-11d in full of all accounts. Paid him also 2s-2d for a large payr of cross [g.........], 1s for 2 door latches, 6d for 2 large gimblets, 3s-4d for 2 papers of lath nails and 9d for a knife. Paid Mr Baldy £15 for Mr Richard Whitpaine which I receiv'd of him in the morning. Robert Gatland workt on the school stairs, so did Standbridge and he yesterday. Paid Weller the chandler 20d for a gross of corks, 16d for a quart of linse seed oyl and 1s for a pint of oyl of turpentine. Paid Stephen Avery the sadler 2s-2d in full of all. Paid Samuel Tourl 4s-3d for ¼lb of bohea. We staid all night, the weather very bad. Expences 4s.

The 24th November 1717 Sunday. A stormy day, rain after. Mr Jeremiah Dodson preacht. I return'd from Lewis, was at Church afternoon. My Wife and I were at Mrs Catherine Beard's after evning prayr.

The 25th November 1717 Munday. A stormy day but little rain. John Edwards ditcht and rakt stubble. John Gun thrasht pease, so did Ned May and Willy etc. John Gun had a bushel of malt. Vallence and Samuel Jarvice workt at Towne and an other man of Old William Brand's workt there part of the afternoon. Mr Scutt and his wife and Mr John Hart supt here. Stephen Bine workt here. Jo Wood workt part of the day on the school stairs.

The 26th November 1717 Tuesday. A dry, gloomy day. John Edwards ditcht. John Gun thrasht pease. Ned May and Willy fetcht 2 small loads of sand home from Michael Stacey's pitt. Thomas Vallence workt at Towne to finish the school stairs. John Pierce workt here. Mrs Ann Dodson and her daughter were here in the afternoon. Nunnery boy came in the evning, brought a ribspare.

The 27th November 1717 Wednesday. A fine day. Ned May thrasht etc. John Edwards ditcht. John Gun thrasht. Willy went to coursing. Vallence workt at Towne cutting stone. Dick          workt there part of the day makeing course stuff for the kitchen ceeling. Samuel Jarvice helpt him. I went to Nunnery in the afternoon.

The 28th November 1717 Thursday. A dry day, frosty. John Gun thrasht, John Edwards ditcht. Two of Old William Brand's men laid the gutter in the back court. I suppose the boys helpt. Willy and Ned May fetcht clay etc for the masons and carry'd one cart load of stubble. My Brother James Ede came to the Nunnery afternoon. Thomas Field had 1700 store fish at Nunnery from 3 to 4 inches long at 3s per 100. I return'd from Nunnery in the evning. John Gurney came.

The 29th November 1717 Fryday. A very wet day. Win'd 3 quarters 3 bushels head and 2 bushels tail of John Gun's pease. Widdow Tully, Ned May and Willy helpt. John Gurney begun work here at 18d per day and his board. John Edwards thrasht wheat. Roach mended shop windows. My Brother Peter had 500 of my bricks for which he is to lend me his 3 horses a journey and to pay what the bricks cost me. My Father Stone lent me all his hitcholls yesterday.

The 30th November 1717 Saturday. A dry day. A Fair at Bolny and East Grinstead. John Gun did not work. John Edwards ditcht. Ned May kept holy day. John Gurney workt. Old William Brand's men struck the kitchen ceeling at Towne. I breakfasted with Mr John Hart. Din'd there also. Paid Old William Brand 10s per my Wife. Put the cows into the Cowfield. Lent my Cousin Thomas Norton 6 sacks per William Norton.

The 1st December 1717 Sunday. A gloomy day. Mr Jeremiah Dodson preacht. We had a parish meeting in the afternoon.

The 2nd December 1717 Munday. A gloomy day. John Gun stript poles. John Edwards thrasht wheat. Ned May did severall jobbs. Willy thrasht pease. John Gurney and Vallence, Thomas Collingham and Samuel Jarvice workt on the back court. Old William Brand lookt on. John Pierce workt here. Reckon'd and clear'd all accounts with John Norton, his bill of meat was 16s-3¾d. Receiv'd of him £4-2-8d. John Snashall was here twice to see John Haslegrove, he gave him phisick. Widdow Tully tended him.

The 3rd December 1717 Tuesday. A dry morning, very wet after. John Gun thrasht oates. John Pierce workt. John Gurney workt in the Towne celler. Win'd 8 bushels head and 1 tail of John Edwards's Rookwood wheat. Paid Isaac Muzzall 4s-2d for a payr of shoes for Willy. Old William Brand's 2 men and 1 boy workt in the back court. Mr Scutt went to Chichester this morning. I desir'd him to speak to Richard Heath's landlord for me to have his farme when he has left it. John Snashall was back to see Jack Haslegrove. My Wife supt and spent the evning at Mrs Catherine Beard's.

The 4th December 1717 Wednesday. A dry day. John Edwards thrasht pease by the day. John Gurney workt at Towne. John Gun thrasht oates. Ned May and Willy did severall jobbs. Put six 3 yearlings to keeping to John Snashall at 10d per week. Mr Jeremiah Dodson spent the afternoon and evning here. Mr John Hart supt here. John Pierce workt here. Vallence, Thomas Collingham, William and Samuel Jarvice workt in the back court 'till noon. Vallence workt sand stone after. Old William Brand helpt about the court.

The 5th December 1717 Thursday. A showry day. John Edwards ditcht. John Gun thrasht. John Pierce workt. John Gurney workt in the Towne celler. Willy went to Nunnery and came home again. Paid John Pierce 4s-8d in tow, being for all his work to the evning. Ned May did severall jobbs. John Edwards had half a bushel of malt. Paid Mr Jeremiah Dodson 2s last night for half a year's tythe of the Towne House.

The 6th December 1717 Fryday. A fine day. John Edwards thrasht wheat, John Gun oates. Ned May did severall jobbs. John Gurney workt. Paid my Brother Henry Faulkoner £4-10s for a year's intrest due about the beginning of August last per Willy. Receiv'd the sacks again of my Cousin Thomas Norton.

The 7th December 1717 Saturday. A dry, cold day. John Edwards thrasht pease by the day. Vallence and Samuel Jarvice workt on the Towne kitchen. John Gun thrasht. Ned May and Willy carry'd 3 cart loads of the stubble by Burt's. My Wife and I spent the evning at Mrs Catherine Beard's. John Gurney workt at Towne and paid T Cox

10d in full of all, he clouted the waggon wheel to day.

The 8th December 1717 Sunday. A fine day, a smart frost last night. Mr Jeremiah Dodson preacht. I was not at Church in the forenoon. My Wife and I were at Mr Richard Whitpaine's after evning prayr. Old William Brand laid poyson for rats this evning.

The 9th December 1717 Munday. A gloomy day. John Edwards thrasht pease by the day. John Gun mended gaps in Tully's lower field and cut bushes. Ned May did severall jobbs. Put 2 runts into the field by Hyder's and 3 into Tully's teary field. Willy, and Will Norton went to Nunnery with Bett Ede. John Gurney workt half the day at Towne, the rest at home. Jack Haslegrove went to John Snashall's this morning.

The 10th December 1717 Tuesday. A fine day. Willy and Will Norton return'd from Nunnery with Bett. John Edwards thrasht pease 'till noon, win'd after. John Gurney workt, Jack Picknall helpt, win'd 3 quarters 4 bushels of pease. John Gun cut bushes in Tully's lower oat earsh. Ned May and Bignall went with 7 horses, met my Father Stone's teem at Warninglid. We carry'd 6 bushels of pease to be sold at Nunnery, 3 bushels to be sent to John Gurney's and 4 bushels of malt for my Father. We brought home timber, aspen board and timber, a copper still and worme tubbe, straw tubbs 2 an iron back etc. We had 3 horses of my Brother Peter's and 8 of Mrs Catherine Beard's and 2 of my own. My Sister Ann Box here towards night.

The 11th December 1717 Wednesday. A gloomy, dry day. John Edwards begun thrash barly. John Gun thrasht oates. John Gurney workt at Towne. Ned May and Willy carry'd 2 cart load of stubble, the last of the field. John Snashall was here twice to see the bay horse, being sick.

The 12th December 1717 Thursday. A dry day. John Edwards thrasht barly, John Gun oates. Ned May and Willy did severall jobbs. John Gurney workt. Paid William Roach 40s towards his bill and he had a sack of malt some time ago which is set down. Frank Marshall was here ~~with~~ to see the bay horse and gave him a drink. Paid him 2s for it. John Snashall was here also. The carpenters and masons drank out their beer that I gave them. Paid John Edwards 10s. Mrs Catherine Beard and her family supt and spent the evning here. One lamb of the great sheep.

The 13th December 1717 Fryday. A dry day. John Edwards thrasht barly, John Gun oates. Ned May and Willy did severall jobbs. John Gurney workt. My Cousin John Lindfield supt and spent the evning here.

The 14th December 1717 Saturday. A fine day. John Edwards thrasht barly, John Gun oates etc. John Gurney workt 'till noon, went home afterwards. Paid Gurney 15s and outset 6s for a bushel of pease, left 9 quarters and one bushel of pease not reckon'd for, which he is to sell for me as well as he can. Ned May and Willy pickt wheat etc. One lamb of the great sheep yesterday and an other to day. I was at Westtowne in the evning there was Mr Scutt, Mr John Hart. John Gurney went home to day. Paid Old William Brand's wife 18s for Old Ede the thatcher.

The 15th December 1717 Sunday. A dry day. Mr Jeremiah Dodson preacht. My Wife and I spent the evning and supt at Mr Dodson. Willy went to Balcombe with my Brother John Box.

The 16th December 1717 Munday. A stormy day, some rain. John Edwards thrasht barly. Ned May did severall jobbs. John Gun thrasht oates. The Gooders were here, I gave them breaking pease. Mrs Catherine Beard gave me a pig. One lamb of the great sheep. I wrote to the Pickstones by the post. Lent Mr Jeremiah Dodson 6 sacks per Nicholas. Stephen Bine was here in the evning. Receiv'd £5 of John Smith jr a Saturday last.

The 17th December 1717 Tuesday. A fine day. John Edwards thrasht barly, John Gun oates. Ben Shave went to Lewis. Ned May and Picknall did severall jobbs. Put 5 young tench into the middle pond which we took out of the Churchfield pond, 8 inches. Willy return'd from Balcombe, brought home a hare.

The 18th December 1717 Wednesday. A fine day. John Edwards thrasht barly. Win'd 6 quarters head of John Gun's oates. Widdow Tully helpt, had a _____ . Paid Mr Picknall of Arundell £3-5s in full of all. 2 lambs of the great sheep ---- 6. Paid Richard Patching 1s for bleeding me. Ned May sick. Willy and Picknall helpt winnow. Paid John Gatland 1s for cleaning the clock. Paid for a payr of shooes for Molly Balcomb 3s-6d. Paid for a payr of stockens for her 1s-6d, to her for pocket money 1s.

The 19th December 1717 Thursday. A fine day. John Edwards thrasht barly, John Gun oates. Brought up the six three yearlings out of the lower ground and put 'em in the Fifteen Acres. George West begun serve the 10 oxen this evning. One lamb of the great sheep -------- 7. Willy and Picknall did severall jobbs. Mrs Ann Dodson and Mrs Courthope were here in the afternoon. Mrs Ann Dodson gave me a pint of strong wine for the pain in my stomach, which has been very much ever since Munday. R Deerling came this evning for Jacky Ede. I wrote to Mr Ede by the post about Pickstone's mony. Receiv'd my sacks again of Mr Jeremiah Dodson.

The 20th December 1717 Fryday. A very fine day. John Gun, Ned May, Willy and Picknall dug and set pease etc. John Edwards thrasht barly. Lent Old William Brand 5 ridge tiles per William Jarvice.
2 lambs of the great sheep ----- 9.
J Pickstone sent for my 4 fatting oxen per Hall's son. Jacky Ede went for Nunnery with R Deerling. Ben Shave went to Lewis for a bottle of claret.

The 21st December 1717 Saturday. A gloomy day. John Gun, Ned May, Willy dug and set beans here and at Towne. John Edwards thrasht barly. George West and Picknall begun plough in the field by Burt's at 1s per acre for George West. 2 lambs of the great sheep ---- 11. I wrote to Mr Cope for Mr John Hart per post. Receiv'd a letter from Mr Ede. Receiv'd a ridion hour letter from Brighton per post. She said she had it of her that was Anne Johnson. My Wife was at Richard Burtenshaw's and bought 17 nail of cheese at 6s.

The 22nd December 1717 Sunday. A dry day.
Mr Jeremiah Dodson preacht. One lamb of the great sheep ---- 12. Mr Scutt and his wife, Mr Richard Whitpaine and his wife Mary, Thomas Norton of Edgly, Mr John Hart, Mrs Courthope were to see me in the evning.

The 23rd December 1717 Munday. A gloomy day. George West and Picknall, Ned May and Willy begun plough in the Bankfield. Paid Richard Burtenshaw's wife £1-2-8d for 17 nail of cheese per Ned May. John Gun thrasht oates, John Edwards barly.
4 lambs of the great sheep ------ 16.
Mr Jeremiah Dodson and my Cousin John Lindfield, Mrs Catherine Beard and her family were to see me. Nick Plaw was here in the morning.

The 24th December 1717 Tuesday. A gloomy day. Some rain in the morning. Ned May and Willy plough'd with the horses 'till noon. Did severall jobbs after. John Edwards thrasht barly, John Gun oates.
One lamb of the great sheep --------- 17.
Receiv'd 7s-6d of Mr Osbourne for 75 store tench which I sent per Jack Picknall.

Xmas. The 25th December 1717 Wednesday. A stormy day. Mr Jeremiah Dodson preacht. John Gun and his mother, John Edwards and his wife din'd here. Paid George West 2s.

The 26th December 1717 Thursday. A very wet day. Counsellor Burrell died. Mr Scutt and his wife, Mr John Hart, Mrs Catherine Beard and her family, my Brother Peter and Sister Bett were here to see me. Receiv'd a letter from Mr Roberds. Mr Richard Whitpaine here in the morning.

The 27th December 1717 Fryday. A fine day. Nick Marchant din'd here. Reckon'd and clear'd all accounts with him. Reckon'd with John Gun and left 20s to pay. Paid him £1-4-8d. Paid Richard Wood £1-7-6d in full of all accounts. Paid Molly Balcomb 1s for pocket money.

The 28th December 1717 Saturday. A dry day. John Edwards thrasht barly, John Gun oates. Mr Richard Whitpaine and Mr John Hart, Mrs Catherine Beard and her family were here in the evning, the latter supt here.
One lamb of the little sheep ---- 1.
Paid J Wood of Cuckfield 2s for a year's Lord's rent for the Towne House per Dick Wood. Joseph Muzzall was here for the Lord's rent for Edgly at the same time, but I did not pay him.

The 29th December 1717 Sunday. A stormy day. After a very stormy night. Mr Jeremiah Dodson preacht. Thomas Jacket and Eliz Cheal din'd here. Mrs Ann Dodson here in the evning.
An other lamb of the little sheep ------ 2.

The 30th December 1717 Munday. A dry day. John Edwards thrasht barly. John Gun oates. Ned May drew some grit into the orchard and rubbish wood etc. Willy put an other runt into the field by Hyder's. Picknall went to mill with a hog grist.

The 31st December 1717 Tuesday. A fine day. A smart frost last night. Dick Mall kill'd 2 hogs for me, one for pork, the other for bakon. Shutt up the two least hogs. John Gun thrasht oates, John Edwards barly. Paid Kingston miller 21d for 14lbs of fine flower.

The 1st January 1717 Wednesday. A fine day. A smart frost last night. Bartlet and his wife, the Widdow Tully and the Widdow Gun din'd here. One lamb of the little sheep ---- 3. Paid Molly Balcomb 6d for pocket mony and for a payr of buttons for her shoes 3d. John Snashall was here in the morning. Richard Herriot here, he offer'd to take some of the Homefield for flax.

The 2nd January 1717 Thursday. A dry day, frosty. John Edwards thrasht. John Gun begun the ditch between Tully's Mead and clover and workt in the garden in the afternoon. Ned May and Willy and Picknall fetcht up the wheat out of Tully's barne. My Wife and I supt at Mrs Catherine Beard's. I wrote to John Gurney per post.

The 3rd January 1717 Fryday. A fine day. John Edwards thrasht and mov'd his heap. John Gun and Ned May fetcht 3 small loads of bushes out of Tully's ground. John Snashall was here to see the grey colt.
One lamb of the great sheep ---- 18. One of the little sheep had 2 lambs ---- 5. My Wife supt at Mrs Catherine Beard's with Danny family.

The 4th January 1717 Saturday. A windy very cold day, frosty. John Gun and John Edwards thrasht. Receiv'd a letter with the bill of return of £50 from Mr Roberds which the Pickstones paid. Ned May and ~~Pickstone~~ Picknall drew home rubbish wood and some Towne dirt into the little orchard. I supt at Mr Jeremiah Dodson's with Mr Richard Whitpaine and Mr John Hart. We settled the account about wood and rent for the school to Christmas last. Paid Mr Hart 25s for a quarter's schooling to day at Christmas last.

The 5th January 1717 Sunday. A dry cold day, frosty. Mr Jeremiah Dodson preacht. I was at Church afternoon. Supt at Mr Scutt's. R Deerling came for Jacky Ede's cloaths.

The 6th January 1717 Munday. A fine day. A lamb of the little sheep --------- 6. My Wife and I and Bett din'd at Mr Jeremiah Dodson's with Captain Whitpaine and Westtowne family and Mr John Hart. Mrs Scutt and _____ Mr Hugh Orlton and Mr Henry Goffe supt there with us. Mr Scutt came after.

The 7th January 1717 Tuesday. A fine day, frosty. 2 lambs of the little sheep ------ 8. Lost one of the twin lambs to day. Nick Plaw was here in the morning. Paid Joseph Muzzall 18s-4d for a years Lord's rent. Ned May carry'd dung in Tully's Mead 10 loads. Paid my Lord Treep 1s in full of all.

The 8th January 1717 Wednesday. A very fine day, thawing, rain in the morning. Paid William Roach 34s-6d in full of all accounts. John Gun thrasht the wheat shatter'd in the floor. John Edwards thrasht barly. Ned May, lame, could not work. Receiv'd a message from John Gurney per Rookwood by which I was ne'er the wiser. Sent my bill of return for £50 on Mr Cockle to Mrs Susan Courthope per John Gun. John Gun had a bushel of malt at 2s-6d.
One lamb of the little sheep ------- 9. My Wife and I supt at Mrs Catherine Beard's with Mr Scutt and his wife, Mr Richard Whitpaine and his wife Mary and Mr John Hart.

The 9th January 1717 Thursday. A fine day, thawing. John Edwards thrasht, win'd 2½ bushels of the Rookwood wheat and as much of that by Burt's, both thrasht by the day per John Gun and John Edwards. Ned May, Willy and Picknall helpt. Paid John Edwards 2 guineas. One lamb of the little sheep -------- 10. Paid my Mother 4 guineas. My Wife, Jacky and I were at Wanbarrow afternoon. Put the Speed ox and the spaid heifer into the Fifteen Acres. One lamb of the great sheep ------- 19.

The 10th January 1717 Fryday. A gloomy day. John Gun and John Edwards thrasht. Jack Haslegrove return'd from John Snashall's. Standbridge and Robert Gatland workt mending the wheat barn's floor. Receiv'd the £50 which Mrs Courthope brought from Lewis per Ralph Beard. Paid Mrs Catherine Beard the 9 guineas which my Wife borrow'd of her. Paid William Dumsday 8s for a payr of stays for Molly Balcomb. Ned May and Willy and Picknall did severall jobbs. Picknall went home to his father's. One lamb of the little sheep ------- 11.

The 11th January 1717 Saturday. A gloomy day. John Gun and John Edwards thrasht. Willy, and Ned May pug'd clover. Took Speed and the heifer into the close again. John Snashall was here and drest the grey colt. John Standbridge work'd 'till noon on the floor, crib etc. One lamb of the little sheep -------- 12.

Molly Balcomb return'd from Henfield and Albourne. I supt and spent the evning at Westtowne.

The 12th January 1717 Sunday. A dry day. Mr Jeremiah Dodson preacht. I was at Church in the afternoon. My Sister Bett din'd here. A lamb of the little sheep ---- 14.

The 13th January 1717 Munday. A gloomy day. John Edwards thrasht. John Gun workt in the Towne Orchard digging etc. Willy too. Took 3 carp and 1 tench out of the Marldfield stew. Took one carp out of the flat stew. John Snashall drest the colt again. John Edwards had half a bushel of malt. Ned May pug'd clover. John Pierce workt here, made Willy's spatterdashes.

The 14th January 1717 Tuesday. A gloomy day. Some rain. John Edwards thrasht. John Gun mow'd apple trees etc. Ned May and Willy pug'd clover. My Grandmother and Mrs Catherine Beard, Mrs Ann Dodson and her daughter and Mr John Hart supt here.

The 15th January 1717 Wednesday. A fine day. John Edwards thrasht. John Gun mow'd trees etc. John Snashall drest the grey colt. Ned May and Willy pug'd clover. Reckon'd and clear'd all accounts with my Cousin John Lindfield, receiv'd £1-1s of him. I ow him for a pound or 2 of lime.

The 16th January 1717 Thursday. A fine day. John Edwards thrasht. John Gun mow'd trees etc. Ned May and Willy carry'd grit into the orchards and fetcht the wood out of the Towne Orchard. My Wife, Willy and I supt at Westtowne with Mr Scutt and Mr John Hart. Paid Tom King 2s in full of all.

The 17th January 1717 Fryday. A smart snow. John Edwards and John Gun thrasht. Willy and Ned May pug'd clover. Paid John Stone £8-10s for half a year of the 3s Land Tax due at Michaelmas last. He told me from the Pickstones that I should pay my Brother Peter the £3 due to them.

The 18th January 1717 Saturday. A gloomy day, a frost. John Gun and John Edwards thrasht. Ned May and Willy pug'd clover. I wrote to Mr Ede by the post. I was at Mrs Catherine Beard's in the afternoon to set out the grates of her stew. John Snashall was here in the evning to see my Wife.

The 19th January 1717 Sunday. A dry day, frosty. Mr Jeremiah Dodson preacht I was not at Church. Mrs Catherine Beard here afternoon. One lamb of the little sheep ------- 15.

The 20th January 1717 Munday. A dry day, frosty. John Edwards and John Gun thrasht. George West and Ned May pug'd clover and fetcht home sheeprack. Receiv'd 9d of Mr John Hart for ℔ of roll tobacco. He supt here. Stephen Bine put up a new mantle piece in the hall. George West made an end of his flax on Saturday and begun work for me again today.

The 21st January 1717 Tuesday. A very fine day. John Edwards and John Gun thrasht. George West and Ned May made an end of pugging clover in the wheat barne, clean'd out the granery etc. Paid Frank Holden 15d for ½ell of canvas to make me an apron. Receiv'd 8d of William Shepard for 9℔ of okum tow at 8s per ____ . Reckon'd with John Bodle for 8 ewes of William Balcomb's at 20d per ewe £1-3s-4d, and 15 lambs at 4s-6d per lamb, £3-16-6d, in all £4. Reckon'd with John Bodle for 8 ewes of William Balcomb's at 20d per ewe 13s-4d, and 15 lambs at 4s-6d per lamb £3-7s-6d, for all £4-0s-10d. The bargain was 14 ewes and 17 lambs at £5 but 6 of the sheep and 2 of the lambs were stol'n. Receiv'd the £4-0s-10d of John Bodle. Paid 6d for beer. Nick Plaw was there at the Swan.

The 22nd January 1717 Wednesday. A very fine day. John Gun thrasht pease, John Edwards barly. Willy, George West and Ned May win'd clover pug and carry'd it into the granery. John Snashall was here in the evning to see the colt. Paid my Unkle Courtness 6d½ for ingredients for a drink bott.

The 23rd January 1717 Thursday. A gloomy day with some rain. John Edwards thrasht. John Gun begun a ditch against the lower side of Tully's Mead. George West begun thrash of the Rookwood wheat. Ned May did severall jobbs. Old John Box and I were at Mr Scutt's in the morning. My Wife and I supt at Mrs Catherine Beard's, Mr Jeremiah Dodson also.

The 24th January 1717 Fryday. A gloomy day, some rain. John Gun ditcht. Win'd 2 bushels of Edward's barly and _____ . A mountebank came to our Towne today, calls himself Dr Richard Harness.

Mr Scutt and I drank with the tumbler, he play'd very well on the fiddle. I were at R Kester's afterwards with Mr Richard Whitpaine, Mr Burry and Thomas Norton of Edgly about putting out parish children.
One lamb of the little sheep ----- 16.
Turn'd the 2 great hogs into the little sty top_____ .

The 25th January 1717 Saturday. A dry day, frost last night. John Gun ditcht, John Edwards thrasht and heav'd some more of his barly. The grey colt would not rise so we knockt him at head in the morning. Sold the skin to Thomas Baker for 2s and clear'd accounts. Ned May and Willy did severall jobbs. Dick Wood mov'd the little horse's 4 shoes.

The 26th January 1717 Sunday. A fine day, frosty. Mr Jeremiah Dodson preacht and went to Newtimber in the afternoon. Mrs Catherine Beard, her mother and Mrs Courthope here afternoon.

The 27th January 1717 Munday. A fine day. John Gun ditcht. Banks and George West ditch in the old hop garden afternoon. George West thrasht etc and Banks mended gaps in the forenoon. Ned May and Willy carry'd dung at Tully's, 10 loads. Jack Picknall came to go to plough but the frost was too hard. Paid my Cousin Peter Marchant of Lewis 20d for the wine he bought. Nick Plaw and he din'd here. Nick Plaw cut my lambs.

The 28th January 1717 Tuesday. A gloomy day, some snow. John Edwards thrasht. George West and Banks ditch'd. John Gun, Ned May and Willy carry'd dung at Tully's, 26 loads, the last of the mixen, in all 46 loads, laid on the mead. William Jarvice return'd from Nunnery whither he went yesterday, he brought a new piece of linnen cloath which my Wife sent for them to get woven. Paid my Unkle Courtness 6d for half a gallon of nutts and 10d for a bunch of very mean clock line.
My Wife in the evning paid a small bill there.

The 29th January 1717 Wednesday. A dry, cold day, frosty. John Gun ditcht. George West and Banks made an end of the hop garden ditch. Ned May and Willy cleft logs. John Edwards thrasht wheat in the afternoon by the day. Borrow'd a saw of Stephen Bine and a hedge and wedges of Standbridge. Sent home Mrs Catherine Beard's shovel per Jack Haslegrove. Mr John Hart din'd here.

The 30th January 1717 Thursday. A snowy morning, thaw towards night. John Gun ditch'd. George West and John Edwards pugg'd clover in the afternoon. Ned May drew logs etc together in the afternoon. Ned May, Willy and I kill'd the boar hog afternoon. My Wife, Willy and I were at Church in the forenoon. I wrote to my Father per post. Paid my Brother Peter £3 per John Pickstone's order. 2 lambs of one of the little sheep -------- 18.

The 31st January 1717 Fryday. A gloomy day, some rain. George West and John Edwards pug'd clover. Ned May carry'd dung for Stephen Bine with one court. John Gun ditcht. Banks thrasht wheat by the day. The mountebank at Towne. John Edwards had half a bushel of breaking pease, 21d a gallon before. Mr Jeremiah Dodson, Mr Ralph Beard and Nick Plaw supt here.

The 1st February 1717 Saturday. A fine day.
Banks thrasht wheat. John Gun ditcht. John Edwards pug'd clover. Ned May carry'd dung for Stephen Bine. George West mended gaps in the forenoon and afterwards he, Willy and I built a stall for the new cow. Markt 10 sheep and 10 lambs of the right ear and 9 of the left, all of the great sheep. Paid Richard White £3-13s-6d for a young milch cow, he brought her home in the afternoon. Banks had half a bushel of breaking pease at 21d.

The 2nd February 1717 Sunday. A fine day.
Mr Jeremiah Dodson preacht. My Wife and I receiv'd the sacrament. I supt at Mr Scutt's with Mr Richard Whitpaine. We had a parish meeting at Church.

The 3rd February 1717 Munday. A very fine day.
Mr Luxford of Ockly buried at Kymer. I was at the funeral. George West and Picknall plough'd with the oxen by Burt's. Ned May and Willy plough'd with the horses in the Bankfield. Banks and I markt 10 little sheep and lambs of both ears. Banks turn'd them into the lower ground, mended the hedge cross the lane etc. John Edwards made an end of pugging clover in the great barne. Stephen Bine and Robert Gatland workt on the granery. John Pierce workt here. Stephen Bine workt but half the day.

The 4th February 1717 Tuesday. A fine day, a frost last night. John Gun ditch. John Edwards thrasht barly. Banks thrasht wheat. 2 lambs of the little sheep ----- 20. Ned May and Willy plough'd, so did Picknall and George

West. Stephen Bine and Robert Gatland workt on the granery. John Gun had half a bushel of oates per Willy.

The 5th February 1717 Wednesday. A fine day. John Edwards thrasht barly. John Gun workt for him self. Ned Burt tackt the vines. George West, Picknall, Ned May and Willy plough'd. Stephen Bine and Robert Gatland workt on the granery. Banks thrasht wheat. Stephen Bine workt but half the day. Mr John Hart and supt *(Ed: sic)* and spent the evning at Westtowne. Nick Plaw came to us, we staid late, and drank too much.

The 6th February 1717 Thursday. A very fine day. John Gun set quick sets in Towne garden. Banks and Willy, George West and Picknall plough'd. Ned May was lame and could not plough, did small jobbs. John Edwards thrasht barly.
2 lambs of the little sheep ------------- 22.
Stephen Bine and Robert Gatland workt on the granery. Jack Haslegrove went to Nunnery yesterday, return'd to day. Nick Plaw was here in the evning about William Balcomb's accounts.

The 7th February 1717 Fryday. A gloomy day, the wind very high. John Edwards thrasht. John Gun sow'd pease in the Bankfield. Banks harrow'd with the ox harrow, Ned May with 2 horses, one of them Old William Brand's mare. George West and Picknall plough'd in the Bankfield. Standbridge and Robert Gatland cut down a spire tree and a pollard in the shaw by Hyder's and 2 or 3 ashes in the orchard. The mountebank at Towne. I spent 4d with my Cousin John Lindfield etc. My Wife and I supt at Mrs Catherine Beard's with Mr Richard Whitpaine.

The 8th February 1717 Saturday. A gloomy day, the wind very high. John Edwards thrasht. Ned May, Banks, Willy, Picknall and George West plough'd. John Gun ditch. Turn'd 2 steers into the close, 2 cows into the Fifteen Acres. Dick Wood set an old shoe at 4d on the bay horse's near foot, before mov'd the other.

The 9th February 1717 Sunday. A very wet day and high wind. Mr Jeremiah Dodson preacht. I was not at Church in the forenoon. I was at Stephen Bine's after evning prayr.

The 10th February 1717 Munday. A gloomy day, thick mist. John Edwards thrasht. Picknall and George West plough'd in the forenoon. Banks ditcht, helpt plough etc. Picknall did jobbs after. Ned May and Willy begun plough in the Rookwood 'till noon, did severall jobbs after. John Gun and my Wife went to Nunnery, Jack Haslegrove with _____ .
One lamb of the little sheep --------- 23.
The long tetted cow calv'd a bull calf. Thomas Vallence did some plaistering about the granery and shop. John Parson's wife lay here with the child.

The 11th February 1717 Tuesday. A stormy day, small driveing rain. John Edwards thrasht. Banks and Willy, Picknall and George West plough'd in the Rookwood. My Wife and John Gun return'd from Nunnery. Mr John Hart supt and spent the evning here. Banks had a bushel of John Edwards's barly. Mr Picknall of Arundell here towards night. Paid George West 1s.

The 12th February 1717 Wednesday. A fine day. John Gun workt in the Towne garden. I was at Westtowne in the morning. Banks and Willy, George West and Picknall plough'd in the Rookwood. Win'd 5½ quarters of John Edwards's barly and 6½ bushels before this time.    Tom Picknall helpt winnow afternoon. Reckon'd with Stephen Bine. Clear'd all his to Candlemas and outset all my carriage. His work was £12-6-0d, my carriage etc £8-15s. He took £3-3s, abated 8s, left £3-6-4d to pay to him for laths etc. He supt here. Put the long tetted cow's calf to White's cow.

The 13th February 1717 Thursday. A gloomy day, rain towards night. Anne Norton marry'd Samuel Stubbs. *(Ed: married Samuel Stubbs at Pyecombe. He was born 1688 in Newtimber, the son of William and Margaret)* Picknall workt. Win'd 6½ quarters head and 4 bushels tail of John Edwards's barly. Banks and George West ditch against the Rookwood in the forenoon. George West went to ringing afternoon and Banks ditcht against the Hovelfield Orchard. Banks's girl tended and set pease in the Bankfield to day and yesterday, so did Widdow Tully yesterday. John Gun workt in the Towne Orchard 'till noon, for himself after. Deliver'd 12 quarters of barly to Harry Wickham per Willy, Ned May, Jack Haslegrove and William Smith. Receiv'd 5s of Richard White for 2 bushels of malt. John Pierce workt here. Borrow'd 10 sacks of Mr Richard Whitpaine yesterday. Sold 2 quarters of pease yesterday to Mr Whitpaine for seed at 25s per quarter to be deliver'd at his request.

The 14th February 1717 Fryday. A very wet, windy day. John Edwards thrasht. Banks did not come. John Gun workt for him self. Win'd 12 bushels barly head and 1 tail of the Rookwood wheat. Banks thrasht it by the day. George West, Picknall, Willy and I winnow'd it. Lent Mr Richard Whitpaine a throat hasp and white leather per John Smith. Sent home his sacks per Jack Picknall. Paid Sanders of Whiteman's Green 1s per Ned May for mending two sievs.

The 15th February 1717 Saturday. A fine morning, small rain after. John Edwards thrasht. Ned May, Willy and Picknall plough'd in the Rookwood. Banks and George West ditch'd and hedg'd in the Rookwood 'till about 3 afternoon, then ditch in the hop garden. I went to Lewis to sell clover seed. Paid Mrs Su Tourl 8s-6d for half a pound of bohea and 3s for ½lb of coffee had December the 17th. Paid Mr Court 20d for a latch for the back door to the Towne house, 4s-8d for 1000 of short bricks, 10d for a bunch of large cat gut for a _____ lath string. Paid Mr Beard of Lewis 1s for a tea pot. Paid my Cousin Peter Marchant 7d for 1lb of powder.

The 16th February 1717 Sunday. A wet day. Mr Jeremiah Dodson preacht. Mr Richard Whitpaine and Mr John Hart supt here. My Cousin John Lindfield here after evning prayr.

The 17th February 1717 Munday. A fine forenoon, wet after. John Edwards thrasht. Ned May and Willy plough'd. Banks hedg'd and ditch't. John Gun ditch't. George West rung 'till noon, helpt Banks after. Receiv'd £12-17-3¾d. Outset £1-13-9¼d for half a year's Land Tax, 2s for a license to cut timber for _____, 5s for mending the chimney and 2s for a River Tax, in all £15 of Thomas Champion sr for half a year's rent for Eastout due at Michaelmas last. My Cousin John Lindfield gave me a bottle of brandy. John Edwards had half a bushel of malt at 15d. I was at John Smith's jr with my Cousin Lindfield and _____ Sold my Brother John Box 4 bushels of clover seed at 16s per bushel. Sold Michael Stacey 4 bushels at the same price.

The 18th February 1717 Tuesday. A gloomy day. John Gun brusht up part of the elms in the Homefield. John Gun had a bushel of malt at 3s-6d. John Edwards thrasht. Banks and George West ditch't against the Rookwood. Ned May and Willy made an end of ploughing the Rookwood, begun the Homefield.

Paid Mr Burry £3-2-2d and outset 15s for the Widdow Tully's rent to Lady Day next and 17s-6d for Jack Haslegrove's board to Easter next, in all £4-14-8d. Paid 2s to Roach's wife for 8 weeks schooling for Molly Balcomb. Bargain'd with a boy from Wivelsfield, his name William Chapman, to come Lady Day at 20s per annum.

The 19th February 1717 Wednesday. A fine day, very wet night. John Gun brusht elms. John Edwards begun the ditch in the lane by Burt's. Banks and George West ditch't and hedg'd against the Rookwood. Ned May and Willy plough'd in the Homefield. Paid Banks 12s-6d and clear'd all accounts to last Munday morning. Mr Ralph Beard here, walkt over the ground, supt and spent the evning here. T Cox workt here makeing here horse harrows.

The 20th February 1717 Thursday. A dry day. John Gun spread dung. John Edwards ditch't. Banks and George West hedg'd in the Churchfield against Rookwood. Ned May and Willy plough'd.
Cox made an other harrow ---------- 2nd day.
The Simons from Woodmancourt here for a Service. Reckon'd with Mrs Storer from Xmas last, paid her 4s-6d for a jack for my Father Stone. Mr John Hart din'd here. Banks had a bushel of barly. Greenaway workt in the Towne Orchard to day and yesterday for my Father.

The 21st February 1717 Fryday. A fine day. John Edwards ditch't. John Gun spread dung. Banks and George West hedg'd. Willy and Ned May plough'd. I supt and spent the evning at Mr Scutt's.
Frank Cox made an other harrow ----- 3rd day.
I was at Westtowne in the morning. Let the Bowling Ally to John Smith for an other year. William Greenaway and his boy workt in the Towne Orchard.

The 22nd February 1717 Saturday. A gloomy day. John Edwards ditch't. John Gun ditto. Banks and George West hedg'd. Ned May and Willy plough'd. Cox came at noon, cut and cleft an ash by the new pond etc ----- 3 ½. Paid Greenaway 8s for this day's work and 3 before in the Towne Orchard for my Father Stone. Paid Mrs Catherine Beard 2s-3d for a cheese for my Father. Reckon'd and clear'd all accounts with Mrs Beard. She is to have 7 pecks of clover seed on demand. She and her family supt here. Sold Harry Wickham all my barly (except what I sow and sell for seed) at 14s-6d per quarter. Sold John Smith 3 barrens of my great sheep _____ . Reckon'd with Mrs Storer yesterday and clear'd all intrest to Xmas last. Paid her 4s-6d for a jack for my Father.

The 23rd February 1717 Sunday. A fine day. Mr Jeremiah Dodson preacht. I was with Mr Richard Whitpaine to see a sick cow. Mrs Courthope was here after evning prayr.

The 24th February 1717 Munday. A gloomy day. Banks and George West hedg'd. Ned May and Willy plough'd. John Gun and John Edwards ditch'd. Dick Smith mended the roof of the great barne. Cox workt on an ox harrow --------- 4 ½ days. Stephen Bine and I went round the ground to look for knees. He din'd and staid the afternoon here. My Brother John Box and Sister were here a while in the evning.

The 25th February 1717 ~~Tuesday~~. Shrove Tuesday. A dry day. Banks and George West hedg'd 'till noon. Ned May and Willy plough'd 'till noon. John Edwards ditcht. John Gun made an end of cutting the coppice, workt on Tully's pond the afternoon. Sam Jarvice and Widdow Tully set tick beans in the Bankfield yesterday and Jarvice and Jack Haslegrove set beans there to day 'till noon. Dick Smith thatcht to day 'till noon. Mr Richard Whitpaine and his wife Mary here towards night. Receiv'd 21d of William Bennet of Oathall for ½ bushel pease. Bargain'd with Banks's son Richard for a year from Lady Day at £-5s certain and if he deserve it he is to have 5s more. Paid George West 1s.

The 26th February 1717 Wednesday. A fine day. John Gun sifted pease 'till 10, workt for himself after. Banks and George West plough'd Homefield. Ned May and Willy begun Tully's 1st field.
John Edwards ditcht, turn'd all the sheep and lambs into the wheat by Wickham. Paid Dick Smith 3s 10½d for work and wifts. Cox workt -------- 5 ½.
Paid my Mother the remainder of her thirds to Michaelmas last, by my Wife. She was at Wanbarrow. Willy spent the evning at Mrs Catherine Beard's. Paid Pierce 20d for making a payr of breeches for Willy. Ned Burt workt in the Towne garden to day and yesterday.

The 27th February 1717 Thursday. A gloomy day. Some rain. John Edwards did not work. Win'd 3 quarters and half a bushel of John Gun's pease, he ditcht forenoon. Willy and Ned May plough'd 'till noon. Ned May helpt winnow afterwards and Willy went to Brighton. Banks and George West made an end of the Homefield about noon, did severall jobbs afterwards. Michael Stacey had a peck of breaking pease per T _____ . Mr Jeremiah Dodson, his wife and daughter, my Cousin Plump and Mr Molly din'd and supt here. Mr Richard Whitpaine came at night. Paid Molly Balcomb 1s for pocket money.

The 28th February 1717 Fryday. A gloomy day with small driveing rain. Paid John Edwards 5s yesterday. John Edwards did not work today. Win'd 13 bushels of John Gun's oates, he made a ladder for himself in the afternoon. Banks did not work. George West helpt winnow in the forenoon, sifted pease afterwards etc. Turn'd 6 working oxen into Tully's close afternoon. Ned May and Willy plough'd. The mountebank here. I din'd at Mr Richard Whitpaine's of Westtowne - it being his birthday, 42 years *(Ed: Richard Whitpaine baptised 7 March 1675 at Hurst, son of Lieutenant Thomas Whitpaine and Ann née Challoner)* with Mr Jeremiah Dodson, his wife and daughter, Mr Ralph Beard, Mr John Hart and Mr Burry. Sold John Smith my 9 weathers at 14s a piece, paid 6d for dying a payr of stockins for Molly Balcomb.

The 1st March 1717 Saturday. A fine day. John Edwards rakt beans in the Bankfield. Sarah Tully and Jack Haslegrove set beans there. John Gun ditcht round the shaw by Hyder's. Banks and George West hedg'd in the Churchfield. Ned May and Willy carry'd 8 bushels of pears to Hand Cross. Receiv'd 28s of P Courtice for the pease per Willy. I was at Lewis market, sold 4 bushels of clover seed to Mr Friend of Portslade and 1½ to his father. It was Nick Friend spoak for his father all at 15s-6d per bushel. I am to deliver it. Left a sample of pease with           Olive, a corne Chandler.

The 2nd March 1717 Sunday. A dry windy day. Mr Jeremiah Dodson preacht. We had a parish meeting. Thomas Turness jr dy'd this morning.
*(Ed: His burial recorded on 4 March in Hurst Parish Register)*
I supt and spent the evning at Mrs Catherine Beard's.

The 3rd March 1717 Munday. A dry day. George West and John Edwards hedg'd in the dry pond. Ned May and Willy made an end of Tully's first field. John Gun ditcht round the shaw by Hyder's. Paid     Marten of Cuckfield 14d for clipping my ewes. My Wife and I din'd at my Brother John Box's.

The 4th March 1717 Tuesday. A dry day. John Gun and George West ditcht. Banks and John Edwards hedg'd. Ned May and Willy begun plough Tully's lower oat earsh. Ned May had 4 bushels of oates for his horses to night. Paid Ned Burt 3s for work in the Towne garden. My Brother James Ede and Nunnery boy came at night. I was at Old Richard Heath's, sold him 3 pecks of clover seed at 12s. Paid him 4s for a cheese at 18d per nail. John Gun had half a bushel of oates. Turn'd the ewes and lambs into the Nine Acres wheat.

The 5th March 1717 Wednesday. A fine day. John Gun and George West begun the hedge on the north side of Tully's Mead. Banks and John Edwards spread grit and mended the hedge round the dry pond 'till noon. Begun the hedge against the lower side of the Bankfield afterwards. Dick Vinall kill'd a hog in the morning. Nunnery boy went home, carry'd 2 bushels of malt. Old William Brand's man begun pitch the ally between Thomas Baker _____ . Mr Ede and I supt and spent the evning at Mrs Catherine Beard's. Standbridge and Robert Gatland cut down timber.

The 6th March 1717 Thursday. A fine day. John Gun and George West hedg'd. Banks and John Edwards hedg'd. Ned May and Willy plough'd. Standbridge and Gatland hew'd timber etc. I was at Brighton. Sold 3 bushels of clover seed to Mr Friend for his sister Kemp at 15s-6d per bushel. Mr Ede, Mr Richard Whitpaine and I were at Mr Brigden's and saw the book discharg'd of all Mr Richard Whitpaine's work. Mr Ede and I came home by Mr Price's. Supt there with Mrs Catherine Beard, her son, Mr Scutt and Mr John Hart. Reckon'd and clear'd all accounts with Mr Ede.

The 7th March 1717 Fryday. A fine day. John Gun and George West hedg'd and John Edwards and Banks hedg'd. Hollingall and Willy plough'd. Hollingall workt for Ned May. My Brother John Box had 4 bushels of pease per T Barnet. Paid John Parsons for shaveing my head and Willy's. Spent 8½d at John Smith's with Mr Ede, Mr Richard Whitpaine, Mr Scutt, Mr William Brett of Lewis and Mr Ralph Beard. My Brother Peter had 9 bushels of pease at 25s per quarter yesterday. Receiv'd 10s of John Gilham for the use of a cow last summer.

The 8th March 1717 Saturday. A drizling morning, dry after. Willy went to Lewis. Ned May drew bushes into the Churchfield and by Burt's. Banks and John Edwards hedg'd. John Gun and George West hedg'd also. Mr Beard, Mr Ede and I went to Copthall to see a fat ox of Henry Wood's. Deliver'd 3 pecks of clover seed to Richard Heath at 16s a bushel per Richard White jr. Receiv'd the cheese I bought there. Receiv'd a cheese from my Cousin William Wood per Jack Haslegrove.

The 9th March 1717 Sunday. A fine day. Mr Jeremiah Dodson preacht. Mr Ede, Mr Beard and I supt and spent the evning at Westtowne.

The 10th March 1717 Munday. A very fine day. John Gun and George West hedg'd. Receiv'd an iron grate of Ned Burt weigh'd 4¾ lb. Lost one of the little sheep in the wheat, overturn'd. Bank and John Edwards made an end of the Churchfield hedge. Ned May and Willy made an end of ploughing Tully's oat earsh. Mr John Hart supt and spent the evning here. Old William Brand's man Thomas Collingham laid the grate on the gutter of the sink and mended the garden wall.

The 11th March 1717 Tuesday. A fine day. John Gun and George West shovel'd the Towne. Banks and John Edwards hedg'd against the lane by Burt's. Ned May and Willy plough'd Tully's little field and orchard. Paid 19d for a payr of gloves for Molly Balcomb per Mrs Courthope. Mr Ede had an other bushel of oates and a half. Dick Wood new made the tines of 2 horse harrows. He laid and steel'd the tines for one harrow and only steel'd the tines for the other, all at 2d per tine, but he has now made them all

The 12th March 1717 Wednesday. A very fine day. Banks and John Edwards hedg'd. John Gun and George West hedg'd part of the day, helpt winnow after and George West sow'd the flax. Sow'd an acre of flax in the Homefield. Sow'd 2 bushels 3 pecks of seed. Ned May and Willy harrow'd and roll'd. Mr Ede, my Wife and Jacky went to ~~Nunnery~~ Lewis. Mrs Catherine Beard was here in the morning. Took the sheep and lambs out of the wheat. William Jarvice went to Nunnery on foot afternoon.

The 13th March 1717 Thursday. A fine day. Banks and John Edwards hedg'd. John Gun and Phillips new planted part of the asparagus. Ned May and George West carry'd some dung to the garden, helpt winnow the Nonsuch and other jobbs. Willy went to Brighton with a sample of Nonsuch. Nick Plaw was here in the evning.

Mrs Catherine Beard and her mother supt here. William Jarvice return'd from Nunnery, brought a letter from my Father that Sir Isaac Shard had been there and they had agreed about the purchase.

The 14th March 1717 Fryday. A fine day. Willy and Ned May, George West and Picknall begun stir the field by Burt's. Banks and John Edwards hedg'd.
John Box's wife buried at Hurst. I was at the funeral.
*(Ed: Hurst Register - "Charity, wife of John Box of Wickham")*
Mr Price preacht. Richard White had a sack of barly, 15s per quarter. John Gun workt for himself.

The 15th March 1717 Saturday. A gloomy day. Banks and John Edwards hedg'd. Ned May and Willy, George West and Picknall plough'd. John Gun poll'd trees. Banks had 2 pecks of malt at 8 groats per bushel. Mr Ede and I supt at Mr Scutt's. Dick Wood fixt the tines in my new ox harrow.

The 16th March 1717 Sunday. A gloomy morning, dry after. Mr Jeremiah Dodson preacht. I was at Mr Scutt's after evning prayr.
We had a meeting about E Ball's child and Thomas Shave. Yesterday Stephen Bine and I measur'd the timber he is to have of me vizt 122 feet of hew'd timber at 8d per foot, 66½ feet of round timber at 30s per load and a pollard as he stands at 9s, in all £6-9-10d.

The 17th March 1717 Munday. A dry day. John Edwards and Banks hedg'd 'till noon, winnow'd afterwards 5 quarters 1 bushel of John Edwards's barly. Ned May and Willy, George West and Picknall made an end of stirring the field by Burt's at noon. Willy and Picknall helpt winnow after. George West mended gaps etc.
Paid Banks a guinea. John Gun faggotted and cut bushes. Paid Goody Roach 2s-6d for Molly Balcomb's schooling. Receiv'd 34s-3d of my Brother Peter for 10 bushels of pease. My Cousin Peter Marchant of Lewis here afternoon. Ned May harrow'd with the ox harrow afternoon by Burt's. Paid the cooper 1s for setting 12 hoops less something to pay. Nunnery boy went home this morning, came last night. John Pierce workt here to day and a Saturday. Deliver'd 4 bushels of clover seed to my Brother John Box at £3-4-0d.

The 18th March 1717 Tuesday. A gloomy day, a showr about noon. John Gun and George West hedg'd 'till noon. John Gun thrasht wheat after. John Edwards poll'd trees 'till afternoon then win'd barly. George West and Picknall helpt winnow. Ned May and Picknall and Willy roll'd and harrow'd in the field by Burt's 'till noon, afterwards Ned May and Willy fetch 3 quarters of lime from Taylor's for my self and 8 bushels for Old William Brand. The Widdow Westover's sale to day. Mr Richard Whitpaine and Mr John Hart supt here.

The 19th March 1717 Wednesday. A wet day after the morning. Mr Jeremiah Dodson's horses helpt us draw a tree out of the pond shaw to Stephen Bine's yard. Paid John Westover 17s-6d for a small clock that was his father's, which I bought of him this morning and 5s-8½d for severall things I bought yesterday.
Win'd 15 quarters and a bushel of John Edwards's head barly and a quarter tail. Ned May, Willy and Picknall helpt winnow. George West did severall jobbs. Ned May, Willy and Picknall harrow'd and roll'd a while in the morning. Thomas Jacket was here in the evning to set my new clock goeing. John Gun poll'd trees 'till noon, thrasht wheat afterwards. John Pierce workt here to day and yesterday.

The 20th March 1717 Thursday. A gloomy day. Win'd 6 quarters 5 bushels of John Gun's oates. George West, Jack and Picknall helpt winnow and John Edwards thrasht barly. Ned May and Willy fetcht 2 very small loads of sand from Michael Stacey's pitt, afterwards drew bushes etc. John Pierce workt here.
Mr Jeremiah Dodson breakfasted here.
The Nunnery heifer calv'd a bull calf this morning.

The 21st March 1717 Fryday. A gloomy morning, dry after. Win'd 4 quarters 6 bushels of Edward's barly. Picknall helpt. John Gun cut out the top of the trees in the dry pond, there was 24 faggots and about ¼ of a cord of wood. He workt 'till noon about it, hedg'd afterwards. George West sow'd Tully's first field in the forenoon with 15½ bushels of oates, hedg'd afterwards. Ned May and Willy harrow'd with the oxen and horses. Picknall workt in the sow field afternoon. Receiv'd 2 quarts of brandy of my Cousin John Lindfield. Mr Brand's man and 2 boys made mortar etc 'till noon.

The 22nd March 1717 Saturday. A dry day 'till towards night. John Edwards workt for himself. George West sow'd 17½ bushels of oates on Tully's second field below the Mead. Ned May and Willy harrow'd. Mrs Ede, my Wife and I set out for Nunnery with Nan Wood etc but (the child being froward) we went but to Danworth and return'd. Mrs Ede went forward. John Gun went with us etc. Paid John Gun four guineas. John Bodle's man had 2 bushels of oates for his master. The long legd cow calv'd a bull calf.

The 23rd March 1717 Sunday. A stormy day. My birthday 41 years. No service at Church because Mr Jeremiah Dodson's chancel was repairing. My Wife and I, Jacky, Molly and Kitty and Jack Gun and Nan Wood, Jack Haslegrove and Ben Shave went to Nunnery.

The 24th March 1717 Munday. A wet day. Jack Gun went but to Warninglid yesterday and came home again. John Gun, George West and Ned May thrasht clover. John Edwards did not work.
Mr Lindfield's Clerk came to Nunnery. My Mother and my Wife sign'd the purchase deeds, Richard Collens and the Clerk Theenden Nevil were witnesses.

## 1718

The 25th March 1718 Tuesday. Lady Day. My Father, Mr Ede, Richard Collens and I went to Darking to meet Sir Isaac Shard to finish the matter about the purchase of Nunnery. Sir Isaac, Mr East, Mr Spencer and I went to Betford to treat with Mrs Arnold to take in her money to which she agreed to take it next Michaelmas, Sir Isaac to pay her £4 per cent 'till then, of which we were to allow him 10 per cent. When we came back we agreed the whole, Mr Richards, Dr John Budgen, Mr Mills, Mr Heathfield and Richard Collens being there. All kept holy day at home.

The 26th March 1718 Wednesday. A dry forenoon, very wet after. Richard Collens went back to Rusper, we finisht the whole affair with Sir Isaac and the remainder (after the mortgages were closed) was paid to Mr Roberds last night, Dr John Budgen and Mr Roberds went for London. Sir Isaac, my Father and Richard Collens seal'd the leases. Sir Isaac paid all the reckoning.

The 27th March 1718 Thursday. A fine day. Scutt thrasht wheat yesterday and to day. John Gun and George West hedg'd yesterday or a Munday. John Edwards mov'd his goods yesterday, poll'd trees part of the day. John Gun and Ben Shave went home from Nunnery a Tuesday, return'd to day and brought my Mother's maid. Willy and Ned May deliver'd 4 bushels of clover seed to Mr Friend of Portslade and 1½ bushels to Mr Friend of Sadlescombe yesterday, and to day they and George West thrasht clover. John Edwards did not work. My Father and I return'd from Darking to Nunnery. Paid for my horse etc 4s-2d. Paid for a new shaul 1s-4d. Receiv'd £1-2-6d for old Mr Friend's seed per Willy, remains due £9.

The 28th March 1718 Fryday. A fine day. We return'd from Nunnery. Young Richard Banks came this morning. George West, Banks and Ned May thrasht clover. John Edwards poll'd. The mountebank at Towne. I talkt with my Cousin John Lindfield at Towne.

The 29th March 1718 Saturday. A fine day. John Gun and George West hedg'd. John Edwards poll'd. Willy sow'd 4 bushels of oates on Tully's little field and almost half a bushel of tail clover seed. Banks harrow'd. Paid Ned May 5s and 2s-6d and a wigg at 2s-6d, in all 10s for his Winter wages so he went away being lame and not able to hold his work. John Gun and George West hedg'd. John Bodle's man had 2 bushels of oates on Thursday. I was at Mr Jeremiah Dodson's in the morning and at Mr Scutt's towards night. Paid E Purvey of Cuckfield 1s for a chuck basket.

The 30th March 1718 Sunday. A gloomy day. No service, the chancel not finisht. Jack Gun went to Nunnery with Nunnery boy. Paid Thomas Picknall 10s for Jack Picknall's work. Left 11d on the score.
Lost one of the little sheep asprung markt on both horns. John Hart came to tell me of it. John Gun carry'd half a bushel of malt to Nunnery.

The 31st March 1718 Munday. A stormy day. Begun sow barly by Burt's. Banks and Willy, Allexander Snatt and Picknall plough'd. George West sow'd and harrow'd. Sow'd about 14 bushels. Paid John Edwards £1-3-6d. He poll'd trees. Old Dick Banks helpt about severall jobbs 'till noon, hedg'd after. John Gun and R Deerling came from Nunnery in the night with a hive of bees. John Gun hedg'd afternoon. Receiv'd half a quarter of bief of John Smith at 18d per nail. Ned Burt workt here. Sarah Woolgar came at 30s per annum. Receiv'd a letter from Mr Picknall of Arundell that he had bought a piece of drugget for me at Salisbury Fair about 38½ yards at £3-10s. Brought the 6 working oxen from Tully's. John Gun, Banks and Widdow Tully win'd 12 bushels of oates in the morning. John Bodle's man had 2 bushels of oates at 10d per bushel.

The 1st April 1718 Tuesday. A gloomy day. Young Dick Banks and Willy, Allexander Snatt and Picknall plough'd by Burt's. George West sow'd and harrow'd, Jack sow'd. Old Dick Banks and John Gun hedg'd, John Edwards poll'd afternoon. Dick Vinall and John Edwards kill'd 2 hogs in the forenoon. Richard White had a quarter of seed barly at 15s per Jack White. Deliver'd 1¾ bushels of clover seed to Mrs Catherine Beard, paid for. My Wife and I supt at Mrs Beard's.

The 2nd April 1718 Wednesday. A stormy day. John Edwards poll'd trees part of the day. Young Dick Banks and Willy, Allexander Snatt and Picknall made an end of ploughing the field by Burt's. George West made an end of sowing him. Sow'd 36 bushels. Old Dick Banks and John Gun thrasht Nonsuch. John Gun had a bushel of malt at 2s-8d. Lent my Cousin John Lindfield my leather bags per William Lindfield. Borrowed his grey horse and harness.

The 3rd April 1718 Thursday. A fine forenoon, stormy after. John Edwards poll'd. Banks and John Gun hedg'd. Young Dick Banks and Willy plough'd in the Rookwood. Allexander Snatt and Picknall's harrow'd etc. George West sow'd 9½ bushels. Deliver'd 20 bushels of seed barly to my Brother Peter. Banks fetch 10 bushels of my malt (straw dried) from Harry Wickham's yesterday. I wrote to Mr Picknall by the post. Sold John Parsons an old door to be valued by Stephen Bine.

The 4th April 1718 Fryday. A gloomy day. John Gun and Old Dick Banks hedg'd. Young Dick Banks and Willy plough'd, George West harrow'd and sow'd. Allexander Snatt faggoted and sometimes helpt harrow. Paid Dick Wood £1-16-9d in full of all accounts. The brindled heifer calv'd a bull calf. Jack Shave bought me an order from Mr Baldy to pay £150 to Mr Slade a woolen draper at the Gold Key in the burrough. Brought home 50 of John Edwards's faggots out of the Churchfield and 29 that Allexander Snatt made.

The 5th April 1718 Saturday. A fine forenoon, very wet towards night. John Gun and Old Dick Banks thrasht Nonsuch. Young Dick Banks and Willy plough'd. George West sow'd 16½ bushels and harrow'd. Allexander Snatt faggoted and helpt harrow. Brought home 25 of John Edwards's faggots. Paid Snatt 6s and left 8d to pay. I went to Lewis. Sent an order from thence to Mr Roberds to pay to Mr Slade pursuant to Mr Baldy's order. Sent a letter to Michael Stacey in the morning per George West to let him know that I insisted on the bargain of clover seed.

The 6th April 1718 Sunday. A dry day. Mr Jeremiah Dodson preacht. We had a parish meeting. John Terry's wife and daughter Sarah din'd here and William Terry's daughter Anne.

The 7th April 1718 Munday. A dry day. Stephen Bine hung the street door at Towne. Young Dick Banks and Willy made an end of ploughing Rookwood. George West sow'd and harrow'd. Sow'd in all 72 bushels. Allexander Snatt faggoted in the forenoon. Deliver'd 3 bushels of clover seed to Mr Kemp at Preston afternoon. John Edwards poll'd, roll'd an hour in the afternoon. Mr Olive of Lewis was here. I sold him 12 bushels of pease at 25s per quarter, to be deliver'd as soon as I can. John Gun and Old Dick Banks made an end of thrashing Nonsuch. There was 4 bushels head and near a bushel tail. Jack Haslegrove went to Nunnery. I was at the Royall Oak in the evning with the officer. Grafted a few russet apples from my Brother Peter's Westtown house in the Hovelfield Orchard.

The 8th April 1718 Tuesday. A gloomy day. Brew'd 10 bushels of straw dried malt yesterday. Young Dick Banks and Willy begun plough the Homefield. Allexander Snatt and George West sow'd the Rookwood with clover and sow'd 9 bushels of barly in the Homefield. John Edwards and Widdow Tully heav'd some barly in the morning, John Edwards poll'd afterwards. John Gun and Old Dick Banks hedg'd. Jack Haslegrove return'd from Nunnery.

The 9th April 1718 Wednesday. A dry forenoon, very wet after. Young Dick Banks and Willy plough'd 'till noon, did jobbs after. Old Dick Banks and John Gun hedg'd 'till noon. John Gun thrasht after. George West and Allexander Snatt sow'd 2 bushels and a peck of tail Nonsuch by Burt's. Did severall jobbs after. John Edwards had half a bushel of malt. So had Snatt. Young Dick Banks and Widdow Tully win'd bushels of tail oates. Receiv'd a summons from J Rowland the baylif to appear at the King's Bench in Westminster on a jury between Jarret Reve, plaintiff and William Trindle, defendant to try the issue joyn'd in Writt of Appeal for murder to by try'd on Wednesday the 7th of May next. Paid John Gatland of Cuckfield 1s for mending my chamber clock.

The 10th April 1718 Thursday. A gloomy day, the wind high. John Edwards poll'd. Young Dick Banks and Willy plough'd. Allexander Snatt harrow'd and thrasht. George West sow'd 10 bushels of barly.
I was at Brighton Market. Paid Thomas Roberds 2s-6d for a cart whip. The least of the 3 yearling heifers calv'd a cow calf. Receiv'd my leather bags again yesterday. Lost one of the great ewes markt on the left horne.

The 11th April 1718 Fryday. A fine day. John Edwards poll'd. Allexander Snatt thrasht. Young Dick Banks and Willy plough'd. George West sow'd and harrow'd. Old Dick Banks and John Gun hedg'd. I grafted some apples in the Hovelfield Orchard. George West sow'd about 9 bushels to day.

The 12th April 1718 Saturday. A gloomy forenoon, fine after. Made an end of sowing. Young Dick Banks and Willy made and end of ploughing. George West and Allexander Snatt sow'd and harrow'd. Sow'd 38½ bushels _. They also sow'd him with tail clover seed. Young Dick Banks fetch the piece of drugget from Brighton. He brought also a basket for Mrs Scutt and a box for Mr Richard Whitpaine. John Edwards poll'd. Paid Allexander Snatt 6s-8d and left 1s to pay. Old Dick Banks and John Gun made an end of the hedge against the Hovelfield Orchard, afterwards thrasht and win'd pease. Turn'd 2 runts into the hop garden. Receiv'd Mr Slade's bill of £180 on Mr Baldy from Mr Roberds per post. I sent Mr Baldy word of it per post. Paid Mr John Hart 25s for a quarter's schooling due at Lady Day last. Put 4 oxen into Tully's close. Paid 6d to Goode Shave for mending cloaths for Molly Balcomb. Paid 13½d for canvas and {..........]to work a payr of shoes for Molly Balcomb, to Mrs Atkinson.

The 13th April 1718 Easter Sunday. A dry day. Mr Jeremiah Dodson preacht. Mr Richard Whitpaine and his wife Mary and Mr John Hart here afternoon.

The 14th April 1718 Munday. A fine day. The parish accounts settled at Church and officers chosen as usual. I din'd at Mr Jeremiah Dodson's with Mr Richard Whitpaine and Thomas Norton. The mountebank here,

his last day. The bay horse's 4 shooes, mov'd. Paid John Westover 34s in full of all accounts. Turn'd 2 runts into the dry pond.

The 15th April 1718 Tuesday. A dry morning, wet afternoon. I went to Nunnery afternoon. Paid George West 5s.

The 16th April 1718 Wednesday. A showry day.
*(Ed: xxx text deleted xxx)*
John Gun poll'd. Young Dick Banks and Willy carry'd 12 bushels of pease to Olive's of Lewis and a quarter of oates to my Cousin Peter Marchant. I return'd from the Nunnery, supt and staid late at Dean House. George West bow'd pease in the Towne Orchard.

The 17th April 1718 Thursday. A dry forenoon, wet after with a smart storm of thunder and hail. Young Dick Banks and Willy carry'd 2 cart loads of hay for Stephen Bine from the Russells to his farme. I am to have nothing for it. George West ground malt and bow'd pease. John Gun poll'd. I know not what John Edwards did this day or yesterday. Receiv'd 27s-6d of John Parson's for his half years rent. Receiv'd a letter from my Brother James Ede per post. My Grandmother and Mrs Catherine Beard here afternoon. My Brother Peter bad me £30 for the Nine Acres next year for flax.

The 18th April 1718 Fryday. A gloomy day. Win'd 18 quarters 5 bushels head and 7 bushels tail of John Edwards's barly. George West helpt. I know not what John Gun and Banks did. Deliver'd 8 quarters to Harry Wickham per Young Dick Banks and Willy and Jack Haslegrove and I was at John Stone's with Mrs Catherine Beard. I bought 2 cow calves at 40s, to fetch them the 12th of May. Mrs Wicks of Cowfold came hither in the evning.

The 19th April 1718 Saturday. A fine day. Deliver'd 4½ quarters of barly to Harry Wickham per Banks and Willy. George West mow'd the grass plots etc. John Edwards workt for himself. Young Dick Banks and Willy carry'd a cart load of hay for Stephen Bine. I went to Lewis with Mrs Wicks. She rode my old horse. Paid my Cousin Peter Marchant a guinea and outset _of oates
in full for a new wigg receiv'd lately. Receiv'd 37s-6d of Mr Olive for 12 bushels of pease. Paid Samuel Tourl 3s for 1⅓lb of coffee and 2s-6d for 2 _.
Paid a blacksmith 1s for 2 shoes to the bay horse.

Receiv'd £150 of Mr Baldy which Mr Roberds paid to Mr Slade in the Burrough for his use. My Wife carry'd 95 guineas to Mrs Catherine Beard to lay up a while for me. Paid 13½d for a yard of stuff for my Cousin John Lindfield, which left 20d to pay at Mr Court's for a knocker to the street door of the Towne House. John Gun set poles in the hop garden.

The 20th April 1718 Sunday. A dry day. Mr Jeremiah Dodson preacht. I was not at Church in the forenoon, a meeting afternoon. Clear'd accounts with my Cousin John Lindfield except intrest. I was to see Mr John Hart after evning prayr.

The 21st April 1718 Munday. A very fine day. Thomas Hamper and John Mills begun work here. Allexander Snatt and George West mow'd the clover pugg. Afterwards George West mended gaps and Snatt helpt John Gun cut hop poles. Young Dick Banks and Willy plough'd for my Brother Peter. Lent Mrs Catherine Beard my bay horse to ride to Brighton. Turn'd an other runt into the hop garden. John Edwards thrasht, Thomas Collingham and William Jarvice workt part of the afternoon on the granery and a wall of the great stables. Sent home my Cousin Thomas Norton's 4 sacks per Jack Haslegrove. Dick Lashmer was here in the evning with his lease.

The 22nd April 1718 Tuesday. A very fine hot day. John Gun poll'd the hogs. John Edwards made an end of thrashing barly. George West mended gaps before noon, helpt John Edwards afternoon. Allexander Snatt did severall jobbs. Eliz Cheal ty'd hops. Thomas Hamper and his boy workt. They finish'd the ladders about noon, then begun on the granery ------- 2 days.
The biggest 3 yearling heifer calv'd a bull calf. Nick Plaw din'd here. Young Dick Banks and Willy plough'd for my Brother Peter. Thomas Collingham and William Jarvice new pitcht the sow's sty. They begun about 9 aclock. My Wife went to Danny afternoon. Paid the Widdow Cecilia Marks 1s and sent her a faggot.

The 23rd April 1718 Wednesday. A fine day. A Fair at Henfield, Nutley and Jolsfield Comon. Win'd 3½ bushels head and 1½ tail of John Edwards barly being the last of the 2 fields, in all 55 quarters 3 bushels. Deliver'd 2½ quarters head and 12 bushels tail to Harry Wickham per Banks and Willy. Allexander Snatt and George West hedg'd against the Rookwood. John Gun poll'd trees. Ed Burt workt here.
Thomas Hamper, his man James and Jack Mills workt on the granery 3rd day. Mr Andrew Laurence's son came for the drugget, he carry'd home 21 yards to make Willy and Jack each of them a suit. Sent home Edgly wanty per Jack Haslegrove. Sent my Cousin Peter Marchant's bridle bit per Young Andrew Laurence.

The 24th April 1718 Thursday. A fine day. Thomas Hamper workt alone on the granery --------- 4th day. Willy roll'd the field by Burt's and the Rookwood. Young Dick Banks carry'd 10 loads of Towne dirt. George West and Allexander Snatt hedg'd. John Edwards did not work. Ned Burt workt. John Gun workt in the garden. Shutt the cows into the dung mixen plott. Mr Richard Whitpaine and Mr John Hart supt here. Thomas Hamper workt 'till 2 aclock then went to the tythe feast. I were to see John Snashall's calves.

The 25th April 1718 Fryday. A fine day. George West and Allexander Snatt hedg'd. Paid John Edwards 5s. He went to Lewis. John Gun and Old Dick Banks hedg'd against Widdow Tully's orchard. Young Dick Banks carry'd 5 loads of Towne dirt. Kept holy day Lent Mr Richard Whitpaine 7 guineas for a note of his hand. Paid Mr Jeremiah Dodson £5-7s for half a year's tythe for Little Park and West Edgly and my Towne House. My Wife and I supt at Mrs Catherine Beard's.
Thomas Hamper workt on the granery ------------ 5th day. Jack Mills workt in the morning 'till about 9 aclock. I were at John Smith's sr with H Wood, John Smith and John Bodle. Drank out our wagers.

The 26th April 1718 Saturday. A very fine, hot day. George West and Allexander Snatt thrasht clover. Reckon'd and clear'd all accounts with John Edwards. John Gun did some jobbs 'till noon, workt for himself after. Young Dick Banks and Willy plough'd for Mr Richard Whitpaine. Thomas Hamper workt on the granery ----------- 6th day. Put my clover thrashing to Snatt at 3s per bushel. Paid Snatt 5d in full of all. I was to buy Snashall's calf. He promis'd I should have him but would not set the price yet. My Unkle Courtness and John Bodle here towards night to take horse keeping. The Albourne heifer, the 2 yearling heifer of Nick Plaw's cow and the Nunnery cow went all to the bull about the time. The long tetted heifer calv'd a cow calf.

The 27th April 1718 Sunday. A fine day. Mr William Martin preacht twice. We had a meeting about the charges of the tryal at Chichester in issuing an order to settle Ed Jarvice here. Mr William Martin put his mare in the Marldfield last night at 18d per week.

The 28th April 1718 Munday. A fine day. Thomas Hamper workt in the granery ------------- 7th day. Young Dick Banks and Willy plough'd for Mrs Catherine Beard. Allexander Snatt and George West mended gaps 'till noon, thrasht clover after. John Gun faggoted, so did John Edwards. My Cousin Weeks came from Lewis. Din'd here and went home. Sent my new wig to Lewis by the man that brought her. I think his name is Austen. Molly Balcomb, Bett and Nan Wood went to Broad Street. I wrote to Mr Ede per post and to Mrs Kettilby which Mrs Catherine Beard sent with hers. Thomas Hamper had 2 rings that is 2 douzen of hoops at 9d per ring. Allexander Snatt had half a bushel of malt at 16d. Receiv'd half a bushel of lime of John Hart. Old William Brand plaster'd the hall chimney

The 29th April 1718 Tuesday. A dry forenoon, showry after. John Gun faggotted. Thomas Hamper workt on the granery ------------- 8th day. Allexander Snatt and George West thrasht wheat and win'd 11 bushels head and 2 bushels tail of the Rookwood wheat. Young Dick Banks and Willy plough'd for Mrs Catherine Beard. John Norton was here with one Pope of Uxbridge to buy my lambs. Did not deal. I went with them to Mrs Catherine Beard and to the Swan. They bought my Brother Peter's 30 out of 32 at 12s-9d per lamb. Paid a guinea in hand to void them 3 weeks in May. John Norton promis'd to see the mony paid. Mr Ralph Beard, Mr Richard Whitpaine and Richard Raimel the salesman was there. Nick Plaw was here in the evning. I gave him a bill of £150 on Mr Roberds for my Lord Dennet and a note for Mr Dennett to sign acknowledging the receit of it and promising the payment of the money when receiv'd.

The 30th April 1718 Wednesday. A dry day. Allexander Snatt and George West thrasht clover. John Gun and John Edwards faggotted. Paid the Widdow Cecilia Marks 1s per Bartholomew's wife. Willy sow'd Tully's lower oat field with about 13 gallons of course clover. Went to a cricket match at Bolny afterwards. Banks roll'd the Homefield, Tully's lower field and the little field by the orchard. Sent home my Cousin John Lindfield's horse per William Lindfield. Mrs Catherine Beard and her mother here afternoon. John Snashall cut open the bay horse's back, being rung. Thomas Hamper and Jack Mills workt on granery ---------------- 9th day.
The sow farrow'd 5 piggs. Lent Thomas Norton of Edgeley 4 guineas for a note of his hand.

The 1st May 1718 Thursday. A fine day. Thomas Hamper and James workt on the granery --- 10th day. Paid George West £1-8-10d and 10s he left in my hand for John Smith being in full of all due to George West. Paid my Brother John Box £15-12-6d in full for all intrest due to him to the 19th day of this month. Receiv'd £6 of him for a load of William Balcomb's wheat which he sold at Darking, 15s for a young ram, £3-4s for a sack of clover, 12s for a sack of pease and 15d for 6 trenchers. His wife and he supt here.
Paid the Widdow Smith 11s, Boniface 12s, markes a faggot. A Fair at Lindfield and Storrington.

The 2nd May 1718 Fryday. A very fine day. John Gun and John Edwards faggotted. Allexander Snatt and George West thrasht clover and win'd 2 bushels head and half a bushel tail. Paid Snatt 4s-6d in full of all. Thomas Hamper workt on the granery ----- 11th day. William Bennet of Oathall and Stephen here to borrow my 3 yearling steers. Banks carry'd Towne dirt. My Cousin Plump here towards night. Paid Widdow Webb 4s, Herriot 4s.

The 3rd May 1718 Saturday. A very fine day. Banks sr thrasht pease etc. John Gun and John Edwards faggotted. Willy how'd beans. Allexander Snatt faggotted. George West thrasht wheat. Thomas Hamper made a gate and did severall other jobbs --------- 12th day. Receiv'd 11s of John Smith for a heifer's calf he kill'd yesterday.
My Wife, Young Dick Banks, Molly Balcomb and Jacky went to Nunnery. Receiv'd 6 douzen of glass bottles from Mr Baldy at 2s per douzen and a basket at 1s, packing and thread 3d per my Cousin John Lindfield's teem. My Cousin John Lindfield call'd here. He brought 2 books for the overseers to keep their accounts in, cost 3s. Henry Marchant of Bourne *(Ed: Henry of Eastbourne, born 1672, was 2nd cousin once removed to Thomas)* came for Molly Balcomb. Receiv'd a table of the Acts of this session of Parliament from Mr Norman.
William Bennett's son and a boy fetcht my steers.

The 4th May 1718 Sunday. A fine day. Mr William Martin preacht twice. A parish meeting as usual. Agreed with Thomas Broad to take Ed May at 50s, the parish to pay 20s and Thomas Muzzall the rest.

The 5th May 1718 Munday. A fine day.
John Gun and John Edwards faggotted. Paid Allexander Snatt 2s-6d in full for makeing 128 faggotts etc. Deliver'd 12 faggotts to my ükle Courtness at 2d per faggott, also 12 to Widdow Cecilia Marks at 2d per faggott. Also 20 to Richard King. He had 6 before all accounted to the _____ . Carry'd 150 to my Father Stone's stack. Paid Robert Cowdry 2s, the Widdow Cecilia Marks 18d and to Boniface's wife 3s for a gowne for Widdow Averd.
Receiv'd a letter from Mr Roberds with Dr John Budgen's inclos'd. Sent an answer per post. Sent my Father's letter to Mr Roberds per Mr Richard Whitpaine. John Chasemore of Horsham bought Mrs Catherine Beard's lambs, 32 and one into the bargain at 12s a piece. He was here to buy mine but we did not deal.
Michael Stacey and William Borer was here with him. Young Dick Banks and Willy carry'd faggots. Allexander Snatt helpt carry the last load and 2 or 3 loads of dung. Willy and Jack Haslegrove went to Brighton with a [etter] John Smith sr bad me £22 for 40 of my lambs.

The 6th May 1718 Tuesday. A dry day. John Gun and John Edwards faggotted. Old Dick Banks thrasht pease, George West thrasht wheat. Young Dick Banks and Willy carry'd 75 faggots to my Father and 100 to the Widdow Tully. Paid R Piony 15s for keeping Mary Morley and sent her to William Greenaway's. My Cousin William Wood din'd here. His wife came towards night. Thomas Hamper workt making doors for the Towne House -- 13th day.

The 7th May 1718 Wednesday. A dry day, till towards night. Mov'd Old William Brand, my Brother's _____ . Old Dick Banks thrasht pease. George West thrasht wheat. John Gun and John Edwards faggoted.
Receiv'd a load of lime from Taylor's per Young Dick Banks and Willy. I took up severall goods for Mr Morley at Mr Courtness. The old butcher promis'd me to stand to the price he bad for my lambs till Saturday night. Paid Thomas Broad as with Ned May. He took him by a payment of his _____ from _____ . John Gun had a bushel of malt at 2s-8d. Greenaway had 3 faggots for Mr Morley. Jack Haslegrove went to Nunnery.

The 8th May 1718 Thursday. A dry day. Thomas Hamper workt till noon ------------- 13½. Ruth Westover buried. *(Ed: Recorded in Hurst Parish Register)*
Win'd 9½ bushels head and 1½ bushels tail of George West's wheat by Burt's. Paid George West 18d in full to this day 10 aclock. Old Dick Banks thrasht pease till 10 aclock, then George West and he begun thrash wheat. Frank Cox put a new axle in the cart wheels outset 16d in his hands and clear'd accounts. John Gun speared mole hills in the Meads. John Edwards faggoted. Young Dick Banks helpt Cox etc in the forenoon, afterwards fetcht 3 small loads of sand from Michael Stacey's pit. Nick Plaw was here in the morning, cut a yearling that came of the peeking cow and a calf that came of the long tetted cow. My Cousin Henry Marchant's son of Bourne *(Ed: Henry jr)* and Young John Marchant fetcht Molly Balcomb to Bourne. Willy went to the Plate Race at Lewis. My Wife and I were at Westtowne in the afternoon. I was to see Mr John Hart in the evning. Jack Picknall helpt winnow in the morning.

The 9th May 1718 Fryday. A fine day. Allexander Snatt and George West thrasht wheat. John Edwards faggoted. John Gun and Young Dick Banks made mortar and emptied the little house afternoon. Thomas Hamper workt on a door till 3 aclock, then begun the new little house at Towne --------- 14½ days. Paid the Widdow Cecilia Marks 18d per my Wife. Paid the Widdow Tully 6s-3d for weeding my wheat. She had half a bushel of malt, clear'd accounts. Return'd the basket to Mr Baldy per my Cousin John Lindfield's teem. Mrs Ann Dodson and her daughter here afternoon. John Shave mow'd the walk and cut the hedges.

The 10th May 1718 Saturday. A fine day. John Gun and John Edwards faggoted. Allexander Snatt workt at Towne and helpt Young Dick Banks carry faggots. Paid Snatt 2s-4d in full. George West thrasht wheat. Carry'd 150 faggots to my Father's stack. Willy and I went to Horsham, thence to Nunnery. Thomas Hamper workt on the little house at Towne ----------- 15½ days

The 11th May 1718 Sunday. A fine day. Mr Beaumont preacht. I agreed with Mrs Chapman of Rusper to take Mary Morley upon tryall. Willy and I return'd from Nunnery.

The 12th May 1718 Munday. A very fine day. John Gun and John Edwards faggoted, win'd _____ bushels of George West's Rookwood wheat and _____ . Paid Allexander Snatt 1s left 2d due for thrashing etc to day. Bignall and Young Dick Banks went for a load of my Father's goods with my Brother's horses and mine. Old Dick Banks thrasht pease. Old William Brand, John Jeoffery, William and Samuel Jarvice stript part of the house and granery. Paid the Widdow Smith 10s-6d due for the month of April. Paid Old William Brand 2s for 100 slatts fetcht for Shoreham _____ .
Thomas Hamper and Jack Mills workt cleaving laths and pales etc ----------- 16½ days.

The 13th May 1718 Tuesday. A very fine hot day. John Gun and John Edwards faggoted. Banks thrasht. Thomas Hamper, James and Jack workt on the house roof ------------ 17½ days. Old William Brand, Thomas Collingham, John Jeoffery, William and Sam Jarvice workt on stone healing. Young Brand, Bignall and I went to meet my Father's teem with a load of goods. I din'd at Dean House as I came back. George Whitpaine was there and bought 1703 hop poles lying on the east side of the gill in the coppice at Pickwell for the Captain at 8s per 100, to be deliver'd at Captain Whitpaine's garden. George West thrasht _____ . My Cousin John Lindfield got me a remit on Mr Virgoe's bill. My Lord Dennet was here in the morning but I was gone from home.

The 14th May 1718 Wednesday. A very fine hot day. John Gun and John Edwards faggoted. Banks made an end of thrashing pease by noon, begun winnow them afternoon. Young Dick Banks helpt. Young Dick Banks and Willy fetcht 1500 tiles from Taylor in the morning. Willy and I fetcht John Snashall's calf. George West thrasht wheat. Old William Brand, Thomas Collingham, John Jeoffery and the 2 boys workt stone healing. Thomas Hamper workt mending the roof ---- 18½ days. Receiv'd a parcell of nailes from Mr Courts yesterday per Jack Haslegrove and a bill with them of 19s-9d. I was at my Lord Dennet's in the morning and receiv'd the £150 which Mr Roberds paid him in London and I lodg'd it at Mrs Catherine Beard's and she had 95 guineas before of mine. Paid the Widdow Cecilia Marks 18d. Paid a bill of 6s-7d to Francis Holden for Molly Balcomb. Paid him also £3-7s-1¾d for my self in full of all accounts.

The 15th May 1718 Thursday. A fine day. John Gun and John Edwards faggoted. George West ~~and Old Dick Banks~~ thrasht in the forenoon and helpt wash the sheep afternoon. Old Dick Banks helpt also. Young Dick Banks and his father made an end of winnowing the pease in the forenoon and carry'd them into Tully's garret 6 quarters 6 bushels the last of the field, in all bushels. Sent Mr Richard Whitpaine my 2 horses to Slaugham. Willy went with them. Old William Brand, Thomas Collingham, John Jeoffery, the 2 boys and an other workt. Thomas Hamper workt on the roof and cleavin ------- 19½ days. I sent Mr Roberds a bill of my expences with a receit to it tho I have not receiv'd the money. Paid Mrs Catherine Beard 27d for 13½ pounds of sheet lead. Paid John Stone 40s per Young Dick Banks for 2 cow calves fetcht new. Paid John Snashall 25s for a bull calf fetcht yesterday. My Wife and my Cousin Plump went to Frize Oak afternoon.

The 16th May 1718 Fryday. A gloomy day, some rain. John Gun and John Edwards faggoted. Old Dick Banks, his son and Willy begun carry dung out of the home close 38 loads. George West went to live at Kester's, thrasht wheat. Old William Brand, Thomas Collingham, John Jeoffery, the 2 boys and the other workt. Paid Old William Brand 2s for 100 slatts. William Jarvice fetcht. Thomas Hamper workt on the roof cleaving laths and at Towne ----- 20½ days. John Westover rode the sorrel horse to Lewis. Jack Haslegrove carry'd 7 of Mr Richard Whitpaine's cole sacks to Nunnery. Receiv'd 19½lbs of the parishes tow from John Hart by Goode Greenaway. Mr Richard Whitpaine rode the bay horse to Henfield yesterday. Borrow'd Mr Richard Whitpaine's tarpaulin to lay over the malt chests and on the house.
Receiv'd 22s-6d of Richard White for 12 bushels of barly. Paid William Greenaway's wife a bill of 22s-6d for Mr Morley per _____ .

The 17th May 1718 Saturday. A gloomy day. John Gun and John Edwards faggoted. Banks, his son and Willy carry'd dung, 38 loads. George West thrasht. Frank Osbourne weeded in the garden. Old William Brand, John Jeoffery and the 2 boys workt stone healing. Thomas Hamper and Jack Mills workt on the roof and at Towne --- 21½ days. Jack Mills fetcht Willy's cloaths from Lewis afternoon. I was at Randalls afternoon to see the mudd slides but Mr Burry was not at home. Old

Dick Banks had a bushel of malt at 2s-8d. Jack Mills brought me 2 large sheets of stampt paper from Cousin Peter's.

The 18th May 1718 Sunday. A showry day. Mr William Martin preacht. I was at Stephen Bine's after evning prayr and at Mrs Catherine Beard's in the evning. Turn'd all John Gun's beasts to pasture.

The 19th May 1718 Munday. A gloomy day with some rain. John Gun and John Edwards faggoted. Old Dick Banks carry'd dung 17 loads. George West thrasht wheat. Young Dick Banks and Willy fetcht a load of tan for John Hart. Thomas Norton's horses and mine joyn'd. Paid Goode Marks 1s. Thomas Hamper workt at Towne putting up palisades at the garden gate and getting 'em ready ------ 22½.
Old William Brand, Thomas Collingham, John Jeoffery and the 2 boys workt stone healing. John Jeoffery stopt up 2 windows here and at Towne. Frank Osbourne weeded in the garden. Richard White fetcht the parish tow to weave 19½ lbs. Receiv'd 24s of Richard Heath by his man in full of all.

The 20th May 1718 Tuesday. A gloomy rainy day. John Gun and John Edwards faggoted. Old Dick Banks carry'd 17 loads of dung. George West thrasht wheat. Young Dick Banks and Allan Savage went with Mrs Catherine Beard's horses and mine to meet my Father's goods. Old William Brand, Thomas Collingham, John Jeoffery, the 2 boys workt healing. Mr John Hart and I spent the evning at Westtowne.

The 21st May 1718 Wednesday. A fine day. John Gun and John Edwards faggoted. Old Dick Banks carry'd dung   loads. George West thrasht wheat. Young Dick Banks and Allan Savage workt as yesterday. Old William Brand and his people as yesterday. Thomas Hamper and Jack Mills workt at Towne, finisht the poles etc.
Paid John Gun a guinea.

The 22nd May 1718 Thursday. A fine day, a tempest of thunder and rain last night. Old Dick Banks thrasht. All the rest kept holy day. I cut the 5 bull calves.
Old William Brand, Thomas Collingham, John Jeoffery and the boys workt as yesterday. My Father sent his 3 steers yesterday with the teem. John Smith sr draw'd 18 lambs and paid me £11. John Smith jr kill'd one runt.

The 23rd May 1718 Fryday. A dry day. John Gun and John Edwards faggoted. Thomas Hamper workt to day and yesterday, and yesterday James and Jack Mills workt with him at Towne ----------- 25½ days.
Old Dick Banks thrasht and carry'd 2 small loads of loam. Young Dick Banks fetcht chucks, faggots and odd ends out of the Towne Orchard and afternoon went to Nunnery with my Wife. George West thrasht wheat. Old William Brand, Thomas Collingham, John Jeoffery and the 2 boys made an end of healing the house. Mr William Martin supt and spent the evning here. Goodman Marten of Cuckfield shear'd my sheep. Paid him 2s for it, there was 41 of them. Willy and Jack Haslegrove helpt the sheep shearer.

The 24th May 1718 Saturday. A very fine day. John Gun and John Edwards faggoted. Old Dick Banks and Willy carry'd 3 small dung cartloads of flints into the Towne per my Father's door. Receiv'd 536 whole tiles of Old William Brand. Paid him a guinea. George West thrasht wheat. Old William Brand, Thomas Collingham and the 2 boys begun tile heal the granery. Thomas Hamper workt 'till noon, James and Jack Mills also that day, Thomas Hamper set up the coolers ----- 26 days.
Drenched the sorrel horse for his cough. James and Jack Mills cut down 5 pollards in Little Park garden. Paid my Lord Treep 5s-6d in full of all. My Wife return'd from Nunnery, Molly Ede with her.

The 25th May 1718 Sunday. A very fine day. Mr William Martin preacht. John Dale came at noon and I went to Nunnery with him.

The 26th May 1718 Munday. A fine day. John Gun and John Edwards faggoted. Old Dick Banks and his son fetcht flints into the highways. Willy went to Horsham Fair from Nunnery. I bought 3 cows of John Brown's son at Rigate. Paid him £7-10s for them, Willy drove them to the Fair and from thence home. George West thrasht wheat. My Brother James Ede and I went to Darkin. Din'd at Dr John Budgen's, settled the accounts. Called at Mr Wood's of Newdigate as we came home.

The 27th May 1718 Tuesday. A very fine day. John Gun and John Edwards faggoted. Old Dick Banks and George West thrasht wheat. Young Dick Banks and Willy went to waymending with the teem. I return'd from Nunnery. Receiv'd £100 of my Father which was paid to him in London. My Father and I sign'd the discharge to the Trustees and the accounts. Thomas Hamper's man James workt on the granery yesterday. Old William Brand, John Jeoffery and the 2 boys workt a Munday all day and Thomas Collingham 'till noon and the old man, John Jeoffery and William Jarvice to day.

The 28th May 1718 Wednesday. A fine day. John Gun mended gaps 'till noon. Ditch'd in the lane afterwards. Old Dick Banks and George West thrasht wheat. Young Dick Banks and Willy fetcht flints into the highways. Mrs Catherine Beard and her family here afternoon. Receiv'd 10s of her for 3 old yoaks and a payr of court dills of William Balcomb. Paid Towner 2s-8d for work, clear'd accounts. Old William Brand, John Jeoffery and William Jarvice workt on the granery.
Thomas Hamper workt from 10 aclock ---- 26 days 2/3. We had a swarm of bees at Towne.

The 29th May 1718 Thursday. A showry day. A Fair at Stenning. John Gun ditcht and John Edwards did not work. Old Dick Banks and George West thrasht wheat. Young Dick Banks and Willy fetcht a load of lime and 1000 tiles from Parker's new kiln *(Ed: Thomas obtained his bricks and tiles from three kilns at St John's Common Marten's, Parker's and Taylor's)*. I am to pay Old William Brand. Paid Taylor 41s-6d in full of all. They fetcht a load of sand also. I supt and spent the evning at Westtowne with Mrs Catherine Beard's family.

The 30th May 1718 Fryday. A gloomy day with rain in the morning. Old Dick Banks and George West thrasht wheat. Young Dick Banks and Willy met my Father's teem with goods. Mr Richard Whitpaine's horses helpt. John Gun faggoted or ditch. John Edwards faggoted. Old William Brand, John Jeoffery and William Jarvice workt. Widdow Tully and Sarah Tully weeded half the day.

The 31st May 1718 Saturday. A very fine day. John Gun ditcht. Old Dick Banks and Willy helpt George West winnow 4 qarters head of the wheat by Burt's and 2 bushels tail. Young Dick Banks went with Mr Richard Whitpaine's horses and mine to meet my Father's goods. Molly Ede went home. Paid Old William Brand for 1550 tiles and a load of lime and 5s-2d over to continue _____ . Mr Sismith here afternoon. My Wife took very ill towards night. Mrs Catherine Beard here. Paid Old Dick Banks 2s-6d. Old Dick Banks, Thomas Collingham, John Jeoffery and the 2 boys finisht healing the granery. Paid Widdow Cecilia Marks 18d.

The 1st June 1718 Whit Sunday. A fine day. Mr William Martin preacht. George West din'd here. We had a parish meeting as usual. Paid Widdow Webb 4s, Widdow Smith 19s, Boniface for keeping Widdow Averd 12s and for making a shift for her 1s.

The 2nd June 1718 Munday. A very fine day. I wrote to John Brand. John Jeoffery laid the granery ceeling. Thomas Hamper and Jack Mills workt at Towne ---------- 27 2/3 days. George West skreen'd 5 qarters of wheat. Old Dick Banks thrasht, all the rest kept holy day. Receiv'd £9 of John Westover and gave him a bill on Mr Roberds for £10, he being goeing to London. My Wife sign'd the discharge to the trustees and the accounts. John Westover and Nan Wood were witnesses and I sent it per John Westover. Receiv'd a letter from Mr Picknall per post. My Cousin Plump supt here. Paid the Widdow Herriot 4s for last month.

The 3rd June 1718 Tuesday. A fine day. A Fair at Lewis. Old Dick Banks and George West mov'd the wheat straw loads into the pare orchard. Afterwards Banks fetcht a load of sand which he dug out of the bank by Snashall's hedge. Young Dick Banks drove my Father's steers to the Fair. Brought home Molly Balcomb. I was at the Fair. Paid David Douglas 6s for a hat for Willy. Paid Mr Andrew Laurence 3 guineas towards his bill. Paid Mr Court 12s-6d for nailes I had now and a half a crown for a bridle and 18d for 3 payr of knives and forkes. Thomas Hamper, James and Jack Mills workt on the chamber floor --- 28 2/3 days.

The 4th June 1718 Wednesday. A showry day. John Gun ditcht, Banks thrasht. Young Dick Banks and Willy carry'd a load of flints to the highway. Old William Brand, John Jeoffery, George Sanders and 2 boys workt _____ . Paid Robert Cowdry for this month 18d. Paid Bartholomew's wife 18d for looking after Widdow Cecilia Marks 6 weeks to Munday last. Paid Mr Dikes 10s yesterday for 2 payr of parish indentures. I went to Nunnery afternoon. Paid Mary Morley 6d for pocket money. I call'd at R Bennet's of Bolny. He sent his boy back to Hurst for some things I had forgot.

The 5th June 1718 Thursday. A fine day. ~~John Gun ditcht.~~ George West thrasht. Young Dick Banks came to Nunnery. Old Dick Banks did not work. John Gun met my Father's teem. ~~My Mother and I~~ I return'd from Nunnery and brought my Mother in their chaese. Thomas Hamper, James and Jack Mills workt Old Towne -------- 29 2/3. Old William Brand *(sic)*

The 6th June 1718 Fryday. A gloomy day, some rain towards night. John Gun made an end of the ditch by the lane and faggoted. Young Dick Banks and his father met my Father's teem. Thomas Hamper, James and Jack finisht the floor at Towne ----------- 30 2/3. Old William Brand and Samuel Jarvice workt here, his man George at Towne. My Father came away from Nunnery.
Mr Richard Whitpaine and his wife Mary, Mr Scutt and his wife, Mr John Hart, George Hugh and Mr William Martin came to wellcome my Father and Mother Stone. *(Ed: John and Eleanor Stone moved from the Nunnery in Rusper to live in Hurst)* Sent 2 fletches of my Father's bakon to Thomas Hamper's. Sold John Smith the py'd runt at £5-10s, to be kill'd by mid June. Receiv'd 5s of John Smith and a tongue. I am to have to keep his mare 3 weeks from this day in the hop garden.

The 7th June 1718 Saturday. A very wet day. I know not what John Gun did. Old Dick Banks and George West thrasht wheat. Young Dick Banks and Willy met my Father's teem. Old William Brand, Thomas Collingham, John Jeoffery and William Jarvice workt at Towne. Brand's man George and Samuel Jarvice workt on the granery 'till noon. Afterwards on Old Lag's shop.

The 8th June 1718 Sunday. A fine day. Mr William Martin preacht. A meeting afternoon about Oliver, Parker and Boniface. The ball'd mare went to Nick Plaw's horse last night.

The 9th June 1718 Munday. A fine day. John Gun and George West begun mow the Churchfield. Old Dick Banks mow'd my Father's orchard etc. Young Dick Banks and Willy met my Father's teem. Old William Brand, George West and the 2 boys workt at Towne. John Gurney came towards night. Receiv'd a letter and notes of £32-19-10d from Mr Roberds. Paid Widdow Cecilia Marks 2s-6d per Bartholomew's wife. My Father sold a steer to John Moor of Rusper at 51s-6d the odd money in hand, to be deliver'd at Roffee and to be allow'd a small debt due to J Moore. Mrs Catherine Beard, her mother and Mrs Kettilby here afternoon.

Thomas Hamper made a frame for a cubbard door in the morning.

The 10th June 1718 Tuesday. A fine day. John Gun and George West mow'd. Banks mow'd thistle. Young Dick Banks workt on the Chuch Hill with a court. Willy and Jack Haslegrove drove the steer to Roffee mentioned yesterday. Clear'd accounts with my Mother to Lady Day last. Old William Brand's man George and Samuel Jarvice workt at Towne. I was to see Mr Richard Whitpaine, he haveing fall'n from his horse.

The 11th June 1718 Wednesday. A fine day, only a smart showr about noon. Young Dick Banks workt on the Church Hill with a dung court. Old Dick Banks and Willy carry'd 175 faggots to King and brought a load home. Young Dick Banks carry'd 21 faggots to John Edwards which _____ . Old Dick Banks and Willy carry'd dung a little while in the morning. John Gun and George West mow'd clover. Jack Haslegrove fetcht the shalloon from Brighton.

The 12th June 1718 Thursday. A fine day. John Gun and George West made an end of the clover. Old Dick Banks, Dick and Willy carry'd the dung out of the fatting close. My Wife and I went to Lewis. Paid Mr Andrew Laurence in full of all accounts. Paid Samuel Tourl 4s-6d for 4 ozs bohea. Abraham Muzzall had a bushel of wheat at 2s-6d.

The 13th June 1718 Fryday. A fine day. John Gun and George West mow'd for John Smith.
Old Dick Banks, Dick and Willy made an end of the fatting close dung      loads. Begun at Tully's. I was at Westtowne afternoon with Mr Friend, Mr Hall and Mr Price etc. Receiv'd in full of Mr Friend for clover seed sold to him, his father and Sister Kemp. Paid Mr Court yesterday 23s in full of all. Paid Watt Brett 3s-8d for 2 large sheets of stampt paper.

The 14th June 1718 Saturday. A fine day. John Gun and George West hay'd etc. Old Dick Banks, his son and Willy carry'd dung 'till 11 aclock. Afterwards carry'd 2 loads of clover out of the Churchfield to Mr Scutt and 2 loads to John Bodle. Receiv'd 40s of Mr Scutt for his hay. Paid George West 6s. Widdow Tully, her daughter and Sarah Surgeant hay'd. Thomas Hamper workt at Town --- 31 days 2/3. Old Dick Banks had half a bushel malt. I was at Westtowne in the afternoon.

The 15th June 1718 Sunday. A fine day. Mr Price preacht twice. My Cousin John Lindfield here after evning prayr.

The 16th June 1718 Munday. A fine day. John Gun and George West mow'd J Reed's grass. Helpt us hay and mow'd in the orchard afterwards. Young Dick Banks, his father and Willy carry'd 7 loads of clover to the horse's ricks behind the hovel, the last of the Churchfield, in all 11 loads. Widdow Tully, her daughter and Sarah Surgeant hay'd. My Wife had a corner cubbard from London at 12s-6d. Paid the Widdow Tully 20d, outset 16d in full for weeding.

The 17th June 1718 Tuesday. A gloomy day. John Gun and George West begun to mow the way mead. Old Dick Banks and his son made an end of dunging. Thomas Hamper finisht the granery ------ 32 days 2/3.

The 18th June 1718 Wednesday. A showry day. John Gun and George West mow'd. Thomas Hamper workt on the granery and shop afternoon --------- 33 days. Paid the Widdow Cecilia Marks 1s and Bartholomew's wife 2s. Old William Brand and George his son carry'd 475 faggots near 200 before in this _____ .

The 19th June 1718 Thursday. A wet day. George West and John Gun thrasht wheat. Old Dick Banks and his son win'd the last of the Rookwood 13 bushels in all carry'd faggots. Thomas Hamper and Jack Mills workt at Towne --------- 34 days. I supt at Westtowne.

The 20th June 1718 Fryday. A gloomy day, some rain. John Gun and George West mow'd the garden court etc. Old Dick Banks, his son and Willy win'd 15 bushels, the last of the Rookwood wheat in all. Old Dick Banks did not work in the afternoon. Young Dick Banks and Willy gather'd cherrys afternoon.

The 21st June 1718 Saturday. A fine day. John Gun and George West mow'd the dry pond. Young Dick Banks and his father fetcht a load of great chalk and a small load of sand, hay'd afterwards. Widdow Tully, her daughter and Sarah Surgeant hay'd. My Father and I were at Westtowne afternoon. Clear'd accounts with John Gurney in the morning. He went home. My Father is to pay me 6s on his account. Turn'd the fatting oxen into the Middle Piece.

The 22nd June 1718 Sunday. A fine day. Mr William Martin preacht.

The 23rd June 1718 Munday. A gloomy day. John Gun and George West begun the Edgly Mead.
Old Dick Banks, his son and Willy carry'd the way mead and the Little Mead below      loads to the fatting ricks. Widdow Tully and her daughter hay'd the afternoon. Sarah Surgeant hay'd all day. My Cousin Peter Marchant and his wife and son din'd here. Mr Price, his wife, Mr Alcock, my Cousin Picket, Mrs Scutt, Mr John Hart's brother Peter here afternoon. Receiv'd £11 of John Smith in full for my lambs, draw'd 26 to day. Paid 8d for a knife and fork for Molly Balcomb.

The 24th June 1718 Tuesday. A fine day. John Gun and George West mow'd. A Fair at St John's Comon. Young Dick Banks draw'd trees 'till noon. Old Dick Banks mended gaps and lay'd the chalk goeing into the dry pond half the day. Paid George West 6s. Paid John Westover 13s-3d yesterday which he lay'd out for me. I was at the Fair and agreed with William Bennet of Oathall that he should keep my steers at £10.
Thomas Hamper workt at Towne ------------ 35 days.

The 25th June 1718 Wednesday. A very fine day. John Gun and George West mow'd. Pay'd Sarah Surgeant 6s in full of all. Sold John Smith jr my 18 great ewes, 2 rams and 2 runts at £23-10s, the runts to be kill'd in 3 weeks and the sheep as they are fat. Receiv'd in hand 10s. Paid Henry Ford 1s for spaying 4 piggs and the sow.
Thomas Hamper workt at Towne ------------ 36 days.
Bought 2 cord of wood of Stephen Bine at 10s per cord at Wineham. Young Dick Banks and Willy drew home some of Stephen Bine's knees in the morning, carry'd hay after. Old Dick Banks did jobbs in the morning. Helpt carry 3 loads of hay out of the dry pond to the rick behind the hovel. Lent Mr Richard Whitpaine a guinea, he supt here. Widdow Tully and her daughter hay'd.

The 26th June 1718 Thursday. A very fine day. John Gun and George West mow'd. Widdow Tully and Sarah Tully hay'd. Dick Banks and Jack went to Brighton with the teem. Brought 66 deals for Thomas Hamper and as many for my self. Thomas Hamper with us. Paid Dean's wife £3-8-6d for my part. They were too [togh] deals.

Old Dick Banks and Willy carry'd a load of hay out of the dry pond, the last 4 in all. Carry'd it to the fatting rick behind the hovel.

The 27th June 1718 Fryday. A very fine day. George West mow'd, John Gun sick. Young Dick Banks and Jack fetch'd a load of spill wood from Wineham to my Father. Carry'd hay after. Old Dick Banks and Willy hay'd and carry'd 5 loads of the Edgly Mead to the fatting rick. Widdow Tully and her daughter hay'd. Thomas Hamper's man hay'd afternoon. Paid Jack White 2s for mole catching. Old William Brand, Thomas Collingham and the boys workt at Towne for my Father. Old William Brand and one boy yesterday also.
Thomas Hamper workt at Towne ------ 37 days.

The 28th June 1718 Saturday. A very fine day. George West mow'd. John Gun sick. Young Dick Banks carry'd a load of Wineham wood to Thomas Hampers. Old Dick Banks carry'd half a cord of my own wood and 50 faggots to the Widdow Herriot and Hambledean. Widdow Tully and Sarah Tully hay'd and Willy all day, the Banks's and Jack afternoon. Old William Brand, Thomas Collingham and the 2 boys workt laying the hall at Towne and hanging the furnaces.
Thomas Hamper workt at Towne ------ 38 days.
Receiv'd a ram lamb of John Smith for which I am to keep his mare 'till Munday fortnight.

The 29th June 1718 Sunday. A very fine day. Mr William Martin preacht. My Cousin John Lindfield, his wife and daughter supt here. Paid Widdow Cecilia Marks 18d.

The 30th June 1718 Munday. A very fine day. John Gun and George West mow'd. Widdow Tully and Sarah Tully hay'd. Old Dick Banks and Willy carry'd 5 loads of hay to the fatting rick. Edgly Mead. Young Dick Banks and Jack fetch a load of Wineham wood to Thomas Hamper's etc. Old William Brand etc workt at Towne. Jacky and I was at Brighton and at Lewis. Had the Land Tax books sign'd. Paid Mr Court 2s-9d. Clear'd all accounts. Paid Mr Friend £1-2s for goods for Molly Balcomb.

The 1st July 1718 Tuesday. A very fine day. George West and John Gun mow'd. Widdow Tully and Sarah Tully hay'd. Old Dick Banks, Willy and Dick Smith carry'd 1 load to the rick behind the hovel and 3 to the fatting. Dick Banks and Jack fetch a load of Wineham wood to my Father's, helpt about the hay afterwards. Paid Mr Picknall of Arundell £6-10s-4d in full for a piece of drugget and shalloon and carriage. He supt and lay here.

The 2nd July 1718 Wednesday. A very fine day. George West and John Gun mow'd. Widdow Tully and Sarah Tully hay'd. Old Dick Banks and Willy carry'd a load of hay to Kester's and 3 loads into Tully's rick steddle. Edgly Mead. Thomas Hamper workt at Towne to day and yesterday and Munday ---------- 41 days.
Dick Banks fetch a load of Wineham wood to my Father. Helpt carry hay after. Thomas Jacket and his daughter and Dick Smith cut pease. Paid the Widdow Smith 19s, the Widdow Herriot 4s, the Widdow Webb 4s and Greenaway's wife 2s-8d for Robert Cowdry's quarters yesterday. Deliver'd 2 ells of linnen to Banks for George Buckwell this last month. Agreed with Mr Henry Scrase's man Blunden to come next week to thrash wheat at 18d per day or 2s-6d per quarter. Southwick miller here to buy wheat, agreed for none. Paid Dick Wood £1-11s in full of all. Paid 20d for a fan for Molly Balcomb that is, I must pay it at Lewis.

The 3rd July 1718 Thursday. A very fine day. John Gun and George West mow'd. Thomas Hamper's maid hay'd afternoon. Willy and Old Dick Banks carry'd 2 loads into Tully's rick the last of the Edgly Mead, in all 21 loads. 18 good loads. Young Dick Banks fetch't a load of Wineham wood to my Father and carry'd ¾ load of my own wood to Mrs Storer's and ½ a load to Widdow Herriot. Thomas Hamper workt at Towne -- 42 days. Thomas Collingham and William Jarvice workt at Towne. Paid Mr Lenilin 10s-2d for my hop duty. John Gun had a bushel of malt at 2s-8d.

The 4th July 1718 Fryday. A very fine day. John Gun and George West mow'd. Widdow Tully and Sarah hay'd. Thomas Jacket, Dick Smith and John Lindfield's wife Elizabeth cut pease. Jo Herriot and his company begun pull flax at noon. John Lindfield's wife helpt pull flax afternoon. Old Dick Banks and Willy hay'd and carry'd 6 loads of Tully's Mead to the rick at the lower end of Tully's Mead.
Thomas Collingham and William Jarvice workt at Towne.
Thomas Hamper workt at Towne ------ 43 days.
My Father and I were a while at Mrs Catherine Beard's. Willy and Mr John Hart went to Wanbarrow towards

night. Receiv'd the guinea lent to Mr Richard Whitpaine June the 25th.

The 5th July 1718 Saturday. A fine day. John Gun and George West made an end of Tully's Mead. Young Dick Banks and Dick fetcht 120 deals from Brighton for Thomas Hamper and for my self. Thomas Hamper workt a little while at Towne after his _____ Old Dick Banks and Willy carry'd 2 loads of hay to the lower side of Tully's Mead and 131 faggots to John Gun. Widdow Tully and Sarah Tully hay'd. Paid Thomas Jacket and Dick Smith 12s for cutting the pease. They did not _____ their waggon. Paid Dick Smith also 1s for part of a day haying. Paid 2s to Mrs Anne Beard for a month's schooling for Molly Balcomb.

The 6th July 1718 Sunday. A gloomy day, some rain. Mr William Martin preacht. A parish meeting as usual. My Cousin John Lindfield supt here. I gave him 12 guineas to buy me a payr of oxen tomorrow.

The 7th July 1718 Munday. A gloomy day, some rain. A Fair at Horsham. John Gun and George West begun mow the little meads. Young Dick Banks and Jack fetcht a chaldron of sea coal and 4 from Brighton for my Father. Paid 28s and spent 6d for 'em per Dick Wood. Allexander Snatt and Old Dick Banks carry'd 4 loads to Tully's upper rick. Heal'd the lower rick, hay'd etc. Widdow Tully and Sarah Tully hay'd. I was at Brighton. Old Dick Banks had half a bushel of malt. Willy went to Horsham Fair, bought nothing. Win'd 10½ bushels of the wheat by Burt's, thrasht by John Gun and George West.

The 8th July 1718 Tuesday. A dry day. John Gun and George West mow'd. Widdow Tully and Sarah Tully hay'd. Old Dick Banks, Allexander Snatt, Young Dick Banks and Willy carry'd a load to back of Tully's ricks, 2 loads of pease into Tully's barne etc. Allexander Snatt hurt himself cutting an alder pole. Paid John Snashall 15s. Clear'd accounts except for the parish. My Father and I were at Vale Bridge Mill pond. My Father and his family went to their house this evning.

The 9th July 1718 Wednesday. A fine day. John Gun and George West mow'd. The Tullys hay'd afternoon. Young Dick Banks and Willy fetcht 1000 bricks from Taylor's for John Pierce and 1000 for my self. Paid Thomas Westover the 200 bricks that I borrow'd of him. Old Dick Banks did some jobbs, hay'd afterwards. I were at Dr Woodward's in the morning. My Father and I and our wives spent the afternoon with Mr John Hart. Paid Mr John Hart 25s for schooling to mid Summer last.

The 10th July 1718 Thursday. A very fine day. John Gun and George West mow'd. Goodman Blunden of Withing begun thrash wheat at 18d per day or 2s-6d per quarter which he chooses. Allexander Snatt cut poles, turn'd the flax etc. The Tullys hay'd. Young Dick Banks fetcht a load of Wineham wood to Dick Wood. Willy went with him. Old Dick Banks and Snatt they carry'd one load out of Tully's Mead to the rick in the Fifteen Acres, the last of the mead, in all loads. They carry'd 4 loads out of the Little Meads to the lean oxen's rick. Paid Abel Muzzall 20d for a new yoak. Thomas Ilman was here in the afternoon.

The 11th July 1718 Fryday. A fine day. John Gun and George West mow'd. The Tullys hay'd. Old Dick Banks, Allexander Snatt, Young Dick Banks and Willy did jobbs in the morning, carry'd 1 load of pease to Tully's and 5 into the great barne. Blunden thrasht. John Smith kill'd my 4th runt yesterday. Paid Widdow Webb 2s for spinning 6lbs of tow, for the _____ . Young Dick Banks carry'd 37 faggots to John Edwards and 25 to Mr _____ .

The 12th July 1718 Saturday. A fine day. John Gun and George West made an end of mowing. Young Dick Banks and Jack fetcht a load of spill wood from Wineham to [S...........]. Old Dick Banks, Allexander Snatt and Willy carry'd a load of pease to Tully's and 3 into the great barne and 3 loads of hay. Dick helpt afternoon. The Tullys hay'd all day, Moll King and Tom afternoon. Paid Blunden 4s-6d for this day and 2 before.
The mowers helpt cock about an hour. Receiv'd 2 ram lambs of Jack Smith at 10s and a weeks keeping for his mare. I am to have an other at 5s.

The 13th July 1718 Sunday. A very fine day. Mr William Martin preacht. I din'd at my Father's with Richard Collens of Rusper. Receiv'd £6-19s of Richard Collens for a load of wheat he sold for me at Darkin. Paid him 6s for the carriage from Warninglid (back carriage) to Rusper 3s from thence to Darkin and 2s-6d for selling. He also paid my Father £10-2s-7½d. Mr Litchford's charity was paid at Church to Michaelmas 1717.

The 14th July 1718 Munday. A gloomy day. Blunden thrasht. The Tullys hay'd. Allexander Snatt, John Gun, George West, Old Dick Banks, his son and Willy cut the fatting rick. Carry'd 2 little loads of flax and 3 loads, the last of the pease into the great barne, in all 15 loads. Snatt had half a bushel of malt. Mr Lun, the danceing master, begun teach at Kester's. Paid John Stone £8-10s for the last half year of Land Tax for the year 1717. Goode Beard of Brighton first came hither to wash my Father's parcell of matting which he receiv'd a Saturday from London, weigh'd 38 lbs.

The 15th July 1718 Tuesday. A gloomy day, the wind high. The Tullys hay'd afternoon. John Gun cut ricks 'till noon, cut wood after. Old Dick Banks cut ricks and carry'd a load of hay in the forenoon, hay'd after. George West cut ricks forenoon, fisht Hyder's pond after. Young Dick Banks and Willy helpt carry a load to the oxen's rick etc. Draw'd trees, helpt fish etc afternoon. Sold my Cousin Peter Marten *(Ed: Peter was married to Elizabeth Marchant, Thomas's 1st cousin once removed)* the young mare at £4 to fetch her tomorrow. Richard Webb was here with him. Receiv'd £13-6s-3 ¾d of Thomas Champion and outset £1-13-8¼d for the Land Tax which makes £15 for half a year's rent for Eastout due at Lady Day last. Thomas Hamper's man James and Jack Mills workt on the barne's floor so did Thomas Hamper a little while, the rest of the day for my Father -- 44 days.

The 16th July 1718 Wednesday. A gloomy morning, wet after. Blunden thrasht. John Gun and George West did not work. Paid George West 31s. Clear'd accounts. Thomas Hamper, James and Jack workt on the barne's floor _____ . Paid John Parsons 6d for shaveing my head. Receiv'd £4 for the young mare. She went away to day. Old Dick Banks, his son and Willy carry'd 4 loads the last of the Little Meads, in all     loads to the oxen's rick. Made an end of haying. They did some jobbs before.

The 17th July 1718 Thursday. A showry day. Blunden thrash'd and win'd. Young Dick Banks drew knees and helpt Blunden winnow 3 quarters 1 bushel head of the wheat per Burt's. Paid Goodman Paine of Pyecombe 5s-6d for a bore pigg. I was there, came home by Wanbarrow to see my Brother's oxen. My Father and Mother Stone din'd here. Paid Old Dick Banks £3-11s clear'd accounts to this day. John Gun, George West nor Banks did not work. Let them my wheat to reap a Tuesday at £3-15s being 15½ acres. Receiv'd 4 quarters of brandy of my Cousin John Lindfield per Willy. Paid 2s for Holland for 2 caps for Molly Balcomb. Paid Blunden 6s in full for thrashing.

The 18th July 1718 Fryday. A very ~~stormy~~ wet day after the morning. Old Dick Banks skreen'd wheat afternoon. John Gun grubb'd part of the day. Helpt George West knock flax afterwards. Young Dick Banks and I fetcht 59½ feet of Thomas Hamper's rough timber from [R...............]. I was with Mr Richard Barcroft in the evning at the Swan about [Rickmans?]. Mr John Hart was here in the evning.

The 19th July 1718 Saturday. A gloomy day, some showers. John Gun and George West knockt flax. Young Dick Banks and William Gorman carry'd a load of wheat to Warninglid and brought some of Thomas Hamper's timber home in the waggon. I came home with them. Din'd at Dean House. John Mark came thither in the evning to tell him that Bide's daughter was come from London and fallen sick of the smallpox.

The 20th July 1718 Sunday. A fine day.
Mr Price and Mr Bird preacht. A meeting in the afternoon about the smallpox. Paid Cowdry 14d, Widdow Cecilia Marks 3s. I supt at Mrs Catherine Beard's. James Chapman of Rusper lay here.

The 21st July 1718 Munday. A dry day. A Fair at Henfield, yesterday this day. The reapers went to the Fair. Young Dick Banks unloaded the timber etc. J Cox put a yellow in one of the old fore wheels. Widdow Reed went to tend Widdow Cecilia Marks afternoon. My Father and Mother Stone and my Wife and I were at Wanbarrow. Mr Roberds of London came to us. He, my Father and I supt at Westtowne. I talkt with Goodman White in the morning and he consented that I should have Goodman Heath's farme, and on that account I let him my Father's field against Edgly Sandfield from this time to Allhallantide at 30s and from next Lady Day to Michaelmas following at 30s more.

The 22nd July 1718 Tuesday. A dry day. John Gun, George West and Old Dick Banks begun reap the Nine Acres. Young Dick Banks and James Stiles fetcht 59 feet of Thomas Hamper's timber. Willy and Jack Haslegrove fetcht the bore pigg from Pycomb. Thomas Hamper and

Jack Mills workt on the barne's floor -------- 46 days.
The Widdow Cecilia Marks died this afternoon.

The 23rd July 1718 Wednesday. A fine forenoon, smart rain after. The reapers workt 'till it rain'd. Young Dick Banks and Willy mow'd straw etc. The Widdow Cecilia Marks buried. (*Ed: Recorded in Hurst Register as Cecilia widow of John*) Thomas Hamper and James workt on the floor ------ 47 days. Dr Woodward, his wife and niece, Mr Smith of [Ashurst] and Mrs Catherine Beard's family supt here. John Gun had a bushel of malt.

The 24th July 1718 Thursday. A dry day. The reapers laid out flax in the morning 'till 10, reapt afterwards. Sarah Surgeant, Towner's wife, Tully and her daughter laid out flax. Young Dick Banks workt clearing out the wheat barne. Paid George Wickham 2s-6d for finding the sheep. Thomas Hamper, James and Jack workt on the floor 'till 10, afterwards at Towne --------- 48 days. John Smith kill'd my last runt. I took an inventory of Widdow Mark's goods. I wrote to Mr Richard Barcroft per post.

The 25th July 1718 Fryday. A gloomy morning, fine after. A Fair at Lindfield and Shoreham. The reapers workt after the morning. Thomas Hamper workt at Towne 'till 10, on the floor afternoon ---- 49 days.
Willy and Young Dick Banks went to the Fair at Lindfield. Brought home a payr of oxen at £14 bought of Mr Middleton of Hurstbarnes.

The 26th July 1718 Saturday. A fine day. Richard Heath died. The reapers win'd the flax 6½ bushels in the morning and reapt afterwards. Young Dick Banks and Willy carry'd half a cord of wood to Old Hyder, half a cord they brought home and 57 faggots to John Gun. Brought home     hop poles. They carry'd 5 loads of the Nine Acres wheat to Tully's barne. I was at Nick Plaw's in the morning. Paid the Widdow Tully 22s in full for her self and daughter. Mr John Hart supt here, I went with him to my Father's. I was at Richard White's just afternoon.

The 27th July 1718 Sunday. A gloomy day, fine after. Mr Springet and Mr Bare preacht. I went to Arundell in the morning, sent to Mr Richard Barcroft.

The 28th July 1718 Munday. A very fine hot day. The reapers workt. Thomas Hamper and Jack Mills workt on the floor to day and yesterday ------ 51 days. Young Dick Banks and Willy carry'd 3 loads of the Nine Acres wheat etc. Mr Richard Barcroft came to me at Mr Picknall's. We agreed for Richard Heath's farme at £18 per annum, the landlord to pay Land Tax and Lord's rent. I am to plough 12 acres yearly, to enter at Michaelmas next, to have a lease for 8 years. He is to put it in repair and I am to keep and leave it so and I am to have the close and one field 'till the 10th of May after the end of the lease to sowe. I lay at Mr Picknall's and came home this evning.

The 29th July 1718 Tuesday. A gloomy day, some rain. The reapers did not work. Willy and Dick did severall jobbs. Thomas Hamper and James and Jack workt on the floor ------ 52 days. John Gun helpt Dick and Willy cut the pea mow towards night. Goodman White was here. Richard Heath buried.
(*Ed: Recorded in Hurst Parish Register*)

The 30th July 1718 Wednesday. A very fine, hot day. The reapers reapt. Young Dick Banks and Willy did severall jobbs and carry'd 3 loads of the Nine Acres wheat into the great mow of the wheat barne and fetcht up that I set in Tully's barne. Thomas Hamper's man James workt on the floor 'till near 2 aclock. I was with Sir Robert Fagg in the morning. I was at the Widdow Heath's in the evning with Thomas Norton, John Oliver and John Marchant. I read Mr Richard Barcroft's letter to her and they consented that I should come on the ground to plough etc. My Wife and John Mills went to Lewis.

The 31st July 1718 Thursday. A fine day. The reapers made an end of the Nine Acres. Young Dick Banks and Willy carry'd 2 loads of Stephen Bine's wheat and 2 loads of the Nine Acres the last of the field, in all     loads. I was to see my Cousin John Lindfield in the morning. My Father and Mother Stone din'd here. Thomas Hamper's man James finisht the barne's floor. Paid my Cousin John Lindfield 28s due for the oxen. Paid 18d for a ribband for Molly Balcomb's hat.

The 1st August 1718 Fryday. A gloomy, hot day. The reapers begun the field per Wickham's. Willy carry'd one load thence to the North Mow. Young Dick Banks, James Stiles and I fetcht a load of Thomas Hamper's timber. I din'd at my Cousin John Lindfield's, he was ill.

The 2nd August 1718 Saturday. A fine day. The reapers workt. Young Dick Banks and Willy reapt beans and carry'd 3 loads of wheat. I was at the assizes, talkt with Sir Constantine Phipps.
*(Ed: Born: 1656, probably at Reading, Berkshire, Lord Chancellor of Ireland, died: 9th October 1723 at the Middle Temple, Westminster, Middlesex)*

The 3rd August 1718 Sunday. A fine day. Mr Jeremiah Dodson preacht. We had a parish meeting as usual, but settled no accounts. Paid William Beaty by order of the Vestry 10s.

The 4th August 1718 Munday. A gloomy day, some rain. The reapers workt in the garden etc half the day. Young Dick Banks and Willy did severall jobbs. Nick Plaw cut the bull and the boar. Paid Mr Scutt £4-10s for the parish.

The 5th August 1718 Tuesday. A fine day. The reapers reapt. Young Dick Banks and Willy workt in my garden and carry'd 2 small loads of wheat. Dr White's man fetcht 2 large carp and a tench. My Father and Mother Stone din'd here. Paid Mr Ede 10s and clear'd all accounts.

The 6th August 1718 Wednesday. A fine day. The reapers mow'd and reapt. Young Dick Banks and Willy carry'd 1 load of wheat and fetcht a load of chalk into my Father's close. Mr Ede went away. Thomas Hamper workt at Towne for my Father ------ 53 days.

The 7th August 1718 Thursday. A gloomy day. The reapers made an end. Young Dick Banks and Willy carry'd a load of wheat, the last of the field by Wickham's, in all 7 loads. I was at Dean House, went to Pickwell to get out one of his oxen that was mired. I was at the Widdow Heath's and they would give me no answer 'till Sunday whether I should enter.

The 8th August 1718 Fryday. A very fine day. The reapers made an end of the Homefield barly. Young Dick Banks and Willy did severall jobbs and carry'd [2] jobbs of the Homefield barly. West Mow. I din'd at my Father's. Harry Chapman and John Box were there towards night and Mr Ede and Mr Gratwick of Jarvice. Mr John Hart rode my Father's horse to Mr Orton's jr. Willy carry'd the malt sieve to Whiteman's Green. He promis'd to new bottom it by Munday sennight.

The 9th August 1718 Saturday. A very fine day. The reapers mow'd the oates. Young Dick Banks and Willy carry'd a load of the Homefield barly and did severall other jobbs. Sarah Surgeant turn'd flax in the forenoon and helpt _____ barly after to day and yesterday. Mrs Catherine Beard and her family and Mrs Gratwick here afternoon. John Pierce workt here mending my cloaths, he had 125 bricks of me. Eliz Surgeant came yesterday.

The 10th August 1718 Sunday. A very fine, hot day. Mr Shave preacht. I was at Westtowne after evning prayr. There was Mr Peter Courthope, Mr Shave, Mr Smith, Mr Beard and Mr John Hart. I were likewise a while at my Lord Treep's with Mr Courtness and his son William, Edward Burry, Jude Storer, W Sturt, T Reeve. Richard Collens was at my Father's. He took the draught of my Father's lease.

The 11th August 1718 Munday. A very fine day. A Fair at Hurst and Arundell but yesterday is the day. The reapers made an end of mowing the oates and begun mow the seed clover. I were at the Widdow Heath's and wrote to Mr Richard Barcroft per post. Young Dick Banks and Willy carry'd 4 loads of the Homefield barly, one of 'em to the East Mow. Sarah Surgeant, Widdow Tully and her daughter helpt. Receiv'd £13-7s of Harry Wickham and clear'd accounts. William Bennet of Oathall was here. I bought a load and a half of seed wheat of him at £6 per load if I like it and he is to bring it home. I am to tell him before Saturday night. John Gun had a bushel of malt. Paid him half a crown.

The 12th August 1718 Tuesday. A very fine day. The reapers made an end of the seed clover and begun the barly by Burt's. Young Dick Banks, Willy and Allexander Snatt carry'd 7 loads of the Homefield barly, the last of the field, in all 15 loads and a small jobb of the beans. Sarah Surgeant, Widdow Tully and her daughter helpt. Mr William, a bookseller in London breakfasted here. Paid Mrs Mary Gratwick £5 for a year's intrest, due about the beginning of this month, she was here.
Lent Stephen Bine's wife the bay horse to go to Bolny.

The 13th August 1718 Wednesday. A fine day. The reapers made an end of the field by Burt's and begun the Rookwood. Young Dick Banks, Allexander Snatt and Willy carry'd Tully's lower field of oates, 6 loads and did severall jobbs in the morning. Sarah Surgeant, Widdow Tully and her daughter helpt. Thomas Hamper's maid workt in the afternoon. Roach helpt 2 hours. Mr John Hart and I din'd at my Father's.

The 14th August 1718 Wednesday. A gloomy morn, fine after. The reapers reaped in the Rookwood 'till 3 aclock, helpt carry seed. Young Dick Banks, Allexander Snatt and Willy carry'd the rest of the beans, being 2 very small jobbs. Fetcht the wheat up from Tully's barne and helpt carry clover, in all 5 loads of clover. Sarah Surgeant, Widdow Tully and her daughter helpt. I was at William Bennett's of Oathall and agreed to have 60 bushels of his wheat, as at the Fair. Paid Old William Brand 20s per my Wife, he new set up the little _____ .

The 15th August 1718 Fryday. A fine day. The reapers made an end of the Rookwood barly at noon, turn'd barly and tipt the fatting rick. Allexander Snatt, Young Dick Banks and Willy carry'd the rest of the oates, 5 loads. Sarah Surgeant, Widdow Tully and her daughter helpt. My Father and Mother Stone, my Wife and I supt at Westtowne. Paid Mary Burt 8s-11d for Molly Balcomb.

The 16th August 1718 Saturday. A gloomy day, rain towards night. The reapers mow'd stubble in the field by Wickham's. Young Dick Banks, Jack and I fetcht the last of Thomas Hamper's timber and my Father's chaese wheels etc from Warninglid. I din'd at my Cousin John Lindfield's as I came home. Paid John Parsons 6d for shaveing my head.

The 17th August 1718 Sunday. A fine day. Mr Sixsmith and Mr Thomas Chatfield preacht. Paid Thomas Nye 2s for Frank Osbourne.
Mr John Hart and I supt at Mr Price's. The short tetted 3 yearling heifer went to bull per Mr Richard Whitpaine's bull. The 2 yearling heifer that came of the Albourne cow calv'd a cow calf.

The 18th August 1718 Munday. A gloomy day. The reapers mow'd stubble. Young Dick Banks did severall jobbs. Widdow Tully and her daughter and Willy turn'd barly from 11 aclock.
I was at Lewis in the afternoon. Paid Thomas Friend £1-10-6d for 9 yards of drugget etc. Paid 21d at Mr Fissenden's, 2s-1d at Mr Court's. Thomas Hamper workt at Towne for my Father ---------- 54 days.
Old William Brand and the 2 boys workt at Towne.

The 19th August 1718 Tuesday. A very fine day. The reapers mow'd stubble 'till noon, helpt carry barly after. Young Dick Banks, Willy, Widdow Tully and her daughter and Allexander Snatt rakt stubble in the morning, carry'd barly after. William Roach, John Westover and Thomas Hamper's maid helpt. Carry'd the field by Burt's, 11 loads. Lent Richard White 4 oxen to plough. Sent a parcell of shalloon to Danny in the morning to go to Lewis. My Wife was at Wanbarrow afternoon.

The 20th August 1718 Wednesday. A very fine day. The reapers cut mows and helpt carry barly, so did Young Dick Banks, Allexander Snatt and Willy. Sarah Surgeant, Widdow Tully and her daughter rakt stubble in the morning and bore on barly after, Thomas Muzzall from 10 aclock. William Roach and Thomas Hamper's maid helpt afternoon. Carried the Rookwood, 10 loads. Made an end of harvest. Thomas Hamper's maid workt at Towne for my Father ------- 55 days.

The 21st August 1718 Thursday. A fine day. The reapers made an end of mowing stubble. Young Dick Banks and Willy drew home Stephen Bine's timber and tipt ricks etc. Receiv'd a letter from Richard Barcroft per post with an other for Widdow Heath. I were at my Brother John Box's to meet my Aunt Holden and Cousin Hayne etc. Bought 27 bushels of seed wheat of my Brother John Box at 3s-3d per bushel.

The 22nd August 1718 Fryday. A fine day. The reapers cut the home rick, the oat mow and took up one load of flax. Young Dick Banks, Willy and Allexander Snatt fetcht 2 loads of hay from Broad Street for Old William Brand. Willy went to Balcombe with my Sister Bett towards night. Paid the reapers 2 guineas a piece.
One          Rupson of Lewis came to see the bay horse for Mr Pelham, the lowest price I made was £18.

The 23rd August 1718 Saturday. A fine day. John Gun cut hedges half the day. Old Dick Banks thrasht wheat in the forenoon and helpt George West take up flax afternoon. Young Dick Banks fetcht a load of chucks for John Lindfield. Gather'd the Burgaine pares and carry'd the flax. Reckon'd with John Gun for all his work etc to this day except bullock serving. I deliver'd Mr Richard Barcroft's letter to Matt Heath yesterday. Jack Haslegrove fetcht my coat from Lewis. Willy return'd from Balcombe, brought home a hare and the malt sieves from Sanders for the bottoming he paid 20d.

The 24th August 1718 Sunday. A very fine day. Mr Beaumont and Mr Healy preacht. My Cousin John Lindfield and his wife Elizabeth din'd here. Jude Storer, my Brother Peter and I were at the Swan. Jude supt and lay here.

The 25th August 1718 Munday. A gloomy day, some rain. None of the workmen workt. Young Dick Banks and Willy begun stir the Bankfield etc. Reckon'd with my Father Stone, due to me £7-3-9d. Paid Old William Brand a guinea. Jude Storer lay here last night. The Widdow Heath sent her man to tell me I should plough etc. I went and talkt with her and agreed that 2 men should settle matters between us to morrow.

The 26th August 1718 Tuesday. A dry day. John Gun faggoted, George West begun dress flax. A Fair at Agdean and Brighton yesterday, Sunday the day. Receiv'd the £7-3-9d of my Father due on the reckoning yesterday. Receiv'd £5 of my Daughter Bett yesterday for which I gave her a note of my hand to pay her 5s per annum on 10th August. Receiv'd six guineas of Mr John Hart last night for which I gave him an order to take it of Mr William Roberds. Old Dick Banks thrasht wheat. I am not certain whether he thrasht yesterday or not. Young Dick Banks, Willy and I catcht 10 partridges last night in John Stone's wheat earsh by Hyder's. My Cousin John Lindfield met Richard Ifield and Goodman Coulstock at the Widdow Heath's and agreed that I should give the widdow 30s for the pasture which is left at Michaelmas and the dung and she is to take no beasts to keep. My Cousin John Lindfield was here in the evning. Mr Picknall of Arundell here afternoon.

The 27th August 1718 Wednesday. A very fine day. Old Dick Banks thrasht wheat. Young Dick Banks and Willy fetcht 500 bricks and a load of lime for Old William Brand. John Gun faggoted, George West drest flax. My Wife, Bett, Jack, Mr Scutt's boy and I went to Chichester.

The 28th August 1718 Wednesday. A fine day. Old Dick Banks thrasht, George West drest flax. Young Dick Banks and Willy fetcht 2 loads of sand, 1000 of tiles and, I think, a load of lime for Old William Brand. John Gun faggoted.

The 29th August 1718 Fryday. A fine day. Crawley Fair. Banks thrasht. John Gun faggoted. Young Dick Banks mow'd the weeds on Heath's _____ . Willy went to Crawley Fair bought 10 runts at      per runt of which I am to have 5. Mr Richard Barcroft and I seal'd a lease at Mr Wakeford. Paid Mr Wakeford 5s for my part and left both parts with Mr Wakeford at Mr Richard Barcroft's request 'till I enter on the farme which is to be at Michaelmas next.
Mr Packham and we supt at Mr Libbard's.

The 30th August 1718 Saturday. A gloomy day, dry after. Banks thrasht. John Gun faggoted. George West drest flax. Young Dick Banks and Willy fetcht 1000 bricks for Old William Brand. My Wife and I, Jacky and William Fryer return'd from Chichester, left Bett at Mr Libbard's for change of air. Din'd at Mr Picknall's of Arundell. I talkt with Mr Peckham of Arundell about Tanbridge and gave him 5s. We lay at Mr Peckham's the apothecary whilst at Chichester. Paid Mr Lee of Chichester 3s-6d for a large map of Europe, 1s a piece *(Ed: xx text deleted xx)* for other prints and 6d a piece for 6 small metrotinto prints, all for my Father. Paid him also 18d for 4 quires of writing paper and 15d for a pocket book and 6d for a comb.

The 31st August 1718 Sunday. A dry day. Mr Price and Mr Bare preacht. My Brother John Box and Sister were here after evning prayr. Paid my Cousin John Marchant of Lox £4 for a year's intrest for the Widdow Weller of Horsted.

The 1st September 1718 Munday. A gloomy day. Horsted Fair. John Gun and George West and Old Dick Banks begun mow the Churchfield clover. Willy went a coursing with Mr Scutt. Young Dick Banks and Jack carry'd tub staves to Ditcheling and brought planks and timber etc (the last of the broak) from Old Land for Stephen Bine at 7s. Paid my Cousin John Lindfield £17-10s for 5 runts from Crawley Fair. Young George Hill of Rigate was at Dean House with me. My Father went for Horsham and Rusper. Jack Mills was with him on our little horse.

The 2nd September 1718 Tuesday. A gloomy day with some rain. The mowers ended the clover. Young Dick Banks and Will fetcht 500 bricks and a load of lime from Marten's at the Comon for Stephen Bine.
Paid my Brother John Box £100 which Mr Farncombe

of Withing had for a quarter of a year on bond at £5 per 100. I have the bond, 'twas seal'd at the Swan.

The 3rd September 1718 Wednesday. A gloomy day, some rain. The mowers begun mow the stubble in the Nine Acres. Young Dick Banks and Willy fetcht 500 bricks and 1500 tiles from Marten's for Stephen Bine. My Mother, my Wife and I went to Shermanbury Place. Reckon'd with John Smith jr and there is due to me £49-14-0½d. He gave me a note of his hand that I should have his dung as I used to have it, after the 29th September 1719 allowing him straw.
Receiv'd 20s of R Kester for a load of hay yesterday.

The 4th September 1718 Thursday. A showry day. Old Dick Banks and John Gun clear'd Tully's barne floor and win'd the oates, 7 bushels for _____ . They and George West mow'd stubble in the Nine Acres after. Young Dick Banks and Willy deliver'd half a load of wheat straw to Old Kester at 5s etc. Sold John Smith jr my little ewes, 20, at 9s-6d but if they prove too dear I am to abate 5s. Molly Balcomb went to Mr Lun's dancing school. I was with Mr Lun and Mr Chatfield at the Swan. Borrow'd 2 hop bags of Mr Richard Whitpaine per Dick Banks. Jack Mills return'd from Rusper and brought a letter from my Father that he had the gout.

The 5th September 1718 Fryday. A dry day. Old Dick Banks and his son begun plough the pease earsh at Rickman's. George West drest flax. John Gun pull'd poles to the hop pickers. My Cousin John Lindfield and I went up the hill to buy sheep, call'd at Mr Farncombe. He was not at home. We went thence to Stanmer and bought 120 ewes of William Scrase at £50 to be fetch a Tuesday or Wednesday next.

The 6th September 1718 Saturday. A fine day. The mowers mow'd stubble 'till noon, gather'd apples after. Young Dick Banks and Willy plough'd at Rickman's 'till noon, gather'd apples after. Thomas Hamper and his man workt here --------------- 56 days.
They made and hung up the gate beyond Tully's house. Paid Goode Shave 9d for mending Molly Balcomb's cloak. Widdow Tully, Sarah Tully turn'd clover all day, Sarah Surgeant and Sarah Nicholas the afternoon.

The 7th September 1718 Sunday. A fine day. Mr Jeremiah Dodson preacht. We had a meeting as usual but past no accounts. Paid Mr Jeremiah Dodson £5-5s for half a year's tythe due at Michaelmas next. I was there in the evning. Paid 1s for a payr of pockets for Molly Balcomb yesterday.

The 8th September 1718 Munday. A very fine day. John Gun faggoted 'till noon, helpt carry clover after, 4 loads all in the Churchfield. Old Dick Banks and Thomas Jacket mended the hedges at each end of Tully's gate etc, helpt carry clover after. Young Dick Banks and Willy plough'd at Rickman's. Widdow Tully and Sarah Tully rakt clover all day. Thomas Hamper's maid, Eliz Cheal, Thomas Jacket's girl and boy and Boniface's girl from 11 aclock. My Father return'd from Rusper in a cart. John Smith's man went to come home with him. I wrote to Mr Richard Barcroft by the post and gave him an estimate of the charge of repairs on Rickman's, the whole amounting to £5-0-6d not including the thatching. Jack Haslegrove went to Brighton with the letter for Mr Richard Barcroft and a box to go to Bett at Chichester.

The 9th September 1718 Tuesday. A fine day. Old Dick Banks and Willy plough'd at Rickman's. Young Dick Banks carry'd 11 bushels of pares to Brighton and a bushel of apples and bakon but he brought the bakon home again and 3 bushels of salt at 4s-3d per bushel. John Gun went up the hill with Banks and workt 'till noon. George West drest flax. Receiv'd a load and ½ of seed of William Bennett and 20s, and clear'd accounts. Thomas Hamper and his man and Jack Mills workt here -------- 57 days. Mr Chatfield supt here. My Wife went to Brighton. Thomas Jacket bagg'd my hops and rakt stubble, he and his boy.

The 10th September 1718 Wednesday. A dry day. My wedding day, 18 years. Paid Molly Balcomb 10s for entrance to the dancing master, Mr Lun. Young Dick Banks fetcht a load of chucks for William Bartlet. Brought 25 of my watle from Mr Richard Whitpaine's _____ . Mr Harry Morgan, the exciseman, weigh'd my hops and Mr Richard Whitpaine's, one small pocket for my Cousin John Lindfield 11½lbs and one 23lbs for which he charg'd £31 neat. Paid him 2s-7d for the duty before Dick Wood _____ . Thomas Hamper and his man and boy workt on the syder press ------ 58 days. Thomas Jacket and his boy rakt stubble, helpt carry one load. Old Dick Banks and Willy made an end of stirring the pease _____ . John Gun faggoted.

George West drest flax. Nathaniel Turner and Young John Lindfield fetcht the ewes from Stanmer and we shifted them here. Paid Young John Lindfield £24 for my share in the morning. Receiv'd the piggs from my Cousin John Lindfield but they straid back again. Receiv'd 3 bushels of Mr Richard Whitpaine's charcoal to dry my hops with per Thomas Jacket.

The 11th September 1718 Thursday. A fine day. Old Dick Banks, John Gun and Young Dick Banks did severall jobbs in the morning, gather'd apples after. Thomas Hamper's man and Jack Mills workt on the syder mill after. Paid Sarah Surgeant 10s in full of all. Young Dick Banks harrow'd the lower oat earsh and Willy sow'd it with clover.

The 12th September 1718 Fryday. A fine day. John Gun parted and markt the store ewes in the morning. Gather'd apples afterwards. Old Dick Banks and his son and Willy went with 2 teems to Wineham for Stephen Bine, fetcht 2 loads of wood. John Gun had a bushel of malt at 2s-8d. Allexander Snatt and both the young Picknalls made syder for my Father. George West drest flax 'till 3 aclock, made syder after. Old Hyder and John Wickens sign'd their indentures. Spent 3½d at the Swan. Receiv'd 5s of old Hyder for the indentures.
Mary Morley was brought from Rusper and I sent her again and am to pay her Mrs, Mrs Chapman, 1s per week from hence 'till Easter.

The 13th September 1718 Saturday. A fine day. Old Dick Banks, his son and Willy begun ridge at Rickman's. John Gun, Allexander Snatt and Jack Bartlet, rung the hogs and gather'd apples. Paid George West a guinea, he drest flax. The 2 Picknalls helpt, Tom 'till noon, Jack all day. Receiv'd ¼lb of course bohea of Samuel Tourl yesterday per Mr Jeremiah Dodson and an ounce of fine ditto. Receiv'd a letter from Mr Richard Barcroft wherein he allows me £5-0s-6d to do the repairs at Rickman's, not including the thatching. John Smith jr turn'd a cow into my ground yesterday which I am to have at £5 if I like her. My Wife went to Wanbarrow towards night.
Old William Brand drew off a tubb of his beer at my Father's to send to his son John, at Lisbon. Paid Goodman Coulstock 1s for Matt Heath for a piece of hedge and poton.

The 14th September 1718 Sunday. A fine day. Mr William Martin preacht. My Wife and I supt at Westtowne. Mr Richard Whitpaine sign'd Sarah Lindfield's indenture to John Wickens.

The 15th September 1718 Munday. A gloomy day. A Fair at St Johns Comon. George West drest flax. John Gun shovel'd some part of the Towne. Threw up John Smith's _____ . Old Dick Banks, his son and Willy harrow'd and ridged at Rickman's. One of Thomas Hamper's men and Jack Mills cut down 6 pollards at Rickman's and left off at noon. Mr William Martin turn'd his mare into my ground again towards the latter end of last week. My Wife and I went to the Fair. Were both at Mr Norden's but not together. My Cousin John Lindfield sign'd Sarah Lindfield's indentures to John Wickens and paid him 50s, but I did not see it.

The 16th September 1718 Tuesday. A gloomy day, some rain. George West drest flax. Young Dick Banks and Willy plough'd. Old Dick Banks harrow'd and roll'd. John Gun and Thomas Jacket sow'd and harrow'd at Rickman's. Old Dick Banks drew the trees down to the house. My Aunt Gratwick, Mr Lintott and his wife here afternoon. Dr Nick Plaw here a while in the evning. Clear'd accounts with John Edwards.

The 17th September 1718 Wednesday. A dry windy day. Finisht the field at Rickman's haveing sow'd 12 bushels 3 gallons. Young Dick Banks and Willy plough'd. John Gun sow'd and helpt Thomas Jacket and his boy rake the furroughs etc. Old Dick Banks harrow'd and roll'd. Receiv'd 6 ewe lambs from my Cousin John Lindfield (Stanmer _____ ) at 4s-3d a piece. John Smith's cow, that was my Brother John Box's, calved a bull calf. John Smith kill'd the heifer's calf. My Cousin Richard Turner of Old Land and William Wood's wife din'd here.

The 18th September 1718 Thursday. A very fine day. John Gun and Thomas Jacket cast mud out of the pond by Tully's house and made an end of Rickman's wheat furrough. Old Dick Banks made an end of thrashing the wheat in the barne's floor, helpt carry dung after. Young Dick Banks and Willy carry'd did severall jobbs in the morning and carry'd John Smith's dung after, 12 loads. Paid Harry Courtness 6d for 2 letters he had set down and also for severall things for Willy's coat. Sent a letter to Jude Storer by post. Mr Henry Campion and Mrs Courthope here afternoon. Paid Eliz Cheal for hop tying etc 4s-9d.

The 19th September 1718 Fryday. A dry day, John Gun and Thomas Jacket and his boy carry'd stubble by Wickham's, 7 loads to the rick goeing to the fatting close. Old Dick Banks, Young Dick Banks and Willy carry'd dung and dirt out of the Towne,      loads into the Churchfield and      loads into the Rookwood. My Wife, Jacky and I went to Lewis, swapt a saddle with my Cousin Peter, gave 6s-6d to boot. Paid Stephen Avery 6d for new stuffing a saddle. Paid Thomas Friend £2-6s-6d for camlet etc for my Mother Stone and receiv'd 2 guineas again when I came home. Paid Samuel Tourl by my Wife, all that was due. Frank Holden put his mare in my ground at 18d per week.

The 20th September 1718 Saturday. A dry day. John Gun, Banks, Thomas Jacket, Young Dick Banks and Willy carry'd 50 loads of dung into the Churchfield. I were at Danny afternoon, receiv'd Mr Peter Courthope's Poor Tax. Receiv'd 4s of John Snashall jr for Thomas Hart's nest of draws.

The 21st September 1718 Sunday. A gloomy day, some rain. Mr William Martin preacht. I supt at Mrs Catherine Beard's. Were a while at my Father's with Mr Richard Whitpaine and his wife Mary.

The 22nd September 1718 Munday. A fine day. John Gun, Thomas Jacket, Old Dick Banks and his son dung'd, 51 loads into the Churchfield. Reckon'd with William Roach. Paid him 17s, due to me 4s-2d. George Piony found a hare. My Father, Mr William Martin, Mr Beard, Willy and I went to course her, kill'd her.

The 23rd September 1718 Tuesday. A fine day. John Coulstock here in the morning. I gave him a note of my hand to move the hay or sort it out in the close, if the landlord was paid. Old Dick Banks, his son and Thomas Jacket made an end of carrying dung      loads, in all 138 loads in the Churchfield. My Wife, Mr Richard Whitpaine, Jacky and I went to Shiprods to my Cousin Cheal's, din'd there with Mr Richard Carrol, Dr Lintott and Harry Goffe. John Gun cutting the furz hedge etc.

The 24th September 1718 Wednesday. A fine day. John Gun helpt measure apples and cast mud out of the pond by Tully's house. Old Dick Banks and Dick fetch 2 loads of small chalk to Rickman's and brought 2 home. Willy set out for Wayhill Fair with Mr Richard Whitpaine. My Cousin Jenny Libbard came hither afternoon. Receiv'd 31s-6d of Stedman of Horsham for 21 bushels of apples. He had likewise 22½ bushels of my Father. Paid Widdow Tully 12s and clear'd accounts.

The 25th September 1718 Thursday. A dry day. John Gun workt for himself. Old Dick Banks and Dick carry'd 2 loads of chalk to Rickman's, gather'd apples after. Receiv'd a letter of attorney from Mr Richard Barcroft to take the rent for Rickman's at Michaelmas of Widdow Heath. Din'd and supt at my Father's.

The 26th September 1718 Fryday. A gloomy day, smart showr in the night. Richard Heath's sale. Old William Brand and Dick fetcht 2 loads of small chalk and 2 loads of sand to Rickman's. John Gun mended some gaps and scour'd a watring and cut the woods at the tail of the new pond. Receiv'd £32 of John Smith jr and concluded to have his cow at £5. Receiv'd 7s-6d of Old Hyder for half a cord of wood. Receiv'd his Poor Tax and paid him Widdow Reed's rent to Michaelmas. Paid Taylor at the Comon 16s for 1000 of bricks and agreed with him to send in half a load of lime to Rickman's at 1s for the carriage and the comon price for the lime. My Wife and Cousin Jenny Libbard were at Westtowne. Paid Thomas Reeve £1 for my Window Tax due at Lady Day last. Paid at the sale. The smallpox came out on Frank Osbourne.

The 27th September 1718 Saturday. A gloomy day. John Gun did not work. Paid John Gun 30s. Thomas Collingham and Samuel Jarvice heal'd the poarch etc. Old Dick Banks and Dick carry'd 2 court load and a waggon load of small chalk to Rickman's. John Towner and Ja Reed saw'd stuff for the wainhouse. Receiv'd my 10 sacks from Blackstone that went to Darkin.

The 28th September 1718 Sunday. A very wet day. Mr William Martin preacht. George Piony din'd here.

The 29th September 1718 Munday. A dry day. Stenning Fair. John Gun and Old Dick Banks did not work. Paid Young Dick Banks 2 guineas. He kept holy day. Thomas Hamper made a new manger ---------- 59 days. Jack Mills workt 'till noon. John Coulstock here in the morning.

The 30th September 1718 Tuesday. A gloomy day. My Cousin Jane Libbard and Dick Banks and George Courtness set out for Chichester. Thomas Hamper and Jack Mills finisht the manger about 9 aclock. Old Dick Banks carry'd 2 court loads of chalk to Rickman's.

Paid Taylor 6s-6d for half a load of lime deliver'd at Rickman's. Settled the account between Matt Heath and Mr Richard Barcroft and my self receiv'd £5-13-5d, outset 30s for dung and pasture, 12s for clover seed sow'd last Spring and 4s-7d for the repair of Ruckford alias Rickman's Bridge, in all £8 for the half years rent due at Michaelmas last. Took a chamber at Hollingall's for Parker's wife at 12s-6d 'till Lady Day last and past my word for her rent due to _____ . John Coulstock and his son were at Matt Heath's with me and the young man paid the mony. Paid Thomas Ilman the £30 due to him on bond and intrest. Mrs Mary Whitpaine, Mrs Scutt and Mrs Scrase of Stanmer here.

The 1st October 1718 Wednesday. A gloomy morning, very wet after. Bett came from Chichester. Old Dick Banks mov'd to Rickman's to give 40s per annum rent and to keep a hog and to keep a cow at 40d more but to sow the ground into the bargain. John Gun scour'd a pond in Tully's ground 'till it rain'd. Thrasht barly after. Mr John Cheal and his wife din'd at my Father's and Cousin Bodle.

The 2nd October 1718 Thursday. A very wet day. John Gun, Banks and George West mow'd stubble a while in the morning, John Gun begun thrash beans after. Banks did not work, George West drest flax, Young Dick Banks did severall jobbs. Mrs Cheal, Cousin Bodle and my Father and Mother Stone din'd here.

The 3rd October 1718 Fryday. A showry day. Willy return'd from Wayhill Fair. Brought home a black horse colt at £6-10s, 2 years old, coming 3. John Gun, Old Dick Banks and George West mow'd stubble. Young Dick Banks drew trees to the sawpit at Rickman's. Receiv'd a letter from Mr Jeremiah Dodson with one from Mr Kitt Campion to him inclos'd. Turn'd 20 ewes, 2 lambs and 2 rams into Rickman's ground. I supt at my Father's.

The 4th October 1718 Saturday. A dry day. John Gun, Banks and George West made an end of the stubble. George Buckwell set up a payr of barrs at Rickman's, the posts and rails were some that were on the ground before. Dick Banks drew the rest of the trees at Rickman's and Willy and he drove the 6 yearlings thither. I were to see a hare cours'd with severall others. Carry'd 17 sacks to Thomas Jacket's to mending. Lost a ewe at Rickman's last night. Receiv'd Parker's rent yesterday and the 2s I had given her. Paid 13s to Greenaway's wife for Parker's rent.

The 5th October 1718 Sunday. A dry day. Mr William Martin preacht. We had a parish meeting as usual, settled the accounts.

The 6th October 1718 Munday. A very windy, dry day. John Gun, Willy and Young Dick Banks begun winnow the wheat. John Gun thrasht barly after. Young Dick Banks and Willy carry'd 2 loads of Thomas Jacket's flints. Sold Thomas Jacket all my course wheat at 20d per bushel and the skreenings at 10d per bushel measur'd and some in 6 bushels of the wheat and 4½ bushels of the skreenings. Old Dick Banks had away a small cow at £3 if he likes. I was at Mr Burry's to see his fish with Mr Beard, Michael Stacey and John Packham, but they did not get out the water. Thomas Hamper and John Mills workt on the wainhouse from 3 aclock afternoon and 1 day before ------------ 60½ days.

The 7th October 1718 Tuesday. A fine day. Win'd 24½ bushels of the Nine Acres wheat. John Gun and Banks harrow'd and sow'd in the Bankfield after they had win'd the wheat. Young Dick Banks and Willy plough'd. Thomas Hamper, Jack Mills and Marten workt on the wainhouse ------------ 61½ days. Paid Mrs Anne Beard yesterday 7s for 14 weeks for Molly Balcomb, 1s for thread and 3d for washing a payr of gloves. John Pierce workt here to day and yesterday mending _____ . My Wife and I supt and spent the evning at Westtowne.

The 8th October 1718 Wednesday. A stormy day, wet afternoon. Paid Dick Lashmer 2s for digging the sawpitt at Rickman's. John Towner and Ja Reed begun saw there. Young Dick Banks and Willy plough'd 'till near noon, did severall jobbs after. John Gun sow'd and harrow'd 'till noon, thrasht beans after. Old Dick Banks mended gaps and thrasht barly. Thomas Hamper workt on the wainhouse 'till noon and after on a payr of winnowers ------------ 62½ days. Sold John Smith my 4 fatting cows at £17-10s and 2 tongues. Mr William Martin supt and spent the evning here.

The 9th October 1718 Thursday. A very stormy day, thunder last night. Thomas Hamper and Marten and Jack Mills workt on the wainhouse --------- 63½ days. Dick Banks went to Lewis with apples and pares brought 1000 of 3" and 1000 4" nails for which he paid 5s.

Brought also 4 ozs of bohea not paid for. Old Dick Banks did some water furroughing at Rickman's. John Gun did not work. Borrow'd my Cousin John Lindfield's bites. Paid Mr Osbourne 2s for his fees for a licence to cut 3 spire trees on Rickman's and 4d for the Lord of the Manor. John Stone was at Mr Osbourne's with me. Willy and I cours'd a hare George Piony found in Devils Ditch, kill'd her. John Pierce workt here to day and yesterday. Receiv'd 8s of my Cousin Bodle of Hailsham for a payr of stays of my Cousin Molly Balcomb, when she was here.

The 10th October 1718 Fryday. A stormy day. Old Dick Banks made water furroughs at Rickman's. John Gun, Young Dick Banks and Willy carry'd dung into Tully's close. John Towner and Ja Reed saw'd at Rickman's to day and yesterday. George Buckwell hew'd timber there. Thomas Hamper, Marten and Jack Mills workt on the wainhouse ------------ 64½ days. The Widdow Cecilia Marks's sale to day. Thomas Norton jr had 20 bushels of wheat on Mr Richard Whitpaine's account.

The 11th October 1718 Saturday. A gloomy day, little rain, a very wet night. Thomas Hamper, Marten and Jack Mills rais'd the wainhouse ------ 65½ days.
Old Dick Banks thrasht barly. John Gun, Young Dick Banks and Willy carry'd dung and mudd at Tully's etc. Reckon'd and clear'd accounts with Stephen Bine, except wheat carriage. Reckon'd also and clear'd accounts with Richard Wood. Paid my Sister Bett 5 guineas for my Mother.

The 12th October 1718 Sunday. A dry day. Mr William Martin preacht. Mr John Hart return'd out of Stafford Shire. He, Mr _____, Mr Richard Whitpaine, my Father and Mrs Scutt supt here.

The 13th October 1718 Munday. A fine day. John Gun, Young Dick Banks and Willy plough'd _____.
Old Dick Banks thrasht barly and cut ashen rafters. Thomas Hamper and Marten workt on the wainhouse ------- 66½ days. Receiv'd 2 guineas of Old Dick Banks towards his cow. Old William Brand, Sanders and the 2 boys workt on the oven at Rickman's. Receiv'd a letter from Mr Richard Barcroft wherein he allow'd me 20s more towards the repairs of Rickman's.

The 14th October 1718 Tuesday. A dry forenoon, very wet after. Old Dick Banks thrasht. Young Dick Banks and Willy plough'd. John Gun sow'd and Old Dick Banks harrow'd. John Gun carry'd 150 of Old William Brand's bricks to Rickman's. Lent Mr Jeremiah Dodson 2 guineas. He was here in the morning. I din'd with Mr William Martin with Mr Dodson, Mr Storer, Mr Price, Mr Owen, Mr Beaumont, Mr Bird, Mr Chatfield, my Father, Mr Beard and Mr Richard Whitpaine. Mr Scutt and Mr John Hart came after dinner.
Thomas Hamper, Marten and Jack workt on the wainhouse 'till 3 aclock -------- 67¼ days.

The 15th October 1718 Wednesday. A fine day. John Gun and Old Dick Banks mow'd stubble at Rickman's 'till noon, sow'd and harrow'd after. Young Dick Banks and Willy did severall jobbs 'till noon, plough'd after. Lent Mr Richard Whitpaine 4 guineas for a note of his hand. I was at Mr Jeremiah Dodson's afternoon, hir'd his Haybell Croft for 2 crops from next Spring, for the 1st I am to give 55s per acre, for the 2nd 40s per acre, but if when I have plough'd him the 1st time I do not like the ground, I am to lease the ploughing and to be off the bargain. Paid Boniface 4s-8d for spreading 138 loads of dung in the Churchfield.

The 16th October 1718 Thursday. A fine day. Begun a weekly club at the Swan. John Gun, Young Dick Banks and Willy made an end of sowing the Bankfield. Sow'd 16½ bushels of Brother John Box's wheat. Old Dick Banks thrasht barly. Paid Widdow Tully 6d per bushel for picking up acorns. She pickt up 5½ bushels, but the comon price is 4d per bushel.

The 17th October 1718 Fryday. A very fine day. Begun plough Tully's first field below the mead with 2 teems. Paid Old William Brand a guinea. Thomas Hayne was with me from my Aunt Holden. Mr Todd and Mrs Kettilby went for London. Paid Mr John Hart 25s yesterday for a quarter's schooling due at Michaelmas. Receiv'd 5s of Stephen Bine for the carriage of 2 loads of wheat sheavs. Thomas Hamper, Marten and Mills workt at Towne setting up the posts and rails before the house ------ 68 days. I was at the Swan with Mr Price, Mr John Hart and Mr Scutt and George Whitpaine. Receiv'd 18d of Stephen Bine for an ax of William Balcomb's.

The 18th October 1718 Saturday. A very fine day. Plough'd and sow'd as yesterday. Thomas Jacket set the stubble to rights this afternoon and yesterday afternoon. Thomas Hamper and Jack Mills finisht the rails in the

Towne --------- 69 days. I supt at Westtowne with Mr John Hart and Mr Scutt. John Gun had a bushel of malt.

The 19th October 1718 Sunday. A gloomy day. Mr William Martin preacht, no service afternoon. My Brother Peter and Brother Henry Faulkoner here afternoon.

The 20th October 1718 Munday. A gloomy day. Finisht Tully's field haveing sow'd about 10 bushels of my Brother John Box's wheat. Young Dick Banks and Willy harrow'd etc. Old Dick Banks and Thomas Jacket carry'd 4 loads of the Nine Acres stubble to Tully's and helpt plough the headlands. Mrs Mary Gratwick din'd here. Lent my Cousin John Lindfield 25 guineas for a note of his hand. My Wife and John Gun went to Mr Wade's at Henfield.

The 21st October 1718 Tuesday. A gloomy day with small rain. Willy went to Balcombe. Young Dick Banks fetcht 750 bricks from Taylor's for Dick Kidd. John Gun and Old Dick Banks mow'd stubble at Rickman's. I were to speak with John Box sr afternoon. Receiv'd William Game's Poor Tax per John Smith jr. John Smith fetcht one of the black cows. Receiv'd 15s of Thomas Coates for 6 bushels of pease to be deliver'd at his request.

The 22nd October 1718 Wednesday. A fine day. Old Dick Banks made water furroughs etc. John Gun made an end of thrashing beans and win'd on 14½ bushels. Young Dick Banks and Willy carry'd 6 loads of the Nine Acres stubble. Receiv'd £4-10s from Richard Collens and 20s outset for carriage from Warninglid and selling at Darkin per Harry Wickham, also 20s for my Father for part of a load of wheat straw. Sent a letter to my Cousin Hayne per Nick Plaw. Towner had a bushel of pease at 2s-6d per Willy.

The 23rd October 1718 Thursday. A fine day. John Gun thrasht and win'd 6½ bushels of oates. Young Dick Banks and Willy fetcht 750 bricks from Taylor's. Old Dick Banks thrasht barly and drove home 6 young beasts. Paid my Father the mony I receiv'd of Richard Collens yesterday. Mr Price, my Father, Mr Beard and Mr Richard Whitpaine at Mr Scutt's. Carry'd the little round plough to Howell's for new handles.

The 24th October 1718 Fryday. A gloomy day. Old John Smith died last night. Receiv'd the 2 guineas I lent Mr Jeremiah Dodson per his man. Receiv'd likewise the mortar I lent him per Dick Banks. Brought 250 bricks from Towne to the wainhouse. Shut up 5 hogs a fatting and begun feed the white piggs with acorns. Young Dick Banks did severall jobbs. John Gun thrasht oates. Willy went to coursing with my Brother Will. Mrs Catherine Beard had a sack of seed wheat at 12s per Allan Savage.

The 25th October 1718 Saturday. A fine day. Thomas Holden and Dick Smith begun thatch the wainhouse. Old Dick Banks made an end of thrashing the barly that lay in the floor and begun winnow it. John Gun thrasht oates. Young Dick Banks did severall jobbs. Willy went to coursing with my Brother Will. Jack Lindfield and his brother cut 4 pollards.
Mr Richard Whitpaine, my Brother Peter and I were at Lewis about Thomas Westover's and Oliver's apprentice. Mrs Catherine Beard had an other sack of wheat and Towner a bushel of pease. Turn'd the fatting oxen into the cow field and the cows into the Fifteen Acres. John Smith kill'd the Wintermilch's calf.

The 26th October 1718 Sunday. A gloomy day. Mr William Martin preacht. Paid Samuel Tourl yesterday in full 19s-6d in full of all.

The 27th October 1718 Munday. A fine day. Old John Smith buried. *(Ed: Recorded in Hurst Parish Register)*
Old Dick Banks win'd and screen'd his barly 3½ head and about 4 bushels tail and screenings. Begun thrash breaking pease. Holden and Dick Smith thatcht. John Gun thrasht oates. Brand's boys workt 'till a little after noon. Paid Old William Brand a guinea per William and Sam Jarvice. Paid John Westover 36s-6d in full of all accounts. Goodman Richard White and I went to Richard Divall's of Birdshole to treat with A Divall about the herriot but came to no conclusion only White paid him a years rent for which Divall and John Hayne gave him a receit that is for two thirds of the rent for he had (by their consent) paid the Widdow Lintott of Collwood a third part. Simple Dick Lintott's hounds brought a hare through my ground and just by the house to day.

The 28th October 1718 Tuesday. A fine day. Dick and John Gun, kept holy day. Old Dick Banks thrasht pease. Jack Lindfield and his brother William cut the great tree in Tully's orchard and a jobb or two beside. Holden and Dick Smith thatcht. Jack Bartlet faggoted.

Brewed 10 bushels of malt for my Father. My Brother Will and Peter supt here. My Brother John Box and Sister here a while in the evning. Paid my Brother John Box £4-11s for 28 bushels of seed wheat.

The 29th October 1718 Wednesday. A gloomy day. Banks thrasht pease. Jack Lindfield and his brother cut 4 spire trees in Tully's mead and Dick Banks fetcht 6 ridge tiles and half a load of lime from Parker's and brought the plough from Howell's, drew timber afternoon. John Gun, Thomas Jacket and Widdow Tully win'd 29½ bushels of John Gun's oates afternoon. Thomas Hamper workt on the great gates by the Towne ------- 79 days. Holden and Smith thatched.

The 30th October 1718 Thursday. A gloomy day, some rain. Holden and Smith thatched. Jack Bartlet and Dick Banks carry'd 100 faggots to my Father's and a load of straw and pease haum to Rickman's.
Thomas Hamper workt on the Towne gates ---- 80 days. John Gun faggoted and win'd ____ bushels of tail oates. Old Dick Banks and Willy carry'd a load of barly straw to Rickman's, carry'd wood etc for Old Dick Banks and brought up the oates from Tully's. John Towner and Ja Reed saw'd the posts for the Towne gates afternoon. Receiv'd a letter from Mr Richard Barcroft per post, wherein he order'd me to put Rickman's house in tennantable repair, to build a new oven and to do the thatching when I thought fitt. Paid 6d for Mr Richard Whitpaine at the Swan, being his forfiture for the 1st club night. Thomas Holden had part of 2 bushels of pease brought up from Tully's for him per Willy and Jack Bartlet or Old Dick Banks.

The 31st October 1718 Fryday. A gloomy day. Holden and Smith thatcht. He begun pug clover at Tully's. Old Dick Banks did not work. He had a bushel of barly. Holden had 2 bushels of pease.
Thomas Hamper 3, Marten and Jack Mills's 1 workt on the Towne gates ---- 81 days. Dick Banks drew up the gate posts etc. Young John Snashall and his wife, the Widdow Snashall and Mrs Futcher was here afternoon. Mrs Mary Whitpaine and Mr Harry Dodson came towards night. Mrs Gratwick set out for Lewis in my Father's chaese.

The 1st November 1718 Saturday. A gloomy day. John Gun and Old Dick Banks did _____ .

Young Dick Banks kept holy day. Dick Wood dockt the black colt. Thomas Hamper 4, Marten 2 workt on the towne gates ------ 82 days.
Towner had a bushel of pease per Dick Banks. Willy went to Balcombe with his Unkle William.

The 2nd November 1718 Sunday. A fine day. Mr William Martin preacht. My Wife and I supt at Mrs Catherine Beard's.

The 3rd November 1718 Munday. A gloomy day. John Gun workt in the garden. Old Dick Banks and Dick brought home the heifer and _____ . Deliver'd 2 bushels of pease to Thomas Holden per Dick Banks and 3 bushels of barly to Old Dick Banks. John Smith's man kill'd a porker for me. Holden and Smith thatcht on the fatting hovel. Old William Brand, Vallence and William Jarvice workt on the underpinning of the wainhouse. Thomas Hamper 5, Marten 3 and Jack Mills 2 workt on the Towne gates --------- 83 days.
I gave Mr Beard an order on Mr Robert's for the 8een pounds I had in his hands and also my Brother James Ede's receit to Robert Skinner for the £50 which he receiv'd for part of William Balcomb's hops and paid to Mrs Margret Fagg. Mr Scutt, Mr John Hart and I supt at my Father's. Lent Mrs Catherine Beard the iron rake that was at Edgly _____ . Paid the Widdows Herriot and Webb 4s each; Wells and _____ .

The 4th November 1718 Tuesday. A gloomy day. John Gun faggotted. Old Dick Banks did not work. Holden and Smith thatcht on the fatting hovel.
Thomas Hamper 6, Marten 4 and Jack 3, workt on the Towne gates ----- 84 days. Young Dick Banks drew trees etc out of Rookwood and Churchfield and 1 of Tully's. My Wife and Cousin Plump etc went to Lewis to fetch home Mrs Gratwick. I supt at my Father Stone's. Nick Plaw was here with a message from my Aunt Holden. Paid Mrs Atkinson 35s for things for Molly Balcomb when she went to school.

The 5th November 1718 Wednesday. A dry day. Old Dick Banks thatcht and win'd 9 bushels of pease. Deliver'd 6 bushels of pease to Thomas Jacket per Dick, kept holy day after. Paid Holden 19s-2d in full of all. Towner fetcht 3 bushels of pease.
Thomas Hamper 7, Marten 5 and Jack 4, allmost finisht the town gates ---- 85 days. My Cousin John Lindfield supt and spent the evning here.

The 6th November 1718 Thursday. A fine day. John Gun faggoted, Old Dick Banks thrasht. Young Dick Banks and Jack carry'd 9 bushels of pease to Mrs Tweedale's to be sold. Receiv'd 28s-6d of Mr William Martin for keeping his mare. My Cousin Nick Marchant carry'd home a sample of pease. Thomas Hamper's man, Marten finisht the gates an hour or 2 in the morning. My Father, Mr Richard Whitpaine, Mr Scutt, Mr John Hart and I at the club. Old Dick Banks had half a bushel of wheat per Willy. Willy return'd from Balcombe.

The 7th November 1718 Fryday. A fine day. John Gun pug'd clover. Old Dick Banks mended gaps etc. Young Dick Banks fetcht 2 small jobbs of sand and Willy and he carry'd the stubble at Rickman's, afterwards 4 cart loads. Willy was coursing with Mr Richard Whitpaine in the morning. John Box sr, one Thomas Tobut a miller and I were to view the Widdow Hayne's windmill. Paid 1s-4d to Thomas Tobut for his journey and 1s-7d to expences at the George, in all 2s.

The 8th November 1718 Saturday. A gloomy day. A Fair at Howards Heath. I was at Westtowne in the morning. Reckon'd with Mr Richard Whitpaine and there is due to me £9-9-6d for which he gave me a note of his hand.

The 9th November 1718 Sunday. A dry day. Mr Jeremiah Dodson preacht. We had a meeting about Dog Smith's mony. Mr Scutt, Mr John Hart and I supt at Westtowne.

The 10th November 1718 Munday. A gloomy day. John Gun helpt kill 2 hogs in the morning, helpt Old Dick Banks mend gaps after. Old Dick Banks mended gaps. Young Dick Banks and Willy begun plough the Nine Acres. My Father, Mother, Wife and I din'd at my Brother John Box's.

The 11th November 1718 Tuesday. A gloomy day. John Gun and Richard White pug'd clover. Old Dick Banks clear'd 12 bushels of breaking pease. Young Dick Banks and Willy plough'd. Weigh'd my Father's hog 16 nail 6lb at 22d per nail.

The 12th November 1718 Wednesday. A gloomy day, some rain in the morning. John Gun and White pug'd clover. Banks thrasht pease. Young Dick Banks and Willy plough'd. William Courtness and Willy and I went to course a hare. John Gun found it. Din'd and supt at my Father's.

The 13th November 1718 Thursday. A fine day. John Gun and White win'd clover pug, Widdow Tully helpt. Old Dick Banks mend gaps etc. Dick and Willy plough'd. Deliver'd 2 bushels of breaking pease to E Harrodon _____ . Thomas Hamper and Jack workt hewing timber 'till noon ----------- 85½ days.

The 14th November 1718 Fryday. A fine day. John Gun and White win'd and pug'd clover. John Towner and Ja Reed saw'd to day and yesterday. Reed had half a bushel of breaking pease to day at 21d and a bushel of barly yesterday at 2s. Mr Price, my Father, Mr Richard Whitpaine, Mr John Hart and I were at the club last night. Mrs Anne White, her 2 nieces, Mrs Catherine Beard and my Grandmother supt here last night. Receiv'd 28s last night of Mrs Catherine Beard in full for seed wheat. John Box sr and I were this day at Henfield at the King's Head and there sold the windmill that was John Hayne's to one Henry Charman of Billinghurst for £75. He is to pay all charges of writeings etc and to enter at Christmas next and to seal the writeing on Saturday the 13th of December at the White Horse in Horsham. Paid 5s for dinner and expences. Receiv'd 1s in hand. Mr Vans made an Article between us which we left in Thomas Wilson's hands. John Vinall and Mr Vans were witness to the Article. We also talkt with my Cousin John Goffe the butcher and he promis'd to give us a counter bond on William Balcomb's account and Mr Van's was order'd to do it.

The 15th November 1718 Saturday. A wet day. Old Dick Banks and John Gun thrasht pease. Young Dick Banks and Willy plough'd 2 ridge etc. Deliver'd 4 bushels of old pease to Thomas Westover per Dick Bank.

The 16th November 1718 Sunday. A gloomy day some rain. Mr Jeremiah Dodson preacht. Mr John Hart supt and spent the evning here. I was not at Church in the forenoon.

The 17th November 1718 Munday. A gloomy day, some rain. Shut up the fatting oxen. John Gun and Old Dick Banks thrasht pease. Young Dick Banks and Willy carry'd litter into the fatting close and other jobbs. Receiv'd 15s-9d of John Cook of Bolny for 6 bushels of old pease. John Towner and Ja Reed saw'd. Mr Scutt and his wife here afternoon. My Father and Mother Stone supt and spent the evning here. Mr Scutt paid me his Poor Tax.

The 18th November 1718 Tuesday. A dry day. Reckon'd and clear'd accounts with Stephen Bine. Old George Buckwell died to day. Old Dick Banks and Jack clean'd bushels of breaking pease. Mr Courtness had half a bushel of breaking pease ⸳. Receiv'd 5s-3d of Courtice's wife for 2 bushels old pease. Young Dick Banks and Willy plough'd. John Gun begun the ditch in the Middle Piece about noon. My Wife and I supt and spent the evning at Mrs Catherine Beard's.

The 19th November 1718 Wednesday. A driling forenoon, very wet after. Old Dick Banks did not work. John Gun helpt kill a hog in the morning, ditcht a while and win'd 8 bushels of pease of his thrashing. Mr Woodham came to my Father's. Young Dick Banks and Willy plough'd 'till noon. Reckon'd with the Sawyers and clear'd accounts, only Towner is to have 4 bushels of pease and 4 bushels of barly. Old Dick Banks had half a bushel of wheat.

The 20th November 1718 Thursday. A very wet day. Mr Jeremiah Dodson's tythe feast. Old Dick Banks did not work. Young Dick Banks and Willy plough'd a little while. John Gun thrasht pease. My Wife, Molly and Nanny, went to Danny in the chaese. I was at Mr Dodson's tythe feast and paid Mr Dodson my Father's tythe, 2s which my Father paid me again at the club. I were at the club with Mr Price, Mr Osbourne, Mr John Hart, my Father, Mr Richard Whitpaine and Mr Scutt. Paid 6d for Mr Whitpaine at the club. I was at Mr Dodson's likewise in the morning and he did an errand to me from Mr Sixsmith.

The 21st November 1718 Fryday. A showry day. Old George Buckwell buried. *(Ed: Recorded in Hurst Parish Register as "George Buckwell sen)* John Gun ditcht, Old Dick Banks did not work. Young Dick Banks and Willy plough'd. Willy and I were to see a hare course'd which John Grey found, we kill'd her and left her at Danny. Harry Wickham had half a bushel of breaking pease per his boy.

The 22nd November 1718 Saturday. A showry day. Willy and Dick made an end of the Nine Acres. John Gun ditcht. Old Dick Banks did not work. Turn'd the 4 oxen that are to be fatted into Tully's Mead. I made my will to which John Smith, the butcher, John Westover and my man Dick Banks are witnesses. Willy and Bett spent the evning at Wanbarrow.

The 23rd November 1718 Sunday. A fine day. Mr Jeremiah Dodson preacht. I was at John Stone's with Mr John Hart after evning prayr. We supt at Westtowne. My Cousin John Lindfield din'd here and paid me the 25 guineas and I return'd his note.

The 24th November 1718 Munday. A very fine day. Jack Lindfield and his brother begun Tully's garden fence. Paid 2s-9d to a Scotch man John Gracie for a handcerchief for Molly Balcomb. Dick draw'd up posts and nails etc for the fence etc. John Gun ditcht. Old Dick Banks thrasht barly. Receiv'd 2s-7d of Courtice's maid for 2 bushels of old pease and ⸳. My Father and Mother Stone, my Wife and I supt at Westtowne. Willy and William Norton and I went to coursing.

The 25th November 1718 Tuesday. A gloomy day. John Gun workt for himself. Banks thrasht. Young Dick Banks and Willy made water furroughs in the morning. John Gun workt for himself. William Lindfield workt on the garden fence, his brother did not work because his wife was in labour. Receiv'd 17d of Abraham Muzll for 34lb of bakon and 6d for a gallon of breaking pease. Receiv'd Mr Jeremiah Dodson's Poor Tax. My Father had a gallon of pease per S Marten.

~~The 26th November 1718 Wednesday. A gloomy day. Rain towards night. Old Dick Banks thrasht barly, John Gun ditcht and had a bushel of malt. Deliver'd 6 bushels of pease to Jacket per Dick Banks. Willy were to coursing in the morning, Young Dick Banks and he fetcht up a pbb of flax etc afterwards.~~

The 26th November 1718 Wednesday. A very fine day. Old Dick Banks thrasht. John Gun ditcht. Young Dick Banks and Willy carry'd 3 bushels of apples to Brighton, 6 bushels of breaking pease to the postwoman's and 7 bushels to an other woman on Lettice Holden's account. John Smith kill'd the spaid heifer.

The 27th November 1718 Thursday. A gloomy day, rain towards night. John Gun ~~thrasht~~ ditcht. Old Dick Banks thrasht barly part of the day. Thomas Jacket had 6 bushels of old pease and Dick Banks, put 6 bushels of new pease in the tub for the fatting hogs. Mr Vans of Henfield was here and took a coppy of 2 deeds about John Hayne's windmill. Weigh'd the spaid heifer at John Smith's. She weigh'd 91 nail, I am to have 17d per nail for her, 5 quarters. Willy went a coursing with William Norton in the forenoon. Afterwards Dick and he fetch't up flax etc. Mr Ede's horse had a bushel of oates.

The 28th November 1718 Fryday. A stormy day. Old Dick Banks thrasht. John Gun ditcht. Young Dick Banks had the ball mare to Frank Marshall's in the morning. Afterwards Willy and he carry'd 2 loads of flints. Willy and Jack Haslegrove put 2 runts to Rickman's and 3 into the field by Hyder's, the 2 wintermilches into the hop garden, the other 5 cows and the little bullstag into the Cowfield, the lean oxen into the Fifteen Acres and the calves into the Edgly mead. I mended Mr Richard Whitpaine's skreen and sent it home per Jack. I had half a quarter of the spaid heifer weigh'd of which my Father had 4 nails 7lb at 18d per nail.

The 29th November 1718 Saturday. A dry day. John Gun workt for himself, so did Banks. Young Dick Banks carry'd 1½ load of Thomas Jacket's flints etc. Receiv'd 11s of Widdow Wickham per Dick Banks for a sack of old pease. Jack Lindfield and his brother workt on Tully's garden to day or, I think, yesterday. Sent Stephen Bine £2-6s for a note of his hand. Nick Plaw supt here.

The 30th November 1718 Sunday. A dry day. Mr Jeremiah Dodson preacht. Mr Litchford's claim was paid to Lady Day last. Mr Richard Whitpaine his wife and 2 children supt here.

The 1st December 1718 Munday. A very fine day, John Gun begun cut the wheat mow. John Lindfield and his brother finisht Tully's garden fence. Lent Mrs Catherine Beard 50s on bond at 5 per cent and part of it was 6 per cent which Mr Ralph Beard receiv'd of Mr Roberds in London. Kill'd 2 of the pigs I had of my Cousin John Lindfield. They weigh'd about 6 nail a pig. Willy helpt. Young Dick Banks and Willy carry'd an other load of Thomas Jacket's flints and litter into the fatting close etc. Old Dick Banks thrasht. Mr Ralph Beard and I were at Captain Whitpaine's in the evning. Afterwards supt at Mrs Catherine Beard's.

The 2nd December 1718 Tuesday. A stormy day. Old Dick Banks and John Gun thrasht. John Lindfield and his brother set up a gate post in Tully's garden. Mrs Catherine Beard and her son were here in the morning and she seal'd a bond to me for the mony lent yesterday, Mr Ralph Beard and Nan Wood witnesses. Young Dick Banks and Willy begun fallow the field per Wickham's. Paid my Mother 4 guineas and clear'd accounts to Michaelmas last. Old Dick Banks had part of a sack of barly and is to have the rest.

The 3rd December 1718 Wednesday. A dry day. John Gun cut wood. Banks thrasht. Young Dick Banks and Willy clear'd and litter'd the home close and shut up the lean oxen. Thomas Hamper made a gate to hang up by Holden's --- 86½ days. Paid Jack Lindfield 15s-6d in full of all being 10s for the fence round Tully's garden, the rest for other work. They cut and cleft 2 spire trees in Tully's Mead to day. Mr John Hart din'd here.

The 4th December 1718 Thursday. A stormy day. Old Dick Banks thrasht barly. Win'd 10 bushels of John Gun's pease. Young Dick Banks and Willy carry'd more litter into the close. Tipt the lean oxen rick etc. Thomas Hamper, Marten and Jack begun hang up the gate by Holden's ------- 87½ days. I were at the club with Mr Peter Courthope, Mr Price, Mr Scutt, Mr Beard and Mr John Hart.

The 5th December 1718 Fryday. A fine day. Old Dick Banks begun winnow his barly. Young Dick Banks and Willy drew up pales, rails, etc. John Gun thrasht oats. My Cousin John Lindfield and Thomas Skinner of Rigate came to see my oxen but we did not deal. I went with them to Captain Whitpaine's and Thomas Skinner bought his 4 oxen at £37-10s and paid the mony down.

The 6th December 1718 Saturday. A very fine day. Old Dick Banks thrasht pease. My Cousin John Lindfield and Thomas Skinner lay here last night. I sold Skinner my 2 oxen and a steer at £30 to be gone before Christmas. I went with them to Wanbarrow and left them there. John Gun thrasht oates. Young Dick Banks and Willy plough'd 'till noon, broak their plough and fetch water for brewing afterwards.
Thomas Hamper, Marten and Jack finisht the gate by Holden's yesterday and workt on the fence between the stables and house at Towne to day ------------ 89½ days. Sold 10 quarters of barly to William Beard at £8, to be deliver'd next week. Receiv'd a guinea in hand. Receiv'd £20 of John Smith.

The 7th December 1718 Sunday. A dry day.
Mr Jeremiah Dodson preacht. My Wife and I receiv'd the sacrament. We were a while at Mrs Catherine Beard's after evning prayr. We had a parish meeting as usual, settled my accounts. There came a man to my house for work in the forenoon, he said he came out of Kent, near [K........]. George West had 19lb of bakon in the morning at 3s per lb.

The 8th December 1718 Munday. A fine day. Old Dick Banks and John Gun thrasht. Young Dick Banks and Jack carry'd 2 bushels of pease to the postwoman's and 6 bushels to Lettice Holden's field. Receiv'd 10s of the latter. Thomas Hamper, Marten and Jack made an end of the fence between the stables and house at Towne and did some other jobbs -------- 90½ days.
Thomas Howell's man clipt my 2 turnrist ploughs.
Mr Jeremiah Dodson and I were at Church to look on my Wife's seat, which he gave me leave to enlarge as I desir'd.

The 9th December 1718 Tuesday. A dry day. John Gun thrasht oates. Old Dick Banks made an end of thrashing pease and begun winnow them. Young Dick Banks and Willy plough'd.
Allexander Snatt dug bean ground. Thomas Hamper and Marten alter'd my Wives' seat in the Church and made the door of my seat wider -------- 91½ days.
My Father, Mother and I supt at Mr Jeremiah Dodson's. Receiv'd 10 bushels of straw dried malt.

The 10th December 1718 Wednesday. A stormy day. Old Dick Banks, his son and Willy made an end of cleaning the pease, begun yesterday, 20 bushels. Afterwards Thomas Gravet and Old Dick Banks thrasht barly. Young Dick Banks and Willy did some jobbs afterwards. John Bodle had half a bushel of pease at 3s per bushel. Eliz Surgeant went away. John Gun thrasht oates. Allexander Snatt begun the ditch against the Churchfield. My Wife went to Danny afternoon. Dick Wood plated both the turnrist ploughs.

The 11th December 1718 Thursday. A fine day.
Old Dick Banks and Thomas Gravet thrasht. Allexander Snatt and his boy ditcht. John Gun thrasht. Young Dick Banks and Willy plough'd. Thomas Skinner and Richard Edwards of Rigate din'd here. Receiv'd £30 of Skinner for my oxen, Jack Haslegrove drove them to Hand Cross. I went to Danny with them and then return'd hither. I took Mr Scutt's fish out of the flat stew. Receiv'd 10s of the postwoman.

The 12th December 1718 Fryday. A fine day.
Thomas Gravet and Old Dick Banks thrasht 'till noon and afterwards win'd 6 quarters 6 bushels head and 2½ bushels tail of Old Dick Banks's barly. Old Dick Banks had half a bushel of barly wheat. Allexander Snatt and his boy ditcht, Snatt had a bushel of barly at 2s. Reckon'd and clear'd accounts with John Bodle.
Mrs Anne White din'd here. My Wife and she went to Westtowne. Thomas Skinner and Richard Edwards lay here last night and went away to day. Deliver'd 8½ quarters of barly to William Beard per Young Dick Banks and Thomas Gravet. John Bodle had half a bushel of pease and is to have 3 bushels more, paid for. Lodg'd 100 guineas with Mrs Catherine Beard.

The 13th December 1718 Saturday. A fine day. Old Dick Banks and Thomas Gravet thrasht. Young Dick Banks and Willy plough'd. John Gun thrasht oates. Deliver'd the 3 bushels of pease due to John Bodle per Dick. John Box and I went to Henfield to meet Henry Charman about the windmill but we could not make a good title to him so were forc'd to be off. Paid Charman the 1s again which I had had in hand. Paid likewise 18d for half the charges of the article made at our last meeting and expences at 3s-4d. Mr Barret of Billinghurst was there as Charman's attorney. We lett the mill to Charman for 4 years at £5 per annum, he to pay all manner of taxes and repairations and to enter at Christmas. We call'd at Nick Plaw's and at Westtowne as we came home. Mr Richard Whitpaine brought my part of my lease of Rickman's from Chichester, from whence he return'd to day with his eldest daughter.

The 14th December 1718 Sunday. A fine day.
Mr Jeremiah Dodson preacht, no service afternoon, Mr Dodson went to Newtimber. Mrs Anne White din'd here. She, Mrs Gratwick, my Father and Mother Stone and Mrs Susan Courthope spent the afternoon here.
I sent a letter to Mrs Chapman of Rusper per J Borer.

The 15th December 1718 Munday. A dry, cold day, a smart frost last night. Old Dick Banks and Thomas Gravet thrasht. So did John Gun. Allexander Snatt ditcht. Old William Brand, Vallence and the 2 boys workt on the back court at Towne.

Young Dick Banks and Willy plough'd the Towne Orchard and brought away _____ . Sold Harry Wickham 40 quarters of barly at 10s per quarter. Receiv'd 2s-6d in hand. John Stone was here in the evning, Settled accounts for Poor Tax and [rent].

The 16th December 1718 Tuesday. A gloomy day, snow and rain towards night. Old Dick Banks and Thomas Gravet thrasht. John Gun and Allexander Snatt ditcht. Young Dick Banks and Willy level'd the close at Towne etc. Reckon'd and clear'd accounts with John Gun. Paid Elizabeth Towner a bill for work for Molly Balcomb 5s-7½d

The 17th December 1718 Wednesday. A gloomy day, some rain. Old Dick Banks and Thomas Gravet thrasht. Paid Mrs Anne Beard 6s for schooling for Molly Balcomb. Lent John Gun a guinea and a half. He ditcht or thrasht oates. Allexander Snatt half a bushel of wheat and 10d. Young Dick Banks made an end of levelling my Father's close etc. Willy and Jack Haslegrove carry'd 6 bushels of pease to the postwoman's and a bushel to Lettice Holden's friend. My Father gave me an old plough share and colter and about 43 old harrow tines.

The 18th December 1718 Thursday. A gloomy day, some rain. Old Dick Banks and Thomas Gravet thrasht. Young Dick Banks deliver'd 2 bushels of old pease to Towner etc. Frank Marshall had the ball mare home to cure her back. Receiv'd 10s of the postwoman. John Gun ditch. Sent a letter to Jude Storer per post, about the seat etc. Willy and Jack Haslegrove carry'd 6 bushels of pease to Lettice Holden. Thomas Hamper and Jack Mills put up shelves at Tully's etc -------------- 92½ days. I think Allexander Snatt ditcht at Rickman's. Turn'd the 2 cows into the Middle Piece. Mary Anscomb came yesterday afternoon. Receiv'd half a hide of tan leather for harness of John Hart at _____ . Receiv'd 20s of Lettice Holden's friend on outsetting 18d for selling. Receiv'd £3-13-2d of Stephen Bine, being Dog Smith's mony. I were at the club with Mr Price, Mr Scutt, Mr Beard, Mr John Hart and Mr Richard Whitpaine.

The 19th December 1718 Fryday. A dry cold day. John Gun ditcht, Allexander Snatt and his boy at Rickman's. Win'd 11 quarters 2 bushels head and 2 bushels tail of Banks _____ . Young Dick Banks and Willy helpt in the forenoon and in the afternoon. Young Dick Banks begun cut up mole hills in Tully's farther field.

Goodman [Joak] of Newtimber lent me a blind horse as long as I want him, I am only to keep him for his work. Mr Richard Whitpaine was here in the morning, we shifted the _____ . Thomas Hamper and Jack Mills made an end of boarding the east side of the wainhouse and put up the celler windows at Towne ----- 93½ days. Mr John Hart supt and spent the evning here.

The 20th December 1718 Saturday. A dry day, smart frost last night. Allexander Snatt ditch. John Gun helpt kill a hog in the morning. Afterwards he and Willy cutt mole hills in Tully's farther field. Young Dick Banks carry'd 2 loads of loam earth for Stephen Bine. Afterwards carry'd mole hills. Deliver'd 12 bushels of barly to William Beard per Dick being the last of the half score. Receiv'd £2-19s of William Beard towards the barly and a guinea I had in hand. Old Dick Banks and Thomas Gravet begun thrash pease. Old Dick Banks had a bushel of wheat, I was a while with John Hart at John Smith's. He gave me leave to have a way through a field of the Latchets to go to Rickman's. William Norton and Allan Savage were at John Smith's. I were a little while at Mrs Catherine Beard's.

The 21st December 1718 Sunday. A gloomy day, smart frost last night. Mr Jeremiah Dodson preacht. I were not at Church in the forenoon. I were at my Father's after evning prayr with Mrs Catherine Beard's family and my Sister Betty. I supt there but they did not.

The 22nd December 1718 Munday. A dry, cold day, frost. Old Dick Banks and Thomas Gravet thrasht pease. John Gun thrasht oates. Allexander Snatt ditcht at Rickman's. Mr Burry sent his Poor Tax, £3. Paid John Bodle 19s-10d for half a quarter of John Stone's cow at 10d per nail. Receiv'd 2s-6d of Mrs Gratwick for some leather. Young Dick Banks and Willy carry'd a cart load of hay to Rickman's and begun carry dung there into the Sedge Mead, 7 loads. Brought the cows into the Fifteen Acres and turn'd the 5 young beasts into the cow field.

The 23rd December 1718 Tuesday. A gloomy day, rain towards night, smart frost last night. Old Dick Banks and Thomas Gravet thrasht pease. John Gun thrasht oates. Young Dick Banks and Willy carry'd dung at Rickman's, 15 loads. They also drew 2 gate posts out of the upper clover there. I had half a quarter of John Smith's best runt, weigh'd 11 nail 3 lb. Paid John Bodle 9d for a neat's tongue. I saw Mr Richard Whitpaine's

cow weigh'd at John Bodle's, 62 nail 6 lb.
George Buckwell and his boy workt at Rickman's.

The 24th December 1718 Wednesday. A wet day. Win'd 5 quarters 3 bushels head and half a bushel tail of Bank's and Thomas Gravet's pease. Willy and Jack helpt winnow. Young Dick Banks helpt winnow in the forenoon a while and thrasht the cuttings of wheat mow a while. Afterwards fetcht the cart and horses and a few chucks from Rickman's. Sent Mrs Catherine Beard wattles per Allan Savage.

The 25th December 1718 Thursday. Christmas Day. A gloomy day. Mr Jeremiah Dodson preacht. I was not at Church, being lame with the rhoumatisme. My Father and Mother Stone, my Sister Bett, Old Dick Banks, his wife and sons and John Gun din'd here. My Father and Brother Peter supt here.

The 26th December 1718 Fryday. A dry day. Old Dick Banks and Thomas Gravet thrasht barly by the ____ . Allexander Snatt had a bushel of wheat at 2s-6d. My Wife and I din'd at my Father's and supt there with Mrs Catherine Beard and her family.
Charles Garr of Broadstreet came in there in the afternoon and promis'd to pay my Father £10 on demand, being as he said, an order from John Hill so to do.

The 27th December 1718 Saturday. A gloomy forenoon, wet after. Old Dick Banks and Thomas Gravet thrasht barly 'till noon ------------ 1½ days.
Receiv'd 12s of Peter Hill per his boy, for 4 bushels of pease. Sent Willy to my Brother Henry Faulkoner's with £4-10s due for a year's intrest about the beginning of August last. He brought home the oat sieves from Whitmans Green. Paid Joseph Muzzall the quitrent for Edgly and Rickman's and receiv'd his Poor Tax and half a year's Land Tax for his farme and the quitrent, due at Michaelmas last. Sent my Cousin Peter Marchant of Lewis a goose per Jack. He brought home my horse shooes and ¼lb of bohea. I new set my Father's coffee mill and sent it to my Lord Treep's to be case harden'd. Sam Jarvice carry'd it.

The 28th December 1718 Sunday. A wet day.
Mr Jeremiah Dodson preacht. My Father Stone din'd here. Mr Scutt came down and we did not go to Church afternoon.

The 29th December 1718 Munday. A stormy day. Old Dick Banks and Thomas Gravet thrasht ------- 2½ days. John Gun thrasht oates, Snatt spread dung at Rickman's at 8d per score. He took up a few black thorn sets. Young Dick Banks deliver'd 12 bushels of pease to my Unkle Courtness and afterwards Willy and he begun make the pond in the close at Rickman's. George Buckwell and his boy workt on a gate there. I were at Westtowne in the afternoon and brought home my 2 quarts of train oyl which Mr Price sent to London for. I call'd at my Lord Treep's as I went. There was Thomas Norton and Stephen Bine. Receiv'd 2s of SB for carrying earth. Reckon'd and clear'd accounts (except for the parish) with Thomas Westover. He told me that the man's seat in the Church belonging to my house, late Mrs Storer's, was (to his certain knowledge) in the fore seat on the north side of the Old Gallery and the 1st or second from the door.

The 30th December 1718 Tuesday.
A stormy day. Old Dick Banks and Thomas Gravet thrasht barly -------- 3½ days.
Young Dick Banks, Allexander Snatt and Willy workt on the pond at Rickman's half a day. John Coulstock had half a bushel of pease per Old Dick Banks. Mrs Catherine Beard's family, my Brother and Sister Ann Box and my Father supt here.

The 31st December 1718 Wednesday. A dry day. Win'd 4 quarters 6 bushels head and tail of Old Dick Banks's and Thomas Gravet's barly thrasht by the day -------- 4 days. Deliver'd 8½ quarters of barly to Harry Wickham per Dick and Jack. Reckon'd with Mrs Storer and there remains due to her £35, I paid her £5 of the principall mony due to her before and gave her a note of my hand to pay the £35 on demand with legal intrest. Reckon'd and clear'd accounts with my Cousin John Lindfield, he supt here. Nick Plaw din'd here. Jack Hayne of Henfield brought a letter from my Aunt Holden, I sent a letter by him to John Goffe.

The 1st January 1718 Thursday. A very gloomy day, some rain. Ditcheling cooper was here in the morning. I sold him one of my porkers at 20d per nail to be kill'd about a week hence and carry'd to his house. Deliver'd three bushels of pease to Greenaway per Dick. Receiv'd 10s of the postwoman. Paid my Lord Treep 9d for 9lb of shott.

Paid Old Dick Banks 10s yesterday per William Jarvice. My Wife and I supt at my Father's with Mr Scutt and his wife and Mr John Hart.

The 2nd January 1718 Fryday. A very fine day. Old Dick Banks and Thomas Gravet thrasht oates. Deliver'd 5 quarters of barly to Harry Wickham per Dick and Jack. Afterwards Dick drew some logs into the orchard. I was at Rickman's afternoon. Came home by Harry Morley's and spoke for 6 bushels of his master's pease which his wife promis'd I should have at 3s per bushel. My Wife and Willy and I supt at Mrs Catherine Beard's with my Father's Mother and Richard Collens and      Oliver of Rusper.

The 3rd January 1718 Saturday. A dry day. Old Dick Banks and Thomas Gravet thrasht. John Gun, Allexander Snatt, Young Dick Banks and Willy workt clearing Tully's farther field. Jack Mills cut down the tree in the middle etc. Jack Mills workt there half the day.

The 4th January 1718 Sunday. A very gloomy *(sic)*. Mr Jeremiah Dodson preacht. We had a parish meeting, past accounts as usual. Paid Mr John Hart in full for books and schooling to Xmas last. My Cousin John Lindfield sent his accounts per      Herriot I was a little while's at Mr Scutt's and at my Father's after evning prayr.

The 5th January 1718 Munday.
A very wet morning, dry after. Old Dick Banks and Thomas Gravet thrasht. John Gun, Allexander Snatt, Jack Bartlet, George West, Young Dick Banks and Willy workt clearing Tully's lower field. Thomas Hamper and Jack Mills workt there ----------- 94½ days.
Mrs Gratwick here in the evning.

The 6th January 1718 Tuesday. A dry day. Old Dick Banks thrasht barly, John Gun oates. Dick went to see the ball mare. Receiv'd 5s of Old Kester for half a load of straw. Paid Dick Wood £1-8s in full of all accounts. My Wife and Willy and I supt at Mr Scutt's with my Father, Mrs Catherine Beard's family, Mr Richard Whitpaine and his wife Mary.

The 7th January 1718 Wednesday. A dry day, frost last night. Banks and Thomas Gravet thrasht. Young Dick Banks and Willy carry'd 2 loads of furz to Rickman's and brought one load home. John Gun, George West, Jack Bartlet, Thomas Jacket and his boy, Allexander Snatt and Hollingall workt clearing the lower field. Paid Hollingall 1s for his day's work. Thomas Hamper and Jack Mills workt there ----------- 95½ days.
Kill'd the 3 porkers to day per W Chainey and G Wickham. Mr Richard Whitpaine lent me a horse to day.

The 8th January 1718 Thursday. A showry day. Win'd 9 quarters 2 bushels head and 1 bushel tail of Bank's and Gravet's barly. John Gun thrasht oates. Young Dick Banks thrasht part of the cutting of the wheat mows. Towner had a bushel of pease yesterday. Sent a porker to the cooper at Ditcheling per G Wickham, weigh'd 79lb at 20d per nail. I were at the club with Mr Price, my Father, Mr Beard, Mr Scutt, Mr John Hart and Whitpaine. Paid Mr Price 21d for half the gallon of oyl he sent for.

The 9th January 1718 Fryday. A gloomy day. Old Dick Banks and Thomas Gravet thrasht. Allexander Snatt, Thomas Jacket and his boy workt in the lower field to day and yesterday. John Gun workt there yesterday afternoon with George West and he all day to day.

The 10th January 1718 Saturday. A gloomy day. Old Dick Banks and Thomas Gravet thrasht. John Gun and George West grub'd, so did Allexander Snatt and Thomas Jacket and his boy. Thomas Hamper and Jack Mills workt in the lower field ---------- 96½ days.
Young Dick Banks and Willy carry'd mole hills, bushes etc. Mrs Catherine Beard's family and Mr Scutt's and my Father and Sister Bett supt here.

The 11th January 1718 Sunday. A gloomy day.
Mr Jeremiah Dodson preacht. I was a little while with my Cousin John Lindfield at John Stone's. I din'd at my Father's. I talkt with Abel Muzzall about the seat for the Towne House.

The 12th January 1718 Munday. A dry, very warme day. Banks and Thomas Gravet thrasht. John Gun and George West hedg'd against the lower field. Allexander Snatt and Thomas Jacket and his boy grub'd etc. Young Dick Banks deliver'd 8 quarters 2 bushels of barly to HW. Reckon'd with Old William Brand for all the work he has done for me (except at Rickman's) and I paid him 5 guineas and remains due to him £1-0-7d. Let him Widdow Tully's end of Tully's house at £4 per annum and the Hovelfield Orchard at 20s per annum to enter at Lady Day next, but I am to have all the nonpareils at 4d per gallon. Nick Plaw was here in the evning. Thomas Hamper workt in the lower field ----- 97½ days.

The 13th January 1718 Tuesday. A gloomy day. Brew'd 10 bushels of malt. Old Dick Banks, Thomas Gravet and John Gun thrasht. Young Dick Banks and Jack carry'd 10 bushels of pease to the postwoman's and 2 bushels of apples to Lettice Holden's friend. Allexander Snatt and George West hedg'd in the lower field. I promis'd Richard White 4 or 6 bushels of white pease. Thomas Howell was here in the evning about the ploughs. Receiv'd 28½lb of Mr Richard Whitpaine's boar from my Father's. Paid Greenaway's wife for all Cowdry's quarters to the last day of December. Thomas Hamper and Jack Mills workt in the lower ground ----- 98½days.

The 14th January 1718 Wednesday.
A dry day. Win'd 6 quarters 6 bushels head and 2 bushels tail of Bank's and Thomas Gravet's barly. They thrasht a while after. John Gun and George West hedg'd. Allexander Snatt poll'd trees etc. Young Dick Banks carry'd boughs etc out of the lower field. Thomas Hamper and Jack Mills set up a payr of barrs between Tully's farther field and Edgly Sandfield. Afterwards they new hung the grindstone etc. ---------- 99½ days.

The 15th January 1718 Thursday. A fine day. Old Dick Banks and Thomas Gravet helpt get in the clover ricks 'till noon, thrasht barly after. Young Dick Banks and Willy helpt in with the clover, carry'd the litter etc. Allexander Snatt and John Gun hedg'd in the lower field. Receiv'd 16s-8d of the postwoman towards pease. I was at the club with Mr Price, my Father and all the members. My Father had a bushel of wheat to day at 3s, seed wheat. I made a new leather halter for the black colt.

The 16th January 1718 Fryday. A very fine day. Banks and Thomas Gravet thrasht. John Gun and Allexander Snatt made an end of the South hedge by noon against the lower field which they did by the day and begun the north hedge afternoon and they are to have 2d per rod and to make an extraordinary good thing. Deliver'd 5 quarters of barly to Harry Wickham per Dick and Jack. Drencht the sorrel horse and let him bleed, he has (as we suppose) a pain in his head. Thomas Howell's man begun make 2 ploughs -------- 1 day.

The 17th January 1718 Saturday. A very fine day. John Gun and Allexander Snatt thrasht oates and win'd 11½ bushels of John Gun's oates. Old Dick Banks, Thomas Gravet, Dick and Willy finisht the pond at Rickman's, Dick and Willy was but half a day there. George Buckwell, his man and boy workt by the day putting up racks and cribs at Rickman's ------ 1 day.
Thomas Howell's man workt on the ploughs ----- 2 days. Paid my Father 10s ~~towards~~ for half a side of Mr Richard Whitpaine's boar and 3d towards bringing it home. Receiv'd 10d for half a bushel of pease of J Colstock per Bank's wife.

The 18th January 1718 Sunday. A fine day. Mr Jeremiah Dodson preacht. My Father and Mother Stone din'd here. I supt at Mrs Catherine Beard's. Mrs Gratwick gave me a handcerchief.

The 19th January 1718 Munday. A dry day. Banks and Thomas Gravet thrasht. John Gun and Allexander Snatt hedg'd. Young Dick Banks and Willy thrasht the cuttings of the wheat mow etc.
George Buckwell, his man and boy workt on the crib and racks at Rickman's ----- 2 days.
Thomas Howell's man workt on the ploughs ----- 3 days. Paid Frank Marshall 11s for keeping the ball mare dureing the cure of her back. He brought her home. My Wife went to Lewis, John Kneller and Jack with her. Dick begun a sack of oates for his horses last night.

The 20th January 1718 Tuesday. A fine day. Thomas Gravet thrasht. John Gun and Allexander Snatt hedg'd. Young Dick Banks and Willy begun plough Tully's farther field. George Buckwell and his man and boy workt at Rickman's on the cribs etc --- 3 days.
Thomas Hamper workt here ------- 100½ days.
Mr Richard Whitpaine supt and spent the evning here.

The 21st January 1718 Wednesday. A dry day. Banks and Thomas Gravet thrasht. John Gun and Allexander Snatt thrasht 'till noon, hedg'd after. Young Dick Banks and Willy plough'd, broak their plough, had her clipt and plough'd again about half the day in all.
Thomas Howell's man clipt the plough and workt as before ------ 4 days.
George Buckwell and his (sic) workt as yesterd---- 4 days. The widdow Bide was here with a letter from her son-in-law Charles Cosier.

The 22nd January 1718 Thursday. A gloomy day, rain towards night. Old Dick Banks and Thomas Gravet thrasht. John Gun and Allexander Snatt hedg'd. Young Dick Banks and Willy plough'd. Paid Old William Brand 10s per Samuel Jarvice. Thomas Howell's man workt as before ------ 5 days. George Buckwell's man and boy workt as before ------ 5 days. Receiv'd a letter from Jude Storer per post. I was at the club with all but Mr Richard Whitpaine. Clear'd accounts with Thomas Westover and had a new payr of strong shooes at 4s-6d.

The 23rd January 1718 Fryday. A dry day. Banks and Thomas Gravet thrasht. John Gun and Allexander Snatt thrasht 'till noon, hedg'd after. John Gun had a hog weigh'd 28 nail at 2s per nail. We kill'd the last of my hogs, his fleath weigh'd 27 lb. Young Dick Banks and Willy plough'd. George Buckwell, his man and boy workt 'till noon and only the man afternoon and finisht the close at Rickman's --------- 5½ days. Thomas Howell's man workt on the ploughs -------- 6 days.

The 24th January 1718 Saturday. A gloomy day. Win'd 10½ qarters head of Banks and Thomas Gravet's barly and 3 bushels tail. John Gun and Allexander Snatt hedg'd. Young Dick Banks and Willy plough'd. Thomas Howell's man finisht -------- 7 days.
I supt at my Father's with my Brother John and Sister Ann Box (Ed: née Marchant).

The 25th January 1718 Sunday. A fine day.
Mr Jeremiah Dodson preacht. No service afternoon.
My Cousin John Lindfield din'd here.
I supt at Mr Jeremiah Dodson's.

The 26th January 1718 Munday. A gloomy morning, dry after. Thomas Gravet begun thrash wheat. John Gun and Allexander Snatt hedg'd. Old Dick Banks cut bushes etc at Rickman's. Young Dick Banks and Willy plough'd. I wrote and sent a letter to Mr Frank Hicks of Rotherbridge for John Reeve, with the Churchwardens and overseer's hands to it. Mr Jeremiah Dodson, Mr Richard Whitpaine, Mr Scutt and Stephen Bine were here afternoon. We settl'd the accounts about the school, vizt for rent, Wood and Stephen Bine's work and everything to Christmas last. Mr Dodson supt here.
I din'd at my Father's. Paid for a payr of pattens for Molly Balcomb 13d and for a handcerchief 2s-9d.

The 27th January 1718 Tuesday. A showry day. Thomas Gravet thrasht wheat. John Gun, Young Dick Banks and Willy mov'd seed clover at Tully's afternoon. Young Dick Banks and Willy plough'd a while before and John Gun and Allexander Snatt hedg'd. I were at Old John Snashall's to buy fish but they were under size. My Wife and I at Young John Snashall's afterwards. He was not at home. I supt at my Father's.
Old Dick Banks did severall jobbs about half a day.

The 28th January 1718 Wednesday. A fine day. Thomas Gravett thrasht wheat. John Gun and Allexander Snatt hedg'd. Old Dick Banks and George West plough'd. Young Dick Banks and Willy plough'd with the horses, borrow'd Mr Richard Whitpaine's mare to go in the foot. My Father and Mother Stone, my Brother John Box and Sister supt here. Nan Wood and William Gorman went to Lewis. Snatt had a bushel of wheat.

The 29th January 1718 Thursday. A fine day. Thomas Gravet thrasht wheat. John Gun and Allexander Snatt did severall jobbs. Old Dick Banks and George West made an end of ploughing Tully's lower field. Jack Haslegrove and I drove 5 steers and cows downe to Tully's round by the lane and, it being stopt where my way goes into Edgly ground I breackt it open. Paid Frank Holden 4s for 4 ells of canvass. Abraham Muzzall had a bushel of wheat, Banks's. Young Dick Banks and Willy carry'd grit for my Father in the forenoon and begun plough at Rickman's. Mrs Gratwick supt here.

The 30th January 1718 Fryday. A very gloomy day. Thomas Gravet thrasht wheat. John Gun thrasht pease. Old Dick Banks and Allexander Snatt hedg'd and ditcht. Young Dick Banks and Willy plough'd at Rickman's. Paid 3s for Molly Balcomb for 1½ yard of Scotch cloath for a ⌐
Thomas Hamper workt here ---- 101½ days.
My Cousin William Wood and his wife din'd here.
I was not at Church because my head aked very much.
Old Dick Banks's cow calv'd a bull calf.
I had one lamb -------- 1.

The 31st January 1718 Saturday. A gloomy morning, very wet after. Thomas Gravet thrasht. Old Dick Banks and Allexander Snatt hedg'd at Rickman's. John Gun workt for himself.

Thomas Hamper and Jack Mills workt here - 102½ days. Young Dick Banks and Willy plough'd at Rickman's, ended the wheat earsh. My Father, Mr Beard and Mr John Hart supt here. Lost one lamb at Rickman's. Nan Wood went away.

The 1st February 1718 Sunday. A dry day.
Mr Jeremiah Dodson preacht. A parish meeting as usual. Mr Letchford's charity paid to Michaelmas last.
My Brother Peter supt here.

The 2nd February 1718 Munday. A gloomy day, rain in the morning. Thomas Gravet thrasht. Banks and Allexander Snatt thrasht barly. I know not what John Gun did. Paid Taylor at the Comon 24s for 1500 bricks. I wrote to Jude Storer per post. My Father, Mr John Hart, Mr Richard Whitpaine and I were at Mr Price's.

The 3rd February 1718 Tuesday. A showry day.
Allexander Snatt and Banks thrasht barly. Paid Old William Brand 10s, his men begun dig the Hovelfield Orchard. John Gun thrasht pease. Dick Banks jr, Willy and Jack helpt Thomas Gravet winnow 33 bushels head and 1½ tail of his wheat. Mr Beard went to London, I were to look on their ploughing. I planted severall trees in the Hovelfield Orchard. The 3 yearling heifer that came of Nick Plaw's least cow, calv'd a cow calf.

The 4th February 1718 Wednesday. A gloomy day.
Thomas Gravet thrasht wheat, John Gun pease. Young Dick Banks and Willy did severall jobbs. Allexander Snatt and Old Dick Banks hedg'd at Rickman's.
My Cousin John Lindfield was here afternoon.
One lamb in the little Meads -------- 2.
Lost one lamb in a ditch a Sunday last.

The 5th February 1718 Thursday. A showry forenoon, fine after. John Gun thrasht. Allexander Snatt and Old Dick Banks thrasht 'till noon, hedg'd after. Willy and Jack helpt John Gun winnow 16½ bushels head and a bushel tail of pease the last of the field, in all win'd also nine bushels head and a bushel tail of John Gun's oates. Young Dick Banks did severall jobbs.
Thomas Hamper and Jack Mills workt on the wainhouse stable ---- 108½ days. Paid Thomas Gravet 25s. One lamb in the little Meads ------------ 3. Receiv'd 8s of John Towner in full of all. I was a little while at the club where was only Mr Richard Whitpaine. We went from thence and supt at my Father's.

The 6th February 1718 Fryday. A showry day. Thomas Gravet thrasht. My Wife was very ill last night. Dick and Willy did severall jobbs. Receiv'd 6 bushels of pease from Thomas Avery's per Dick. One lamb in the Little Meads and one in Edgly Mead ------------- 5.
I think Allexander Snatt and Banks hedg'd at Rickman's. John Gun thrasht oates. Mrs Catherine Beard and my Grandmother here in the evning.

The 7th February 1718 Saturday. A gloomy day.
Allexander Snatt and Old Dick Banks hedg'd at Rickman's. John Gun thrasht in the forenoon, ditcht after. Young Dick Banks and Willy carry'd bushes at Rickman's and begun plough the field by the house there. Dick brought home 8 bushels of oates for the horses. I wrote to Mr Beard per post about Thomas Shave. 3 lambs in the Edgly Mead -------- 8.
Four lambs at Rickman's in 2 or 3 days last past.

The 8th February 1718 Sunday. A gloomy day.
Mr Jeremiah Dodson preacht. I was not at Church in the forenoon. I call'd a vestry about Thomas Shave.
3 lambs in the Little Meads------------ 10.

The 9th February 1718 Munday. A showry day. Thomas Gravet thrasht wheat. I wrote to Mr Beard about Thomas Shave. Allexander Snatt and Old Dick Banks hedg'd at Rickman's, John Gun cut bushes, took up black thornes etc there. Young Dick Banks and Willy carry'd bushes, boughs etc there. 2 lambs at Rickman's. I were at        Steel's of Sayers Comon, call'd at Westtowne as I came home, Mr Tattersall was there. I supt at my Father's with Mr Jeremiah Dodson and Mr John Hart. Thomas Hamper and his man Marten workt at my Father's.

The 10th February 1718 Shrove Tuesday. A gloomy day. Thomas Gravet thrasht part of the day. Young Dick Banks and Willy deliver'd half a load of straw to R Coster and as much to Ned Burt at 10s per load. Old Dick Banks and Allexander Snatt thrasht. John Gun did not work. I cut out Mrs Catherine Beard's harness. Talk with Emsley of Kymer about his boy. Thomas Hamper, Marten and Jack begun wainescot my Father's parlour.

The 11th February 1718 Wednesday. A showry day. Thomas Gravet thrasht. Old Dick Banks and Allexander Snatt hedg'd 'till noon, cut stakes for a new hedge at Rickman's after. John Gun took up sets etc for the new hedge. Young Dick Banks and Willy carry'd the straw I ow'd Mr Richard Whitpaine and begun plough Tully's 1st Field. Greenaway plaister'd and seel'd a pantry at Towne. Thomas Hamper, Marten and Jack workt on the parlour at Towne ------ 2 days. 2 lambs in the Little Meads and 2 in the Edgly Mead ------- 14.

The 12th February 1718 Thursday. A showry day. John Gun, Banks, Thomas Gravet, Allexander Snatt, Old White and his son Richard begun plant the hedge in the great field at Rickman's. Greenaway and his boy pav'd the new pantry at Towne in the forenoon, helpt about the hedge after. Young Dick Banks and Willy plough'd in Tully's first field. Thomas Hamper, Marten and Jack workt on the Towne parlour. My Father has been 2 days very ill of the gout.

The 13th February 1718 Fryday. A showry day. Thomas Gravet thrasht. John Gun, Banks and Allexander Snatt workt on the ditch and fetching stuff at Rickman's. Thomas Steel at Sayers Comom begun make an edderd hedge in the great field at Rickman's. Thomas Hamper etc workt as yesterday ------- 4 days. Young Dick Banks and Willy plough'd as yesterday. 1 lamb in the Edgly Mead ----- 15. One lamb at Rickman's some days ago.

The 14th February 1718 Saturday. A showry day. Thomas Gravet thrasht. Thomas Steel, Jack Bartlet, John Gun, Banks and Allexander Snatt finisht the new hedge and ditch in the great field at Rickman's, being 33 rod and costs, materials and workmanship 50s. Paid Allexander Snatt 3s and Jack Bartlet 1s. Thomas Hamper etc workt as yesterday -------- 5 days. Paid William Dumsday of Horsham £1-3s-5d for a payr of stays and mending an other payr for Molly Balcomb. Young Dick Banks and Willy finisht Tully's first field and carry'd Ned Burt an other half load of straw.

The 15th February 1718 Sunday. A dry day. Mr Jeremiah Dodson preacht. My Cousin John Lindfield din'd here, we did not go to Church in the afternoon, for which we were much to blame. 1 lamb in the Edgly Mead ----- 16.

The 16th February 1718 Munday. A dry morning, some snow afternoon. Thomas Gravet thrasht. Lost the old long tetted cow last night. John Gun helpt flea her and afterwards Jack Haslegrove and he drove the 6 young beasts round by the lane and in of the way to Tully's, put 3 in the close and the rest in the cow field. John Gun workt for himself afternoon. Allexander Snatt and Banks hedg'd at Rickman's. Young Dick Banks and Willy plough'd by Wickham's 'till noon. Afterwards Banks made water furroughs in Tully's first field and Willy and Jack plough'd. Receiv'd £13-6-3¾d in mony and outset £1-13-8¼d for the Land Tax being £15 for half a years rent of Thomas Champion jr (the old man being dead), for Eastout due at Michaelmas last. Receiv'd a new payr of outseam'd gloves of Thomas Baker. Receiv'd ¼lb of bohea from Samuel Tourl, per Jack Mills.

The 17th February 1718 Tuesday. A fine day, a frost last night and Sunday night. Thomas Gravet thrasht. Allexander Snatt and Old Dick Banks thrasht barly. John Gun workt for himself. Willy and Jack plough'd by Wickham's. Young Dick Banks carry'd 10 loads of Towne dirt into the Rookwood. Paid Harry Morley 18s for 6 bushels of Thomas Avery's pease. I were at Mrs Catherine Beard's and set out her new hedge in the Lye Mead. Thomas Hamper etc workt in the Towne parlour as Saturday --------- 6 days.

The 18th February 1718 Wednesday. A wet day. Young Dick Banks, Willy and Jack helpt Thomas Gravet winnow 56 bushels head and 2 tail of his wheat that grew by Wickham's. Old Dick Banks and Allexander Snatt thrasht barly. Allexander Snatt had a bushel of wheat. John Gun ditcht and thrasht oates. Thomas Hamper etc workt in the Towne parlour ----- 7 days.

The 19th February 1718 Thursday. A gloomy morning, wet afternoon. Thomas Gravet thrasht. Allexander Snatt, Old Dick Banks and John Gun ditcht. Young Dick Banks and Willy plough'd 'till noon, carry'd Mr Scutt half a load of straw after. Thomas Hamper etc workt as yesterday -------- 8 days.
I was at the club with Mr Price, Mr John Hart, Mr Scutt and Thomas Norton of North End.

The 20th February 1718 Fryday. A fine day. John Gun, John Edwards, Young Dick Banks and Willy begun plant the hedge in the Rookwood. Allexander Snatt and Old Dick Banks ditcht at Rickman's. Thomas Gravet thrasht. Jack Haslegrove fetcht 6 bushels of malt from Wickham. 1 lamb in the Little Meads and 1 in Edgly Mead ------ 18.

The 21st February 1718 Saturday. A showry morning, dry after. Thomas Gravet thrasht. John Gun and John Edwards litter'd the closes in the forenoon, ditcht after. Allexander Snatt and Old Dick Banks hedg'd etc at Rickman's.
Thomas Hamper etc workt as a Thursday ----- 9 days. Young Dick Banks fetcht oisters from Brighton etc.
2 lambs in house field and 2 in Edgly Mead ---- 22.
Two lambs at Rickman's this week.

The 22nd February 1718 Sunday. A dry day. Mr Jeremiah Dodson preacht. I were at my Father's after evning prayr with Mr Scutt and Mr Richard Whitpaine.
1 lamb in the Homefield --------- 23.

The 23rd February 1718 Munday. A fine day. Thomas Gravet thrasht. Allexander Snatt and Old Dick Banks hedg'd at Rickman's. John Gun and John Edwards made an end of planting the hedge in the Rookwood by noon. Afterwards John Gun mended the hedge in the Churchfield and John Edwards did not work.
Dr Nick Plaw cut some of my lambs. My Wife and I supt at Mrs Catherine Beard's. Young Dick Banks and Willy begun fallow the Homefield.
Thomas Hamper, Marten and Jack set up the fence against the Hovelfield ---- 104½ days.

The 24th February 1718 Tuesday. A fine day. Thomas Gravet thrasht wheat. John Gun did not work. I don't know what Old Dick Banks and Allexander Snatt did. John Edwards cut wood in the Rookwood. Young Dick Banks had the dung court and harrow stuff to Thomas Howell's. Thomas Hamper's man Marten workt in the fatting close. Thomas Howell's man William mended the old turnrist plough. Paid Thomas Gravet 10s.
Frank Marshall was here and bleeded the bald mare in the thighs, rowel'd her in the forehead and gave her a drink. Paid him 8s for cureing her back.

The 25th February 1718 Wednesday. A dry day. Thomas Gravet thrasht. John Gun ditcht. John Edwards poll'd trees. Paid Allexander Snatt 4s. Banks had half a bushel of wheat. Win'd 8 quarters 2 bushels head and 5 bushels tail of Bank's and Allexander Snatt's barly. Young Dick Banks and Jack and Willy carry'd 5 quarters of barly to Wickham's and brought home 6 quarters of malt and carry'd half a cord of wood to my Father's. Frank Marshall gave the ball mare an other drink to night.
Thomas Hamper's man Marten workt in the fatting close. I were to see Mrs Catherine Beard's ditch in morning. My Cousin Plump and her children supt here with Mr John Hart.

The 26th February 1718 Thursday. A dry day. Thomas Gravet thrasht. John Gun ditcht. Allexander Snatt, Banks and John Edwards poll'd trees. Young Dick Banks and Jack carry'd 5 quarters of barly to Wickham's and brought home 9 bushels of malt so that I had 7 quarters and 7 bushels of malt of the 7 quarters of barly. Markt 10 sheep and 10 lambs of the left ear and the same number of the right ear to the day. 1 lamb at Rickman's 2 or 3 days ago.
1 lamb in the Homefield yesterday ---------- 24.
Thomas Hamper's man Marten finisht the fatting close by noon and workt on the hay bin. Paid George West 5s-9d, clear'd accounts.     Old William Brand and the 2 boys workt here afternoon. Lent Richard White six oxen to plough. I were at the club with Mr Scutt, Mr Beard, Mr John Hart and Mr Richard Whitpaine (Mr Price being gone home) where I paid Mr Beard the 5s order'd him to give Thomas Shave. William Dumsday was here with coates for Molly and Nanny. My Brother Peter here to day.

The 27th February 1718 Fryday. A fine day. Thomas Gravet thrasht. John Gun and John Edwards ditcht. Allexander Snatt and Old Dick Banks hedg'd at Rickman's. 4 lambs on the Little Meads to day and yesterday --- 28. Thomas Hamper set up a gate to the sheep pen in the back court etc ---- 105½ days.
The cooper at Ditcheling and Mr Hallet here in the evning. Young Dick Banks did severall jobbs. Thomas Marshall gave the ball mare an other drink.
Mrs Susan Courthope and Mrs Gratwick here afternoon.

The 28th February 1718 Saturday. A very fine day. Thomas Gravet thrasht. John Gun ditcht. Old Dick Banks and Allexander Snatt hedg'd afternoon. Young Dick Banks did severall jobbs. Turn'd the sheep and lambs into the back field wheat. I were at St John's Comon and at Ditcheling to see after a horse and to talk with Thomas Howell and John Clark. We had news of the Chevalier de St George being taken at Doghoret carry'd into the castle of Milan. I supt at Mrs Catherine Beard's with Nick Plaw. Markt 5 sheep and lambs of both ears. Paid Mr Beard 18d for a snuff box.

The 1st March 1718 Sunday. A fine day.
Mr Jeremiah Dodson preacht. I was not at Church in the forenoon. We had a meeting in the afternoon as usual, settled 2 months accounts and I gave an account of the distribution of Dog Smith's mony. I supt at Mr Scutt's, Mr Richard Whitpaine there before supper.
3 lambs in Tully's lower field some days since -------- 31.

The 2nd March 1718 Munday. A fine day. Win'd 52 bushels head and 2 tail of Thomas Gravet's wheat. Young Dick Banks and J Greenaway helpt winnow. John Snashall senior and Frank Marshall were to see the ball mare yesterday and John again to day. Frank gave her a drink yesterday and John gave her a gentle purge to day. Old Dick Banks spread Towne dirt in the Rookwood and mended a few gaps. Allexander Snatt workt for himself. I were to look on the Hayslecroft and Mrs Catherine Beard's field. I were at Stephen Bine's with Mr Jeremiah Dodson, Mr Scutt and Mr Richard Whitpaine and Mr John Hart. Mr Hart concluded to stay with us to teach our school and Mr Richard Whitpaine promis'd to contribute £7 per annum, Mr Scutt £7 and my self £3 and to be answerable for my Mother's £1 per annum in case she should refuse to continue this. We were likewise at Mr Scutt's before and after, all but Mr Jeremiah Dodson. N.B. Mr John Hart had been sent to teach a school at Deptford. Willy and William Smith carry'd 9 bushels of oates to Lewis which were due to my Cousin Peter. They brought home a mare from John Chatfield's of Ditcheling at £9-1s or I must return her in a day or two.

The 3rd March 1718 Tuesday. A gloomy day, small showrs. Thomas Gravet thrasht. Young Dick Banks and Willy plough'd a while then carry'd half a load of straw to my Unkle Courtness etc. John Gun ditcht. Allexander Snatt workt for himself. My Father had 2 bushels of seed wheat per Dick. Carry'd 25 faggots to the Widdow Reeve's per Dick. I wrote to Mr John Cheal per William Smith, Gorman. Receiv'd 5s of Mr Courtness for half a load of straw.

The 4th March 1718 Wednesday. A fine day, Thomas Gravet thrasht. John Gun ditcht. Old Dick Banks and Allexander Snatt workt for themselves. Frank Marshall was here to see the mare and put a rowel in the sorrel horse's neck. One lamb at Rickman's. Young Dick Banks and Willy carry'd 9 loads of dung into the Bankfield at Rickman's. My Brother Peter and his horse rider, William Clerk were here afternoon. Dick Smith of Albourne was here for a service, but did not fully agree, I bid him 30s.

The 5th March 1718 Thursday. A dry day. Thomas Gravet workt for Mr Jeremiah Dodson. John Gun ditcht, Allexander Snatt and Banks workt for themselves. Young Dick Banks and Willy carry'd 2 loads of dung at Rickman's, in all 11 into the house field, spread it and plough'd afterwards. I were at the club with Mr John Hart, Mr Scutt and Mr Richard Whitpaine, the supervisor came to us, crack brain'd and drunk. Receiv'd 5s of Mr Scutt for half a load of straw. Thomas Hamper and Jack Mills finisht the wainhouse stable etc ------- 106½ days. Mr John Hart din'd here.

The 6th March 1718 Fryday. A very fine day. The ball mare died. John Gun ditcht in the forenoon, flead the mare and dug a pitt to bury her in afternoon. Allexander Snatt and Banks thrasht barly. Young Dick Banks, Willy and William Gorman plough'd at Rickman's. Pay'd Frank Marshall 6s for what he did for the mare. Receiv'd 10s of Richard White for 6 bushels of pease he had to day. Richard White sent home my oxen to day. Took the sheep out of the Bankfield wheat.

The 7th March 1718 Saturday. A showry day. Allexander Snatt and Banks helpt John Gun winnow 45½ bushels head and 7½ bushels tail of his oates. Young Dick Banks, William Gorman and Willy plough'd at Rickman's. Thomas Hamper and his man Thomas Hamper workt, made 3 small cribs and would have made 4 had the stuff been handy --- 107½ days. Dr Nick Plaw was here to drench an ox. I was at Wickham to help Mr Richard Whitpaine sling a cow. Mr Jeremiah Dodson came hither to breakfast with Cousin Plump.

The 8th March 1718 Sunday. A fine day.
Mr Jeremiah Dodson preacht. We had a meeting about Thomas Shave. My Cousin John Lindfield din'd here.
I supt at Mr Beard's with Mr Richard Whitpaine.

The 9th March 1718 Munday. A gloomy morning, fine after. John Gun and Old Dick Banks hedg'd. Allexander Snatt workt in the garden and had a bushel of wheat. Young Dick Banks and Willy made an end of ploughing the house field at Rickman's, William Gorman helpt. I wrote to Henry Scrase per post. Paid Mr Beard 8d for a pint of ink and carryage. Paid Mrs Catherine Beard the remainder and outset her tax and took Mr Dee's receit of her for £12-12s which she paid him for me as part of the tax. I gave John Alcock an order to pay Mr Dee 56s more. The long tetted cow calv'd a cow calf last week. 2 lambs more at home ------------ 33.

The 10th March 1718 Tuesday. A fine day. Willy sow'd 9 bushels of pease on the house field at Rickman's. Dick harrow'd. William Gorman steer'd. Paid Goodman Chapman of Aberton 1s for clipping my ewes 60 being 4d per score. Receiv'd 8 quarters of barly of Thomas Norton of Pycomb on Harry Wickham's account, per Mr Scrase's teem. Willy and Young Gorman fetcht 2 new harrows from the Comon. I was a little while at Thomas Smith's with Mr Michelham, Thomas Friend's man of Lewis. Allexander Snatt and John Shave workt in the garden. John Gun and Old Dick Banks hedg'd in the forenoon, mended gaps in Tully's ground afterwards.

The 11th March 1718 Wednesday. A very fine day. John Gun and Banks hedg'd. Young Dick Banks finisht the pea field at Rickman's, Willy and Jack plough'd in the Homefield. Paid Allexander Snatt 4s-9d and clear'd accounts. My Wife was at my Brother John Box's afternoon.

The 12th March 1718 Thursday. A very fine day. Willy sow'd 15 bushels of the Hovelfield at Rickman's. Dick harrow'd. John Gun and Old Dick Banks hedg'd. John Gun ground malt at night 8½ bushels. Paid Chapman 1s for sheering 12 dry sheep and rams. I was at the club with Mr Price, Mr Richard Whitpaine and Mr Scutt and Mr John Hart. My Wife was at Danny towards night. 2 lambs in the Nine Acres ------------35.

The 13th March 1718 Fryday. A fine day. John Gun went to see his unkle Friend, being very ill. Old Dick Banks poll'd trees. Ned Burt workt in the garden. Young Dick Banks and Willy workt in the Hovelfield at Rickman's, Willy sow'd it with clover etc. George West sow'd a piece by the East side of the wheat at Rickman's with his flax. Paid Stephen Bine £9-1s which he paid John Chatfield of Ditcheling for a mare. Receiv'd 25s-6d of him for pease sent to Mr Tweedale's

The 14th March 1718 Saturday. A gloomy day. Young Dick Banks finisht the field at Rickman's. John Gun and Old Dick Banks hedg'd. Allexander Snatt plough'd in the forenoon, workt a gardening afterwards. Willy and Jack plough'd in the Homefield. Lent Mrs Gratwick a guinea per my Wife. William Terry's daughter Anne was here with her aunt. My Wife bargain'd with Anne for a year at 30s. Ned Burt workt in the garden. The long tetted heifer calv'd a bull calf. I were at Mr Jeremiah Dodson's in the evning. He sign'd a new Poor Book at 9d per lb.

The 15th March 1718 Sunday. A fine day. Mr Jeremiah Dodson preacht. We had a meeting and sign'd the new Poor Book. I supt at Mr Snatts with EB.

The 16th March 1718 Munday. A fine morning, stormy after, snow and hail. My Wife, Jacky and John Kneller went to Lewis. John Gun and Banks hedg'd a while, shovel'd part of the Towne after. Willy sow'd Tully's first field with 14½ bushels of oates. Afterwards Jack and he plough'd in the Homefield. Dick and Allexander Snatt harrow'd etc. Paid John Alcock £50 which he paid to Mr Dee in London for me. Lost a lamb in Nine Acres yesterday and the long cow's calf to day. Paid George Buckwell 2 guineas in exchange of a cow I am to have to morrow. Paid Greenaway 4s, remains a bushel of wheat due to him. Clear'd accounts.

The 17th March 1718 Tuesday. A gloomy, cold day. John Gun thrasht oates. Allexander Snatt ditcht in the forenoon, thrasht barly after. Young Dick Banks and Willy did severall jobbs. Old Dick Banks did not work for me. George Buckwell brought his cow and calf and drove away mine. The cow that was his calv'd a Wednesday last. Thomas Avery's widdow was here towards night. Allexander Snatt had a bushel of wheat.

The 18th March 1718 Wednesday. A fine day, frosty. Old Dick Banks and Allexander Snatt thrasht. Willy went to Balcombe. Young Dick Banks roll'd Tully's first field, Jack and he plough'd on the Homefield part of _____ . I were at Danny, at Habboys, the Widdow Wickham's and Richard Lashmer's. Paid Sanders of Whiteman's Green 4s per Willy for bottoming 2 sieves.

The 19th March 1718 Thursday. A fine day. Thomas Gravet thrasht wheat. Willy sow'd clover in Tully's first field and afterwards Young Dick Banks and he begun plough Mr Jeremiah Dodson's Hayselcroft. Old Dick Banks and John Gun hedg'd in the forenoon, shovel'd part of the Towne after. I were at the club with Mr Price, Mr John Hart and Mr Burry.

Went from thence to Mr Scutt's and staid a little while with Mr Richard Whitpaine etc.

The 20th March 1718 Fryday. A dry windy day. Thomas Gravet thrasht. John Gun and Old Dick Banks hedg'd. Young Dick Banks, Allexander Snatt, Willy and I plough'd in Mr Jeremiah Dodson's Hayselcroft. I drove 'till noon, R Hollingall after. I din'd at Mr Burry's with my Wife and Mrs Stacey. Receiv'd Mr Burry's 2s Poor Tax and half a year's Land Tax. John Ovenden and George Whitpaine there afternoon. Mrs Catherine Beard's heifer calved a bull calf. A very great light in the air about the space of half a minute or more, last night between 7 and 8.

The 21st March 1718 Saturday. A dry windy day. George West sow'd 4½ bushels of my Cousin John Lindfield's flax seed on Mr Jeremiah Dodson's Hayselcroft. Dick harrow'd with the ox harrow. Allexander Snatt fetcht the seed and harrow and helpt Willy plough the headlands. Paid John Gun 10s. Old Dick Banks and he hedg'd. John Snashall was here in the morning for grafts for Mr Norden.

The 22nd March 1718 Sunday. A fine day. Mr Jeremiah Dodson preacht. My Cousin John Lindfield din'd here.

The 23rd March 1718 Munday. A dry day. My birthday 42 years. John Gun and Old Dick Banks hedg'd. Allexander Snatt and Young Dick Banks harrow'd with the 2 ox harrows in the Nine Acres. Agree'd with Stephen Bine for part of his house for the Widdow Gorrman at 20s 'till Michaelmas. Thomas Hamper and Marten begun make a ox harrow etc and one day before Thomas Hamper made a dib etc --------- 109½ days. I were at Henry Scrase's and receiv'd both his Poor Tax and half a years Land Tax. I call'd at Danny with R Hollingall about Habboy's horse.

The 24th March 1718 Tuesday. A fine day. Thomas Gravet thrasht wheat. John Gun and Old Dick Banks ditcht against the wheat. Young Dick Banks, Willy, Allexander Snatt and Jack plough'd in the morning. I were to see Mrs Gratwick in the afternoon and spent the evning with Mr Jeremiah Dodson and Mr John Hart and Mr Beard.
Thomas Hamper and Marten finish the ox harrow by noon and mended a gate afterwards ----- 110½ days.

Paid Molly Balcomb 2d per week since last Lady Day, 8s-8d for spending mony.

## 1719

The 25th March 1719 Wednesday. Lady Day. A wet day. Old Dick Banks came to Tully's at £ per annum for his part of the house and £ per annum for the Hovelfield Orchard. The Widdow Tully mov'd to Danworth. Old Dick Banks and Dick Smith mov'd the Widdow Tully. Young Dick Banks went to Horsham for my Father. John Gun and Allexander Snatt workt for themselves. William Roach mended the sink windows. I lent Mr Scrase 6 oxen to draw them up the Church Hill with a load of Old William Brand's goods. John Smith's son Dick of Albourne came from Thomas Fowl's of Albourne to live with me at 30s per annum.

The 26th March 1719 Thursday. A gloomy day, some rain. Thomas Gravet thrasht. Old Dick Banks thrasht barly. Nick Plaw din'd here, staid the afternoon. Win'd 6 bushels head and 1 quarter tail of John Gun's oates. Willy and the 2 Dicks helpt. Paid John Snashall jr 1s for drawing a tooth of Polly's. John Snashall sr was here to see the bay horse twice. I talkt with White about the Harwells. With Allexander Snatt I agreed for Hollingall to live in part of his house at £ 'till Michaelmas next. I were at the club with Mr Beard and Mr Scutt. Jack Haslegrove went to Lewis with butter.

The 27th March 1719 Fryday. A fine day.
Mr Jeremiah Dodson preacht. Willy begun sow Tully's lower field with pease and oates. Young Dick Banks and Dick Smith harrow'd with the ox harrow and 2 horse harrows. John Gun and Old Dick Banks ditcht, Thomas Gravet thrasht. Mrs Susan Courthope, my Sister Sarah and Bett din'd here. Paid my Sister Sarah a years intrest, she gave me a guinea. Thomas Hamper and Marten workt here ---- 111½ days.
Receiv'd Captain Whitpaine's 2 Poor Taxes and half a year's Land Tax and 20d for half a bushel of tick beans.

The 28th March 1719 Saturday. A fine day. Willy made an end of sowing Tully's farther field with     bushels of pease and     bushels of oates. Young Dick Banks and Dick Smith and Allexander Snatt harrow'd.
Thomas Hamper and Marten finish the gate into the

Edgly Mead and the barrs at the lower end part of the day -----112 days. John Gun and Old Dick Banks ditcht, I think Thomas Gravet thrasht. Paid Young Dick Banks £-8s and £-2s he had before in full for his last years wages. He begun an other year at £. I was at John Snashall's ȷ̇ in the evning. Paid John Clark at the Comon £-11s-11d in full of all. Ja ck and I brought the 2 runts and the young bull from Rickman's after.

The 29th March 1719 Sunday. A fine day. Mr Jeremiah Dodson preacht. Scutt and I supt at Westtowne.

The 30th March 1719 Munday. A fine day. Allexander Snatt, Thomas Gravet and Jack Greenaway win'd 4 quarters 2 bushels of Gravet's wheat. _about noon, did not work afterwards. Dick Smith finisht Tully's lower field etc for which I gave him 6d. Paid Thomas Gravet 32s-6d and clear'd accounts. He has earn'd of me £-16s-6d. We settled accounts at Church as usual. Paid George Buckwell £-17s-6d in full for work done at Rickman's. Supt at Westtowne with my Cousin John Lindfield and John Hart the tanner. Receiv'd 10d of Thomas Hamper for William Balcomb's auger.

The 31st March 1719 Tuesday. A gloomy morning, wet afternoon. All kept holy day. Paid Thomas Hamper £1-14s in full of all, his bill was £7-0-0d. My Cousin Plump and Mr John Hart din'd here. Mr John Hart and I spent the evning at my Father's. Turn'd 2 runts to grass in the dry pond. Richard White ȷ̇ and Mary Tully married this morning. *(Ed: Recorded in Hurstpierpoint Parish Register)*

The 1st April 1719 Wednesday. A fine day. Old Dick Banks and Allexander Snatt made an end of thrashing barly and win'd    bushels head and    bushels tail. John Gun cut half a cord of wood in the forenoon and set up wood at Tully's after. Young Dick Banks and Jack, Dick Smith and Willy fagoted. I were a while at the Swan with John Rice, Chapman and after my Wife and I were at Thomas Norton's at the North End, he not at home. Paid 2s-6d for a payr of stockens for Molly Balcomb.

The 2nd April 1719 Thursday. A gloomy day. John Gun and Banks hedg'd. Young Dick Banks and Willy plough'd in the forenoon, the 2 boys with them after. Allexander Snatt and George West clean'd the flax seed in the morning. Allexander Snatt workt in the garden afterwards. Deliver'd half a cord of wood to my Father per Mr Jeremiah Dodson's teem. My Cousin Wicks came hither in her way to Lewis. I were at the club with Mr Scutt and Mr Burry.

The 3rd April 1719 Fryday. A dry day. Young Dick Banks and Willy, Jack and Dick plough'd. John Gun and Old Dick Banks hedg'd. Allexander Snatt poll'd trees in Tully's lower field. My Wife and I supt at Mr Jeremiah Dodson's with Mr Richard Whitpaine and Mr John Hart. William Clark gave the sorrel horse a purge. Mrs Courtness din'd here. My Sister Ann Box here afternoon. My Cousin Wicks went to Lewis, William Gorman with her.

The 4th April 1719 Saturday. A dry day. Win'd 18 bushels head and 2 tail of John Gun's oates afternoon. Old Dick Banks helpt. They hedg'd and ditcht in the forenoon. Young Dick Banks and Willy plough'd all day, Jack and Dick part of the forenoon. Jack went to Lewis afternoon. Dick helpt winnow etc.
Allexander Snatt poll'd as yesterday. William Clark workt off the sorrel horse's purge. Receiv'd 17s-6d yesterday of my Cousin John Lindfield for 8½ yards of drugget, 10s-10d for 6½ yards of shalloon. He came hither to advise me in my flax season etc. Paid my ñkle Courtness's bill £-5-4½d in full. Receiv'd his Land Tax.

The 5th April 1719 Sunday. A fine day.
Mr Jeremiah Dodson preacht. My Wife and I receiv'd the Sacrament. We had a parish meeting. My Cousin John Lindfield supt here.

The 6th April 1719 Munday. A dry cold day. Willy and William Michell sow'd about 5 quarters of oates on 7 acres of the Nine Acres, harrow'd and roll'd. My Cousin John Lindfield's man William helpt with 5 horses. Allexander Snatt and Dick Smith harrow'd also, so did Young Dick Banks. John Gun and Old Dick Banks hedg'd against the Middle Piece. Mr Jeremiah Dodson and Ralph Beard supt and spent the evning here. Mr Scutt lent me his horse to ride about the ground.

The 7th April 1719 Tuesday. A gloomy day. Allexander Snatt, Young Dick Banks, Willy and Dick Smith harrow'd and roll'd in the Nine Acres. John Gun and Old Dick Banks hedg'd. Mr Richard Whitpaine and his wife Mary and daughter supt here. Paid Dick Wood bill £-12s-2d. Receiv'd his ta xes. Richard and William

Jarvice workt here most part of the day.

The 8th April 1719 Wednesday. A very fine day. John Gun and Banks hedg'd. William Michell sow'd about 5 bushels of flax and 2 bushels of clover seed on the Nine Acres. Young Dick Banks, Allexander Snatt and Willy harrow'd and roll'd. Paid William Michell 2s for this day and yesterday. Thomas Hamper and Marten workt on the Towne parlour. Mr Jeremiah Dodson and Dick Wood were here in the morning to talk about Wood's gutter etc. Paid Mr Dodson half a year's tythe for Little Park etc and half a year's tythe 16s for R Burry. Agree'd with Mr Dodson for the tythe of Rickman's at 32s per annum for so long as we live together. Dr Nick Plaw here this evning. Receiv'd 14 guineas of my Father for Mrs Price. Outset Mr Dodson's Poor Tax. Old Hyder's too etc.

The 9th April 1719 Thursday. A fine day. Young Dick Banks and Willy finisht the Nine Acres and carry'd Mr Richard Whitpaine what straw was due. John Gun and Old Dick Banks hedg'd. Allexander Snatt and Dick Smith plough'd. I went to Rusper to treat with Mrs Pryaulx about my Father's business. Agreed for a reference at Hand Cross when my Father could come. I clear'd accounts with Mrs Chapman about Mary Morley and she offer'd to keep her an other year at 50s per annum but I offer'd her but 40s. Jack Haslegrove went with me. I call'd at Mr Robert's at Cowfold as I came home there was Mr Michell and Thomas Vinall.

The 10th April 1719 Fryday. A very fine day. John Gun and Old Dick Banks hedg'd. Dick Smith and Willy plough'd. Young Dick Banks harrow'd a fallow. Paid my Father his 14 guineas again which I receiv'd yesterday. I were with Thomas Steel at Sayers Comon to come to hedge for me and he promis'd to come a Wednesday. William Clark gave the sorrel horse an other purge. I talkt with John Box sr at John Smith's about John Balcomb's comeing to Mr John Hart's to school. My Wife went to Wanbarrow afternoon. Allexander Snatt ditcht.

The 11th April 1719 Saturday. A very fine day. John Gun and Old Dick Banks hedg'd. Allexander Snatt and Young Dick Banks carry'd bushes. John Edwards faggoted. Willy and Jack plough'd. Dick roll'd by Wickham's. Clear'd accounts with John Snashall sr, he supt here. I had 3 throat hasps at Westtowne, he not at home. Thomas Hamper set up some posts and rails between the Homefield and Middle Piece about half a day --- ½ day. Mr William Martin's mare came this evning at 2s per week. John Pierce workt here.

The 12th April 1719 Sunday. A very fine day. Mr William Martin preacht twice. My Brother Peter and Mr William Martin here after evning prayr. I were at Tott after dinner, my Cousin John Lindfield din'd here.

The 13th April 1719 Munday. A fine day. Begun sow barly by Wickham's, Young Dick Banks and Jack Haslegrove, Willy and Will Lindfield plough'd, George West and Dick Smith sow'd and harrow'd. Allexander Snatt and Old Dick Banks hedg'd. Paid Allexander Snatt 16s. My Cousin John Lindfield lent me 4 oxen. Deliver'd 8½ quarters of barly to Harry Wickham per Young Dick Banks and Jack. Receiv'd 2 quarters of Thomas Norton's barly and 8 quarters before. Jack Balcomb begun go to school to Mr John Hart and William to Abraham Muzzall.

The 14th April 1719 Tuesday. A very fine day. Old Dick Banks and Allexander Snatt hedg'd. John Gun cut stakes etc. George West sow'd and roll'd. Young Dick Banks and Jack, Willy and William Lindfield plough'd. Dick Smith harrow'd. Marten and Jack Mills hew'd a little timber and set up the stile to the Churchfield afternoon. Richard White sr took a horse coller, loss for me. Paid Thomas Roberds of Brighton 7s in full of all.

The 15th April 1719 Wednesday. A dry day. Thomas Steel and John Gun begun the hedge by Greenaway's. Allexander Snatt and Old Dick Banks mended hedges 'till noon, helpt John Gun and Thomas Steel after. Jack Mills and Jack Haslegrove, Willy and William Lindfield plough'd. George West and Dick, harrow'd and sow'd. Young Dick Banks harrow'd with the ox harrow in the Homefield with 3 horses. Deliver'd 3 quarters of barly to Mr Richard Whitpaine's men, John Smith and Dick King. Receiv'd 44s of Mrs Cheal, per my Wife, in full for hops. Old Dick Banks had half a bushel of wheat.

The 16th April 1719 Thursday. A very fine day. John Gun and Steel hedg'd. Richard Hart and Dick Smith, Willy and William Lindfield plough'd. George West sow'd and harrow'd. Young Dick Banks roll'd and harrow'd in the Homefield. Jack went to Lewis. Allexander Snatt and Old Dick Banks hedg'd. My Cousin John Lindfield din'd here. I gave him my receits from Mr Dee for £72-12s to carry to show to the reciever at Cuckfield. My Sisters Sarah and Betty here afternoon.

The 17th April 1719 Fryday. A gloomy day, some rain towards night. Richard Hart and Jack Haslegrove, Willy and William Lindfield begun plough the Homefield. George West and Young Dick Banks sow'd and harrow'd. John Gun and Thomas Steel hedg'd. Allexander Snatt and Old Dick Banks hedg'd against Tully's wheat. Paid 1s for Tabby for Molly Balcomb to work a purse. Thomas Howell's man William made 2 payr of court dills. Paid Mr Picknall of Arundell 45s in full of all. Dick Hart and Jack broak my old plough in the morning and I borrow'd one of his mother. I were at the club last night with Mr John Hart, Mr Richard Whitpaine, Mr Scutt and Thomas Norton North End. Dick Smith thwartled and finisht the field by Wickham's, George West has sow'd there 4 quarters 3 bushels. Mr Waller of Brighton was here to enquire what I had done with my last years wool.

The 18th April 1719 Saturday. A windy day with a showr or 2 in the morning. John Gun and Thomas Steel made an end of the Rookwood hedge by the lane and begun the new planted hedge. Allexander Snatt and Old Dick Banks ditch in the Nine Acres. Richard Hart and Jack, Willy and William Lindfield plough'd. George West and Dick Smith sow'd and harrow'd. Young Dick Banks harrow'd and roll'd in the forenoon and ground 7½ bushels of malt afternoon. Ned Burt made a hot bed in the upper garden.

The 19th April 1719 Sunday. A fine day. Mr William Martin preacht. No service afternoon. Mrs Courthope and my Sister Betty din'd here. I din'd and spent the afternoon at Dean House. Mrs Weeks came here from Lewis towards night.

The 20th April 1719 Munday. A showry day. The smallpox came out on Sarah Norton yesterday. Richard Hart and Jack, Willy and William Lindfield plough'd. George West, Dick Banks and Dick Smith harrow'd, sow'd and John Gun poll'd and faggoted. Old Dick Banks and Allexander Snatt hedg'd. Allexander Snatt had a bushel of wheat, Old Dick Banks half a bushel of wheat and as much barly. Paid William Clark 2s for working off the sorrel horse's purges and I am to pay John Snashall jr for the purges. Receiv'd 7 guineas and 4d towards my Brother Peter's Land Tax, remains 36s. Nick Marchant and he here afternoon. Thomas Hamper and his men made an end of wainscotting the Towne parlour. Paid Richard Hart 4s for his 4 days ploughing. Paid my Unkle Courtness 5s for 3 yards of thicksett, 3s and 6d for 3 yards of white fustian and 3d for mohair.

The 21st April 1719 Tuesday. A gloomy morning, dry after. George West made an end of sowing the Homefield with 5 quarters 3½ bushels of barly. Young Dick Banks, Dick Smith, Willy and William Lindfield plough'd and harrow'd. William Lindfield went home. Old Dick Banks and Allexander Snatt hedg'd. John Gun poll'd and faggotted. John Towner and Ja Reed sow'd to day and yesterday. Mr Richard Whitpaine supt and spent the evning here, reckon'd and clear'd all accounts with him. Mrs Gratwick and Mrs Catherine Beard here afternoon. Jack Haslegrove had Mrs Wicks to Fryland. Agreed with Jack Smith for 3¼d per lb for my barren sheep etc.

The 22nd April 1719 Wednesday. A fine day. William Michell sow'd 2 bushels of Nonsuch on the Homefield. Young Dick Banks, Dick Smith, Willy and Jack harrow'd, roll'd and finisht the field. Clear'd accounts with John Towner and Ja Reed. Their sawing came to 8s-4d. Outset Reed's Poor Taxes and ½ year Land Tax. Old Dick Banks and Allexander Snatt made an end of hedging. John Gun poll'd.

The 23rd April 1719 Thursday. A fine day. A Fair at Nutley (famous for barrens) at Henfield and at Jolsfield Comon. Young Dick Banks and all the Family did a jobb or 2 in the morning. Kept holy day after. Clear'd accounts with John Snashall jr in the morning. Mr John Hart din'd here. John Gun and Allexander Snatt poll'd. I were to see Mrs Gratwick afternoon with my Father etc. I were at the club with Mr Price, Mr Dunstall and Mr Osbourne and Mr John Hart.

The 24th April 1719 Fryday. A fine day. Old Dick Banks begun thrash wheat yesterday. John Gun and Allexander Snatt poll'd. Old Dick Banks thrasht. Young Dick Banks and Willy fetcht a cart load of bushes and an other of boughs from Rickman's into the Rookwood. Dick Smith roll'd the barly by Wickham's. John Pierce brought home my thick set breeches. My Wife went to my Brother John Box's.

The 25th April 1719 Saturday. A fine day.
A Fair in the Cliffe of Lewis. Old Dick Banks thrasht. John Gun and Allexander Snatt roll'd. Deliver'd 10 bushels head and 9 tail of barly to Harry Wickham per Dick. I din'd at Mr Jeremiah Dodson's with Mr John Hart. Mrs Cheal was at Hurst this afternoon.
Paid Old Dick Banks 5s, he had a bushel of head barly.

The 26th April 1719 Sunday. A fine day.
Mr William Martin preacht. My Wife had a fitt of an ague. I was not at Church afternoon. My Father and Mother Stone and sister Bett here afternoon.

The 27th April 1719 Munday. A very fine day. I wrote to John Reeve's ‗. James Aux of Darkin and John Snashall j̇ were here a while in the forenoon. Young Dick Banks and Dick Smith carry'd 25 faggots to the Widdow Reeve, fetch't up a cart load of hay from Tully's etc. Dick Smith harrow'd in the Towne Orchard afternoon. Old Dick Banks thrasht. John Gun and Allexander Snatt faggotted. I were at Oathall afternoon. Turn'd the least Wintermilch to pasture, the old one bulling. Receiv'd the 36s of my Brother Peter which remain'd of his last Land Tax.

The 28th April 1719 Tuesday. A very fine day.
John Gun, Young Dick Banks, Willy, the boys and I begun the raddled hedge across the Rickman's.
Old Dick Banks thrasht. Allexander Snatt faggotted. Thomas Hamper workt on my closset window shutters --------- 1½ days. My Father din'd here. Mr John Hart and Mr William Martin here night.

The 29th April 1719 Wednesday. A very fine day. John Gun finisht the Rookwood hedg's by noon. Old Dick Banks thrasht, Allexander Snatt faggoted. Young Dick Banks and Willy fetcht 2 loads of boughs from Rickman's and carry'd Thomas Hamper 50 faggots. Jack carry'd 21 fleeces of wool to Thomas Friend's £44. Thomas Hamper put up my window shutters -- 2½ days. Reckon'd and clear'd accounts with William Roach. He put up a window 6½ feet in the new buttery at Towne. Mrs Gratwick and Frank Holden's wife *(Ed: nee Mary Marshall)* here afternoon. Paid John Gatland of Cuckfield 13d for mending the ‗.

The 30th April 1719 Thursday. A fine day.
Mr Jeremiah Dodson's tythe feast. John Gun and Richard White j̇ workt clearing the hedge by Patching's. John Gun left at noon, went to his cousin Friend's afterwards. Young Dick Banks fetch up some wheat for Richard Hart and carry'd 25 faggots to Richard King. Willy and the boys helpt about the hedge. Jack carry'd my chamber clock to John Gatland's and a letter to my Brother Henry Faulkoner. Dr Nightingale was to see my Sister Sarah. Thomas Hamper and Marten set up a payr of barrs in the Rookwood etc. Thomas Hamper workt till 3 afternoon, Marten till noon ------- 3 days.
Paid Thomas Steel 5s for hedging. Clear'd accounts with George West. Let John Gun and Richard White my home clover to thrash and pugg at 4s per bushel, Tully's at 4s-6d.

The 1st May 1719 Fryday. A fine day. A Fair at Lindfield and Storrington. Mr John Hart, my Wife and I went to Lewis and Jacky clear'd accounts with Thomas Friend, Samuel Tourl and Mr Court. I din'd at my Cousin Peter Marchant's. My Sister Betty went away with John Courtness last night. *(Ed: They married next day at Fleet Prison – Betty was 18 years old. Their daughter Elizabeth was baptised at Hurst on the following 25 February)*

The 2nd May 1719 Saturday. A fine day. Banks thrasht. Allexander Snatt faggoted. John Gun, Richard White, Willy and Dick Smith begun the hedge to Church ‗. Young Dick Banks carry'd 11 loads of Towne dirt into lower part Rookwood. I were at Wanbarrow in the forenoon, at Mr William Martin's after. Clear'd accounts with Thomas Howell £2-15s-10d. Mr Todd and Mrs Kettilby came down yesterday.

The 3rd May 1719 Sunday. A fine day. Mr William Martin preacht twice. We had a parish meeting, settled accounts as usual. I was at Mrs Catherine Beard's after evning prayr.

The 4th May 1719 Munday. A fine day. John Gun and Willy made an end of the hedge by Patching's. Old Dick Banks thrasht. Young Dick Banks carry'd    loads of Towne dirt into the Rookwood, 2 loads to Mr John Hart and Dick Smith and he fetcht up a cart load of hay from Tully's. Win'd 5 bushels of John Gun's oates in the morning. Dick Wood, Old William Brand and I measur'd the ground for Dick Wood gutter etc but did not conclude. Turn'd 6 oxen into the Fifteen Acres.

5 young steers into the Marldfield and 3 heifers into the lower orchard. I were at Westtowne, he being sick, I lookt over the ground for him etc. Richard White faggoted. Allexander Snatt did not work, his wife sick.

The 5th May 1719 Tuesday. A very fine day.
Young Dick Banks went to Cuckfield to his sister's child's Christening and is to work a holy day for it. Old Dick Banks did not work. Turn'd the 6 oxen into the Nonsuch with the cows. John Gun and Dick Smith poled the hop garden. Willy mended gaps in the Slip etc. Mrs Gratwick breakfasted here, she gave me an order to pay her intrest to Mr Lintott and went away from Mrs Catherine Beard's afternoon. Richard White faggoted. Allexander Snatt did not work. I talkt with John Marchant of Lox at John Bodle's. John Bodle's horse was put into the Rookwood a 2s-6d for this week and 2s per week afterwards. Anne Terry came this evning at          per annum.

The 6th May 1719 Wednesday. A very fine day, a showr in the night. A Fair at Bolny. Young Dick Banks and Willy carry'd      loads of Towne dirt into the Rookwood and 1 load to Mr John Hart. John Gun poled in the hop garden etc Dick Smith helpt. Dick Smith and Jack drove the long cow to Nick Plaw's bull and Mrs Catherine Beard's heifer with her. Jack carry'd butter to Lewis in the morning. Receiv'd Frank Holden's Taxes.
I din'd at my Father's. Old Dick Banks did not work. Dick White faggoted.

The 7th May 1719 Thursday. A fine day, only a showr afternoon. A Fair at Brighton, at Darkin and at the Dicker. My Wife and I din'd at Mr Heely's. All the servants kept holy day. Old Dick Banks thrasht. Dick White faggoted. Thomas Hamper workt on the benches in the porch ------------- 3½ days.

The 8th May 1719 Fryday. A fine day.
Captain Whitpaine died afternoon *(Ed: Mr Thomas Whitpaine buried 11th May at Hurst according to Parish Register)*. Young Dick Banks and Willy carry'd Towne dirt. Dick and Jack tied hops etc. Old Dick Banks thrasht. John Gun, Allexander Snatt and Dick White faggoted. My Father, Mother and I were at Wanbarrow afternoon. Thomas Hamper and Jack Mills set up the gate into the Hovelfield etc ---------- 4½ days.
I set out 3 trees at Rickman's.

The 9th May 1719 Saturday. A gloomy day.
John Gun and Allexander Snatt faggoted. Old Dick Banks spread dirt. Young Dick Banks carry'd dirt into the little Rookwood. The boys ty'd hops. Turn'd the fatting oxen to pasture by Hyder's. My Wife and Willy went to Shermanbury. Receiv'd 2lbs of roll tobacco and a letter from John Brand from Lisbon.

The 10th May 1719 Sunday. A wet morning, dry after. Mr William Martin preacht. My Cousin John Lindfield supt and spent the evning here. My Cousin John Marchant of Lox here after dinner.

The 11th May 1719 Munday. A gloomy day.
Young Dick Banks made an end of carrying the Towne dirt etc. The boys workt in the garden etc. Reckon'd and clear'd accounts with Old Dick Banks. John Gun, Allexander Snatt and White faggoted. Old Dick Banks thrasht.          I were at Lewis about the Window Tax. Paid Thomas Friend 3s-6d for my Cousin John Lindfield. My Cousin John Lindfield had 9lb of hops here in the morning per his son John. He is to give me 21d per lb.

The 12th May 1719 Tuesday. A showry day. My Wife and I, Young Dick Banks and Jacky went to my Brother Henry Faulkoner's. Old Dick Banks and the boys spread Towne dirt etc. John Gun, Allexander Snatt and White faggoted.

The 13th May 1719 Wednesday. A windy forenoon, wet after. John Gun, Allexander Snatt and White faggoted if they workt. Young Dick Banks and Dick Smith had the waggon to Thomas Howell's and brought home the dung court with 500 bricks and 2 bushels of lime from Parker's, the brick to Rickman's. They carry'd 2 ploughs to John Clarks and a harrow. My Father and Mother Stone supt and din'd here. Bought a payr of large burden boxes, cast iron, of Jack Clark at 2s-6d. Left 4 old shares there weigh'd 26lb for which I am to have 1½d per lb. Young Dick Banks and Dick Smith fetcht also a load of sand. Agreed with George Buckwell to frame and raise the stable at Rickman's at 10s.

The 14th May 1719 Thursday. A gloomy day, wet last night. Win'd 7 quarters head and 5 bushels tail of Old William Brand's wheat. Willy and the boys helpt to day and yesterday, Jack Picknall helpt part of yesterday, Old Dick Banks helpt skreen it to day etc about 2⅔ of the day. John Gun, Allexander Snatt and White faggoted. Young Dick Banks did severall ꝑbbs. My Sister Mary Faulkoner *(Ed: Mary Marchant married Henry Faulkoner at Balcombe 5th June 1711)* din'd here. My Sister Betty Courtness was down here. George Buckwell begun frame the stable at Rickman's. I was at Mrs Brand's afternoon and my Wife. Thomas Hamper primed my closset.

The 15th May 1719 Fryday. A showry day. Young Dick Banks and the boys ground 7½ bushels of malt in the morning etc, in the afternoon he and Willy workt at Rickman's cleaning the ponds. Dick Smith roll'd the Towne dirt in the Rookwood and afterwards stickt pease etc. My Brother John Courtness was down here in the morning and promis'd to demand no intrest for the mony I was to pay him of his wive's portion. *(Ed: i.e for Thomas's sister Betty – now newly wed)* Old Dick Banks thrasht, John Gun, White and Allexander Snatt fagotted. I din'd at my Father's. Thomas Hamper laid the 2nd colour on my closset. The red heifer went to bull. Paid 5 for 2 yards of linen for a pettycoat for Molly Balcomb.

The 16th May 1719 Saturday. A dry day. John Gun, White, Young Dick Banks, Willy and Dick Smith carry'd dung out of the home close. George Buckwell and his boy set up some posts and rails and stopt 3 windows at Rickman's. Mr John Hart supt and spent the evning here. Old Dick Banks ditcht at Rickman's. Drove 2 barrens and a runt to Rickman's.
Mr Beard and J Chainey of Arundell were here with a proposall for printing some [ꝑp........] effigies etc but I did not subscribe. Old Plaw was at my Father's and had the mony Mrs Pryaulx demanded for tythe.

The 17th May 1719 Sunday. A dry day. Mr William Martin preacht. I was not at Church in the forenoon. Not well. We had a vestry afternoon in John Reeve's rooms. My Wife was to see my Sister Ann Box in the forenoon.

The 18th May 1719 Munday. A fine day. All kept holy day. I were at Thomas Howell's in the morning. Paid Parker 7s for lime and ridge tiles I had last year. My Father, Mr John Hart, my Wife and I went to Mr Price's afternoon and I were forc'd to come away before them being haveing an ague.

The 19th May 1719 Tuesday. A fine day. All kept holy day. Paid Allexander Snatt 10s.

The 20th May 1719 Wednesday. A fine day. Old Dick Banks thrasht. John Gun win'd        bushels of his oates, faggoted the rest of the day. Young Dick Banks and Willy fetcht 1000 bricks and a load of lime from Taylor's for Mr Scutt. Mrs Catherine Beard and her family here afternoon. The heifer that suckled the young bull, calved yesterday at Rickman's, a cow calf. My Sister Sarah here towards night.

The 21st May 1719 Thursday. A very fine day. Old Dick Banks thrasht and mow'd a little grass in the Edgly Mead. John Gun faggoted. Young Dick Banks and Dick Smith fetcht half a load lime and 750 bricks from Taylor's for Stephen Bine and brought home about 25 faggots out of the Hovelfield. My Cousin John Box here. Willy bought a ꝑ........]of Old Nicholas of Ardingly for 50d at Cuckfield Fair.

The 22nd May 1719 Fryday. A very hot fine day. Banks mended gaps etc. John Gun and White made an end of faggoting. Paid and clear'd accounts with Richard White, left 3s-10d in his hands. Allexander Snatt faggoted. Dick Smith water'd trees etc. Willy and Young Dick Banks carry'd a small load of straw to Rickman's and fetcht half a load of lime and 750 bricks from Taylor for Stephen Bine. Paid John Snashall sr 2s in full of all.

The 23rd May 1719 Saturday. A very hot, fine day. Old Dick Banks did severall ꝑbbs. John Gun and White made an end of oat thrashing and win'd 9 bushels in all. Allexander Snatt faggoted. Young Dick Banks and Willy fetcht half a load of lime and 700 of bricks for Stephen Bine, also half a load of lime for my self and 750 bricks for Mr Scutt. John Hill of Rigate, son to Old George Hill bought my lambs, 40 at £20 to be gone by midsummer. Receiv'd ten guineas of Harry Wickham.
My Father, Mr William Martin and Mr Scutt here afternoon. John Reeve sign'd a bill of sale here to the officers of his goods for the sum of £11-7s.
Thomas Hamper, John Hill and _ Thomas Hamper workt here on severall ꝑbbs ---- 5 ½ days. Deliver'd the mony left in White's hands yesterday. Paid Richard Patching 1s for bleeding me.

The 24th May 1719 Sunday. A fine day. Mr William Martin preacht. We had a vestry afternoon about John

Reeve. My Cousin John Lindfield was here after evning prayr, Mr Scutt and Brother Peter before and Cousin John Lindfield too.

The 25th May 1719 Munday. A very fine, hot day. Old Dick Banks thrasht. Young Dick Banks and Willy fetcht 1000 bricks for Mr Scutt and a load of sand for my self. John Gun and Young thrasht clover. Allexander Snatt faggoted. Thomas Hamper made a frame for the chirm, finisht the porch etc ------- 6 ½ days. I were at the Comon in the evning. My Wife was at my Brother John Box's afternoon. Paid my U kle Courtness 3d for 1lb of small and 7d for 2lbs of white lead. Receiv'd 17s-6d of Stephen Bine in full for carriage.

The 26th May 1719 Tuesday. A very fine hot day. Old Dick Banks thrasht. Young Dick Banks, John Gun, White and Willy carry'd 40 loads of dung. John Gun and Dick Smith made out half a load of lime in the morning. Allexander Snatt faggoted. My Wife, Jacky, Molly and I were at the christening of my Brother John Box's daughter Mary *(Ed: Recorded in Albourne Parish Register)*. Thomas Hamper workt on my cubbord ------- 7 ½ days. Thomas Hamper's man painted my closet once over and ground more colour etc.

The 27th May 1719 Wednesday. A very fine day. Old Dick Banks thrasht. John Gun and White thrasht clover. Allexander Snatt faggoted. Young Dick Banks, Willy and Dick Smith fetcht 1250 bricks from Taylor's for Mr Scutt and brought home the other waggon with a new payr of fore wheels and the hind wheels new iron'd. Paid Mr Durrant £4-5-6d for cloaths for Molly Balcomb.

The 28th May 1719 Thursday. A very fine hot day. Mrs Wicks, Molly Balcomb, Bett, young William Beard and I went to Lewis yesterday brought home Mrs Wick's eldest son, in order to go to school to Mr John Hart. Young Dick Banks, Willy, John Gun and White carry'd 47 loads of dung. Old Dick Banks thrasht. Allexander Snatt faggoted. My Aunt Holden, Cousin Hayne and her son John here. I gave her a note on Thomas Champion to take £3 for a quarter's annuity due at Lady Day last. My Father and Mother Stone din'd here.

The 29th May 1719 Fryday. A very fine day. A Fair at Stenning. Young Dick Banks, Old Dick Banks, Willy and Dick Smith carry'd 32 loads of dung out of the fatting close. John Gun and White thrasht clover. Allexander Snatt faggoted. I went to the Fair, bought a payr of oxen of Thomas Lidbeater of Bramber at £17. Jack Haslegrove went with me. I supt at Westtowne as I came home. The cow I bought of George Buckwell went to bull.

The 30th May 1719 Saturday. A very fine day. Old Dick Banks, John Gun and White thrasht. Paid Allexander Snatt 10s-6d. He faggoted. Old Dick Banks had half a bushel of wheat. Thomas Hamper's man painted my clossett with the last colour. Young Dick Banks, Willy, Dick, Jack and I fetcht flints for the highway with 2 teems. George Buckwell rais'd the stable at Rickman's. Ed Rusbridger and his wife, Widdow Sumersel, John Dale's wife, my Father and Mother Stone and Mr John Hart here in the evning.

The 31st May 1719 Sunday. A very fine day. Mr William Martin preacht, my Cousin John Lindfield's wife Elizabeth din'd here. My Sister Sarah and John Courtness here after dinner. Did not go to Church afternoon.

The 1st June 1719 Munday. A very fine day. Old Dick Banks, John Gun and White thrasht. Paid Chapman of Aberton 1s for washing 59 sheep. Young Dick Banks carry'd grit from Stephen Bine's celler and into my Father's close etc. The boys helpt wash the sheep etc.

The 2nd June 1719 Tuesday. A very fine day. Old Dick Banks thrasht. John Gun and White thrasht clover. Allexander Snatt did not work. Young Dick Banks and Willy carry'd a load of great chalk to Taylor's at the Comon at 6s and brought home 750 bricks for Mr Scutt and 6 paving tiles and 2 bushels of lime and 2 bushels of lime for my self. The boys did severall jobbs. My Wife went to Danny afternoon. William Lashmer's widdow buried. Receiv'd 36s of Mr Scutt for carriage and 4s for 250 of my bricks.

The 3rd June 1719 Wednesday. A very fine day. Old Dick Banks carry'd dung at Rickman's. Young Dick Banks, Willy, the boys and I fetcht flints with 2 teems. My Father, Mother and Sister Sarah din'd here. Mrs Mary Gratwick of Reeds and Sister Betty Courtness here afternoon. John Gun and White thrasht clover.

The 4th June 1719 Thursday. A very fine day. Old Dick Banks fetcht a load of building flints and a load of small chalk. Will Gorman helpt. Young Dick Banks and Dick Smith carry'd a load of great chalk to Taylor's etc and brought home 500 bricks, half a load of lime and 20 paveing for Mr Scutt. Paid Chapman 2s-6d for sheering 59 sheep. Willy helpt afternoon. John Gun and White workt in the garden. A cricket match in the Sandfield. Paid H Kord 8d for spaying and receiv'd his taxes.

The 5th June 1719 Fryday. A very fine day. My Brother James Ede and his daughter Katherine came last night. She lay at my Father's. My Brother, my Wife and I were at Rickman's, came home by White's. Bought 15 young ducks of White at 4d a piece and 16 at 2d a piece to be outset in the rent of my field. Young Dick Banks carry'd a stock of board to Jo Wood for Mr Scutt at 16s per 100. Young Dick Banks, the boys and Willy carry'd a small load of straw and a load of small chalk to Rickman's. Old Dick Banks carry'd dung at Rickman's in the morning and went to the chalk pitt afternoon with my teem for 2 loads of great chalk. Drew it down to Edgly lower gates. Paid the chalk diggers 2s in full of all. Thomas Hamper was here and my Father paid him £3-5s towards wainscotting the parlour and other works etc 10s towards his man's painting.

The 6th June 1719 Saturday. A very fine day. John Gun pugg'd clover at Tully's. Old Dick Banks clear'd the close at Rickman's, in all         loads. Young Dick Banks, Dick and Willy carry'd 2 loads of great chalk to Taylor's and brought home 1000 bricks for Dick Wood and 160 gutter bricks and 500 tiles for John Pierce. They afterwards carry'd 2 loads of small chalk to Rickman's. Paid Parker at the Comon 8s-6d, remainder due to him 4d. John Gatland of Cuckfield brought home my chamber clock and I paid him 1s for mending it and 1s for mending Mrs Gatwick's coffee mill. He carry'd home my watch to clean. It was a Wednesday last he was here.

The 7th June 1719 Sunday. A very fine day. Mr William Martin preacht. A parish meeting but no accounts settled. I deliver'd Ned May's indentures to him out of the chest but kept Thomas Muzzall's assignment to Thomas Beard. I was at Mrs Catherine Beard's after evning pray'r. Receiv'd a new hat from Lewis a Saturday per Harry Wickham, I am to give 7s for him. My Brother James Ede carry'd away his daughter Bett early this morning.

The 8th June 1719 Munday. A fine day. John Gun and Willy thrasht clover. Young Dick Banks, Old Dick Banks, Willy and Dick Smith carry'd 4 loads of chalk into the close at Rickman's. I sent an intry of my wool per Widdow Dennet. I were to meet my Cousin John Lindfield at Sarah Hart's. He came but would not stay. My Wife went to my Brother John Box's towards night. Receiv'd £3-10s of John Smith.

The 9th June 1719 Tuesday. A fine day, thunder showers towards night. Old Dick Banks thrasht wheat, John Gun and White clover. Young Dick Banks, Willy, Dick and I carry'd 4 loads of chalk in Rickman's. Old Dick Banks's daughter weeded by Wickham's to day and yesterday, Jack with her now and then. Paid Boniface's wife 5s for 24 ducks. My Cousin John Lindfield and his wife Elizabeth here towards night.

The 10th June 1719 Wednesday. A very fine day. Old Dick Banks thrasht wheat, John Gun and White clover. Young Dick Banks, Dick and Willy carry'd 4 loads of chalk to Rickman's. Thomas Holden and John Edwards begun thatch the stable at Rickman's. George Buckwell's boy put on the eve laths there. Old Dick Banks's girls weeded by Wickham's. Picknall's boys pickt up flints in the Nonsuch yesterday. I were to talk with Mr Jeremiah Dodson in the morning. Paid for 6 yards of edging at 21d per yard, 10s-6d for 3 quarters and half yard of muslin for cap and ruffles and to graft an apron 5s-9d *(Ed: xxx text deleted xxx)*, in all 15s-9d to John Gracie a Scotchman for Molly Balcomb. Item 2s for a payr of gloves for her some time since Christmas which I forgot to set down, bought at Lewis and 13d for an other payr bought very lately.

The 11th June 1719 Thursday. A gloomy day and a little rain. Old Dick Banks thrasht. John Gun and White thrasht clover. Holden and John Edwards thatcht. Young Dick Banks, Willy and Dick carry'd 2 loads of chalk to Rickman's and as much into the fatting close. Mr Bernard Heasman of Cuckfield was here, I sold him my wool at a guinea per todd and a packet of old hopps at 21d per lb. He likewise left his mare here and rode home the sorrel horse, both for tryall and to exchange if we like. I were at Westtowne with him. My Sister Sarah came hither.

The 12th June 1719 Fryday. A wet day.
Old Dick Banks thrasht. John Gun and White thrasht.

Young Dick Banks, Willy and Dick fetcht 2 loads of great chalk in the waggon, 1 load of small chalk in the dung court to Rickman's and 1 load of great chalk in the dung court brought home and left in the court. Thomas Hamper workt on a ladder and my Wive's closet --- 8 ½ days. My Cousin John Lindfield and I took an inventory of Mrs Hart's goods.

The 13th June 1719 Saturday. A dry day. Old Dick Banks, John Gun and White thrasht. Nick Plaw here in the morning, cut calves etc. Thomas Hamper workt on my Wive's closet ------ 9 days. Young Dick Banks, Willy and Dick carry'd a dung court load of great chalk to Rickman's that was left at home last night. They also carry'd 2 loads of chalk to Taylor's and brought home 1500 bricks for Stephen Bine. My Sister Sarah went to Balcombe, my Sister Mary Faulkoner being sick and sent for her.

The 14th June 1719 Sunday. A wet forenoon, dry after. Mr William Martin preacht. I was not at Church in the forenoon.

The 15th June 1719 Munday. A fine day. Old Dick Banks faggoted. John Gun and White helpt Old William Brand about his tomb. Young Dick Banks and Willy carry'd 2 loads of straw to thatch my Father's stable, Holden begun it. They carry'd 500 of my bricks to John Pierce and a court load of flints to Old William Brand. Sent 43lbs of hopps to Mr Bernard Heasman per Dick Banks and he return'd Willy's horse. Thomas Hamper workt on the garret stairs -------- 10 ½ days. Dick Wood begun lay his gutter. Receiv'd lb of bohea from Samuel Tourl. Paid my Mother her thirds to Lady Day last.

The 16th June 1719 Tuesday. A very fine day. I were at Shoreham Market. Sold 2 loads of wheat for 3 if I please to Benjamin Hayler at £5-5s per load to be deliver'd a Saturday next. Young Dick Banks drew home Stephen Bine's knee, one piece to Thomas Hamper and one piece to my sawpit, helpt winnow afternoon. Old Dick Banks, Willy and the boys win'd 71 bushels of Old Dick Banks's wheat. Thomas Hamper finisht the garret stairs and made a ladder -------- 11 ½ days.

The 17th June 1719 Wednesday. A very fine day. Old Thomas Surgeant and Sarah Picknall marry'd yesterday *(Ed: Recorded in Hurst PR).* John Gun and George West mow'd in the Churchfield yesterday and to day Old Dick Banks faggoted at Rickman's. Young Dick Banks, Dick and Willy fetcht 1500 bricks from Taylor's for Old William Brand, gather'd cherrys after. Thomas Hamper workt on my Wive's closet --------- 12 ½ days.
The 2 boys ground 7½ bushels of malt afternoon. I were to make an end of the Widdow Hart's inventory at the tanyard.

The 18th June 1719 Thursday. A gloomy day, rain towards night. Old Dick Banks faggoted, John Gun and George West mow'd. Holden and John Edwards thatcht. Young Dick Banks and Willy went with the teem for stones for Old William Brand's tomb. The boys gather'd cherrys. Thomas Hamper and his man Thomas Hamper workt on my Wive's closet --------- 13 ½ days.
Mrs Ann Dodson here afternoon.

The 19th June 1719 Fryday. A wet forenoon, dry after. Old Dick Banks faggoted. John Gun and George West mow'd. Holden and John Edwards thatcht. Thomas Hamper's man workt on the beds etc. Young Dick Banks and Willy loaded the waggons etc. John Smith's man kill'd the calf this evning. The boys gather'd cherrys. John Parsons shaved my head and face. Sent my Mother a basket of cherrys per Jacky and E Lintott.

The 20th June 1719 Saturday. A very fine day. John Gun and George West mow'd clover. Young Dick Banks and his father carry'd 2 loads of wheat to Shoreham and brought home 2 loads of boulders. Thomas Hamper's man planed boards for my Wive's closet. I were at Shoreham, bought a winsheet of Dick Smith at 17s-6d and the boulders at 3s. Paid 6d and left 20s to pay. I came home by Brighton. Paid 6d for a Let Pass for my wool to Mr Waller's daughter and she promis'd to send it by post here. Waller not at home. Willy, Will Beard, Thomas Hamper's maid, Jack, Dick Smith and Old William Brand's maid hay'd afternoon in the Churchfield. I bought a salt fish at Shoreham at 1½d per lb. The calf weigh'd 16½ qarter.

The 21st June 1719 Sunday. A very wet morning, dry after. Mr Thomas Wilkinson came the _. Mr William Martin preacht. I was not at Church in the afternoon.

The 22nd June 1719 Munday. A dry day. John Gun and George West mow'd. Banks faggoted. Young Dick Banks and Jack carry'd 4 qarters 6 bushels of wheat to Shoreham, brought home 28lbs of sea bisqet from

Mr R Hayler's. I were there too. Mr Pelham's man was to look on my bay horse in the morning. He bid me 15 guineas for him. The boys gather'd cherrys etc. Sold all my ewes to John Smith at 10s-6d per ewe, 10 of my culling lambs at 8s per lamb. He is to give me 5s and 2 neat's tongues over and to stand to all loss after Michaelmas. Mrs Catherine Beard and Mrs Kettilby here towards night. Mr John Hart supt and spent the evning here. Mr Mills of Greatham came to Mr Scutt's.

The 23rd June 1719 Tuesday. A showry day. John Gun and George West mow'd. Banks faggoted. Richard White workt on the ditch from Richard Wood's gutter. Thomas Norrice and his boy workt here for Old William Brand. Young Dick Banks, Willy and the boys gather'd cherrys etc. Jack carry'd my wool to Cuckfield. I were at my Brother Henry Faulkoner's, came home via Cuckfield. Receiv'd £7-14-0d of Bernard Heasman for my wool and hops and paid him 4s for a payr of stockens for my self. My Wife supt at Westtowne. Allexander Snatt and his boy faggoted to day and yesterday.

The 24th June 1719 Wednesday. A gloomy day. A Fair at St John's Comon. Old William Brand and his 2 boys, Norrice and his boy workt at Rickman's. Young Dick Banks and Dick Smith carry'd 50 faggots to Parker. I din'd at Mr Scutt's with Mr Mills, Mr Wheeler and Mr Richard Whitpaine and Dr Vincent. They all supt here. Willy bought 5 lambs at the Fair of Nick Friend at 4s per lamb, putt 'em at Rickman's. Mr Cheal and Mr Farncomb were at Mr Scutt's afternoon. John Mills markt my lambs and lay here. Paid my Brother John Courtness £125 in full for that part of his wive's portion which I were obliged to pay. John Snashall jr witness to the receit.

The 25th June 1719 Thursday. A fine day. Old Dick Banks, Allexander Snatt and White faggoted. John Gun and George West mow'd. Holden and John Edwards thatcht. Paid Holden 27s for thatching my Father's stable and the stable at Rickman's. There was 736 foot, I think on my Father's stable and 340 at Rickman's. Sarah Marten, Will Beard, Young Dick Banks, Willy, Dick Smith and Sarah Banks hay'd afternoon. Mr Cheal here in the evning. William Jarvice finisht the underpinning of the stable at Rickman's.

The 26th June 1719 Fryday. A gloomy day. Allexander Snatt, White and Old Dick Banks faggoted. Receiv'd £20 yesterday of John Hill for 40 lambs. John Gun and George West mow'd. Marten, Jane Tully, Old Sarah, William Beard and Allexander Snatt hay'd afternoon. Young Dick Banks, Willy and Dick carry'd 6 loads of clover to the horse's rick. Thomas Norton, his wife and daughter, Mr William Martin and Mr John Hart here towards night. John Smith had half a bushel of wheat, clear'd accounts.

The 27th June 1719 Saturday. A wet forenoon, dry after. Old Dick Banks thrasht. John Gun and George West mow'd part of the day. I know not what Allexander Snatt and White did. William Jarvice struck the ceeling in the porch. Young Dick Banks and Dick clear'd my Father's close. John Smith kill'd one of my sheep that was ailing. Turn'd the fatting oxen into the cow field. My Wife was at my Brother John Box's afternoon.

The 28th June 1719 Sunday. A fine day. Mr Price preacht. He was here after dinner. My Father and Mother Stone din'd here. My Cousin John Lindfield and his wife Elizabeth supt here. We had a parish meeting afternoon about Thomas Penfold that now lives at Worth.

The 29th June 1719 Munday. A fine day. Old Dick Banks thrasht. John Gun and George West mow'd. Young Dick Banks, Willy and Dick carry'd a load of faggots in the morning. Afterwards a small load of clover, in all 6 loads out of the Rookwood and 3 great loads out of the way mead and Little Mead below it, being all was in them. Thomas Hamper workt on my Wive's closet ----- 14½. William Jarvice workt here plastering etc. Mr Peter Courthope had 6lbs of hops at 2s per lb, not paid. My Wife went to Westtowne with Thomas Norton's wife. Banks's girl and Jack turn'd hay swarths in Edgly Mead.

The 30th June 1719 Tuesday. A very fine day. George West and John Gun mow'd. Old Dick Banks thrasht 'till noon. Young Dick Banks and Willy fetcht a load of great chalk in the morning, carry'd hay after. Old Dick Banks and Dick Smith and William Beard helpt carry 6 loads of the Edgly Mead. Jane Tully, James Banks, Thomas Hamper's maid and Jack hay'd all day, Parker afternoon. Samuel Jarvice rode old Duke horse to Lewis, brought my Mother's cloaths per Molly Balcomb.

The 1st July 1719 Wednesday. A very fine day. John Gun and George West made an end of the Edgly Mead. Young Dick Banks and Willy fetcht a load of great chalk and carry'd 4 loads of the Edgly Mead, the last, in all 10 loads. Paid my Unkle Courtness a bill of £1-6-3d for Molly Balcomb. William Beard, S Marten, Sarah Banks and Parker hay'd. My Cousin John Bodle went to Lewis and brought word that Mr Pelham had purchased my bay horse by his man Samuel Brown yesterday at 16 guineas. I receiv'd a guinea in hand yesterday of the man and Mr Pelham promis'd my Cousin Peter Marchant to pay the remaining 15 guineas to him according to my order. I gave Mr Pelham's man 5s. Dick and Jack hay'd and helpt carry. Old Dick Banks thrasht. The heifer that suckl'd the bull went to bull to day.

The 2nd July 1719 Thursday. A very fine day. John Gun and George West mow'd. Banks thrasht. Young Dick Banks, Willy and Dick Smith fetcht a load of great chalk from the pitt, carry'd 2 loads to Taylor's and brought home 750 bricks for Old William Brand and 750 tiles and 500 bricks for my self. Banks's girl hay'd. Sold John Smith a heifer at £5. He kill'd her to day and drove the 3 runts to Rickman's. I supt and spent the evning at Mrs Catherine Beard's. My Sister Sarah here afternoon. Jack fetcht and borrow'd a thing from Sander's of Cowfold to put on the cow's neck to prevent her sucking her self.

The 3rd July 1719 Fryday. A very fine day. John Gun, George West and Banks as yesterday. Young Dick Banks, Willy and Dick fetcht 2 loads of small chalk into my Father's close. Afterwards carry'd the hay of the dry pond - 2 loads. Banks's girl hay'd all day, William Beard half. Paid Mrs Catherine Beard 12s last night in full for oates. Turn'd 30 ewes and the young horse into the Churchfield.

The 4th July 1719 Saturday. A fine day. John Gun and George West mow'd. Old Dick Banks made an end of thrashing and helpt hay, I think about half the day. Young Dick Banks, Willy and Dick carry'd 5 loads of hay etc. William Beard, Banks's girl, ____. Paid the hatter at Lewis 7s for my hat and spoke for 2 more for the boys. Paid my Cousin Peter Marchant a guinea towards a wigg he is making for me. Receiv'd 15 guineas of him which Mr Pelham paid to him for my horse. Paid Samuel Tourl in full of all. Paid Mr Walter 1s for seeing my Aunt Margret's will.

The 5th July 1719 Sunday. A fine day. Mr William Martin preacht. Mrs Ede, my Wife, Kitt Ede and I were at Newtimber Church and Mr Osbourne afternoon.

The 6th July 1719 Munday. A gloomy morning, fine after. John Gun, George West, Young Dick Banks, Willy, Dick Smith, William Beard begun pull flax in the Hayslecroft all day, Thomas Hamper's man half the day. My Father and Mother Stone, Mrs Ede, Kitt Ede, Bett and I went to Shiprods. John Kneller attended, left them there.

The 7th July 1719 Tuesday. A fine day. John Gun and George West mow'd. Old Dick Banks, Sarah Banks, Young Dick Banks, the boys, Willy, William Beard, Parker's wife and Betty Westover made an end of drawing the Hayslecroft flax. William Roach mending the windows of my Wive's closet and the new chamber.

The 8th July 1719 Wednesday. A fine day. Old Dick Banks cut pease 'till noon, helpt carry hay after. John Gun and George West mow'd. Young Dick Banks, Sarah Banks, William Beard and Dick Smith hay'd. Young Dick Banks, his father, Dick and Willy carry'd 4 loads of hay out of the Little Mead. Richard White begun mow the winter oates at 1s per acre. Receiv'd 1s of my Mother which I paid to Mr Walter. Paid Mr Jeremiah Dodson 10s-6d for coffee and tea. He breakfasted here. I sent a letter yesterday to Mr Sixsmith per Mr John Hart. My Cousin Hayne sent her girl to ____ here to day to tell me Thomas Miller was leaving the windmill.

The 9th July 1719 Thursday. A fine day. John Gun and George West mow'd. White mow'd oates. Young Dick Banks and Jack went to the Rock with a load of tree nailes for Stephen Bine. Old Dick Banks, his girl and William Beard cut pease and hay'd. Dick helpt afternoon. I din'd at Westtowne, were at Dr Nick Plaw's and he here in the evning. Thomas Hamper's man Thomas Hamper workt here half the day on the porch.

The 10th July 1719 Fryday. A gloomy morning, fine after. John Gun and George West mow'd, win'd 3 quarters 6 bushels head and 2 bushels tail of Old Dick Banks's wheat. He and White begun cast the mud out the tail of the pond by the house afternoon. Young Dick Banks,

Nick Plaw and I drencht the great stagg and drest his kibes and afterwards Young Dick Banks, ~~his father and Dick~~ helpt scour the pond. I went to Mr Cheal's to fetchhome my Father etc. Paid Abel Muzzall for makeing a payr of _____ .

The 11th July 1719 Saturday. A gloomy morning, fine after. John Gun and George West mow'd 'till noon, cast mud after. Old Dick Banks and White cast mud all day. Paid Old Dick Banks 10s-6d. He had half a bushel of wheat. Young Dick Banks cast mud a while in the morning. Afterwards he, Willy and Dick Smith carry'd 3 loads to the lean oxen's rick and one to R Kester's, last of the Little Meads, in all 12 loads. William Beard hay'd half the day, Sarah Banks all. Sold John Smith my 3 runts at £18 to be kill'd when they are fat. My Sister Sarah here afternoon.

The 12th July 1719 Sunday. Mr William Martin preacht. I was not at Church, not being well. Mr Burry supt here.

The 13th July 1719 Munday. A fine day. John Gun, George West and Old Dick Banks begun reap in the Bankfield at 4s-6d per acre to reap and pitch. Young Dick Banks, Willy and Dick carry'd part of Tully's Mead, 5 small loads. William Beard and Sarah Banks hay'd all day, Parker and Jane Tully a little above half. My Father and Mother Stone, Mr Ede and his daughter, John Kneller and Jack Haslegrove went to Brighton.

The 14th July 1719 Tuesday. A very fine day. The reapers turn'd flax 'till between 9 and 10 and reapt afterwards. William Beard helpt turn flax and bore on oates after. Sarah Banks [.........pt] pease and rakt oates afterwards. Young Dick Banks, Willy and Dick carry'd Rickman's pease, 5 small loads and 1 load of the winter oates. I supt at Westtowne with Mrs Catherine Beard's family and Mr Ede. Paid Mr Courtness 1s for a bottle of claret.

The 15th July 1719 Wednesday. A very fine day. The reapers reapt. Young Dick Banks, Willy and Dick carry'd the rest of the winter oates, in all 5 small loads. They carry'd up Stephen Bine's wood, faggots and roots. I receiv'd Mr Peter Courthope's Land Tax and Mrs Catherine Beard's. Mr Beard went with me to Danny. Bought a bay horse of John Smith at £7-13s and 100 faggots. He is 6 or 7 years old.

The 16th July 1719 Thursday. A fine day. John Gun and Old Dick Banks reapt. George West helpt take up the Hayslecroft flax. Young Dick Banks and Willy carry'd the flax, 2 great loads. Towner's wife, Eliz Cheal, Thomas Hamper's maid, Sarah Banks, Frank Holden's maid helpt take up flax afternoon, Parker's wife all day. The boys helpt in the forenoon and Dick sifted wheat afternoon. Paid a man, Young Marks, 8d. Chapman sent for sheering lambs, Jack helpt him. Receiv'd my Brother Peter's tax and the 1st half year of John Stone's. I were at Dean House and left £40 with my Cousin John Lindfield's wife Elizabeth, part of the Land Tax. Mrs Scutt and Mrs Mary Whitpaine here towards night.

The 17th July 1719 Fryday. A very fine hot day. The reapers reapt at Tully's. Young Dick Banks, Willy and the boys sifted malt and wheat and unloaded the flax. Eliz Cheal and Banks's girl pull'd flax in the Nine Acres all day, Towner's wife the afternoon.

The 18th July 1719 Saturday. A gloomy morning, fine after. The reapers as yesterday. Young Dick Banks, Willy and Dick carry'd the Bankfield wheat, 5 great loads and 1 load of Tully's. Towne, Eliz Cheal, Sarah Banks pull'd flax all day, Jack and Thomas Hamper's maid half the day.

The 19th July 1719 Sunday. A very wet morning, fine after. Mr John Hart preacht. I supt at Mr Scutt's with Mr Orlton and his clerk and Mr Beard. I was not at Church in the morning.

The 20th July 1719 Munday. A fine day. The reapers mow'd Tully's first field of oates and made an end of Tully's first field of oates and made an end of Tully's wheat and Banks and George West drew flax about 2 hours. Eliz Cheal and Sarah Banks drew flax all day, Thomas Hamper half. The boys and Willy drew flax part of the day. Young Dick Banks carry'd 2 loads of sand to Frank Holden's for Old William Brand. Afterwards Willy and he carry'd 3 of Tully's wheat, 3 loads in all. Receiv'd Old John Snashall's Land Tax. Young John Snashall's wife, sister and aunt here. I were at Nick Plaw's in the morning.

The 21st July 1719 Tuesday. A fine day. Nan Westover marry'd at Lewis. *(Ed: she married Thomas Burt at St Anne's)* The reapers and Willy and Jack reapt oates at Rickman's. Towner's wife and Sarah Banks drew flax.

William Jarvice workt on the wainhouse stable. Young Dick Banks and Dick sifted wheat. I was at Mr Courtness's with Mr Cheal. Supt at Mrs Catherine Beard's. John Pierce made me a payr of houseing, 6d. Paid Frank Holden 4½d for ferret for binding. Paid Mr Courtness 9d for more ferret.

The 22nd July 1719 Wednesday. A gloomy day, some rain. The reapers made an end of the oates by 11 aclock. Young Dick Banks fetcht a load from the Comon for Stephen Bine and a load of chalk to Rickman's. Towner's wife and Sarah Banks drew flax and the boys part of the day. I were at Lewis paid £100 of the Land Tax, £60 being my Cousin John Lindfield's mony. Paid Thomas Friend 13s for Willy's breeches and 2s-9d for small nailes at Court's. Receiv'd 28s of Thomas Avery for tythe which I am to pay Mr Jeremiah Dodson for him.

The 23rd July 1719 Thursday. A fine day. The reapers begun the wheat at Rickman's, Young Dick Banks and Willy and Dick sifted wheat, Willy and Dick carry'd 2 small loads of Rickman's wheat. Sarah Banks and Jack pull'd flax 'till noon. My Wife and Jack went to Cuckfield afternoon.

The 24th July 1719 Fryday. A gloomy morning, a smart showr about noon, fine after. Young Dick Banks and the boys drew flax 'till noon and Banks and Jack sifted wheat at Tully's after. Willy and Dick begun stir the pease earsh at Rickman's and carry'd a load of wheat there. Thomas Hamper's man Marten set up a falling post to Tully's gate next Edgly and a fence at the corner of the garden. The reapers as yesterday. Receiv'd a receipt of Mr Jeremiah Dodson per Old William Brand for Thomas Avery's tythe 28s which I receiv'd of Thomas Avery at Lewis and sent per Brand to day. My Wife and Mrs Wicks went to Danny afternoon. John Smith kill'd one sheep out of the Churchfield. Paid George West 15s.

The 25th July 1719 Saturday. A fine day.
A Fair at Shoreham and Lindfield. The reapers made an end of all my wheat. Willy and Dick plough'd a while at Rickman's and then carry'd the wheat thence, 3 small loads, in all 4 good middling loads. Young Dick Banks cut the _____ in the forenoon and reapt in John Gun's room afternoon while John Gun mow'd the court and walk and cut the hedge. Ned Burt helpt cut the hedges afternoon. My Wife was at Danny afternoon, Mr Peter Courthope's birthday his being 80 years old. Paid John Gun 5s.

The 26th July 1719 Sunday. A fine day. Mr William Martin preacht. Mr Peter Courthope, Mr Willard of Bourne and his wife, Mrs Susan Courthope and Mrs Catherine Beard and her mother here after evning prayr. I went by Stephen Bine's with Mr Peter Courthope and Mr Willard and after they were gone home I supt at Mrs Catherine Beard's.

The 27th July 1719 Munday. A very fine day. Young Dick Banks and Dick made an end of pulling the flax and afterwards Willy and he carry'd the oates at Rickman's, 3 loads, laid them on the pease. Paid the reapers 1s for helping bind them. They begun mow the field by Copthall. Parker's wife, the 2 boys, John Edwards and Sarah Banks bore on. Paid John Edwards 6d for helping bear on. John Smith's boy helpt an hour or 2 hours. Stephen Bine was here in the morning to look on a tree or 2.

The 28th July 1719 Tuesday. A showr in the morning, fine after. The reapers mow'd grass at Rickman's. Young Dick Banks, Willy and the boys mov'd the calf house in the morning etc, afternoon carry'd 3 loads of Tully's upper oates. I went to Shoreham. Sold Mr Ben Hayler all my wheat in the calf house (about 2 loads ) at a guinea per quarter. Receiv'd £14-7-6d and 2s-3d outset for 28lbs of bisquet and 20s paid for me to Richard Smith, in all £15-9-9d of Mr Ben Hayler for 14 quarters 6 bushels of wheat. Clear'd accounts.

The 29th July 1719 Wednesday. A fine day. The reapers mow'd grass and begun Tully's lower oates. Young Dick Banks and Jack took up some flax in the forenoon and afternoon. John Gun, Willy and Dick Smith carry'd the last of Tully's upper oates, 4 great loads. Sarah Banks hay'd at Rickman's, our people helpt towards night. Willy and Dick plough'd in the forenoon at Rickman's. John Edwards pickt floyts. M Osbourne (the Duke of New Castle's huntsman) here about noon.

The 30th July 1719 Thursday. A very fine day. The reapers mow'd Tully's _____ . Young Dick Banks, Willy and Dick carry'd 2 loads of the _____ the field by Copthall and 3 loads of the clover at Rickman's. Richard White helpt hay there and Young Dick Banks and he carry'd a load of clover haum thither out of

Tully's barn. Parker's wife, Sarah Banks, Nan Terry and my Mother's maid helpt hay at Rickman's. Paid Parker's wife 2s-2d in full for work. George West went home sick from brewing. Carry'd allmost a load of Edward's flints at Rickman's.

Thomas Hamper and Jack Mills workt here makeing a case for my chamber clock ------------ 15½ days.

The 31st July 1719 Fryday. A gloomy day. The reapers made an end of Tully's oates and begun mow them in the Nine Acres. Old Terry, Willy and Dick carry'd 2 loads of hay at Rickman's and carry'd and took up the flax after. Young Dick Banks, Jack, E Row and my Mother's maid helpt about the flax. Thomas Hamper and John Smith finisht the clock case at noon, so the case stands me in (deals and all) 8s-6d [16........]. My Cousin Libbard of Chichester, Mrs Scutt and my Father din'd here. Richard White begun mow the sedge mead at Rickman's.

The 1st August 1719 Saturday A gloomy day. The reapers mow'd in the Nine Acres. Terry, Young Dick Banks, Jack and I skreen'd 2 loads of old wheat and loaded it, gather'd pares after. Willy and Dick plough'd at Rickman's. Paid John Pierce 5s 11d for Molly Balcomb. Clear'd account. Richard White mow'd in the sedge at Rickman's.

The 2nd August 1719 Sunday. A fine day. Mr William Martin preacht. We had a meeting. Settled accounts as usual. My Cousin John Lindfield supt here. Young Dick Banks, Willy and I took 12 partridges last night in the sedge at Rickman's.

The 3rd August 1719 Munday. A very fine day. The reapers made an end of the Nine Acres oates and begun the Homefield barly. Young White mow'd. Goodman Flint, Willy and Dick carry'd 3 loads of Tully's lower oates. Parker and Sarah Banks helpt. Young Dick Banks and I went with 2 loads of wheat in one waggon to Shoreham for Benjamin Hayler. Paid Richard Smith 10s-6d for 6 bottles of brandy and 1s for the bottles and 1s for the boulders. Dr Nick Plaw brought home the brandy for me. I din'd at Benjamin Hayler's. Came home with Mr Richard Whitpaine.

The 4th August 1719 Tuesday. A gloomy day. The reapers made an end of the Homefield barly. Terry, Flint, William Lashmer, Young Dick Banks, Willy, the 2 boys, Rowland and Ned May, Parker, Jack Mills, S Marten, Banks's wife, Vildor's wife bore on and carry'd the Nine Acres of oates in part of the Nine Acres, 19 or 20 loads, 4 loads to Tully's barne and the rest in the last mow of the great barne William Gorman made the mow. My Cousin John Lindfield sent a teem per Rowland and Ned May _____ . Sent 6 partridges yesterday to Mr Jeremiah Dodson from Shoreham per Mrs Tweedale's maid. My Father and Mother Stone din'd here. Richard White mow'd at Rickman's.

The 5th August 1719 Wednesday. A wet morning, fine after. The reapers mow'd a while by Wickham's, play'd the fool after. Flint, Terry, Young Dick Banks, Willy and the boys cut the oat mow and the fatting rick and carry'd 2 loads of hay out of the sedge at Rickman's. Paid Flint 5s-6d in full for work. Paid my Sister Betty Courtness 5s which her husband paid to Jude Storer.

The 6th August 1719 Thursday. A fine day. The reapers made an end of mowing barly. Terry, Young Dick Banks, Willy and the boys win'd 9 bushels of the Nine Acres oates, carry'd 2 small loads of the last of the sedge (4 in all) at Rickman's, gather'd and corkt the brook meads there and carry'd 2 loads of the Homefield barly at home. Parker's wife and Richard White helpt from between 3 and 4 aclock. White faggoted before. My Father and Mother Stone, my Wife and I were at Danny afternoon. Mr Osbourne and Mr Piggot there. Paid Mrs Susan Courthope £6-5-5d of which I receiv'd 10s-4d of my Father. John Parsons shav'd my head and face. Receiv'd 2 bushels of malt of Harry Wickham. Paid Mr Peter Courthope also 14s for my whip (a fool and his mony parted). Receiv'd 20d of Vildor's wife for a bushel of course old wheat. Thomas Hamper's man Thomas Hamper painted the porch 'till 11 aclock.

The 7th August 1719 Fryday. A dry day. The reapers, Young Dick Banks, Willy and the boys cut the oxen's rick and the horse's rick afterwards. They carry'd 8 loads of the Homefield barly (10 in all). Parker and Banks's girl helpt bare on from 10 aclock. Richard White cut wood in Tully's lower ground. Terry helpt cut the ricks and carry the barly. Jack *(Ed: most probably Jack Mills)* went to Lewis afternoon and brought home a hat for Jacky and one for Willy too little.

The 8th August 1719 Saturday. A fine day. ~~The reapers, Terry, Parker, Sarah Banks.~~ Old Dick Banks and George

West brought home 400 faggots out of the home ground and 100 from Rickman's. Young Dick Banks and Willy fetcht a small load of hay from Rickman's and John Gun and Young Dick Banks laid it on Tully's ricks afternoon and cut the ricks and carry'd some wood together. Willy and Thomas Wilkinson went to wash in the sea afternoon. Mr Richard Whitpaine and I met at the Swan to settle the Widdow Smith's thirds between Thomas Smith and she. We settled it at 45s per annum without deduction but they both desir'd time to consider of it.

The 9th August 1719 Sunday. A very fine day. Mr William Martin preacht. I were at Mr Scutt's after evning prayr. Mr John Hart was here in the evning haveing been at Brighton with Mr Green his tutor and Mr Price.

The 10th August 1719 Munday. A very fine day. Hurst Fair. Mr Benjamin Hayler and Richard Smith din'd here. After dinner Mr Hayler and I went to Mrs Catherine Beard's. There was Mr Farncomb, Mr Short, Mr Cheal, one Mr Chatfield of London, Harry Standbridge, Mr Giles and Mr Ives. Mr Hayler bid me £5-10s for my wheat. I was at Mr Scutt's in the evning with Mr _____ and his son, Mr Gratwick of Reeds, John Box sr, Dr Nick Plaw, Poynings miller etc. Dr Clerk was here with the sorrel horse. I saw Thomas Holden of Henfield in the Fair and told him we would pay the mony William Balcomb was bound with John Goffe for when the half year was ended of which he promis'd to give me notice. Paid Isaac Muzzall a guinea. Paid John Gun 2s and George West 5s.

The 11th August 1719 Tuesday. A very fine, hot day. George West did not work, John Gun and Banks carry'd 300 faggots at Rickman's for Banks and 150 and 28 lath faggots to John Gun at Tully's to day and yesterday. They brought home 200 faggots yesterday of Tully's ground and 100 from Rickman's. Workt half the day yesterday and half the day to day carrying faggots and barly afterwards. Young Dick Banks and Dick Smith carry'd 100 faggots to Old Surgeant, 100 to King, 100 to Widdow Herriot and 50 to Widdow Hambledon, carry'd 4 loads of barly by Wickham's afterwards, Willy, Sarah Banks, the boys helpt. George West helpt carry faggots yesterday half the day.

The 12th August 1719 Wednesday. A gloomy day. I made an end of harvest. John Gun, Old Dick Banks, George West, Sarah Banks, the boys and Willy carry'd 6 loads of barly of the field by Wickham's, 10 in all, the last of the field. Willy went to Balcombe after. Paid Ellis the fuller 13s-6d for dressing 27 yards of Irish linsy. Jude Storer of Guildford here afternoon. My Wife and Mrs Courthope went to Lewis afternoon. Paid Richard White jr £2-6-4d in full of all.

The 13th August 1719 Thursday. A fine day 'till towards night then thunder and rain. John Gun went to Lewis for my Wife. Paid him 10s-6d. George West cut the wheat mows half the day, knockt flax after. Young Dick Banks and the boys helpt cut the mows, skreen'd about 15 bushels and loaded 39 bushels of wheat to go to Shoreham. Old Dick Banks carry'd chucks for himself at Rickman's. My Wife return'd from Lewis, brought me ¼lb of bohea, spurs and Acts of Parliament.

The 14th August 1719 Fryday. A dry day. William Clerk came with the sorrel horse and an other. George West knockt flax at 2s per hundred bundle. Young Dick Banks and the boys cut Tully's mows, John Gun helpt afternoon. Old Dick Banks carry'd chucks etc for himself at Rickman's. Mr John Hart and his wife, Mr Minshall etc here afternoon. I were at Nick Plaw's in the forenoon, he sick.

The 15th August 1719 Saturday. Gloomy day. Young Dick Banks and Smith carry'd 39 bushels of wheat to Benjamin Hayler's mill and brought home a small load of marl from Poynings pitt. Old Dick Banks cut the marl at Rickman's. John Gun did a small jobb, sick after. George West knockt flax the forenoon, loaded water into the flat stew after. Paid George West 2 guineas, receiv'd due to him 7s-11½d. I were at Nick Plaw's afternoon. Jack went to Lewis for Bett's cloaths.

The 16th August 1719 Sunday. A gloomy day. Mr William Martin preacht. I was not at Church in the forenoon. Mrs Anne Beard din'd here. Mr William Roberds of London and his wife came to Westtowne last night. They were at my Father's after evning prayr. I were there with them and Mr Richard Whitpaine and his wife Mary.

The 17th August 1719 Munday. A fine day. George West knockt flax, Young Dick Banks and Smith carry'd 300 faggots to John Smith and 100 to John Parsons. Old Dick Banks did severall jobbs at Rickman's. Win'd the cuttings of the mows, there and sold it to him at 5s. John Gun mow'd in Tully's Mead. I were at Nick Plaw's with John Box sr. He paid John Box £50 of William Balcomb's mony. Mrs Catherine Beard and her family, Mr Roberds and his wife and Mrs Mary Whitpaine came here towards night. [C............] and Willy were a shooting at Randalls coppice. They shot a cock pheasant.

The 18th August 1719 Tuesday. A fine day. George West knockt flax. Old Dick Banks begun make a gripe in the lane by Rickman's. John Gun made an end of mowing the east part of Tully's Mead. Young Dick Banks and Smith carry'd 400 faggots to my Father's. Willy and Jack hay'd in Tully's Mead afternoon. My Father, Mother, my Wife and I at Westtowne. Measur'd a tree at Thomas Hamper's 15 foot great measure.

The 19th August 1719 Wednesday. A fine day. George West knockt flax. John Gun scour'd the stew. Old Dick Banks workt on the gripe half, carry'd hay the rest of the day. Young Dick Banks, Willy and Smith carry'd 100 faggots to my Father and 2 small loads of the east quarter of Tully's Mead. I din'd at my Father's with Mr Roberds etc. I was at Westtowne in the morning with Mr Thomas Pelham of Lewis and my Cousin Peter Marchant. They call'd here but I was not within. Reckon'd and clear'd accounts with Mr Roberds, receiv'd of him £1-18-10d. I was at the Swan towards night with Mr Roberds, his wife, my Father, Mother, Mrs Catherine Beard etc. A mountebank's man here the second time.

The 20th August 1719 Thursday. A fine day. George West knockt flax. John Gun went to Lewis. Old Dick Banks did severall jobbs in the stew etc. Willy and Smith plough'd at Rickman's 'till noon. Young Dick Banks carry'd mortar to my Father's. Afterwards Smith and he carry'd 3 cord of wood to my Father's and 500 of faggots he had before. Lay'd the load of marl in the middle of the Homefield. John Norrice and one of Brand's boys workt at Towne. Thomas Hamper workt there part of the day ------ 16½ days. Paid John Gatland 20d Tuesday for mending my chamber clock and cleaning the other. Paid William Clark 10s for paceing the sorrel horse, 4s for keeping 18d for a set of shoes and 6d for moveing them, he went away this morning. Paid John Pierce the Widdow Smith's rent to Lady Day last and receiv'd his taxes for last year. Jack Haslegrove fetcht 4 bottles of claret from Shoreham for Mr John Hart for which he paid me 6s this morning.

The 21st August 1719 Fryday. A fine day. Old Dick Banks begun the thrashing wheat at Rickman's. George West knockt flax. John Gun sick, Young Dick Banks too. Willy went to coursing with Mr Roberds, came home sick. John Norrice and his brother workt at Towne. Mr Roberds, his wife and Mrs Mary Whitpaine here towards night. Mr Green and Mr John Hart and Mr Scutt breakfasted here.

The 22nd August 1719 Saturday. A fine day. George West knockt flax. John Gun sick. Old Dick Banks mow'd orchards. Jack went to Lewis for Willy. Smith gather'd pares etc. Young Dick Banks sick. I were at Westtowne in the morning. Mr Green and Mr John Hart there, I went to Mr Price's with them. Din'd there, Mr Beaumont too.

The 23rd August 1719 Sunday. A fine day. Mr Green preacht. We had a parish meeting about E Ball. I were at Mr Scutt's in the evning cum multis _____ .
Paid George West 9s-11d in full of all the last reckoning.

The 24th August 1719 Munday. A fine day. A Fair at Brighton and Rodean. Paid Boniface 5s-2d for mowing stubble in the Marldfield __ . George West knockt flax, all the rest kept holy day. Willy went to coursing with Mr Roberds in the forenoon. Mr John Hart rode the bayard mare to Cuckfield with Mr [G........] and Mr Price.

The 25th August 1719 Tuesday. A fine day. George West begun knock flax at Tully's. Old Dick Banks thrasht wheat. John Gun faggoted. Young Dick Banks and Smith carry'd a load of wood to my Father's, brought me home, gather'd apples or pares after. John Westover rode the young horse to Lewis. I were at Shoreham. Din'd at Benjamin Hayler's. Paid John Snashall jr 1s for 2 papers of lozenges from London and 6½d for a bottle of _____ . Paid Richard Smith 6s-8d for 4 bottles of wine and the bottles.

The 26th August 1719 Wednesday. A fine day. John Gun begun mow seed clover in Rookwood. Old Dick Banks thrasht wheat. George West knockt flax Tully's. Young Dick Banks and Smith carry'd 75 faggots to Richard King. They brought home 4 loads of wood.
The mountebank here again, his name Charles Smith.

Dr Lintott and his wife and Dr Vincent din'd at my Father's. They were down here a while in the morning. My Wife was very ill last night. Mr Beard's dog at Thomas Hamper's bitt one of my sheep yesterday so that John Smith kill'd it. Dr White's man was here to day.

The 27th August 1719 Thursday. A fine day. John Gun mow'd clover. George West knockt flax. Young Dick Banks, Smith and I fetcht the piece for a roller from Twineham Green. They gather'd apples after. My Father and Mother Stone din'd here. Old Dick Banks thrasht. Dr White's man was here and had 2 carp and a tench. My Sister Betty Courtness supt here.

The 28th August 1719 Fryday. A fine day. Old Dick Banks thrasht wheat, George West knockt flax. John Gun made a little stubble in the Bankfield and begun scour the pond by Tully's house. Young Dick Banks, Willy and the boys cut the rick at Rickman's and gather'd apples and some elder berrys afterwards. Dick Wood made me a new spitter from this wood. I made the wood my self. Paid Isaac Muzzall 6s-6d in full of his bill, paid a guinea before. Mr Roberds and his wife, Mr Richard Whitpaine and I supt here.

The 29th August 1719 Saturday. A gloomy day, some rain. George West knockt flax. Old Dick Banks thrasht wheat. John Gun helpt scour the Edgly Mead pond and stopt holes in the thatch afterwards. Young Dick Banks and Willy helpt John Gun. The boys rakt between the swaths of the seed clover.
My Wife and I supt at Mr Scutt's.

The 30th August 1719 Sunday. A gloomy day.
Mr William Martin preacht. I had a severe fitt of an ague. Paid the hatter at Lewis 10s-6d for 2 hatts for the boys and a box. He was here in the morning.

The 31st August 1719 Munday. A dry day. Old Dick Banks thrasht. George West knockt flax. John Gun and Willy made an end of cutting the barly mow. Stopt holes in the thatch after. Young Dick Banks and Smith carry'd 175 faggots from Rickman's to Old William Brand's and a cord of wood from home to the school. Paid my Cousin John Marchant of Lox £4 for the Widdow Wells of Horsted. He is to pay it to her for me. My Father, my Wife and I were at my Cousin John Lindfield's a while towards night.

The 1st September 1719 Tuesday. A gloomy day.
A Fair at Horsted. Old Dick Banks, his son, Smith and Willy went to Balcombe with two teems for Stephen Bine, I am to have a guinea. John Gun mended the thatch, George West knockt flax. I had an ague again.

The 2nd September 1719 Wednesday. A gloomy morning, fine after. George West knockt flax. John Gun scour'd the Marldfield stew. Old Dick Banks thrasht. George West made an end of knocking flax at 2s per 100 bundles but he cheated me, for the comon price is but 18d per 100 and my bundles were much smaller than usual too. Thomas Hamper's man and Jack Mills cut a large tree in the pond shaw for bucket timber, workt 'till noon. Receiv'd 30s of R Kester for a load of hay.
Mr Scutt, Mr Woodcock etc supt here. Young Dick Banks and Willy went to Balcombe with the teem for Stephen Bine, brought slabs etc as before.

The 3rd September 1719 Thursday. A dry day, smart showr last night. Old Dick Banks thrasht. John Gun, George West and the boys win'd flax in the forenoon, turn'd clover and gather'd pares afterwards. Young Dick Banks and Willy went with the teem as yesterday and carry'd 10 foot of my bucket timber to Sanders. My Sister Ann Box and Sister Sarah din'd here. Agreed with the China woman to carry her things to Cuckfield for 3s.

The 4th September 1719 Fryday. A dry day. John Gun and George West carry'd a load of the Hayslecroft flax into Tully's oat earsh and afterwards carry'd a load of the Rookwood clover to the Rutt barne being all sold to my Cousin John Lindfield. Old Dick Banks mended a gap or 2 in the morning, loaded wheat after. Young Dick Banks and Smith fetcht a load for Stephen Bine as yesterday. Clear'd accounts with John Bodle for horse keeping and meat. Receiv'd 5s-9d of my Cousin John Lindfield for 3 bottles of brandy he had this day. Sold him all the clover in the Rookwood in the hand at 6 guineas. Paid William Nicholas 15d for helping about the clover to day and half a day's work _____ .

The 5th September 1719 Saturday. A dry day. George West begun lay out flax. Old Dick Banks helpt lay out flax and mended gaps. John Gun mow'd clover half the day, carry'd a parcell of hay out of the orchard to Kester's and gather'd pares the rest of the day. Young Dick Banks, Smith and Willy went to Balcombe for Stephen Bine as yesterday. Receiv'd a letter from

Mr Benjamin Hayler and sent an answer. I wrote also to Thomas Gratwick of London and RB. John Pierce workt here to day and yesterday.

The 6th September 1719 Sunday. A fine day.
Mr William Martin preacht. We had a parish meeting, settled accounts as usual. My Cousin John Lindfield din'd here.

The 7th September 1719 Munday. A showry day.
John Gun, George West and Banks mended hedges, laid out flax etc. Young Dick Banks, Smith and Willy went to Balcombe for Stephen Bine and carry'd away the China woman for which she pay'd me 3s per Banks. I sent 4 partridges to Benjamin Hayler of Shoreham and Cheesman the miller of Southwick. Young Dick Banks, Willy and I catcht 8 young birds in the Nine Acres last night. I din'd at my Father's. Reckon'd with John Smith and there is due to me £3 and 8 sheep not reckon'd for. Mr Gratwick came to my Father's and Mrs A Lintott.

The 8th September 1719 Tuesday. A fine day.
A Fair at Cuckfield and Stenning. Young Dick Banks and Willy went for Stephen Bine as yesterday. John Gun mended gaps. George West laid out flax. Old Dick Banks no work. John Smith kill'd a sheep to day which makes 9 not reckon'd. Mrs Gratwick, my Father and Mother Stone here afternoon. Paid George West 4s.

The 9th September 1719 Wednesday. A fine day.
George West laid out and win'd flax. John Gun mended gaps and win'd flax. Old Dick Banks _____ .
William Jarvice workt underpinning the wainhouse. Young Dick Banks, Smith and Willy to Balcombe as yesterday. My Cousin John Lindfield and I went to Stanmer and bought 60 store ewes at 7s-6d per ewe. Paid William Scrase £11-5s for my part. Receiv'd £10 of Harry Wickham per my Wife.

The 10th September 1719 Thursday. A fine day. My wedding day 19 years. John Gun and Banks mended hedge. George West laid out flax. William Jarvice workt as yesterday. Young Dick Banks, Willy and Smith went to Balcombe with 2 teems, clear'd the broak, 11 journeys in all. My Brother Will came at night. Mr John Hart supt here. We had our harvest supper tonight. I din'd at my Father's with Mr Gratwick.

The 11th September 1719 Fryday. A dry day. George West and Old Dick Banks laid out flax and carry'd clover. Young Dick Banks and Smith carry'd 25 faggots to Old William Brand and carry'd the rest of the Rookwood clover to my Cousin John Lindfield, fetcht a small load of sand and a little straw from the Danworth barn. I were at Ditcheling. Sold 21 bushels of flax seed to Ed Harrodon at 3s per bushel to be deliver'd at the Cliffe to Thomas Beard. I were at Nick Plaw's towards night. John Gun did not work. John Norrice and Samuel Jarvice pitcht the wainhouse stable in the forenoon. William Jarvice helpt and workt there all day.
Mr Gratwick, his wife, my Father and Mother Stone breakfasted here.

The 12th September 1719 Saturday. A gloomy morning, very wet after. Reckon'd and clear'd accounts with John Gun, paid him £4-4-3d. He mow'd stubble part of the day. Old Dick Banks and George West carry'd the flax that grew in the Nine Acres into the Rookwood, laid out there part of the day. Dick Smith laid out flax. Young Dick Banks and Jack went to Lewis with 21 bushels of flax seed to Thomas Beard in the Cliffe. Borrow'd a horse of Nick Plaw to help thither. I were at Nick Plaw's afternoon. Paid Thatcher Holden 4s-6d for severall jobbs. Weigh'd the Cuckfield Fair cow yesterday at John Smith's, she weigh'd 49 nail 4lbs the 4 quarters at 16d per nail, 5 quarters.

The 13th September 1719 Sunday. A fine day.
Mr Price preacht. My Cousin John Lindfield din'd here. I was at Church afternoon but not in the forenoon. My Cousin John Lindfield and I was at Frank Holden's after evning prayr about Young Bide.

The 14th September 1719 Munday. A fine day. John Gun mow'd stubble Tully's. Old Dick Banks and George West laid out flax. Young Dick Banks and the boys laid out flax and gather'd pares. Paid William Brand 10s-6d in full for his son's work.

The 15th September 1719 Tuesday. A fine day.
John Gun mow'd stubble. A Fair at St John's Comon. Paid William Vinall £6-15s for 20 ewes and a ram. He lives at Court House in St John's parish near Lewis. Old Dick Banks laid out flax 'till 1 aclock. George West laid out flax the same and turn'd flax after. Young Dick Banks did severall jobbs with the cart. Willy and Smith begun stir the lower oat earsh at Tully's.

The 16th September 1719 Wednesday. A dry day 'till towards night. Old Dick Banks mow'd stubble at Rickman's. Young Dick Banks and Smith plough'd in Tully's farther field. George West turn'd flax 'till noon. The mountebank here. John Gun mow'd stubble. Jack Haslegrove carry'd 3 partridges to Old Jenner's and fetcht my Brother Will's dog from Balcombe. Jack Mills mended the stile into the Churchfield. Receiv'd 7 bushels of malt of Harry Wickham at 2s-6d per quarter. Thomas Jacket mended my partridge net this morning.

The 17th September 1719 Thursday. A dry morning, wet afternoon. Old Dick Banks mow'd stubble. John Gun workt for himself. ~~George turn'd flax 'till noon, thrasht~~ George West clear'd the barne etc 'till noon, thrasht wheat after. Willy and Smith plough'd 'till noon, Smith ground malt after. Young Dick Banks carry'd boulders to Rickman's, brought home some wheat thence that was only heav'd. Allan Savage brought my sacks from Shoreham. Jack Mills workt here most part of the day. My Father and Mother Stone din'd here, we had a hare. Sold 8 ewes and a ram for the stock at Rickman's and 5 ewe lambs.

The 18th September 1719 Fryday. A wet forenoon, dry after. John Gun and Terry thrasht clover. George West thrasht oates 'till noon, wheat after. Win'd 4 quarters 3 bushels head and 3 bushels tail at Rickman's. Young Dick Banks and the boys helpt and laid stubble on the fatting rick. Paid Mr Picknall 2s-6d for soap and candles. I supt at Westtowne with Mr John Hart, Mr Price and Mr Picknall. Receiv'd a quarter of bief of John Smith at 14d per nail, weigh'd I think 7 nails.

The 19th September 1719 Saturday. A very fine day. John Parsons begun his year last Tuesday. He is to shave my face twice a week and my head once a fortnight and I am to give him 100 faggots per annum. Young Dick Banks and Smith plough'd. Old Dick Banks mow'd stubble forenoon, mended gaps after. John Gun and Terry thrasht clover at Tully's. George West turn'd flax 'till 4 aclock. Dick Wood set 2 new shoes on my bay horse's forefeet. John Gun and Terry stript the hop poles and stackt 'em and thrasht oates after they had made an end of Tully's clover, in all about 3 hours. Jack pickt some hops in the hop garden and hedges.

The 20th September 1719 Sunday. A cold stormy day. Mr William Martin preacht. Willy carry'd 8 birds to Old Jenner's in the forenoon.

The 21st September 1719 Munday. A cold windy day. Richard Patching the weaver had his leg cut off this morning by John Snashall. John Gun and Terry thrasht oates and win'd      bushels of the oates. Win'd 7 bushels of George West's Bankfield wheat. He, Nan Kester, E Westover and William Gorman took up flax after. Young Dick Banks and Jack helpt winnow and carry'd half a cord of wool and 70 faggots to Mrs Storer and the flax after. Old Dick Banks mow'd stubble at Rickman's. Willy and Smith plough'd in Tully's lower field. My Brother John Box was here towards night. He gave me a receit for Mr Farncomb's intrest and I gave him a receit for Mr Farncombe. Paid Mr Scutt 19d for a blank bond.

The 22nd September 1719 Tuesday. A dry, windy day. Begun sow wheat at Rickman's. Young Dick Banks, Willy, Old Dick Banks and Smith plough'd etc. John Gun and Terry workt in the garden. George West thrasht and win'd 3 bushels head and a bushel tail of the Rookwood wheat. Thomas Hamper and Jack Mills workt on the rollers -------- 17½ days. I was at John Clerks at the Comon. He made me a payr gudgons to my great roller, weigh'd 15½ lbs. Richard Patching died this afternoon. *(Ed. Goodman Richard Patching buried at Hurst next day)* My Wife and Mrs Mary Whitpaine went to Danny. I gave Stephen Bine an order to take mony of Benjamin Hayler.

The 23rd September 1719 Wednesday. A windy day, some rain. Plough'd and sow'd as yesterday. John Gun and Terry workt in the garden 'till noon. Begun thrash clover after. Thomas Hamper and Jack Mills workt on the rollers ------------ 18½ days. George West begun dress flax. The mountebank here. I were a while at Mr Scutt's. Sent my Father Stone a guinea a Munday.

The 24th September 1719 Thursday. A wet morning, fine after. Finish'd the wheat field at Rickmam's. Sow'd 8 bushels under furroughs. Willy, Young Dick Banks and Smith workt there.
John Gun and Terry thrasht clover. George West drest flax. Old Dick Banks mow'd stubble. Thomas Hamper and Jack Mills finish'd the 2 rollers ---------- 19½ days.

My Father, my Wife and I went to Broadwater to Mr Jeremiah Dodson's.

The 25th September 1719 Fryday. A fine day. Willy and Smith made an end of stirring. John Gun and Terry thrasht clover. Old Dick Banks rakt stubble. George West drest flax. Young Dick Banks (Ed: xxx text deleted xxx) made water furroughs at Rickman's.

The 26th September 1719 Saturday. A fine day. Young Dick Banks and the boys skreen'd wheat, rakt stubble etc. John Gun and Terry thrasht clover. Old Dick Banks rakt stubble at Rickman's. George West drest flax part of the day. We return'd from Broadwater.

The 27th September 1719 Sunday. A fine day. Mr William Martin preacht. My Cousin John Lindfield and his wife Elizabeth din'd here. I supt at Mr Scutt's. Mr Wilkin was there before supper.

The 28th September 1719 Munday. A fine day. Begun sow the field by Shiprods. Young Dick Banks, Willy and Smith plough'd etc. John Gun and Terry thrasht clover. George West drest flax. Old Dick Banks rakt stubble at Rickman's. Receiv'd 8 guineas of E Harrodon for flax seed. Paid Richard White in full for clover thrashing. Paid Mr Dobbs 2d for my hop duty. He supt here with my Father, Mother and Mr John Hart. Sent the colt that came of the founder'd mare to my Cousin John Lindfield at £3-13-6d per Old Terry. If she have a colt he is to pay for the keep 10s.

The 29th September 1719 Tuesday. Michaelmas. Dry day. A Fair at Stenning and Chichester. Willy, Old Dick Banks and Smith plough'd, sow'd etc. Young Dick Banks, John Gun and Terry did not work. Paid George West 21d in full for all work except flax dressing. I think he drest flax to day. Paid _____ Bowen £9-19-6d for 4 steer runts and a heifer. Allan Savage brought home 2 at £6 for his Mrs with Jack Haslegrove.

The 30th September 1719 Wednesday. A fine day. John Gun and Terry thrasht clover. George West, Young Dick Banks, Willy and Smith plough'd and sow'd. Old Dick Banks rakt stubble. Receiv'd £4 of Mr Jeremiah Dodson for 5 quarters of my Cousin John Lindfield oates. He supt here. Settled accounts with my Sister Sarah. I talk't to Mrs Catherine Beard for Allan Savage, about her horse that was seized by the officers at Brighton running brandy. John Smith's 2 horses came into my ground at 18d per week for each horse.

The 1st October 1719 Thursday. A dry day. John Gun and Terry thrasht clover. Young Dick Banks, Willy and Smith plough'd etc. George West drest flax. Old Dick Banks ditcht _____ close at Rickman's. My Wife and I din'd at my Cousin John Lindfield's and settl'd accounts for the colt and the £4 receiv'd of Mr Jeremiah Dodson. Mr Bernard Heasman was there and Dick Edwards of Rigate and John Bart. I supt at Mrs Catherine Beard's.

The 2nd October 1719 Fryday. A fine day. Mr Jeremiah Dodson din'd here. John Gun and Terry thrasht clover. George West drest flax. Old Dick Banks, Willy and Smith plough'd, sow'd etc. Receiv'd a colt from Wayhill. Young Dick Banks sick. My Father and Mother Stone din'd here. Mrs Scutt, her mother and sister Woodcock here afternoon. Boniface's wife here in the morning about Widdow Averd.

The 3rd October 1719 Saturday. A fine day. John Gun and Terry thrasht clover. George West drest flax. Old Dick Banks thrasht wheat at Rickman's. Dick Smith fetcht a payr of wheels new iron'd from TH. Dick Banks sick. Dick Wood dockt the new colt. Paid my Cousin Libbard's son John 26s for soap, candles and starch. He din'd here. My Wife and Mrs Woodcock went to Brighton.

The 4th October 1719 Sunday. A fine day. Mr William Martin preacht. We had a parish meeting. Settled accounts as usual.

The 5th October 1719 Munday. A fine day. John Gun and Terry thrasht clover. Old Dick Banks thrasht wheat. George West drest flax. Thomas Hamper workt here _____ rack and close -------------- 20½ days. I were at my Father's with Mr Jeremiah Dodson and his wife. Lent my Father 2 guineas per my Wife. Young Dick Banks and Smith plough'd and sow'd part of the day.

The 6th October 1719 Tuesday. A very fine day. My Cousin John Libbard went away. John Gun and Terry thrasht clover, George West turn'd flax. Reckon'd and clear'd accounts with Old Dick Banks to Michaelmas last only he owes me for 200 faggots. Reckon'd and clear'd accounts with Harry Wickham. Smith and Willy finish'd the lower wheat field haveing sow'd 18 bushels in him. Young Dick Banks fetcht home rubbish wood. My Wife went to Danny afternoon.

The 7th October 1719 Wednesday. A fine day. John Gun and Terry thrasht clover. George West turn'd flax part of the day. The mountebank here. Old Dick Banks thrasht or faggoted at Rickman's. Young Dick Banks fetcht home rubbish wood. Jack went to Rusper for the writeings that were sent to Darkin. Carry'd Mr Morley three shifts. I were at John Snashall's in the evning. Dick Smith fetcht the dung court and some rubbish wood from Rickman's. William Jarvice underpinn'd the hog trough.

The 8th October 1719 Thursday. A fine day. John Gun and Terry thrasht oates at Tully's. George West drest flax 'till noon, took up flax after. Nan Kester helpt. Old Dick Banks, Willy, Smith and Young Dick Banks carry'd dung. My Cousin John Lindfield was here about E Ball's bastard, she being run away last night. I were at Danny towards night. Paid Old John Snashall's wife 1s for a bottle of Elixir Propietatus. Clear'd accounts with Dick Wood only I owe him 7 bushels of mortar.

The 9th October 1719 Fryday. A gloomy morning, fine after. George West drest flax. John Gun and Terry thrasht oates and win'd     bushels, cut wood after. Old Dick Banks and Smith carry'd 100 faggots to Widdow Webb and brought back a load of chalk. Young Dick Banks sick. Mov'd the Widdow Averd to Widdow Brook's. Reckon'd and clear'd accounts with Stephen Bine. My Father and Jack Haslegrove went for Horsham. Receiv'd £5-10s for Mr Peter Courthope's Poor Tax per John Smith. Receiv'd ¼lb of bohea from Samuel Tourl per Mr Dobb.

The 10th October 1719 Saturday. A gloomy day. John Gun and Terry, Old Dick Banks and Smith dung'd. Receiv'd £15-17-3d of Mr Benjamin Hayler in full of all accounts. Mr Hayler din'd here. William Chapman, his factor came with John Gun from Lewis and went away before dinner for London. I sent Jack Picknall with him to Hand Cross. Allan Savage likewise receiv'd what mony was due to his Mrs from Mr Hayler. Bernard Heasman came towards night and I paid him £2-11s for cloaths for Molly Balcomb and £5 for my self.
Mr Osbourne kept a Court Barron at the Royall Oak for the manor of Hurstpierpoint.

The 11th October 1719 Sunday. A showry day. Mr John Hart preacht. I was at Mrs Catherine Beard's a while after evning prayr. Mrs Storer and her daughter din'd here. Clear'd accounts with Thomas Howell yesterday.

The 12th October 1719 Munday. A showry day. John Gun, Terry and Old Dick Banks dung'd. George West drest flax. Young Dick Banks sick. Willy same. Paid Mr Beard 13d for 2 quires of paper. Young Smith helpt dung. I wrote to John Brand by Mrs Woodcock. Young Dick Wood let my bay horses bleed in the shoulder vein.

The 13th October 1719 Tuesday. A showry day. Thomas Howell's man begun mend a plough. John Gun and Terry cut wood and thrasht clover. George West drest flax. Old Dick Banks and his son sick. Willy and Young Smith plough'd a while in the Churchfield, made water furroughs after in the lower field. Towner and his mate saw'd here. Jack Mills hew'd timber part of afternoon. Paid William Wood 10s for weaving the cloath for a bed.

The 14th October 1719 Wednesday. A dry day. Old Dick Banks, Willy and Smith plough'd. John Gun and Terry thrasht clover. George West drest flax. Young Dick Banks sick.
Thomas Howell's man as yesterday ---- 2 days.
I was at John Stone's afternoon. The mountebank here. Receiv'd 5 bushels of malt of Harry Wickham. Towner and his mate saw'd as yesterday.

The 15th October 1719 Thursday. A showry day. John Gun and Terry thrasht. Old Dick Banks, Smith and Willy plough'd and sow'd. Thomas Howell's man made an end of the ploughing about noon, did some jobbs after. Mr Pickstone here towards night with John Smith.

The 16th October 1719 Fryday. A wet day. Win'd 13½ bushels of wheat at Rickman's yesterday. Old Dick Banks thrasht. Young Dick Banks did severall jobbs,  the boys helpt. I were at the Swan with J Osbourne etc. John Gun and Terry thrasht clover Bankfield. George West drest flax to day and yesterday. Ned Pickstone was here in the morning, bad me £43 for my 4 oxen. I din'd with him at the Swan.

The 17th October 1719 Saturday. A dry day.
John Gun and Terry thrasht clover. Old Dick Banks drove plough afternoon. George West drest flax. Willy and Smith plough'd, sow'd and harrow'd. Paid Mrs Anne Beard 24s-6d for Molly Balcomb's schooling etc. Mr John Hart din'd here, my Brother Peter here towards night. My Brother William sent me a hare yesterday or Thursday per Old George Haslegrove of Cuckfield.

The 18th October 1719 Sunday. A fine day. Mr William Martin preacht. I went to Dean House afterwards. My Father and Jack Haslegrove return'd from Horsham.

The 19th October 1719 Munday. A dry day. John Gun and Terry thrasht clover. George West drest flax, Old Dick Banks and his son plough'd. Willy and Smith sow'd afternoon. Willy went a coursing with Mr Scutt in the morning. Kill'd a hare. Thomas Howell's man mended my Father's chaese about half the day. John Westover helpt about it most of the afternoon. Ellis the fuller fetcht the cloath for a bed, to dress it. Receiv'd 4 guineas of my Father which were lent to him.

The 20th October 1719 Tuesday. A fine day.
John Gun and Terry thrasht clover. Old Dick Banks thrasht wheat. George West drest flax. Young Dick Banks, Willy and Smith plough'd and sow'd etc. Jack Smith and I supt at Westtowne. Receiv'd 16s-8d in part of his Land Tax. Clear'd accounts with Thomas Baker.

The 21st October 1719 Wednesday. A fine day.
John Gun and Terry thrasht clover. George West drest flax. Old Dick Banks, Willy and Smith plough'd and sow'd. Young Dick Banks went to Lewis. My Wife and I went to Lewis. Din'd at my Cousin Peter Marchant's. Paid Mr Dee £5 towards the Land Tax. Clear'd accounts with Samuel Tourl. Paid Mr Scutt 7s-3d for severall goods. Clear'd accounts with Mr Norman.

The 22nd October 1719 Thursday. A fine day.
Sold Ed Pickstone my 3 oxen and my best stagg at £43. I am to send 2 of them to Hand Cross tomorrow and he is to fetch the other 2 in a month. He was here in the morning with John Smith and Michael Stacey. I were at the Swan with Ed Pickstone, Mr Richard Whitpaine, Michael Stacey, John Smith and Mr Scutt and Dr Vaux. Young Dick Banks, Willy and Smith plough'd and sow'd. John Gun and Terry thrasht clover 'till 2 aclock and turn'd flax after. George West drest and turn'd flax with 'em. Win'd 8 bushels of Old Bank's wheat at Rickman's.

The 23rd October 1719 Fryday. A fine day.
Young Dick Banks and Willy made an end of ploughing and sowing of Churchfield with 28 bushels of wheat. John Smith and Thomas Greenfield drove 2 of my oxen and a steer that John Smith bought of Mrs Catherine Beard to Hand Cross for Ed Pickstone. Deliver'd them at P Courtice's. Terry thrasht oates at Tully's. John Gun sick. George West drest flax. Old Dick Banks thrasht wheat 'till noon. Mended gaps after. Holden and John Edwards thatcht at Rickman's. I supt and spent the evning at Mrs Catherine Beard's last night. Ed Burt workt the garden to day and yesterday.

The 24th October 1719 Saturday. A very fine day. Old Dick Banks thrasht wheat at Rickman's. John Gun and Terry thrasht oates 'till noon, took up flax after. Young Dick Banks carry'd 2 loads of Picknall's \_\_\_\_ the flax after. George West drest flax 'till noon, took up flax after. Two of Dick Wood's girls, both Stephen Bine's sons, my Father's maid, Frank Holden's maid and the boys helpt take up flax and Samuel Jarvice. Willy went a coursing and helpt carry the flax. My Wife, Jacky and Polly went to my Brother John Box's afternoon. I wrote to Mr Wilkin by post.

The 25th October 1719 Sunday. A fine day.
Mr Jeremiah Dodson preacht. Mrs Catherine Beard, Mrs Mary Whitpaine and my Cousin John Lindfield's wife Elizabeth din'd here.

The 26th October 1719 Munday. A fine day.
Smith and Willy begun plough the field by Burt's. John Gun and Terry thrasht and win'd 32 bushels of oates. Ned Burt workt in the garden to day and Saturday. Old Dick Banks thrasht wheat. George West drest flax. Young Dick Banks carry'd the rest of Picknall's flints, four loads in all. My Brother Peter and Sarah Moore's husband supt here, his name is Holter. Paid Thomas Holden £2-1-2d for thatching 16 squares and 46 foot on the barne at Rickman's and 4d for mending a hole in the roof of the hovel there. Paid George West a guinea. Paid my Unkle Courtness 4s for 3½ yards of strong linnen for a flock for Willy and 3d for thread and stay tape.

The 27th October 1719 Tuesday. A fine day. Young Dick Banks and Willy plough'd. ~~John Gun and Terry thrasht clover.~~ George West drest flax. Nick Plaw din'd here. Mr Richard Whitpaine supt here.
*(Ed: xxxx text deleted xxxxx)*

The 28th October 1719 Wednesday. A fine day. Young Dick Banks and Picknall plough'd. Picknall and Smith helpt Old Dick Banks winnow 13 bushels of wheat yesterday. Smith harrow'd and Willy sow'd to day. John Gun and Terry workt in the garden. George West drest flax. Thomas Hamper's man Thomas Hamper workt here. Old Dick Banks thrasht wheat.

The 29th October 1719 Thursday. A very fine day. Thomas Avery of Hamsey call'd here. Young Dick Banks and Picknall plough'd. George West drest flax. Willy and Smith sow'd and harrow'd and mended gaps. John Gun and Terry did not work. Old Dick Banks thrasht wheat. My Cousin John Lindfield and Thomas Friend here towards night. I were at Church. Mr Shave sr preacht.

The 30th October 1719 Fryday. A fine day. John Gun and Terry carry'd 11 loads of dung into my Father's orchard. George West drest flax. Young Dick Banks and Picknall plough'd. Smith and Willy sow'd etc. Win'd 11 bushels of Old Dick Banks wheat at Rickman's, the last of the field, in all 10 quarters 7½ bushels. Mr John Hart supt and spent the evning here. Receiv'd 10s-6d of John Bodle for his horse keeping. Paid my Unkle Courtness 6s for a rope. My Brother Peter here in the morning.

The 31st October 1719 Saturday. A dry day. Finisht my wheat season. John Gun and Terry workt at my Father's. George West drest flax. Young Dick Banks and Picknall plough'd. Smith and Willy harrow'd etc. Sow'd 19½ bushels on the field by Banks's. Old William Brand, William and Samuel Jarvice workt on the gutter and causey by the back door at my Father's. Borrow'd a flat stone of Mr Richard Whitpaine.

The 1st November 1719 Sunday. A dry day. Mr William Martin preacht. Mr Richard Whitpaine supt and spent the evning here.

The 2nd November 1719 Munday. A dry day. John Haslegrove begun dress flax here. Young Dick Banks did severall jobbs and went to Lewis with my Wife, return'd and left her there. Reckon'd with Thomas Jacket and there remains due to him 11s-4d and the sack mending not reckon'd. Willy went a coursing with his Unkle John Box, brought home a hare. Lent Mr Richard Whitpaine a dung court per Richard King. He has likewise 2 of my mud casters. I wrote to Mr Ralph Beard by post. R Smith helpt Old Dick Banks carry 5 cart loads of stubble at Rickman's. Shut up the other 3 hoggs to fatting in the sow's pound. Dick Wood shoo'd my bay horse round and the old horse.

The 3rd November 1719 Tuesday. A dry day. Young Dick Banks and I went to Lewis for my Wife. Paid Mr Norman 3s for a paper book. Paid Thomas Friend 3s for 3 handcerchiefs and the same to Mrs Durrant. Young Dick Banks fetch a load of sand in the morning. Smith carry'd 2 cart loads of stubble, 7 in all at Rickman's.

The 4th November 1719 Wednesday. A wet day. Return'd from Lewis, lay at my Cousin Marchant's. Call'd at Nick Marchant's Ditcheling, he sick. Paid his wife 5s towards spinning. Paid Thomas Burt at Lewis 11s for severall goods. Paid Thomas Friend £2-15s for camlet etc by my Wife. Paid all due at Mr Tourl's. Paid Mr Andrew Laurence for making a coat long ago and 1s for altering it. Smith helpt Old Dick Banks at Rickman's.

The 5th November 1719 Thursday. A wet day. All kept holy day. Reckon'd and clear'd account with my Father to Michaelmas last, except Old William Brand's work.   I supt here with Mr Scutt. Receiv'd £3 of Mr William Martin last night for keeping his mare 30 weeks. He supt here.

The 6th November 1719 Fryday. A wet day. A Fair at St Leonard's. Thomas Muzzall kill'd 2 hogs for me. Young Dick Banks and the boys did some jobbs. My Father and Mother Stone din'd here. Mr Scutt here afternoon. Terry and John Gun begun thrashing the other clover at _____ a day. Nan Terry went away sick. John Gun begun serve young beasts in Tully's ground on _____ .

The 7th November 1719 Saturday. A wet day. Young Dick Banks and the boys thrasht. Did severall jobbs. Clear'd accounts with Frank Holden to the 22nd of September last. Paid him £1-5-7d for Molly Balcomb.

Paid him my Window Tax to. Receiv'd all his taxes. I supt at Mr Scutt's, clear'd accounts with him.

The 8th November 1719 Sunday. A wet day. Mr Jeremiah Dodson preacht. His family came from Broadwater last night. We had a meeting about Nan Pelling. I supt at Mr Jeremiah Dodson's with Mr Richard Whitpaine.

The 9th November 1719 Munday. A very fine day. I talkt with Old Hyder and desir'd him to stop up the way through the middle of my field out of his orchard, he refus'd. My Father had a bushel of my Rickman's wheat. Paid Thomas Holden 10d for sparrs and mending thatch to day. Young Dick Banks and Smith cast the stable dung and made an end of scouring the Hovelfield stew. Old Dick Banks had half a bushel of head wheat. Receiv'd Mrs Catherine Beard's Poor Tax, handled her oxen.

The 10th November 1719 Tuesday. A fine day. I begun build my Father's cubbard shelves. Young Dick Banks and the boys and Willy tipt ricks etc. Willy went to Balcombe after. I was a while at the Swan with my Brother John Box and his son Willy and John Stubbs. John Gilham was here in the evning. Sent the yearlings to Rickman's.

The 11th November 1719 Wednesday. A dry day. Young Dick Banks and Smith carry'd Towne dirt. Mr Richard Whitpaine and I measur'd Mr Jeremiah Dodson's Hayslecroft and it is (the pond deducted) 2 acres wanting 6 rods. Paid Mr Jeremiah Dodson his rent and all my tythes to Michaelmas last. Receiv'd his Poor Tax and clear'd accounts to, (all but his Land Tax) and there is due to him 4 douzen of 8d tire and 4 douzen of 4d tow. I supt there with Mr Richard Whitpaine etc. I sent a letter to Mr Sixsmith per Jack Haslegrove. Ditcheling cooper brought a new upright barrel for my Father which I spoak for. John Smith kill'd one of my runts.

The 12th November 1719 Thursday. A fine day. Mr Jeremiah Dodson's tythe feast. I din'd there. Young Dick Banks and Smith helpt carry Towne dirt 'till noon and dung out of Tully's close afterwards.
Receiv'd £10-13-0d in mony, 2s-6d outset for 2 River Taxes and £3 for a quarters annuity he paid to my Aunt Holden, in all £15 for half a years rent for Eastout due at Lady Day last past. My Cousin William Bull of Albourne brought word from Ed Pickstone that I would drive my other 2 oxen to Hand Cross to morrow.
Receiv'd a letter from Mr William. Receiv'd 13s-6d of Thomas Surgeant sr for 100 faggots

The 13th November 1719 Fryday. A fine day. John Gilham begun work here at 20d per day. Reckon'd and clear'd accounts with Old Terry. Young Dick Banks and Smith carry'd dung. Old William Brand and his 2 boys workt at Towne in the morning, here after. Paid John Haslegrove 15s. He left off for the present. My Cousin John Lindfield spent the evning here last night and Ellis the fuller. Sent my other 2 oxen to Hand Cross for Ed Pickstone per Jack Haslegrove and Nick Smith.

The 14th November 1719 Saturday. A gloomy day. John Gun win'd 8 bushels, oates __ . Old William Brand and his boys workt by the brewhouse.
John Gilham workt on the henroost -------------- 2 days. Young Dick Banks and Smith helpt carry dung at Tully's. Paid Abraham Muzzall 2s-6d, clear'd accounts. Old Dick Banks had a bushel of oates and pease.

The 15th November 1719 Sunday. A dry day, the wind very high. Mr Jeremiah Dodson preacht. My Father and Mother Stone, my Brother Peter Marchant and Brother John Box supt and spent the evning here.

The 16th November 1719 Munday. A showry day. Old Dick Banks had ½ bushel wheat. John Gilham finisht the henroost ------- 3 days.
Young Dick Banks and the boys did severall jobbs. Willy and I were to see a hare cours'd, kill'd her. John Smith kill'd my least bull stagg.

The 17th November 1719 Tuesday. A fine forenoon, wet towards night. Young Dick Banks and Smith carry'd 4 quarters 2 bushels and 3 pecks of William Balcomb's wheat to Shoreham from Nick Plaw's mill. Receiv'd £3-0-10½d of Mr Benjamin Hayler for the wheat and for carrying it thither 8s. Very well worth 12s. Paid Mr Hayler 40s for a hundred weight of new raisons of the sun, 5s for the bag and portrage and 6d for the carriage down to Shoreham. John Gilham workt here ---- 4 days. I din'd at Mr Hayler's. My Father supt here. Mr Hayler gave me some sail cloath to cover my flax house.

The 18th November 1719 Wednesday. A wet day. Young Dick Banks sick. The boys helpt John Gun winnow 3 quarters ½ bushel of oates and pease. I gave part of the stagg that John Smith kill'd to the Gooders against Xmas 4lbs for my self and 2lbs for my Father. John Gilham workt here --------------- 5 days. Mr John Hart supt and spent the evning here.

The 19th November 1719 Thursday. A wet day.
Young Dick Banks and the boys did severall jobbs.
I were at the Swan with Ed Pickstone, Harry Wood, Mr Richard Whitpaine, Brother Peter, Jack Smith and Stephen Carter and Jack Alcock.
Receiv'd a bill of return of Ed Pickstone for £50. Paid to Mr Wilkin by my order, vizt £48 for my oxen and £8.
I am to set off to Jack Smith. Receiv'd a gun of Ed Pickstone here. Sold and deliver'd a hog to Jack Haslegrove at 2s per nail. John Gilham here ------ 6 days.

The 20th November 1719 Fryday. A very fine day.
Dr Vaux marry'd yesterday. Receiv'd £19-0-6d of John Smith and clear'd accounts for the last years ewes 5 _____ of the last reckoning. John Gilham finisht the Bankfield stiles ------------ 7 days. Young Dick Banks and Smith mov'd Parker's wife etc.
Weigh'd John Haslegrove's hog 183lbs at 2s per nail.
Dr Vaux and John Snashall here afternoon and my Father. Mr John Hart supt and spent the evning here.
My Wife and Mrs Ann Dodson went to Danny.

The 21st November 1719 Saturday. A fine day.
Young Dick Banks sick. Smith did severall jobbs.
Paid Abraham Muzzall 7s-6d for schooling of William Balcomb. John Gilham put up the water shoot by the brewhouse ------- 8 days. Jack Haslegrove went to Lewis.
Paid John Clark £2-0-6d in full of all accounts.

The 22nd November 1719 Sunday. A dry day.
Mr John Hart preacht, no service afternoon. My Cousin John Lindfield din'd, supt and spent the evning here.
Receiv'd 4s of him for 4 nails of the stag bief. I sent a letter to Nick Plaw in the morning.

The 23rd November 1719 Munday. A gloomy day, some rain. Young Dick Banks went to his father's yesterday sick. My Wife and I were to see Nick Marchant.
My Brother Will din'd and spent the evning here. Willy and he kill'd a hare. Receiv'd a letter from Mr Wilkin that he has receiv'd £50 of Ned Pickstone per Robert Skinner for my Wife. Turn'd 2 of my runts into the field by Hyder's yesterday.

The 24th November 1719 Tuesday. A dry day.
My Father, my Wife and I went to the Thomas Norton's.
Paid Nick Marchant's wife yesterday and 5s before for spinning 6lbs of tire at 6d per lb. Turn'd the lean oxen into the Fifteen Acres. Willy carry'd my Cousin John Lindfield a hare.

The 25th November 1719 Wednesday. A very fine day.
Put the runt heifer into the field by Hyder's.
Mrs Ann Dodson and her daughter and Mrs Catherine Beard's family supt here. Young Jack Lindfield came home with Willy last night. Receiv'd 5½ bushels of malt of Harry Wickham.

The 26th November 1719 Thursday. A gloomy day.
Willy and Smith spread dung. Receiv'd 3½ bushels of malt of Harry Wickham. Mr John Hart din'd here.
Paid Stephen Reeve 2s-6d for weaving 10 yards of tow cloath for _____ . Dr Nick Plaw call'd here towards night.
I wrote to Mr Jeremiah Dodson and Mr Ede by post.

The 27th November 1719 Fryday. A gloomy day, some rain. The boys helpt John Gun winnow      bushels of oates etc. My Brother Will and Brother John Box spent the evning here. Paid my Mother her thirds to Michaelmas last.

The 28th November 1719 Saturday. A gloomy day.
The boys spread dung etc. My Cousin Nick Marchant of Ditcheling buried this afternoon, died a Wednesday night last.
John Gilham here to day and yesterday ------ 10 days.

The 29th November 1719 Sunday. A dry day. Mr John Hart preacht, no service afternoon. My Cousin John Lindfield din'd here. I set my hand to a sort of petition in the nature of a certificate for Thomas Hart the butcher in order to his being taken into some noble man's service. He was here likewise a Fryday evning but then I refus'd it and wish I had done so again.

The 30th November 1719 Munday. A dry, cold day.
A Fair at East Grinstead and Bolny.
John Gilham finisht the water shoot and set up a stile against Tully's orchard ----------- 11 days.
Paid John Westover 2 guineas to Stephen Bine's wife.
I supt and spent the evning at Mr Scutt's. I was at Westtowne in the morning. Sent some errands to London by Mr Richard Whitpaine. Sent Mr Ede's

receit for 50lbs of R_____ to be exchanged for Mrs Margret Fagg's. Went to Mr Ede for part of William Balcomb's rent.

The 1st December 1719 Tuesday. A fine day.
The boys spread dung. Paid John Gun £2-9-9d, clear'd accounts. Clear'd accounts with William Roach, paid him 5s. Reckon'd with John Smith for the stag and there is due to me for that £1-13-1½ d. Receiv'd his taxes.
John Gilham workt here ------ 12 days.
John Smith fetcht the last runt.

The 2nd December 1719 Wednesday. A wet day.
The boys mow'd oates at Rickman's.
John Gilham here ----------- 13 days.
Receiv'd £1-7-6d of Taylor the brickmaker, clear'd account.
My Cousin Wicks supt here. Shut up the 4 fatting oxen.

The 3rd December 1719 Wednesday. A showry day. The boys fetcht oates from Tully's etc. John Gilham here 14 days.

The 3rd December 1719 Thursday. A fine day.
Molly Balcomb and I went to Brighton. I agreed with Noah Gates a miller there that Mrs Catherine Beard should send him a load of her wheat before Munday night at £6-10s if she pleas'd or she might let it alone. I left a sample with him. Receiv'd Mr Harry Scrase's taxes. The boys spread dung.

The 4th December 1719 Fryday. A fine day, a frost.
Win'd 3 bushels of the cuttings of the mows at Rickman's. John Gilham here ------------------ 14 days.
Willy took physick. The boys helpt winnow. John Pierce workt here loading cloaths. Receiv'd a letter from Henry Lintott per William Roach, sent an answer.

The 5th December 1719 Saturday. A fine day, frosty. The boys win'd wheat. John Gilham set up a payr of barrs at the lower side of the further Marldfield --------- 15 days.
Paid my Unkle Courtness 1s yesterday for buttons.
Reckon'd 2 boxes of sugar from Mr Cousins of London.
My Lord Treep put a ferrel and pick in my stick.

The 6th December 1719 Sunday. A gloomy day, some rain. Mr John Hart preacht. My Cousin Thomas Norton North End din'd here and his wife.

The 7th December 1719 Munday. A showry day.
The boys and Old Dick Banks made an end of winnowing 8 quarters 5 bushels, all that grew in Tully's field and did severall jobbs afternoon. John Gilham workt in Tully's ground ------------- 16 days.
Thomas Jacket mended the chamber clock. Deliver'd a sack of oates and a sack of pease and oates to Thomas Jacket per Old Dick Banks.

The 8th December 1719 Tuesday. A dry day.
I was at Shoreham market. Paid Henry Lintott £5 for Mrs Mary Gratwick, I went that way to Shoreham.
Benjamin Hayler bought 3 loads of wheat of Mr Scutt of Brighton at Candlemas price. Shoreham Market to be the rate. My Father and Mr John Hart supt here. I left a sample of my wheat at Mr Benjamin Hayler's, he not at home.

The 9th December 1719 Wednesday. A gloomy day. The boys drew home timber. John Gilham saw'd timber and made 2 rolls ------------ 17 days.
Nick Plaw here to see an ox. Towner and his mate saw'd. Will thrasht barly to day and yesterday.

The 10th December 1719 Thursday. A wet day. The boys shovel'd the close etc. I made a new tack in the hovel for the harness. Paid Frank Holden £14 for a bed cord for the back. Will thrasht barly.

The 11th December 1719 Fryday. A fine day. My Cousin Peter Marchant din'd here. Will and Jack Hill begun fallow by Wickham's. Dick Smith carry'd dung out of the home close etc. My Cousin Marchant spent the evning at Mr Scutt's. I supt and spent the evning at Westtowne.
Receiv'd the receit he had of Mr Dee's agent for £40 paid of my mony from Mr Wilkin, here with his wife. Mr Ede's note which Mr Richard Whitpaine had of me. Mr John Hart had a new wigg of my Cousin Peter Marchant.

The 12th December 1719 Saturday. A dry day. Willy and Jack plough'd. Young Smith carry'd dung out of the close. John Haslegrove left of flax dressing for a while. Robert Hurst of Horsham brought my Father a great coat. He and my Father supt and spent the evning here.

The 13th December 1719 Sunday. A dry, cold day.
Mr Jeremiah Dodson preacht. I supt and spent the evning at Mr Jeremiah Dodson's with Mr Richard Whitpaine.

The 14th December 1719 Munday. A gloomy, cold day.
I were at Tott in the morning. Harry Wickham din'd
here, I sold him 20 qarters of barly at 26s per qarter.
Willy and Smith and Picknall begun fallow the
Hayselcroft. Jack carry'd a letter to Mr Sixsmith.

The 15th December 1719 Tuesday. A fine forenoon,
snow after. I were at Shoreham Market. The boys
plough'd in the Hayselcroft.
John Gilham workt here ---------- 18 days.

The 16th December 1719 Wednesday. A very cold day.
Thomas Sawyers left off yesterday. Young Smith spread
dung etc. My Cousin John Lindfield here in the evning.
Nick Plaw here about William Balcomb's accounts.
I were at Tott in the morning. Paid Mrs Anne Beard 6s
yesterday for Molly Balcomb's schooling. Sent a letter to
Mr Evelin's steward at East Grinstead per R Kester jr
and my Cousin John Lindfield sent an other to Mr
Faulkoner. He is to have 5s for his jurney.

The 17th December 1719 Thursday. A dry day, a small
frost. The boys drew trees. Thomas Howell here to look
on elms by Old Hyder's and brought us word that Old
Hyder had stopt and hedg'd up the stiles into my field.
Paid R Kester 5s for his jurney. He brought a letter
from Mr Nathan Moore, Mr Glanvill's steward.
Mr Evelyn's name is, by Act of Parliament, chang'd to
Glanvill. John Gilham workt here -------- 19 days.
Will thrasht barly. Paid John Gun £10. My Father and I
were at Mrs Catherine Beard's.

The 18th December 1719 Fryday. A gloomy day.
John Gun went to East Grinstead with a letter
afternoon.
John Gilham here ------ 20 days.
Receiv'd 7 guineas of Mr Jeremiah Dodson and clear'd
accounts. The boys did severall jbbs. Will thrasht barly.
My Cousin John Lindfield supt and spent the evning
here. Seal'd the mortgage with my Father for the
payment of his annuity. Paid Mr Beard 2s _____ for my
part and _____ bond.

The 19th December 1719 Saturday. A gloomy day.
John Gun return'd from Grinsted about noon, thrasht
after. John Gilham workt here --------- 21 days.
Dick Banks came again, Smith and he carry'd faggots in
the forenoon etc, sick at night. Will and Jack plough'd.
I went part of the way to my Cousin John Lindfield.

The 20th December 1719 Sunday. A dry day.
Mr Jeremiah Dodson preacht. I spent the afternoon at
Dean House. My Cousin Lindfield sent her man to
Grinsted.

The 21st December 1719 Munday. A dry day.
Stephen Bine here in the morning. The boys carry'd
some stubble etc. I begun let out the new pond. Mr
Jeremiah Dodson and Mr Sixsmith here in the evning.

The 22nd December 1719 Tuesday. A fine day.
I were at Lewis to appeal in the Window Tax, got off.
*(Ed: xxx word deleted xxx)* Rickman's. Paid Samuel Tourl
sr 3s-9d for 4lbs of bohea. Paid Norman 8s in full of all.
Smith spread dung etc.

The 23rd December 1719 Wednesday. A dry day.
Will and Jack begun fallow the barly field. John Gun,
George West and Smith win'd      bushels of oates and
pease, the last of the field, 1 in all. Paid Thomas Hamper
56s-6d, clear'd accounts. I went over Mrs Catherine
Beard's farme. Din'd there.

The 24th December 1719 Thursday. A fine day.
Will and Jack plough'd Smith fallow'd.
John Gilham set up barrs etc -------- 22 days.
I were at Brighton. Sold Mr Gates of Beeding a load of
_____ at £5-15s. Receiv'd £5-19s of Noah Gates of
Brighton for a load of Mr Ward's wheat. Sent the mony
to Mrs Catherine Beard per Willy.

The 25th December 1719 Fryday. Xmas. A dry day.
Mr Jeremiah Dodson preacht. My Father and Mother
Stone and workmen din'd here. Mr Burry and Brother
Peter supt and spent the evning here. Dick Banks went
home again sick.

The 26th December 1719 Saturday. A gloomy day.
Chose surveyors as usual. My Cousin John Lindfield
din'd here. Paid Ellis the fuller 27s for dressing and
dyeing the blew cloath for a bed at 1s per yard.
He carry'd home cloath wastcoat to dress and scour.

The 27th December 1719 Sunday. A dry cold day.
Mr John Hart preacht. My Cousin Peter Marchant and
his wife came afternoon. Mr Scutt, his wife and Mr John
Hart here in the evning.

The 28th December 1719 Munday. A dry day, frost.
My Cousin Peter Marchant went home. My Cousin

Marchant's wife Sarah, my Wife and I din'd at my Father's. Mrs Catherine Beard's family supt there. I were at Mr Jeremiah Dodson's to borrow a dung court and he told me that Mr Osbourne of Newtimber had very lately promis'd him solemnly that I should have the forsakeing of Newtimber Farme whenever he lett it. Paid George Buckwell 16s-4½d in full of all accounts. Old Ned May came this evning at 2s per week. Reckon'd and clear'd accounts with Allexander Snatt, only due to me 21d.

The 29th December 1719 Tuesday. A gloomy day.
I din'd at Danny with my Wife and Cousin Marchant. Ned May, Smith and Will carry'd dung at Rickman's.

The 30th December 1719 Wednesday. A fine day.
My Wife, Will and I din'd at Thomas Norton's North End. Ned May and Smith made an end of the dung at Rickman's and brought home Parker's faggots.

The 31st December 1719 Thursday. A dry day.
Will and I din'd at Mrs Catherine Beard's. Ned May and Smith carry'd 3 loads of grit to my Father's ____ faggots afterwards. Paid Richard Wood 16s, clear'd accounts for work and taxes.

The 1st January 1719 Fryday. A fine day. Fisht the new pond. Young Dick Banks din'd here. Mrs Ann Dodson and her daughter, Mr Richard Whitpaine and his wife Mary, my Father and Mother Stone supt here.
John Gilham was here a Thursday and begun cover the great chair in the hall.

The 2nd January 1719 Saturday. A stormy day. Ned May and the boys carry'd 2 cart loads of stubble, measur'd a load of wheat etc. John Gilham finisht the great chair. Paid Joseph Muzzall the Lord's rent for Edgly and Rickman's and receiv'd the Land Tax for the mannor.

The 3rd January 1719 Sunday. A fine day. Mr Jeremiah Dodson preacht. My Wife and I receiv'd the sacrament. We had a parish meeting, settled accounts as usual.

The 4th January 1719 Munday. A dry day. Reckon'd with Old William Brand and there is due to me £2-16-6d for which he gave me a note of his hand.
John Gilham here -------- 23 days.
Paid Gilham 1s for covering the great chair in the hall. Deliver'd half a load of wheat to Shoreham for Mr Gates of Beeding per Ned May, Dick Smith, _____ Smith.

The 5th January 1719 Tuesday. A gloomy day.
Deliver'd the other half load of wheat to Mr Gates per Ned May etc as yesterday. I gave Michael Stacey an order to pay his Poor Tax to Stephen Bine. Sent a goose to Mr Wilkin per Smither the carrier. He took it last night, I paid 8d for carriage and portrage. Put 3 runts into Tully's Mead. John Gun had away his hog this afternoon. Paid £9-11-4d for my half year's Land Tax due at Michaelmas last, to my Cousin John Marchant of Lox.

The 6th January 1719 Wednesday. A very fine day after the morning. Thomas Norton and his wife and two daughters, my Cousin John Lindfield and his daughter, Mr John Hart, my Brother and Sister Betty Courtness and my Father and Mother Stone din'd here. My Brother Peter, my Cousin Jack Lindfield and Mr Scutt and his wife came towards night. I deliver'd to my Cousin John Lindfield all my receits for the Land Tax of which I have paid £214-12s-0d. Paid my Unkle Courtness 18d for 4 glasses, 2s for 12 lemons per my Cousin John Lindfield and 1s for 6 more per Jack Haslegrove and also for all the tobacco and pipes had to day. Borrow'd 2 bottles of brandy of my Father.

The 7th January 1719 Thursday. A gloomy day, wet towards night. Kill'd the 2 piggs. Weigh'd John Gun's hog 25 nail 7lbs at 2s per nail.
John Gilham here ------ 24 days. Will and Jack plough'd. Ned May and Smith carry'd 2 loads of stubble and 2 loads of grit to my Father's. Shutt up 2 piggs to fatting. Lent John Smith £4 yesterday for a note of his hand.

The 8th January 1719 Fryday. A very windy day. Willy and Jack plough'd. Ned May and Smith carry'd a cart load of stubble. Drew 3 trees at Rickman's and helpt Dick Banks winnow 4 bushels of his pease there.
John Gilham here ---- 25 days.
Receiv'd 10s of John Parsons for faggots and clear'd all accounts to Michaelmas last.

The 9th January 1719 Saturday. A fine day. Ned May and Will plough'd in Hayselcroft. Dick Smith litter'd Tully's close etc. John Smith's man kill'd a hog for me. Shut up John Gun's 5 beasts in Tully's close.
Gilham's man and he workt in Tully's close ----- 26 days.
Receiv'd the £4 of John Smith, which I lent him.

The 10th January 1719 Sunday. Fine day. Mr Jeremiah Dodson preacht. I was not at Church haveing a violent cold. Thomas Norton's wife North End and daughter to din'd here.

The 11th January 1719 Munday. A fine day.
Will, Smith and Nick Gorman made an end of fallowing the Hayselcroft. George Buckwell and his boy begun set up the crib in the hovel at Rickman's ------ 1 day. Win'd Dick Banks's pease there, in all 3 quarters 6 bushels.
I supt at Mr Jeremiah Dodson's with severall people.

The 12th January 1719 Tuesday. A fine day.
Will and Smith plough'd.
George Buckwell and his boy as yesterday ------ 2 days.
My Cousin Peter Marchant lay here last night, carry'd away his daughter to day.

The 13th January 1719 Wednesday. A fine day.
Win'd 15 bushels of Old Dick Banks's oates. Deliver'd a quarter of oates to my Cousin Peter Marchant per Jack Smith. Receiv'd ¼lb of bohea of Samuel Tourl per Jack Haslegrove. One black lamb in Tully's wheat earsh.
John Gilham here -------- 27 days.

The 14th January 1719 Thursday. A very wet day.
Dick Wood set 2 new fore shoes on my horse.
John Gilham here ---- 28 days.
John Gun hung up two flitches of our bakon in the evning. I was at Mr Jeremiah Dodson's and settled the account about the school to Christmas last. There was only Mr Richard Whitpaine and I. Mr Scutt is to pay me 19s-4½d.

The 15th January 1719 Fryday. A dry morning, wet after. Gilham made a wheelbarrow for my Father ---- 29 days. My Father, my Wife and I supt at Westtowne.

The 16th January 1719 Saturday. A dry day. John Gun and Will kill'd the boar. Smith spread dung. George Buckwell and his boy workt at Rickman's 'till noon.

The 17th January 1719 Sunday. A gloomy day.
Mr Jeremiah Dodson preacht. We had a meeting about Mr Litchford's mony. My Cousin John Lindfield din'd here. We settled our accounts about the Land Tax.
He paid me £6-19-6d. One lamb in Tully's ground.

The 18th January 1719 Munday. A dry day. Smith spread dung at Rickman's.

George Buckwell workt at Rickman's all day ------ 4 days. His boy workt 'till noon. Mrs Catherine Beard's family supt here. She paid me 50s for a year's rent due to me at hand and 19s for 12lbs of tire.

The 19th January 1719 Tuesday. A dry day. Will and Smith begun ploughing Tully's wheat earsh.
John Gilham here ----------- 30 days.
Mr John Hart supt and spent the evning here. Receiv'd 12 bushels of straw dried malt. Old William Brand rode the old Duke horse to Lewis.

The 20th January 1719 Wednesday. A gloomy day, some small rain. Paid John Westover 13s for a new payr of boots which he brought home to day. Drove the four fatting oxen to Rickman's. Smith and Will spread the dung there etc. John Gilham here ---------------- 31 days.
Sold George Buckwell 4 bushels of oates and pease at 9s-6d. He carry'd home 2 bushels. I were at The Swan with Mr Peter Courthope, Mr Jeremiah Dodson, Mr Beard, Mr Scutt, Mr Burry, Thomas Norton North End and Mr Richard Whitpaine. We sign'd the assignment of a mortgage for Mr Litchford's mony and Mr Richard Whitpaine paid the mony, £100 to Mr Peter Courthope. Spent 5s on the parish account. Paid Allexander Snatt 4s.

The 21st January 1719 Thursday. A fine day.
Will and Smith plough'd at Tully's. Gilham finisht my wheelbarrow ------ 32 days. George Buckwell and his boy at Rickman's ------ 6 days. I sent Mr Jeremiah Dodson five mean carp per Jack Haslegrove. Mr Sparks the Excise man here to gauge barrels for me.
Young Dick Banks told me he intended to go away.

The 22nd January 1719 Fryday. A gloomy day. Smith and Jack begun set beans etc.
George Buckwell and his boy at Rickman's -------- 7 days. Receiv'd £6-15s of Mr Gates for my wheat per Brother Peter. Nick Plaw here all the afternoon and evning. John Gilham here -------- 33 days.

The 23rd January 1719 Saturday. A fine day. Smith and Will plough'd. George Buckwell and his boy half day at Rickman's stable ------------ 7½ days.
My Wife and Molly at Danny afternoon. Paid Allexander Snatt 2s. Jack set more beans. One lamb in the Little Meads.

The 24th January 1719 Sunday. A dry day.
Mr Jeremiah Dodson preacht. I were not at Church in the forenoon.

The 25th January 1719 Munday. A dry day. Old William Brand and his 2 boys pitcht the stables at Rickman's. I was a while at Mrs Catherine Beard's in the evning with Mr Friend of Portslade and Mr Baldy and Will. Smith and Will made an end of Tully's wheat earsh.

The 26th January 1719 Tuesday. A gloomy day. Fisht the great pond. John Harland and Allexander Snatt helpt. Paid them 18d each and their dinner. Will and Jack plough'd by Wickham's. Put 103 large carp into the new pond, 104 the next size into the flat stew, 70 the largest tench into the Hovelfield stew, 363 small tench into the Marldfield stew and 110 small carp into the hole in the Middle Piece, 2 large carp in the upper pond and 12 small eels there also.

The 27th January 1719 Wednesday. A stormy day. Mr Picknall of Arundell here. Paid him 10s in full of all. Win'd Rickman's oates 12 quarters 5 bushels. Will, Old Dick Banks and Jack helpt winnow. Smith and I got the middle pond ready. Mr Burry here towards night. The horned ram kill'd the other old ram.

The 28th January 1719 Thursday. A gloomy day. Fisht the middle pond. Put 51 large carp in the new pond, 4 large and 47 under size in the flat stew, 27 large tench in the hovel field stew and 450 store tench in the Marldfield stew. Put 70 small eels into the pond again. Paid Harland and Allexander Snatt 19d each for fishing and _____ . Will and Jack plough'd. Smith helpt fish.

The 29th January 1719 Fryday. A fine day. Din'd at Dean House with Mr Norden, Thomas Norton, Mr Beard etc. Paid Mr Norden 6s in full of all accounts. Will and Jack plough'd. Will came to Dean House after. Smith carry'd my Wife to Dean House.

The 30th January 1719 Saturday. A gloomy day, small rain. I were at Church in the forenoon and at Oathall afternoon. Sold Mr Shirly 100 store tench at 7s-6d. He is to send for 'em a Saturday next.

The 31st January 1719 Sunday. A fine day. Mr Jeremiah Dodson preacht. My Cousin John Lindfield din'd here. I supt and spent the evning at Mrs Catherine Beard's. Dick Smith fetcht Mrs Heard from Cuckfield Mill for Mrs Scutt. Mrs Catherine Beard had two stray ewes cry'd which were mine, 7 lambs last week.

The 1st February 1719 Munday. A dry day. Deliver'd 3½ quarters of barly and as much oates to Harry Wickham to be malted for my self. I were at Westminstone, at Ditcheling and at Danny, Mr Peter Courthope spoke for 12 large tench. I supt at my Father's with Mr Beard, Mr John Hart etc.

The 2nd February 1719 Tuesday. A stormy day. Smith and I mov'd some fish. My Brother Peter here a while in the evning. I were at Mrs Catherine Beard's after supper. Staid late.

The 3rd February 1719 Wednesday. A fine day. Will went to Balcombe. Smith and Jack did severall jobbs. 5 - 6 lambs since Sunday. Receiv'd 3s-6d of Mr Richard Whitpaine for 109 store carp and 9 tench.

The 4th February 1719 Thursday. A fine day. Smith carry'd a crock of lard to Nick Plaw's, weigh'd 22 lbs. He had one before, must be return'd. Young Dick Banks and Jack helpt winnow 6 quarters 3 bushels head of Old Dick Banks Bankfield wheat. Paid John Westover 8d for a hand bill. I din'd at my Father's.

The 5th February 1719 Fryday. A fine forenoon, wet towards night. My Wife and I went to Lewis, din'd at my Cousin Peter's. Paid Mrs Punty £1-9-6d for makeing cloathes etc. Molly Balcomb _____ it to Thomas Friend for a payr of stockings for her 2s and for silver lace for a purse 8d for her. Paid Mr Scutt 2d for 1¾lb of hair line for the horse. Paid Mr Durrant 2s for 2 handcerchiefs for Mr John Hart _____ .
Paid Samuel Tourl 7s-6d for ½lb of bohea and 1s to Norman for binding. Paid Eliz Towner a bill for 6s-2d for work for Molly Balcomb.

The 6th February 1719 Saturday. A wet forenoon, stormy after. The boys did severall jobbs. Return'd with Thomas Jacket and there is due to me £1-2-6. Receiv'd 19s of Dick Wood for a flitch of old bakon. Left a piece of a flitch at John Smith's 2s-4½d at 3s-[..d] per nail for Dick Wood.

The 7th February 1719 Sunday. A dry day. Mr Jeremiah Dodson preacht. We had a meeting. Sign'd the new Poor Book. I were at Wanbarrow after evning prayr. Supt at Westtowne with Harry Goffe and Thomas Barker.

The 8th February 1719 Munday. A stormy day. Reckon'd with Old Dick Banks and there is due to me 5s ____ for 200 of faggots. Will and Smith plough'd by Wickham's. John Gilham and his man here ----- 34 days. Mr Scutt etc and my Sister Ann Box here. 13 lambs since Wednesday last.

The 9th February 1719 Tuesday. A dry, cold day. I were at Shoreham market. Offer'd Mr Friend some clover seed at 19s per bushel. Staid a while at Sadlescombe. Supt at my Father's with Thomas Norton North End and his wife. John Gilham and his man here --- 35 days.

The 10th February 1719 Wednesday. A stormy day. Receiv'd 7s-6d of Mr Shirly's man for 100 store tench, gave him 20 into the bargain. Paid Frank Marshall 18d for drenching the buck horse. John Gilham's man here 'till noon ------ 36½ days. Gilham's man here all day. Fetcht my 2 sheep out of Mrs Catherine Beard's ground.

The 11h February 1719 Thursday. A dry, cold day. I were at Brighton. Will and Smith carry'd roots and Jack. John Gilham and his man workt on a rick in the home close ------------ 37½ days. Paid 3s-8d for a handcerchief for Molly Balcomb to a Scotchman.

The 12th February 1719 Fryday. A fine forenoon, wet after. Mr Scrase of Withing din'd here, bid me 2s per bushel heap measures for 50 quarters of oates at my barne door. Mrs Ann Dodson here afternoon. John Gilham and his man finisht the racks in the close about noon on the north end of the wainhouse outlet after ------------ 38½ days. Will and Smith carry'd more roots and Jack. I saw an ox of my Cousin John Lindfield weigh'd at John Smith's, weigh'd 103 nail 4lbs the four quarters. Mr Peter Courthope sent for 6 tench. I did not think it worth my while to take them.

The 13th February 1719 Saturday. A showry day. Will and Smith drew bushes.
John Gilham and his man here ------------ 39½ days. Paid Gilham 2 guineas. My Father, Mother and Sister Betty Courtness din'd here. Thomas Muzzall kill'd one of the porkers. My Wife went to Danny afternoon.

The 14th February 1719 Sunday. A fine day. Mr Shave preacht afternoon, no service forenoon. William Bennett of Oathall din'd here. My Cousin John Lindfield here after evning service, staid late.

The 15th February 1719 Munday. A fine day. Will and Smith stackt faggots etc.
John Gilham here ------ 40½ days. Molly Balcomb went to my Cousin Thomas Norton's yesterday.

The 16th February 1719 Tuesday. A dry day. I were at Mr Scrase's of Withing. Sold him all the oates I can spare at 16s per quarter, 9 for 8 and he is to fetch them at my barne. Went from thence to Shoreham.
Call'd at Mr Friend's of Portslade as I came home with Mr _____ . Old Mr Friend and Nick Friend, Will, Smith and Thomas Gravet carry'd boughs, bushes etc.

The 17th February 1719 Wednesday. A gloomy day. Will and Jack begun plough the long field and Tully's coppice.
John Gilham and his man set up a gate here -- 41½ days. My Brother Henry Faulkoner din'd here, spoke for store fish.

The 18th February 1719 Thursday. A gloomy morning, fine after. I were at Brighton market. Sold Merchant Cook 4 ½ bushels of clover seed at £3-18-6d, I am to send. Will and Smith plough'd. I wrote Mr Picknall per post. I left a sample of my seed with Mr Gold.

The 19th February 1719 Fryday. A fine day. Deliver'd the seed to Merchant Cook per Will and Jack Haslegrove. Left 2 sacks there. Bargain'd with Dick Smith for next year part of Randalls house with all the orchard below the way into Mr Peter Courthope's field, at 40s certain by as much more as I think he deserves. I din'd at my Father's. My Wife din'd at Danny. Gilham workt here -- 42½ days.
The cow I had of Mrs Catherine Beard (when a calf) calv'd 2 calves, a bull calf, the other a cow calf.

The 20th February 1719 Saturday. A gloomy morning, dry after. I were at Lewis. Sold 6 bushels of clover seed to Mr H Farncombe of Withing at 17s per bushel. Paid Samuel Tourl 3s-9d for ¼lb of bohea. Paid Norman 2s-6d for a pocket book. The red heifer calv'd a bull calf. Will and Smith plough'd.

The 21st February 1719 Sunday. A gloomy day, rain towards night. No service in the forenoon. Mr Base preacht in the afternoon, a funeral sermon for Henry Heath. I were at Mrs Week's in the evning.

Nick Plaw was here to draw away a cow's clean. Brought home the fatting oxen last night.

The 22nd February 1719 Munday. A fine day. Mr Peter Courthope had 12 large tench. Deliver'd 6 bushels of clover seed to Mr H Faulkoner per Dick Banks and Young Botting. Receiv'd John Stone's first Poor Tax. He supt here. My Brother Henry Faulkoner's man fetcht 150 store carp about 7½ inches and 100 store tench.

The 23rd February 1719 Tuesday. A dry day. I were at Shoreham. Receiv'd £3-19-6d of Merchant Cook for 4½ bushels of seed. Will, John Box sr and Thomas Norton North End went to coursing. Paid E Purvey at Ansty Cross 1s for a basket per Dick Banks.

The 24th February 1719 Wednesday. A gloomy day. Put the fish in order. Mr Healy's man fetcht a crock of butter from home. Dr White and Young John Snashall here for a while. The Dr was sent for to my Unkle Courtness. John Gilham here half the day a Munday ------ 43 days.

The 25th February 1719 Thursday. A dry day. I were at Brighton. Sold a load of wheat to Harry Standbridge at £6-15s. I were at Mr H Farncombe's as I came home. Will and Smith plough'd to day and yesterday. Frank Osbourne here in the morning with R Buckwell. My Sister Betty Courtness brought to bed of a girl yesterday or a Tuesday.

The 26th February 1719 Fryday. A very fine day. Paid William Nicholas 9s for grubbing half 4 cord of oaken stems at 5s per cord, half 4 cord 6 foot a bush roots at 3s-6d per cord. 6d for his boys picking cherrys etc, 6d for cutting bushes. Reckon'd with Widdow Patching's Land Tax for the year 1718. Will, Smith, Jack and Young Dick Banks helpt Old Dick Banks winnow 86 bushels head oates. Paid Parker's wife 6s. Had Botting help winnow after. Old Dick Banks and Botting's boy din'd here. Turn'd all my sheep and lambs into the Churchfield wheat. There is 10 sheep and lambs of the right ear and 9 of the left and 9 of _____ .

The 27th February 1719 Saturday. Dry forenoon, very wet after. I were at Lewis. Paid Mr Court 11s-0d in full and 6s for 12lbs soap, 2s-6d for a quart of oyl and 2s for _____ to my Cousin Marchant. Will and Smith plough'd. Thomas Howell's man put a new chip and wing to the horse round plough.

The 28th February 1719 Sunday. A gloomy day, much snow last night. Plaw's heifer calved a bull calf a Thursday last. Mr Heard din'd here. I were at Mrs Catherine Beard's in the evning.

The 29th February 1719 Munday. A gloomy day, some snow. Smith drew logs to the faggot stack. Reckon'd with Ditcheling cooper. Clear'd accounts. Paid the cooper 9s for an upright 30 gallon barrel for my Father. Old Dick Banks had a bushel of wheat. John Smith sent his blind mare to me and Thomas Greenfield at a guinea.

The 1st March 1719 Shrove Tuesday. A dry day, thawing. Dick and the boys jobb'd 'till noon. Paid Dick White 2s-6d in full for mole catching. Paid John Gun 5s. John Haslegrove hitcholl'd to day and yesterday.

The 2nd March 1719 Wednesday. A stormy day. Deliver'd 2 loads of oates to Mr Scrase per his brother Hamshire and 4 men. Reckon'd and clear'd accounts with John Haslegrove. Mr John Hart supt and spent the evning here.

The 3rd March 1719 Thursday. A gloomy day. I were at Brighton. Paid William Nicholas 2s-7½d for cleaving a cord and 2 foot of crown wood. Thomas White's fat'd heifer calved a bull calf last night. Old William Brand, his son, Will and Ned Botton win'd 11 quarters of barly head and 9½ tail of the Nine Acres oates. Mr Edwards the plastrer came at noon to set up and make up the blew cloath bed. Brought up the 4 three yearlings out of Tully's close. Receiv'd 5 guineas of Mr Richard Whitpaine which I lent him at 22s on Thomas Jacket's account.

The 4th March 1719 Fryday. A fine day. Deliver'd 20 quarters of oates to four of Mr Scrase's men. Stephen Davis and Thomas Roberds of Brighton were here to buy alder poles. Davis bid me 24s per 100 [flaid] and deliver'd at Brighton. Did not deal.
Gilham here ------- 44 days.
Mr Beard, my Father and Harry Wickham here towards night. Paid Thomas Roberds 10s in full of all accounts.

The 5th March 1719 Saturday. A dry day. Dick Banks, Dick Smith and Nick Gorman carry'd 21 bushels of wheat, by mistake to Ben Hayler's mill which should

have been carry'd to Harry Standbridge's vessel. Paid
Mr Edwards 30s for work and materials about the bed.
Paid E Towner for work for Molly Balcomb 6s.
John Gilham here about the bed ---------- 4s.

The 6th March 1719 Sunday. A gloomy day. Mr Jeremiah
Dodson preacht. We had a meeting as usual but settled
no accounts. I were a while at Mr Scutt's after evning
prayr and afterwards at Mr Jeremiah Dodson's. Thomas
Smith at Ansty Cross carry'd home an auger of mine to
new bit. Molly Balcomb came here.

The 7th March 1719 Munday. A very fine day. Deliver'd
a load of wheat (all but 4 bushels which was thrown into
the water) to ~~Harry Standbridge~~ Richard Smith at
Shoreham for Harry Standbridge at Brighton. They left
the 4 wet bushels with R Smith. Thomas Howell's man
made a horse harrow here. Ned Botting helpt winnow
barly. John Gilham here half the day cutting ash for
shovel trees etc --- 4s½.
My Wife were at Westtowne afternoon.

The 8th March 1719 Tuesday. A fine day. I were at
Shoreham and at Stephen Robert's race at Portslade,
Mr Beard went with me. We were at Mr Benjamin
Hayler's. Will and Jack were at the race. Ned Botten
helpt winnow barly. Paid Isaac Muzzall 6s-6d for a
payr of spatterdashes.

The 9th March 1719 Wednesday. A very fine day.
Deliver'd 22 quarters of barly to Harry Wickham and
William Wickham, Dick Banks and Jack Haslegrove
brought home 36 bushels of seed barly. Harry Wickham
lent me his waggon and 3 horses. R Botten helpt me.
I gave his malter and William Wickham 1s each. Put the
sheep into the Churchfield wheat again.

The 10th March 1719 Thursday. A fine day. I were at
Brighton. Sold 5 bushels of clover seed to Mr Douglas
of Bletchington at 16s per bushel. Receiv'd £24-5s of Mr
Scrase in part for oates. Receiv'd £5-2s of Mr Farncomb
in full for clover seed. Stephen Davis bid me 25d per
100 for poles, I refused it. Young Dick Banks and the
boys did severall jobbs.

The 11th March 1719 Fryday. A very fine day. Will sow'd
16 bushels of oates out the field below Tully's Mead,
Smith and Young Dick Banks harrow'd. Jack and I
carry'd 5 bushels of clover to Mr Douglas. Receiv'd £4
of Mr Douglas for the seed. I call'd at Mr Scrase's of
Withing as I came home, bid him 4 quarters of oates for
a cart, he refus'd it.

The 12th March 1719 Saturday. A dry day. Will sow'd the
field below Tully's Mead with clover. Young Dick Banks
and Smith harrow'd. Smith spread a load of pidgeon's
dung on an acre of the north edge of the long field by
Tully's coppice. Paid George West 6s. Thomas Whiteing
of Blackstone and an other here. They bid me 18s per
cord for alder wood deliver'd at Blackstone Street. Old
Mrs White, Mrs Barbara Campion and Mrs Willard here
etc. Win'd 3 quarters bushel head, 1 bushel tail, the last
of the barly. The little runt heifer went to Bull.

The 13th March 1719 Sunday. A dry cold day.
Mr Jeremiah Dodson preacht. Mrs Anne White and
my Cousin John Lindfield din'd here. I supt at
Mrs Catherine Beard's.

The 14th March 1719 Munday. A dry cold day, some
snow.
My Cousin Thomas Norton of Edgly and Thomas
Howell here. Will and Young Dick Banks plough'd at
Rickman's, broke in the colt. George West sow'd an acre
of flax by Tully's coppice, Smith harrow'd.
My Brother Peter here in the evning.

The 15th March 1719 Tuesday. A dry, cold day.
Young Dick Banks and Will sow'd. Smith plough'd with
Will afternoon. Banks had an ague. Paid Frank Holden
19s-6d and left 30s to pay for 5 buck skins and some
other things for which 30s he is to have 200 faggots in
the Sumer. Sold Thomas Howell a parcell of pollard ash
at 7½d per foot or 8d at most to be deliver'd at his
house.

The 16th March 1719 Wednesday. A stormy day, the
wind very high and _____ last night. Young Dick
Banks and John Gun bound the thatch on the barnes
etc. The boys did severall jobbs. John Pierce begun make
me a payr of buckskin breeches. Turn'd the sheep out of
the Churchfield wheat.

The 17th March 1719 Thursday. A fine day.
Deliver'd 10 quarters head barly and 9 bushels tail to
Harry Wickham per Banks and Willy. Receiv'd 6 quarters
seed barly of him. Deliver'd likewise 4 bushels of flax
seed to him at 10s per bushel. Mr Sixsmith din'd here.

I promis'd to allow 1000 of bricks towards paving the parsonage stables at Rusper. My Father and Mother Stone din'd here with him.
John Pierce workt on my breeches ------- 2 days.
I receiv'd a summons to serve in the Grand Jury at the assizes at East Grinstead on Munday the 28th of this month. Young Rowland deliver'd it to my Wife.
John Gun is to begin serve the calves but once a day to morrow morning. Mr William Martin, his brother and Mr John Hart breakfasted here.

The 18th March 1719 Fryday. A dry day.
Will and Young Dick Banks plough'd at Rickman's. John Pierce finisht my buckskin breeches -------- 3 days. Deliver'd a load of bush roots to the school. I supt and spent the evning at Westtowne. I were at the Oak with R Smith the painter and Stephen Bine.

The 19th March 1719 Saturday. A fine day.
I were at Lewis Market. Paid Samuel Tourl 8s-9d for ¼lb of bohea. Paid Mr Mitchell 2s-6d to have me excused from the assizes. I gave him also a pint of wine. Paid Stephen Avery the saddler 3s for new covering my leather bags. Jack Haslegrove return'd from Rusper, he went yesterday. Will and Young Dick Banks made an end of ploughing at Rickman's.

The 20th March 1719 Sunday. A dry day.
Mr Jeremiah Dodson preacht. We had a meeting on Abraham Muzzall's account. My Cousin John Lindfield din'd here.

The 21st March 1719 Munday. A fine day. Brickhouse sale. Mr Norden din'd here. Will sow'd the last of the long field by Tully's coppice with 4 bushels of oates and pease, 7 bushels of white pease and near a bushel of flax seed. Young Dick Banks and Smith harrow'd. Jack Haslegrove went to Lewis for my Father's hat etc.

The 22nd March 1719 Tuesday. A dry day.
Begun sow barly at Towner's. Sold Old George Hill of Rigate all my ewes and lambs together with Will's ewes, lambs and taggs and the lambs at 10s-9d a head and a guinea over in the whole, I to have the wool, the lambs to be gone by Midsumer and the ewes by Michaelmas as usual. Receiv'd a guinea in hand. H Bull of Bolny was here with him. P Hill bid me £18 for one of my oxen and a runt. Receiv'd 2 bottles of brandy from Mr Hayler at £2-10s.

The 23rd March 1719 Wednesday. A gloomy day. My birthday, 43 years. I din'd at Wanbarrow with divers others. I were to see Mrs Catherine Beard's sheep and lambs with George Hill and H Bull. They lay here last night. Will, the boys and Banks plough'd and sow'd.

The 24th March 1719 Thursday. A showry forenoon, wet after. I were at Brighton. Young Dick Banks, Will and Smith plough'd and sow'd part of the day. Harry Standbridge appointed to pay for his _of wheat next Thursday. Paid Mr Jeremiah Dodson half a year's tythe which is due to morrow, £6-1s for Little Park, Edgly and Rickman's. Paid him also for coffee, tea and faggots.

## 1720

The 25th March 1720 Fryday. Lady Day. A showry day. A Fair at Ditcheling. Dick Banks went away. Clear'd accounts. Mr Jeremiah Dodson, Mr John Hart, my Father and Mother Stone here afternoon. Paid Molly Balcomb 2s per week since Lady Day last for spending mony 8s-8d.

The 26th March 1720 Saturday. A wet day.
Richard King came at £3-15-6d certain and 5s more if he deserves it for a year. Will, Thomas Gravet and Smith plough'd and sow'd one warp. Put 10 carp about six or seven inches and ten tench the same size into the pond at the northwest corner of Rickman's farme. George Haslegrove was here from my Sister Sarah. Thomas Burt's wife of Lewis here in the forenoon.

The 27th March 1720 Sunday. A fine day.
Mr Jeremiah Dodson preacht. We had a meeting afternoon about an indightment on the parish.
I supt and spent the evning at Mrs Catherine Beard's.

The 28th March 1720 Munday. A gloomy day, some rain. The boys plough'd and sow'd. Paid Chapman 1s for clipping my sheep and Will's at 4d _.
Mrs Scutt, her sister, my Father and Mother Stone here towards night. Order'd John Gun to give his calves no more hay. Turn'd 2 cows and calves into the Marldfield. Turn'd 2 runts to pasture in the hop garden.

The 29th March 1720 Tuesday. A wet day. Turn'd John Gun's 5 bullocks down to Rickman's close. Sold the old Duke horse's skin to Thomas Baker at 2s-6d. Sent 2 sacks of oakum tow to West's a weaver at St John's

Comon per Richard King, weigh'd 68½ lbs sacks and all. John Smith the butcher agreed to have the Bowling Ally an other year at 22s-6d per annum.

The 30th March 1720 Wednesday. A fine day. Reckon'd and clear'd accounts with my Father to Lady Day last. John Gilham here --------------- 46½ days.
Old William Brand and Norris here for 2 alder poles. The boys plough'd and sow'd barly 'till noon, cross harrow'd and sow'd Nonsuch after. My Father and Mother Stone din'd here, supt also and Mr John Hart with them.

The 31st March 1720 Thursday. A fine day. I were at Brighton, staid late. Receiv'd £6-1-6d of Harry Standbridge for 4 quarters 4 bushels of wheat. Receiv'd £8 of Henry Scrase in full for oates. The boys plough'd and sow'd barly.

The 1st April 1720 Fryday. A fine day. George West and the boys plough'd and sow'd. Will went to coursing with his Unkle William. Will Terry was here with his boy Ned, left the boy here.
Gilham workt ¾ of the day yesterday --------- 47¼ days. The long tetted cow calved a bull calf ~~yesterday~~ last night. Old William Brand finish his tomb stone.

The 2nd April 1720 Saturday. A fine day.
The boy made an end of the field by Towner's, sow'd him with Nonsuch. My Cousin John Lindfield here towards night, 2 lambs to day.

The 3rd April 1720 Sunday. A fine day. Mr Jeremiah Dodson preacht. A parish meeting, settled accounts as usual. My Cousin John Lindfield and his wife Elizabeth here after evning prayr.

The 4th April 1720 Munday. A fine day. Will sow'd the wheat earsh at Rickman's with 3 acres of oates and an acre of flax. John Gilham here --- 48¼ days.
Reckon'd and clear'd accounts with Gilham.
John Pierce begun make buckskin breeches for Will. The cow at Rickman's calved a cow calf last night. Paid Gilham 36s-6d in full of all.

The 5th April 1720 Tuesday. A dry day. Finisht the wheat earsh at Rickman's with clover. Begun the Bankfield with barly. Sent a letter to John Brand yesterday. John Pierce workt on the breeches ------2 days. My Wife went to Susan Bradford's at Kymer and to Old Land. Will Meads of Blackstone was here to shave some of his alder wood. Nick Plaw was here and drew a cow's clean. Receiv'd 27s-6d of him for flax seed and 3s-6d for bief and payrs.

The 6th April 1720 Wednesday. A wet morning, dry after. Gilham set up a little seat for a child in my Wive's seat. Dick Banks workt here with him, clear'd accounts again. Paid John Pierce 10s in full for work. He finish Will's breeches about 3 aclock. Paid Dick Wood a guinea, closed account. The boys plough'd and sow'd most of the day in the Bankfield. Sold a steer runt to Henry Dubbins and Thomas Stone at £5-10s a Munday last and their man fetcht him a Tuesday deliver'd by John Gun.

The 7th April 1720 Thursday. A dry day, wet evning. The boys plough'd and sow'd. My Wife and I were at Danny afternoon. Receiv'd Mr Peter Courthope's Poor Tax and 10s-6d for 12 large tench. Turn'd 2 runts into the dry pond yesterday.

The 8th April 1720 Fryday. A gloomy day.
The boys plough'd and sow'd. Receiv'd Mrs Catherine Beard's Poor Tax. Mr Beard and I were at Mr Burry's. Sent Mr Friend of Portslade 2 bushels of clover per Jack. Paid Thomas Gravet a guinea.

The 9th April 1720 Saturday. A fine day.
The boys plough'd and sow'd. Lent John Stubb's £25 for a note of his hand. Paid Thomas Gravet 23s-3½d and a bushel of oates, clear'd accounts.

The 10th April 1720 Sunday. A fine day.
Mr John Hart preacht. Mr Samuel Beard, Mr Ralph Beard, Mr Samuel Kemp, Mr Richard Whitpaine and Thomas Norton of Pycomb here after evning prayr, Mr John Hart and Mr Scutt also.

The 11th April 1720 Munday. A fine day.
The boys plough'd and sow'd. I din'd at my Father's. Thomas Terry here towards night, I gave him 1s to go to Mary Morley.

The 12th April 1720 Tuesday. A fine day. The boys finisht the Bankfield with clover. Dick King harrow'd with the ox harrow in the Hayselcroft afternoon. Receiv'd £14 of Young George Hill of Rigate for an ox, he had him away to day, sold to his father. Turn'd the 5 calves into the Rookwood and clear'd Tully's Mead.

The 13th April 1720 Wednesday. A fine day.
The boys begun plough and sow the Hayselcroft. Jack went to Lewis with butter. Mr Beard went with my Wife and I to Old Land, Jack came to and brought home half an anchor of brandy for which I paid Samuel Beard a guinea. Samuel Beard and William Birch of Arundell were there. Receiv'd 23s-6d of Ashfold of Poynings for 1½ bushels of clover seed per Willy.

The 14th April 1720 Thursday. A very fine day.
The boys made an end of barly sowing. Jack went to Lindfield to my Brother John Courtness for ribb'd fustian etc for a frock for me. I were at John Stone's and receiv'd his Poor Tax

The 15th April 1720 Fryday. A showry morning, fine after. The boys laid up the plough harrow etc and went to church. I were at the Royall Oak with my Cousin John Lindfield and Stephen Bine. Jack went to Warninglid, brought a letter from Mrs _____ .

The 16th April 1720 Saturday. A very wet day. The boys oyld the horse harrow and other jobbs. Dick King carry'd 2 bushels of the seed barly to Harry Wickham's. Reckon'd and clear'd accounts with Mr Burry, John Ha......] and John Snashall sr paid him 25s for a bull calf.

The 17th April 1720 Easter Sunday. A showry day.
Mr Jeremiah Dodson preacht. We had a meeting afternoon about Dog Smith's mony. I supt and spent the evning at Mrs Catherine Beard's.

The 18th April 1720 Munday. A very fine day.
All kept Holy Day. Past accounts and chose officers as usual. My Cousin John Lindfield and Thomas Norton North End din'd here. Jack went to Lindfield and brought 8 yards of fustian for a frock for Willy. Paid John Westover a guinea, he set out for London.

The 19th April 1720 Tuesday. A very fine day. My Wife and I and the boys went to Lewis. Will and I chang'd 2 payrs of silver shoe buckles allowing 2s per payr for the exhange. Clear'd accounts with Thomas Friend. Paid Abraham Muzzall 4s yesterday for 10 weeks schooling for William Balcomb and 4d for work etc for Molly Balcomb.

**(Ed: Gap in diary from 20th April until 1st May 1720)**

The 1st May 1720 Sunday. A fine day.
Mr Jeremiah Dodson preacht twice.
Yung John Lindfield din'd here. My Wife and I receiv'd the sacrament. Danny family and Mrs Catherine Beard here after evning prayr. My Cousin John Lindfield here a while. A parish meeting.

The 2nd May 1720 Munday. A dry day.
My Cousin John Lindfield and I went to Rotherfield. The boys did severall jobbs. Will went to Lindfield Fair, bought a barren of William Bennet for 59s.

The 3rd May 1720 Tuesday. A gloomy day, small rain.
A Fair at Ukfield. My Cousin John Lindfield and I lay at Mr Thomas Butcher's of Rotherfield last night, came home to day. Paid Thomas Butcher £3-4s for cloath etc for a suit for Will, brought home likewise a suit for Yung John Lindfield and I, my Cousin John Lindfield paid for them.

The 4th May 1720 Wednesday. A gloomy day, some rain.
Mr Jeremiah Dodson here in the morning. Paid him all the rent for the Hayselcroft for this year to come, outset his Poor Tax for last year.
George Buckwell here about E Ball. My Father and I supt and spent the evning at Mr Dodson's.

The 5th May 1720 Thursday. A wet forenoon.
The boys did severall jobbs. Supt and spent the evning at Mrs Catherine Beard's with my Father.

The 6th May 1720 Fryday. A wet morning, dry after.
The boys got ready for dunging. Paid Molly Balcomb 6s a Thursday last to go to John Hubbard's wedding
*(Ed: John married Mary Hobbes on 3rd May at Clayton).*
Paid John Snashall sr 10s due from the parish for setting E Chapman's girls away. George Buckwell went to Lewis with E Ball. Turn'd the working oxn down in Tully's lower ground. Receiv'd 2 qires of paper of Mr Beard.

The 7th May 1720 Saturday. A gloomy dry day.
The boys carry'd 25 loads of Kester's dung into my Father's orchard. John Pierce made Will a fustian frock. Bought a barren cow of John Snashall at £3-15s to fetch her next week and if I don't like her at fortnight's end I am to loose the keeping and return her.

The 8th May 1720 Sunday. A fine day.
Mr Jeremiah Dodson preacht twice. We had a parish meeting. My Cousin Elizabeth Norton North End

(*Ed: née Smith, married Thomas Norton 1705 in Hurst*) and her 2 daughters here after evning prayr. Mr Beard and Brother Peter spent the evning, staid late.

The 9th May 1720 Munday. A fine day.
My Wife, 2 girls and I went to Lewis. Paid Norman 16d for this book, clear'd accounts. Clear'd accounts with Samuel Tourl and Mr Court. John Hart and I were sworne Church Wardens. Carry'd cloath etc to Mr Andrew Laurence to make a suit of cloaths for Will.

The 10th May 1720 Tuesday. A very fine day. Ned Terry drove 2 oxn to Hand Cross for London.
Paid P Courtice 6s to drive them from thence to Robert Skinner's ground, 2s for their hay on the road and 4s for staying to see the market and I ordered him if they would not yield £13 a piece to bring 'em home again. Dick King and Smith carry'd 5½ loads of Kester's dung 30½ in all. My Cousin Elizabeth Norton North End went to Lewis. Her daughter Betty (*Ed: born 1706 Hurstpierpoint*) rode our little horse with her.

The 11th May 1720 Wednesday. A dry forenoon, wet after. The boys and I went to Lewis and the boys went home again, I staid there. I din'd and supt at Dr White's. Turn'd the fatting ox that was left at home to pasture and fetch John Snashall's cow.

The 12th May 1720 Thursday. A gloomy day. My Wife and I lay at Dr White's last night. The boys came for us and we return'd home with the children. My Father and Mother Stone here towards night. Ned Terry ty'd hops. Dick Smith's mother bury'd yesterday. (*Ed: Albourne Parish Register shows "Ann wife of John Smith buried"*)

The 13th May 1720 Fryday. A gloomy day, some rain. The boys carry'd 27 loads of dung out of the home close. Turn'd one ox 2 steers and John Snashall's cow into the field by Hyder's. Receiv'd £26 of John Smith in full of the last reckoning so that he owes me for nothing but the little cow runt at £4. Shut up one of the twins and put George Buckwell's cow's calf to the Wintermilch that I had of Mr Burry. Will begun goeing to school to Joseph Muzzall yesterday or the day before, to learn arithmatick.

The 14th May 1720 Saturday. A fine day. Smith had the brown mare that I had of John Smith to Yorkshire Stephen's horse at Gline; brought home Will's cloaths from Lewis. E Terry went to Hand Cross and brought an account of my 2 oxn sold yesterday at London, one at £14, one at £12-10s, I don't think I were well used. Dick King went to Shoreham with Rutter, sold at 5d per lb. I din'd at Westtowne. Receiv'd 18s-4d½ of Mr Scutt on the school account. Dick Wood set 2 new shooes on my horse's fore feet.

The 15th May 1720 Sunday. A fine day. Mr John Hart preacht, no service afternoon. The child's seat in my Wive's seat was pull'd down, I suspect by Thomas Norton's order or by himself. I were at Mrs Catherine Beard's a while in the afternoon with Mrs Courthope.

The 16th May 1720 Munday. A fine day. The boys and John Gun carry'd 32 loads of dung. Dick King went to Fletching yesterday, came home to day after noon. John Friend of Abbots in Wiston parish din'd here. Mr Conly a painter here about painting the church.
Paid Jo Chapman £1-0-8d for Mr Chapman of Rusper for keeping Mary Morley and for necessarys for her, with what she had before is £3-4-1d in all.

The 17th May 1720 Tuesday. A very fine day only a showr afternoon. Will went to a Plate Race at Lewis. The boys carry'd 20 loads of dung. Shut up the sucking cows calf.

The 18th May 1720 Wednesday. A very fine, hot day. Mr Peter Courthope went through our ground for London. The boys carry'd (as they say) 30 loads of dung. Will went to a second Plate Race at Lewis. Lent John Godly and _____ at the Comon an oxn pole. John Smith the butcher went for London to day. Turn'd the blind mare out to the fatting oxn.

The 19th May 1720 Thursday. A gloomy day, with small rain. Washt the sheep. Paid John Hart of Fulking 1s for washing 3 score sheep and 1s for a sheep hook. Dick Smith went to Lewis _____ . The boys helpt wash the sheep and Dick King carry'd 5 loads of dung after and Terry weeded flax at Rickman's. Reckon'd with John Gun and paid him £1-0-3d in full of all. Mr John Hart and I were at Edgly in the evning about the seat.

The 20th May 1720 Fryday. A very fine day.
The boys finisht the home close 23 loads. Receiv'd £20 part of John Norman's mortgage of Nick Plaw and £10 more being 5 years interest due from Nick Plaw to

William Balcomb on a bond of £40. My Sister Sarah here afternoon. The branded heifer calved a cow calf yesterday.

The 21st May 1720 Saturday. A dry day. The boys carry'd dung in the forenoon, only Dick King in the afternoon out of the fatting close 15 loads. Dick King went to Fletching after 5 aclock. Ned Terry weeded barly in the Hayselcroft after noon. My Father, Mr John Hart, my Wife, Mrs Mary Whitpaine, Jack and I went to Brighton afternoon.

The 22nd May 1720 Sunday. A fine day. Mr John Hart preacht, no service afternoon, Mr Jeremiah Dodson sick. Mr Beard here in the morning, he set out for London after dinner. Paid him half a guinea for a saddle and gave him a note to take what he pleas'd of my mony of Mr Wilkin in London. Mr Richard Whitpaine here towards night We went to see Mr Dodson.

The 23rd May 1720 Munday. A fine day.
The boys carry'd 20 loads of dung out of the fatting close. Mr William Martin brought his mare into the ground at 2s per week. Paid Chapman 2s-6d for sheering 61 sheep. Sent an entry of the wool to Mr Waller per post. Mrs Catherine Beard shovel'd part of the towne. I desir'd Mr Jeremiah Dodson to write to the Lord of the Mannor to renew my lease of the soyl and to offer him 2 broad pieces. Receiv'd 31s-6d of Mr Blunt's man for 450 store tench 7 inches. William Bennet of Oathall here afternoon and Brother Peter.

The 24th May 1720 Tuesday. A fine day.
The boys finisht the fatting close 9 loads. Terry weeded barly afternoon. Smith went to Lewis for SM. Reckon'd and clear'd accounts with Richard White sr.

The 25th May 1720 Wednesday. A dry day.
The boys begun clear Tully's close 16 loads. Sold young George Hill of Rigate a runt at £6-10s certain if he is sold in London for £7 I am to have 5s more; to be gone in the Whitsun week. The bayard mare went to Mr Scrase's house at Withing; gave the carter 2s. Brother Peter washt his sheep here. Dick Smith had the mare to horse. Old Dick Banks begun clear Rickman's close at 4s by the _____ . Paid John Pierce 50s for Widdow Smith and Parker's rent to Lady Day last.

The 26th May 1720 Thursday. A dry day. All kept Holy Day after the _____ . My Wife and I rode to Rickman's etc. Will and William Norton went to Findon Fair. My Cousin John Lindfield supt and spent the evning here.

The 27th May 1720 Fryday. A gloomy day.
Dick King and Terry carry'd dung at Tully's 'till noon, Dick King after, 15 loads. Smith King and Terry weeded. I spent the evning with Mr John Hart, there was Mr Piony and _____ Woolgar.

The 28th May 1720 Saturday. A dry day. Dick King clear'd Tully's close 10 loads; 41 in all. Reckon'd and clear'd accounts with Banks. Mr Richard Whitpaine din'd here. My Wife and I supt at Westtowne. Will's cow, bought at Crawley Fair, went to bull. Banks made an end of clearing Rickman's close yesterday. 57 loads.

The 29th May 1720 Sunday. A fine day.
Mr William Martin preacht. Mrs Courthope and my Cousin Thomas Norton's wife Elizabeth North End here after evning prayr.

The 30th May 1720 Munday. A fine day.
Horsham Fair. I were at Shermanbury with my Wife and Molly Balcomb. Paid Dick Smith 5s. Terry carry'd 7 loads of Towne dirt.

The 31st May 1720 Tuesday. A fine day.
Dick King carry'd a load of Towne dirt to Mr John Hart out of the hop garden and 7 out of the Towne for me. Terry and Smith did several jobbs.

The 1st June 1720 Wednesday. A gloomy day.
Carry'd the rest of the alder wood, 1¼ cord in all; receiv'd 22s-6d of Thomas Whiteing for it. E Terry helpt John Gun mend the bay of the hovelfield stew.
Smith and 2 boys hay'd in the lower part of Nine Acres. My Wife and Jacky went to Danny towards night.

The 2nd June 1720 Thursday. A gloomy morning, wet after. The boys fetcht up 2 loads of roots out of Tully's middle lane, clear'd the bares etc. I was at Mrs Catherine Beard's a while afternoon. John Snashall's cow was bulling and we brought her to the bull. Turn'd the sheep out of the homefield into Tully's Winter oat earsh.

The 3rd June 1720 Fryday. A gloomy day, small rain.
The boys did several jobbs. Drew John Smith's flocks. Mr John Hart, my Brother Will and Mr Burry here in

the eve. Reckon'd with Harry Wickham and there is due to me £22-5-6d for which he gave me a note of his hand to which Mr Hart is witness. Turn'd the 2 Nunnery steers to fatting.

The 4th June 1720 Saturday. A showry day.
The boys carry'd roots and faggots. Paid my Brother John Courtness 14d for buttons and mohair.

The 5th June 1720 Sunday. A wet day.
Mr William Martin preacht. I was not at Church in the morning. We had a meeting, settled no accounts. I was Mrs Catherine Beard's in the evning.

The 6th June 1720 Munday. A fine day.
I went to Shiprods with my Father and Mother Stone, Mr Richard Whitpaine, his wife and daughter they went in my waggon. The boys kept Holy Day.

The 7th June 1720 Tuesday. A very fine day. Cliffe Fair. Receiv'd the £50 and intrest of Mrs Catherine Beard on bond. Lent John Westover £4 for a note of his hand. Sent the runt sold to George Hill to H Bull of Bolny.

The 8th June 1720 Wednesday. A showry day.
The boys carry'd 200 faggots to Frank Holden and 100 to John Smith; brought several home, cut the calves, ground 8 bushels of malt. Paid Stephen Avery 12s in exchange and 2 old saddles for a new saddle. Sold John Smith a runt at 20d per _____ 5 quarters, to be kill'd in her _____ . Receiv'd £14-17s of George Hill jr. He markt 27 sheep, lambs and rams which I am to send to Bolny to morrow. John Smith kill'd a calf of mine.

The 9th June 1720 Thursday. A showry morning, fine after. My Cousin _____ went home. Dick King fetcht a load of lime for Briers at the Comon, a load of sand out of the lane by Randiddles ground. Clear'd accounts with John Smith for the calf he kill'd yesterday and sold him the saddles I bought of Mrs Catherine Beard and for which he paid me 14s-6d. Sent the 27 sheep and lambs and rams to Bolny per Nick Gorman with Jack Haslegrove.

The 10th June 1720 Fryday. A dry day.
Went to Shoreham with a load of tree nails for Stephen Bine for which I am to have 10s-6d. Clear'd accounts with Mr Benjamin Hayler. Will and Terry hay'd.

The 11th June 1720 Saturday. A very fine day.
The boys did severall jobbs, hay'd afternoon.
Will went to Broadwater Fair. Mrs Mary Whitpaine and her daughter here in the evning.
John Gilham and Richard Banks workt here ----- 2 days.

The 12th June 1720 Sunday. A showry day.
Mr William Martin preacht. We had a parish meeting about Jack Haslegrove and _____ I supt at Westtowne.

The 13th June 1720 Munday. A showry day.
Fetcht my Father and Mother Stone from Shermanbury Place. Din'd there. The boys did severall jobbs.
John Gilham and Richard Banks here --------- 3 days.

The 14th June 1720 Tuesday. A showry day.
Dick King and Terry carry'd 200 faggots. Smith hay'd etc. Gilham and Banks here -------- 4 days. My Wife and the children were at Thomas Norton's North End.

The 15th June 1720 Wednesday. A gloomy day.
The boys carry'd 300 faggots to my Father's, 100 to John Smith and 100 to William Roach. Mr William Martin here towards night, supt here. My Cousin John Lindfield, supt here, reckon'd with him and there is £13-13-6d due to me on the parish account. He paid me his intrest to Midsumer 1720.

The 16th June 1720 Thursday. A fine day, only rain towards night. The boys carry'd 2 loads of the Nine Acres and 4 of Tully's first field into Tully's rick steddle. Gilham and Banks here ---------- 5 days.
John Westover made me a new belly girt for the fore horse. I were a while at Mr Scutt's towards night. John Hart brought me 6 new tassels and a yard of fringe from Thomas Roberd's of Brighton.

The 17th June 1720 Fryday. A wet day. The boys carry'd John Smith 100 faggots, 400 in all. They fetch a load of sand out of the lane by Randiddle's ground. Smith went to Shermanbury and afterwards to Brighton to have a coller fitted to the blind mare but the fool sent him home again without doing anything to it. Gilham and Banks here --- 6 days. Ned Penfold workt here --- 1 day.

The 18th June 1720 Saturday. A gloomy morning, dry after. The boys helpt scour a pond at Rickman's, hay'd after. ~~Gilham and Banks here~~. Ned Penfold here 2 days.

The 19th June 1720 Sunday. A dry day.
Mr William Martin preacht. I were not at Church being very bad with the toothache. There was a meeting about the _____ . Mr Peter Courthope here towards night.

The 20th June 1720 Munday. A fine day. The boys carry'd 6 loads of the Rookwood to the horse rick. Old William Brand and his boys set up a broyler in the kitchen. Gilham and Banks made a hen coop for my Father ------------- 7 days. Ned Penfold here 3 days.

The 21st June 1720 Tuesday. A fine day, only a small showr at night. Carry'd 4 loads of the oat earsh at Rickman's. Paid John Gilham a guinea in full of all. Ned Penfold finisht my waistcoat ------- 4 days.

The 22nd June 1720 Wednesday. A very fine day. The boys finisht the Rookwood 4 loads, 10 in all and a small jobb of the Little Mead. George Buckwell here last night about the Goal Tax.

The 23rd June 1720 Thursday. A fine day. The boys carry'd 1 load of Tully's first field 5 in all and a load of Tully's field by the orchard. West's wife had 12lbs of cherrys at 4d per 1b.

The 24th June 1720 Fryday. A fine day.
Bought 5 of Stanmer lambs of William Scrase at the Fair at 4s per lamb for _____ . Mr Richard Whitpaine and I came home together. The boys workt 'till noon, went to the Fair after.

The 25th June 1720 Saturday. A very fine day.
The boys hay'd, cut Tully's rick in the morning. Will Baker helpt hay a while towards night. I were at Mrs Catherine Beard's a little while towards night. My Wife and Ned Terry went to Balcombe.

The 26th June 1720 Sunday. A very fine day.
Mr William Martin preacht and read the brief for Oksted church.    I was not at Church. My Cousin John Lindfield din'd here. My Cousin Thomas Norton North End, his wife and daughter, my Brother Peter here after evning prayr.

The 27th June 1720 Munday. A very fine, hot day.
The boys carry'd 7 loads to the fatting rick, all of the way mead and mead below.
Receiv'd £20 of Mrs Susan Courthope for which I gave her a note on Mr Wilkin for the same _____ .

The 28th June 1720 Tuesday. A very fine day.
Will not well. The boys gather'd cherrys in the forenoon, carry'd 2 loads of hay to John Smith after and one to the fatting rick all of the Edgly Mead. Mr Lintott etc came to my Father's. Lent Mr Ralph Beard 20 guineas for a note of his hand. West's wife had 64lbs of heart cherrys and 10lbs of other.

The 29th June 1720 Wednesday. A showry forenoon, dry after. Dick King and Smith fetcht 1000 brick from Taylor's for my Father. I din'd at my Father's with Dr Lintott. I supt at Westtowne with Dr Lintott, my Father etc. John Smith fetcht a runt at 20d per nail.

The 30th June 1720 Thursday. A very fine day.
The boys carry'd 1 load of hay to John Smith and 2 to John Bodle.

The first July 1720 Fryday. A fine day. Dr Lintott and his wife din'd here and Mr Richard Whitpaine, his wife and daughter etc. Dr Lintott went home. Turn'd the sucking cow out of the dairy. Weigh'd the runt at John Smith's 58 nail 4lbs the 4 quarters at 20d per lb. Goody West had 8lbs of cherrys.

The 2nd July 1720 Saturday. A fine day. I went to Lewis with my Wife, Mrs Wicks and Jo Wood.
Clear'd accounts with Norman and Mr Michelbourne. The boys carry'd 5 loads of the Edgly Mead to the fatting rick.    I din'd at Dr White's with Mr Board of Lindfield. I talkt with Mr Sixsmith at the Starr. Clear'd accounts with Mr Andrew Laurence.

The 3rd July 1720 Sunday. A fine day.
Mr William Martin preacht. We had a parish meeting. I din'd at my Father's with Mr Richard Whitpaine and his wife Mary and daughter. Dick Smith had the old horse to Dr White's.

The 4th July 1720 Munday. A fine day. The boys fetcht a load of sand to pave my Father's causey and carry'd 3 loads of the Edgly Mead to the fatting ricks. Clear'd accounts with John Westover and Richard Wood.
Dr White, his sister and daughters din'd here. The Dr and I were at Edgly and at John Stone's to see horses. We went after to Mr Osbourne's. The Dr went thence home.

The 5th July 1720 Tuesday. A showry day.
Mrs Agnes White and her niece lay here last night.

Din'd and went to Danny. Young George Hill fetcht 30 lambs and a tagg. Receiv'd of him £16. The boys and Old Dick Banks carry'd a load of hay to the fatting rick and one to the horses rick of the Edgly Mead. My Aunt Holden and Cousin Hayne here afternoon. Ned Penfold workt here to day and yesterday.

The 6th July 1720 Wednesday. A wet day The boys did severall jobbs and carry'd 100 faggots to John Gun. Mr Norden's son and John Lindfield jr here afternoon. Ned Penfold here ---------- 3 days.
Mr Richard Whitpaine here a while towards night. Mrs Catherine Beard and her mother supt here with the Mrs Whites.

The 7th July 1720 Thursday. A dry, windy day. The boys hay'd part of the day and mow'd weeds etc. My Wife, the Mrs Whites and I supt at Mrs Bea were at *(Ed: xxx text deleted xxx)* Mr Norden supt at Mrs Catherine Beard's. Paid William Wickham half a guinea for 15 snag bells, I am to have 3s again.

The 8th July 1720 Fryday. A dry, windy day.
I carry'd 2800 tree nails to Shoreham for Stephen Bine. Paid Richard Smith 3s for 4 bushels of seacoals. Will and Old Dick Banks carry'd 3 loads of the Edgly Mead into Tully's rick steddle. The Mrs Whites and my Wife din'd at Danny and they went thence home.
Mr Richard Barcroft and his sister came in the evning.

The 9th July 1720 Saturday. A wet forenoon, dry after. Mr Richard Barcroft, his sister, Bett and I were at Rickman's. Reckon'd with Mr Richard Barcroft and clear'd accounts to Lady Day 1720. Paid him £8-12s. My Brother James Ede here a while in the forenoon. Receiv'd £7-6s of Thomas Champion and outset £6 for half a year's annuity to my Aunt Holden, £1-13s for half a year's Land Tax and 1s for a River Tax, in all £15 for half a year's rent for Eastout, due at Michaelmas last past. The annuity also due at Michaelmas last. Sold John Smith my 4 cows which I bought of my Lord Dennet, a steer runt and a cow of Will's at 18d per nail reckoning five quarters as usual. Receiv'd 8 runts from my Cousin John Lindfield at £7-15s which he bought for me at Horsham Fair.

The 10th July 1720 Sunday. A fine day.
Mr William Martin preacht, no service afternoon. Mr Richard Barcroft went to Church.

The 11th July 1720 Munday. A fine day.
Mr Richard Barcroft and his sister went away.
The boys carry'd 5 loads of Edgly Mead, 25 in all. My Wife and John Kneller went to Lewis. I were at Mrs Catherine Beard's afternoon.

The 12th July 1720 Tuesday. A fine day, wet towards night. The boys hay'd at Rickman's in the morning, carry'd 3 loads of the [p......] to the lean oxen's rick afternoon. My Mother Stone and my Wife reckon'd. Paid George West 6s. Turn'd 20 ewes into Tully's lower field. Sold John Smith the steer runt (one of the late bargain) £5-5s, he drove him away to day. Paid John Pierce 20s for my Window Tax at Dick Wood's.

The 13th July 1720 Wednesday. A dry day. The boys cut the fatting rick and carry'd 1 load of the dry pond to the oxen's rick, 4 in all. Ned Terry sick afternoon. My Sister Ann Box here afternoon.

The 14th July 1720 Thursday. A fine day, wet towards night. The boys tipt the horse's rick and carry'd 3 loads of hay of the sedge at Rickman's. Frank Holden here in the evning.
Paid Stephen Avery of Lewis 20s in exchange for an other saddle. I had a bridle with the new saddle.

The 15th July 1720 Fryday. A dry day. The boys carry'd 3 loads at Rickman's. My Wife, Kitt Ede and I went to Lindfield, I bought a payr of stockens for my self at 4s. Paid my Brother John Courtness £2-11-6d for things for Molly Balcomb. Bought severall other things. We are to settle the accounts to morrow, he is to come to Hurst. I were at W Brett's after black cherry trees, he not at home. John Haslegrove begun pull my flax yesterday at 6s per acre, his sister and Goody Keg helpt him.

The 16th July 1720 Saturday. A gloomy morning, fine after. The boys carry'd the rest of the sedge at Rickman's, 8 loads in all etc. Mr Jeremiah Dodson din'd here, Mr John Hart here after. Paid Mr Dodson 13s-8d in full for things from Mr [B..............].
My Unkle Richard Turner and Aunt Sarah *(Ed: née Chatfield)* here to buy the Rusper liveing. Paid my Cousin John Marchant £9-11-4d for the Land Tax. Jack Haslegrove and his company made an end of pulling my flax. My Brother John Courtness here but (haveing company) we did not settle the account between us. Receiv'd the 20 guineas of Mr Beard which I lent him.

The 17th July 1720 Sunday. A fine day.
Mr William Martin preacht. My Cousin John Lindfield and his wife Elizabeth din'd and supt here. Receiv'd 50s of William Charman for half a year's rent for Henfield windmill due at Midsumer 1719.

The 18th July 1720 Munday. A fine day.
The boys hay'd in Tully's Mead. George Buckwell and his boy set up a horse gate at Rickman's.
Paid Mrs Anne Beard 4s-6d for Molly Balcomb's schooling between Lady Day last and Midsumer last.
Receiv'd 2 guineas of John Bodle for a load of hay.

The 19th July 1720 Tuesday. A fine day, rain towards night. The boys carry'd 6 loads of Tully's Mead. John Smith here towards night. I talkt with my Cousin Thomas Norton of Edgly again and he consented that I should set up the child's seat again, allowing him just half what the seat was made longer. I sent Dr John Budgen ½lb of tobacco per William Norton. Paid Mr Bartholomew 5s a Munday for his boy's work.

The 20th July 1720 Wednesday. A dry day.
The boys carry'd Old Kester a load of hay out of Tully's Mead and one to the rick at the lower side of the mead and 2 loads of the barne field at Rickman's. Molly Balcomb went to Henfield Fair.

The 21st July 1720 Thursday. A gloomy day.
The boys carry'd an other load of Tully's Mead to Kester's and a load to the rick as yesterday; fetcht home 50 faggots.

The 22nd July 1720 Fryday. A wet day. The boys did some pbbs etc. R Smith had the blind mare (she being horseing) to the dun horse at Gline. I talkt with Thomas Norton of Edgly again and he refus'd to let me set up the seat as I desir'd. I proposed an exchange of seats with my Unkle Courtness of which he desir'd to consider. John Gilham and his man here ----- 1 day.

The 23rd July 1720 Saturday. A wet day. The boys cut pease some part of the day. Clear'd out the garret etc. John Gilham and his man here ---------- 2 days.
We went up to the Church but did nothing. Receiv'd 23s of Stephen Bine for 2 purneys to Shoreham.

The 24th July 1720 Sunday. A gloomy day.
Mr William Martin preacht. My Wife and I supt at Mrs Catherine Beard's. Mrs Barbara Campion here a while after evning prayr.

The 25th July 1720 Munday. A gloomy day.
The boys cut pease and hay'd. Ned Penfold was here. Will not well. John Gilham and his man here ---- 3 days.
I was at Mr Jeremiah Dodson's in the evning.

The 26th July 1720 Tuesday. A dry day.
Mr Jeremiah Dodson breakfasted here, we went up to the Church and he consented that I should set up a seat for Thomas Norton in his chancell. Paid Mr Dodson 23s-8d for part of his old pump at 12s-6d per _____ .
Lent him 3 guineas for a note of his hand. We din'd at Westtowne together. The boys carry'd 4 loads of Tully's Mead.

The 27th July 1720 Wednesday. A fine day. The boys carry'd    loads of Tully's Mead, in all 22 loads and one load of the Little Mead to James Holden.
Richard Lashmer helpt the afternoon and his girl.
Bought 2 piggs of Jo Picket at 22s, he to bring 'em home. Mr Richard Whitpaine and his wife Mary din'd here. Paid my Brother John Courtness 2 guineas.
He and his wife Betty (Ed: TM's sister) here.
Paid John Haslegrove 6s for drawing    acre of my flax and 6s-6d for Will's. John Gilham, his father and Dick Banks made an end of reaping Will's wheat.

The 28th July 1720 Thursday. A very fine day.
John Marchant of Lox buried. He died a Sunday morning. I were at the funeral, my part of the family of Fulkin were here after they came from Church. Receiv'd £9 of Harry Courtness on Mr Jeremiah Dodson's bill of return. The boys carry'd a load of the Little Meads to a rick at Tully's and a load to the lean oxen's rick. They also carry'd Tully's flax 2 loads. Richard Lashmer workt till noon.

The 29th July 1720 Fryday. A fine day. The boys etc begun a rick in the Fifteen Acres, carry'd 4 loads of Tully's pease etc. Richard Lashmer helpt all day, his girl above ½ and Towner ½. John Pecket brought home the 2 piggs bought a Wednesday. Paid him 22s for 'em by my Wife.

The 30th July 1720 Saturday. A fine day. The boys and Towner carry'd Rickman's wheat, 8 small loads and 4 loads to the 15 Acre rick. The mowers helpt.

I were at Lewis at Dr White's etc. Paid J S Tourl 8s in full and Norman in full. Talkt with Mr Mitchell the attorney. Carry'd Stephen Avery the last saddle due to him in exchange and an old one to cover. George Courtness went with me, I gave him a comon prayr book at 3s. Mr Mitchell promis'd to get the faculty I desir'd ____ 2 guineas at most. Paid Thomas Friend 7s-6d for 1¼ yards of cloath for a saddle cloath for my self and in full for all due. Left my wive's side saddle cloath at Stephen Avery's.

The 31st July 1720 Sunday. A fine day.
Mr William Martin preacht. Stephen Bine call'd a meeting about an indictment with which Henry Scrase threaten'd the parish.

The 1st August 1720 Munday. A gloomy hot day, some raine towards night. The reapers begun by Burt's. The boys carry'd 2 small loads of hay out of the brook meads at Rickman's and 4 out of the Little Meads at home to the oxen's rick. Towner helpt. Lent Young John Marchant of Lox £100 of Molly Balcomb's mony for six months at £4-10s per cent per annum. Mr John Hart and Sarah Packham witnesses. Lent Mr Richard Whitpaine £8 for a note of his hand. My Unkle Richard Turner and Aunt Sarah here towards night. I was with Mr Jeremiah Dodson in the morning and with Mr Beard atimes. Lent Mr Dodson the blind mare to carry John Shave to the assizes. Paid Susan Bradford 14s for a pound of bohea and 6d for her day's work. She hay'd. Receiv'd a letter from John Brand from Lisbon with an account of wines and tobacco sent to London for me, for which I am to pay Old William Brand when I have receiv'd the goods. Paid for 12lb of tire for Molly Balcomb, 14s her grandmother promis'd to spin some of it. Paid Towner 3s-6d in full of all. _____ spinning the other 4lb at 14d per lb, 4s-8d her grandmother spun but 6 lb.

The 2nd August 1720 Tuesday. A wet forenoon.
The boys clean'd oates and carry'd two quarter to Mr Burry's which he promis'd to carry to Shoreham for me tomorrow. I were at Mr Burry's, Wanbarrow, Westtowne and Mr Scutt.
The smallpox came out on Mr Jeremiah Dodson's man and he was mov'd to Broadwater towards night.

The 3rd August 1720 Wednesday. A gloomy dry day.
The boys carry'd 2 loads of the Little Meads to the lean oxen's rick etc. Mr Burry's man carry'd my oates to Shoreham 1 quarter to Mr Bridger and 1 quarter to Mr Tenner, brought me 32s for 'em. My Brother Will here in the evning.

The 4th August 1720 Thursday. A dry day.
The boys cut the oxen's rick stirr'd flax, hay'd etc. Mr Jeremiah Dodson din'd and supt here, I were at his house afternoon with John Box sr and Goodman Young. Mr Dodson bargain'd with Young for a month from Munday next. Young to find 3 horses and their harness, to go with them himself at £5-10s. Mr Dodson to board him and his horses. Receiv'd the 3 guineas of Mr Dodson lent him some time ago.

The 5th August 1720 Fryday. A wet day. The boys carry'd 2 loads of oaken roots to Stephen Reeve at 10s per load. John Gilham and his man workt the afternoon on the seat for Thomas Norton ------- 3½ days.

The 6th August 1720 Saturday. A very wet day.
The boys took up the season'd boards in the garrett by their chamber door and laid down green ones in their room etc. My Cousin John Lindfield din'd and supt here. John Smith here in the afternoon, he bought 3 cows of my Cousin John Lindfield at £17-10s and sold him a saddle at 15s. Left £17 to pay for the cows. Receiv'd a letter from Mr Woodcock.

The 7th August 1720 Sunday. A showry day.
Mr William Martin preacht we had a parish meeting. Lost a Ewe last night.

The 8th August 1720 Munday. A showry day.
Will and Terry mow'd oates at Tully's. Dick King fetcht 2 deals from Brighton. Tom Greenfield 2 more. Bought of Derrick Pain at 18d per deal. Thomas Stone paid for 'em. Smith carry'd 4lb of loaf sugar to my Cousin John Lindfield at 8d per lb. I supt at Westtowne. I wrote to Mr Woodcock per post. Borrow'd or bought my Fathers syth.

The 9th August 1720 Tuesday. A fine day.
The boys cut the 15 Acre rick and afterwards turn'd flax, hay'd and Will and Terry mow'd.

The 10th August 1720 Wednesday. A showry day about noon. Dr White here to see Kitty. She sick. The boys carry'd a load of hay of the Little Meads and went to Rickman's to take up Will's flax, not dry, turn'd the Nine

Acres oats after. Goodman Oliver here. Agreed for Daniel Bide at 6d per day when I want him.

The 11th August 1720 Thursday. A fine day.
The boys carry'd 6 loads of the wheat per Burt's, Will's flax 2 loads and the head land of pease in the Bankfield. Mr Pain jr of Lewis, Mr Beard and my Cousin Peter Marchant din'd here. Paid George West 10s and John Gun had a bushel of oats.

The 12th August 1720 Fryday. A wet day.
Receiv'd a cask of red wine from Mr Woodcock at London, sent from Lisbon by John Brand and 8lb of tobacco for Dr John Budgen, both per Smither. There is about half a hogs head of the wine. I were at Mr Scutt's towards night, Mr John Hart sick.
Smith went to Dr Tabor for him on the blind mare. The boys did severall jobbs, carry'd the few oats in the pea field, 2 small jobbs in the morning. John Smith kill'd the heifer's calf at 14s.

The 13th August 1720 Saturday. A very wet forenoon, showry after. The boys mow'd oates at Rickman's afternoon. I were to see Mr John Hart afternoon, he sick.

The 14th August 1720 Sunday. A dry day.
Mr William Martin preacht, no service afternoon. My Cousin John Lindfield and his wife Elizabeth din'd here.

The 15th August 1720 Munday. A dry day. The boys made an end of mowing Will's oates, carry'd 2 loads of wheat by Burt's and one of the Churchfield. Receiv'd £11 of young George Hill, he drew 17 ewes and 2 lambs.

The 16th August 1720 Tuesday. A dry day.
The boys mow'd barly by Wickham's and carry'd 2 loads of the Churchfield wheat and one by Burt's. My Wife, William Baker, George Courtness and I went to Lewis afternoon, paid Mr Court 6s-8d for 4 doz of pint bottles. Chang'd a payr of gloves with Thomas Friend. Borrow'd an Act of Parliament etc of Mr Norman. Paid William Baker 6d for his journey.

The 17th August 1720 Wednesday. A wet day.
The boys mow'd by Wickham's part of the day. Will went to Wanbarrow afternoon, brought home a young lamb. I were with Goodman Towner towards night, he sick. Thomas Hamper here in the evning, askt 25s to do Cousin John Lindfield's seat. Will Lindfield here with a letter about the seat.

The 18th August 1720 Thursday. A fine day 'till towards night. The boys mow'd barly in the forenoon, carry'd two loads of the Winter oats after to Tully.
Return'd Norman's Act of Parliament per Rick Wood jr.

The 19th August 1720 Fryday. A fine day 'till towards night. Thomas White begun reap at noon at 8d per day. I found a hare in John Gun's room, he [thatcht]. Will and the boys mow'd etc.

The 20th August 1720 Saturday. A fine day.
The boys and Dick Hart made an end of the field by Wickham's and carry'd 4 loads of the Nine Acres oates Thomas Smith, Will Baker and others helpt bear on.

The 21st August 1720 Sunday. A fine day. Mr John Hart and Mr William Martin preacht. My Cousin John Lindfield din'd here. I were at Westtowne towards night.

The 22nd August 1720 Munday. A fine day.
The boys etc carry'd 7 load's of oates and 4 small loads of the Churchfield wheat. Dick Hart workt here in the forenoon and Dick King and he went to carry John Hart's wheat afternoon. John Westover, William Baker, Thomas Roach, Thomas Greenfield, Thomas Picknall sr and Ned Burt helpt. Mr Libbard of Chichester came afternoon. Mr Richard Whitpaine here afternoon.
My Wife was to see John Towner in the evning.

The 23rd August 1720 Tuesday. A gloomy day, hot and dry. Will mow'd. My Cousin Libbard lay here last night, went home to day. The boys and Dick Hart carry'd four loads the last of the Winter oates, in all 17 loads. Carry'd 2 great loads of the Churchfield wheat into the barly barne and a load of the field by Burt's, 15 in all. Paid Thomas Hamper 12s-11d for his own and his man's work (3 days wanting an hour) for the seat in the chancel for my Cousin Thomas Norton and materials, part of the materials I mean. I din'd at Westtowne with Mr Wilkin, Mr Beard, Mr William Martin and Mr John Hart. Mr Wilkin, Mr Jeremiah Dodson and Mr Beard supt here. Paid Mr Dodson 11s-4d for bread and wine for Whitsuntide and Trinity Sunday.

The 24th August 1720 Wednesday. Very wet day.
The boys and Richard Hart cut the mows at Tully's, a little above half the day. Weigh'd a runt cow at John

Smith's 46 nail 6lb at 10d per nail. Spent 6d at the Swan with John Smith. Mr Beard had his bridle again per Thomas Beard.

The 25th August 1720 Thursday. A dry day.
The boys mow'd and carry'd 2 loads of the Churchfield wheat into the great barne. William and Sam Jarvice made up the pavement in the Church near ½ a day. Mrs. Courthope here afternoon. Old William Brand here. Mr Picknall of Arundell here in the evning. Paid the cooper for hooping.

The 26th August 1720 Fryday. A gloomy dry day.
The boys and Dick Hart mow'd and carry'd 2 loads of the Churchfield, in all 17 loads. I were at Westtowne in the morning. Mr William Martin and Brother Peter here in the evning. Paid Dick Lashmer 3s-6d in full. I think 'twas a Thursday last. Lent Mr Richard Whitpaine eight sacks a Wednesday per Crooked Stool.

The 27th August 1720 Saturday. A gloomy day.
Dick King and 3 horses workt for John Hart. Will made an end of mowing barly. Afterwards he, Dick King and Dick Hart carry'd 2 loads of Tully's wheat. Dick Hart came about 3 aclock afternoon. Mr Richard Whitpaine supt and spent the evning here.

The 28th August 1720 Sunday. A showry day.
Mr William Martin preacht. I supt and spent the evning at Mrs Catherine Beard's.

The 29th August 1720 Munday. A gloomy day.
The boys cut a rick in the morning. Carry'd 2 loads of Tully's wheat after. Goodman White and his son John reapt afternoon. Richard Hart reapt afternoon. The post brought news that Mr Henry Campion was come to London. My Wife and Mrs Mary Whitpaine at Danny afternoon.

The 30th August 1720 Tuesday. A very fine day.
The reapers made an end about 3 aclock. John White reapt in Banks's roome about 4 hours he being sick. The boys cut the rick in Tully's Mead, carry'd 1 load of Tully's wheat. Carry'd 4 loads of Tully's oates. Goodman White and his daughter cockt part of William's oates afternoon. Abraham Muzzall turn'd barly and bore on oats. Dick Hart helpt from 10 aclock.

The 31st August 1720 Wednesday. A fine day.
Carry'd William's oates, 5 loads. Carry'd the rest of Tully's oates, 2 Jarvices, William Baker, Jack White and Thomas White.

The 1st September 1720 Thursday. A fine forenoon, showry after. My Cousin John Lindfield sent me a teem to help in with my barly and 6 people with it. Will Baker the 2 Jarvices, John and Thomas White, John Pierce, John Gun, George West. Daniel Bide and our own people carry'd 12 loads of the barly by Towners, the last of the field 15 loads in all. Carry'd also 2 loads of the Bankfield barly. I talkt with Mr Jeremiah Dodson and Mr Richard Whitpaine. Paid John Snashall jr 1s for bleeding me.

The 2nd September 1720 Fryday. A fine day.
Made an end of harvest, all but the Hayselcroft barly. John White, Thomas White, John Pierce, Abraham Muzzall, William Baker, the 2 Jarvices. My Cousin John Lindfield's people etc helpt. Carry'd 10 loads more of the Bankfield, in all 12 loads. Carry'd also 4 small loads of the Hayselcroft into Mr Richard Whitpaine's rick house barne. Paid John White 8s in full for his work.

The 3rd September 1720 Saturday. A very fine day.
Will, Smith and Terry carry'd the rest of the Hayselcroft, 4 jobbs, 8 in all. William Jarvice helpt in the afternoon. Richard King sick. Mr Henry Campion came home this evning about 9, haveing been gone from Danny five years and six weeks. Mr William Martin, Mr Beard, Mr Richard Whitpaine, Mr Scutt and Stephen Bine went part of the way to London to meet him.

The 4th September 1720 Sunday. A fine day.
Mr William Martin preacht. My Cousins Susan and Sarah Lindfield din'd here. Brother Peter and Goodman White here towards night.

The 5th September 1720 Munday. A fine day.
The boys fetcht the spoil'd hay, 2 loads out of the Little Mead etc. Thomas Hamper mended the horse dill My Brother Will and Cousin John Lindfield here towards night. Dick Wood mov'd 13 shoees on the cart horses and mended the iron of the horse dill.

The 6th September 1720 Tuesday. A fine day. The boys fetcht home wood and faggots. Carry'd 10 bales and 50 of the coppice faggots to Old Dick Banks's. I were at Sander Bridges's to see a large cistern. I bid him 18d per bushel he askt 2 guineas by the [lump] or 2s per bushel.

The 7th September 1720 Wednesday. A fine day.
The boys carry's 15½ bushels of pares to the post woman's at Brighton and 7 bushels of my Father's, all at 16d per bushel. Derrick Pain of Brighton offer'd me two hundred of 10 foot deal, six score to the hundred, at £7 per hundred. Receiv'd £5-4s of Henry Dubbins, 6s before of Thomas Stone, all in full for a runt.
Paid Thomas Ridge 13s-6d for 3 bushels of salt.

The 8th September 1720 Thursday. A fine day.
Will and Smith begun stir Tully's pease earsh. Dick King and Terry carry'd faggots. Mr Jeremiah Dodson and Mr Sixsmith din'd here. Mr Dodson and I were at Danny in the evning. Daniel Bide made an end of working here.

The 9th September 1720 Fryday. A wet day. The boys made an end of the faggot stack and cut mows at Rickman's. Will went to coursing. Paid George West 11s-11¾d and clear'd accounts. I were at Stephen Bine's in the evning. Paid John Bodle 5s for a store ewe lamb. Sent 3 todd and 20lb of wool to Bernard Heasman's of Cuckfield per Smith at a guinea per todd.

The 10th September 1720 Saturday. A showry day.
The boys clear'd Tully's and Rickman's floors. Will and Smith plough'd. Mr John Hart and Mr Beard here in the evning. Lent Mrs Wicks my horse to ride to Lewis.

The 11th September 1720 Sunday. A fine day.
Mr William Martin preacht. My Cousin John Lindfield and Brother Peter here afternoon.

The 12th September 1720 Munday. A dry day.
Will and Dick King plough'd. Terry and Smith did severall jobbs. Thomas Hamper workt here mending the dog kennel ---- 1 day. Paid John Gun 4s. Dr Nick Plaw here to see a cow.

The 13th September 1720 Tuesday. A fine day.
Dick King and Terry plough'd. Will went to coursing. Smith and S Peckham hay'd afternoon at Rickman's. I wrote to Mr Bernard Heasman per Nan Surgeant. Thomas Hamper here, built a little house for the children ----- 2 days.

The 14th September 1720 Wednesday. A fine day.
Dick King and Smith fetcht 22cwt of wet cole from Shoreham for Harry Wickham. Terry gather'd a tree of pares at Rickman's etc. I were at Mr Osbourne's of Newtimber, he not at home. I spoke to his wife for the farme. Will went to coursing with his Unkle William.

The 15th September 1720 Thursday. A fine day.
Ned Terry mow'd clover afternoon. Smith turn'd grass at Rickman's afternoon. Dick King carry'd my Wife etc to Dean House in the waggon, from thence to the Fair. I din'd there. Will went to Slough Green with birds.

The 16th September 1720 Fryday. A very fine day.
The boys hay'd at Rickman's. I were at Mr Jeremiah Dodson's in the evning and at Mr Scutt's.
Paid Mrs Catherine Beard 9s-6d in full of all accounts.

The 17th September 1720 Saturday. A gloomy morning, fine after. The boys and John Gun carry'd 4 loads of hay at Rickman's. I din'd at Mr Osbourne's of Newtimber with Mr Jeremiah Dodson, Mr Osbourne of Poynings and Mr Charles Osbourne. Dick King and George West carry'd 10 loads of Towne dirt. Bought one hundred weight of hops of Mr Osbourne, Mr Richard Whitpaine to set the price. William Norton here. He paid my Wife 33s from Dr John Budgen for tobacco.

The 18th September 1720 Sunday. A fine day.
Mr William Martin preacht. My Cousin John Lindfield here after evning prayr. Goodman Stenning of Westminstone here. He promis'd to come to work between this and the first of November.

The 19th September 1720 Munday. A fine day.
Will, the boys etc ended haying at Rickman's. Carry'd three loads. Brought home a jobb of Will's flax. Sold John Smith two cows to be kill'd before Xmas, £12. Dick King carry'd 6 loads of Towne dirt.
Paid William Baker 5s-6d in full for harvesting.

The 20th September 1720 Tuesday. A gloomy day, wet towards night. Will Jarvice and Samuel Terry etc gather'd apples. Dick King carry'd 7 loads of Towne dirt. Will went to coursing.

The 21st September 1720 Wednesday. A fine day.
My Wife, Will, Jacky etc at Lewis Fair. Cattle very dear. Ewes sold at 10s. Paid Avery 5s for a whip. Will.
Paid Court 16d for a pad lock.

The 22nd September 1720 Thursday. A fine day.
The boys carry'd a load of stubble and gather'd apples.

I were at Danny after Mr Burry. The 2 Jarvices gather'd apples. Turn'd 2 steers to the fatting oxen.

The 23rd September 1720 Fryday. A fine day.
Carry'd the clover in the Nine Acres, 6 loads and 2 loads of Tully's first field. Richard White and his sons and daughter and Thomas Gravet pick't _____ . Paid Jack White 9d for his afternoon's work. I were at Westtowne in the morning. Receiv'd my 2 guineas of _____ . Will, John Smith and Mr Burry went up the hill to my ewes for me. They bought 50 ewes and a ram of Mr John Penfold of Broadwater at 10s a piece and 20 for Mrs Catherine Beard. John Smith paid for them.

The 24th September 1720 Saturday. A fine day. The boys carry'd a load of roots to Old Dick Banks's, brought home Will's flax, carry'd a load of wood to my Father's etc. Thomas Jacket's wife and daughter, three of Dick Wood's girls, Ned Botting and George West spread flax afternoon. Receiv'd £8 of Mrs Mary Whitpaine due to me on a note. Mr William Martin and John Smith here in the evning.

The 25th September 1720 Sunday. A gloomy day.
Mr William Martin preacht. I were not at Church in the forenoon. Mrs Barbara Campion, Mrs Courthope and Mrs Mary Whitpaine here towards night.

The 26th September 1720 Munday. A fine day.
Dick King harrow'd with the ox harrow. Flax laid out as a Saturday. Paid my Brother Henry Faulkoner a year's intrest due, I think, about the beginning of August last. Terry threw over wood etc. My Wife, my Father and I din'd at Shermanbury. I carry'd them a hare. Yesterday was a Sennight Thomas Barber of Park Farm drown'd himself in the river just by Windham bridge.

The 27th September 1720 Tuesday. A dry day.
The boys harrow'd, rol'd and gather'd pares. I were at Shoreham market receiv'd 34s of Mr Friend for two bushels of clover seed. Call'd at Sadlescombe with Mr Friend there was Mr Turner and Mr Cockersum. Paid my Sister Sarah £12 per Willy.

The 28th September 1720 Wednesday. A dry day.
Will and Smith plough'd. Dick King and Terry carry'd a load of wood to my Father's and an other to the school etc. Clear'd accounts with Thomas Smith and Kester for hay. Harry Wickham and John Westover here. Kester, I think, and Thomas Smith here after.

The 29th September 1720 Thursday. A wet day.
I went to Stenning Fair. Bought six steer runts of Meredith Bowen at £19-15s. and a cow runt of an other man at 50s. Sent an empty hogshead to Mr Osbourne's per Ned Terry to be fill'd with hops.

The 30th September 1720 Fryday. A gloomy morning, fine after. Dick King and Smith plough'd.
Will and Terry tipt ricks etc. Paid Elie Towner a bill of 4s-4d for Molly Balcomb. Mr William Martin and I collected a brief about the Towne. Receiv'd the 32s of Mr Beard per my Wife for sheep. John Hart here in the evning. My Cousin John Lindfield din'd here.
Paid Molly Balcomb 2s towards her 2d per week for spending mony for this year.

The 1st October 1720 Saturday. A wet day.
The boys plough'd in the morning, cut the barly mow at Brickhouse after. Will went to coursing. Mr William Martin and my Brother Will here towards night. Paid Brother John Courtness a guinea in full of a bill of £3-0s-1½d. He din'd here.
Agreed with Mr Jeremiah Dodson yesterday for the Hayselcroft next year to sow flax. If I have a crop I am to give him 55s per acre, if not, I am to give but 50.

The 2nd October 1720 Sunday. A dry day.
Mr William Martin preacht. We had a parish meeting as usual. I supt at Mr Scutt's. Allow'd the Widdow Heath 4s per month from this time. Paid Mr Woodcock's bill for my duty etc of my claret.

The 3rd October 1720 Munday. A gloomy morning fine after. Dick King and Smith plough'd.
Will and Terry tipt the 15 Acre rick, turn'd clover etc. Receiv'd a letter from Mr Colbron per post. Mr Scutt, Mr Woodcock, Mr Randall, Mr John Hart and my Father supt and spent the evning here.

The 4th October 1720 Tuesday. A gloomy day.
Will and Smith made an end of stirring Tully's long field. Dick King ground pares in the morning. Afterwards Smith and he fetch us a jobb of my flax from Tully's. Paid Dick Wood bill to Michaelmas. I were at some of the houses in the North End for a brief. Ned Terry fetcht Mrs Colbron from Brighton.

The 5th October 1720 Wednesday. A wet forenoon, dry after. The boys did severall jobbs. Mr Colbron came towards night. My Father and Mother Stone here.

The 6th October 1720 Thursday. A dry day 'till towards night. The boys did severall jobbs, carry'd a load of wood to my Father's. Mr Colbron and his wife etc din'd at my Father's. Will went to coursing. Ned Botten here.

The 7th October 1720 Fryday. A dry day, the wind exceeding high. Will and Dick King begun plough the Nine Acres. Terry, Smith and Ned Botten turn'd clover etc. Mrs Catherine Beard and her mother here afternoon. Mr Richard Whitpaine spent the evning here. Paid George West 5s. Mr Colbron went home this morning.

The 8th October 1720 Saturday. A dry day 'till towards night. Will and Dick King plough'd. and sow'd. Smith harrow'd. Old Dick Banks turn'd flax an hour. Brought a large copper drinking pot of my Unkle Courtness for which I am to fetch his hops from John Peckham, or to do half a crowns worth of work more with my teem, in all 5s-7d.

The 9th October 1720 Sunday. A fine day.
My Unkle Richard Turner buried at Ditcheling, died last Sunday. Mr Ivers preacht his funeral sermon. I were at the funeral. *(Ed: Richard Turner of Oldland buried in front of altar in Ditchling church)*
Mr William Martin preacht at Hurst.

The 10th October 1720 Munday. A fine day.
Will and Dick King plough'd. Terry, Smith, Botten and John Gun turn'd flax mended gaps etc. My Wife and Mrs Colbron went to Danny afternoon.

The 11th October 1720 Tuesday. A fine day, rain towards night. Kitt Ede, Bett and I went to Shoreham.
Paid Mr Sleech 10s-6d for a ladder pole. Mr Ben Hayler was with me. Mr Hayler promis'd to take care of the pole and, Mr John Friend of Portslade promis'd to bring it to John Peckham's. My Cousin John Libbard of Chichester came hither. Will and Dick King plough'd. Terry and Smith helpt John Gun and Ned Botten helpt gather stubble etc. George Hill's son here to mark the sheep.

The 12th October 1720 Wednesday. A wet day 'till towards night Will and Dick King plough'd allmost 'till noon. Terry, ~~King and~~ Botten and Smith helpt winnow etc. Dick King and Smith carry'd a load of wood to my Father. Thomas Surgeant and William Nicholas made syder for my Father. Ned Penfold workt here.
Mr Colbron came towards night. My Brother John Box here in the evning. I gave him a receit for Mr Farncomb for a year's intrest and took a receit of him.

The 13th October 1720 Thursday. A wet day.
Dick King and Smith carry'd 2 loads of wood to my Father's and one to the school. Terry cut wheat mow. My Cousin John Libbard went home after dinner.
My Father and Mr John Hart din'd here. Will went to Slough Green. Paid Taylor the 10s for 1000 bricks for the causey at my Father's. Paid Parker 11s for a load of lime.

The 14th October 1720 Fryday. A fine day.
Mr Colbron and his wife went home. I din'd at my Father's with Mr Colbron etc. Will and Dick King plough'd. Terry helpt Banks in the morning, went home with Mrs Colbron afternoon.

The 15th October 1720 Saturday. A fine day.
Will and Dick King plough'd. Smith and Terry helpt winnow the cutting of the wheat mows, 2½ bushels. Turn'd and took up flax after.
Receiv'd a letter from Mr Richard Barcroft per post.

The 16th October 1720 Sunday. A fine day. Mr John Hart preacht. I were not at Church. John Smith's bitch bitt one of my piggs that we were forc'd to kill it. My Cousin John Lindfield and Brother Peter supt here.

The 17th October 1720 Munday. A fine day.
The boys plough'd etc. I were at Wanbarrow to look on his turnips. Took up and carry'd Will's flax.

The 18th October 1720 Tuesday. A dry day.
The boys sow'd and harrow'd in the Nine Acres. Terry and Botten turn'd clover. Dr Nick Plaw here, drencht and bleeded my calves, they being almost spoil'd with eating clover. I were at the Swan with my Father and Mr Arnold of Horsham, about the Rusper liveing.

The 19th October 1720 Wednesday. A dry day.
They made an end of ploughing the Nine Acres. Terry, Smith and Botting helpt Banks winnow 9 bushels wheat. Smith and I fetcht some turnips from Wanbarrow.

The 20th October 1720 Thursday. Dry morning, very wet after. Will and Dick King begun ridge Tully's long field. Lost one of my calves last night. Dick King and Smith and John Gun win'd my flax afternoon, 9½ bushels. Dick Wood shoo'd the cart horses 5 new shooes and 10 removes. The white pigg from Peckett went to hog yesterday.

The 21st October 1720 Fryday. A dry day.
Will and Dick King plough'd. Terry and Smith helpt John Gun winnow flax etc. Nick Plaw here about William Balcomb's account. Lost an other calf. I had a quarter of bief of John Smith at 17d per nail.

The 22nd October 1720 Saturday. A fine day.
Will went to coursing. The boys carry'd dung for the garden, carry'd my Unkle Courtness's hops and a load of the seed clover. Mr Henry Campion and Mr Beard spent the evning here. Ned Terry carry'd the other calves skin to the tanner.

The 23rd October 1720 Sunday. A fine day.
Mr William Martin preacht. I were not at Church in the forenoon. Molly Balcomb came home from Dean House.

The 24th October 1720 Munday. A gloomy day.
John Gun made an end of sowing the Nine Acres. Terry harrow'd. Smith jobb'd. George Hill sent for my sheep, 33 per John Title and an other man. Dick Smith helpt them out of my ground. Thomas Hamper and his boy here from 9 aclock making an apple cracker ------ 3 days. Brother Will and Peter here in the evning and Mr John Hart.

The 25th October 1720 Tuesday. A gloomy day, wet towards night. Will and Dick King plough'd. Smith and Terry did severall jobbs. Thomas Howell's man mended the little round plough etc. I were to see Sir Robert Fagg's fat runt.
Thomas Hamper finisht the apple cracker this morning which made yesterday up a full day ---------- 3 days.

The 26th October 1720 Wednesday. A fine day.
I were at Thomas Barber's sale. Will and Dick King plough'd, Terry and Smith did severall jobbs. My Wife and I supt and spent the evning at Westtowne and Will. Receiv'd £10 in full of all accounts of Harry Wickham.

The 27th October 1720 Thursday. A fine day.
Will, the boys and John Gun made an end of ploughing Tully's long field and sow'd all but the head lands. Struck up the furroughs and in the Nine Acres. Young Botten gather'd clover afternoon at Rickman's.
Mrs Catherine Beard and her mother here afternoon. Let Harry White at Cuckfield the kitchen part of Tully's house at 40s per year, a Munday last. He is to enter at Lady Day next, to keep no hog!

The 28th October 1720 Fryday. A very wet forenoon, dry after. Dick King and Terry helpt John Gun winnow 12 bushels of oates, kept holy day after. Smith went to Lewis. Ned Terry went to Slough Green afternoon.
Mr John Hart din'd here.

The 29th October 1720 Saturday. A very fine day.
Will and Dick King begun plough the Hovelfield at Rickman's. Terry, Smith and Botten carry'd the clover there, 2 loads. Turn'd the working oxen into the Edgly Mead. I went to Lewis, carry'd our Michaelmas presentments paid 3s-2d for staying above a month after Michaelmas. Paid Samuel Tourl 4s for ¼lb of bohea. Paid Mrs Skinner 12s for 4 handcerchiefs.

The 30th October 1720 Sunday. A gloomy day.
Mr William Martin preacht. Mrs Susan Courthope and my Cousin John Lindfield din'd here. Mrs Anne Beard and her mother here after evning prayr.

The 31st October 1720 Munday. A fine day.
Will and Dick King plough'd at Rickman's. Terry and Smith chang'd beasts. Win'd and took up flax. Mr Cheal's son came to school to Mr John Hart, his mother and Mrs Weeks here.

The 1st November 1720 Tuesday. A wet day.
Will and Smith plough'd at Rickman's. Terry made water furroughs in Nine Acres 'till noon. Reckon'd with Old Dick Banks, clear'd accounts. Lent John Smith 52s-6d. Paid Goodman Oliver 13s-6d in full for Daniel Bide's work.

The 2nd November 1720 Wednesday. A fine day.
John Gun sow'd the headlands of the long field by Tully's coppice. Dick King harrow'd it. The boys made water furroughs, unloaded the clover etc. Thomas Howell's man workt to day and a Munday. Clear'd accounts with my Lord Treep. Will went to coursing.

The 3rd November 1720 Thursday. A fine day.
My Wife, Jacky and I went to Lewis. Smith carry'd 2 old side saddles to Lewis, came home again. Dick King rode before my Wife. Clear'd accounts with Stephen Avery. Paid him 20s in exchange and the 2 old side saddles for my wives new side saddle. Supt at Dr White's. Clear'd accounts with J S Tourl and Mrs Skinner.

The 4th November 1720 Fryday. A fine day. Will sow'd the Hovelfield at Rickman's with ____ bushels of wheat. The boys harrow'd. We lay at my Cousin Marchant's, return'd to day. Clear'd accounts with Mr Michelbourne.

The 5th November 1720 Saturday. A fine day. Made an end of sowing at Rickman's. Will, Terry and Jacky went to coursing. Receiv'd the 52s-6d of John Smith which I lent him a Tuesday last. Paid Dick King half a guinea.

The 6th November 1720 Sunday. A fine day.
Mr William Martin preacht. I supt at Mrs Catherine Beard's. Mr Henry Campion there a while.

The 7th November 1720 Munday. A fine day. The boys did severall jobbs. Receiv'd £18 of Young George Hill at St Leonards Fair. I spoak with Mr Bray of Balcombe there. Frank Marshall drencht the buck horse, etc. George West came to board here at 4s per week. He is to get his linnen washt himself.

The 8th November 1720 Tuesday. A fine day.
Goodman Stenning came to make shovel trees etc. Smith carry'd 2 bushel of apples to Mr Colbron's. Will and Terry made water furroughs Dick King did severall jobbs. Frank Marshall here to drench the buck horse again. My Wife went to Danny. At Mrs Catherine Beard's in the evning. Receiv'd 7½ bushels of malt of Harry Wickham yesterday.

The 9th November 1720 Wednesday. A gloomy day.
Will went to coursing. Terry made water furroughs. Dick King and Smith jobb'd. Thomas Hamper's 2 boys workt half the day. Frank Marshall drencht the horse again, paid him 5s for a dung court and dills which was left at Heath's, which I bought of his brother Thomas Marshall. Paid my Brother Peter £14-15s for a payr of oxen which he bought at St Leonard's Fair.

The 10th November 1720 Thursday. A gloomy day.
The boys jobb'd. Frank Marshall drencht the horse again. I supt at Danny with Mr Boyce, Mr Alford, Mr Shave. I went to talk with Mr Boyce about the Rusper liveing.

The 11th November 1720 Fryday. A very fine day.
John Paine fisht the lower pond, the boys helpt, etc. Mr Richard Whitpaine and my Father supt here. Jack Mills here 'till noon mending the hen coop.

The 12th November 1720 Saturday. A gloomy day.
Fisht the middle pond, the boys and John Pain did it. Stenning went home. Put 142 of the lower pond fish into the new pond yesterday and 110 to day of the middle pond. Put 48 large tench into the Hovelfield stew. Put a great number of very small store carp yesterday into the Edgly Mead pond and about 150 or more to day into the Churchfield pond.

The 13th November 1720 Sunday. A fine day.
Mr John Hart preacht. No service afternoon. My She Cousin Lindfield din'd here. I sent my Cousin John Lindfield a hare per John Herriot.

The 14th November 1720 Munday. A gloomy day.
Fisht the upper pond. Paid John Pain 3s for this and his 2 other day's work. Put 94 large carp into the new pond, 6 large carp and 10 large tench into the Hovelfield stew, 80 carp about 5 inches, 9 tench the same size and 16 small tench into the middle pond and 50 eels. Put 70 small eels into the upper pond again. Frank Marshall drencht the buck horse again. Ned Terry went to Balcombe yesterday.

The 15th November 1720. A gloomy day.
The boys carry'd --- 25 faggots to Old Dick Banks and as many to Mrs Storer. Will and his Unkle went to coursing, he supt here. My Brother Henry Faulkoner's man here. I sent some eels. Goodman Stenning came again this afternoon.
Thomas Hamper mended the Penstock ----- 3¾ days.

The 16th November 1720 Wednesday. A dry day.
Stephen Carter here. I sold him 300 carp at 4 guineas per hundred. He is to take 50 at a foot and the rest he is to take the best I have which I think are about 13, 14 and 15. Receiv'd 6 guineas in hand. My Wife sold him 15 _____ fowls at 20s to be deliver'd a Saturday sennight at Horsham. Receiv'd all the money. The boys rakt stubble in the Churchfield etc. My Father and Mr Burry supt here with Stephen Carter.

The 17th November 1720 Thursday. A fine day.
Mr Jeremiah Dodson's tythe feast. Stephen Carter went away this morning. The boys rakt and carry'd 3 loads of stubble. Will went to the tythes feast with his tythes. William Roach begun set up my new pump. Old William Brand and his 2 boys here. Thomas Hamper here the afternoon --------- 4¼ days. Weigh'd the last cow runt at 18d per nail to John Smith.

The 18th November 1720 Fryday. A dry day.
Will and Dick King begun fallow the Churchfield. Dick King and Smith carry'd Bett to Dr White's. They brought me ½lb of bohea from Samuel Tourl. Roach and his boy finisht the pump by noon. Clear'd account with Roach, his works about the pump came to 15s-2d. Old William Brand and Samuel Jarvice made good the paving in the sinks afternoon. I supt and spent the evning at Mr Jeremiah Dodson's. Paid 3s to John Snashall for an ounce of the bark for Molly Balcomb. Paid 2s-6d at Lewis for a payr of clogs and a payr of gloves for Molly Balcomb.

The 19th November 1720 Saturday. A wet morning, dry after. Lost the 4th calf and sent 2 skins to John Hart per R Smith. The boys did severall jobbs. Will, his Unkle and the boys went to coursing. Paid John Westover 17s-6d in full of all. Paid Frank Marshall 11s-6d for looking after the buck horse. Turned the cows into the cowfield. Goodman Stenning went home afternoon.

The 20th November 1720 Sunday. A very wet, stormy day. Mr Jeremiah Dodson preacht. I was at Church afternoon.

The 21st November 1720 Munday. A dry morning, showry after. Will and Dick King plough'd 'till noon. John Gun and his boys mended thatch. Will and I went to course a hare George Piony had found. Supt at Randalls. Goodman Stenning came again at night.

The 22nd November 1720 Tuesday. A fine day.
Will went to coursing. The boys helpt clear the great barn's floor and carry'd a cart load of stubble to Brickhouse Barn and 1 into the fatting close. Thomas Hamper and his boy here -------- 5¼ days. Harry Wickham din'd here. Lent Mr Burry a scythe.

The 23rd November 1720 Wednesday. A fine day.
Will and Dick King plough'd. Thomas Hamper, his man and least boy here ------ 6¼ days. Thomas Carter and his tunn came. Paid my Brother John Courtness 2 guineas in full.

The 24th November 1720 Thursday. A very wet morning, dry after. The tunn went away with 300 carp for which I receiv'd 12 guineas at _____ . Harry White of Cuckfield came and desired to be off his bargain to _____ . I sold Stephen Carter a basket at 1s and 2 brace of old carp at 2s and gave him a brace of tench. Will's cow was weigh'd 63 nail 1lb at John Smith's.

The 25th November 1720 Fryday. A dry day 'till towards night. Will went to coursing. The boys helpt John Gun winnow etc. Borrowed a crate to carry fowls of Old Hyder and an other of Hollingham.

The 26th November 1720 Saturday. A dry day. Terry and Smith carry'd 15 fowls to Horsham. Sold to Stephen Carter at 20s. Will and Dick King plough'd in the Churchfield. Will carry'd Mr Jeremiah Dodson a hare in the evning.

The 27th November 1720 Sunday. A dry day.
Mr Jeremiah Dodson preacht. My Cousin John Lindfield and his son John din'd here. I were not at Church in the afternoon.

The 28th November 1720 Munday. A wet day.
John Lindfield and Will went to coursing. Young George Hill came towards night. Reckon'd and clear'd accounts with George Hill. Paid him 3s-9d which he had paid me too much for the sheep and lambs. Receiv'd a steer of John Smith at £3 and 3 bushels of oates, the steer was Mrs Catherine Beard's. Shut the fatting oxen up in the close, 6 of 'em.

The 29th November 1720 Tuesday. A very wet day.
Shut up the working oxen. Jack Lindfield and Will kill'd 2 hares. George Hill went away this morning. Ned Terry thrasht with Banks. Dick King and Smith jobb'd.

The 30th November 1720 Wednesday. A stormy, showry day. Old Bank and the boys win'd 20½ bushels of wheat. Jack Lindfield went home in the evning. Carry'd home a hare. Mr Jeremiah Dodson had a carp and a tench.

The 1st December 1720 Thursday. A dry day.
Kill'd one hog. The boys carry'd 2 loads of stubble per Burt. Goode Parker and E Charman rakt stubble.

Mr Jeremiah Dodson and his wife supt here. Dick Smith went to Lewis, carry'd Dr White a hare. Brought ¼lb of bohea from Samuel Tourle. He brought also a coat for Jack.

The 2nd December 1720 Fryday. A dry day.
The boys carried stubble per Burt. I were at my Unkle Richard Turner's sale at Friar's Oak. Paid 9s-5d for a payr of old wheels to Richard Turner. John Clerk the smith bought the wheels. I gave him 6d for his bargain.

The 3rd December 1720 Saturday. A dry day.
The boys carry'd 25 faggots and half a cord of wood to Mrs Storer. Carry'd also some stubble into the fatting close etc. Mrs Catherine Beard and her family supt here. We gave Mrs Beard a hare. Will and his Unkle went to coursing. They kill'd a leash of hares and a couple of conys. John Clerk here in the evning.

The 4th December 1720 Sunday. A dry day.
Mr Jeremiah Dodson preacht. We had a parish meeting. Settled accounts as usual. I were at Mrs Catherine Beard's a little while.

The 5th December 1720 Munday. A wet day.
The boys did severall jobbs. _____ furrough'd. I were at the Swan in the forenoon on the parish account. There was Thomas Norton, Edgly, John Hart, Mr Scutt, John Wood the tanner at Woodmancourt, Isaac Muzzall and Thomas Norton. Lent a traveller whose wife lay in at the Swan, 15s on the parish account. I think John Wood, the smith and Mr Scutt witnesses. My Cousin Peter Marchant din'd here. Mr Richard Whitpaine and his wife Mary, Mrs Scutt, Mr John Hart and my Father supt here. Mr Scutt came after supper.

The 6th December 1720 Tuesday. A very wet day.
The boys drew 3 trees out of the Marldfield and did some other jobbs. Terry thrasht with John Gun. The traveller mentioned yesterday his name is Robert Hobbes, belongs as he said to the parish of St George's in the borough of Southwark, was born there and likewise apprentice to one Adds, a packthread spinner in that parish and never had any settlement elsewhere. Thomas Howell here to tell me his cow was sold. John Smith brought 32 sheep hither to keeping. Paid John Gravies a Scotchman 3s-2d for a handcerchief and edging for Molly Balcomb. Paid yesterday. Paid Goodman Stenning 10s-6d.

The 7th December 1720 Wednesday. A dry day 'till towards night. Will and Will Norton went to coursing and Dick King workt in my Father's garden. Terry thrasht with John Gun and Smith jobb'd. I din'd at my Father's. Supt at Mr Jeremiah Dodson's. Mr Burry there. I were at Mrs Catherine Beard's in the morning to put a thing on their chaese mare to keep her from breaking _____ .

The 8th December 1720 Thursday. A dry day.
Will and Smith helpt winnow at Rickman's afternoon. Dick King workt as yesterday. Terry thrasht barly. Richard White helpt thrash barly afternoon. I was a while at my Father's in the evning. Shut up 2 runts into the closes at Rickman's. Towner and his mate saw'd here, rafters for the chaese house.

The 9th December 1720 Fryday. A showry day.
The boys helpt Old Dick Banks winnow. Jacky thrasht barly with Young White. Towner and his mate saw'd. Clear'd accounts with Goodman Stenning for making shovel trees etc.

The 10th December 1720 Saturday. A very wet forenoon.
The boys did severall jobbs. Terry thrasht barly. Smith went home. I were at the Swan with John Farncomb, Mr Doyle, Harry Wickham, Mr Scutt, Mr Sparkes and John Smith.

The 11th December 1720 Sunday. A fine day.
Mr Jeremiah Dodson preacht. My Father, Mother and Mr Beard din'd here. I were at Westtowne in the evning with Mr Scutt. Harry White was here. Promis'd to come to work.

The 12 December 1720 Munday. A gloomy day.
Henry White came, to have 12d per day, lodging and small beer. Terry sick. Dick King thrasht barly with Henry White. Smith did severall jobbs. I din'd at my Father's. Wrote to Mr Richard Barcroft by post. My Wife was at Danny towards night.

The 13th December 1720 Tuesday. A fine day.
My Wife, Mr H Dodson and I went to Lewis. I din'd at my Cousin Peter Marchant. Paid J S Tourl 8s in full of all accounts. Dick King and Smith went to Lewis with us. Terry thrasht barly with Harry White.

The 14th December 1720 Wednesday. A gloomy day.
Will and Dick King plough'd. Terry thrasht barly ½,

thrasht wheat with Harry White ½. I din'd at my Father's with Mr Cheal, Mr John Hart and Mr Scutt. Thomas Hamper and Jack Mills put up the rafters to the chaese houses ------- 7½ days

The 15th December 1720 Thursday. A gloomy morning, fine after. I were at Brighton. Will and Dick King plough'd. Terry and Smith begun winnow barly.

The 16th December 1720 Fryday. A dry day.
A public fast on account of the plague. My Cousin Thomas Norton's wife Elizabeth North End din'd here. I were at Church in the afternoon. Reckon'd and clear'd all manner of accounts with my Cousin John Lindfield except money on bond and intrest. I sent a letter to Poynings to Mr Sixsmith by Smith. Shut Mr Burry's cow's calf up a weaning.

The 17th December 1720 Saturday. A gloomy day, small rain. The boys win'd 9 quarters 1½ bushels of barly. Borrowed 2 sacks of Mr Jeremiah Dodson.
Paid E Purvey of Ansty Cross 1s for a basket per White. I was a while at Mr Dodson's in the evning.

The 18th December 1720 Sunday. A gloomy, windy day, some rain. Mr Jeremiah Dodson preacht. My Cousin John Marchant of Lox din'd here. We were not at Church afternoon. Nick Plaw here in the morning to see a hog and calf.

The 19th December 1720 Munday. A wet, stormy day. I were at Rose Land in Wivelsfield. Bought either half a bag of new hops of Mr Pilbeam (he boards there) at £3-7s per cwt or the whole bag at £3-5s or else a packet of old hops which are now at Little Ease house at 50s per cwt. He is to call at my house a Thursday next and then I am to tell him which of the three I will have. Paid John Gun 2s-6d for nursing a dog. Deliver'd the 2 cows to John Smith per R Kester jr. Sold at £12. Dick Smith helpt Kester out of the ground with the cows. Lent Mr Jeremiah Dodson Will's horse for his son to ride to Broadwater. My young boar died (we drown'd him) which John Smith's bitch bitt.

The 20th December 1720 Tuesday. A dry day.
Will and Dick King plough'd. Smith went to Lewis. Lost the 5th calf. Terry and White carry'd a load of stubble thrasht after. I were at Thomas Hamper's in the evning

with Mr my Father, John Marchant Lox, John Bodle and John Box.

The 21st December 1720 Wednesday. A dry day. Stephen Pilbeam here. Reckon'd and clear'd accounts with Mr John Hart to this Xas. Paid Mr John Hart 7s-5d for books and £3-10s for seven months schooling for John Balcomb ending this Christmas. Will went to coursing. He and his Unkle kill'd a fox in my Brother John Box's ground. Dick King had an ague. Terry and Smith thrasht barly. John Smith fetcht the 2 Nunnery steers by W Chainey.

The 22nd December 1720 Thursday. A dry day.
Dick King and Will plough'd ½, Terry and Dick King gather'd stubble after. Smith workt for J _
Mr Sixsmith here, XMy Father and Mother Stone here in the evning. My Cousin John Lindfield's teem came through the ground.

The 23rd December 1720 Fryday. Will and Smith plough'd _. Dick King and Terry carry'd seven quarters of barly to H Williams to be malted. Paid my Cousin John Lindfield £4-15s which he is to pay William Lindfield of Grubbs for a Wintermilch for me. Am to fetch her about a week hence. I talkt with Abel Muzzall about a hog he is to have of my Cousin John Lindfield at 2s-4d per nail. Thomas Muzzall kill'd a hog.

The 24th December 1720 Saturday. A wet forenoon, dry after. Smith went to Lewis. Paid my Cousin Box the £6-10s which he paid Mr Richard Barcroft in London. John Smith had kill'd 3 of my young oxen. Paid Harry White 7s in full for his work. John Smith put a runt to keeping at Rickman's at 18d per week.

The 25th December 1720 Xas day. A gloomy day.
Mr Jeremiah Dodson preacht. My Father and Mother Stone din'd here and the workmen as usual. There was a vestry call'd. I were not at Church afternoon.

The 26th December 1720 Munday. A dry day.
My Wife and I din'd at my Father's. Receiv'd £10 of Mr Richard Barcroft's tennant John Freeman. We supt at my Father's with Mr Scutt and his wife. One of Abraham Combes's sons was here with Freeman.

The 27th December 1720 Tuesday. A fine day. Harry White came again to thrashing. Ned May din'd here. I were at Mr Jeremiah Dodson's in the morning.

Nick Plaw sent me word he was goeing to London on next Thursday. Paid Joseph Muzzall the Lord's rent for Rickman's and West Edgly. The boys went to hunt our tame hare with spaniels. William and Jack's horses both got away from 'em. Clear'd all accounts with Joseph Muzzall.

The 28th December 1720 Wednesday. A fine day.
Will and Terry went after the horses and brought them home. Paid my Mother a year's thirds due at Michaelmas last. My Wife and I were down there afternoon.

The 29th December 1720 Thursday. A gloomy day.
My Wife and I and Jacky went to Shermanbury. The boys carry'd stubble etc.

The 30th December 1720 Fryday. A gloomy day, some sun and rain. My Wife and I return'd from Shermanbury. Mr Cheal din'd there with us. The boys plough'd etc. I were at the Royall Oak with Sir Robert Fagg. He spoak to me about the Duke of Norfolk.

The 31st December 1720 Saturday. A gloomy day, small rain. Will and Smith plough'd. Dick King and Terry jobb'd. I supt at Mr Scutt's with my Father. Mr Lindfield and his son brought home a cow and calf at £4-15s. My Brother John Courtness here in the morning.

The 1st January 1720 Sunday. A fine day. Mr Jeremiah Dodson preacht. We had a parish meeting as usual. A guinea was ordered to Thomas Shave. I were at my Father's with Mr Scutt after evning prayers. My Brother Will din'd here.

The 2nd January 1720 Munday. A fine day. Will went to hunting with the hounds. Terry and Smith scour'd Wood's gutter. Thrashed barly afternoon. Let Stephen Reeve the kitchen end of Tully's house at 49s per annum to enter at Lady Day next.

The 3rd January 1720 Tuesday. A fine day. I went to Petworth with Mr Scutt. Will and my Wife went to Danny. Mr Scutt and I din'd at Greatham. Mr Mill not at home. I were at the Duke of Somerset's in the evning. Terry thrasht barly. The rest jobb'd. *(Ed: Charles Seymour, 6th Duke of Somerset, Baron Seymour of Trowbridge, son of Charles, 2nd Baron of Trowbridge, born 1662 in Preshute, Wiltshire, died 1748 at Petworth. Married Baroness Elizabeth Percy, daughter of Jocelyn Percy, in 1682. He was largely responsible for the Revolution in 1688 and for the accession of George I in 1714 thus securing the Hanoverian dynasty. Because of his arrogance he was known as "The Proud Duke". Jane Seymour, wife of Henry VIII, was a member of the same family)*

The 4th January 1720 Wednesday. A fine day.
Win'd 11 bushels of wheat. The boys rakt stubble etc. I talkt with the Duke of Somerset. He bid me £100 per annum and a house to live in to be his steward but we did not agree because I could not go immediately. We lay at the Half Moon last night, return'd to Greatham.

The 5th January 1720 Thursday. A fine day. Will went to coursing. The boys rakt stubble. Smith came to meet me at Stenning. Mr Scutt went from thence to Broakwood and I came home. Call'd at John Box's.

The 6th January 1720 Fryday. A fine day.
All kept holy day. I were to talk with Sir Robert Fagg. My Father and Mother Stone din'd here.

The 7th January 1720 Saturday. A fine day.
Ned Terry went to Horsham with chickens. Smith served the beasts etc. Mr John Hart, my Wife, Children and I din'd at Dean House. Harry White went home.

The 8th January 1720 Sunday. A fine day.
Mr John Hart preacht. My Cousin John Lindfield din'd here. My Brother Peter supt here.
I were at Mrs Catherine Beard's a little while. They sent for me about Edmund Norris and their maid.

The 9th January 1720 Munday. A gloomy, dry day.
The boys helpt John Gun winnow 4½ quarters of oates at Tully's. I were at Danny afternoon with Mr Jeremiah Dodson. Receiv'd a letter from Ri Scutt of Petworth.

The 10th January 1720 Tuesday. A fine day.
I fetcht Bett from Lewis. Sir Robert Fagg and I both went to the Duke of Somerset from Lewis. Staid all night. Came home with Mr Bodle. The boys carry'd the last of the Churchfield stubble.

The 11th January 1720 Wednesday. A gloomy day.
Will and Dick King plough'd. Terry thrasht barly part of the day. Smith did some small jobbs. My Cousin Peter Marchant's daughter Bett came home with my girl yesterday.

The 12th January 1720 Thursday. A wet afternoon. The boys plough'd forenoon. My Father and Mother Stone, Mr Scutt and his wife and Mr John Hart supt here.

The 13th January 1720 Fryday. A fine day, a very wet stormy night last night. Will and the boys fetcht home my malt from Harry Wickham's. Deliver'd 2 quarters of barly to him.

The 14th January 1720 Saturday. A stormy day. Dick King went sick to his father. Paid Harry White 15s-6d, clear'd accounts. Thomas Muzzall kill'd a small porker here. Goodman Nick Weeks the miller buried this afternoon. *(Ed: Hurst Parish Register shows Goodman Nicholas Wicks)*

The 15th January 1720 Sunday. A fine day, stormy towards night. Mr Jeremiah Dodson preacht. My Wife and I were at Wanbarrow afternoon. My Cousin John Marchant of Lox came home with us. Ned and William Norton and John Burry here.

The 16th January 1720 Munday. A fine day, small frost last night. Will and his Unkle went to coursing. Ned Terry thrasht barly. Smith jobb'd. John Smith took away his sheep.

The 17th January 1720 Tuesday. A stormy forenoon, dry after. My Cousin John Lindfield and his wife Elizabeth, my Cousin Thomas Norton and his wife, John Marchant of Lox, Mr Beard, my Brothers and my Father and Mother Stone here. I sent my great ox for London by John Smith and Allan Savage and John Smith took my 2 steers at £20. Put 2 steers into Tully's close, 2 into the cowfield and 2 heifers into the Fifteen Acres. Paid half a years Land Tax to my Cousin John Marchant due, I think, at Michaelmas last £9-11-4d.

The 18th January 1720 Wednesday. A dry day. The boys helpt Old Dick Banks begin winnow the wheat at Rickman's. My Cousin John Lindfield and his wife Elizabeth lay here last night. My Cousin John Lindfield went home this afternoon. Receiv'd the 5 guineas of Mr Jeremiah Dodson lent him some time ago.

The 19th January 1720 Thursday. A fine day. The boys and Old Dick Banks made an end of winnowing 5 quarters of head and 5½ bushels tail wheat at Rickman's. Brought home 2 bushels head. Will and Smith made an end of fallowing the Churchfield. Turned the two old oxen into the fatting closes. Paid William Dumsday of Horsham £1-3s for a payr of stays for Molly Balcomb. I din'd at my Father's. Supt at Mrs Catherine Beard's.

The 20th January 1720 Fryday. A dry day. Will went to coursing with his Unkle. Terry thrasht barly. Smith went to Lewis. Brought me a new hat and one dyed for my Father. Return'd a bible to Norman's. The white faced 4 yearling heifer calved a cow calf a Wednesday to day and the py'd heifer a bull calf to day. My Sister Sarah here a while afternoon.

The 21st January 1720 Saturday. A fine day. Terry thrasht barly and Dick King came again. Will and Dick King rakt stubble at Burt's. I were at Albourne Place in the morning. Talkt with Sir Robert Fagg. Paid 8 for a letter for Old William Brand.

The 22nd January 1720 Sunday. A fine day. Mr Jeremiah Dodson preacht. Dr Nick Plaw here afternoon. We did not go to Church.

The 23rd January 1720 Munday. A dry day. Dick King, Smith, my Wife and I set out for Shermanbury. Terry thrasht. Will and his Unkle went to coursing. Receiv'd £8 of John Smith at Frank Holden's.

The 24th January 1720 Tuesday. A gloomy day. Mr Gratwick of Jarvice buried. My Wife and I lay at Shermanbury last night. Went to the funeral to day. I went thence to Wallhurst. My Wife lay at Jarvice. Will and Terry begun fallowing the field by Burts.

The 25th January 1720 Wednesday. A gloomy forenoon, wet after. Dr Lintott and I at Mr Mitchell's of Brooks in the evning. Will and Terry plough'd half the day. Terry thrasht after. Smith rakt stubble and saw'd wood.

The 26th January 1720 Thursday. A fine day. Will and the boys carry'd a load of stubble. Plough'd after. Smith came to us. I din'd at Jarvice and my Wife and I return'd to Wallhurst.

The 27th January 1720 Fryday. A stormy day, very wet towards night. Will and Terry plough'd. My Wife and I return'd from Cowfold. Din'd Shermanbury. Came home after.

The 28th January 1720 Saturday. A very fine day. The boys carry'd stubble. Receiv'd £20 of John Smith for the 2 steers. He jobb'd. Receiv'd likewise £5-6-10d and £8 I recieved before it in full for the ox he drove to London for me.

The 29th January 1720 Sunday. A dry day.
Mr Jeremiah Dodson preacht. My Cousin John Lindfield din'd here. My Cousin Peter Marchant Lewis came later.

The 30th January 1720 Munday. Frosty morning, snow after. The boys kept holy day. Lent John Westover 3 guineas for a note of his hand. Paid Molly Balcomb 4s-6d for spending money at Xmas at 2d per week. I wrote to the Duke of Somerset per post to Petworth. Smith carry'd something to Mr Gratwick of Jarvice.

The 31st January 1720 Tuesday. A frost day.
Dick King and Terry thrasht barly. Cousin Peter Marchant din'd here and my Father and supt. Lent my Cousin Peter Marchant £10 for a note of his hand.

The 1st February 1720 Wednesday. A fine day.
My Father and Mother Stone, my Wife, Mr John Hart and I din'd at Mr Jeremiah Dodson's. Mr Russell the non-juror came there in the evning. Dick King and Terry thrasht barly. Smith went to Sadlescombe about my ladder pole. I were at John Stone's in the morning. 2 lambs tonight and 2 before.

The 2nd February 1720 Thursday. A fine day, frosty.
Dick King helpt Old Dick Banks winnow and is to have Saturday for it. The rest kept holy day. The runt cow went to bull. I din'd at my Father's with my ñkle Courtness. I supt at Mrs Catherine Beard's. Harry Goffe there and at my Father's. George Buckwell set up a stile at Rickman's a Tuesday.

The 3rd February 1720 Fryday. A dry day, frosty.
Will and Dick King plough'd. Terry thrasht. Smith did severall jobbs. Thomas Hamper and my Lord Treep mended my Father's chaese. Mr Phillip Cheal and Mr Beard and my Father and Mr John Hart supt here.

The 4th February 1720 Saturday. A fine day.
My Wife and I and Jacky went to Lewis. My Wife and I went in the chaese. Paid the hatter 7s for my hat and 1s for dressing and dyeing my Father's. Paid Norman 3s-6d for a bible for Ned Terry. Mr Michell made me an instrument in writeing for Mr [Sh.............]. Mr Jeremiah Dodson to sign about the seat.

The 5th February 1720 Sunday. A fine day, frosty.
Mr Jeremiah Dodson preacht. My Cousin John Lindfield din'd here. A parish meeting.

The 6th February 1720 Munday. A fine day, frosty.
Will and Terry plough'd. Lent John Smith £5 for a note of his hand. Gave Mr Jeremiah Dodson the writeing aforementioned a Saturday and the deed from the Lord Goring's son to Stephen Norton of a lease of Little Park etc. Dick King had this day for Candlemas day. Smith and E Row helpt John Gun winnow oats. Mr Dodson carry'd the deed mentioned on the other side in order to get a new lease of the Towne dirt.
*(Ed: In the original diary the first part of this entry is on the preceding page)* Paid Mr Jeremiah Dodson 2s-6d for keeping six oxen a week with oat straw.

The 7th February 1720 Tuesday. A frost, snow towards night. Smith and Sarah Packham helpt John Gun winnow oates. They winnowed to day and yesterday 6 qarters 3 bushels. Dick King and Terry carry'd 25 faggots to Abraham Muzzall on the school account and ten to the other school. Will and Dick King plough'd a while in the afternoon. Smith ground my Father's malt afternoon. Mr Richard Whitpaine here afternoon. He supt here.

The 8th February 1720 Wednesday. A fine day, frost.
The boys begun dunging. Carry'd 19 loads into the field per Towner. Smith went to Mr _____ . Turn'd the ewes into the Edgly Mead and Little Meads. Mrs Scutt here towards night. Brew'd 8 bushels of malt for my Father Stone, 6 pounds of hops. Clear'd accounts with John Smith about the brandy.

The 9th February 1720 Thursday. A fine day, frosty.
John Gun and the boys carry'd 29 loads of dung. Will went to Dean House. Mr Norden din'd here. Plaw's cow calved a cow calf. Brought up 2 steers out of Tully's close.

The 10th February 1720 Fryday. A fine day, frosty.
John Gun and the boys carry'd 25 loads of dung into the field by Towner's and 3 into the orchard. Dick King sick afternoon. Paid to Wood's wife yesterday for work etc for Molly Balcomb 10s-5d.

The 11th February 1720 Saturday. A fine day frosty.
The long tetted cow calved a cow calf. John Gun and the

boys carry'd 20 loads of John Smith's dung and one from my own mixen _____ into the field per Towner's. 3 lambs to day in the Little Meads.

The 12th February 1720 Sunday. A fine day, frosty. John Hart preacht.
My Cousin John Lindfield and his son John din'd here. Will return'd from Dean House. Thomas Hamper and his man Thomas Hamper and boy workt here. Set up a stile lower side way mead etc --- 8¼ days.
2 lambs to day and 2 at Rickman's yesterday.
My Wife and I were at Wanbarrow.

The 13th February 1720 Munday. A fine day, frosty. Will and I went to Twineham Place. There was my Cousin John Lindfield and his son and Mr Sackvile, a London butcher. I gave my Cousin John Wood my stick. The boys carry'd 25 faggots to [John Gun] and half a cord of wood to Thomas Hamper's. Thrash'd after.
John Stone brought Stephen Reeve's goods to Tully's.

The 14th February 1720 Tuesday. A gloomy day, frosty, some snow, Dick King and Terry thrasht.
Paid Mr Picknall of Arundell £2-1s in full of all.
Thomas Hamper workt here --------- 9¼ days.
4 lambs since Sunday. One at Rickman's.

The 15th February 1720 Wednesday. A dry day, frosty. Dick King and Smith carry'd 11 loads dung Rickman's. Terry thrasht barly with White. My Father and Mother Stone supt here. Reckon'd with George West and there is due to me 15s-6d a Munday morning next.
Pay'd Mr Bernard Heasman of Cuckfield 10s for 5 yards of Irish cloth for Molly Balcomb yesterday.

The 16th February 1720 Thursday. A windy day, frosty. The boys made an end of carrying dung at Rickman's, in all 23 loads in the _____ . Smith and Terry helpt Old Dick Banks begin winnow. My Wife and I were at Westtowne afternoon Harry Wickham.

The 17th February 1720 Fryday. A dry day, frosty. Will and Terry helpt Old Dick Banks winnow oates at Rickman's. Dick King drew logs etc. Smith also.
My Wife and I supt at Mrs Catherine Beard's. Terry and I cleft logs afternoon. George West went away from boarding with me. A flax dresser from Harry Wickham here in the morning.

The 18th February 1720 Saturday. A gloomy day, frosty. Dick King and Smith drew home logs, rotten wood etc. Terry thrasht with Banks.
Receiv'd of Thomas Champion £7-7s in money, outset £6 for half a year's annuity paid to my Aunt Holden out of Eastout and £1-13s for half a year's Land Tax for Eastout, in all £15 in full for half a year's rent for Eastout, all due at Lady Day last. Paid Harry White 6s for all his work. XXX.
17 lambs since Tuesday last. 3 at Rickman's, 6 in all.

The 19th February 1720 Sunday. A gloomy day, thawing. Mr John Hart preacht. We had a meeting about work in the forenoon. No service afternoon. My Cousin Thomas Norton's wife Elizabeth North End din'd here.

The 20th February 1720 Munday. A gloomy day, some rain. The boys ground malt etc. Terry thrasht barly with Banks at Brickhouse.
Thomas Hamper and his boy workt here ------ 10¼ days. Receiv'd the 3 guineas I lent to John Westover and the 5s I lent John Smith. Stephen Bine here in the evning and John Westover a while.

The 21st February 1720 Shrove Tuesday. A gloomy day, rain afternoon. Terry thrasht barly with Banks 'till noon. Dick King and Will plough'd 'till noon. Paid Thomas Muzzall 6d for killing 2 hogs. Smith helpt. Paid Stephen Reeve 10s-6d for weaving 18 ells of linen cloth for Molly Balcomb. My Father and Mother Stone din'd here. Thomas Hamper and his boy here ------------ 11¼ days. Old William Brand's boys did a jobb in the forenoon.

The 22nd February 1720 Ash Wednesday. A dry day. Will and Dick King plough'd in the forenoon. Fetcht home the ladder pole from Saddlescomb. Terry thrasht with Banks. Smith jobb'd.
Thomas Hamper and his boy here ------ 12¼ days.
My Brother Will here in the evning. My Brother John Courtness here afternoon.

The 23rd February 1720 Thursday. A fine day, small frost. Will and Dick King begun plough the wheat earsh by Hollinghams. I were at Brighton market afternoon. E Daws of Cowfold was here for Mr Gratwick's things. Thomas Hamper and his boy here ---------- 13¼ days. Lost a ewe this afternoon. Terry thrasht with Banks. Smith set beans. My Wife was at Danny afternoon.

The 24th February 1720 Fryday. A fine day, frosty.
Will and Smith plough'd. Dick King sick. Terry thrasht with Banks, mov'd dung at Kester's afternoon.
Thomas Hamper and his boy here ---------- 14¼ days.
Thomas Hamper fetcht a large press from my Father's.
John Gun begun serve Smith's beasts this evning.

The 25th February 1720 Saturday. A fine day, frosty.
Will and Smith plough'd. Terry mov'd dung at Kester's with Banks in the forenoon and both thrasht in the great barn afternoon. I din'd at my Father's. Harry Wickham carry'd me there. We went thence to the Swan, there I sold him all my barly at 10s per quarter with the liberty to sell that in Brickhouse Barn to William Beard if I will. There was Mr Burry, John Snashall jr, John Smith, John Box sr.

The 26th February 1720 Sunday. A fine day.
Mr Jeremiah Dodson preacht. We had a meeting about Wicks. Concluded to pay their debts due to Ed Harland. I were at Mrs Catherine Beard's in the evning with Mr Orlton, Mr Daw, Mr Scutt, my Father and Mr Richard Whitpaine.

The 27th February 1720 Munday. A fine day.
Will and Smith plough'd. Moll Terry's father lay here. Went home this morning. Mr Orlton etc din'd here. My Wife and I supt at Thomas Norton's North End. Terry thrasht with Banks in the great barn.

The 28th February 1720 Tuesday. A fine day, frosty.
Terry and Old Dick Banks win'd 4 quarters of barly in the great barn and Terry carry'd it to Harry Wickham's and brought home 4 quarters of seed barly. Will Botten helpt. Will and Smith plough'd. My Wife and I went to my Cousin Marchant of Ditcheling. I bought 2½ bushels of flax seed of Young Jacob Hubbard at 17s to fetch it this week. We were at my Aunt Sarah Turner's.

The 1st March 1720 Wednesday. A very fine day, frosty.
Will and Smith made an end of ploughing Tully's wheat earsh by Hollingham's. Terry thrasht with Banks at Brickhouse. Ned Burt workt in the garden.

The 2nd March 1720 Thursday. A very fine day, small frost. Will and Smith begun plough the Hayselcroft. Terry thrasht with Banks at Brickhouse. I were at Wanbarrow and at Brother Box's in the morning. Ned Burt workt in the garden with John Gun. I supt at Stephen Bine's with Mr Jeremiah Dodson, Mr John Hart and Mr Burry.

The 3rd March 1720 Fryday. A fine day, frosty.
Will and Smith plough'd a while. Smith helpt John Gun winnow after, 4 quarters. Old Dick Banks bought the two fatting oxen from Rickman's. Terry thrasht barly with Banks at Brickhouse.
Thomas Hamper here to day ---- 15¼ days.
John Towner and Ja Reed saw'd here. My Brother John Courtness here. I were at Kester's with him and Mr Beard and at his father's in the evning. Harry Wickham and Joseph Muzzall here afternoon.

The 4th March 1720 Saturday. A very fine day, frosty.
Terry and Smith carry'd 4 quarters of barly to Harry Wickham's. Brought home as much seed barly Will helpt. Old Dick Banks made an end of thrashing barly at Brickhouse barly. Old Dick Banks scour'd the fatting close watring after. I were at Wanbarrow in the morning. At Mrs Catherine Beard's after with my Brother John Courtness. I din'd at my Father's with Mr Cheal. My Brother Will supt and spent the evning here.
Thomas Hamper workt here ------------ 16¼ days.
John Towner and Ja Reed saw'd here.

The 5th March 1720 Sunday. A fine day, frosty.
Mr Jeremiah Dodson preacht. We had a meeting afternoon. overseers not there. My Wife and I receiv'd the sacrament.

The 6th March 1720 Munday. A very fine day.
Will and Terry jobb'd. Lent Mr Jeremiah Dodson £5 for a note of his hand. Paid Mr Courtness 3s for 7 glass bottles, 2 quarts. Paid John Gun 7s.

The 7th March 1720 Tuesday. A stormy day, thawing.
Will and Smith plough'd Rookwood. Terry, Thomas Greenfield and Abraham Muzzall carry'd 8 quarters and 7 bushels of the Hayselcroft barly to Harry Wickham and brought home 3½ quarters of seed barly. Win'd all the Hayselcroft barly and there was 9 quarters 5 bushels head and 7 bushels tail. Paid Goodman Parker 6d for helping winnow. Left 7 sacks with Thomas Jacket's wife to mend.

The 8th March 1720 Wednesday. A gloomy day.
I were at Stenning monthly market. Staid all night.

Will and Smith plough'd. Terry did severall jobbs.
Thrasht with Banks after.

The 9th March 1720 Thursday. A fine day.
Will and Smith plough'd. Terry thrasht with Banks. My
Cousin John Wood of Twineham Place supt and spent
the evning here.

The 10th March 1720 Fryday. A very fine day.
Will and Smith plough'd. Terry dugg, set beans etc.
John Gun made an end of carrying Kester's dung to my
Father's yesterday. There was 25 loads of it. I agreed for
it at 5s per load.

The 11th March 1720 Saturday. A fine day.
Will and Smith plough'd. Terry helpt John Gun mend
gapps round the orchard. My Wife and I at Westtowne
towards night.

The 12th March 1720 Sunday. A dry day.
Mr Jeremiah Dodson preacht. I were not at Church in
the forenoon. My Cousin John Lindfield and his wife
Elizabeth din'd here. We had a meeting at Church about
the indictment on the highways. Lost a lamb.

The 13th March 1720 Munday. A very wet day.
The boys did severall jobbs. Terry thrasht barly with
Banks. Went to Ditcheling. Will Wickham and Dick
Banks here in the evening. 11 lambs since the 18th
February, 1 at Rickman's. 7 in all. Bottled some syder in
the morning. Paid Thomas Jacket 1s for cleaning the hall
clock.

The 14th March 1720 Tuesday. A gloomy day, some rain.
Will and Smith plough'd. John Gun fetcht Bett from
North End towards night. I were at Harry Wickham's in
the forenoon, pruned trees after. Terry spread dung with
Banks per Towner's. John Haslegrove here in the
evning.

The 15th March 1720 Wednesday. A stormy day.
Will and Smith finisht the Rookwood. Smith fetcht 5
bushels of flax seed from Dean House. Terry spread
dung with Banks. Finisht by Towner's. Reckon'd with
John Smith and there is due to me £10-2s-4d besides 2
cows from Rickman's but there is 14s-4d to be set off on
Old William Brand's account. Paid Chapman 1s for
clipping 56 sheep.

The 16th March 1720 Thursday. A wet day.
The boys win'd barly, 8 quarters. I were at William
Nicholas's in the morning, teaching him to make ox
harness. Dick Wood shooed the cart horses. Thomas
Hamper's man hew'd a tree. Paid Old Dick Banks 1s for
his son for mending 2 augers.

The 17th March 1720 Fryday. A gloomy day, wet towards
night. The boys carry'd 8 quarters of barly to Harry
Wickham. My Wife and I din'd at Dean House, he not at
home. We call'd at North End goeing and coming. John
Towner and Ja Reed saw'd here.

The 18th March 1720 Saturday. A stormy day.
The boys win'd barly and 18 bushels of wheat. Reckon'd
and clear'd accounts with Old Dick Banks all but bullock
serving, rent and cow keeping. Mr John Hart spent the
afternoon here. Mr Plaw here a while. Lost a lamb to
day. The cow I had of Mr Beard calved a bull calf.

The 19th March 1720 Sunday. A fine day.
Mr Jeremiah Dodson preacht. An other meeting about
the highways. Agreed to make a tax at 4d in the £.

The 20th March 1720 Munday. A very fine day.
Will sow'd the Hayselcroft with 4½ bushels of flax. Nick
Plaw here all the afternoon. Stephen Bine here for grafts.

The 21st March 1720 Tuesday. A very fine day.
Will sow'd 16¼ bushels of pease in the Rookwood.
Will fetcht 1¾ bushels of pease from Wanbarrow. Smith
and Terry harrow'd. Mr Jeremiah Dodson and Mr John
Hart supt and spent the evning here.

The 22nd March 1720 Wednesday. A fine day.
Will sow'd Tully's lower field with 30 bushels of oates.
Smith and Terry finisht the Rookwood and begun
harrow Tully's field. I were at John Godly's sale at St
John's Comon.

The 23rd March 1720 Thursday. A very fine day.
My birthday, 44 years. Receiv'd 9s and a neat's tongue of
John Smith for a calf he is to kill between this and
Munday and I am to have a hindquarter into the bargain.
Terry and Smith harrow'd in Tully's field. My Wife and I
spent the evning at Young John Snashall's.

The 24th March 1720 Fryday. A showry day.
Will and Terry carry'd the stubble at Rickman's etc.
Smith finisht the field by Hollingham's. John Godly

here. William Jarvice workt in the orchard. I were at John Snashall's sr in the morning. He from home.

## 1721

The 25th March 1721 Saturday. A fine day. My Wife, the boys and I at Lewis. Paid all due at Mr Court's.

The 26th March 1721 Sunday. A cold windy day. Mr Jeremiah Dodson preacht.
I were at Mrs Catherine Beard's in the evning. Paid her £3-18s which I receiv'd of Thomas Bart at Lewis for 5 bushels of her clover seed. My Cousin John Lindfield din'd here. Receiv'd £3-10s of him for cloath etc which I bought of Thomas Butcher last spring.

The 27th March 1721 Munday. A fine day.
Will and the boys begun the Churchfield. I were at Westtowne afternoon with John Marchant and Mr Webb of Brighton a taylor etc about deals. John Smith kill'd the calf mentioned a Thursday last.

The 28th March 1721 Tuesday. A very fine day.
Lawyer Thomas Whitpaine's widdow buried. Will and Smith plough'd. Terry harrow'd fallow. Deliver'd 3 quarters of barly to Harry Wickham per Terry and Abraham Muzzall jr. My Wife and I were at the funeral. *(Ed: Hurst Parish Register shows burial of Mrs Elizabeth Whitpaine)* 30 faggots for the Widdow Hambledon.

The 29th March 1721 Wednesday. A wet day.
Henry Packham's wife of Hayly was buried yesterday. The boys and Will Jarvice win'd and ground 8 bushels of malt in the forenoon. Cleaned the pidgeon house afternoon. Fisht the Hovelfield stew etc. Susan Bradford's husband here about noon. He promis'd to come to thrashing of wheat. Thomas Hamper sr here in the morning about deal. Paid Harry Morley 27s for thatching etc at Rickman's.

The 30th March 1721 Thursday. A gloomy day, some rain. Will sow'd about 10 bushels of barly in the Churchfield. Terry and Smith harrow'd. Win'd barly in the morning. Paid Mr Richard Whitpaine £6-5s at my Father's to be sent to Norway for deals between Mrs Catherine Beard, Goodman Thomas Hamper and I.

The 31st March 1721 Fryday. A gloomy day. The boys plough'd and sow'd about 6 bushels more in the Churchfield. My Cousin John Lindfield lent me a horse.

Thomas Field's son Robert brought him in the morning. Mr Jeremiah Dodson and I din'd at Mr Burry's. Receiv'd £2-1-8d of Mrs Catherine Beard as a third share of the money mentioned yesterday for deals. Sold William Nicholas a parcell of wood yesterday at 16s.

The 1st April 1721 Saturday. A showry day.
The boys win'd barly etc. Smith went to Lewis. Will Jarvice has workt here all this week. John Smith and I were to see the beasts at Rickman's but could not deal for them. Terry carry'd 6 bushels of the Hayselcroft barly to Harry Wickham's. I grafted 2 cherry trees and Jacky 2 apple trees.

The 2nd April 1721 Sunday. A wet morning, showry after. Mr Jeremiah Dodson preacht. We had a meeting as usual.

The 3rd April 1721 Munday. A gloomy day.
The boys plough'd and sow'd. Receiv'd £2-1-8d of Thomas Hamper towards deals. He is to go a third with Mrs Catherine Beard and I, recv'd yesterday.
I din'd at Mr Jeremiah Dodson's with Mr Beaumont, Mr John Hart, Mr Richard Whitpaine and Mr Burry. Receiv'd a box of sugar loaves from Mr Baynes, London. Will Jarvice workt here. Paid Dick Wood £1-0-6d in full of all.

The 4th April 1721 Tuesday. A very fine day.
The boys plough'd and sow'd bushels. Thomas Hamper and his boy here -- 17½ days. Cut the trees in Tully's ground. Will Jarvice here a digging and setting beans etc.

The 5th April 1721 Wednesday. A dry day.
The boys plough'd and sow'd      bushels.
Thomas Hamper workt part of the day --- 17½ days. Sold John Smith 2 runts at Rickman's and a cow at £17-10s and the cows tongues. I were at John Westover's a while afternoon. Clear'd accounts with Brother Peter on the parish account. Mr Richard Whitpaine and he supt here.

The 6th April 1721 Thursday. A gloomy day, some rain. The boys plough'd and sow'd part. Will Jarvice and John Gun fisht the Edgly mead stew pond. John Snashall had about 200 store fish of which I am to have one in 5 when he takes them out again. Thomas Norton of Edgly had 100 of which I am to have one in 7 when he takes them out again. Put 44 carp about 7 inches into the

upper pond and 26 about 8 inches.
I was at Mr Jeremiah Dodson's with Mr Richard Whitpaine and Mr John Hart reckon'd and clear'd accounts at the school to Christmas. Mr Scutt and Mr Richard Whitpaine are to pay me per 19s each. Paid Mr Jeremiah Dodson £1-1-4d on the parish account. Borrowed 10 guineas of my Brother Will. He din'd here.

The 7th April 1721 Good Fryday. A stormy day.
Mr Jeremiah Dodson preacht. The boys plough'd part of the day and went to Church. Jarvice and John Gun fisht the pond by Tully's old hovel place and the Churchfield pond. My Wife and I were at Church.

The 8th April 1721 Saturday. A stormy day.
The boys made an end of sowing the Churchfield. Sow'd 47 bushels of barly. My Wife and I were to see my Brother John Box afternoon. Will Jarvice here all this week.

The 9th April 1721 Easter Sunday. A showry day.
Mr Jeremiah Dodson preacht. My Cousin John Lindfield din'd here. We went not to Church afternoon.

The 10th April 1721 Munday. A showry day.
The boys carry'd 7½ quarters of barly to Mr Wickham's. Passt accounts and chose officers at Church as usual. Mr John Hart and my Brother Peter here in the evning. Paid my Unkle Courtness, my Lord Treep and William Nicholas in full on the parish account.

The 11th April 1721 Tuesday. A wet forenoon.
I met James Wood and my Cousin John Lindfield at Thomas Wood's to value Thomas Wood's stock on Burry Land Farme. It was agreed at £95 and a guinea, my Cousin John Lindfield to enter at Lady Day last. He paid £20 and a guinea to Thomas Wood's wife in hand. My Wife went to Dean House and back again. The boys kept holy day.

The 12th April 1721 Wednesday. A dry day. The boys and Old Dick Banks win'd 40 bushels of head and 2 bushels of tail wheat. Receiv'd £4 of John Stone on John Reeve's account and there is £4 more due to me on the account. Receiv'd 1s of John Wood of Twineham Place for 150 very small store carp. John Stone, John Wood and he that has taken Wanly Farm were here together. I had a ewe overturned yesterday. John Smith _____ .

The 13th April 1721 Thursday. A very fine day.
The boys plough'd by Burt's. Turn'd 2 runts to pasture in hop garden. Mrs Scutt here in the afternoon. Paid Dick King £2 and 3d in full of all. Sent home my Cousin John Lindfield's lanthorns per Dick King.

The 14th April 1721 Fryday. A gloomy day.
Will and Smith, King, George West plough'd. Thomas Hamper and his man mend'd wattles ---------- 18½ days. My Cousin Thomas Norton's wife Elizabeth North End and her daughter here. Cousin Plump here. My Father and Mr Burry supt here.

The 15th April 1721 Saturday. A gloomy day, fine after.
Plough'd as yesterday. George West _____ at 11. Paid Mr Jeremiah Dodson all my tythes due at Lady Day. Likewise all the rent for the Hayselcroft for the crop now on the ground.
My Wife and I supt at Mrs Catherine Beard's. Lost a [hive] in Tully's ground. One of the tags farrow'd this week.

The 16th April 1721 Sunday. A gloomy day, some rain.
Mr John Hart preacht twice. Receiv'd £12-5s of John Smith and a cow at £2-15s which is in all £15 in part of what is due to me.

The 17th April 1721 Munday. A showry day.
The boys made an end stirring the field at Burt's. Harrow'd, roll'd etc. Terry helpt John Gun make a hot bed afternoon. Turned 2 runts into the ponds yesterday.

The 18th April 1721 Tuesday. A very wet day 'till towards night. Will, King and Terry helpt John Gun winnow oates. Young Dick Banks helpt Smith fetch 3 loads of barly straw from Brickhouse into the fatting close. Paid him £6 for it. The great old cow calved a cow calf.

The 19th April 1721 Wednesday. A showry day.
The boys and George West plough'd 'till noon. King and Terry thrasht oates after.
Thomas Hamper and his man here ---------- 19½ days.
Mrs Ann Dodson here afternoon. John Smith also.

The 20th April 1721 Thursday. A stormy wet day. The boys thrasht oates ½. King and Smith jobb'd afternoon. Terry helpt John Gun mend gapps afternoon in Tully's ground. Thomas Hamper and his man here --- 20½ days. Paid Thomas Muzzall 6d for killing 2 small porkers.

The 21st April 1721 Fryday. A showry day.
The boys did severall jobbs. The branded heifer calved a bull calf. My Wife and I were at Westtowne afternoon. Mr Rawlins there.

The 22nd April 1721 Saturday. A showry day.
The boys laid out flax in Tully's Mead. Dick Wood's three girls helpt lay out flax almost a day. Smith helpt John Gun cut 2 trees in Tully's Mead. John Gun poll'd three trees. Goode West carry'd some butter to Lewis for me. Paid Molly Balcomb 4s-4d for spending money at 4d a week from Christmas last to Lady Day last.

The 23rd April 1721 Sunday. A showry day.
Mr Jeremiah Dodson preacht twice. We had a meeting afternoon about Parker's wife. My Cousin John Marchant of Lox and I at the Swan.

The 24th April 1721 Munday. A gloomy day.
King and George West mov'd the ground wheat to Mr Jeremiah Dodson's barn where George West is to thrash it at 6d for every 12 sheaves. Will and E Terry went to Nutley Fair. Bought 2 barrens at £5-13-6d. Left them at Dick Bull's. Mrs Catherine Beard and her mother supt here. John Gun fisht Tully's dipping pond. Paid him 6d for it.

The 25th April 1721 Tuesday. A fine day.
Will went to Cliffe Fair. Bought nothing. Receiv'd the £10 which I lent my Cousin Peter Marchant. Terry fetcht the 2 cows from Dick Bull's. Smith and George West carry'd two jobbs of wheat to Mr Jeremiah Dodson's barn to be thrasht there. King went home sick last night. I were to see Mr John Hart afternoon. My Father there.

The 26th April 1721 Wednesday. A fine day, only a small showr or two. Will and Smith plough'd. Terry jobb'd. William Barr pretends to come from Carford begun thrash with John Gun, lodges with Thomas Smith at the Swan. My Brother Will came hither last night.

The 27th April 1721 Thursday. A showry day.
The boys plough'd and sow'd. My Brother Will went for Cuckfield afternoon. I were at Mr Jeremiah Dodson's in the evning, had tythe feast to day. Drove 4 cows to Rickman's, 2 to hay and 2 to grass.

The 28th April 1721 Fryday. A gloomy morning, wet after. The boys jobb'd. I went to Beeding to meet Mr Penfold of Broadwater to view the repairs of the glebe lands in William Burfield's hands. We agreed for all but the thatch and the fence round the closes. I din'd at Mr Reckwood's of Court Farm. George Courtness went with me. Sent £6 to my landlord Richard Barcroft to Chichester by Mr Newlin who went thither soon after I came to Mr Reckwood's. Mr Reckwood gave me half a guinea by Mr Newlin's order. I left the account of our proceeding with Mr Reckwood. There was likewise at William Burfield's Natt Hobbes and one Meers (I think his name was) a carpenter from Thacum on the part of the executrix and Richard Backshall on Mr Newlin's part to view the great bridge over the river and they valued repair of it at £5 which I think too little by £50. But Richard Backshall did not in the least agree to it. Mr Williams was likewise there on behalf of Mr Allan's executrix and behaved himself (I think) not well, endeavouring to influence the _____ more than he ought to have done. There was a kind of certificate drawn up by Mr Penfold importing that the barns were in good repair all save one door and some underpinning and likewise that the repairs of the bridge might be done for £5 which was sign'd by Hobbes and Meers.

The 29th April 1721 Saturday. A gloomy day.
The boys helpt Banks winnow 36 bushels head and 3 bushels tail wheat. Terry fetcht my malt from Harry Wickham's. Sold John Smith a quarter of wheat at 3s per bushel. Sold Parker at the Comon 20 bushels of wheat at 3s per bushel which I am to deliver next week, and to take it in bricks, lime etc. I may likewise carry 4 bushels each to Frank Holden and Ri Pierce if I will, at the same price. Lost one ewe to day.

The 30th April 1721 Sunday. A dry day.
Mr Jeremiah Dodson preacht twice. We had a meeting about Sarah Brooker etc. My Cousin John Lindfield din'd here. I supt at Mr Dodson's.

The 1st May 1721 Munday. A dry forenoon, wet after.
Thomas Westover's wife buried. *(Ed: Shown in Hurst Parish Register as Catharine wife of Thomas Westover)* Thomas Hamper and his man and boy here, Thomas Hamper but 'till 2 aclock -------- 21 days. Will and Smith harrow'd in the morning. Terry roll'd in Rickman's field. Paid a rope maker at Lewis 16s for a lot of bell ropes. Paid Dick Smith 2s-6d.

The 2nd May 1721 Tuesday. A fine day. Will and Smith plough'd and harrow'd. Terry helpt John Gun and Barr winnow 26 bushels of wheat. Mr Jeremiah Dodson went to London. I went to Heath's with him. I were at Westtowne afternoon. Supt at Mrs Catherine Beard's. Nick Plaw here in the evning to see a cow. John Smith fetcht the second runt from Rickman's.

The 3rd May 1721 Wednesday. A dry day.
The boys did severall jobbs. Deliver'd 2 qarters of wheat to John Smith at 3s per bushel and 4 bushels to James Holden at the same price. Deliver'd my deed from my Lord Goring to Stephen Norton on the soil of the town etc to Mr Ralph Beard which he promis'd to carry to London to Mr Jeremiah Dodson. There was likewise an instrument for Mr Shaw to sign *(Ed: as patron of the Living)*, in it relating to my new seat in the church. Turned the red runt into the hop garden.

The 4th May 1721 Thursday. A very fine day.
The boys plough'd etc. My Wife and I and Mr John Hart at Wanbarrow afternoon. I wrote to Mr Jeremiah Dodson per post. Dick Clerk peekt plough.

The 5th May 1721 Fryday. A dry day. The boys plough'd and sow'd. Dick Clerk helpt the boys. A mountebank man was here the 2nd time. I were at Thomas Smith's with Edward Burry, Thomas Norton etc.

The 6th May 1721 Saturday. A fine day. The boys made an end of sowing barly. My Cousin's wife here afternoon. Will Baker and little Abraham Muall went to Lewis for my Cousin Peter Marchant's wife.
Mr William Martin brought his mare into the ground at 2s per week. Old Dick Banks drove the cow runt to Rickman's.

The 7th May 1721 Sunday. A fine day.
Mr William Martin preacht twice. A parish meeting afternoon. John Gun allowed 200 faggots. My Cousin Marchant, my Wife and I at Westtowne.

The 8th May 1721 Munday. A fine day.
Deliver'd 20 bushels of wheat to Parker per Terry and Smith. Had the waggon and 17 strakes to Thomas Howell's. John Marchant's teem help us along part of the way.

The 9th May 1721 Tuesday. A fine day.
Will and Abraham Muall went to Lindfield. Brought cloaths for Will. The boys fetcht home faggots etc. John Smith here at night. An excise man put his horse in my ground yesterday. Frank Holden's mare came yesterday at 18d per week.

The 10th May 1721 Wednesday. A dry day. Will roll'd barly. Terry sow'd flax etc. Smith and I fetch'd a payr of wheels from Frieoak.
Thomas Hamper mended court Dill's ------ 21½ days.
Will Haslegrove and Dick Wood's 3 girls spread flax afternoon in Tully's little field. Thomas Butcher din'd here. A 8 yearling heifer calved a bull calf a Munday night.

The 11th May 1721 Thursday. A gloomy day.
Turned all John Gun's beasts to pasture. The boys did severall jobbs. Dick Wood's girls laid out flax part of the afternoon. Mrs Mary Whitpaine, her daughter and Mr Bernard Heasman here.

The 12th May 1721 Fryday. A fine day. The boys and John Gun carry'd Towne dirt. Terry sick. Turn'd the 6 working oxen to Rickman's and turn'd 2 bullocks to pasture there. Turn'd 3 fatting oxen to pasture at home. Left 2 in the close. Paid George West 2s-4d in full for thrashing. A mountebank at Towne. His name (as he says)William Luby. I agreed to keep a horse for him at 2s per week.
Thomas Hamper, 2 men and a boy here ------ 22½ days.

The 13th May 1721 Saturday. A cold, windy day.
The boys carry'd Towne dirt. Reckon'd and clear'd accounts with Banks all but runt and bullock serving. I were at Wanbarrow in the evning with Mr Pierce.

The 14th May 1721 Sunday. A dry cold day. Mr William Martin preacht twice. I din'd at Mrs Catherine Beard's. Receiv'd a book of Mr Reed.

The 15th May 1721 Munday. A dry day, only a showr towards night. The boys shut up 3 calves a weaning. Carry'd a load of flint at Rickman's. Left the horses there. Turned the mountebank's horse to Rickman's. Will went to Lewis, carry'd a suit of cloaths thither to be made.

The 16th May 1721 Tuesday. A fine day.
The boys plough'd at Rickman's. Terry did severall jobbs. Harry Morley and his children begun thatch.

Sold John Smith 2 tags at Rickman's at a guinea and the wool of one of them. I were at Mr Scutt's a while towards night. Thomas Howell's man William was here. I helpt him to 5 wheel bonds and 4 boxes and 2 small bolts with roundles.

The 17th May 1721 Wednesday. A fine day.
The boys plough'd at Rickman's. Terry did severall jobbs. Will, Jacky and John Gun went to a race at Lewis. Thomas Hamper and his man, Thomas Hamper made 2 deal ladders --- 23½ days. Mrs Catherine Beard and her mother were here afternoon. Receiv'd 3 calves of John Snashall at £4. Paid John Snashall 20s towards the calves.

The 18th May 1721 Thursday. A fine day. The boys kept holy day. Will and Terry went to a cricket match at Henfield. Smith did severall jobbs for which I gave him 6d. My Father and Mother Stone supt here. Dick Wood dresst a steer which broke off his horns.

The 19th May 1721 Fryday. A fine day. Will plough'd 'till noon and begun sow oates in the field by Rickman's house. Terry harrow'd etc. Smith drove plough etc. Turned Mr William Martin's mare to Rickman's.

The 20th May 1721 Saturday. A fine day, only a showr towards night. Will and Smith plough'd and sow'd at Rickman's. Terry went to mill in the morning, harrow'd after. Turned the working oxen to pasture at Heath's. Sent a pig to my Brother John Box per Mr Willet.
Mr Jeremiah Dodson return'd from London. I talkt with him at his house and took a bill of 35s-9d which he paid for me in London in part of £3-16d due to me.
Mr William Martin there. I drank with the mountebank yesterday at the Swan. Dick Wood's 3 girls and Sarah Banks helpt take up flax.

The 21st May 1721 Sunday. A fine day.
Mr William Martin preacht twice. I were not at Church haveing a very bad cold. Will and William Baker went to Cuckfield to see my Brother Will afternoon. Mrs Susan Courthope and my Aunt Courtness here after evning prayr.

The 22nd May 1721 Munday. A very fine day. My Wife, Jacky, Mrs Hart and I went to Shiprods. The boys made an end of sowing oates and clover at Rickman's. Nick Plaw cut the calves and the young bull in the morning.

The 23rd May 1721 Tuesday. A very fine day.
Joe return'd from Shiprods, left Jacky there. Din'd at Nick Plaw's as we came home. The boys carry'd Towne dirt. Jack Smith fetcht the white faced steer at 18s per nail.

The 24th May 1721 Wednesday. A fine day.
Will and Terry fetcht a new waggon from Howell. Smith fetcht geese from Henfield. Thomas Hamper and his man begun colore the waggon and 2 ladders. Mr Jeremiah Dodson and Mr John Hart supt here.

The 25th May 1721 Thursday. A fine day. The boys did severall jobbs. A cricket match between Hurst and Henfield in Danny Sandfield. Hurst won. Receiv'd £6-9s of my Cousin John Lindfield to be paid to Mr Jeremiah Dodson for his half-year's tythe which I did accordingly and took a receit. Mr Beard supt here.

The 26th May 1721 Fryday. A very fine day.
Old Dick Banks and the boys carry'd dung out of the home close, 43 loads. The mountebank's servants here. My Father, my Wife and I supt at Mrs Catherine Beard's.

The 27th May 1721 Saturday. A fine day. The boys and Old Dick Banks carry'd 43 loads of dung out of the fatting close to the mixen. Reckon'd with Harry Wickham and there is due to me £4-13-9d. He paid me ten guineas. Dick Wood dresst the steer's horns in his penthouse. Thomas Whiteing of Blackstone carry'd home my plush breeches to make a Thursday last and the pattern.

The 28th May 1721 Whit Sunday. A very fine day.
Mr William Martin preacht. Mr William Martin din'd here. I went to Dean House afternoon, he sick.

The 29th May 1721 Munday. A fine day.
Sent my Brother Henry Faulkoner 175 store carp per Terry. I were at Mr Osbourne's. Thomas Farncombe here. I were at Dean House afternoon. Dr Waller there.

The 30th May 1721 Tuesday. A very fine day.
My Wife, Jacky and I at Lindfield, bought cloaths for Jack. My Sister Sarah there.

The 31st May 1721 Wednesday. A fine day.
The boys carry'd the last of the fatting close dung, 37 loads, in all 80 loads. I were at Dean House afternoon. Turned the 2 heifers to Rickman's again.

The 1st June 1721 Thursday. A fine day.
The boys helpt John Gun winnow 61 bushels of wheat. I went to Cuckfield Fair. Clear'd accounts with Mr Bernard Heasman. I was with my Brother William at Hunt's.   He gave me a writeing to lay up for him. I brought 2 pairs of stockings from Mr Heasman's. One I paid 4s for and the others are to be return'd.

The 2nd June 1721 Fryday. A gloomy day.
Old Dick Banks and the boys carry'd      loads of dung in the home close to the mixen. Paid Chapman 10d for washing 51 sheep. Terry helpt. The mountebank took away his little mare and sent an other.

The 3rd June 1721 Saturday. A gloomy day, some rain. The boys and Old Dick Banks carry'd 28 loads of the home close dung. A cricket match in the Sandfield between Stenning and our parish, the latter won at one inning. Receiv'd £25 of John Stubbs being the money lent to him for a note of his hand, part of my Brother John Box's money and 25s for intrest. I promis'd him 5s for the use of it to Michaelmas next for a friend of mine.

The 4th June 1721 Sunday. A fine forenoon, some rain towards night. Mr William Martin preacht, no service afternoon. My Cousin Peter Marchant and his son lay here last night. My Brother John Courtness here afternoon.

The 5th June 1721 Munday. A dry forenoon, wet towards night. The boys helpt Old Dick Banks carry thatch and load of dung. Paid Chapman 2s-3d for shearing 51 sheep which is more per score than ever I gave him before. My Father and Mother Stone, my Wife and I were at North End afternoon. Sold John Smith a calf at 10s to be kill'd tomorrow.

The 6th June 1721 Tuesday. A dry morning, very wet after. Old Dick Banks and the boys carry'd dung 'till noon. The boys sifted wheat after. Will went to Stenning with the rest of our parish to play a cricket match but the weather so bad they could not. A little stone horse from Chichester or near went with little mare last night.

The 7th June 1721 Wednesday. A gloomy day, rain towards night. Old Dick Banks and the boys carry'd 2 loads of wheat into Tully's ground. Made up 77 faggots to Stephen Reeve. James Banks and E Wood weeded barly half the day. Mrs Catherine Beard and her mother here afternoon.

The 8th June 1721 Thursday. A dry day.
The boys carry'd dung. Paid Frank Holden a bill for severall things for Molly Balcomb, £11.

The 9th June 1721 Fryday. A dry day.
Mr Scrase of Withing here. I sold him 2 loads of wheat at £11 to be deliver'd at the Rock a Munday next. I were at Dr Vincent's in the evning. Paid John Gracie 2s-6d for a handcerchief for Molly Balcomb.

The 10th June 1721 Saturday. A gloomy day, some rain. Paid William Barnet 10d for spaying. Will and Jack went to Ifield Green to see a cricket match but they did not play. My Father, my Cousin John Marchant of Lox, Mr Richard Whitpaine and Mr John Hart and Dr Vincent here towards night.

The 11th June 1721 Sunday. A fine day.
Mr William Martin preacht. My Cousin John Lindfield, Thomas Butcher of Rotherfield, John Hart and Mr Lockier of Rotherfield here afternoon. Paid John Hart for briefs in my hands.

The 12th June 1721 Munday. A showry day.
Smith and Terry went to the Rock with the teem. We and John Marchant's teem carry'd 2 loads of wheat to the Rock for Henry Scrase at £5-10s per load. Mrs Catherine Beard's teem went with us. We all brought home deals.  I brought a load for John Marchant in lieu of his carrying a load of my wheat. I were at Mrs Catherine Beard's in the evning. Paid Harry Morley an other guinea. He made an end of thatching for the present. He says there is 2171 feet.

The 13th June 1721 Tuesday. A dry day. The boys carry'd dung. I were at Mr Henry Scrase's of Withing afternoon.

The 14th June 1721 Wednesday. A fine day. Smith, Terry and I went to Brighton for deals. I likewise left an entry of my wool, 51 sheep with Mrs Waller.
I din'd at Mrs Colbron's. Carry'd 6lbs of tyer thither. Receiv'd 96lbs of Old Wheel tier of the Wheeler at Brighton which I bought of Mr Gold at 1½d per pound. I wrote a letter to Mr Jeremiah Dodson to let him know that Mr Norton had given notice to Mr Jeremiah Dodson's servants that he must come to tything

tomorrow if this day proved fine. Paid Goode Muzzall 18d for knitting a payr of stockings for Molly Balcomb.

The 15th June 1721 Thursday. A very wet day.
Terry drove a runt to Hand Cross for J Skinner. Smith fetcht some yarne from Henry Scrase's. Dr Lintott and his wife and my Father and Mother Stone din'd here and Mr John Hart supt here.

The 16th June 1721 Fryday. A fine day.
I were at Wanbarrow in morning. Told my Brother Peter I were ready to go on Mr Norton business. Will begun mow clover. Smith did severall jobbs. Terry return'd from Hand Cross. I supt at my Father's. Settled our accounts with Mr Webb. Paid him £3-13s-7d apiece in full for deals. John Bodle is to have 60. The mountebank at town. A smock race in our field.

The 17th June 1721 Saturday. A fine day.
The boys helpt John Gun winnow. My Wife and I went to Lewis with Jack and Molly.

The 18th June 1721 Sunday. A wet day.
Mr William Martin preacht. I were at All Saints Church at Lewis afternoon. Lay at my Cousin Marchant's last night. Were at Dr White's after evning prayr.

The 19th June 1721 Munday. A fine day.
The boys helpt Old William Brand winnow. My Wife and I return'd from Lewis. Din'd at my Cousin Marchant's with Mr Reed of Arlington. Paid Mr Court in full of all and Mr Norman. Left material for cloaths with Mr Andrew Laurence. The bayard mare went to Mr Scrase's blind horse a Saturday last.

The 20th June 1721 Tuesday. A fine day.
The boys carry'd 50 faggots John Parsons, and to John Gun and 64 home. Did some other jobbs.

The 21st June 1721 Wednesday. A fine day.
I wrote to Mr Jeremiah Dodson per Wickham. I were at Wanbarrow afternoon. Offer'd my Brother Peter to go about Mr Norton's business which he refused and said he was very busy and would see Mr Norton first if he could. The boys carry'd wheat into Tully's garret etc. Paid Mrs Mary Punty at Lewis 14s for work for Molly Balcomb.

The 22nd June 1721 Thursday. A fine day.
My Father and Mother Stone went to Shermanbury in my waggon, Bett with them. A cricket match between our parish and Cowfold in the Sandfield, the latter lost. Terry and Sarah Banks and our maids hay'd. Receiv'd £19 of George Hill. He drew 40 lambs. My Brother Peter sent John Haslegrove to tell me that he had sent him JH had been at Stuckles by my Brother's order to know if anybody would show us the ground etc and they, Mr Norton's servants told JH that they had no order about it from their master, that they were very busy and did not care to go after it without their master's order.

The 23rd June 1721 Fryday. A very fine day.
The boys carry'd 3 loads of the Bankfield clover to the horse ricks. Sarah Banks and our maids hay'd. Receiv'd 12s of Dr Luby for keeping his mare 6 weeks. Paid my Unkle Courtness 8d for 2 rakes.

The 24th June 1721 Saturday. A fine forenoon, gloomy after. I went to St Johns Comon Fair with Molly Balcomb. Paid William Scrase 20s for 5 ewe lambs. Receiv'd the guinea of Mr John Hart which I lent him some time ago. The boys carry'd 4 loads of the way mead to the fatting ricks and 2 loads of clover to the close rick.

The 25th June 1721 Sunday. A fine day.
Mr Jeremiah Dodson preacht. I were not at Church afternoon. Mr Dodson and Brother Peter here after evning prayr. Paid Molly Balcomb 4s-4d for a quarter's spending money at 4d per week due and paid yesterday.

The 26th June 1721 Munday. A very fine day.
The boys, maids and Sarah Banks hay'd. Our parish plaid a cricket match with Cowfold on Ashendean Green, ours beat them again. Thomas Hamper here in the evning. Borrowed Frank Holden's mare for Will to ride to Cowfold.

The 27th June 1721 Tuesday. A fine day.
The boys carry'd 3 loads of the way mead and Little Mead below to the fatting rick. Carry'd also 2 loads of the fatting Bankfield clover. I were at the Swan with Mr Jeremiah Dodson, Mr Norton, my Brother Peter and Mr Scutt. Mr Norton and Mr Jeremiah Dodson sign'd bonds of reference to me and Brother Peter under the penalty of £500 if we could not agree it. James Wood of Twineham to do it.

The 28th June 1721 Wednesday. A gloomy morning, very fine afternoon. The boys carry'd 2 small loads of the Bankfield clover, 2 loads of Edgly mead to Kester's at a guinea per load and 2 loads to the fatting ricks. Brother Peter and I viewed Mr Norton's tythes. Peter came hither afternoon but we could not agree. Dr Woodward and his wife, Mrs Catherine Beard and her mother and Mr John Hart supt here. Dr Woodward brought his son Henry to school to Mr John Hart.

The 29th June 1721 Thursday. A gloomy morning, very fine after. The boys carry'd 3 loads of hay thus, one to the horse rick, 2 to the 15 Acre rick. My Wife and I were at Brighton. Abraham Muzzall sr fetcht _____ and some of my cloaths from Lewis.

The 30th June 1721 Fryday. A fine day.
The boys carry'd 5 loads to the 15 Acre rick and 1 to the fatting rick. James Banks and the maids hay'd. Smith, my Wife, Nanny and I went to Shermanbury to fetch my Mother home. I call'd at James Wood's as I came home about Mr Norton's tythe.

The 1st July 1721 Saturday. A fine day. Smith and I fetcht a load of seacoal from the Rock for John Snashall jr and two bushels for my self. The boys and William Haslegrove carry'd 2 loads of hay to the fatting rick etc. I were at Mr Jeremiah Dodson's in the evning.

The 2nd July 1721 Sunday. A fine day.
Mr Jeremiah Dodson preacht twice. We had a meeting at Church afternoon, passt the overseers accounts as usual. My Brother Peter here after evning prayr.

The 3rd July 1721 Munday. A fine day.
Smith and I fetcht an other load of seacoal from the Rock for John Snashall jr and 2 bushels for my self. Paid Combes 5s-6d for 9 bushels for my self of which I have had 4. The boys and William Haslegrove carry'd 7 loads of the Edgly mead hay to a rick in Tully's rick steddle. I gave an account of Mr Norton's tythe to my Brother Peter which he promis'd to carry to James Wood to day.

The 4th July 1721 A fine day. Tuesday.
Smith and I fetcht a load and 4 bushels of seacoal for John Clerk at the Comon and 5 bushels for my self so that I have now a quarter of a chaldron for which I paid Combs 5s-6d. Will and Terry carry'd 3 loads of the Edgly mead to Tully's, the last.

The 5th July 1721 Wednesday. A fine day.
Smith and I fetcht a load of seacoal from the Rock for John Clerk.   I were at Shoreham. Wrote to Mr Jeremiah Dodson from thence. I were at Mr Scutt's towards night with James Wood about Mr Dodson and John Norton's business. James Wood sent for me thither. The boys carry'd 2 loads of hay in Tully's Mead. Richard Banks hay'd.

The 6th July 1721 Thursday. A fine day.
Smith and I fetcht an other load of seacoal from the Rock for John Clerk. The boys carry'd 2 loads more of Tully's Mead.
Thomas Hamper and his man here ------ 24½ days

The 7th July 1721 Fryday. A showry day.
Smith and I fetcht the 4th load of seacoal from the Rock for John Clerk. Sarah Banks hay'd 'till noon. Return'd Mr Scrase's horse per Dick Clerk. He also fetcht a horse from Mr Gold's which he lends me. Paid Dick Clerk 7d for his day's work. Paid Dick Wood £1 5-0d in full of all accounts. Will went to Horsham Fair. My Father and Mother Stone here in the evning.

The 8th July 1721 Saturday. A gloomy morning, fine after. Smith and I carry'd a load of seacoal to John Clerk's and brought 773 plain tiles and 6 ridge tiles from James Parker's. John Clerk here towards night. Carry'd some old wheel strakes to Thomas Howell's.

The 9th July 1721 Sunday. A fine day.
Mr William Martin preacht twice. Mr Beard and my Father supt here. I call'd a vestry to consult about the repairs of the church.

The 10th July 1721 Munday. A fine day.
A new Fair at Trusslehouse Hill in Albourne. The boys carry'd 7 loads of Tully's Mead. Smith drove 4 cows to the Fair. Sold the black cow runt at the Fair to John Smith at £3-12-6d _____ . Sold also the 2 cows from Nutley Fair to Henry Dubbins and Thomas Stone at £8 to be fetcht this day fortnight. Receiv'd 20s of George Wickham for a load of hay.

The 11th July 1721 Tuesday. A fine day.
Smith and I carry'd a load of seacoal to John Clerk's. Brought home 500 bricks from James Parker's. Begun put flax in the Hayselcroft. Receiv'd 50s of George Hill in full for      lambs and one ewe, he had to go along

with the lambs. George Hill lay here last night.
Mr Jeremiah Dodson here this morning. I deliver'd James Wood's award between John Norton and he with the bond and a copy of the article in Mr Pierce's hands. Will, John White and Terry carry'd 5 loads of Tully's Mead.

The 12th July 1721 Wednesday. A fine day. Smith and I were way mending. Will and Jack White carry'd 5 small loads of Tully's Mead. Also they pulled flax as yesterday. Reckon'd with my Father and clear'd accounts for rent and his annuity to Lady Day last and for all other things to this day. John Smith fetcht the second runt.

The 13th July 1721 Thursday. A wet day.
Smith and I carry'd my Cousin Marchant's deals afternoon. Receiv'd 40s of Mr William Martin for keeping his mare last year.

The 14th July 1721 Fryday. A showry day.
Smith and I fetcht Old Sergeant's chucks which is to pay for his stubble mowing last year. Will, Jack White and Terry workt on the ricks etc. Mr John Hart supt and spent the evning here. Mrs Kettilby came to Hurst last night.

The 15th July 1721 Saturday. A dry day.
My Wife and I went to Balcombe. My Brother Henry Faulkoner and I were at Nayland. William Virgoe promis'd to pay me 30s for keeping Mary Terry the last year ending soon after Lady Day last. We brought Jacky Faulkoner home with us. Will and Jack White workt on the ricks. Smith and Harry White were way mending.

The 16th July 1721 Sunday. A fine day, only a showr or two towards night.
I were not at Church in the forenoon. My Wife and I were at Ditcheling to see my Cousin Nick Marchant's widdow being ill. We were at Church and at my Aunt Turner's. Mr Porter of Chayley preacht, Mr Ivers sick.

The 17th July 1721 Munday. A fine day.
Smith and I way mending. Carry'd 71 alder faggots to Stephen Reeve. Will, Jack White, Terry and the maids and SB hay'd. I were at Mrs Catherine Beard's towards night. Mr William Martin came there and desired my hand to a kind of certificate or commendamus to be shown to the Byshop in relation to the matter between Mr Jeremiah Dodson and he, which I refused. Receiv'd a payr of spatterdashes of Mr Richard Whitpaine for which I am to give him 2s.

The 18th July 1721 Tuesday. A fine day. Smith and I were way mending the 4th day. Paid my Cousin John Marchant £9-11-4½d for the Land Tax and receiv'd my legacy of 40s given me by my Cousin John Marchant deceased. Paid Mr Richard Whitpaine 2s for the spatterdashes mentioned yesterday. Paid John Westover 6d for mending them. Paid Thomas Whiteing 4s-3½d for lineing etc and 3s for making a payr of plush breeches. John Smith kill'd the white-faced heifer's calf at 10s. John White helpt carry 4 loads of the pond etc.

The 19th July 1721 Wednesday. A wet day.
Smith and I went to the Comon with a load of seacoal. Terry brought the mare to us afternoon. We brought home the waggon with chowl wheels from Thomas Howell's. I din'd at Clerk's. Howell's man clouted the wheels of the horse waggon. Brought home 500 bricks from James Parker's. Will, White and Terry topt the square ricks in Tully's steddle. Parker will have lime Tuesday or Wednesday next.

The 20th July 1721 Thursday. A gloomy day.
The boys hay'd afternoon. I were very much out of order else should have gone to Mr Price's afternoon. Sold John Smith 2 ewe lambs at 15s to be kill'd next week. Paid Chapman 1s for sheering 12 lambs unwashed. Paid Dick Smith 3s. He went to Henfield Fair towards night to fetch Jacky home.

The 21st July 1721 Fryday. A gloomy morning, fine after. Smith, Terry and I went to way mending with 2 teems. Carry'd a load each and carry'd 7 loads of the Little Meads hay after. Reckon'd with George West in the morning and he left 4s in my hands towards what was unpaid for his board. My Cousin Bodle of Hailsham call'd here in her way to Shermanbury. Mr Wicks here afternoon.

The 22nd July 1721 Saturday. A fine day.
The boys and I fetcht a load of great chalk and they carry'd 5 loads of the Little Meads to the ox rick.

The 23rd July 1721 Sunday. A fine day.
Mr Hawes preacht here this being his first Sunday of his officiating here. I were at Clayton church in the forenoon. Din'd at Mr Rick's. Went to Ditcheling

afternoon to see my Cousin Marchant, at Old Land afterwards.

The 24th July 1721 Munday. A gloomy morning, fine after. The boys hay'd and carry'd 1 load to Tully's and 2 home, of the Little Meads. Smith and Terry and I fetcht a load of great chalk in the forenoon and Smith and White fetcht 2 loads of sand from the bank by John Snashall's ground afternoon. Richard Wood mended one of the court wheels.

The 25th July 1721 Tuesday. A showry day. White and Smith fetcht one a load of sand from John Snashall's ground and one load out of Stephen Bine's pit. They and Terry winno'd wheat after. John Parsons shaved my head.

The 26th July 1721 Wednesday. A gloomy day, a showr or two. The mowers made an end of mowing grass yesterday at Rickman's. Harry White made an end of wheat thrashing. Terry, Smith and I deliver'd a load of chalk to Parker at the common and receiv'd 2 loads of lime and     bricks. Terry and James Banks drove the calves to Rickman's.

The 27th July 1721 Thursday. A gloomy morning, fine after. Smith and I carry'd half a load of alder wood and 50 faggots to Mrs Storer. Smith helpt carry hay after. CNI - The boys and the mowers carry'd 8 loads of the Little Meads being the last of our hay at home. Dick Wood repaired the ox waggon, comes to 3s-4d.
H Ockenden return'd the steers I lent him.

The 28th July 1721 Fryday. A fine day but a thunder showr in the evning. Smith, Clerk and I fetcht a load of building flints from Standean. *(Ed: South west of Ditchling).* The boys etc carry'd 8 loads of the clover at Rickman's. My Brother Will din'd here, went home towards night. Mr Coppard of Alciston here towards night. Paid Harry Woolven of Twineham 2s-6d for killing an otter in our parish. John Smith's boy kill'd a ewe for me.

The 29th July 1721 Saturday. A gloomy morning, fine after. Smith, Terry, Clerk, Harry White and I fetcht 2 loads of building flints from Standean, gave Mr Scrase's or Hamshire's men 6d to draw us out of the bottom. Mr Gratwick of Shermanbury, my Father and Mother Stone and Dr Vicent and Mrs Wicks din'd here. John Smith cut out my ewe this morning and she weigh'd 14½lbs per quarter, great weight. Paid Harry White 36s in mony and goods and clear'd accounts.

The 30th July 1721 Sunday. A dry day. Mr Hawes preacht twice. My Cousin John Wood of Twineham Place here. The brief for Cosby, John Alcock and H Chatfield was read and I kept the brief and money 8s-5d in John Hart's hands. My Wife and I were at Wanbarrow towards night.

The 31st July 1721 Munday. A fine morning, very wet after. Smith, Clerk and I went with our teem to Slaugham for stone for Mr Richard Whitpaine. Mrs Catherine Beard's teem, Harry Wickham's, Thomas Norton's Edgly and one teem of his own. Will and Terry did some jobbs at home. Mrs Bodle's man came for her towards night. Mr Picknall of Arundell here.

The 1st August 1721 Tuesday. A fine day.
Smith, Clerk and I fetcht a load of building flints from Standean. I were at Westtowne with Mrs Gratwick, Mrs Cheal, my Father and Mother Stone and Mrs Wick. Mr William Martin came towards night. We supt there. The boys etc carry'd 2 loads of flax of the Hayselcroft.

The 2nd August 1721 Wednesday. A fine day.
The boys and Jack White carry'd     loads of hay at Rickman's, Smith etc carry'd 2 jobbs, the last of the Hayselcroft flax. I were at Wanbarrow in the morning and after at the Swan with Mr Orlton, his brother John, Mr Beard and Mr Scutt. Three men with musick here. They said they lived at Hampton Court. George Hill jr of Rigate here to offer North Country lambs, I spoke for 10 and a ram. Thomas Hamper here --------- 25½ days

The 3rd August 1721 Thursday. A very fine day.
The boys made an end haying. They carry'd     loads of the sedge and of the Brooksmead. I were at Brighton. Receiv'd £11 of Mr Scrase etc for 2 loads of my own wheat and £11 for 2 loads of my Brother Peter's barly. Receiv'd likewise £5 of Mr Scrase, William Hamshire and Mr Scutt of Brighton for a load of wheat between them which I am to deliver tomorrow. I were at the New Ship with Mr Henry Campion, Mr Beard etc.
William Jarvice begun a flint wall --------- 1 day.

The 4th August 1721 Fryday. A fine day.
Smith and I deliver'd the load of wheat sold yesterday. Left Mr Scutt's at Mr Scrase's. Smith brought home a small load of flints out of a bottom northeast of

Patcham. Sent my Brother Peter's £11 which I receiv'd yesterday. Jack and Will went to Twineham Place afternoon. Will Jarvice and John Sanders workt on the flint walls ------- 2 days. Terry sifted wheat. The reapers begun reaping in Tully's long field by the coppice.

The 5th August 1721 Saturday. A very fine day. Smith and I fetcht ¾ of a cord of wood from Balcombe to John Smith's. Paid my Brother Henry Faulkoner 50s and 30s. He is to take of Balcombe's officers, in all £4 for a year's intrest. I din'd there. Will Jarvice workt on the wall alone ---------- 3 days. Will and Terry begun cut pease in the Rookwood.

The 6th August 1721 Sunday. A fine day. Mr Jeremiah Dodson preacht twice. I were at Wanbarrow afternoon with Mr Jeremiah Dodson. My Cousin Peter Marchant of Lewis here.

The 7th August 1721 Munday. A fine day. Will and Old Boniface begun mow oates. My Father, Mother, Widdow Somersoll, Cousin Rosbridger and his wife, my Wife and I and 2 girls din'd at Mr Colbron's of Brighton. I were at Harry Standbridge's. Also at Rogers's with Robert Skinner, George Hill etc. Will and Samuel Jarvice workt on the wall --------- 4 days. My Brother James Ede and Kitt Ede came to my Father. Paid my Cousin Peter Marchant 18s-6d for Will's wig.

The 8th August 1721 Tuesday. A fine day. Will and Bonny mow'd oates. Terry and Smith sifted wheat and Smith and Samuel Jarvice carry'd a load of wood to my Father's towards night.
Will and Jarvice cut pease ------------- 5 days.
I were at Wanbarrow in the morning. Receiv'd 20d of my Mother for a bottle of claret and the bottle. John Gold sent for his horse by Jack Bignall.

The 9th August 1721 Wednesday. A very fine day. Smith and I fetcht an other load of wood from Balcombe to John Smith. I din'd at Dean House. There was Robert Skinner, his wife and Young George Hill. Carry'd half a load of chalk to my Brother Henry Faulkoner. My Wife and I were at Wanbarrow towards night. Will, Terry etc cut pease. Will and Samuel Jarvice workt on the wall -------- 6 days. I saw Phineas Curtis of Hand Cross at Cuckfield and agreed with him for 1½ cord of wood at 9s per cord and to fetch it in the Annise Wood where I have the faggots.

The 10th August 1721 Thursday. A fine day. Smith and I carry'd the 4th and last load of John Clerk's coals and brought 400 coaping brick and 200 tiles from Taylor's at the Comon. Paid Taylor 8s for them. Paid my Cousin Libbard £1-18-6d in full of all accounts. Will and Samuel Jarvice finisht the wall about noon ------------- 6½ days. Receiv'd 40s of Nick Plaw for a year's intrest due on bond to William Balcomb. Thomas Campion here but not haveing brought the right receits we did nothing. Nick Plaw cut my bull for which I gave him 2s. He was here again in the evning to see him.

The 11th August 1721 Fryday. A fine day.
Will and the boys carry'd a load of pease etc. The bull cut yesterday bled to death in the night. I were at Counsellor Osbourne's for a licence to bring off my wheat from my copyhold. The counsellor not at home. I left a note with his brother Will. I were at Patcham to get market for my bull bief. I were also about Pyecomb Street. I supt at Mrs Catherine Beard's with my Father and Mother Stone and Mr Ede.

The 12th August 1721 Saturday. A gloomy morning, fine afternoon. I marketed my bull at John Smith's. Sold him at 10d per nail. John Smith went with Dick Smith to Patcham with 2 quarters of the bull and sold it all. The boys carry'd 3 loads of wheat by Tully's coppice. They also carry'd 4 loads of the Nine Acres.

The 13th August 1721 Sunday. A gloomy day. Mr Hawes preacht twice. I din'd at Mrs Catherine Beard's with Mr Ede. Mr Hawes read a brief for a churching. John Hart took the money.

The 14th August 1721 Munday. A fine day. The boys did severall jobbs. Carry'd 2 loads of pease. Fetcht home some faggots etc. Will and Boniface begun mow the Churchfield barly. Sarah Banks begun lay out the flax. Richard Wood's 2 girls helpt ½ the day. Sold John Smith Mr Burry's cow at 15d per nail and the tongue or the cheeks, to be kill'd this week. My Father and Mother Stone din'd here. Mr Picknall of Arundell here in the evning. Receiv'd 10s of John Smith for my bull's hide. John Hart here in the morning, brought a calfskin dresst.

The 15th August 1721 Tuesday. A wet morning, fine afternoon. The boys helpt Will Haslegrove clean flax seed, spread flax after. My Wife, Kitt Ede, Molly Balcomb, Smith and I went to Lewis afternoon. Paid Mr Andrew Laurence £2 in full of all accounts. Paid Mr Norman 14d for a book and all accounts. I were at Wanbarrow in the morning. Paid Mrs Durrant 8s for 3 handcerchiefs.

The 16th August 1721 Wednesday. A gloomy day, some rain. The boys did severall jobbs. Terry laid out flax. Reckon'd with my Cousin John Lindfield for the flax seed, intrest to midsummer last etc. John Smith kill'd the cow I had of Mr Burry at 15d per nail 5 quarters. My Sister Betty Courtness here.

The 17th August 1721 Thursday. A showry day. I were at Brighton. Sold a load of wheat to Thomas Gates of Beeding to be deliver'd at Shoreham at £5. I may carry 2 loads if I please. The boys did severall jobbs. Paid Mr Gold 10s-6d for Old Wheel tire. Weigh'd my cow I had of Mr Burry at John Smith. Her 4 quarters weigh'd 66 nail 7lb at 15d per nail 5 quarters.

The 18th August 1721 Fryday. A showry day. The boys did severall jobbs. Weaned the backward ram lambs 5. Mrs Minshall etc came to Mr Scutt's. My Father, Mr Ede, Mr Beard here in the evning. Mrs Catherine Beard's family here afternoon. Receiv'd £7-7s of Thomas Champion yesterday and outset half 2 year's annuity to my agent Holden with the Land Tax, in all £15 for half a year's rent for Eastout due at Michaelmas 1720.

The 19th August 1721 Saturday. A gloomy morning, fine after. The boys jobb'd. Smith and I fetcht a load of wood from Balcombe. Mr William Martin brought the parish register etc this morning.

The 20th August 1721 Sunday. A fine day. Mr Hawes preacht twice. My Cousin John Lindfield jr din'd here.

The 21st August 1721 Munday. A dry forenoon, wet towards night. The boys and Will Haslegrove carry'd a load of wheat and 2 loads of pease. Carry'd the pease to Tully's barn. Dr Vincent rode about the ground with me afternoon. Mrs Mary Whitpaine and Mr Picknall's daughter Mary came here. John Hart the tanner here in the morning. I exchanged a calf's skin with him. I am to pay for the corder's work. John Hart carry'd a calf's skin home with him. Newly lost.

The 22nd August 1721 Tuesday. A wet day. Mr Ralph Beard, Mr Ede and Will went to Balcombe to shooting. Shot 5 pheasants and 3 partridges in my Brother Will's ground. The boys mow'd wheat, straw etc. I sent a calf's skin and an old payr of housing to Stephen Avery's at Lewis per Abel Muzzall jr. I were at John Knight's in the evning with John Wood and Thomas Butcher jr. Receiv'd 10s-6d of JS for one of my ewes he kill'd to day. Receiv'd ¼lb bohea from Sam Tourl per AM. Receiv'd 2000 of 4d nails and 1000 6d from Mr Court's.

The 23rd August 1721 Wednesday. A dry day. The boys and Jack White cut ricks at Rickman's in the forenoon. Carry'd 1½ loads of wheat and 2½ loads of pease at home. Jack White did not help at home. Paid Thomas Hamper £3-8s, clear'd accounts, only there is 2 bushels of wheat due to him. Markt the tags at Rickman's.

The 24th August 1721 Thursday. A dry day. The boys cut pea mow and carry'd 2 loads of pease and a load of Tully's oates. Jack White helpt 'till noon. Mr Hawes and Master Jeremiah Dodson supt here. I were at Wanbarrow in the morning. Bought my Brother Peter's bull stag at £4.

The 25th August 1721 Fryday. A fine day. The boys made an end of Tully's oat field and 2½ loads, 4½ in all. Carry'd 6 loads of the Churchfield barly and two loads of the Nine Acres wheat. John Westover and John Kneller helpt carry barly. John White and Sarah Banks helpt carry barly. Sent a letter to Sir Robert Fagg which I receiv'd of Mr Henry Campion's coachman yesterday.

The 26th August 1721 Saturday. A fine day. The boys, Thomas Smith etc carry'd 8 loads of the Churchfield barly. John Smith drew out my fat sheep for London. Oliver had 1 bushel of the wheat due to Thomas Hamper.

The 27th August 1721 Sunday. A fine day. Mr Beaumont preacht twice. My Cousin John Lindfield supt and spent the evning here.

The 28th August 1721 Munday. A gloomy day, some rain. I were at a new Fair at Jolsfield Comon. Bought 5 runts of John Jenkins at £3-5s per runt, and afterwards

Nick Plaw and I bought 5 more of the same man at 58s per runt of which I am to have 3. Young Dick Banks begun his week at 6s and his board. He and the rest carry'd 5 loads of the Churchfield barly and 100 faggots to my Father. I call'd at Shermanbury as I came home from the Fair. Paid Nick Plaw 7 guineas towards the runts between us.

The 29th August 1721 Tuesday. A gloomy day, rain towards night. The boys and Dick Banks carry'd 2 loads of wood to my Father's and 3 loads of the Churchfield barly after. My Father and Mother Stone supt here. Receiv'd 4s-6d of John Smith for 4 rotten ewes.

The 30th August 1721 Wednesday. A very wet day. The boys screen'd 2 loads of wheat etc Richard Banks made a horse to saw wood on. Dick Smith fetcht the five runts from Nick Plaw's.

The 31st August 1721 Thursday. A wet day. Dick Banks and the boys fetcht some wood and did some other jobbs. Mr Burry din'd here. Mrs Scutt, her mother and Mrs Woodcock here afternoon. Paid Old Bony 6s-1d in full of all. The boys and Richard Banks carry'd a load of wheat into Tully's garret.

The 1st September 1721 Fryday. A gloomy morning, dry after. The boys turned some flax and carry'd 3 loads, the last of the Churchfield barly. Dick Smith went with four horses to help Mr Burry fetch a load of wood from Rivers Wood. Mr Phillip Cheal and Mrs Cheale of Shiprods din'd here. Mr John Hart here afternoon. My Father din'd here. Will fetch the other 3 runts from Plaw's.

The 2nd September 1721 Saturday. A fine day. The boys, Thomas Picknall _____ up the flax turned some barly etc. Will and Jack White carry'd the wheat at Rickman's. I were with Mr Burry in the morning at Thomas Smith's. I were at Randalls in the afternoon. I bid him £84 per annum for Randalls without the coppices. Mr Scutt there. Receiv'd 10s of Mr Burry for 9 of William Balcomb's sacks.

The 3rd September 1721 Sunday. A fine day. Mr Jeremiah Dodson preacht twice. We had a vestry afternoon. Settled accounts. My Cousin John Lindfield supt here. I borrowed £10-12s of him for a note of my hand dated the 4th.

The 4th September 1721 Munday. A dry day. Smith, Mr Burry's man and I went with 2 loads of wheat to Shoreham. Deliver'd it into Captain Boon's vessel for Mr Gates, one load at £5 the other at £5-5s. Will etc carry'd 5 loads of barly by Burt's. Mr Jeremiah Dodson supt here. I paid him my tythe due at Michaelmas next £6-1s and £6-10s for 42 bushels of seed wheat brought home. Paid Mr _____ at Shoreham 2s-6d for an other ladder pole. Paid Mr Pierce 4s-6d for 3 tare tubbs.

The 5th September 1721 Tuesday. A fine day. My Wife and I went to Broadwater. Call'd at Mr Burry's father's at Sounting. Din'd there. Mr Jeremiah Dodson went with us. I there bad Mr Burry £85 per annum for ~~Randiddle~~ Randalls. He insisted on 86 but I am to have it if he leaves it. The boys, Jack White etc tipt ricks and carry'd 4 loads of the barly by Burt's.

The 6th September 1721 Wednesday. A fine day. I were to see some ewes of Mr Penfold's at a farm call'd Burvells but we could not agree for 'em. I were at Natt Hobbes's towards night. The boys carry'd 2 loads more of the barly by Burt's.

The 7th September 1721 Thursday. A fine day. My Wife and I return'd from Broadwater. I were at Randalls in the evning and afterwards at Mrs Catherine Beard's. Terry begun carry dung out of Tully's close into Tully's long field, 8 loads. Terry drove 40 fat sheep yesterday to Dean House for London.

The 8th September 1721 Fryday. A fine day. I were at Cuckfield Fair and there bought a payr of oxen of John Hill's of Horsted Keynes servant at 16 guineas, the fuller brought them to Dean House. John Hill's man's name is George Ellis but I paid Hill's brother-in-law. Terry and Smith carry'd dung at Rickman's, 15 loads.

The 9th September 1721 Saturday. A fine day. The boys carry'd 13 loads of dung. I din'd at Dean House. My Cousin John Lindfield set out for part of the way to London. I brought home my new oxen with me. Receiv'd a new black saddle from Stephen Avery.

The 10th September 1721 Sunday. A fine day. Mr Hawes preacht twice. My wedding day, 21 years. My Father and Mother Stone din'd here. Goodman Daniel Groombridge of Horsham, carpenter brought my Father £20 from his tennant Rogers, for which ____ £14 brought some time ago by Rogers's boy, £34 in all. My Father gave a receit as in part for arrears of rent.

The 11th September 1721 Munday. A gloomy day. The boys did severall jobbs. My Wife and I din'd at my Father's. Paid Will Haslegrove a guinea. Borrowed twenty guineas of my Father.

The 12th September 1721 Tuesday. A showry day. Will and Jack White went tipping of ricks for my Brother Peter. Receiv'd and clear'd accounts with John Gun to this day all but rent and that to Lady Day last. Paid John Gun £3-17-2d. John Smith put 3 horses into my earshes last night at 3s per week. The boys carry'd dung at Rickman's 12 loads. Had home my Cousin John Lindfield's oxen and horses. Receiv'd 2 quarters of seed wheat of Mr Jeremiah Dodson. Nick Plaw here to see a sick hog.

The 13th September 1721 Wednesday. A dry forenoon, wet towards night. The boys did severall jobbs, gather'd apples afternoon. Thomas Hamper workt here, made a deal ladder ---------- 1 day. I were at Randalls afternoon. John Cook came home with us (with my Wife and I). I let Cook part of Randalls house with all the orchard below the way into Mr Peter Courthope's field, to keep a hog but no poultry at 45s per annum. He is to have a penny a week per bullock for serving the cattle when he works by the great but when he works by the day he is to serve the beasts into the bargain.

The 14th September 1721 Thursday. A dry forenoon, wet after. Smith and Terry fetcht 2 loads of wood and faggots from Dean House to my Father's. Reckon'd with Old Dick Banks to this day, only his runt and cow keeping was reckon'd but 'till Lady Day last. Left to pay to him £4. I receiv'd my accounts of my sheep market of my Cousin John Lindfield with 7s-6d in money and a bill of £14 on Frank Holden one sheep lost by the way. Harry Morley thatched at Tully's to day and yesterday.

The 15th September 1721 Fryday. A fine day. I were at St John's Comon Fair, bought 2 oxen of John Faulkoner at Bridge _____ . Paid him 13 guineas for them. Old Dick Banks brought 'em. Terry and Smith fetcht the dung carts from Rickman's. Carry'd 12 loads of dung up into the field by Botting's. Receiv'd the £14 of Frank Holden which I paid for him in London.

Harry Morley thrasht at Tully's. Bought 4 bushels of head wheat of John Gold as he sold the rest.

The 16th September 1721 Saturday. A gloomy morning, fine after. The boys and Old Dick Banks carry'd 13 loads of dung at home and 2 loads of oates at Rickman's. I were at Albourne Place in the morning to see a horse. He was too small. I were afternoon at Randalls. Offer'd Mr Burry to carry a load of wheat for him to Shoreham or Beeding for buying the 40 ewes. Agreed with Goodman Rick of Pyecomb, he is to have the kitchen part of my Tully's house at 35s per annum, to keep no hog nor poultry, to enter at Michaelmas next and each to give the other a quarter's notice when we design to part.

The 17th September 1721 Sunday. A fine day. Mr Hawes preacht in the forenoon, Mr John Hart afternoon. My Wife and I were at Wanbarrow after evning prayr. I sent a letter to James Wood per Smith.

The 18th September 1721 Munday. A wet morning, fine after. The boys carry'd 16 loads of dung into the field by Botting's. My Cousin James Wood, my Cousin John Lindfield and I were at Randalls. They valued things between Mr Burry and I. H Peckham came but did not stay. Young George Hill brought 11 North Country lambs at 10s a piece.

The 19th September 1721 Tuesday. A fine day. The boys carry'd 5 loads of dung. Paid 3s-6d for a handcerchief for Molly Balcomb. The boys made an end of harvest at Heath's, 2 loads oates. My Brother Peter and I were at William Hamshire's to see store ewes. Paid George Hill £5-10s for 11 store lambs.

The 20th September 1721 Wednesday. A very fine day. I were at Horsted. Paid the Widdow Weller £4 for a year's intrest due at midsummer last. Came home by Sayers of Chayley Comon to buy a horse, but bought none. My Father and Mr John Hart supt here. The boys carry'd 15 loads of dung. ~~Sarah Banks~~ Old Dick Banks and the maids turned the seed clover.

The 21st September 1721 Thursday. A fine day. I were at Cliffe Fair. Bought a payr of oxen of Thomas Kemp of Horsted Keynes at £14-10s. Paid him for 'em. Borrowed 20 guineas of Dr White for a note of my hand. Bought a horse of Mr Pollington at 3 guineas paid.

Paid Samuel Tourl and Stephen Avery in full. John Gun and the boys carry'd 27 loads of dung into the field at Bottings.

The 22nd September 1721 Fryday. A fine day.
My Wife and I were at Mr Kelsy's sale at the Bull in Cuckfield. We bought severall goods which we left for the most part unpaid. The boys, John Gun and Banks carry'd 30 loads of dung into the Bankfield.

The 23rd September 1721 Saturday. A fine day.
The boys and I went to Balcombe for a load of wood and brought our goods from Cuckfield. Will went to coursing with John Box sr. John Gun and Banks carry'd loads of dung into the Bankfield.

The 24th September 1721 Sunday. A fine day.
Mr Hawes preacht. No service afternoon. My Cousin Jack Lindfield jr din'd here.
I din'd at Mrs Catherine Beard's with Mr Wilkin of London. I were at Mr Scutt's afternoon, he not at home.

The 25th September 1721 Munday. A fine day.
The boys did severall jobbs. Reckon'd and clear'd account with Harry Morley the thatcher.
Mr Wilkin here in the morning. I receiv'd £5-6-6d of him which Mr Davenport paid to him for my Brother Peter in my name. Mrs Nordon din'd here. John Haslegrove here hitcholling. I deliver'd him £55. Paid my Brother Peter the money receiv'd above mentioned. I were at Randalls afternoon. Divided the ewes between my Brother and I, he 42 and I 63 with the rams. I call'd at Mr Jeremiah Dodson's as I came home. Appointed to go to Beeding a Wednesday next on Mr Newlin's account. John Hart here about noon.

The 26th September 1721 Tuesday. A fine day.
Mr Picknall and Mr Howes here. Smith and White begun stirr the little fallow at Randalls. Joe carry'd 3 loads of Tully's seed clover afternoon. We had our harvest supper this evning. Mr Hawes supt here. John Gun and Rick carry'd     loads of dung at Randalls. Terry had my new horse to Sam Hart's yesterday and brought home Sam's colt in exchange, I gave a guinea to boot which I am to outset with John Smith.

The 27th September 1721 Wednesday. A gloomy forenoon, fine after. Rick and Banks carry'd loads of dung at Randalls. I were at Beeding again about Mr Newlin's matter with Mr Penfold. Did not agree, referred it to James Wood.

The 28th September 1721 Thursday. A fine day.
Moved Stephen Rick and a load of Stephen Reeve. I were at Randalls in the morning. Mr Scutt there too. We gave him instructions for a lease. Paid Mr Burry £16 towards the 40 ewes I had of him. Receiv'd £19-19s in money of John Smith and outset a guinea on Samuel Hart's account, in all £21.

The 29th September 1721 Fryday. A fine day.
I went to Stenning Fair with my Cousin John Lindfield etc. Bought 10 runts of David Williams at £4-10s per runt. He is to bring them to my house tomorrow. Will and Terry plough'd in the Rookwood. Banks and Smith fetcht a load of seacoal from Shoreham for my Lord Treep.

The 30th September 1721 Saturday. A fine day.
Will and Terry plough'd in the Rookwood. Smith etc carry'd dung at Randalls, 38 loads. David Williams and his man brought the runts into Randalls ground. They were here a while. Promis'd to bring the runts hither tomorrow. My Cousin John Lindfield here. Receiv'd £3-10s of my Cousin John Lindfield for 7 of the North Country lambs from George Hill. Paid Molly Balcomb 4s-4d for a quarter spending money at 4d per week due yesterday.

The 1st October 1721 Sunday. A fine day.
Mr Jeremiah Dodson preacht. My Wife and I receiv'd the sacrament. A parish meeting afternoon as usual. Mr Williams brought our runts home and we paid him.
I supt and spent the evning at Mr Dodson's.

The 2nd October 1721 Munday. A fine day.
My Father, Mother, my Wife and I went down and din'd at Randalls. Smith etc carry'd dung there, 47 loads. The last of the mixen. My Cousin John Lindfield here afternoon.     We shifted our runts and lambs. He is to have but 5 lambs but I did not return the money I had receiv'd for them. John Packet here with a mare and colt. I bad him two guineas for the colt but we did not deal.

The 3rd October 1721 Tuesday. A fine day.
Smith drove plough at Randalls. Terry, Jack White and Will sow'd and harrow'd in Rookwood. I din'd and supt

at Randalls. Thomas Hill the butcher at Stenning din'd there.     Jack Smith there in the evning.

The 4th October 1721 Wednesday. A fine day.
Will and Terry finisht the Rookwood. Sow'd 14 bushels of Mr Jeremiah Dodson's wheat on it. Jack White and Dick Smith begun ridge the little field at Randalls. Bought a parcell of horse harness of Mr Burry at 20s. Borrow'd £20 of John Snashall jr for a note of my hand. Borrowed 10 guineas more of my Father Stone. Paid Old Dick Banks £3 of the £4 due when we reckon'd.

The 5th October 1721 Thursday. A fine day.
My Wife and I went to Lewis. The boys and Jack White sow'd the old hop garden at Randalls with the 4 bushels of wheat from John Gold's. Paid Dr White the 20 guineas I borrowed of him.

The 6th October 1721 Fryday. A fine day.
The boys and Jack White plough'd and sow'd at Randalls. Finisht the old hop garden. I were at Twineham Place. Gave James Wood an account in writeing of Mr Newlin's matter and appointed to go Wednesday next. Receiv'd £10 of John Smith per my Wife. Paid my Father Stone the last 10 guineas I borrowed of him.

The 7th October 1721 Saturday. A gloomy day.
The boys and Jack White plough'd and sow'd at Randalls. Richard Banks jr helpt them afternoon. Abraham Muzzall carry'd a saddle and leather to Lewis with a saddle I borrowed. Brought 100 faggots home from Randalls. Will Haslegrove ran his knife into his thigh unloading 'em. Dick Smith went to Broadwater with Bett.

The 8th October 1721 Sunday. A wet morning, dry after.
Mr Hawes preacht. I were at my Father's a while in the evning.

The 9th October 1721 Munday. A fine day.
I were at Mr Virgoe's of Cuckfield with Mr Ives. Borrowed £100 of H Burtenshaw for a year at £5 per 100. Din'd at Dean House as I came home. The boys and Jack White and Dick Banks plough'd and sow'd at Randalls. Mr Burry and his 2 brothers supt here. They came to Randalls with 3 teems.

The 10th October 1721 Tuesday. A showry day.
Plough'd at Randalls with one teem, the other teem mov'd Cook's goods and carry'd some of ours to Randalls. Mrs Catherine Beard and her family at Randalls afternoon. Mr Hawes with them. Paid John Snashall the £20 which I borrowed of him and £30 to John Smith to carry to Henry Scrase tomorrow, brought 50 faggots from Randalls yesterday.

The 11th October 1721 Wednesday. A fine day.
The boys plough'd at Randalls. I din'd at Mr Reckwood's of Beeding with Mr Newlin and my Cousin James Wood. We viewed the repairs of the close thatch and left him, James Wood to consider of _____ . We were at Mr Newlin's house afterwards. Mr Newlin sent a messenger to Stenning for Mr Penfold of Broadwater but he was not to be found, nor William Birdfield.

The 12th October 1721 Thursday. A wet day.
The boys did severall jobbs. Paid my Cousin Libbard of Chichester £1-2 6d in full of all accounts and 2s-6d for spatterdashes. John Gun helpt Banks winnow all the wheat at Rickman's etc. There was 3 quarters 1 bushel head and 4 bushels tail. Paid Henry Scrase £30 yesterday per John Smith for my part of the ewes between Brother Peter and I. Paid Dick Wood £1-8-6d yesterday in full of all.

The 13th October 1721 Fryday. A very wet morning, fine after. Mr Libbard lay here last night. Went home this morning. Dick Banks jr and the boys and Jack White plough'd half the day at Randalls. Rob Leach begun thatch a hay rick at Randalls. I supt at my Father's.

The 14th October 1721 Saturday. A dry day.
Banks, White and the boys made an end of ploughing and sowing at Randalls. Thomas Hamper and his man workt at Randalls ----------------- 2 days.
The teem brought a jobb of Jack Parker's stuff for Thomas Hamper as they came home from Randalls.

The 15th October 1721 Sunday. A fine day.
Mr Jeremiah Dodson preacht. Mr Phillip Cheal din'd here. We were at Westtowne afternoon. Mr Dodson supt here.

The 16th October 1721 Munday. A fine day.
Banks and White begun plough by Wickham's. Smith cross harrow'd and finisht the field at Randalls. Mr John Hart supt and spent the evning here. I din'd at my Father's. My Brother John Box here in the morning.

We exchanged receit about H Farncomb's money. Will King and one of Thomas Hamper's men workt at Randalls. Paid Mr Jeremiah Dodson £4-17-6d for 30 bushels more of seed wheat. He is to send it home.

The 17th October 1721 Tuesday. A gloomy day, rain towards night. Paid Will King 1s for my part of the work at Randalls. I din'd at Randalls with Mr Burry. Banks, White and the boys plough'd and sow'd at Wickham's. My Father, Mother, Mrs Hart, my Wife and I supt at Westtowne, and the Flabberchops Bruite his wife pick't a quarrel with my Wife because she *(Ed: Mrs Mary Whitpaine)* had kept my Brother Will's dog by force.

The 18th October 1721 Wednesday. A wet morning, dry after. My Cousin John Wood of Twineham din'd here. I invited my Cousin John Lindfield but he did not come. Richard Banks and the boys and clear'd the great barn's floor. Win'd oates with John Gun etc. Receiv'd 2 quarters of wheat of Mr Jeremiah Dodson yesterday. Paid Thomas Hamper 20s for my Window Tax yesterday.

The 19th October 1721 Thursday. A very wet day. Richard Banks and the boys did severall jobbs, cutting mows etc. Will and Terry drove 8 runts to Randalls. I were a while at the Swan with Stephen Bine, Edgly Norton, John Westover and William Beard. Dick Wood put on new fashioned tuggs to two payr of horse dills. He is to have 2s for it. Edgly Norton gave me a letter from Mr Burry.

The 20th October 1721 Fryday. A showry day. The boys and Banks made water furrows at Randalls etc. I went to course a hare George Piony had found in Randalls ground but she was gone. I supt and spent the evning with Mr John Hart.

The 21st October 1721 Saturday. A dry day 'till towards night. The boys, Richard Banks, White etc plough'd and sow'd. Jacky and I went to Lewis. Din'd at my Cousin Bl......'s. Paid 4s-6d for a cart saddle, a crooper dock etc. Paid Stephen Avery 4s-6d for covering a saddle. Left Mr Gold's sack at my Cousin Peter Marchant's. Return'd a sack to Thomas Friend which I borrowed.

The 22nd October 1721 Sunday. A dry day. Mr Hawes preacht. My Cousin John Lindfield, Mr Beard and Cousin Peter Marchant din'd here. Mr Scutt and his wife supt here.

The 23rd October 1721 Munday. A very wet day. Richard Banks and Smith went to Shoreham ferry with a load of Mr Burry's wheat and brought home a load of seacoal for Mr Scutt.

The 24th October 1721 Tuesday. A fine day. Mr Sixsmith din'd here. I supt at my Father with Mr Sixsmith. Mr Price here and afterwards at my Father's. Richard Banks and White and the boys plough'd and sow'd.

The 25th October 1721 Wednesday. A dry day. Made an end of sowing the field by Wickham's etc. Mr Sixsmith lay at my Father's last night.

The 26th October 1721 Thursday. A fine forenoon, wet after. The boys win'd skreenings etc. Smith and I went to Broadwater. Call'd at Mr Burry's of Sounting. Paid him 20 guineas for his [S............]. I were at Mr Penfold's a while towards night. Mr Jeremiah Dodson and his wife went to dine with Mr Wills. My Son Will's birthday, 20 years.

The 27th October 1721 Fryday. A dry day. Smith and I return'd from Broadwater. Richard Banks, Terry and Rick carry'd 22 loads of the stable dung into the Bankfield. I came home by Shoreham.
Went to J Bromfield's sale at St Johns Comon after I came home.

The 28th October 1721 Saturday. A dry day. Richard Banks etc carry'd 11 loads of the stable dung and 15 of John Smith's into the Bankfield. Paid Richard Banks 12s for 3 weeks work. Dick Wood set 2 steeld shoes on my horse's forefeet.

The 29th October 1721 Sunday. A fine day. Mr Hawes preacht.

The 30th October 1721 Munday. A gloomy day. My Wife and I were at Ditcheling. Din'd at my Cousin Marchant's. Went to see Mr Ivers's goods and bought as much as came to 15s-3d. Paid Mr Nath Osbourne for it. The boys etc carry'd dung.

The 31st October 1721 Tuesday. A dry day. The boys and John Gun carry'd dung. Put the fatting oxen into the Fifteen Acres. Borrowed 20 guineas of

Frank Holden for a note.
I supt at my Father's with Mr Scutt and Mr John Hart. Reckon'd with John Smith yesterday and there is due to me £17-7-7¾d. Reckon'd with Mrs Storer to day and clear'd her intrest and all our accounts to Michaelmas last and gave her a fresh note for £30 with intrest.

The 1st November 1721 Wednesday. A gloomy day, some rain. Will and Terry begun fallow at Randalls. Smith kept holy day. I were at Mr Ivers's sale at Ditcheling. Paid my Brother John Courtness a bill of £10-8-8d and £1-1 0d on my Mother's account. Paid him also £1-9-6d for Molly Balcomb.

The 2nd November 1721 Thursday. A gloomy day, rain towards night. Will and Terry plough'd at Randalls. Smith did severall jobbs. My Wife and I supt and spent the evning at John Stone's.

The 3rd November 1721 Fryday. A showry day. The boys did some jobbs. Thomas Hamper made a new door into the parlour out of the sink ------- 3 days.
I was at Mr Hawes in the evning. Afterwards at Thomas Smith with Mr Arnold of Horsham.

The 4th November 1721 Saturday. A dry day. Young Dick Banks and Smith went to Shoreham Ferry with a load of Mr Berry's wheat and brought home a load of seacoal for Mr Scutt. I were at Shoreham with Mr William Martin.

The 5th November 1721 Sunday. A wet day Mr Jeremiah Dodson preacht. Dr White came to my Mother Stone.

The 6th November 1721 Munday. A showry day. Dr White lay at our house last night, went away this morning. I went to St Leonard's Fair, bought a Lancashire bull at £4 and heifer at £4-15s of David Williams, also a culling runt of my Cousin John Lindfield's parcell of Evan Bowen at 45s. Mr William Martin here in the evning. I sold him the Rusper liveing at £700 and 5 guineas over to enter at Michaelmas past and to pay all the money by Xmas next and to allow intrest for it from Michaelmas last.

The 7th November 1721 Tuesday. A gloomy day. Terry lay at my Cousin John Lindfield's and brought home the beasts from St Leonard's to day. I were at Mr Jeremiah Dodson's in the evning. Smith did severall jobbs.

The 8th November 1721 Wednesday. A gloomy day. The boys and I went to Ditcheling with the horse teem for feeds. I went thence to Mr Sixsmith's, he not at home. I went to Falmer and borrowed £50 of Margret Bradford for a note of my hand. Paid Frank Holden 20 guineas which I borrowed. I were a while at Mr Jeremiah Dodson's. My Cousin John Lindfield, John Stapley and Mr Burt of Brook Street call'd here in the evning.

The 9th November 1721 Thursday. A dry day. Mr Jeremiah Dodson's tythe feast. I were at Mr Scutt's and at Thomas Smith's with Mr William Martin. Will and Smith plough'd at Randalls.

The 10th November 1721 Fryday. A gloomy day, some rain. Will and Terry went to coursing. Smith did some jobbs. Mr William Martin and I went to Lewis, staid very late. Paid Mr Court 6s for 6 knives and as many forks. Also 4s-6d for a lock for the parlour door. Clear'd accounts with Norman.

The 11th November 1721 Saturday. A gloomy day, some rain. Will and Smith plough'd at Randalls. Terry spread dirt etc. Paid John Parsons 6d for shaveing my head. My Brother John Courtness here a little while afternoon. Paid Thomas Whiteing 9s for fustian and making it into a payr of breeches. Paid him at John Parson's shop. Mrs Catherine Beard and Mrs Kettilby here afternoon.

The 12th November 1721 Sunday. A gloomy day. Mr Jeremiah Dodson preacht. A parish meeting afternoon about the Widdow Wicks. My Cousin John Lindfield and his son din'd here.
I was at Mr Jeremiah Dodson's and Mr Scutt's in the evning. Lent Mr Dodson £3-5s for a note of his hand. He was here just before evning prayr.

The 13th November 1721 Munday. A wet morning, fine afternoon. Dr White here to see Kitty. John Kneller went for him. Will and Smith plough'd at Randalls. Terry helpt Rick thrash 9 bushels of oates. Thomas Hamper set on a lock to the parlour door. The heifer of Dr Nick Plaw's cow was bulling and the Lancashire bull was with her. Whether she went to bull or not I can't tell. Bought 5 quarters of grey pease of Mr Jeremiah Dodson for seed at £6 to be brought home at my request.

The 14th November 1721 Tuesday. A gloomy day. Will and Smith plough'd. Terry did severall jobbs.

The 15th November 1721 Wednesday. A showry day. Will and Smith plough'd as yesterday. Terry carry'd a great coat to Cuckfield to day or yesterday which Willy borrowed of Yung Hunt.

The 16th November 1721 Thursday. A dry day. Will and Terry were a coursing in Danny ground. Thomas Burtenshaw quarrel'd with them and Yung Godly and Hollobone also. Mr Jeremiah Dodson here in the morning in his way to London. I were at Randalls. Sent Cook after a lost sheep. Stephen Reeve brought home a small piece of sacking at 4s6d the weaving.

The 17th November 1721 Fryday. A gloomy morning, fine after. Will went to coursing with John Marchant of Lox. The boys did severall pbbs. Mr Ralph Beard and my Brother Peter supt here.

The 18th November 1721 Saturday. A fine day. Mr Ralph Beard and I were at Danny afternoon. Mr Middleton there. Will and Smith plough'd at Randalls. Terry pbb'd. Receiv'd 8s1d of John Bodle for my part of his deals. Paid my Father Stone 10 guineas of the 20 that I ow'd him on a note per my Wife.

The 19th November 1721 Sunday. An excessive wet day. Mr John Hart preacht. I were not at Church. I were at Mr Scutt's in the evning and at my Father's.

The 20th November 1721 Munday. A dry day. Will and Smith made an end of fallowing Randalls Sandfield. Terry ground malt etc. Thomas Jacket here in the evning. Paid Cook 1s for 2 half day's work. Mr William Martin here in the morning. Receiv'd a letter from Mr Newlin to which I wrote an answer to be carry'd tomorrow. I were at Mr Scutt's to meet Mr William Martin etc but nobody came.

The 21st November 1721 Tuesday. A fine day. I were at Shoreham. Bought a Cheshire cheese of Mr B Hayler at 3d per lb and paid for 'em. Agreed with Richard Smith to carry him a load of wheat at £5 10s. Terry helpt Old Dick Banks winnow oats at Rickman's.

The 22nd November 1721 Wednesday. A very fine day. My Wife and I at Lewis. Smith and John Gun screened wheat and had it to Randalls.

The 23rd November 1721 Thursday. A gloomy day, thick mist. I were at Shoreham expecting my teem to come but they were a stand at the foot of Mr Osbourne's Holt Hill *(Ed: Newtimber)* and like blockheads left the load there. Terry thrasht a little barly. I were at Mr Scutt's in the evning with Mr William Martin and Mr Richard Whitpaine.

The 24th November 1721 Fryday. A dry day. Rick, Smith and I carry'd a load of wheat to Shoreham to Richard Smith at £5 10s. Brought home a load of seacoal for Mr Scutt and 200 weight of cannel coal for my self which I bought of Mr Benjamin Hayler at 2s per hundredweight for my self. Brought also 3 Cheshire cheeses at 3d per lb.

The 25th November 1721 Saturday. A dry day. The boys did severall pbbs. Smith carry'd home Mr Friend's dills which we borrowed yesterday. I were at Mr Scutt's in the evning and seal'd articles with Mr Scutt and Mr Richard Whitpaine for the advowson of Rusper lieving and receiv'd 20s in hand and am to have £699 more when we seal the conveyance or security for it and the money in 3 months. Receiv'd the £50 of my Cousin John Lindfield which he ow'd me on bond and clear'd accounts. He supt here. My Cousin John Lindfield and Frank Holden were witnesses to the articles between Mr Scutt etc and I.

The 26th November 1721 Sunday. A dry morning, very wet after. Mr John Hart preacht, no service afternoon. Mr Ede and an other went through the ground this morning. John Smith kill'd the last year's Wintermilch a Thursday last at 14d per nail. She weigh'd 62 nail 3lb the 4 quarters.

The 27th November 1721 Munday. A fine day. Will and Smith plough'd. Terry went to Lewis for my Father. Dr Vincent paid Thomas Burt 18d per Terry for 4 bushels of salt which I am to have by my Cousin John Lindfield's teem. I were at Thomas Howell's at the Comon. Receiv'd 2s1d of Goodman Taylor for bull bief. I were at Mr Scutt's in the evning.

The 28th November 1721 Tuesday. A very wet day. The boys pbb'd. Agreed with Henry White of Cuckfield to work for me from Lady Day next. He is to live in the Cobb's Croft house which I am to take of Goodman White the weaver. Mr John Hart and Mr Burry here in the evning. Paid Mr Courtness sr a bill of £1 2s 3d for Molly Balcomb. Paid him also £1 2s 3d for my self.

The 29th November 1721 Wednesday. A dry day.
Mr Burry lay here last night. He and I went to Randalls
to see the Foxhole pond fisht but they could not get the
water out. We were at Mr Scutt's in the evning.

The 30th November 1721 Thursday. A fine day.
The boys kept holy day. Mr Burry lay here last night.
We fisht the Foxhole pond to day. He gave me 5 carp.
I went from Randalls to Wanbarrow, my Wife there.
I were at my Father's in the evning. Mr Burry went
home. Paid Mr Burry 15 guineas.

The 1st December 1721 Fryday. A fine day.
Will sick. Thomas Hamper and his man fitted on a new
payr of horse dills in the morning and the Smiths and I
put on the irons after. John Smith kill'd my calf. My
Wife and I din'd at my Father's. Mr William Martin came
there in afternoon. Mrs Ann Dodson and her daughter,
Mrs Catherine Beard and her family here afternoon.
Terry helpt John Gun make syder. Smith and Rick had
the teem to Randalls and loaded the tares for tomorrow.

The 2nd December 1721 Saturday. A fine day, hard frost.
Rick, Smith and I went to Beeding with a load of Mr
Burry's tares. Paid Chapman 1s for greasing my ewes
and sheering the 11 Northamptonshire lambs some time
ago.

The 3rd December 1721 Sunday. A fine day, frosty.
Mr Hawes sr of Berwick preacht. A meeting afternoon
but no business done. My Wife and I supt at Mr ____'s.

The 4th December 1721 Munday. A fine day, frosty.
Smith carry'd some goods to Randalls and brought home
50 of Mr Burry's faggots. Lent John Smith the butcher
£8. Kitt Vinall here and said her aunt was bid £10 for
her barn. I agreed with John Smith that he should have
my calf which he kill'd last week at a guinea.

The 5th December 1721 Tuesday. A fine day, frosty.
The boys and John Gun carry'd dung at Tully's into the
wheat earsh by the coppice, 17 loads. John Smith's man
fetcht a runt from Rickman's. My Wife was at Thomas
Norton's North End. Nick Plaw and Mr William Martin
here in the evning. Will went to Cuckfield.

The 6th December 1721 Wednesday. A gloomy day, frost
thawing towards night. I were at Randalls in the
forenoon. My Cousin Richard Turner's wife Jane of Old
Land, my Cousin Picket etc din'd here. Carry'd dung 13
loads. Mr Beard and Mr William Martin here, Mr Beard
brought word that the living of Rusper was vacated by
Mr Sixsmith. A dancing master at my Father's last night.
Paid John Parsons yesterday 19s for a year's shaveing my
Son William. Clear'd accounts. Paid Old Dick Banks 3s.

The 7th December 1721 Thursday. A gloomy day, snow
in the evning. I sign'd a presentation to Mr William
Martin of Rusper leiving to resign when either of my
Sons are in orders. Took a bond of him for it. The boys
and John Gun carry'd dung at Tully's 15 loads. My Wife
and I supt at John Box's sr.

The 8th December 1721 Fryday. A gloomy day.
A public fast. Mr John Hart preacht afternoon.
The boys and John Gun carry'd dung at Tully's, 13 loads,
in all of the close 58. My Cousin John Lindfield here.
Will and he coursed a hare. Receiv'd the £8 due from
Henry Dubbins per John Smith.

The 9th December 1721 Saturday. A gloomy day, some
snow. Smith and Mr Scutt's boy went to Lewis. They
brought home a saddle new covered from Stephen
Avery etc, 4 bushels of salt from Thomas Burt's, paid for
etc. My Father and Mother Stone supt here. Receiv'd a
letter from my landlord Burry with an account of the
death of his father etc. I sent an answer by the
messenger. R Piony begun thrash barly in the Foxhole
Barne one day this week.

The 10th December 1721 Sunday. A gloomy day, some
snow, rain towards night. No service at Church. Thomas
Howell here in the morning. John Stone's man and
Thomas Nye followed a hare into our New Orchard.
Will and Terry followed from thence and kill'd her not
far from Abby's. I din'd at my Father's, William
Charman came to me there and appointed me to meet
John Box sr at Towne tomorrow night.

The 11th December 1721 Munday. A gloomy day,
thawing. The boys helpt Old Dick Banks winnow 8
quarters and ½ bushel of barly which he thrasht by the
day. Receiv'd a letter from Sixsmith to acquaint me that
Rusper leiving was void for that he was instituted to
Street on Fryday the 1st day of this month. In the evning
I were at Thomas Smith's with John Box, Nick Plaw and
William Charman about Henfield windmill. and (with
much ado) persuaded him to continue in her promising
him to abate 2s per annum for the year ensuing if wheat

in the compass of the year be when sold hereabouts at 4s per bushel. Spent 18d. Paid Nick Plaw 27s due for runts at Jolsfield Fair.

The 12th December 1721 Tuesday. A fine day.
The boys carry'd litter into the fatting close. Brought home some faggots etc. Mr Beard here in the morning. Left a watch with Will. Nick Plaw came last night to look on an ox, not _____ . I were at Mr Scutt's towards night.   My Wife and I supt at Mr [Dodson's].

The 13th December 1721 Wednesday. A showry day.
The boys carry'd 7 quarters of barly to be malted at Harry Wickham's. Brought home 7 bushels of malt. Paid Mr Courtness 8d for 2 wanty ropes per Tom and 4d yesterday for a serving rope my self.

The 14th December 1721 Thursday. A gloomy day.
The boys did severall jobbs. Thomas Muzzall kill'd 2 porkers afternoon. Paid him 6d for ____ . My Father and Mother Stone din'd here. Dick Banks workt afternoon for his victuals.
Thomas Hamper and his man here ----- 4 days.

The 15th December 1721 Fryday. A gloomy morning, wet afternoon. Receiv'd £8 of John Smith for the note of his hand. Dick Banks begun at 2s-6d per week and his board. Will and he drew furroughs in Tully's ground. He loaded the wheat at Randalls afternoon, Banks and Smith [ded]. Terry did severall jobbs. Sifted flax seed and deliver'd 21 bushels at Thomas Smith's for Harry Wickham for which I am to have 23s per quarter. Paid my Unkle Courtness 2s for an old saddle.

The 16th December 1721 Saturday. A dry day.
Richard Banks and Smith carry'd a load of Mr Burry's wheat to Shoreham, brought home an 100 weight of cannel coal for my Father and an other for Mrs Kettilby. Terry and Will helpt John Gun winnow oates. I put on two locks at Randalls Lime Kiln Field.

The 17th December 1721 Sunday. A dry day.
No service in the forenoon. Mr Healy preacht afternoon. I were at Mrs Catherine Beard's in the evning with Mr Henry Campion.

The 18th December 1721 Munday. A gloomy day.
I were at Lewis with my team for Goodman Roach for which I am to have 7s-6d. There was about 3 hundred weight. Paid a bill of £2-19s to Aunt Galloway for wine for my Father, Mrs Kettilby etc. Brought a stove for my Father at 20s to be return'd if not liked. The boys helpt John Gun winnow oates.

The 19th December 1721 Tuesday. A very fine day.
I was at Twineham Place to talk with my Cousin John Wood about Mr Newlin's Molly. Richard Banks carry'd dung out of the rick steddles and Terry spread dung by Tully's coppice. Smith fetcht 20 ewes from Randalls etc. Mrs Ann Dodson supt here. I were at Mr Jeremiah Dodson's in the morning. Paid him £4-17-6d which he paid to Mr Cossins in London for me. Lent Mr Dodson 4 guineas more for a note.

The 20th December 1721 Wednesday. A very fine day.
My Cousin Hayne, Widdow of Henfield died yesterday. Thomas Hayne here to day. Terry did some jobbs. Helpt Old Dick Banks to winnow afternoon. Richard Banks and Smith mov'd some flax, went to Randalls. A man from Lewis here to be a gardener to Mr Jeremiah Dodson.

The 21st December 1721 Thursday. A fine day, frosty.
Richard Banks and Smith went to Shoreham with an other load of Mr Burry's wheat and brought home 228lbs weight of cannel coal. They carry'd 100 weight to my Father's and 200 weight to Mrs Kettilby which were brought home ____ times before so that there was 300 weight then and 200 of a quarter now and none of them paid. Receiv'd £5-10s of Richard Smith of Shoreham for my load of wheat deliver'd the 24th of November last. Terry did severall jobbs.

The 22nd December 1721 Fryday. A fine day, frosty.
Mr Sixsmith here to day and yesterday. I were with him at Mr Scutt's and was witness to a note under Mr William Martin's hand to him for, I think, £7 or thereabouts, for some hangings etc left in Rusper parsonage. I was also witness to a discharge from Mr William Martin to Mr Sixsmith for all dilapidations. Reckon'd with Stephen Rick and clear'd accounts all but ditching and thrashing at Randalls. Thomas Hamper and his man workt at Randalls yesterday and his man and boy workt there all day to day and Thomas Hamper but half. They cut down some trees and hew'd them and set up a jack and some small matters for me. Lent Mr Jeremiah Dodson £3-5-6d more on a note. I was with a man Thomas         there. Mr Jeremiah Dodson bargained to give him £6 per annum and he is to come

on New Year's Day. Harry Wickham here in the morning. Agreed for a quarter of breaking pease at 28s.

The 23rd December 1721 Saturday. A dry day, frosty. Richard Banks and Smith went to Brighton with the teem for a load of timber for William Roach. I went with them. Paid Mr Masters 20s for 12 bushels of pease which I am to have on demand.

The 24th December 1721 Sunday. A dry day, frosty. Mr Jeremiah Dodson preacht. I were not at Church in the forenoon. My Unkle Courtness buried afternoon.
*(Ed: Hurst Parish Register shows Mr Courtness as buried)*

The 25th December 1721 Xmas. Munday. A gloomy day, thawing. Mr Jeremiah Dodson preacht. Our workmen din'd here. John Harden and Ned Terry's brother Jack here. Paid Harden a bill of £1-14-6d for P Curtis for wood and faggots. Receiv'd £1-7-0d of Mrs Kettilby for wines, coal etc. I supt and spent the evning at Mrs Catherine Beard's.

The 26th December 1721 Tuesday. A dry day. We chose surveyors as usual. My Cousin John Lindfield, John Stone and his wife spent this evning here. Paid John Westover 2s and I think 17s-6d in full.

The 27th December 1721 Wednesday. A dry day. Thomas Packham offer'd me his son John's malthouse. Receiv'd £7 of John Smith the butcher. My Sister Sarah and Nanny Faulkoner din'd here. Paid Molly Balcomb 4s-4d for spending money to Xmas day.

The 28th December 1721 Thursday. A dry day. My Wife and I din'd at Danny with severall others. Young Peter Hill of Reeds and our boys ferreted at Randalls, caught 4 rabbits.

The 29th December 1721 Fryday. A gloomy, dry day. The boys win'd 4 quarters and 3 bushels of oates at Rickman's. Richard Banks fetch't home part of William Roach's load and the oates from Rickman's. I gave Frank Holden an order to pay £7 of my money to Mr Wilkin at London for my landlord Mr Richard Barcroft and to pay a small bill to Mr Wilkin for me and to take the remainder for his own use by way of return. I sent 2 oxen to my Cousin John Lindfield yesterday for London and return'd his old horse. I supt at my Father's with Mrs Catherine Beard's family. I talkt with Mr John Packham in the evning at the Swan. Paid Joseph Muzzall 18s-4d Lord's rent for West Edgly due at Michaelmas last, £1-2s for Rickman's with 3s outset for the Land Tax and 6d for Randalls.

The 30th December 1721 Saturday. A gloomy day. Sent 20 bushels of pease to Lindfield per Richard Banks. Terry went after Randalls sheep.

The 31st December 1721 Sunday. A showry day. Mr Jeremiah Dodson preacht, no service afternoon. Goodman Jacket here afternoon. I were at my Father's in the evning with Mr Scutt.

The 1st January 1721 Munday. A wet day. Goodman Jacket and I were at John Packham's to look on the malthouse etc. Mr Beard and my Brother Peter here in the evning. Paid Dick Wood's bill and clear'd accounts. He had 3 cheeses at 18d per nail. Receiv'd 6d of Dick Wood for his part of the land, part for his house, as part of the Black Lyon. Richard Herriot here in the morning. John Haslegrove carry'd away 48lbs of swingled stuff to dress.

The 2nd January 1721 Tuesday. A dry day. Richard Banks and W Parker went to Brighton for 2 quarters of pease of Mr Kester. Paid 1s too much for one sack, the rest were paid for before. John Box and I were at Thomas Hamper's about the windmill. Mr Phillip Cheal is to get a bill of sale. Paid, that is, spent 2s there at the George on William Balcomb's account. We were at Harry Wickham's a while as we came home. Thomas Howell's man workt here on the wheel plough.

The 3rd January 1721 Wednesday. A dry day. The boys and Banks mov'd some of the seed clover ricks etc. Howell's man finisht the plough. Paid John Alcock 4s yesterday in full of all accounts. I supt at Mrs Catherine Beard's with severall others. My Cousin John Lindfield sent me word that my 2 oxen were sold for 1 guinea.

The 4th January 1721 Thursday. A fine day. The boys harrow'd at Randalls. Smith fetch't a box of candles from Henfield. Paid Chapman £3 for greasing sheep 3 times. Cook turned the Randalls ewes into the grubb'd field and workt all day for me on severall jobbs. I supt and spent the evning at my Father's. £6-8s paid my Brother Peter the Poor Tax for my Father.

The 5th January 1721 Fryday. A very fine day.
Richard Banks and the boys harrow'd stubble at Randalls as yesterday. Paid the Pionys 8s towards barly thrashing. The py'd cow and the whitefaced cow have each a bull calf about a week old. Smith rak'd the rows of stubble at Randalls.

The 6th January 1721 Saturday. A gloomy day.
Richard Banks and the boys all kept holy day. They went to Brighton. I supt and spent the evning at Mr Jeremiah Dodson's. My Father and Mother Stone din'd here. Paid Mr Jeremiah Dodson 11s-4d for bread and wine at Xmas. Lent him £3 more for a note of his hand.

The 7th January 1721 Sunday. A gloomy day.
Mr Jeremiah Dodson preacht. We had a parish meeting afternoon. My Wife and I receiv'd the sacrament. Paid Mr Jeremiah Dodson 6d for the postage of Dog Smith's letter.

The 8th January 1721 Munday. A fine day.
The boys and RB harrow'd stubble and fetcht some malt from Harry Wickham's. I was at Wanbarrow with Mr Jeremiah Dodson, supt etc. Thomas Jacket came to see me at Randalls. I were a little while with John Packham at the Swan.

The 9th January 1721 Tuesday. A fine day.
Richard Banks and the boys carry'd 2 loads of stubble at Randalls and begun plough. Paid Thomas Howell £7-15-0d in full on all accounts. I were at Mr Jeremiah Dodson's in the morning. Lent him a plough. Drove 4 working oxen to Randalls. My Wife and I supt and spent the evning at Mrs Catherine Beard's. A Burt of Wick and Thomas Whiteing here about noon with 3 hounds which they had up to Towne.

The 10th January 1721 Wednesday. A gloomy day.
Richard Banks and the boys begun plough and carry stubble at Randalls. My Brother Henry Faulkoner brought his son John again. My Wife and I din'd and supt at Mr Jeremiah Dodson's. I were at the Swan with John Packham, Thomas Reeve etc. My Cousin John Lindfield sent a letter to John Smith to let him know that he they had made a mistake in their reckoning, there was due to my Cousin John Lindfield 4s more than they had accounted for which John Smith readily owned when I showed him the letter and that it was a parcell of sheep that were forgotten. Goodman Cook helpt the boys yesterday at Randalls.

The 11th January 1721 Thursday. A fine day, frosty.
My Brother Henry Faulkoner lay here last night, was at Mr Jeremiah Dodson's with me in the evning. Din'd here to day and went away to my Brother John Box's. The boys, Richard Banks and John Cook plough'd and carry'd stubble at Randalls. Mr Beard and Mr John Hart supt here.

The 12th January 1721 Fryday. A fine day.
The boys, Richard Banks and John Cook plough'd at Randalls. Borrowed £11-5s of Frank Holden's wife *(Ed: née Mary Marshall)*, which I paid for him in London. Will, Bett and I din'd and supt at Dean House. I were at Mr Scutt's in the morning with Mr William Martin and appointed to meet there again next Thursday. Paid Old Dick Banks 13s-8d, reckon'd.

The 13th January 1721 Saturday. A gloomy day.
Richard Banks, John Cook and the boys plough'd at Randalls. Will staid at Dean House last night. I wrote to the parishoners of Balcombe by my Brother Henry Faulkoner's man. Sent him a service tree. My Wife and I were at John Snashall's in the evning.

The 14th January 1721 Sunday. A fine day.
Mr Jeremiah Dodson preacht. We had a parish meeting afternoon. I talkt with Stephen Bine at the Swan. My Cousin John Lindfield and his son din'd here. Paid my Cousin John Lindfield 4s-3d due about the London market.

The 15th January 1721. A dry day.
The first day Mr Beard etc went to hunting with their hounds. Terry and John Cook plough'd at Randalls. Receiv'd £5 of Mr Richard Whitpaine part of the purchase money for the advowson of Rusper. Richard Banks, Smith and William Haslegrove mov'd the rest of the clover rick and brought home some faggots. They also carry'd Stephen Rick half a cord of wood. Dick Wood jr let the sorrel horse bleed in the thigh veins. Paid my Father Stone 10 guineas, the last that I ow'd him on a note of my hand. Sent Harry Wickham 5 guineas yesterday for a note of his hand.

The 16th January 1721 Tuesday. A dry day. Mr Pointin of Henfield begun teach Will Marchant mathematics.

He is to come 3 times a week and to have 2s-6d per week. Mr Burry came and Mr Scutt and he were here in the evning. The boys, Richard Banks and John Cook plough'd.

The 17th January 1721 Wednesday. A dry day.
The boys, Richard Banks and Rick plough'd at home and at Randalls. Mr Burry lay here last night. We were at Stephen Bine's and after at Randalls. Bought the hop poles at 45s. Mr Richard Whitpaine with us. Mr Burry offer'd me his tares at 2s per bushel.

The 18th January 1721 Thursday. A fine day. Terry and Rick plough'd at Randalls. Banks and Will plough'd at home. Paid my Aunt Courtness 15s due on the books. I were at Mr Jeremiah Dodson's in the evning.
Mr Pointin here again. Thomas Hamper and his man and boy workt at Randalls to day and yesterday.

The 19th January 1721 Fryday. A showry day.
We seal'd the writeings for Rusper liveing at Mr Scutt's. I took a bond of Mr William Martin, Mr Richard Whitpaine and Mr Scutt for £700 and a note of Mr William Martin's hand for the five guineas over.
I likewise took an assignment of a mortgage on Thomas Smith's house the Swan for £140 in part for which I gave a receit. Receiv'd 20 bushels of tares of Mr Jeremiah Dodson at 40s. Richard Banks fetcht in 133 faggots, carry'd out some wood, helpt kill 2 hogs etc. The boys helpt Old Dick Banks winnow 11½ quarters of barly hay. Lost a lamb in the Fifteen Acres, the first.

The 20th January 1721 Saturday. A dry day. Richard Banks and Terry made an end of ploughing the Lime Kiln Field at Randalls. Paid R Piony 17s which made 25s with what he had before. My Wife and I din'd at my Father's. Will and John Gun plough'd. Receiv'd 10 sacks from Harry Wickham's landlord at 2s-4d.

The 21st January 1721 Sunday. A gloomy day.
Mr Jeremiah Dodson preacht. No service afternoon. John Hunt here from my Brother Will. 3 lambs of Sadlescombe sheep.

The 22nd January 1721 Munday. A showry day. I took Thomas Reeve's Malthouse at £8 per annum to enter at Michaelmas 1722. Richard Banks and Terry begun plough for tares at Randalls. Rick, Will and Abraham Muzzall plough'd in Tully's wheat earsh. William Hart and John Hart, farmers, din'd here. Old John Box, his son and daughter and little Balcombs supt here.

The 23rd January 1721 Tuesday. A gloomy day.
I were at Cuckfield Towne. Paid my Brother Will 10 guineas which I borrowed of him. Receiv'd £4 of Elliot Wood in full for a cow. Receiv'd likewise £6-10s of him for my Brother Peter. Richard Banks and the boys went to hunting. Harry White appointed me to come for his goods a Candlemas Day.

The 24th January 1721 Wednesday. A fine day.
Richard Banks and Will plough'd. Terry and John Cook plough'd at Randalls. Receiv'd £45-3s of Mr Richard Whitpaine toward Rusper liveing. Dick Smith could not plough because lame. 4 lambs of Sadlescombe sheep since Sunday. Mr Beard and Peter Marchant of Lewis at Randalls in the forenoon. Shut up 3 pigs to fatting. Chapman here to grease the sheep.

The 25th January 1721 Thursday. A wet forenoon, dry afternoon. The boys did severall jobbs. Richard Banks and Will plough'd afternoon. Terry sifted wheat etc, helpt John Gun winnow pease. 7 lambs more of Sadlescombe sheep. I were at Mrs Catherine Beard's towards night. Mr Pointin here in the evning. William Baker here with him.

The 26th January 1721 Fryday. A dry morning, very wet after. Terry and John Cook plough'd at Randalls half the day all most. Richard Banks and Will plough'd in Nine Acres. Reckon'd and clear'd accounts with Frank Holden to Munday last. Sold John Smith 2 steers at £14-10s to be kill'd in a month.

The 27th January 1721 Saturday. A gloomy day.
Richard Banks and Will and Smith plough'd. Terry and John Cook plough'd at Randalls. Receiv'd £7-6-0d of Thomas Champion and outset £1-1s for half a year's Land Tax £6 for half a year annuity paid to my Aunt Holden and 1s to the wood reeve William Woolgar for setting out trees for repairs. In all £15 for half a year's rent for Eastout all due at Lady Day last. 5 lambs since Thursday last in Sadlescombe sheep.
Mr Pointin here ----- V times.

The 28th January 1721 Sunday. A dry day. Mr Jeremiah Dodson preacht. A meeting afternoon. Ordered Thomas Shave a guinea.

The 29th January 1721 Munday. A dry day.
Terry and Richard Banks plough'd at Randalls. Will, Smith and James Banks plough'd in Nine Acres. I were at Will Wood's of Broad Street, bought 20 quarters of seed oates of him at £10. I am to fetch them at his house. I bought also a wheel plough at 10s which I am to return if I don't like her when I have tried her. Lost one lamb to day.

The 30th January 1721 Tuesday. A dry day.
Richard Banks fetcht a wheel plough from William Wood's and Smith went to Balcombe with a letter. Terry mended gaps etc. 1 lamb at Randalls and one at home of Patcham sheep, 5 lambs since Saturday of Sadlescombe sheep. Receiv'd 3 quarters of straw dried malt of Harry Wickham per Banks.

The 31st January 1721 Wednesday. A dry day.
Richard Banks and Samuel Everset plough'd in Churchfield. Will, Smith and James Banks plough'd in Nine Acres. My Wife and I at Randalls afterwards.

The 1st February 1721 Thursday. A fine day.
Terry and Samuel Everset plough'd in Churchfield. Richard Banks and Smith plough'd at Randalls. Paid Thomas Woolgar £7-7s for 2 steers which Thomas Champion bought for me, both here. Paid Thomas Champion 40s for 3 bushels of clover. William Wood of Broad Street here. Thomas Howell's man here altring the wheel plough. The 2 strangers at Kester's supt here. They call themselves Edward and Thomas Fisher and pretend to come out of Essex. Mr Pointin here vi times.

The 2nd February 1721 Fryday. A very fine day.
Fetcht Harry White's goods from Cuckfield to Cobb's Croft. My Cousin John Lindfield's teem and driver went for it. Mr Pointin staid to day------ vii times. Ned Terry flead the old roan horse at Randalls. My Wife and Mr Jeremiah Dodson went to Danny. The hare kill'd yesterday by the hounds (being the 1st) was sent to Danny by the huntsman.

The 3rd February 1721 Saturday. A wet forenoon, gloomy after. Richard Banks and the boys win'd clover pug and had the waggon to Randalls. _____ Mr Burry's pease for [seeding]. My Wife and I at Wanbarrow afternoon. Receiv'd £5-3s of Harry White for 1½ bushels of pease. Carry'd to Cuckfield yesterday for Goodman Davis. Dick Wood shooed the cart horses.

The 4th February 1721 Sunday. A wet forenoon, dry after. Mr Jeremiah Dodson preacht. We had a parish meeting. I receiv'd £5-13s from the parish for Betty Storer due from Wick's decea'sd. Stephen Bine and I were at Thomas Smith's towards night. My Wife was down at Harry White's at night.

The 5th February 1721 Munday. A dry day.
Richard Banks and Smith plough'd with the horses in the Churchfield. Terry and John Cook plough'd at Randalls. Will went to hunting. Mr Jeremiah Dodson's teem carry'd Mr Burry's pease.

The 6th February 1721 Shrove Tuesday. A fine day.
I din'd at Brickhouse at Mr William Martin's treat. Receiv'd 6 guineas of Mr Henry Campion for my Cousin John Lindfield. Richard Banks and Samuel Everset plough'd in Churchfield. Will, Smith, James Banks plough'd in Nine Acres. Terry did severall jobbs at home. The Lancashire heifer calved a Sunday last.

The 7th February 1721 Wednesday. A gloomy day, small driving rain. Richard Banks and Samuel Everset plough'd in Churchfield. Terry and John Cook plough'd at Randalls. Will, Smith and James Banks plough'd in Nine Acres 'till noon. Afternoon Will and Jacky went to Lewis to see a prize fought between Harris and an other and Smith ground a quarter of malt for summer beer.

The 8th February 1721 Thursday. A dry day.
John Cook and Terry plough'd at Randalls. Will, Smith and James Banks plough'd in Nine Acres. Richard Banks sick. Will Haslegrove in the garden to day and yesterday. 6 lambs of Sadlescombe sheep since Tuesday sennight last.      6 lambs at Randalls more of the Patcham sheep --- vii and at home ----- vii. Mrs Ann Dodson and her daughter supt here.
Receiv'd a letter from Mr Richard Barcroft.

The 9th February 1721 Fryday. A wet morning, dry after. Richard Banks and Samuel Everset plough'd half the day in Churchfield. Will and Smith plough'd in Nine Acres part. Ned Terry did severall jobbs. Mark't sheep and lambs with a fork on the right ear 10 on the left and 10 on both all Sadlescombe. I were at Broad Street to see a horse.

The 10th February 1721 Saturday. A gloomy morning, dry afternoon. My Wife and I and Molly Balcomb were at Lewis, Jack also. Paid Dr White 10s-6d for his advice for Molly Balcomb. Paid my Cousin John Lindfield the 6 guineas yesterday, receiv'd of Mr Henry Campion. Paid Mr Norman 4s for binding a bible. Paid Stephen Avery 4d for a lash to my Wife's whip. We carry'd some tow or tire to Thomas Burt. Return'd a stove to Mr Court's and paid all due there.

The 11th February 1721 Sunday. A fine day.
Mr Jeremiah Dodson preacht. My Cousin John Lindfield din'd here. I were at the Royall Oak after evning prayr with the two Fishers.

The 12th February 1721 Munday. A very fine day.
John Cook and Terry plough'd at Randalls. Dick Banks and James Banks plough'd in Churchfield. Smith and Will plough'd by Harry White's. My Wife and I were at Randalls. Will Haslegrove workt at my Father's.
A travelling woman pretended to be (or was really) in labour. Put her in at Kester's. Mr Sixsmith here in the evning. Mrs Scutt also. Thomas Greenfield fetcht a child of my Cousin Peter Marchant. Return'd Mr Friend's buckskinns all but two. 21 lambs at Randalls since Thursday last ------------ xxv

The 13th February 1721 Tuesday. A very fine day.
Terry and White plough'd at Randalls. Richard Banks and James in the Churchfield. Will and Smith plough'd by Harry White's. I were at Megrum's bank with Mr Richard Whitpaine. Mr Sixsmith din'd here, so did Mr Richard Whitpaine. Mr Sixsmith receiv'd his note from Cousin John Lindfield.

The 14th February 1721 Wednesday. A gloomy day.
Terry and White plough'd. Richard Banks and James Smith and Will plough'd as yesterday. Paid Young Nick Plaw 24s for 8lbs of tea from London. Will Haslegrove dresst flax to day. Workt at my Father's yesterday.

The 15th February 1721 Thursday. A very fine day.
Richard Banks and Smith finisht the Churchfield. Terry and White plough'd at Randalls. I were at Lindfield and at Sheffield to buy horses. I din'd at my Brother John Courtness's. He went with me to Sheffield. Will went to hunting.
Thomas Hamper and his boy here -------------- 5 days.
Mr Pointin here ------------- viii times.

The 16th February 1721 Fryday. A very fine day.
White and Terry plough'd at Randalls. Will and Smith plough'd by Harry White's. Dick Banks helpt winnow etc. WH dresst flax. John Snashall here to see the Duke horse. Dick Wood gave the horse a purge about noon.

The 17th February 1721 Saturday. A fine day.
Will begun sow the Lime Kiln Field at Randalls with Mr Jeremiah Dodson's grey pease. Terry, Smith and White harrow'd. Richard Banks lookt after the Duke horse in the working of his purge. My Father and Mother Stone din'd with us at Randalls. Mr Scutt came to us afternoon. WH dresst flax. Mr Pointin here ----------- ix times

The 18th February 1721 Sunday. A gloomy day.
Mr Jeremiah Dodson preacht. My Cousin John Lindfield jr din'd here. My Wife and I were at Mr Jeremiah Dodson's in the evning.

The 19th February 1721 Munday. A very fine day.
John Cook finisht sowing pease in the Lime Kiln Field at Randalls. They sow'd 30½ bushels of Mr Jeremiah Dodson's pease. Terry harrow'd and White. Will and Smith plough'd. Paid R Piony 48s for a 2 yearling heifer. The 2 Fishers came to me at Randalls and after supt with us here. Richard Banks jobb'd. Kill'd 2 hogs. Lent Mr Dodson six guineas more.

The 20th February 1721 Tuesday. A dry day.
Richard Banks and White plough'd Randalls. Terry cross harrow'd and finisht the Lime Kiln Field. Smith and Will finisht the field by Harry White's. Will Wood of Broad Street here. John Smith fetcht the red bull stag.

The 21st February 1721 Wednesday. A dry day.
I were at Balcombe. Paid Mr Burt of Brook Street 9 guineas for a mare I bought of him to day, 6 years old this next summer. Abraham Muzzall jr with me. Will, White etc begun sow and harrow tares at Randalls. I supt at Dean House as I came home.

The 22nd February 1721 Thursday. A fine day.
Made an end of sowing the tares at Randalls per John Cook ½ the day, Banks and Smith all day. Terry and White plough'd. Brought home the waggon from Randalls. Mr Burry sent his boy with sacks etc.

The 23rd February 1721 Fryday. A dry day.
Richard Banks and Smith begun plough the wheat earsh at Rickman's. Terry and White plough'd at Randalls.

Took out fish for Mr Burry, I had 3. Paid John Snashall jr 1s for bleeding me. Bett Bodle went home this morning. Mr Pointin here a Thursday ------ x times. Let William French the kitchen part of my Tully's house at 40s per annum to move at Lady Day.

The 24th February 1721 Saturday. A fine day.
I were at Lewis. Din'd at the Star. Paid John Gold for a sack of wheat. Paid Mr Court 15s-3d for a black stove and plate for my Father Stone. Clear'd accounts. Paid Mr Friend 15s for Will's buckskins. Receiv'd £5-17s of R Weeden's son for my Brother Peter. Richard Banks and R Smith plough'd at Rickman's. Terry did severall jobbs.

The 25th February 1721 Sunday. A very fine day.
Mr Jeremiah Dodson preacht. My Wife and John Peckham and Jacky and Jack Cheal went to Shermanbury. Turned the sheep and lambs into the Rookwood wheat yesterday.

The 26th February 1721 Munday. A dry, cold day.
Terry plough'd Randalls. Richard Banks and Smith plough'd at Rickman's. Paid Thomas Smith 8s for 3 horse collars etc I were at Mrs Catherine Beard's afternoon.

The 27th February 1721 Tuesday. A dry, cold day.
Will and James Banks begun plough Mr Courtness's old hop garden for Richard Herriot. Richard Banks and Smith plough'd at Rickman's, Terry at Randalls. Mr Scutt here in the evning with the lease of Randalls.

The 28th February 1721 Wednesday. A dry day.
White and Terry plough'd at Randalls. Will and James Banks plough'd for Richard Herriot. Richard Banks and Smith plough'd at Rickman's. Let John Haslegrove 1½ acres of the wheat earsh at Rickman's at £3 per acre. I am to lend him a teem to carry flax. Dick Wood set 2 new shoes on my horse before and mov'd the hind shoes.

The 1st March 1721 Thursday. A dry day. Will went to hunting. Terry and White plough'd ½ the day at Randalls. Sifted pease afterwards. Smith and Richard Banks plough'd at Rickman's. John Cook mended gaps at Randalls afternoon. Paid my Lord Treep in full of all. Sent my Brother Peter's money per Jack Haslegrove.

The 2nd March 1721 Fryday. A fine day. Will and James Banks plough'd. R Smith and Richard Banks plough'd at Rickman's. Terry and White sifted pease and White carry'd 7½ bushels of pease into Lindfield to Brother John Courtness. Mr Pointin here yesterday ----- xi times. Thomas Hamper's man and boy cut some timber. Mrs Catherine Beard's family here yesterday afternoon.

The 3rd March 1721 Saturday. A gloomy day, some rain.
Will and James Banks plough'd. Terry and White plough'd at Randalls. Richard Banks and R Smith plough'd at Rickman's. Reckon'd and clear'd accounts with Rick only he left 6s in my hands towards his rent. My Father and Mother Stone din'd here.
Mr Pointin here ------------- xii times.
Eliz Cheal left 8s in my hand towards wood.

The 4th March 1721 Sunday. A dry day. Mr Jeremiah Dodson preacht. A parish meeting. Settled accounts as usual. My Wife and I supt at Mrs Catherine Beard's.

The 5th March 1721 Munday. A wet day.
Terry and White plough'd a while. Will and James Banks plough'd a while. Richard Banks begun harrow the wheat earsh at Rickman's. My Cousin Wood of Broad Street here in the evning. Lost a lamb at Randalls. Paid Mr Jeremiah Dodson 14d for 2 quires of paper. Mr Dodson went for London, took my old lease of the Towne soil and a writeing about the seat with him.

The 6th March 1721 Tuesday. A gloomy day, small rain.
Richard Banks and Smith carry seaven quarters of barly to be malted for my self and 4 quarters for Harry Wickham. Terry and White made an end of fallowing at Randalls. John Smith here in the evning.

The 7th March 1721 Wednesday. A wet day.
Richard Banks and Smith fetcht 60 bushels of seed oates from Broad Street. Will and Terry helpt Old Dick Banks winnow 6½ quarters of barly. Thomas Hamper's man Friend workt here 3 hours. Paid Chapman 2s for clipping or tailing 117 ewes and rams and 6d for greasing them some time ago. Receiv'd 5s of Lamberd's wife towards pease he is to have. Bargain'd with Ned Terry to stay an other year at £4 certain and 5s more if I think he deserves it.

The 8th March 1721 Thursday. A showry day.
Richard Banks and Smith drew some trees -- 20.

Terry went to Randalls in the morning, to mill after. Will went to hunting in the morning but the wet drove 'em home. Thomas Hamper and his man here ------ 6 days.

The 9th March 1721 Fryday. A fine day.
Richard Banks and Terry drew some trees etc. Smith went to Wortleford with me, went home by the Comon, Old Land etc. I went to Horsham. Talkt with Mr Arnold, [D............], Rossel, Foreman etc.

The 10th March 1721 Saturday. A wet forenoon, gloomy after. Thomas Foreman seized John Rogers's goods for rent due to my Father Stone, I was at Tanbridge. I left my Father's account with Mr Arnold. I lay at the White Horse. Came home part of the way with Thomas Vinall. I spoke to Stephen Carter for housing for 6 cart horses and am to give 2s each. They are second hand. Receiv'd Mr Jeremiah Dodson's tythe for Little Broadwater of mills, Soughton and 2 more £4 in all. Rossel told me he had taken 6 acres of Tanbridge of Rogers for flax at 50s per acre.

The 11th March 1721 Sunday. A dry day. Mr Hawes preacht. I supt at Mr Smith's. Mr Pointin here.

The 12th March 1721 Munday. A fine day.
Richard Banks, Harry White and Terry carry'd 24 loads of Towne dirt. Will and Smith plough'd. William Joanes, a turner, came and cleft some ash.

The 13th March 1721 Tuesday. A dry forenoon, very wet after. Richard Banks, Terry and White drew home ash. Carry'd Towne dirt etc. Thomas Hamper's man set up a turning lathe at my Father's. Mr John Hart supt and spent the evning here.

The 14th March 1721 Wednesday. A dry day.
Mr Scutt and I went to Ruston to Mr Burry's. Went by Stenning monthly market. Call'd at Mr Wills's. The boys and Richard Banks plough'd etc.

The 15th March 1721 Thursday. A fine day.
Mr Burry and I sign'd our leases for 21 years from Michaelmas last. We din'd there and came home. Mr Scutt and Jude Wood witness to the leases. Richard Banks and Smith fetcht oates from William Wood's.

The 16th March 1721 Fryday. A gloomy day.
Will, Banks and the boys sow'd     bushels of oates on Tully's field by the coppice and harrow'd it in part.

My Wife and I at Randalls. I supt at my Father's. John Rogers came here in the evning. I lost one of the Sadlescombe ewes a Wednesday.

The 17th March 1721 Saturday. A fine day.
The boys finisht the field by Tully's coppice and begun the Nine Acres. Receiv'd half a rheam of paper from London which Mr Jeremiah Dodson bought at ___ .
Thomas Hamper workt here ------------- 7 days.
John Smith kill'd 3 porkers for me.

The 18th March Sunday. A dry day.
Mr Hawes preacht.  I was at Mr Scutt's and my Aunt Courtness with William Courtness etc. I was at Mrs Catherine Beard's a little while.

The 19th March 1721 Munday. A dry, windy day.
Richard Banks and the boys sow'd, harrow'd etc in the Nine Acres. Thomas Hamper and his man here -- 8 days. Receiv'd the rest of J Lamberd's money for 5 bushels of pease.

The 20th March 1721 Tuesday. A fine day.
Smith and Will finisht the Nine Acres with clover. Will went to Lewis after. Richard Banks harrow'd at Rickman's. Smith helpt after.
Thomas Hamper and his boy hew'd timber ------ 9 days.
Terry deliver'd Lamberd's pease, ground malt etc. Paid H Courtness 15s-6d for fustian etc for a frock for Will.

The 21st March 1721 Wednesday. A wet day.
Will and Old Dick Banks, James Banks and E Terry win'd 18 quarters and 2 bushels of Old Bank's barly. Richard Banks and White mow'd. Eliz Cheal to Randalls. I was at Mr Jeremiah Dodson's in the morning.

The 22nd March 1721 Thursday. A wet forenoon, dry after. The boys and Richard Banks oil'd the harness. Fetcht wood, scour'd furroughs. Thomas Roach new made the pidgeon house window. Towner and his mate sow'd etc one day before.

The 23rd March 1721 Fryday. A dry day.
My birthday, 45 years. Richard Banks and Smith drew home trees. R Smith at Church. Terry at Church in the forenoon, after the runts afterwards. Towner and his mate sow'd. Bottled some beer. Harry Wickham here in the morning. William Dumsday here.

The 24th March 1721 Saturday. A dry day.
Richard Banks, Smith and I went with the teem to Cuckfield for Harry White's wood. Terry and Will went to hunting. Sent a hare to Mr Osbourne's at Newtimber. Paid John Cook for all his work.

1722

The 25th March 1722 Lady Day and Easter Sunday.
A dry day. Mr Jeremiah Dodson preacht. I were at the Swan with Stephen Bine and Brother Peter.

The 26th March 1722 Munday. A fine day.
All kept holy day. A meeting at Church, past accounts and chose officers as usual.
Receiv'd a letter from Mr Burry. Sent an answer.

The 27th March 1722 Tuesday. A gloomy, dry day.
All kept holy day. I din'd at my Father's, Mr Roots of Fletching there to take Tanbridge of my Father.

The 28th March 1722 Wednesday. A fine day.
Mr Roots lay at my Father's, went home to day. Richard Banks and the boys carry'd Kester ½ load wood, Thomas Hamper a cord etc. My Wife and I and the Children at my Brother John Box's afternoon.

The 29th March 1722 Thursday. A fine day.
Richard Banks and Smith carry'd 4 quarters of barly to Randalls etc. Terry drove 2 oxen to Dean House in their way to London etc.

The 30th March 1722 Fryday. A fine day.
Will sow'd the field by Harry White's. Banks and Smith harrow'd. Thomas Hamper and his boy here ---- 10 days. Thomas Howell here, carry'd home bonds for a payr of wheels.

The 31st March 1722 Saturday. A very hot day.
Will and Terry finisht the lower field with clover. Thomas Hamper and his boy here -------------- 11 days. Richard Banks and Smith plough'd in the Churchfield. Paid Mr William Dumsday 3s for mending a payr of stays for Molly Balcomb. The red heifer that came of the broken horn'd cow calved a bull calf.

The 1st April 1722 Sunday. A fine day. Mr Jeremiah Dodson preacht. I were at Mr Jeremiah Dodson's after evning prayr.

The 2nd April 1722 Munday. A very fine day.
The boys, Richard Banks, Will sow'd and harrow'd the pease and Jack Haslegrove flax and an acre of my own flax at Rickman's. Receiv'd 23s of Richard Herriot for ploughing and harrowing 3 acres of flax ground. Thomas Hamper and his man and boy here -------------- 12 days. Lost one ewe yesterday.

The 3rd April 1722 Tuesday. A fine day.
The boys, Richard Banks and Will begun the Churchfield.
Thomas Hamper and his man here -------------- 13 days. William Jarvice and Jack Howard workt on the stables. Mr Jeremiah Dodson, Mr John Hart, my Cousin John Marchant and his wife of Lox and Mrs Catherine Beard's family supt here. Receiv'd £2-0-3d of Mrs Catherine Beard for 11½ bushels of pease.

The 4th April 1722 Wednesday. A fine day.
Richard Banks and the boys plough'd and sow'd barly in Churchfield with 2 teems. My Wife and John Snashall's wife at North End afternoon.

The 5th April 1722 Thursday. A fine day.
The boys etc plough'd and sow'd in Churchfield.
My Brother William call'd here in his way to Wanbarrow.

The 6th April 1722 Fryday. A gloomy day.
The boys plough'd and sow'd as yesterday. Nick Plaw here to see a cow.

The 7th April 1722 Saturday. A fine day.
The boys plough'd and sow'd as yesterday. Paid Dick Wood 35s in full. I was at Kester's with Thomas Reeve etc a Thursday and agreed fully about the Malthouse. Nick Plaw here again to day. Brother Peter and Will came.

The 8th April 1722 Sunday. A fine day.
Mr Jeremiah Dodson preacht twice. We had a parish meeting. Mr Peter Courthope paid the intrest of Mr Litchford's charity to Lady Day last.

The 9th April 1722 Munday. A fine day.
The boys begun plough the Sandfield at Randalls. Will Michell sow'd the Churchfield with 2 bushels of clover. My Cousin Peter Marchant's wife and Mr Burry came. My Wife and I were at Ditcheling afternoon.

The 10th April 1722 Tuesday. A fine day.
Mr Burry lay here last night. Paid Mr Burry £3-2-0d and am to pay Ned Burt 6s for him which is in full for all the stock and takling I bought of him at Randalls. The boys, Will and French plough'd at Randalls. Brought home four runts from Randalls.

The 11th April 1722 Wednesday. A fine day.
The boys at Randalls as yesterday. Lent my Cousin Peter Marchant's wife £10. She went home.
Thomas Hamper and his man here -------- 14 days.

The 12th April 1722 Thursday. A very fine day.
Plough'd at Randalls. Thomas Hamper and his man cut timber at Randalls. Thomas Butcher din'd here. Old William Brand's man and Parsons workt on the stable.

The 13th April 1722 Fryday. A fine day.
The boys plough'd and sow'd as yesterday. Old William Brand's man and 2 labourers workt on the stable.

The 14th April 1722 Saturday. A fine day.
The boys plough'd and sow'd at Randalls.
Paid Mr Pointin 6s-6d for a book and teaching Molly Balcomb arithmetick. Will Jarvice workt till 3 aclock and Thomas Jenner and John Parsons all day on the stables. Paid Mr Pointin likewise 15s for teaching Will with what he had before and 2s-6d for teaching Bett and 6d for a book for her.

The 15th April 1722 Sunday. A fine day.
Mr Jeremiah Dodson preacht.

The 16th April 1722 Munday. A fine day.
I were at Beeding. At Mr Newlin's with Mr Jeremiah Dodson. This was a court kept by the college to whom the living belongs. The boys harrow'd etc at Randalls. Richard Banks carry'd a load of Mr Burry's wheat to Shoreham.

The 17th April 1722 Tuesday. A wet day.
The boys did severall jobbs. Thomas Hamper and his man workt on the stable --------- 15 days.

The 18th April 1722 Wednesday. A fine day after the morning. The boys harrow'd etc at Randalls.
Thomas Hamper and his man again -------- 16 days.
My Brother John Courtness had £50 this morning for his bond and his mother's. Mr Beard made the bond.

The 19th April 1722 Thursday. A fine day.
Mr Jeremiah Dodson's tythe feast. The boys etc begun plough and sow the Whapplegate field at Randalls with barly. Thomas Hamper's man Friend workt on the stable. Mr Roots was at my Father's. Paid Mr Novis for a payr of stays for Molly Balcomb £1-14-0d.

The 20th April 1722 Fryday. A wet day. The boys etc workt at Randalls till noon, jobb'd after. Thomas Hamper and his man on the stable --------- 17 days.

The 21st April 1722 Saturday. A wet day.
The boys did severall jobbs. Old William Brand's man and a labourer on the stable. Thomas Hamper's man Friend on the stable ½ the day.

The 22nd April 1722 Sunday. A dry day.
Mr Jeremiah Dodson preacht twice. My Sister Sarah din'd here.

The 23rd April 1722 Munday. A showry day.
The boys, Banks and Will plough'd at Randalls. Thomas Hamper's man here and for Eliz Cheal. Paid French 5s yesterday. He went to Horsham for my Father to day.

The 24th April 1722 Tuesday. A fine day.
Plough'd and sow'd as yesterday. Receiv'd the 5 guineas of Mr William Martin which he was to give my Wife in the purchase of Rusper liveing. Receiv'd likewise 38s of him in full for keeping his mare. Mr William Martin told me that my Brother Will was married a Thursday last at Warnham near Horsham. *(Ed: William married Ann Orglas at Warnham 19 April 1722)*

The 25th April 1722 Wednesday. A fine day.
Plough'd and sow'd at Randalls. Thomas Jacket brought his goods to Randalls yesterday. He is to pay me half a year's rent to Michaelmas next. Turned out 2 calves weaned.

The 26th April 1722 Thursday. A very fine day.
Will went to a cricket match on Broadwater Green. The boys plough'd and harrow'd at Randalls.

The 27th April 1722 Fryday. A very fine day.
Plough'd and sow'd at Randalls. I were at Poynings to see some calves. Paid John Gun Mr Litchford's money for his brother.

The 28th April 1722 Saturday. A dry, gloomy day.
Will etc made an end of sowing at Randalls.

Receiv'd £12 of John Smith the butcher. Mr Richard Whitpaine's man John Smith died this morning. Turned 2 runts into the hop garden.

The 29th April 1722 Sunday. A gloomy day.
Mr Jeremiah Dodson preacht.

The 30th April 1722 Munday. A dry day.
Will and the boys weeded wheat. Richard Banks drew some trees at Randalls etc. Receiv'd £40 of Mr Richard Whitpaine towards Rusper liveing. I were at Goodman Oliver's to see some calves.

The 1st May 1722 Tuesday. A fine day.
I were at Lindfield Fair and bought a payr of oxen at 15 guineas of the Widdow Wood's man near St John's Comon. Bought likewise a barren at 50s of one that lived, I think, in Plumpton parish. I din'd at my Brother John Courtness's. The boys kept holy day.

The 2nd May 1722 Wednesday. A dry day.
I were at Stenning on Mr Newlin's matter. Richard Banks drew timber at Randalls. Will and the boys harrow'd and roll'd there.

The 3rd May 1722 Thursday. A fine day.
My Wife and I were at Shermanbury, Dick Smith and Dick Banks with us. Paid Mr Lintott £5 for a year's intrest due to Mrs Mary Gratwick which he is to pay to Mr Phillip. Harry White brought his cow home yesterday or a Tuesday last. I bought a yearling steer of John Snashall a Tuesday night.

The 4th May 1722 Fryday. A fine day. My Wife and I at Thomas Bull's sale and at Nick Marchant's widdow's funeral. The boys did severall jobbs.

The 5th May 1722 Saturday. A fine day. The boys etc did severall jobbs. Bought a calf of Goodman Lamberd yesterday at 28s, I am to fetch him a Whit Munday.

The 6th May 1722 Sunday. A fine day.
Mr Jeremiah Dodson preacht twice. A parish meeting. Settled accounts as usual. My Cousin John Lindfield din'd here.

The 7th May 1722 Munday. A fine day.
The boys weeded, roll'd etc. Lost a two yearling steer. Dr Nick Plaw here. Cut the 2 twelve monthing bulls. I were at Mr Jeremiah Dodson's in the morning.

Reckon'd and paid him all my tythes to Lady Day last as follows.

| | |
|---|---|
| For Little Park and West Edgly the half year | £ 5- 5-0d |
| For Randalls half a year | £4- 0-0d |
| For Rickman's half a year | £ 0-16-0d |
| in all | £ 10 - 1-0d |

but there still remains due to me fifteen pounds for which he gave me a note of his hand. Paid Terry and Smith all their last year's wages.

The 8th May 1722 Tuesday. A very fine day.
The boys did severall jobbs. Richard Wood's 2 girls begun weed wheat. Sold John Channel at Albourne what barly I have at 12s per quarter. Sent 3 oxen to Randalls. Mr Burry's boy here about noon.

The 9th May 1722 Wednesday. A gloomy day, wet towards night. Will, Wood's girl and Terry weeded. Smith and Banks did severall jobbs. Had the teem to Randalls afternoon. Loaded a load of wheat for Shoreham. Turned 2 runts and a barren heifer to Rickman's. Paid the 2 Pionys in full for all their work. Borrowed 5s of Cook.

The 10th May 1722 Thursday. A gloomy day.
Richard Banks and Smith carry'd a load of Mr Burry's wheat to Shoreham. Terry and Richard Wood's girls weeded. Will and our parish went to Newick to play a cricket match, our parish won. Mr Richard Barcroft came hither. We reckon'd and clear'd all accounts to Lady Day except the Land Tax. Paid him £8-4s-0d money. He gave me a tree and likewise gave me leave to let the farm to Goodman White but would not assign the accept of an assignment of the lease. We went to Danny.

The 11th May 1722 Fryday. A fine day.
Richard Banks and Smith went to Shoreham with an other load of Mr Burry's wheat. Will, Wood's girls and a girl of Hollingall's weeded. Terry went to Findon with me to meet Mr Downer of Pagham near Chichester and I receiv'd of him £10-5s due to my Father Stone on bond and a note for £5-13-6d all in full for principal and intrest on John Rogers's account. Mr Richard Barcroft went with me to Findon in his way home. Paid Goodman Croskey £1-3-6d for a calf by my Wife.

The 12th May 1722 Saturday. A dry day, only a showr towards night. Will etc weeded at Randalls. Smith carry'd 5 quarters of barly to John Channel at Albourne at 12s per quarter. Richard Banks roll'd the barly under the hill at Randalls. Goodman Richard White here in the evning. I let him the rest of my lime in Rickman's to begin at Lady Day last for which he is to give me £13-10-0d and I am to have my acre of flax now on the ground and if (at the end of the lease) I can get any allowances from the landlord towards what I am out of ~~repair~~ pocket about the repairs he is not to have any thing of it allowed to him. Receiv'd in hand 10s and his son John and he are to give me each 2 day's work in harvest.
Paid my Father Stone £5 of the money I receiv'd at Findon of Mr Downer. Frank Holden's mare came to keeping yesterday at 10d per week.

The 13th May 1722 Sunday. A fine day.
Mr Hawes sr preacht twice. The 2 Mr Fishers and my Brother Peter here afternoon.

The 14th May 1722 Munday. A showry day.
All kept holy day. Henfield boys and ours plaid a cricket match in our Bankfield, Henfield won. Paid my Cousin John Lindfield £22 for six two yearling steers he bought of Mr Peter Courthope for me. Paid J Lamberd 28s at the cricket match for a calf, fetch to day.

The 15th May 1722 Tuesday. A very fine day.
All kept holy day. Richard Banks carry'd some harness to Brighton to be mended. My Wife and I were at Wanbarrow to see my Sister Sarah, she being sick. Lost a ewe at Randalls.

The 16th May 1722 Wednesday. A fine day.
Will, the boys, Wood's girls etc weeded flax at Rickman's half the day. Paid William Lindfield of Grubbs £2-4-0d for 2 calves per Terry. He and Abraham Muzzall fetch them. The branded heifer calved a bull calf yesterday. Richard Banks fetch a load of lime and 1000 tiles from Marten's at St Johns Comon.

The 17th May 1722 Thursday. A very fine day.
Cuckfield Fair. Chapman shore the dry sheep at Randalls. Deliver'd 325 faggots to my Father Stone per Banks. Towner and his mate saw'd here.

The 18th May 1722 Fryday. A showry day.
Richard Banks fetch 2 loads of sand from Stephen Bine's pit and 75 faggots out of Tully's coppice to my Father's. Richard Wood's girls, Hollingall's and James Banks weeded ½ in the Nine Acres. Turned 11 yearlings to Randalls. Receiv'd 6 two yearling steers from my Cousin John Lindfield which he bought for me at Danny and paid for. Thomas Reeve and I seal'd our leases for his malthouse at the Royall Oak, for 6 years from Michaelmas next. Paid Isaac Muzzall 6s-6d for my part of the leases.

The 19th May 1722 Saturday. A gloomy forenoon, wet after. Will and the girls weeded. Banks and Smith carry'd 3 loads of wood to my Father's etc. Terry weeded part and severall jobbs. Put the last heifer's calf to the Lancashire. Turned the 5 fatting oxen to pasture per Hyder's. Mrs Beard of Brickhouse here afternoon.

The 20th May 1722 Sunday. A showry day.
Mr Hawes sr preacht twice. My Cousin John Lindfield here after evning prayr. My Brother Henry Faulkoner's man here.

The 21st May 1722 Munday. A gloomy morning, fine after. My Wife, Molly Balcomb and I went to Lewis. Paid Mr Wheatly 10s-6d for a hat and 6d carriage. Item 1s for 2 doses of pills, 1s for a bottle of elixir p_____ and 3d for some radix cacnana. Paid Rebecca Jones 11s-8d for a hoop petty coat for Molly Balcomb. Item to Eliz Rose for a fan for her 5s. We bought some cloaths for Molly Balcomb of Mr Friend which were set down. Paid Mr Court and Stephen Avery in full. Paid William Rapson 5 guineas for a horse colt a year ¾ old. Took a note of my Cousin Peter Marchant's hand for ten pounds lent him some time ago per his wife. Paid Mrs Shed, my Cousin Laurence and Mr Norman in full. Paid Mr Newdigate 10-6 for his advice in Molly Balcomb's business.

The 22nd May 1722 Tuesday. A fine day.
Mr Ede and his son John at my Father's. Will, Wood's girls, Hollingam's girl and James Banks weeded. Richard Banks and Smith laid up the tools, harrows etc at Randalls and brought Mr Burry's flax to John Haslegrove's. Carry'd some dung after. White helpt 'em. Towner and his mate saw'd. Paid John Cook in full for bullock serving and all other work. Gave him notice to go out of Randalls house at Michaelmas next. I met Thomas Reeve and Thomas Jacket at the Malthouse. My Wife and I were at Wanbarrow in the morning.

The 23rd May 1722 Wednesday. A gloomy forenoon, wet after. Newick men came to play a cricket match but did not play. My Cousin Stephen Ridge din'd here. Turned the last of John Gun's beasts to pasture.

The 24th May 1722 Thursday. A wet day.
Richard Banks and the boys did severall jobbs. Thomas Hamper and his man here -------- 18 days. Mr Paine jr, Mr Beard and Mr Fisher here in the morning. My blind mare went to Mr Beard's horse. I am to give him a guinea if she have a colt.

The 25th May 1722 Fryday. A fine day. The boys and Richard Banks carry'd dung. My Father and Mr Hawes supt here. Thomas Hamper here ----------- 19 days.

The 26th May Saturday. A stormy day.
My Father Stone and I were at Lewis. Richard Banks and the boys carry'd dung in the home close. Thomas Hamper and his boys here, hung up a gate at the end of the hovel ---- 20 days. I spoke to Mr Sixsmith about the chantry ground as I went to Lewis.

The 27th May 1722 Sunday. A fine day.
Mr Hawes preacht, no service afternoon. Receiv'd 24s of Richard White for a quarter of grey pease. My Wife and I and my Mother Stone at Wanbarrow afternoon.

The 28th May 1722 Munday. A fine day. The boys and Banks made end of the home close, 160 loads without the stable dunghill. My Wife and I were at Randalls afternoon. Paid John Westover 36s in full of his book. Sent Young Abraham Muzzall to Dean House to invite him to dine at Mr Jeremiah Dodson's a Saturday next.

The 29th May 1722 Tuesday. A showry day towards night. I were at Stenning Fair with 4 beasts, sold none. Receiv'd 1s of Mr R Masters due to me about the pease. Sold 7 barren ewes to George Hill jr at 11s per ewe. Mr Hall who formerly taught our parish to sing psalms lay here with George Hill, went away this morning.

The 30th May 1722 Wednesday. A fine day.
The boys etc carry'd dung. Will and the girls weeded. Dr Vincent here towards night. Turned the Wintermilch and the white cow out of the dairy.

The 31st May 1722 Thursday. A showry day.
Banks and Smith fetcht home faggots out of Tully's coppice. John Hart of Fulking washt my sheep and Mrs Catherine Beard paid him 4d per score for washing mine. Thomas Hamper's 2 men workt here, new hung the gate at Botten's. Will and the girls and James Banks weeded. Mr Henry Campion and Mrs Catherine Beard here in the evning. Deliver'd the 7 ewes above-mentioned to George Hill and drove per T_____ .

The 1st June 1722 Fryday. A fine day.
Banks and Terry stacked faggots. Smith did severall jobbs. All went to the cricket match. Will went to a cricket match at Henfield. I were at Lewis about the Window Tax, did nothing. Paid Stephen Avery and Norman in full of all. Mr Jeremiah Dodson here in the evning with my Father and Mr Hawes. John Bodle kill'd one of my rams in the evning for me.

The 2nd June 1722 Saturday. A fine day. Richard Banks and Terry made an ending of stacking faggots for the house, 1200. Will and the girls weeded and Ja. My Wife and I din'd and supt at Mr Jeremiah Dodson's. My Father there a while. Shut up the broken horned cow's calf a weaning. Sold John Bodle 4 rams, 2 weathers at 3d per lb only. I am to abate 3s in the whole. Ja Willet and William Carpenter, 2 Brighton butchers here after.

The 3rd June 1722 Sunday. A storm of thunder and rain forenoon, fine after. Mr Jeremiah Dodson preacht twice. My Wife and I receiv'd the sacrament. A parish meeting, passt accounts as usual.

The 4th June 1722 Munday. A dry forenoon, stormy after. Mr Jeremiah Dodson and his son Jerry breakfasted here in their way to London. Lent Mr Dodson 2 guineas which he sent to Jane for Mr Hawes. My Wife and I and John Bodle and his wife went to Lox, he not at home. George Piony and Dick Smith begun carry dung at Randalls.
Thomas Hamper, 2 men and boy here ------ 21 days.
Old William Brand's men begun the healing at Towne. Chapman begun sheer the sheep afternoon. Paid Abraham Muzzall 15d for 5 weeks schooling for William Balcomb.

The 5th June 1722 Tuesday. A fine day. I was at my Father's with John Rogers and wrote a receit from my Father ____ Rogers for £20 which my Father receiv'd of Mr Saxby some time ago and Rogers gave my Father an order to take £14-1s more of Mr Saxby. I likewise wrote a coppy of Foreman's bill of charge on making a distress on Rogers's goods for rent at Tanbridge, there was 2 dis_____ . Paid Chapman 4s-6d for sheering 90 sheep and for sheering 3 dry sheep at Randalls. Thomas Hamper and his boy here ---- 22 days. The sawyers here to day and yesterday. Old William Brand's men at Towne again to day. The new blacksmith at Albourne here and I agreed to go to Lewis to morrow for him with my teem at 12s-6d to bring a tun weight.

The 6th June 1722 Wednesday. A fine day. Mr Burry lay here last night. Paid him 20 guineas towards Lady Day. I went to Wanbarrow with him and there talkt with Thomas Hamper about frameing the wainhouse etc. My teem went to Lewis to day for Albourne _____ . George Piony and Smith carry'd dung at Randalls. Will and Wood's girls weeded in the Churchfield. Old William Brand's man at Towne again to day.

The 7th June 1722 Thursday. A fine day. I din'd at Shiprods and my Wife at Shermanbury. Smith carry'd dung with Piony at Randalls, Terry at home. Will and the girls weeded. Old William Brand's man at _____ . Thomas Hamper and his boy here -------------- 28 days.

The 8th June 1722 Fryday. A fine day.
My Wife and I went to Lewis. Din'd at my Cousin Peter's. I were at Mr Paine's about Ovendean Farm. Paid Mr Court 11s-6d for nails. Piony, Smith and Banks carry'd dung at Randalls. Richard Banks fetcht tiles from the Comon. Terry went to Lewis with us. Old William Brand's men workt at Towne part.

The 9th June 1722 Saturday. A fine day.
Piony, Smith and Old Dick Banks made an end of the Foxhole close 157 loads. Paid George Piony 7s for his weeks work. Paid John Gun in full of all his work to this day except thrashing oates and pease. Old William Brand's men workt at Towne, some of 'em. Receiv'd Stephen Rick's Lady Day rent.

The 10th June 1722 Sunday. A fine day. Mr Hawes preacht twice. We had a meeting afternoon about the highways. My Cousin John Lindfield din'd here.

The 11th June 1722 Munday. A fine day. Will and Bett went to Broadwater Fair. Dick Banks went with the sorrel horse. Reckon'd and clear'd accounts with Old Dick Banks. Thomas Hamper workt here ------ 24 days. Mr John Hart and my Father here towards night. Turned 2 runts to Randalls per Terry. Will Jarvice and Jack Howard workt at Towne. Turned the hop garden 5 runts into the Homefield. Receiv'd £3-17s for the 7 ewes sold to George Hill per my Brother John Box. He came with it in the evning.

The 12th June 1722 Tuesday. A fine day.
George Piony, the boys and _____ begun carry the dung from the home close Randalls. Mr Scutt turn'd his horse to Randalls a Sunday last. John Smith turned 3 horses thither one day last week. Turned 2 great runts to Randalls yesterday.

The 13th June 1722 Wednesday. A fine day.
The boys, Piony and _____ carry'd dung at Randalls. Will Jarvice set up the well cirb at my Father's. Receiv'd 50s of Mr Scutt yesterday for the carrying of 5 loads of seacoal I am to fetch for him from Shoreham this week. Receiv'd to day of my Lord Treep 44s to pay for 2 loads I am to fetch for him. Mr Ward of Whitechapel here to buy my lambs but we did not deal.

The 14th June 1722 Thursday. A fine day. We went to Shoreham with 2 teems for seacoal. Carry'd 2 sacks of wheat. Sold a load to Harry Standbridge at £5-15s to be deliver'd at Shoreham. Mr Hawes turned his mare into my ground at 2s per week yesterday.

The 15th June 1722 Fryday. A fine day.
The boys did severall jobbs. Richard Banks and Smith went to Shoreham for coal. My Wife and I din'd at Dean House. Thomas Reeve came there. I bought 3 loads of wood of my Cousin John Lindfield at 13s per load.

The 16th June 1722 Saturday. A fine day.
White, Smith and I went to Shoreham with the teem. Brought ¾ load of coal for my Lord Treep and ¼ for my self. Paid       Coom for Treep's coal and my own 22s per load. My Wife and I supt at Mrs Catherine Beard's. Paid Richard Smith 6s for cannel coal I had last year and 2s for a piece of old sail I had to day.

The 17th June 1722 Sunday. A fine day.
Mr Hawes preacht. My Cousin John Lindfield and his wife Elizabeth din'd here. They were here after evning prayr, Mrs Barbara Campion and Mr Richard Whitpaine here also.

The 18th June 1722 Munday. A very fine day. Thomas Smith drew 65 lambs for me and markt them. I carry'd my Mother Stone to Shiprods in the waggon. Receiv'd 12s-6d of Albourne Smith for fetching cole and iron from Lewis. Carry'd load to Shiprods for Roach and brought old load back for Mr Cheal. Paid Mr Scutt £25 (being my Brother John Box's money) yesterday which Mick Monk had to day.

The 19th June 1722 Tuesday. A fine day.
_____ Care of Hand Cross drove 66 of my lambs for London. Will etc carry'd 7 loads of the Edgly Mead to the fatting rick. Dr Vincent and Strade to Randalls towards night. My Wife and Mrs Woodward there.

The 20th June 1722 Wednesday. A fine day. Will etc carry'd 5 loads to the ricks in the Fifteen Acres and 1 to the fatting rick. Richard Banks etc fetcht a load of seacoal for Mr Scutt from Shoreham. Paid Mary Wood 6s for making a gown and petticoat for Mary Balcomb.

The 21st June 1722 Thursday. A dry day. We carry'd 3 loads of hay for Mr Jeremiah Dodson and _____ of the Edgly Mead. Paid French 5s and he had a bushel of wheat. John Goffe's daughter and one of Norman's daughters of Henfield here to see Molly Balcomb.

The 22nd June 1722 Fryday. A fine day.
Richard Banks and Smith fetcht a load of coal from Shoreham for Mr Scutt, in all 5¼ loads at 10s per load. Receiv'd 50s some time ago. Will, the girls etc hay'd.

The 23rd June 1722 Saturday. A wet day.
Richard Banks went with the waggon to Shermanbury for my Father etc. My Wife and I went with the waggon. The boys ground 8 bushels of malt. Will and Smith helpt French winnow _____ bushels of wheat. My Cousin Peter Marchant and his wife came this evning.

The 24th June 1722 Sunday. A fine day.
Mr Hawes preacht. I was not at Church afternoon. My Cousin Peter Marchant and his wife and I were at Wanbarrow towards night. Paid Brother Peter the expence of the lambs on the road.

The 25th June 1722 Munday. A gloomy day, some rain.
The boys carry'd a load of hay etc and went to the Fair after. My Cousin Peter Marchant and his wife, my Wife and I din'd at my Father's. They went home. He left his old mare here, had away the sorrel horse.

The 26th June 1722 Tuesday. A gloomy day.
Richard Banks carry'd a cord of wood to my Father. He carry'd hay after. Finisht the Tully's Mead 12 loads.

The 27th June 1722 Wednesday. A fine day.
Carry'd a load of hay for Mr Jeremiah Dodson and 4 loads of chalk in the highway. Reckon'd with my Sister Sarah and gave her a note of my hand for £8 which clears the intrest to Michaelmas last. Sent 8 guineas to my Mother per my Sister Sarah. Jack Faulkoner went home yesterday. Mrs Packham of Chichester, Mrs Scutt and Mr John Hart supt here.

The 28th June 1722 Thursday. A gloomy day.
Will and the boys carry'd the ponds load and loads of the clover per Burt's to the horse's rick. Richard Banks and Smith carry'd 3 loads of chalk in Randalls land. Paid Daniel Hodge the 9s, he promis'd to come this day. Paid William Barnet 4d for spaying a sow and 4d for 2 pigs. Mrs Cheal, my Father and Mother Stone din'd and slept here. Lent Mr Jeremiah Dodson's man and waggon and 2 oxen.

The 29th June 1722 Fryday. A wet forenoon, gloomy after. Daniel Hodge, John Parsons came at noon, at 6s per week for 2 weeks and 7s per week after, 'till harvest is in. Paid Thomas Norton of Edgly 5s in hand for a loan of his horse on the bayard mare he is to have 5s more when she has a colt. The boys, Banks etc did severall jobbs. My Wife and I supt at my Father's.

The 30th June 1722 Saturday. A wet forenoon, dry after. Daniel Hodge mow'd thistles ½ thrasht ½. Richard Banks jobb'd and fetcht 1 load of chalk into Randalls lane, Smith with him. Will and Terry plough'd in the Bankfield.

The 1st July 1722 Sunday. A dry day.
Mr Jeremiah Dodson preacht. A parish meeting. Settled accounts as usual.

The 2nd July 1722 Munday. A dry day. The boys carry'd 4 loads of the clover by Burt's, 6 in all. Daniel Hodge could not work. Richard Banks fetcht 20 geese from Henfield. I was at Mr Jeremiah Dodson's in the evning. With Mr Bullen, Mr Newcomb and Mr Hawes.

The 3rd July 1722 Tuesday. A stormy day.
The boys did severall jobbs. I were at Lewis at the

visitation. I were at Dr White's. Bett went with me to Lewis.

The 4th July 1722 Wednesday. A dry day.
Will and Terry plough'd. Richard Banks carry'd 3 loads of chalk into Randalls lane. Thomas Hamper and his man Thomas Hamper here ---------- 25 days.
Goodman Cripps swingled flax     Cripps of Horsham.

The 5th July 1722 Thursday. A fine day.
The boys, Richard Banks etc carry'd the Nonsuch at Randalls 5 loads and a load at the lower side of the wheat there. Smith fetcht Bett from Lewis. Paid John Stone the Land Tax for my own land, Rickman's and Randalls all due at Lady Day last.

The 6th July 1722 Fryday. A wet day after 10 aclock.
Will and Terry begun fallow the Nonsuch at Randalls. Richard Banks and Smith carry'd 3 loads of chalk into the Randalls lane. Paid Dick Wood £1-19-6d in full. Did not outset the well cirb or materials. Goodman Cripps went away sick to his sister's.

The 7th July 1722 Saturday. A gloomy morning, fine after. Mrs Cheal and Mrs Vincent at my Father's, I din'd there. Richard Banks and Smith plough'd at Randalls. Will and Terry plough'd in the Bankfield. Paid Samuel Nichols 3s-6d for haying, left 3d to pay.

The 8th July 1722 Sunday. A dry day.
I were at Balcombe church. Receiv'd 20s of Ja Feldwick, my Brother Henry Faulkoner and an other of Balcombe officers towards cloathing Mary Terry. My Wife and I din'd _____ . We call'd at Biggs's as we came home. Balcombe officers agreed to give at the rate of 30s per annum for keeping Mary Terry for the time she came to me 'till Michaelmas 1723.

The 9th July 1722 Munday. A wet day.
Richard Banks and Smith plough'd at Randalls. Terry and Will plough'd at home 'till noon. Will went to Lewis after. Thomas Hamper's man Friend workt mending the old waggon I had of Mr Burry. Daniel Hodge did severall jobbs. Receiv'd 2 pigs of George Piony last week at 10s, not paid for.

The 10th July 1722 Tuesday. A gloomy morning, fine after. I were at Albourne Fair. Sold Sam Hart 2 runts at £10-15s. He is to kill one next week. Paid Ed Hill of Holmbush 3 guineas for a yearling colt I bought of him to day at the Fair. Receiv'd E West's money for sow 4s-6d of George Wickham. The boys etc plough'd as yesterday 'till noon. Will to the Fair. E Hill said the colt was foaled in May 1721. Paid Molly Balcomb 4s-4d for a quarter's spending money to Midsummer last.

The 11th July 1722 Wednesday. A dry day.
Will, Richard Banks, Daniel Hodge etc hay'd and carry'd the Randall mead __ loads. Thomas Hamper's man Friend workt here.

The 12th July 1722 Thursday. A showry day.
My Father and I and Bett went to Lindfield to meet Mr Roots. The boys etc carry'd hay etc.

The 13th July 1722 Fryday. A wet day.
Richard Banks and Smith fetcht a load of laths from Mockbridge for Jo Wood. Paid Thomas Roberds 5s-5d in full of all. Thomas Hamper's man Friend here. Thomas Howell's man workt here. The boys, Will, Jack White etc at Randalls. The mowers rung the hogs towards night. I agreed with Goodman Cripps to pull the acre of flax at Rickman's at 6s. Paid Ned Burt the 6s due from Mr Burry. I agreed with Old Smither to bring the body of a chaese from London for 10s.

The 14th July 1722 Saturday. A gloomy morning, dry.
The boys etc plough'd and cut the Fifteen Acres ricks, carry'd hay and hay'd after at Randalls. My Cousin Picket met my Wife at Randalls afternoon. Thomas Smith handled my lambs. We did not deal. Dick Wood set 2 new fore shooes on my horse. Mended the dill neb of the old Randalls waggon.

The 15th July 1722 Sunday. A wet day.
Mr Stedman preacht afternoon. I were not at Church in the forenoon. My Father receiv'd a letter from Dr John Budgen. My Brother James Ede died a Fryday last in the evning at Darkin.

The 16th July 1722 Munday. A wet forenoon.
The men did severall jobbs. Sold 20 lambs to William Fowle's son Thomas per Thomas Borer of Yeovel at £7-15s to be drawn this day sennight. Receiv'd in hand 15s. Mrs Ann Dodson din'd here. Paid George Piony 10s for the 2 pigs I had of him.

The 17th July 1722 Tuesday. A showry day.
Daniel Hodge and Terry plough'd. Will and Smith plough'd at home. Richard Banks had the horse waggon

to the Comon. Brought home 2 loads of lime for Thomas Reeve. Borrowed Old Hyder's horse. Mr Jeremiah Dodson and Nick Plaw here in the evning.

The 18th July 1722 Wednesday. A showry day.
Daniel Hodge and Terry plough'd. Will and Smith plough'd 'till noon. Smith fetcht some heifers to the bull from Randalls. Receiv'd £5-15s of Samuel Hart for a runt he fetcht to day. Richard Banks fetcht a load of lime from James Parker's to Mr Burry, 250 bricks for Thomas Reeve and half a load of lime for my self. Mrs Peckham here.

The 19th July 1722 Thursday. A dry day.
Richard Banks fetcht a load of sand from Randalls. Carry'd hay after. Will and the boys etc hay'd and carry'd hay, 8 loads Randalls Riddons. My Father and Mother Stone, Mrs Ann Dodson and Mr John Hart din'd with us at Randalls.

The 20th July 1722 Fryday. A gloomy day, some rain.
My Wife and I, Jacky and Molly Balcomb went to Henfield Fair. Din'd at Mr Phillip Cheal's. Jacky Cheal with us. Receiv'd Charman's bill of sale of Mr Cheal.

The 21st July 1722 Saturday. A wet day.
Reckon'd with Harry White and paid him all to this day and lent him a guinea. Richard Banks etc did severall jobbs. Jacky Faulkoner came again this evning. Towner and his mate saw'd here. I set my hand to a tax book of 6p per £ towards remending the highways. Mr Beard brought it. Will shot a pheasant I think in Thomas Norton's ground.

The 22nd July 1722 Sunday. A fine day.
Mr Hawes preacht. I were at Church afternoon. Mrs Ann Dodson got harm by a fall from her horse yesterday nere Sadlescombe. Receiv'd £7 of John Lintott of Crawley for the lambs sold to Fowle and Borer a Munday last.

The 23rd July 1722 Munday. A dry day. I went to Horsham to meet Mr Roots about takeing Tanbridge. Will, the boys etc hay'd and carry'd hay at Randalls.

The 24th July 1722 Tuesday. A fine day.
I return'd from Horsham. Met Mr Roots on this side St Leonard's pond. I measur'd the pale fences at Tanbridge etc. John Gurney went with me to Tanbridge.
Mr Reynolds minister of Horsham was buried last night.

Will, the boys etc made an end of haying at Randalls all to a little in the lagg which was spoiled in the wet.

The 25th July 1722 Wednesday. A wet day.
All kept holy day. Dick Banks drove the 2 Henfield steers to Lindfield Fair. Receiv'd 7s of my Father for my charges at Horsham. James Banks begun cut pease at noon. Goodman Cripps, Eliz Cheal and Samuel Nicholas begun cut pease at 2s-6d per acre at Randalls. Paid Dick Banks a guinea.

The 26th July 1722 Thursday. A dry day.
My Wife, Jacky, William Baker and I went to Broadwater with Mr Jeremiah Dodson. Richard Banks and Smith with the teem to the Comon. Will, Jack White and Terry cut ricks etc.

The 27th July 1722 Fryday. A wet day.
We din'd at Broadwater with Mr Jeremiah Dodson, went to Ruston in the evning. Richard Banks and Smith went to the Comon with the teem.

The 28th July 1722 Saturday. A dry day.
We came home from Ruston. Paid Mr Burry £12-17-6d with money paid before and carriage, makes £48 in full for half a year's rent due at Lady Day last. He gave Jacky a lamb that is at Randall's. Clear'd all other accounts to this day. Will, Terry etc did severall jobbs. Richard Banks and Smith went to the Comon with the teem.

The 29th July 1722 Sunday. A wet day.
Mr Hawes preacht. Paid Daniel Hodge 2s in full of all. He says he was married to Sarah Harland a Thursday last at Wickenholt church near Greatham per Mr Steward *(Ed: The SFHG Sussex Marriage Index shows a wedding at Upper Beeding between butcher Daniel Hodges of that parish and Sarah Hart, spinster of Hurst)*.

The 30th July 1722 Munday. A wet day.
Richard Banks and the boys went to the Comon with 2 teems. Fetcht 1225 bricks to the Malthouse. Daniel Hodge did severall jobbs. Frank Marshall came to dress my Father's horse's back. Mr Hawes here in the evning. John Clerk told me that his iron cost him £19 per Tun at a forge near Maresfield.

The 31st July 1722 Tuesday. A dry day.
Richard Banks and Smith at the Comon with the teem. Daniel Hodge cut pease etc. Mr Roots at my Father's agreed _____ for Tanbridge for 7 years from Xmas

next at £35 per annum and Strood at £10 per annum and to enter as soon as my Father can put Rogers out. Robert Hurst of Horsham here.

The 1st August 1722 Wednesday. Showry afternoon. Mr Hurst lay here last night. We went to Randalls in the evning. The reapers begun reap in the Rookwood. Receiv'd 4 guineas of Samuel Hart. He fetcht the last runt that I sold him at Albourne Fair. Frank Marshall here to dress my Father's horse.

The 2nd August 1722 Thursday. A showry day. Mr Hurst lay here last night. Went away before noon. Paid Hollingam's wife in full for her girls work. The boys etc mov'd the straw out of the barns. Dick Banks drew trees at Randalls in the morning.

The 3rd August 1722 Fryday. A wet day. Banks and Smith with the teem. Reckon'd and clear'd accounts with French. Lent him 20s, no rent reckon'd for. Paid William Ball 55s in full for oates. Thomas Harrison of Albourne here with him.

The 4th August 1722 Saturday. A fine morning, dry after. Will, Daniel Hodge and Terry mow'd the oates by the coppice. Mr Beard and Richard Wood's girls hay'd afternoon. John Clerk of St John's Comon here. He brought a bird for my Wife from Mr Wade of Henfield. Thomas Hamper and his man here ½ -------- 25½.

The 5th August 1722 Sunday. A gloomy day. Mr Jeremiah Dodson preacht. We had a meeting. Settled accounts as usual. Kitt Ede and Bett Ede came to my Father's last night. Mrs Susan Courthope here after evning prayr. My Cousin John Lindfield din'd here.

The 6th August 1722 Munday. A showr afternoon. Will etc carry'd 6 loads of the way mead and mead below. Elliot Wood of Cuckfield din'd here. I sold him 3 runts in the hop garden at £14-10. Sold my Cousin John Bodle 4 lambs at Randalls at 30s to be kill'd in a little time. Reckon'd with Mr Jeremiah Dodson and he gave me a receit for my tythes that will be due at Michaelmas next and a note of his hand for £5. Reckon'd also with Harry Wickham of Albourne and there is due to me £8-17-3d for which he gave me a note of his hand.

The 7th August 1722 Tuesday. A wet day. Richard Banks and Smith fetcht half a load of wood and 50 faggots out of Thomas Avery's ground. Carry'd bricks and mortar to Tully's. Thomas Vallence and Daniel Bide begun make an oven at Tully's. Thomas Hamper and his man Thomas Hamper at Tully's part -------- 26 days. Will, Daniel Hodge, Terry and White mow'd oates per White's. Reckon'd with Old Dick Banks and John Gun.

The 8th August 1722 Wednesday. A fine day. Carry'd 8 loads of pease at Randalls. Thomas Vallence workt on the oven at Tully's. Will, Daniel Hodge, Terry and White mow'd oates in the morning. Ended field per White. George Wickham put his horse in the field by Burt's at 15d per week.

The 9th August 1722 Thursday. A fine day. Will etc carry'd the rest of the Lime Kiln field of pease, in all 15 loads. Carry'd the Rookwood wheat, 4 loads. Thomas Vallence finisht the oven at Tully's.

The 10th August 1722 Fryday. A very fine day. Mr Phillip Cheal din'd here. Lent him £50 for a note of his hand. Receiv'd £100 of Mr Scutt in part for Rusper liveing. Mr Madgwicke of Jarvice here afternoon. Mr Sixsmith and Mr John Hart here a little while. Will, the boys etc carry'd 7 loads of the Little Mead. Richard Banks carry'd Jack Haslegrove's flax. Lent Mr Jeremiah Dodson's man Old Hyder's horse.

The 11th August 1722 Saturday. A very fine day. Will etc carry'd hay out of the Little Mead and    loads of wheat at Botten's. Cripps etc took up Rickman's flax, 150 bundles. Richard Banks and Daniel Hodge helpt the reapers for which they are to work for me as much. Jack Faulkoner went this evning to board at Wanbarrow. My Cousin Picket here and Richard Vinall. My Father and Mother Stone din'd here. Dr Vincent here afternoon.

The 12th August 1722 Sunday. A fine day. Mr Hawes preacht. My Cousin John Lindfield, wife and daughter din'd here.

The 13th August 1722 Munday. A fine day. Will, Daniel Hodge, Terry and Richard Banks begun mow the Churchfield barly. Carry'd hay after, 2 loads to Kester. Mr Picknall of Arundell here in the evning.

The 14th August 1722 Tuesday. A fine day. Will etc carry'd a load of hay to Kester's and a small load to Frank Holden's. Carry'd 2 loads of wheat at Randalls and 3 loads of oates at Tully's afternoon. Paid a bill of

£3-11-0d at my Aunt Courtness's. Mr Thomas Fisher din'd here.

The 15th August 1722 Wednesday. A fine day.
Carry'd the oates by the coppice, 3 loads more, in all 6 loads and a load of the field by Harry White's. Will and Jack went to a Plate Race at Lewis. Richard Banks and Smith carry'd 2 loads of Randalls wheat under the hill.

The 16th August 1722 Thursday. A fine day.
Will, Daniel Hodge etc mow'd in the morning, carry'd 8 loads of the Nine Acres oates to Tully's. Kill'd a ewe yesterday, weigh'd 11½lbs per quarter. Paid R Walker 1s for this afternoon's work, he is to give me 2d again.

The 17th August 1722 Fryday. A wet forenoon, dry after.
Richard Banks and Smith went to Shoreham for a load of seacoal for Thomas Smith. Will etc did severall jobbs and mow'd barly afternoon. My Father and Mr Roots seal'd articles for Tanbridge.

The 18th August 1722 Saturday. A gloomy day.
Thomas Hamper rais'd the wainhouse at Randalls. Reckon'd and clear'd all accounts with John Smith the butcher except his horse keeping and marketing a bull for me. Will and Terry carry'd 3 jobbs of wheat at Randalls. Richard Banks, Daniel Hodge etc carry'd 2 jobbs of Tully's oates. They finisht mowing the Churchfield barly in the forenoon.

The 19th August 1722 Sunday. A showry day.
Mr John Hart preacht twice. I were at my Father Stone's afternoon.

The 20th August 1722 Munday. A gloomy morning.
Will etc did some jobbs in the morning. Daniel Hodge and Banks reaped ½, Richard Banks and Smith fetch 50 faggots and a _____ of wood from Thomas Avery's ground for French. Will and Smith carry'd a load of wheat at Randalls. Turned the calves, yearlings and sheep into the pease earsh at Randalls. Mr Wilkin and Mr John Hart here in the evning.

The 21st August 1722 Tuesday. A showry day.
Gather'd pares, carry'd out the flax and wheat into Tully's garret. Daniel Hodge reapt in John Gun's room whilst John Gun heald his oven. Paid Mr John Hart 15s-6d last night for John Balcomb's schooling. I was at Mrs Catherine Beard's in the morning. Gave Mr Wilkin instructions to get my building ensur'd.

The 22nd August 1722 Wednesday. A wet day.
Richard Banks and Smith fetcht 50 faggots and a cord of wood from Thomas Avery's ground. Thomas Hamper and his man here ------------------ 27 days. Paid J Boniface 12s for mowing and 8d for helping raise the wainhouse. The Wintermilch calved a cow calf last night.

The 23rd August 1722 Thursday. A dry day.
Will, Daniel Hodge and Smith carry'd 4 loads of Randalls wheat. Richard Banks fetcht 75 faggots from Randalls to A Muzzall. carry'd 3 small loads of Tully's lower oates, Crips and Boniface helpt.
Thomas Hamper here --------- 28 days.

The 24th August 1722 Fryday. A gloomy forenoon, dry after. My Father, my Wife and I, KE, EE and O went to Brighton Fair. Din'd at Mr Colbron's. Receiv'd £5-15s of H Standbridge for a load of wheat. The boys kept holy day.

The 25th August 1722 Saturday. A fine day.
The reapers made an end of reaping at Randalls and helpt carry oates. Daniel Hodge and Jack White helpt reap 'till noon and a little more. Carry'd 7 loads of the Nine Acres oates and a small jobb, the last of Tully's lower field. Bony mow'd stubble ½, helpt carry oates after.

The 26th August 1722 Sunday. A fine day.
Mr Hawes preacht twice. My Cousin John Lindfield and his wife Elizabeth din'd here.

The 27th August 1722 Munday. A very fine day.
Turned barly and made an end of carrying the Nine Acres oates, in all 22 loads. Dick Banks etc carry'd 2 loads of oates for S Hyder. The reapers begun mow the barly under the hill. Bonny mow'd stubble ½, helpt harvest after.

The 28th August 1722 Tuesday. A dry forenoon, wet after. Richard Banks, Terry and Smith carry'd oates for Old Hyder. John White, Daniel Hodge, James Banks and Old Bonny cut tares part. Begun dig the foundations for the new oast at Thomas Reeve's malthouse. Thomas Reeve and W King here afternoon.
Paid John Haslegrove 18s for 12lb of tire.

The 29th August 1722 Wednesday. A gloomy day.
Richard Banks and Smith fetcht half a load of lime for my self and 100 tiles for the malthouse, all from Parker's.

Fetcht a load of great chalk likewise to the malthouse. Daniel Hodge, Bonny, Jack White, James Banks etc cut tares. The mowers made an end of mowing barly. Thomas Hamper and his man here / made Tully's barn doors ----------- 29 days.

The 30th August 1722 Thursday. A fine day. Richard Banks and Smith fetcht 600 tiles for the malthouse and a load of lime for King. Carry'd 4 loads of the Sandfield barly, cut tares in the morning. Jack White, Bonny etc helpt. Receiv'd £7-6s of Thomas Champion, out £6 for half a year's annuity to my Aunt Holden, 1s-1d for a River Tax and £1-13s for half a year's Land Tax, all due at Michaelmas last. My Father and John Bartholomew's boy set out for Horsham. Paid my Father 3 guineas and a half.

The 31st August 1722 Fryday. A fine day. Carry'd 12 loads of the Sandfield barly. John White, Bonny, Eliz Cheal helpt cut tares in the morning. Daniel Hodge and James Banks and Samuel Everset helpt after.

The 1st September 1722 Saturday. A showry day. Richard Banks and Smith fetcht 2,000 tiles and ridge tiles from James Parker at the Comon for the malthouse. Jack White, Bonny, Daniel Hodge etc made an end of cutting tares. Sold Nathaniel Turner at the Comon a runt at £4-15s and the tongue, to be kill'd against their Fair. Receiv'd 1s in hand. William Jarvice and John Rowland paved Tully's brewhouse. Paid Daniel Hodge £1-3s, he helpt the masons at Tully's.

The 2nd September 1722 Sunday. A fine day. Mr Jeremiah Dodson preacht. We had a parish meeting as usual. I supt at my Father's. He return'd from Horsham, lay at Fryland last night. Dick Smith went for him. My Cousin John Marchant of Lox and his wife din'd here.

The 3rd September 1722 Munday. A fine day. Ended carrying the Sandfield at Randalls      loads, in all      loads. Carry'd 4 loads of the Churchfield barly. Towner and his mates helpt, Jo Wood and his man, Daniel Hodge half the day. Clear'd accounts to him in the morning. Bonny workt all day. Mrs Barbara Campion etc here afternoon. My Cousin John Lindfield here in the evning.

The 4th September 1722 Tuesday. A very fine day. Carry'd 12 loads of the Churchfield. Daniel Hodge helpt ½, Thomas Jenner, John Standbridge and Elliott Wood of Cuckfield fetcht the 2 runts, paid him £50 for my Brother Henry Faulkoner and £50 more. He promis'd to pay to my Brother Faulkoner to morrow for me.

The 5th September 1722 Wednesday. A very fine day. Carry'd 13 loads of the barly under the hill at Randalls. Carry'd also 2 loads of the last of the Churchfield, in all 18 loads. Will King and his man, Thomas Jenner etc helpt. Mrs Packham, my Nieces Edes etc pick't hops. Paid Mr Jeremiah Dodson 12s for 2lb of bohea he promis'd to get me at Broadwater.

The 6th September 1722 Thursday. A fine day. Jack White, Daniel Hodge etc carry'd 10 loads of tares etc at Randalls with Old Bonny and James Banks.

The 7th September 1722 Fryday. A gloomy morning, fine after. Richard Banks, Smith and White made an end of harvest, carry'd 2 loads of tares, in all 12 loads. Jack White helpt cut a rick half the day. Carry'd ½ a load of Mr Burry's flints to the malthouse.

The 8th September 1722 Saturday. A fine day. Richard Banks and James Banks fetcht a load of flints to the malthouse. Towner had my teem, 10 oxen, to fetch a load of ___ . John Snashall dresst my young bull's eyes.

The 9th September 1722 Sunday. A showry day. Mr Hawes preacht. John Clerk at the Comon din'd here.

The 10th September 1722 Munday. A dry day. Richard Banks and Smith fetcht a load of flints. Receiv'd £4-15s of Nathaniel Turner for a runt. Terry begun plough at Randalls. Sold my Cousin John Bodle the py'd cow at 14d per nail 5 quarters and I am to have her tongue. My wedding day ------- 22 years.

The 11th September 1722 Tuesday. A dry day. We had our harvest supper. Richard Banks and Smith fetcht a load of flints to the malthouse. John Bodle and Dick Vinall markt 50 sheep for London. Let John Bodle the Malthouse Field at 40s per annum and a neat's tongue and I am to carry the hay for him. Changed one of my great lambs for 3 of his and I am to give him 5s to boot.

The 12th September 1722 Wednesday. A fine day.
Richard Banks and Smith fetcht a load of salt for Frank Holden and one for S Courtness. I had 10s per load and a sack of salt at the price they gave for it out of the vessel, which was 4s-2d per bushel. Daniel Hodge scoured drains in Edgly Mead afternoon. I were at Nathaniel Turner's. Borrowed £50 for a month for a note of my hand and sent the money to Elliot Wood per my Cousin John Lindfield. Paid Nathaniel Turner 5s for the use of it. My Cousin John Lindfield here in the evning. Thomas Hamper and his man here------- 30 days.

The 13th September 1722 Thursday. A gloomy day.
Richard Banks and Smith got the waggon ready and loaded Jack Haslegrove's flax seed. Terry and Old Dick Banks plough'd to day and yesterday.
Thomas Hamper and his man here on the waggon and Will Chamber -------------------- 31 days. Frank Holden here in the evning. Nanny sick of the measles.

The 14th September 1722 Fryday. A gloomy day.
Richard Banks and Smith fetcht an other load of salt for Frank Holden and carry'd the flax seed. My Cousin Peter Marchant and Mr Landon of London came hither. Receiv'd 16s-8d of my Cousin John Lindfield for a sack of salt.

The 15th September 1722 Saturday. A gloomy day.
Richard Banks fetcht a load of flints and some mortar to the malthouse. Smith and White plough'd at Randalls. Terry went to Lewis with my Wife and I, we din'd at my Cousin Peter Marchant's. Mr Landon went with us. Paid all due at Thomas Friend's except on Molly Balcomb's account. Paid for girt buckles and a hammer at Mr Court's. Paid also 2s-9d for a horse whip for Jacky. My Cousin Peter Marchant's wife Sarah came home with us.

The 16th September 1722 Sunday. A dry day.
Mr Hawes preacht. We had a meeting about D Dine, the vestry did not agree to give a certificate for him. Ned Terry went home with my Cousin Sarah Marchant.

The 17th September 1722 Munday. A fine day.
Richard Banks and Smith fetcht a load of flints and carry'd Mr Burry's mortar to the malthouse. Terry and Banks plough'd at Randalls. Receiv'd 40 tags of John Burry which I am to keep till Lady Day next at 2s per tag for as many as live till that time. My Wife and I were at Old Land afternoon.

The 18th September 1722 Tuesday. A fine day.
My Wife, Bett Ede and I at Lindfield. Richard Banks and Smith fetcht 2 loads of lime to the malthouse.
Will *(Ed: xxx text deleted xxx)* gather'd apples after.

The 19th September 1722 Wednesday. A fine day.
Docked all the 3 colts. Richard Banks and Smith fetcht a load of seacoal from Shoreham for Thomas Smith. Terry and Banks plough'd at Randalls. Receiv'd £50 of Mr Jeremiah Dodson on Mr Richard Whitpaine's and Mr William Martin's account if they consent to it tomorrow. Will etc a hunting. They kill'd a hare in my Brother Peter's ground. He gather'd apples after. Thomas Field went through the ground with his teem.

The 20th September 1722 Thursday. A fine day.
Terry and Old Dick Banks mov'd Stephen Rick to a house in Fulking. Richard Banks and Smith fetcht the third load of coal from Shoreham for Thomas Smith, 1 paid for. Receiv'd £50 more of Mr Richard Whitpaine part of the purchase money for the Advowson of Rusper, being the money mentioned yesterday. Clear'd all accounts with Mr Jeremiah Dodson except the colour Receiv'd 20s, all that was due from John Reeve.

The 21st September 1722 Fryday. A dry day.
I were at Lewis Fair. Bought 20 ewes of Samuel Lullham, Mr Farncomb's shepherd at £6-19s. Bought 19 ewes and a ram of John Hossel. They were Mr Scutt's sheep of Brighton, at £6-15s paid for all. Paid all due at Mr Court's. Din'd at my Cousin Peter's. Banks and Smith fetcht a load of flints to the malthouse.

The 22nd September 1722 Saturday. A gloomy day.
Richard Banks and Smith fetcht a load of seacoal from Shoreham, ½for my Father, ½for my self. Terry and Old Dick Banks made an end of stirring the pease earsh at Randalls. Fetcht the waggon plough wheels etc from the Comon after. Took up the flax. Mr William Martin din'd here.

The 23rd September 1722 Sunday. A fine day.
Mr Hawes preacht, no service afternoon. My Cousin John Lindfield din'd here.

The 24th September 1722 Munday. A gloomy day.
Richard Banks and Smith fetcht a load of tiles from the

Comon to Mr Osbourne's for my Brother Peter. Receiv'd £5-14s yesterday of my Cousin Peter Marchant and clear'd accounts with him. Allowed him 5 guineas for the old mare and I had but 19s for my blind horse. Terry and Banks begun stir the tare earsh. Thomas Hamper and his man here --------- 32 days. Will went to kill a hare for Mr Burt of Wick. Receiv'd £40-6-6d more of Mr Richard Whitpaine, in part for the Advowson of Rusper.

The 25th September 1722 Thursday. A fine day.
Richard Banks fetcht 500 bricks from Marten's for Thomas Reeve and a load of lime for my self carry'd to Randalls instead of that which they used before. Paid Marten £1-19-6d in full of all that I owe him. Paid John Snashall for the yearling I bought of him and bought his barly at Candlemas price. Will and Terry plough'd at Randalls. Thomas Hamper and his man here ----------- 33 days. Win'd 4 bushels of the Nine Acres oates. John Snashall dresst the young bull's eye. Receiv'd 40s yesterday for a year's intrest due to William Balcomb's accounts on bond of Nick Plaw.

The 26th September 1722 Wednesday. A fine day.
All went to hunting except Smith. Moved Eliz Cheal and fetcht a load of wood for Banks. Paid Mr Sixsmith £30 and clear'd all accounts. Bought 42 bushels of seed wheat of him at £7 if I like the wheat when I see it. Mrs Catherine Beard's and her family here afternoon. Kitty sick of the measles. Molly just recovered of it.

The 27th September 1722 Thursday. A fine day.
Richard Banks fetcht 1600 tiles from Marten's to the malthouse. Brought also the plates from John Clerk's for the oast. I were to see Mr Sixsmith's wheat and concluded to have it. I am to send a man to winnow it. Harry White and Smith mov'd French, Daniel Hodge etc did some jobbs. Drove 2 runts to my Cousin John Lindfield's for London. Gather'd apples after. Thomas Fowle, Thomas Borer and Ed Parr of Yovel here.

The 28th September 1722 Fryday. A fine day.
I met John Marten at Warninglid. Call'd at Dean House as I came home. Richard Banks etc mov'd his father to Randalls. Will gather'd apples etc.

The 29th September 1722 Saturday. A fine day.
I went to Stenning Fair. Bought 10 steer runts of    at £3 a runt, and one heifer at 28s. Mr Beard bought 4 at £7-15s. Receiv'd £20 of Edwards at Beeding for my Cousin John Lindfield. Molly Balcomb sick of the measles. Richard Banks fetcht 650 bricks from Parker's to the malthouse. Terry and Will plough'd.

The 30th September 1722 Sunday. A fine day. Mr Hawes preacht. Thomas Butcher here about Mary Morley.

The 1st October 1722 Munday. A fine day.
Richard Banks and the boys got dung courts etc together and begun carrying dung into the Bankfield. Will and Mr Wood's son of Newdigate went hunting. John Clerk and his man laid down the iron plate at the malthouse. Paid Eliz Cheal 2s-11d and clear'd accounts except in cutting. Receiv'd a new payr of traises from John Clerk. Weigh'd 20lb a Saturday last. Paid John Clerk 10s for the traises to day. Clear'd accounts with John Cook for his rent at Randalls etc.

The 2nd October 1722 Tuesday. A dry day.
Dr White here to see Bett. She was taken very ill last night. Richard Banks, Terry etc carry'd 26 loads of my dung and 14 loads of John Smith's dung all into the Bankfield. Smith went for Dr White.

The 3rd October 1722 Wednesday. A fine day.
Dr White here again. Richard Banks etc carry'd    loads of dung into the field by Burry's. Sent the £20 to my Cousin John Lindfield which I receiv'd of Edwards per Will. Smith went for the Doctor. Richard Banks went to Brighton afternoon.

The 4th October 1722 Thursday. A fine day.
Terry and Smith etc carry'd dung into the field per Burt's. 39 loads and 4 loads of mud. James Banks and I set out 6 trees at Randalls. My Cousin John Lindfield here, we settled the account about my sheep and 2 runts and I gave him a note of my hand for £20 which he paid in London for me to Mr Tholly and Longley and £30 of my own money, £50 in all for the use of Mr Phillip Cheal of Henfield. Drove the fatting oxen to Randalls.

The 5th October 1722 Fryday. A fine day.
Terry, Will etc carry'd 14 loads of the hop garden mud and 28 loads of dung. I were at John Farncomb's of Patcham. Bought 40 ewes of him at 8s-6d per ewe. I am to run out 45 and turn back 5. Paid him 4s in hand, remains 16 guineas. Richard Banks and Smith fetcht a load of salt from Lewis for my Aunt Courtness and

carry'd my wool to Mr Friend at 16s per todd. They brought home also 7 doz of glass bottles from Aunt Galloway's.

The 6th October 1722 Saturday. A fine day.
Richard Banks fetcht 625 or 650 bricks from Marten's for my self. James Banks, E Crundel and I fetcht 42 ewes from Patcham. Sold Mrs Catherine Beard 10 of the Brighton ewes. Terry, Smith etc carry'd     loads of dung, gather'd pares after. Receiv'd camlet etc for a coat from my Brother John Courtness yesterday. My Brother Courtness here to day.

The 7th October 1722 Sunday. A fine day.
Mr Jeremiah Dodson preacht. A parish meeting, settled accounts as usual.

The 8th October 1722 Munday. A dry day.
Terry etc carry'd 30 loads of dung of Tully's close into the field by the coppices. Reckon'd with Harry White and clear'd all accounts to Michaelmas last and lent him 2 guineas. Reckon'd and clear'd accounts with Thomas Hamper. Mr Jeremiah Dodson here in the morning in his way to London.

The 9th October 1722 Tuesday. A dry day.
Richard Banks fetcht a load of timber from Bolny for Jo Wood and so he did yesterday. Old Bonny thrasht a sack of oates. Reckon'd and clear'd accounts with Dick Wood. Will, Terry etc carry'd 25 loads of dung of Tully's close. Sent 3 runts to Hand Cross for London. My Sister Mary Faulkoner here afternoon. I were at Nathaniel Turner's, he not at home.

The 10th October 1722 Wednesday. A fine day.
Terry and Old Dick Banks begun plough in the Bankfield. Smith harrow'd. Will, Banks and James tipt ricks at Randalls. My Wife and I at Westtowne afternoon. Old Bonny thrasht oates.

The 11th October 1722 Thursday. A fine day.
Richard Banks and James carry'd the roof of the malthouse down and fetcht a load of flints. Smith etc plough'd. I were at Mr Price's and paid him a guinea for 2 pigs and a young hog.

The 12th October 1722 Fryday. A gloomy morning, fine after. Will begun sow wheat in the Bankfield. Richard Banks harrow'd. Terry, Smith etc plough'd with 2 teems. Will Jarvice workt here copeing the upper garden walls.

My Sister Mary Faulkoner here in her way home. Receiv'd 5 guineas of Frank Holden in part of the mony I am to pay for him in London. 6 young beasts straid out of Randalls ground yesterday or the night before. Bonny and Mr Price's man brought my pigs. Paid Daniel Hodge in full for all his work to this day. My Cousin John Bodle kill'd the Wintermilch's calf at 2½d per pound.

The 13th October 1722 Saturday. A fine day.
Plough'd etc in Bankfield. William Jarvice and Dan Bide here on the wall. My Wife and I at Shermanbury afternoon.

The 14th October 1722 Sunday. A dry day.
Mr Hawes preacht. We had a meeting about Old William Brand's diall. Thomas Muzzall's wife buried. *(Ed: Mary Muzzall's burial recorded in the Hurst Parish Register)*

The 15th October 1722 Munday. A fine day.
Mov'd Thomas Jacket to the malthouse. Richard Banks fetcht 80 corner tiles and 1500 plain tiles from Marten's. Sold Nathaniel Turner 2 runts at 14d per nail and their tongues. Paid him £10 in part of the £50 that I ow'd him on a note of my hand and took in that note and gave him a fresh note for the £40 which remained unpaid. Receiv'd £10 more of Frank Holden in part of money return'd.

The 16th October 1722 Tuesday. A gloomy day, some rain. Finisht the Bankfield with wheat. Terry etc carry'd loads of mud into the field at Burt's. Reckon'd with my Brother Peter and there is due to him £2-9-0d. Win'd to day and before 5 quarters 2 bushels of Bonny's oates. Thomas Hamper and his man and boy workt for me at Randalls in the home close -------- 1 day. Daniel Hodge helpt Banks cut mows at Randalls to day and half the day yesterday. Sent my camlet to Robert Hurst at Horsham by Abraham Muzzall.

The 17th October 1722 Wednesday. A gloomy day, some rain. Richard Banks and Smith fetcht 42 bushels of seed wheat from Mr Sixsmith. Paid my Cousin John Lindfield £8-13-6d for wood and faggots, coals, oates and 10 Northamptonshire lambs at 8s-6d per lamb. Mrs Cheal, my Father and Dr Vincent din'd here. Paid Old Bonny in full for all his work. Receiv'd 5 guineas of John Bodle. Receiv'd 33s of Frank Holden in full of the money return'd. Dr Nick Plaw here to see the young bull.

The 18th October 1722 Thursday. A gloomy day. Richard Banks with the teem fetcht 700 bricks from Parker's for Mr Burry. The rest carry'd mud to day and yesterday. Mr Cheal here. I went to Dr Vincent's with him.

The 19th October 1722 Fryday. A fine day. Richard Banks fetcht 1050 rubbish tiles and 950 good tiles from Parker's for my self. Terry etc carry'd 10½ loads of Thomas Smith's dung and 10½ loads of John Bodle's dung into the field by Burt's. I am to give John Bodle 6d per load for his. Win'd 15 bushels head and 1 bushel tail being all that grew in the field by the Sandfield pond Randalls. Win'd also 2 bushels of the mow cuttings there. Abraham Muzzall went to Horsham again.

The 20th October 1722 Saturday. A fine day. Richard Banks fetcht 700 bricks to John Bodle for Old William Brand. I were at Lewis. Weigh'd my wool at Thomas Friend's. It weigh'd 10 todd 16 pound. Borrow'd £30 of John Bradford of Falmer for a note of my hand. Paid Mr Norman in full of all. Terry etc carry'd loads of dung at Randalls.

The 21st October 1722 Sunday. A fine day. Mr Hawes preacht, no service afternoon. I din'd at my Father's.

The 22nd October 1722 Munday. A gloomy day. My Wife and I din'd at my Cousin John Lindfield's. Richard Banks fetcht 700 bricks more to John Bodle's. The boys etc carry'd 28 loads of dung into the cooper's croft at Randalls. Hodges workt with Richard Banks.

The 23rd October 1722 Tuesday. A fine day. Two men from Ashford in Kent had the two Mr Fishers as they call'd themselves arrested for debt. Their names are Edward and Thomas Elvey and not Fisher. They paid the money and were discharged. Richard Banks etc carry'd 4 waggon loads of chalk and 2 dung court loads into the Randalls lanes and 1 load each into Randalls closes.

The 24th October 1722 Wednesday. A fine day. Richard Banks fetcht 700 bricks from Parker's to the malthouse. Terry etc carry'd 25 loads of dung into the cooper's croft. Paid Mr Shaw £2-12-3d for briefs, he was here. Mr John Hart with Mr Shaw. My Brother John Box here, exchanged receits for Mr Farncomb as usual.

Thomas Field sent me a dish of fish out of the pond of Lie.

The 25th October 1722 Thursday. A fine day. Richard Banks fetcht 700 bricks from Parker's to the malthouse and boards from Thomas Hamper. Terry etc carry'd dung 22 loads of the mixen in the fallow.

The 26th October 1722 Fryday. A dry day. My Son William 21 years old. He went to West Grinstead to hunting with the Lintotts of Hickstead. Dick Banks fetcht a load of slabs for John Bodle at 1_____ . I din'd at my Father's with Dr Lintott, his wife etc. King's man workt at Randalls to day and yesterday. Paid Thomas Peckham 12s yesterday for his son's old old oast hairs at 5s for his bushel. Turn'd all the runts to Randalls yesterday.

The 27th October 1722 Saturday. A wet forenoon. Mr Newlin, Mr Jeremiah Dodson and Mr Hawes breakfasted here. Receiv'd £26 of Mr Dodson on Mr Scrase's account. Nick Plaw here to see young bull. Richard Banks and boy did severall jobbs.

The 28th October 1722 Sunday. A dry day. Mr Hawes preacht. Jacky carry'd a fat goose to Mr Colbron's of Brighton.

The 29th October 1722 Munday. A fine day. Mrs Cheal din'd here. Paid Mr Ives £5 for a year's intrest due to his unkle Henry Burtenshaw on bond. My Cousin Richard Turner and his wife here. Her Unkle William Holden and Aunt Susan (*Ed: née Turner*) here also. Dr Vincent and my Father here in the evning. My Father told me he had sent to enquire of Mr Roots and he was gone away with an other man's wife. Terry etc carry'd 40 loads of dung at Randalls. Richard Banks drew 6 trees to the sawpit at Randalls and carry'd 15 bushels of seed wheat to John Hart's at 3s-9d per bushel. My Lord Treep here with Mr Pointin's draught of a dial for Old William Brand's tomb. He carry'd it away again.

The 30th October 1722 Tuesday. A showry morning. Mr Burry lay here last night. Paid him a guinea for the 3 ewes at Randalls. Were at Westtowne. Terry carry'd 24 loads of dung at Randalls. Thomas Hamper's 2 men cut down trees in Tully's ground.

The 31st October 1722 Wednesday. A gloomy day. Terry etc carry'd loads of dung at Randalls.

Sold Ed Parr and Young Thomas Fowle of Yovel 30 sheep at 7s apiece. I gave Parr an order to pay the mony to Mr Wilkin. Paid my Brother John Courtness £37 in full of all.

The 1st November 1722 Thursday. A fine day.
Richard Banks, Terry and Old Dick Banks begun plough in the Lime Kiln Field. Dick Smith roll'd. Receiv'd £17 yesterday of Mr Jeremiah Dodson on Old Scrase's account. My Wife and I spent evning at Mrs Catherine Beard's.

The 2nd November 1722 Fryday. A fine day. Plough'd at Randalls. Dr Nick Plaw here again to drench the steer. Thomas Hamper and his man at Tully's again ---- 3 days. Mr John Hart spent the evning here. I told Mr Richard Whitpaine of the money Mr Jeremiah Dodson paid me.

The 3rd November 1722 Saturday. A fine day.
Richard Banks etc plough'd and sow'd etc with 2 teems in the Lime Kiln Field. Thomas Hamper and his man at Tully's ---------- 4 days. Paid Old Hyder 4s-6d in full for his boy's work.

The 4th November 1722 Sunday. A fine day.
Mr Jeremiah Dodson preacht. My Wife and I receiv'd the sacrament. We had a parish meeting. Settled accounts as usual. Receiv'd 16s of Richard White for the tythe of Rickman's. I gave Mr Dodson a receit last night for £50 on Mr Scrase's account for Mr William Martin and Mr Dodson gave me a note of his hand for £7 of the money.

The 5th November 1722 Munday. A very wet forenoon. The boys and Banks did severall jobbs at home and Banks carry'd tiles to Randalls from the malthouse. Thomas Hamper and his man at Tully's ----- 5 days. Paid my Cousin John Lindfield the £20 which he paid in London for me. His son John here for it.

The 6th November 1722 Tuesday. A wet day.
Richard Banks, the boys etc plough'd a while at Randalls. Harry White lookt after 8 of the North Country lambs being straid away.

The 7th November 1722 Wednesday. A dry day.
The boys etc plough'd and sow'd. I went (by mistake) for Howard's Heath Fair. Went no further than St Johns Comon. I lookt after my lambs that were astray. My Wife and I at my Brother John Box's in the evning.

The 8th November 1722 Thursday. A fine day.
I were at Howard's Heath Fair, bought 3 cow runts of at £5-19s. Bought also a payr of oxen of James Gibb nere Howards Heath at £12-10s. The boys etc plough'd and sow'd at Randalls.

The 9th November 1722 Fryday. A gloomy day, some small rain. The boys etc plough'd and sow'd at Randalls. Thomas Howell's man chipt one of the wheel ploughs. A chair bottomer here, he calls himself William Branson. Paid him 8½d. He is to come again a Munday. Harry Morley sheer'd 14 lambs.

The 10th November 1722 Saturday. A dry day.
Plough'd and sow'd as yesterday. My Wife and I at Lewis. My Cousin Bodle carry'd my Wife. Paid Mr Friend £2-6-8d in full for cloath for a coat for my self, the cloath 13s-4d per yard and a bill of other goods. Paid Mr Baldy the charitable use money etc for our parish for the year 1721 £1-16-2d. Paid Mr Taylor 13s-10½d yesterday for Mr Jeremiah Dodson's hop duty.

The 11th November 1722 Sunday. A dry day.
Mr John Hart preacht, no service afternoon. My Cousin John Lindfield din'd here. My Father and Mother Stone here afternoon. Dick Banks went for Darkin for my Father.

The 12th November 1722 Munday. A gloomy day.
Will, the boys etc plough'd and sow'd at Randalls. I was at Pyecomb at Thomas Norton's and Pangdean. Bett was at Mr Beaumont's. Nick Plaw here in the evning. William Jarvice workt at Tully's. Receiv'd £20 more of John Bradford a Saturday which made £100 for which I gave bond to him and sister Margret or Mary and took in my note for £50. *(Ed: John born 1681 and Margaret born 1680 were children of John Bradford and his wife Susan née Neaves of Falmer/Preston)*

The 13th November 1722 Tuesday. A fine day. Plough'd and sow'd at Randalls.

The 14th November 1722 Wednesday. A dry day.
Plough'd and sow'd at Randalls. Mr Richard Whitpaine and his wife Mary here afternoon. My Father and Mother Stone with him.

The 15th November 1722 Thursday. A gloomy day.
I were at Brighton morning. Bought 5 quarters of pease of Mr Masters at £4-10s. I am to fetch them. My Wife

and I supt at Danny. My Cousin John Lindfield's teem begun plough in the field by Bankfield. My teems plough'd and sow'd at Randalls. Paid Robert Hurst for makeing my camlet coat.

The 16th November 1722 Fryday. A showry day.
Made an end of ploughing at Randalls. Richard Banks fetcht 3 quarters of seed wheat from Sadlescombe. Paid Harry Morley 4s for sheering some lambs and thatching the haystraw at Tully's. My Cousin William Wood of Sadlescombe was here.

The 17th November 1722 Saturday. A gloomy day.
Begun sow the field at Burt's. My Cousin John Lindfield's teem went home at night. Richard Banks made an end of the field under the hill. John Towner and Ja Reed saw'd at Randalls.

The 18th November 1722 Sunday. A dry day.
Mr John Hart preacht, no service afternoon. My Wife and I were at Wanbarrow afternoon.

The 19th November 1722 Munday. A gloomy morning, wet afternoon. The boys, Richard Banks etc plough'd and sow'd part by Burt's. I were at Dr Vincent's in the evning with Mr Henry Campion etc.

The 20th November 1722 Tuesday. A wet day.
Plough'd as yesterday a while, Smith carry'd home Nick Friend's sacks. Shut up 4 hogs to fatting. Receiv'd a second letter yesterday from Jude Storer in relation to the Duke of Somerset.

The 21st November 1722 Wednesday. A showry day.
The boys, Banks etc made an end of sowing by Burt's.

The 22nd November 1722 Thursday. A showry day.
The boys, Richard Banks etc did severall jobbs. Young Dick Wood shoed the black colt. Mr Henry Campion, Mr Beard and my Father supt and spent the evning here. Paid John Turner £2 clear'd accounts.

The 23rd November 1722 Fryday. A gloomy day.
Richard Banks carry'd 15 bushels of my mortar to the malthouse and fetcht a load of wheat straw to Randalls from Paine's of Pyecomb. R Smith jobb'd. Terry lame.

The 24th November 1722 Saturday. A dry day.
Richard Banks carry'd Eliz Cheal faggots and fetcht a load of wheat straw from Thomas Norton's to Randalls. Smith went with Banks, brought in the black horse colt yesterday. Nathaniel Turner of the Comon here all day. Paid John Clerk's bill for all my own work, he here in the evning. I supt at my Father's with Dr Vincent.

The 25th November 1722 Sunday. A dry day.
Mr John Hart preacht, no service afternoon.

The 26th November 1722 Munday. A fine day, snow last night. Richard Banks and Smith did severall jobbs, helpt Richard Banks winnow 6 bushels tares and 6 bushels of pease in the Foxhole Barne. Deliver'd the 6 bushels of pease to Harry White. Reckon'd with my Father Stone and there is due to me £4-8-3¼d, that is for his rent, his annuity and horse keeping to Michaelmas last. I also gave him bond for £100 which I receiv'd of Mr Downer of Pagham the 11th of May last outset and half a year's intrest for it in the reckoning above mentioned and likewise allowed £2-12-6d towards a new chaese that is to be bought between us. My Wife and I were at my Brother John Box's towards night.

The 27th November 1722 Tuesday. A frost.
Richard Banks and Smith tipped a rick at Randalls, had 8 oxen thither. My Wife and I at Mr John Hart's new house afternoon with a Mr Penderhill, Mr [Goffe] _____ . Mr Scutt there. He said the Dutchess of Somerset was lately dead. *(Ed: née Elizabeth Percy, daughter of Jocelyn Percy, 11th Earl of Northumberland, born 1672 at Petworth, died 23rd November 1722, buried at Salisbury Cathedral)* Mr Richard Whitpaine there too.

The 28th November 1722 Wednesday. A fine day, frosty.
My Brother John Box's youngest girl, Frances, died this morning and his eldest, Mary, died yesterday morning or in the night before, both haveing had the measles. Richard Banks, Smith and Terry cleft logs etc. The Widdow Gorman workt here mending cloaths.

The 29th November 1722 Thursday. A fine day, frosty.
RB etc drew trees.

The 30th November 1722 Fryday. A very fine day.
My Brother John Box's 2 girls buried both in one coffin at Albourne Churchyard, my Wife and 2 girls there. *(Ed: Albourne Parish Register shows "Mary and Frances, daughters of John and Ann Box buried")* Richard Banks kept holy day. Terry helpt winnow Mr Jeremiah Dodson's barly. Reckon'd and clear'd accounts with Thomas Jacket for all at Randalls.

The 1st December 1722 Saturday. A wet day.
Richard Banks carry'd 5 quarters 3 bushels of Mr Jeremiah Dodson's barly to the malthouse, wet 4 quarters. He brought home 4 quarters 3½ bushels head and ½ bushels tail of pease from Randalls of the Piony's thrashing. Win'd 4 bushels of White's wheat at home. Sent an entry of my malthouse to Mr Taylor the exciseman per Thomas Jacket.

The 2nd December 1722 Sunday. A wet forenoon, dry after. Mr John Hart preacht afternoon, no service in forenoon. We had a parish meeting.

The 3rd December 1722 Munday. Gloomy morning, wet afternoon. All went to hunting. Reckon'd and clear'd accounts with James Parker for all the goods I have had on my own account. Receiv'd £9 of Mrs Mary Beard widdow on Elliot Wood's account. She and Mr John Hart supt here. I sent an answer to Jude Storer per post.

The 4th December 1722 Tuesday. A dry day. Richard Banks carry'd 1½ loads of Mr Burry's old wood to the malthouse and 20 bushels of Randalls Sandfield barly. William King, Thomas Jacket and Thomas Hamper's man Jo mesur'd ___ wood. Mr Beard here in the evning.

The 5th December 1722 Wednesday. A fine day. Richard Banks and Smith carry'd dirt out of the home close. Drew out Mrs Catherine Beard's teem. John Towner and Ja Reed saw'd here and 2 days before. Thomas Reeve here in the morning. I saw him at Westtowne and he promis'd to fetch some farras to mend the cistern. Mr Richard Whitpaine gave me the policies for ensuring my Father's house, he brought it from London.

The 6th December 1722 Thursday. A gloomy day, small rain. Richard Banks carry'd the rest of the dirt out of the home close and mov'd Eliz Cheal to Mr John Hart's. We brewed for Mr John Hart. Paid Samuel Hart 13s, clear'd accounts. Will and Terry shut up the fatting oxen. Thomas Piony left off thrashing. William Jarvice workt at Tully's.

The 7th December 1722 Fryday. A dry day.
Richard Banks and Smith carry'd 1500 of my tiles to Randalls and fetcht ½ cord of Thomas Jacket's wood. Terry did severall jobbs. Paid Thomas Marten 10s-4d for 650 bricks, clear'd accounts. Mr Ives and Richard Lintott call'd at the gate this evning.

The 8th December 1722 Saturday. A fine day.
Will Jarvice new set the parlour stove. Richard Banks and Smith helpt White winnow 2 quarters 5 bushels of head wheat and 2 bushels tail. Smith ground my Father's malt after. Will and Terry begun fallow in the field by Botten. Mr Jeremiah Dodson breakfasted here. Lent him 3 guineas more which he set down on the former note.

The 9th December 1722 Sunday. A fine day.
Mr Jeremiah Dodson preacht. My Wife and I supt at Mrs Catherine Beard's.

The 10th December 1722 Munday. A gloomy, dry day. Richard Banks and Smith rakt stubble. Terry jobb'd and carry'd my Wife to my Sister Ann Box, she being taken very ill. William Jarvice here and a Saturday.
Receiv'd 9s-5¼d for 3 cheeses of John Clerk at the Comon. One ___ Burtenshaw near Harvest Hill in Cuckfield, his house burnt down a Saturday night last. Brew'd a quarter of malt for my Father Stone.

The 11th December 1722 Tuesday. A very wet day.
Richard Banks and the boys did severall jobbs. Helpt French winnow 7 quarters 1 bushel head and 2 bushels tail of the Churchfield barly. Paid Eliz Cheal 8s-6d for Sarah Nicholas and her pease cutting.

The 12th December 1722 Wednesday. A gloomy day, some rain. The boys and Richard Banks kept holy day. Thomas Fowle and Thomas Borer fetcht the 30 ewes which I sold to Thomas Fowle and Ed Parr. Parr and his wife have had the smallpox since; his wife dead. Thomas Fowle gave me Mr Wilkin's note for the money. Receiv'd 45s of Old Kester for 3 small loads of hay and 4s for the hay of the Bowling Ally.

The 13th December 1722 Thursday. A wet day.
Richard Banks carry'd 6 quarters of barly to the malthouse and fetcht up 4 quarters of oates from Tully's. The boys helpt John Gun winnow oates and French barly. Receiv'd of Nathaniel Turner in full for the 2 runts. Paid Taylor at the Comon 25s in full for tiles etc.

The 14th December 1722 Fryday. A dry day.
Richard Banks and the boys carry'd 2 loads of stubble at Botten's etc. Paid John Snashall jr 34s in full. Rob Leach begun thatch Randalls wainhouse.

The 15th December 1722 Saturday. A gloomy day. Richard Banks and Smith carry'd 2 qarters of barly to the malthouse and carry'd stubble at Randalls. Brought home 4 bushels of tares and 7 _. Laid 36 bushels in Randalls parlour chamber. Shut up 5 steers in Tully's close, 2 yearlings.

The 16th December 1722 Sunday. A dry day. Mr Jeremiah Dodson preacht. My Cousin John Lindfield din'd here. My Father Stone and Dr Vincent and Mr Beard here in the evning.

The 17th December 1722 Munday. A rainy day. Richard Banks and Terry thrasht. Smith did severall jobbs. My Cousin John Lindfield jr came this morning. My Wife and I at Mr John Hart's towards night.

The 18th December 1722 Tuesday. A fine day. All went to hunting but Sam. Thomas Hamper and his man Thomas Hamper workt here, made a hatch for the stairs ------------ 6 days.

The 19th December 1722 Wednesday. A gloomy day, very wet evning. Banks and Terry thrasht, Smith jobb'd. Thomas Hamper here ---------- 7 days.
Reckon'd and clear'd accounts with Mr Scutt in the evning. Harry Lintott here. Jack Lindfield went home. Weigh'd R Piony's heifer at John Bodle's. She weigh'd 64 nails 7lb at 13d per nail.

*(Ed: The next two entries are inverted in the diary)*

The 21st December 1722 Fryday. A dry day. Richard Banks and Smith carry'd 5 qarters of the Churchfield barly and 4 qarters of the Foxhole barly and nere a cord of wood to the malthouse. Paid the Pionys a guinea towards their work. Will and Terry plough'd by Botten's. James Banks peeckt.

The 20th December 1722 Thursday. A dry day. Richard Banks helpt winnow, so did Terry. Receiv'd £9 of John Marchant of Lox for 2 years intrest of Molly Balcomb. Paid him 50s for 2 half anchors of brandy. Clear'd account. I supt at Mr Jeremiah Dodson's.

The 22nd December 1722 Saturday. A dry forenoon, wet after. Banks thrasht in the forenoon with French. Carry'd litter after. Terry cleft wood forenoon, helpt Banks after. Will, Smith and James Banks plough'd at Botten's. John Harland and R Haslegrove begun grub bush roots at Randalls at 3s-6d per cord. Mr Beard carry'd 4 qarters of barly to my malthouse yesterday to be malted.

The 23rd December 1722 Sunday. A very fine day, hard frost. Mr Jeremiah Dodson preacht. My Wife and I and Mrs Weeks went to Mr Phillip Cheal's wife's funeral. We din'd at Mr John Cheal's and came back thither in the night. I spoke to Old James Holden in Henfield Churchyard about the money William Balcomb was bound for.

The 24th December 1722 Munday. A gloomy day, wet towards night. Return'd from Shiprods call'd at Westtowne. Left Jack at Shiprods. Richard Banks drew some trees to the sawpit. Terry thrasht with French.

The 25th December 1722 Tuesday, Xmas. A gloomy day. Mr Jeremiah Dodson preacht. My workmen all din'd here and my Father Stone.

The 26th December 1722 Wednesday. A dry day. My Wife and I din'd at my Father's.

The 27th December 1722 Thursday. A dry day. My Wife and I din'd at Danny. Mr Paine jr and Cousin Peter Marchant here in the evning with Will.

The 28th December 1722 Fryday. A dry day. Cousin Peter lay here last night. Went to Mr Osbourne's this morning. Came back to dinner.

The 29th December 1722 Saturday. A dry day. My Cousin Peter went home *(Ed: xxx text deleted xxx)* Mr Paine and Mr Beard here in forenoon. Will and I din'd at Mrs Catherine Beard's and my Cousin Peter with us. Mr Jeremiah Dodson and his wife and daughter supt here. Banks and Terry thrasht with 2 of the workmen. Paid John Westover in full of all yesterday.

The 30th December 1722 Sunday. A dry, cold day. Mr Jeremiah Dodson preacht. My Wife and I, Will and Bett receiv'd the sacrament.

The 31st December 1722 Munday. A fine day. Yung Peter Hill of Reeds was here, ferreted at Randalls, catcht 2 rabbits, Richard Banks and Smith fallowed at Botten's, James peekt. Terry helpt ferret and so did Will. Old William Bennet of Plumpton din'd here. Paid Dick Wood in full of all and receiv'd 6d of him for his part of a year's land rent for the Black Lyon.

Paid Molly Balcomb 40s which with 10s she had before makes 50s for half a year's spending money and to find herself clothes from midsummer last to this Christmas.

The 1st January 1722 Tuesday. A fine day.
All kept holy day but Smith. He and James Banks plough'd by Botten's with Will. Reckon'd with my Brother John Box and clear'd all mesure of accounts to this day. Receiv'd £2-10-3d of him for a bed etc of William Balcomb. My Sister Sarah, my Father and Mother Stone and Mr John Hart here.

The 2nd January 1722 Wednesday. A dry day. Henry Courtness buried. *(Ed: Recorded in Hurst Parish Register)* Lent Mr Jeremiah Dodson £6-15s more for a note of his hand and paid him a bill of £1-17-9d. Sold him also 28 bushels of tares at 2 guineas and a half which I am to deliver at his house. Those tares were sold yesterday to my Brother John Box. Will Wood of Broadstreet here. Paid Nick Friend of Sadlescombe 4 guineas for 3 qarters of seed wheat which Thomas Norton bought for me. John Parsons shaved my head to day.

The 3rd January 1722 Thursday. A dry day, frosty. Richard Banks and Smith plough'd in the barly earsh under the hill to day and yesterday. Terry, Will and James plough'd by Botten's. My Brother Peter here in the evning. The Padderish steer died last night.

The 4th January 1722 Fryday. A gloomy day, frost. Terry helpt Old Dick Banks and Daniel Hodge winnow barly. Smith had a day for himself. Ill'd 2 hogs. I supt at my Father Stone's with Brother John Box etc. I were at John Westover's with Mr Beard etc. My Wife at Danny to see Mr Harry Campion.

The 5th January 1722 Saturday. A gloomy day, frost. Richard Banks and Smith carry'd a jobb of straw and 8 qarters of barly to the malthouse and 8 qarters 6 bushels yesterday, brought home 3 qarters of malt to day and 6 yesterday being the malt of 8 qarters of barly. Dick Vinall carry'd home the steer's hide yesterday. Paid Daniel Hodge 2s for helping winnow to day and yesterday.

*(Ed: Gap in diary from 6th January 1722 until 30th March 1727)*

## 1727

The 30th March 1727 Thursday. A showry day. Drew trees etc.

The 31st March 1727 Fryday. A dry day. To Church etc.

The 1st April 1727 Saturday. A gloomy day.
Planted the hedge at the lower corner of Tully's first field and made the ditch to let the water from the stew etc with the cowfield etc.

The 2nd April 1727 Easter Sunday. A dry day.
Mr John Hart preacht. Mr William Martin at Aberton and Newtimber. John Turner went to Stenning to Mr William Martin.

The 3rd April 1727 Easter Munday. A dry day.
Chose officers as usual and settled accounts. I din'd at John Snashall's with my Cousin John Lindfield and Stephen Bine. Plough'd and sow'd at Reeve's.

The 4th April 1727 Tuesday. A dry day.
Plough'd and sow'd. I went to Scotches]and bought 2 barrens of Thomas Vinall at £6-17-6d which he is to bring home tomorrow morning.

The 5th April 1727 Wednesday. A dry day.
Plough'd and sow'd. Receiv'd £7 of William Fleet towards the mare and sheep he is to give me 10d per week to keep his horse. Thomas Vinall brought the cows and I paid him for 'em.

The 6th April 1727 Thursday. A dry day.
I were at Mr J Lea. There was Mr William Martin, my Wife, Mr John Hart, Mr Richard Whitpaine, Mr Scutt and John Bodle. I lookt on 2 barrens of J Flint's, I bad him £8-5s for 'em, we did not deal. I were at Mr Scutt's in the morning with my Cousin John Lindfield and Stephen Bine. Mr Prat of Petworth came there. I went with him to Dean House in his way to Cuckfield.

The 7th April 1727 Fryday. A dry day.
Plough'd and sow'd by Burt's. I was at Dr Vincent's with Mr Madgwick, Mr Phillip Cheal, Mr Offe etc.
Paid R Madgwick all that was due on Mrs Mary Gatwick's bond and receiv'd my wive's legacy and clear'd all accounts.

The 8th April 1727 Saturday. A dry day.
Mr Madgwick breakfasted here and Dr Vincent and Mr Beard.

The 9th April 1727 Sunday. A dry day.
Mr William Martin preacht. We had a vestry afternoon, put John Coulstock in John Marchant's room for overseer if the justices think fit.

The 10th April 1727 Munday. A fine morning, gloomy towards night. Paid Godman Harden £3-10s for a barren cow. He brought her home afternoon. Mr William Martin went home this morning. Fetcht 4 qarters more of seed barly from William Norton's. Bought a barren cow of      Eager at the Comon at 43s.

The 11th April 1727 Tuesday. A very fine day.
Plough'd and sow'd. Paid      Eager 49s for his cow per John Gn and Ned Crunden. Mr Norton of Stuckles here, lent me his stone potter. Turned the 2 milk cows to pasture in the Bowling Ally.

The 12th April 1727 Wednesday. A very fine day.
Plough'd and sow'd. Thomas Hamper and his son here jobbing. Eager's cow went to bull.

The 13th April 1727 Thursday. A dry, warm day.
Plough'd etc. My Wife went to Shiprods and came home again in the waggon that came for Phillip Cheal. I were at Mrs Weeks. Dr Tabor came there and Mrs Cheal came for Phillip Cheal. Receiv'd £16 of my Mother Stone towards paying her fine for Tanbridge.

The 14th April 1727 Fryday. A very fine day.
Plough'd and sow'd. I went to Horsham, lookt over Tanbridge Farm etc, went to my Brother Will's.

The 15th April 1727 Saturday. A dry day.
I was at the Court with Mr Phillip Cheal. He was admitted as attorney for my Mother Stone and the fine was £50. Paid £15 in part of the fine and gave a note of my hand for £35 to be paid in a month. Paid £1-4-4d for the fees to the steward and 1s to the reeve. John Stubbs came home with me from Horsham. I ordered one Jones a mason to hanging the windows at Tanbridge to bring 'em yonder and order'd Daniel Goombridge to cut some timber for Wickenden.

The 16th April 1727 Sunday. A dry day.
Mr William Martin preacht.

The 17th April 1727 Munday. A dry day.
The men jobb'd.

The 18th April 1727 Tuesday. A gloomy day.
My Wife and I at Lewis. Paid Thomas Friend £6 and gave him a note for £7-9s which is all that is due to him on the accounts. Bought a suit of cloathes for Will, cost £5-5s-5d. Left the cloaths with Mr Andrew Laurence to make.

The 19th April 1727 Wednesday. A dry day.
John Gn mov'd part of his goods to Tully's yesterday and the rest to day.

The 20th April 1727 Thursday. A dry day.
Sent William Fleet's horse home per John Pelham. Marrian Edwards thrasht 3 qarters of oates this day. My Cousin Richard Turner and Thomas Turner din'd here.

The 21st April 1727 Fryday. A gloomy morning, fine after. My Wife to Shiprods, Marrian Edwards with her. I were to look on Stephen Bine's 2 runts and ewes, could not deal, he here in the evning. Thomas Hamper and his boy here setting up a corner post to the yoaking hovel

The 22nd April 1727 Saturday. A dry day.
The men jobb'd and thrasht.

The 23rd April 1727 Sunday. A fine day.
Mr William Martin preacht, came on foot yesterday. We had a vestry and afterwards sign'd William Bealy's indentures to E May

The 24th April 1727 Munday. A fine day, very hot.
I were at Nutley Fair. Paid Mr Lindby of East Ginstead £14-17-6d for a payr of oxen I bought of him there and likewise £3-7-0d for a barren heifer to the Widdow Sayers of Ditcheling Comon which I bought as I came home from the Fair. Jack Bartlet went with me and Mr Monk and helpt him along with the oxen and the cow. Godman Heather's son of St John's Comon brought home 2 young heifers which I bought of his father for which I paid 5 guineas.

The 25th April 1727 Tuesday. A fine day.
I were at Lewis Cliffe Fair. Godman Holman of Wivelsfield brought home a cow for _. I paid him £2-2s. I din'd at Mr Wheatly's, talkt with Mr Stephen Johnson.

The 26th April 1727 Wednesday. A very fine day. One of the heifers that I bought of Godman Heather calved a bull calf yesterday. The Lancashire cow calved a bull calf a Saturday last. Rl'd two hogs a Munday afternoon. Sold Mr Henry Campion's man Stamford a load of oates for his master at £6 to be deliver'd next week. Wash'd the 13 weathers this afternoon. Receiv'd a douzen of D Locks a Saturday last from Mr Court at 5d a piece.

The 27th April 1727 Thursday. A fine day.
All jobb'd and fagoted.

The 28th April 1727 Fryday. A fine day, very hot.
Mr Beaumont and his wife and Mr Scutt breakfasted here. I met Stephen Bine at Thomas Norton's of North End. We receiv'd £20-2-11d of him due to us from the parish as church wardens, my part is £11-0-1d. Will to fishing with Mr Naldritt at Valebridge.

The 29th April 1727 Saturday. A fine day, very hot.
My Brother Peter and my Son Will were at Mr Palmer's of Changton or Chinting but he were from home. Will and his ukle din'd at Seaford. *(Ed: xxx text deleted xxx)* Will shore 13 weathers to day of which I sent notice in writing to Mr Waller of Brighton per post. Thomas Bank's young cow calved a bull calf yesterday.

The 30th April 1727 Sunday. A fine day.
Mr William Martin preacht. I din'd at Dean House and spent the afternoon there. Mr Stapley there.

The 1st May 1727 Munday. A very fine hot day.
I were at Lindfield Fair. Bought a barren heifer of Ed Hayler at 5s. Paid him for her. Paid the Widdow Weller a year's intrest due at midsummer last. I went thither towards night. H Bull and I din'd together at an ale house. T Stephens of Rigate and Yung Shave came to me.

The 2nd May 1727 Tuesday. A fine day.
I were at the visitation at Lewis. Paid all the briefs and deliver'd them. Receiv'd four fresh briefs. Mr John Hart and I went and came home together and talkt with Mr Dilck.

The 3rd May 1727 Wednesday. A fine showr, fine after.
John Pelham fetcht my Cousin Peter Marchant's wife Sarah from Lewis. Marrian Edwards thrasht, John Gn fagoted, so did White. Thomas Hamper's man Jo hew'd some timber and Old Boniface ditched. My Brother Peter here in the morning.

The 4th May 1727 Thursday. A dry day.
Mr Jeremiah Dodson's tythes feast. Paid Mr William Martin £6 for my half year's tythe for Mr Dodson's tythe some days ago. Richard Smith of Shoreham, my Brother James and Sister Sarah Burt *(Ed: James Burt married Sarah Marchant 7th December 1724 at Slaugham)* and my Sister Mary Faulkoner din'd here. Sold Thomas Skinner and Richard Edwards 12 weathers at £7-10s to be fetcht next Wednesday senight. Receiv'd 50s of Henry Burtenshaw for a year's intrest due to William Balcomb's children on bond.

The 5th May 1727 Fryday. A gloomy day.
My Wife and I din'd at Mr Martin's at Stenning. Dr Mitchell with us. John Gn fa goted, White helpt Marrian Edwards and John win'd 12½ qarters of oates the last of the Marldfield. Bony ditched. John Towner and Ja Reed saw'd.

The 6th May 1727 Saturday. A very wet forenoon, gloomy after. I went to Lewis, met and talkt with Mr Palmer of Chinting. Deliver'd a load of oates to Mr Henry Campion for which I am to have £6. I appointed to meet Mr Palmer at Lewis Fair.

The 7th May 1727 Sunday. A dry day.
Mr Jeremiah Dodson preacht. We had a vestry meeting as usual. My Wife was at Wanbarrow afternoon.

The 8th May 1727 Munday. A wet day.
John Snashall sent here. I went thither. Thomas Elvey with me. I bought 3 bull calves at 30s per calf (very dear) and an old cow and a calf about 2 weeks old at 3 guineas certain and if I have good luck with her I am to give 2s-6d more, or 5s if the bargain will bare it. Robert Adams here. Jack Bartlet had the mare colt to Pulborough and brought home my Wife's old horse.

The 9th May 1727 Tuesday. A showry day.
Fetcht the old waggon etc from the Comon afternoon. Carry'd a load of hay to Thomas Smith's and half a load of straw, Mr Scutt's. My Wife and I supt at Mr John Hart's.

The 10th May 1727 Wednesday. A showry day.
Begun clean the home close. Shut up the Bank's cow's

calf. This day or tomorrow is my Wife's birthday, she being 48 years old.

The 11th May 1727 Holy Thursday. A fine day.
I were at Brighton Fair, at William Fleet's and at Mr Masters's. The men kept holy day. I din'd at the Ship.

The 12th May 1727 Fryday. A gloomy day.
Carry'd 40 loads of dung. Paid Ja Hayler 4d for fetching a crab from Brighton. John Snashall sr sent home my 3 calves with the calf and cow that I bought of him at 3 guineas yesterday.

The 13th May 1727 Saturday. A wet day.
Carry'd dung etc.

The 14th May 1727 Sunday. A dry day.
Mr William Martin preacht.

The 15th May 1727 Munday. A gloomy day.
Carry'd dung etc.

The 16th May 1727 Tuesday. A gloomy day.
My Wife and I and Molly and John Pelham went to Stenning in our way for Chichester.

The 17th May 1727 Wednesday. A wet day.
Mr William Martin and we went to Chichester. Din'd at Arundell. *(Ed: xxx text deleted xxx)*

The 18th May 1727 Thursday. A wet day.
Mr Picknall and his daughter Anne came to us.

The 19th May 1727 Fryday. A gloomy morning, fine afternoon. Mr William Martin, Mr Picknall, his daughter Molly and I and John Pelham went to Portsmouth. Saw all the stores and the fortifications and went on board the Royal William a first rate Man of War being as large as any in the Navy and a very fine sight as I think. Return'd to Chichester in the evning. Din'd at the Two Fighting Cocks in Portsmouth.
*(Ed: The Royal William was launched in 1719 and was of very advanced design as the framing was charred to prevent rot. Equipped with 104 guns the vessel remained in commission until 1813).*

The 20th May 1727 Saturday. A gloomy day.
We came home from Chichester. Din'd at Arundell at Mr Picknall's and supt at Mr Martin's at Stenning. Mr Picknall showed me a horse which he is to buy for me.

The 21st May 1727 Sunday. A dry day.
Mr William Martin preacht.

The 22nd May 1727 Whit Munday. A dry day.
All kept holy day.

The 23rd May 1727 Whit Tuesday. A showry day.
Will and I went to Lewis Fair and Mr Palmer of Chinting there and went home with him. Samuel Ridge of West Dean went with us.

The 24th May 1727 Wednesday. A gloomy day.
We din'd at Chinting, Came home after. Paid Mr Andrew Laurence 4s-6d for spoiling Mr Martin's great coat.

The 25th May 1727 Thursday. A dry day.
The men carry'd dung. Sold Richard Edwards of Rigate 50 lambs at 9s per lamb to be drawn the Tuesday before midsummer, also a weather and a barren ewe at a guinea. Receiv'd in hand 6 guineas. Dick Edwards lay here last night.

The 26th May 1727 Fryday. A dry day.
The men carry'd dung.

The 27th May 1727 Saturday. A dry day.
Harry White carry'd Nanny to Staplefield.

The 28th May 1727 Sunday. A fine day.
Mr John Hart preacht in the forenoon. My Wife and I receiv'd the sacrament. I were at Shiprods, at Shermanbury and at Mr Bare's, sent a letter to Jack by him he being goeing for Oxford tomorrow morning which was then occasion of my goeing thither.

The 29th May 1727 Munday. A fine day.
The men kept holy day after ten or eleven aclock. Will went to hunting about 10 aclock. Mrs §ept]and Olive Eversfield and Mrs Catherine Beard's daughter here. Reckon'd with William Haslegrove and paid him in full of all. Receiv'd 10s of Harry Wickham per Joseph Muzll.

The 30th May 1727 Tuesday. A showry day.
The men carry'd dung and the grit from above the horse blocks. Reckon'd and clear'd accounts with Mr Martin yesterday. He went to Stenning this morning on the old horse and Jack Bartlet went to fetch the horse back again. Will return'd late from Chinting.

The 31st May 1727 Wednesday. A dry day. John Herriot here in the morning. Mr John Hart supt here.

The 1st June 1727 Thursday. A wet forenoon, showry after. Paid my Aunt Courtness in full of all and outset a year's intrest due to me. I was at Harry Wickham's towards night.

The 2nd June 1727 Fryday. A very fine day. I din'd at Mr Scutt's with Mr Hugh Orlton. A cricket match in the Sandfield.

The 3rd June 1727 Saturday. A fine day. I sent a letter to Mr Palmer in a letter to Richard Vinall, by a young fellow that came from Lewis. An other cricket match in the Sandfield between Hurst and Henfield, Henfield lost.

The 4th June 1727 Sunday. A fine day. Mr Jeremiah Dodson preacht. A vestry afterwards, settled accounts as usual. Receiv'd £7-14s in money of Thomas Champion and outset £1-2s for half a year's Land Tax, £6 for half a year's annuity he paid my Aunt Holden and 4s for a River Tax. In all £15 in full for half a year's rent for Eastout Farm and was all due at Lady Day 1726. We gather'd a pretty many Flemish Cherries afternoon.

The 5th June 1727 Munday. A very fine day. Begun mow clover.

The 6th June 1727 Tuesday. A very fine day. Carry'd in the wheat ricks. William Michell helpt in with the ricks for which I paid him 1s. Thomas Vallence and his prentice here yesterday and half to day. Will and our parish went to play a cricket match at Henfield.

The 7th June 1727 Wednesday. A fine day. Fetcht 1500 tiles from James Parker's. Let John Snashall's old cow and Nick Heaver's heifer bleed.

The 8th June 1727 Thursday. A dry day. I were at Brighton market. Paid Nat the coller maker 8s-4d in full of all. I talkt with Mr Daniel Beard and Mr Swan about sending to Cheshire for cheese etc receiv'd £6-15s of William Fleet in full of all demand. Receiv'd a letter from Mr Picknall, that he had bought me 2 horses at £14 and the grooms fees 12s-6d more.

The 9th June 1727 Fryday. A fine day. Peckney cut the grey colt and John Snashall sr was here to overlook him. Dick Wood jr dockt him at the same time. Mr John Hart supt here. Thomas Vallence and his men workt on the healing of house.

The 10th June 1727 Saturday. A fine day. I went to Lewis, came home sick. Nick Plaw came home with me.

The 11th June 1727 Sunday. A fine day. Mr William Martin preacht. I were not at Church not being well. My Cousin Thomas Norton and his wife din'd here. John Stone and his wife and daughter here after evning service.

The 12th June 1727 Munday. A very fine day. I had a fitt of an ague. John Herriott came here.

The 13th June 1727 Tuesday. A fine day. Hay'd. My Wife went to Lewis. My Cousin Bodle with her. Paid Prosthummer Belchamber 3s for shearing 64 sheep.

The 14th June 1727 Wednesday. A gloomy day. I had my ague again. Thomas Elvey here yesterday making up the wool and to day haying. Pross Belchamber stay'd here. My Wife spent the afternoon at her Aunt Beard with Dr Woodward's family etc. Thomas Vallence and his prentice here to day and yesterday. Thomas Hamper and his prentice here cleaving laths etc.

The 15th June 1727 Thursday. A fine day. Mr Palmer of Chinting here and Robert Adams.

The 16th June 1727 Fryday. A very fine day. Carry'd 8 loads of hay to the fatting ricks. I had my ague again. Mr Price of Clayton here and Mr John Hart. Mr Henry Campion came down to 'em. Paid him the £35 which he paid for my Mother Stone in London. Paid Pross Belchamber yesterday 2s for 2 day's work outset 2 loads of oates with Mr Henry Campion.

The 17th June 1727 Saturday. A dry day. Carry'd hay etc

The 18th June 1727 Sunday. A dry day. Mr John Hart preach'd here in the forenoon, no service afternoon. I were not at Church. Were at Mrs Catherine Beard's after dinner. Mr Henry Campion set out for London.

The 19th June 1727 Munday. A fine day. I mist my ague yesterday. Borrow'd 10 guineas of Thomas Hamper for a note of my hand.

The 20th June 1727 Tuesday. A very fine day.
My Wife, Mrs Wheatly and I met Mr Picknall of Arundell at Stenning. Paid Mr Picknall £14 and I think 16s for 2 horses and expences which he brought for me of the Duke of Norfolk. R Crunden went with us to bring the horses home. I were at Dean House yesterday and borrow'd twenty guineas of my Cousin John Lindfield for a note of my hand.

The 21st June 1727 Wednesday. A fine day.
Carry'd my Cousin John Bodle 2 loads of hay at 2 guineas. Mr Richard Barcroft and his brother came at noon. Mr Price and John Ovenden here towards night. King George the Second was proclaim'd at Stenning whilst we were there, his father haveing been dead above a week. He died somewhere on the road goeing to Hanover. Mr Richard Barcroft and his brother and I rode over Rickman's.

The 22nd June 1727 Thursday. A fine day.
Thomas Skinner of Rigate drew my lambs etc and drove 'em away. Receiv'd £17-5s in full for them.
Paid Mr Richard Barcroft £8 in part of rent. Mrs Barbara Campion and Mrs Catherine Beard's family here afternoon. Carry'd   loads of hay to Thomas Smith's.

The 23rd June 1727 Fryday. A very fine hot day.
Mrs Wheatly and my Wife went to Mr Osbourne of Newtimber, John Ovenden with them. Vallence, Thomas Hamper and Roach about the healing.
Nick Gatland of Ditcheling here, bad me 6 guineas for my new black horse.

The 24th June 1727 Saturday. A showry day. I were at St Johns Fair.

The 25th June 1727 Sunday. A showry day.
Mr William Martin preacht. Mr John Hart supt here. Mr William Martin came yesterday. I were at Mrs Catherine Beard's after evning service. Mr Beard gave me my receits for my insurance to Midsummer next.

The 26th June 1727 Munday. A showry day.
Carry'd faggots to Towne. I wrote to Jude Storer and to Mr Picknall and my Wife wrote to Jack. Old William Brand here, paid George West in full of all his work yesterday or a Saturday. Kill'd a weather to day.

The 27th June 1727 Tuesday. A dry gloomy day.
I were at Shoreham market. Sold a load of wheat to Richard Smith at £7-10s. Mr Leaks of Erringham died, I think, last night. Thomas Smith has had 5 loads of hay and John Bodle 2.

The 28th June 1727 Wednesday. A showry day.
Oyld the harness etc. Receiv'd a gallon of train oyl from Mr Pierce yesterday, I think 'twas at 3s.

The 29th June 1727 Thursday. A showry day.
Will and the rest of our parish went to Patcham to play a cricket match, 'twas wrangled off. Mr William Martin came last night.

The 30th June 1727 Fryday. A dry day.
Reckon'd with Mr William Martin and paid him £7-14s in part of a bill of £10 I receiv'd of Mr Jeremiah Dodson, on a banker in London. Drawn by Mr Sturgson and put into Robert Adams's hands to recieve. Clear'd all board with Mr William Martin to this day. Edward Elvey rode to Lewis with my Wife.

The 1st July 1727 Saturday. A fine day.
I were at Lewis. Paid John Snashall £6 for John Snashall of Randiddles in part rent and took a receit accordingly. Receiv'd 6 guineas of JS in the morning to pay it with. Paid Mr Wheatly 9s due from   Worffold. I receiv'd it of John Snashall jr in the morning. I din'd at Mr Wheatly's. with Mr Palmer of Chinting. Left Will's saddles at Stephen Avery's to be new covered.

The 2nd July 1727 Sunday. A fine day.
Mr Jeremiah Dodson preacht I were not at Church afternoon. There was a vestry. Thomas Norton's wife and daughter here, Sarah din'd here.

The 3rd July 1727 Munday. A showry day. All jobb'd.

The 4th July 1727 Tuesday. A wet day.
I were at Shoreham Market. Deliver'd a load of my wheat to Richard Smith and brought a load of seacoal thence for Thomas Smith. Receiv'd 10 guineas of Richard Smith on account. Sold Richard Smith an other load of wheat at £7-10s.

The 5th July 1727 Wednesday. A fine day.
Richard Wood jr rowel'd my old horse under the belly and let him bleed in the breast. Jack Bartlet at Lewis, carry'd the portmantue to Stephen Avery's to be mended. Carry'd some leather. Fetcht up all the malt

from Tully's. Paid Mr Wait a stay maker from London £3-17-6d in full for 2 payr of stays.

The 6th July 1727 Thursday. A gloomy day. Carry'd hay etc.

The 7th July 1727 Fryday. A very fine, hot day.
I were at Horsham Fair. Din'd with Mr H Gale and Mr W White. Paid J Baterly 10s-6d for a pocket pistol. Came home with Thomas Field and his son. Will bought a payr of oxen at £14-14s.

The 8th July 1727 Saturday. A gloomy hot day. Hay'd etc.

The 9th July 1727 Sunday. A fine day. Mr William Martin preacht. Borrow'd five guineas of my Brother Peter.

The 10th July 1727 Munday. Some rain. I fetcht the oxen bought at Horsham Fair from Thomas Butcher's. My Wife went to Lewis in the chaese. Mrs Anne White and her maid came home with her, brought Will's saddles new cover'd from Stephen Avery's and a new male pillion.

The 11th July 1727 Tuesday. A fine day.
Carry'd hay at Rickman's. Jonathan Walls of Mousecomb here yesterday. Mrs Barbara Campion and Mrs Catherine Beard's family supt here.

The 12th July 1727 Wednesday. A fine day.
Mrs Fuller, Mrs White and Mrs Short came hither from Lewis to breakfast. Jack Bartlet fetch 4 of my pease hooks from Stanmer. Left one hook behind.

The 13th July 1727 Thursday. A gloomy day, some rain. Begun cut pease.

The 14th July 1727 Fryday. A fine day.
Carry'd the first load of flax. Lee begun Denshire of New Orchard. Met the carpenters at Church about a new gallery. Mr Henry Campion with me. Went thence to Mr [H.........]. Deliver'd the half load of wheat to Nick Plaw to day or yesterday per John Pelham.

The 15th July 1727 Saturday. A fine day.
Carry'd 2 loads more of Richard Herriot's flax. Paid George West 21d in full of all.

The 16th July 1727 Sunday. A fine day.
Mr William Martin preacht. Mr Henry Campion and Mr Beard here after evning service.

The 17th July 1727 Munday. A dry day.
Carry'd flax. My Cousin P Mills here afternoon. Sent Harry Wickham 6lbs of turnip seed I had from Stephen Carter of Rigate. Thomas Surgeant jr reapt here at 2s-6d per day. Sold William Fleet the grizled heifer at £5-5s, to be kill'd in a month and 3 tags at 25s. Receiv'd £5-5s of Richard Herriot for the flax ground.

The 18th July 1727 Tuesday. A very wet day.
Carry'd one load of flax. Sent Thomas Howell the sack of malt I ow'd him per Jack.

The 19th July 1727 Wednesday. A showry forenoon, dry after. Will sow'd part of the Bankfield with turnip seed. Mrs White and my Wife at Mrs Catherine Beard's afternoon. I think John Gun and Old Surgeant begun reap.

The 20th July 1727 Thursday. A fine day.
Sold a load of wheat to Mr Bridger at £8 if I can deliver it by Saturday se'night at the Rock. Mrs White and my Wife went to see the Widdow Wickham at Barestake.

The 21st July 1727 Fryday. A dry day. John Pelham set out to fetch John Marchant from Oxford. Paid him 5s. Mrs White, my Wife and I supt at Mr John Hart's.

The 22nd July 1727 Saturday. A fine day.
Mrs White went home. Reckon'd and clear'd accounts with Goodman Lee. Paid Thomas Vallence all his bill except 40s. Win'd all Goodman Lee's wheat. Yesterday William Fleet had away 3 tags at 25s. 3 lambs at 19s all paid for and 2 ewes at 22s which he did not pay for.

The 23rd July 1727 Saturday. A fine day.
Mr John Hart preacht here in the forenoon. No service afternoon. My Wife was to see my Mother afternoon.

The 24th July 1727 Munday. A fine day. Carry'd hay etc.

The 25th July 1727 Tuesday. A fine day.
Lindfield Fair etc. I were at Mr John Hart's afternoon with Mr Healy and his brother and 2 other gentlemen from Oxford and Mr Bare and his wife etc. John Marchant came home from Oxford in the evning.

The 26th July 1727 Wednesday. A fine day.
Sent a load of wheat to Richard Smith of Shoreham and brought home a load of seacoal for Thomas Smith.

The 27th July 1727 Thursday. A fine day.
Thomas Smith went to see Jonathan Walls's 8 lambs for me, but they did not deal.

The 28th July 1727 Fryday. A fine day.
Begun carry the wheat rick together. Kill'd a tag.

The 29th July 1727 Saturday. Fine day.
Carry'd some more wheat. Thomas Muzll, R Geer and Thomas Dancy reapt. John Penden mow'd the grass plots etc.

The 30th July 1727 Sunday. A fine day.
Mr William Martin preacht. I were at Mr Beard's after evning service. There was Mr Turner and Mr Gratwick's brother. Molly and Mrs Wheatly went home to Lewis.

The 31st July 1727 Munday. A fine day. All reapt.
Receiv'd a letter from Mr Pelham per the speaker.

The 1st August 1727 Tuesday. A smart showr. I were at the clubb.

The 2nd August 1727 Wednesday. A fine day. Reapt etc.

The 3rd August 1727 Thursday. A very fine day.
Reapt and carry'd wheat. My Wife went to Lewis yesterday and stay'd all night.

The 4th August 1727 Fryday. A very fine hot day.
Ended reaping in Rookwood. Greenaway and his boy. Thomas Muzll, Dancy, reapt.   Will carry'd his wheat at Rickman's and carry'd all our own at home. I were at Wanbarrow.

The 5th August 1727 Saturday. A fine day. Carry'd some barly, topt up the wheat rick and made it ready for the thatcher and he, Harry Morley, begun thatch it.

The 6th August 1727 Sunday. A fine day.
Mr Jeremiah Dodson preacht. We had a vestry as usual. Settled accounts and chose William Bartlet in the Widdow Nicholas's rooms to recieve Mr Litchford's Charity. I were at Mr Beard's afternoon.

The 7th August 1727 Munday. A fine day.
Carry'd barly. Harry Morley workt on the wheat ricks. Sold William Fleet the Widdow Sawyers's cow at £4-4s. He had her away with him and paid for her.

The 8th August 1727 Tuesday. A fine day.
Carry'd barly and some oats. Paid Harry Morley 10s-6d for thatching the wheat rick, receiv'd 20 tags of Jonathan Walls and his sheppherd at £3-10s.

The 9th August 1727 Wednesday. A very fine day.
Carry'd barly and we kill'd a tag in the evning.

The 10th August 1727 Thursday. A very fine day.
♃ Fair. Richard Lintott and Daniel Groombridge here and paid my Mother Stone her rent to midsummer. Sold Samuel Hart Nick Heaver's heifer at £4 and her tongue, to be kill'd in a week or two.

The 11th August 1727 Fryday. A very fine day.
I were at Lewis. There was a Plate Race. I were at Mrs White's. Carry'd Mrs Wheatly some _____ . Paid Mr Court 4s-4d for 2 locks for the pantry closet.

The 12th August 1727 Saturday. A very fine day.
I were at the third race at Lewis. Mr Penfold's son of Broadwater came home with Mr William Martin.

The 13th August 1727 Sunday. A very fine day.
Mr Penfold preacht. Mr William Martin preacht at Woodmancourt. Mr Penfold lay here last night, din'd here to day.

The 14th August 1727 Munday. A very fine day.
Carry'd barly in the Churchfield. William Fleet fetcht the cow at £5-5s. J Johnson with him.

The 15th August 1727 Tuesday. A very fine day.
Carry'd barly

The 16th August 1727 Wednesday. A very fine day.
Ended harvest in the field at Burt's. Paid Thomas Muzll in full. He helpt bear on.

The 17th August 1727 Thursday. A very fine day.
I were at the Election of Knights of the shire at Lewis. There was no opposition. Spencer Comton and Mr Henry Pelham were chosen. I came home with Dr Woodward. Paid Goodman Lilliot in full for all his work in the morning and outset his faggots

The 18th August 1727 Fryday. A fine day.
Dr Woodward etc here.

The 19th August 1727 Saturday. A fine day.
I were at Horsham talkt with John Rogers in the goal. E Courtice with me. John Stubbs and I came home together.

The 20th August 1727 Sunday. A fine day.
Mr William Martin preacht.

The 21st August 1727 Munday. A fine day.
Win'd Bony's wheat 5 quarters 1 bushel head, 2 bushels tail. Yung Harry Morley begun thatch the barly rick.

The 22nd August 1727 Tuesday. A dry day.
I were at Shoreham. Receiv'd £8 of Mr Harry Bridger for a load of old wheat. Deliver'd this day. Sold him an other load at £8. Mr Hill's son came here to see Jack.

The 23rd August 1727 Wednesday. A fine day.
Carry'd 2 loads of chalk to Lox per White and John Pelham. John Bodle kill'd William Vinall's brandled heifer. Phillip Cheal at Henfield and Nanny Cheal here. I were at Dr Vincent's with him and Mr Beard.

The 24th August 1727 Thursday. A fine day.
I went to Arundell to see Mr Picknall. Paid him £3-4-6d in full of all. The men kept holy day.

The 25th August 1727 Fryday. A fine day.
I return'd from Arundell. Carry'd my Mother Stone her faggots this week. In all 400 at 16s per 100.

The 26th August 1727 Saturday. A fine day.
I were at Lewis. Paid Mr Andrew Laurence in full of all. Drank with Mr Palmer at the Starr. William Ridge order'd Mr Wheatly to come to my Mother Stone.

The 27th August 1727 Sunday. A fine day.
Mr Beaumont preacht. George Whitpaine buried afternoon. *(Ed: Recorded in Hurst Parish Register)*
Mr Wheatly din'd here. The Widdow Somersell from Rusper came before noon with John Gun to be with my Mother Stone. Borrow'd Edward Elvey's mare for John Gun to ride and Goody West's mare for her. Clear'd accounts with Mr William Martin this morning for all his board. He rode the old horse and went to Abberton etc.

The 28th August 1727 Munday. A fine day.
Carry'd 2 loads of chalk to Lox.

The 29th August 1727 Tuesday. A fine day.
I were at Crawley Fair. Paid Mrs Godderd's man £21-17-6d for a payr of oxen and a steer and £14-5s to one Gates of Warnham for a payr of oxen. It was not my Cousin Gates. Supt at Dean house as I came home. I think the men carry'd 2 loads of chalk more to Lox.

The 30th August 1727 Wednesday. A gloomy morning, very fine after. The teem carry'd one load of chalk into the highways, one to Lox and brought an other home. Receiv'd £4 of Sam Hart for a fat heifer. Dick Vinall markt a score of fat ewes to go for London to morrow with my Brother Peter's. John Gun carry'd the Widdow Somersell home. Sold Sam Hart 15 of my ewes to be fetch'd the week after Michaelmas at 9s per ewe ready morning.

The 31st August 1727 Thursday. A dry day.
Win'd a load of Bonifort head wheat and 2 bushels tail.

The 1st September 1727 Fryday. A showry day.
John Pelham had my rydeing horse to Bramber to meet Mr Picknall's man with a little mare which he brought home for me to ride whilst Mr Picknall rides my horse. My Mother Stone died this morning about one aclock.

The 2nd September 1727 Saturday. A fine day after a wet night. I were at Lewis to bespeak things of Mr Friend for my Mother's funeral. Richard Banks and Jack Bartlet carry'd a load of wheat to Southwick to Harry Bridger at £8, brought a load of chalk home.

The 3rd September 1727 Sunday. A dry afternoon.
Mr Jeremiah Dodson preacht. There was a vestry. I were not at Church. John Stubbs brought a new Poor Book hither after the vestry which I sign'd at 18d per … .
Mr Thomas Friend and Jonathan Walls din'd here.
Mrs Cheal at my Mother Stone's house. Sent to Stenning and Henfield to invite Mr William Martin and Mr Phillip Cheal to the funeral. I appointed to go to Jonathan Walls's next Saturday.

The 4th September 1727 Munday. A fine day.
Plough'd with 2 teems. Sent to Rusper per   Mowgridge. James Chapman came hither towards night. Receiv'd 10 guineas of E Ede's that was my Mother's.

The 5th September 1727 Tuesday. A fine day.
James Chapman return'd upon Thomas Elvey's mare which I borrow'd yesterday.

The 6th September 1727 Wednesday. A showry day.
My Mother Stone buried at Rusper. Thomas Friend found a horse and paid Andrew Laurence jr a guinea and half for making Will and Jack each a suit of mourning which he brought home this morning.
Mr John Hart, Mr William Martin, Dr Lintott,

Dr Vincent, Mr Ralph Beard and Mr Phillip Cheal carry'd the pall, had each a payr of gloves and a hat band and are to have _____ . Mr Henry Campion was so kind to lend us his chariot and four horses to carry Mrs Catherine Beard and my Wife to Rusper. Mr John Hart, Mr William Martin, Jack and I return'd in the evning. Will came home before us. Madam Lintott carry'd E Ede in her coach and 4 Jades. Kitt Ede and Matt Ede were there.

The 7th September 1727 Thursday. A dry day.
Plough'd, gather'd apples etc.

The 8th September 1727 Fryday. A fine day.
Plough'd gather'd services, apples, grapes, walnuts etc.

The 9th September 1727 Saturday. A showry day.
Jack fetcht Thomas Elvey's mare from Hand Cross, had her to the common. Mr William Martin came towards night. I were at Lewis, return'd some gloves to Thomas Friend's and took 5 payr [so..d] shammes. I went via Jonathan Walls and din'd there, bought his ewes 30 at £11-5s. He went to Lewis with me. Paid him £3-10s for 20 tags I had from him. Return'd my Cousin Marchant's sacks.

The 10th September 1727 Sunday. A dry day.
Mr William Martin preacht We had a vestry afternoon. My Cousin John Lindfield din'd here. My wedding day, haveing been marry'd 27 years.

The 11th September 1727 Munday. A gloomy day.
Plough'd etc. Paid John Snashall sr £7 in full for 4 calves and an old cow. My Wife and I supt at Mr John Hart's.

The 12th September 1727 Tuesday. A dry day.
My Wife and I at Lewis. Paid Mr Larner 4s-6d and £1-8s-8d to Mr Walter for proving my Mother Stone's will. Paid Molly Balcomb £4-10s yesterday in the Bankfield towards finding her self cloaths.
Samuel Beeching call'd me out to her.

The 13th September 1727 Wednesday. A gloomy forenoon, wet after. Will and Jack went to Major Moore's to hunting. Mr Picknall of Arundell here in the morning. I went to Edgly with him, my Cousin Thomas Norton from home. White and Jack Bartlet to way mending.

The 14th September 1727 Thursday. A gloomy day, some rain. Gather'd walnuts etc. Wrote to William Fleet per post. Paid R Cox 10s-6d towards his turnip howing.

The 15th September 1727 Fryday. A dry day.
I were at St John's Fair. Sold Mr Harry Bridger an other load of old wheat at £8 to be deliver'd at Southwick a Munday next. Mr Jeremiah Dodson here in the evning and reckon'd with Mr William Martin to Michaelmas last and I am to pay my tythe to Mr William Martin to Michaelmas next etc.

The 16th September 1727 Saturday. A showry day.
Win'd 5 quarters 2 bushel of Bonny's wheat and loaded the waggon. Fetcht half a load of lime from Danny to the Church and 24 ridge tiles for my self. I were at Mr John Hart's afternoon with Mr Healy and his brother, Mr Bear etc. Invited them to dine here a Wednesday next.

The 17th September 1727 Sunday. A showry day.
Mr William Martin preacht. No service afternoon. He preacht at Abberton. He rode the black horse to Stenning. Jack Bartlet fetcht him home.

The 18th September 1727 Munday. A wet morning. dry after. Carry'd a load of wheat to Mr Harry Bridger at Southwick. Receiv'd £8 of his wife for a load we carry'd some time ago and am to have the same price for the load we carry'd now. I din'd at William Haslegrove's. Cheapen'd a tomb stone. He askt 3s-6d per foot when cleans'd and a penny a letter for the inscription, but R Smith offer'd me some much cheaper, I think at or about 2s-2d per foot, the inscript the same.

The 19th September 1727 Tuesday. A fine day.
Will begun sow wheat at Rickman's. John Gun fetcht the wheat from William Norton's. Paid Bonny in full for all his work to this day. *(Ed: xxx text deleted xxx)*

The 20th September 1727 Wednesday. A dry day.
Jobb'd etc. Mr Bear and Mr Clark, Mr Healy and his brother, Mr John Hart and Mr G Beard din'd here. Mr William Martin came at night, loaded some goods for him in Mr Jeremiah Dodson's waggon.

The 21st September 1727 Thursday. A gloomy day, some rain. I were at Lewis Fair. Receiv'd £8 of Mr Bridger for a load of wheat and sold him an other at the same price.

The 22nd September 1727 Fryday. A gloomy day.
Mr Thomas Middleton and the boys to hunting to day and yesterday. He came with the hounds early yesterday morning. Will Norton here in the evning.

The 23rd September 1727 Saturday. A misty morning, very fine after. To hunting as yesterday and Mr Thomas Middleton went home in the evning. Mrs Anne Beard the schoolmistress had a bushel of Towne House apples per Marrian Edwards. Mr William Martin came _____ afternoon. Ned Crunden kill'd a tag yesterday morning. White and John went to way mending to day. Paid Richard White jr 1s for 24 peaches.

The 24th September 1727 Sunday. A fine day.
Mr William Martin preacht. I were a while with Mr Henry Campion in the evening.

The 25th September 1727 Munday. A fine day. To way mending. I had a letter from Mr Picknall. I were at Wanbarrow in the evning.

The 26th September 1727 Tuesday. A gloomy day.
Gather'd some apples.

The 27th September 1727 Wednesday. A gloomy day.
Jobb'd etc.

The 28th September 1727 Thursday. A gloomy day.
Reckon'd and clear'd accounts with John Snashall jr and receiv'd £7-18s of Thomas Champion, outset £6 for half a years annuity to my Aunt Holden and 22s for half a year's Land Tax, makes in all £15 for half a year's rent for Eastout and all due at Michaelmas last past.

The 29th September 1727 Fryday. A showry day. Win'd 41 bushels of Bony's head and 2 bushels tail. Loaded the waggon with a load for to morrow. Clear'd accounts with John Pelham, he went away.

The 30th September 1727 Saturday. A wet day.
Mr Osbourne of Newtimber buried at Newtimber.
Mr Henry Campion and Mr H Farncomb, Mr Beard and Mr Scutt, Dr Vincent and my self carry'd the pall. A very wet evning. Mr Baldy serv'd the funerall and owes me a payr of gloves because he had none fitt. Receiv'd a letter from Jude Storer appointing me to go to Petworth Munday or Tuesday next. Kill'd a tag this morning.
Mr William Campion and Mr Beard supt here.
Mr William Martin came yesterday. Paid Henry Osbourne's son Thomas 15s for rideing the young bay mare, 1s for catching her in Pullbarrow and 1s I gave him over and above. Henry White of Marrian Edwards carry'd a load of old wheat to Harry Bridger at Southwick Green, for which I am to have £8.

The 1st October 1727 Sunday. A showry day.
Mr Jeremiah Dodson took sick at Church.

The 2nd October 1727 Munday. A dry forenoon, wet after. Jack and I din'd at Stenning and Mrs Sopkin Everfield and Molly, Jack and I went forward to Petworth, hir'd one Holloway alias Hobly to guide us from Gretham thither, paid him 2s for his pains.

The 3rd October 1727 Tuesday. A wet day.
I talkt with his Grace the Duke of Somerset and agreed to serve him as a Land Steward for which he is to give me £100 per annum, a house to live in and he is to keep me one horse in the stable all the year and an other at grass and I am not to go above 6 miles from home. We din'd with Mr Elder etc. William Clerring supt with us at our lodging and kept us company a great part of the time we were in Towne.

The 4th October 1727 Wednesday. A fine day.
We return'd from Petworth, din'd with Mr William Martin, came by Wiston. Breakfasted at Peter Lutman's. Went down this morning to see the house I am to have of his Grace, which I found much to my liking.

The 5th October 1727 Thursday. A dry day.
Thomas Hamper and his man here. Receiv'd £5 of William Fleet per our tanner.

The 6th October 1727 Fryday. A dry day.
Marrian Edwards helpt begin scour the pond by Hyder's orchard. Thomas Hamper's man James and his boy here setting up the fence at the end of the Slip. John Bodle kill'd my bull a Munday last at 1s per nail 4qtrs and he weigh'd 92 nail 7lb. Molly and I din'd at Dean House yesterday with Mr Lockier sr.

The 7th October 1727 Saturday. A showry day.
Thomas Box and I went to Horsham. Talkt with Mr Pilford and I promis'd him all that was due for John Balcomb's cloaths at Xmas next which will be about 9 or £10. We went to Rusper to James Chapman's.

The 8th 8ober 1727 Sunday. A dry day.
Mr William Martin preacht here. Thomas Box, James Chapman and I were at Mr William Martin's of Rusper afternoon and to see Mrs Pryaulx after evning prayr. Din'd at James Chapman's.

The 9th 8ober 1727 Munday. A dry day.
Discharged all that was due at Rusper on account of my Mother Stone's funerall and divided the pall to Dame Somersell and Joan Longhurst. Paid Mr Salmon 8s-6d Goodman Moore 2s, left with James Chapman for the mason 2s-6d. Paid James Chapman 50s forfeited to the poor for burying in linnen.
Receiv'd £2-12s-2d at Horsham of Mr Parham and J Foreman in full for the goods of John Roger that was distreined for rent 5 guineas receiv'd before of Mr Beard by Mr Perkin's order charges did.

The 10th 8ober 1727 Tuesday. A showry day.
Plough'd and sow'd in Fifteen Acres. Mr John Hart supt and spent the evning here. Stephen Bine here with Mr John Hart. Came to consult about ringing to morrow.

The 11th 8ober 1727 Wednesday. A very gloomy day.
King George the Second crown'd. We order'd the ringers 10s. Sold Elliot Wood 4 cowes at £18 and 8 tongues all to be kill'd in 5 weeks. Thomas Elvey here. Plough'd and sow'd as yesterday. Turn'd the young mare out to night. Receiv'd 10s-6d of Elliot Wood for a calf sold some time ago.

The 12th 8ober 1727 Thursday. A dry day.
I din'd at Mr Healy's with Mr Bare, Mr Price and Mr John Hart etc. Marrian Edwards jobb'd, plough'd part etc.

The 13th 8ober 1727 Fryday. A fine day.
I din'd at Mr Price's with Mr Cannon of Tillington. Plough'd and sow'd. Sent Thomas Elvey to Brighton on the young mare for a Let Pass but the son of a bitch made an other excuse so that he sent him home again without it.

The 14th 8ober 1727 Saturday. A fine day.
Plough'd and sow'd. Mr William Martin came to dinner. Mr Waller sent a Let Pass per post.

The 15th 8ober 1727 Sunday. A dry day.
Mr William Martin preacht. Mr Henry Campion, Mr Beard and Dr Vincent spent the evning here.

The 16th 8ober 1727 Munday. A fine day.
Marrian Edwards and White went to Lewis with _ bushels of turnips and 5 Todds of wool being _ fleeces to Thomas Friend. I spent the evning at Mrs Catherine Beard's with Mr Henry Campion and he gave me a small book of timber measures etc by Isaac Keay and E Hatton. Thomas Hamper and his little boy here. My Wife and Jack Marchant at Shiprods and receiv'd £15 being the remainder of her mother's legacy of £20 from Mrs Gratwick deceased.

The 17th 8ober 1727 Tuesday. A very fine day.
My Wife and I at Lewis. I din'd at the Starr, my Wife at Thomas Friend's. Mr Indike told me Robert Adams and Molly Balcomb were marry'd at Berwick last Fryday was sennight brought Molly from Mrs Wheatly's *(Ed: Robert of Stanmer married Mary of Chiddingly 6th October 1727 at Berwick).* Jack Marchant came in the evning to meet us and came quite to Lewis, borrow'd a pillion girt of John Ledgeter and a pillion at the Starr. Brought a new bridle from Mr Court's for which I am to give him 8s-6d if I keep him.

The 18th 8ober 1727 Wednesday. A gloomy wet morning, dry after. Mr Thomas Middleton, Mr Tree and Mr Dennet came in the morning with Mr Moore's hounds, Will and Jack to hunting. I din'd at Mr John Hart's with Mr Healy etc. Spent the afternoon with them at Mr Scutt's. Thomas Hamper's man Jo laid the boards without the graynery door.

The 19th 8ober 1727 Thursday. A fine day.
Plough'd and sow'd. Molly went to Shiprods with Mr John Hart. Hannah went away in the evning from brewing without anybody knowing it.

The 20th 8ober 1727 Fryday. A dry day.
Plough'd and sow'd. Sent George Wickham to Withing to Hannah's mother to see if she were gone thither. Paid him 1s for goeing. She not there. Sent Thomas Elvey to Mr Bridger's. He from home. My Brother Peter here in the evning. Paid Boniface in full of all yesterday. Paid Mrs Storer all her intrest to Michaelmas last and gave her a new note for £15 principall.

The 21st 8ober 1727 Saturday. A very fine day.
Plough'd and sow'd. Sent Harry White to Kymer to see after Hannah. She had been there and was gone to her mother's. Thomas Elvey lay here last night.

The 22nd 8ober 1727 Sunday. A dry day.
Mr William Martin preacht. I were not at Church in the morning. My Cousin John Lindfield and her daughter, Sarah din'd here.

The 23rd 8ober 1727 Munday. A fine day.
Mr William Martin rode the young mare home this morning. Receiv'd a letter from Jude Storer per post, sent an answer by the same. Goodman Ailner of Poynings had a bushel of turnips here and paid but 19d for 'em. Mr Thomas Middleton and Mr Tree came to hunting kill'd a hare and brought her home. Borrow'd Thomas Box's drawing mare again.

The 24th 8ober 1727 Tuesday. A dry day. By a small showr. I were at Shoreham Market, sent 80 bushels of turnips to Brighton, left 'em at William Fleet's. Receiv'd £8 of Mr Bridger in full of all accounts. Goodman Gibson went with Harry White because of the smallpox.

The 25th 8ober 1727 Wednesday. A fine forenoon, showry afternoon. Paid Goodman Gibson 1s last night for his journey. Bought a cheese of R Smith, 2s-2d per nail, weigh'd 9lb. I have 10 sacks at Harry Bridger's of Southwick. Moll Knapp's grandmother buried at Pyecomb yesterday. Thomas Hamper and his man ½ mending Tully's lower rick steddle. Receiv'd 33s-3d of Joseph Muzzall for 9½ bushels of old oates.
Paid Mrs Storer 2 guineas by her son Jude's order in a letter dated the 20th of 8ober 1727. Paid 4 boys 10d between them for pulling turnips. Paid Ned Burt 1s for the same. Paid my Son John £5-4s towards his expences at 8ord. My team brought 5 hundredweight of coal from Brighton yesterday for which I intend to have 5s.

The 26th 8ober 1727 Thursday. A wet morning, very fine after. John Marchant and Marrian Edwards set out for 8ord. They went to call Dr Healy and he was gone without them so they came back again and set out again after dinner. I din'd at Mr John Hart's with William 8bourne of Poynings. I spent the evning there and reckon'd with Mr John Hart and there is due to him £6-8-10½ Mr Norton of Chestham call'd on me there. Lent Mr Naldrit 2 books of the Game Law.

The 27th 8ober 1727 Fryday. A fine day.
The teem carry'd 30 bushels of turnips to Stenning. Richard Banks and John Gun went with it. My Brother James Burt and Sister Sarah (*Ed: née Marchant*) din'd here. Ed Burt cut turnips. 2 schoolboys also.

The 28th 8ober 1727 Saturday. A dry cold day.
Pull'd turnips. Mr William Martin came at noon. Brought the young mare home lame in the shoulder. Sold him the mare at £6-15s which was due to him. All accounts clear'd whatsoever to the 2nd of November next. Reckon'd with Richard Smith of Shoreham and there is due to him £2-1s-0d and left with him 31 bushels of turnips to sell for me, the turnips not reckon'd for.

The 29th 8ober 1727 Sunday. A showry day.
Mr William Martin preacht in the forenoon, went to Newtimber afternoon. No service here.

The 30th 8ober 1727 Munday. a gloomy day.
Marrian Edwards return'd from 8ord.

The 31st 8ober 1727 Tuesday. A dry day.
Cut turnips etc. I went to Elliot Wood's at Cuckfield. Brought 30 ewes at £13, he is to send 'em home.

The 1st November 1727 Wednesday. A gloomy day.
Went to see Danny Sandfield pond fisht but they could not get the water out. I went to Danny with Mr Beard etc, Stephen Bine there and bought all Mr Henry Campion's barly (except what he had bought before) at a guinea per quarter. I got drunk, fie upon 't. Elliot Wood's man brought the ewes to Lox and had home one of the cowes I sold him.

The 2nd November 1727 Thursday. A fine day.
I went and saw the pond fisht. Din'd at Danny with Mr Price etc. John Gun thrasht oates, White sick, Bony pull'd turnips. Marrian Edwards and the boy jobb'd. Yung Dick Wood put a new set of shooes on my horse. Lent Thomas Elvey £3 yesterday.

The 3rd November 1727 Fryday. A fine day, frosty.
Loaded 34 bushels of turnips. Thomas Box sent for his mare. Harrow'd with the ox harrow in Bankfield. Thomas Hamper did a jobb towards night. John Gun, Bony etc mov'd some of the barly, cut turnips etc. Harry White continued sick, his boy here.

The 4th November 1727 Saturday. A fine day. Begun plough the Bankfield. Reckon'd with Thomas Smith and clear'd all accounts only he owes me a bottle of claret, paid me for all the sheep he is to have that is 25.

Receiv'd a letter from Sir Isaac Shard about Nunnery. My Lord Burt here to look on the Towne House. I offer'd to let it him, which he said he would consider of.

The 5th November 1727 Sunday. A gloomy day.
Mr Jeremiah Dodson preacht we had a vestry, past accounts as usual. My Cousin John Lindfield and his wife Elizabeth din'd here.

The 6th November 1727 Munday. A gloomy day.
I were at Street Fair. Bought ten runts of Evan Shelley at £3-17-6d per runt and gave a note of my hand for £20, which I am to pay to Mr Horner, Mr Killman, goldsmith at the Angel and Crown in the Strand, about St Andrew. Paid him £18-15s-0d at the Fair. Borrow'd it of my Cousin John Lindfield at the same time. Jack Tully brought the runts home to Dean House. I return'd to Dean House, met my Wife there.

The 7th November 1727 Tuesday. A gloomy morning, fine after. We din'd at Dean House. Lay there last night. Reckon'd for all accounts with my Cousin John Lindfield and there remain'd due to him for wood and everything £20-19s-0d. I paid him £1-12s-0d for Harry White's 2 loads of wood. I gave him a note of my hand for the whole £30-19s-0d. Thomas Elvey was there and came home with my Wife. They call'd at North End.

The 8th November 1727 Wednesday. A gloomy day, some rain. Sent about 35 bushels of turnips and 2 bushels of apples to William Fleet at Brighton per WH and Goodman Gibson and they brought home some sand. My Cousin John Lindfield lent me 4 horses. I were at Mr Beard's and askt his opinion about Sir Isaac Shard etc.

The 9th November 1727 Thursday. A gloomy day.
My horse helpt my Cousin John Lindfield's carry oates to John Smith. Will Lindfield and John Gun went with them. I were at John Bodle's in the evning with John Stone and J Byshop and Will. Sent an answer to Sir Isaac Shard's letter and an other letter to Jude Storer and to Mr Picknall's.

The 10th November 1727 Fryday. A dry day.
Plough'd and sow'd I think.

The 11th November 1727 Saturday. A dry day.
I were at Lewis. Paid Stephen Avery 7s in exchange for a saddle. Paid Mr Norman 6s-6d for 2 books. Paid Mr Court 18d for a cubberd lock. Paid Mr Guipin for a new spring to my watch.

The 12th November 1727 Sunday. A dry day.
Mr William Martin preacht. We were at Mr Scutt's in the evning. Mr William Martin came yesterday.

The 13th November 1727 Munday. A dry day.
Mr William Martin went away this morning early. Lent him a guinea. Wrote to Mr Picknall per post and my Wife to Jack. Edward Elvey told me yesterday that his brother design'd to have 8 quarters of barly at 21s-6d per quarter.

The 14th November 1727 Tuesday. A fine day.
My Wife and I went to see Robert Adams at Stanmer. They from home. John Bodle carry'd my Wife. Came home via Mr Beaumont's. Din'd there.

The 15th November 1727 Wednesday. A dry day, frosty.
Carry'd 250 faggots of my Mother Stone's stack to John Snashall and din'd at Snashall's jr. Sold John Bodle 2 cowes, one at 1s per stone and the other at 13d, both 5 quarters, yesterday.

The 16th November 1727 Thursday. A fine day, frosty.
I din'd at Wanbarrow. My Brother Peter marketed an ox which he kill'd very fat. I din'd there. Carry'd 46 faggots to J Goble and 30 to John Bodle. Receiv'd a letter from Jack and an other from Sir Isaac Shard.

The 17th November 1727 Fryday. A gloomy day.
All jobb'd.

The 18th November 1727 Saturday. A gloomy day.
Robert Adams here appointed to come again a Tuesday next and to go to Sir Robert Fagg's together. Reckon'd and clear'd all manner of accounts, except what belong'd to his wife since marrying. Mr William Martin came at noon and brought home the black horse with a letter from J Peck.

The 19th November 1727 Sunday. A dry day.
Mr William Martin preacht. We had a vestry about a fresh demand of 30 and odd pounds towards Lewis bridge by an order of the Sessions. Never were people more heartily curst all the country over, nor never any better deserved it for I think it cost us much about as much before.

The 20th November 1727 Munday. A gloomy day.
Mr William Martin went away early. Win'd 4 qarters 2 bushels of barly. Will Davy and John Gun brought a hive of bees from Rusper last night.

The 21st November 1727 Tuesday. A dry day.
I were to talk with Sir Robert Fagg. Mr Adams here to look into our accounts of William Balcomb's business. Din'd here. Nick Plaw here in the evning about the same. Thomas Butcher of Chayley came hither last night, being forc'd to go assises for catching partridges. He lay here, mended hedges to day. Receiv'd a letter a Munday per post from Jude Storer from Mr Peckwell and took one for Mr William Martin.

The 22nd November 1727 Wednesday. A wet day.
John Westover here the afternoon mending harness etc. Jack Bartlet went to Shiprods, carry'd a cock. Will drove his 10 store ewes to Rickman's of the West Country sort. Lost a tag.

The 23rd November 1727 Thursday. A gloomy day.
All jobb'd or plough'd.

The 24th November 1727 Fryday. A gloomy day. Jobb'd or plough'd.

The 25th November 1727 Saturday. A gloomy day, very thick mist. I went to Lewis, call'd and din'd at Stanmer. Robert Adams not at home. Drank with John Goldsmith at Lewis. Receiv'd 24s of a woman at Lewis for turnips and 16s of Thomas Bart. My Cousin Sarah Marchant did not pay me for hers. Mr William Martin came afternoon.

The 26th November 1727 Sunday. A dry day.
Mr William Martin preacht. No service afternoon, he went to Aberton. The old Widdow Pierce buried this evning.*(Ed: Recorded in Hurst Parish Register)*
Paid Mr Norman 6d for reading of a book yesterday and for severall other things. Paid Mr Friend 18d for an ounce of silk.

The 27th November 1727 Munday. A dry day.
Marrian Edwards and Jack plough'd. Will went to Horsham with young Treadcrofts.

The 28th November 1727 Tuesday. A gloomy day.
Win'd 4 qarters 2 bushels of pease. Jack went to Horsham, carry'd a share and colter to Shave's for a plough and brought home 12 broomes from my Brother William. Receiv'd £14 of Nanny Courtness for which I gave a note of my hand, am to pay it in London. My Brother John Courtness din'd here. I were to see Dr Vicent a Munday evning.

The 29th November 1727 Wednesday. A dry day.
The folk jobb'd etc. *(Ed: xxx text deleted xxxx)* Paid £19 to my Cousin John Lindfield by his daughter Sarah, he not at home.

The 30th November 1727 Thursday. A gloomy day.

The 1st December 1727 Fryday. A gloomy day.
My landlord Richard Barcroft came towards night.

The 2nd December 1727 Saturday. A stormy day.
Borrow'd 5 guineas of my Cousin Bodle.
Paid Mr Richard Barcroft 7 guineas towards the Michaelmas half year's rent, outset no taxes nor anything else. Receiv'd £4-6s of Thomas Elvey (I think yesterday) for the next 4 qarters of barly he is to have. Sold him 8 qarters more at 22s per qarter.

The 3rd December 1727 Sunday. A showry day.
Mr Jeremiah Dodson preacht. We had a vestry and we paid Mr Litchford's intrest to Michaelmas last. John Smith the butcher died Thursday morning. I was at Mrs Catherine Beard's in the evning. Mr Richard Barcroft went away in the morning. Jack Bartlet went with him to Bramber thence to Stenning. Brought home my wives old horse from Mr William Martin's.

The 4th December 1727 Munday. A wet day.
Jack Bartlet had Will's mare to Horsham to him. I were at John Snashall's jr, wrote to Jude Storer per post. Supt at Mr Scutt's, went about killing his hog.

The 5th December 1727 Tuesday. A dry day.
Ended carrying in the barly rick. John Smith the butcher buried this afternoon. *(Ed: Recorded in Hurst Parish Register as "Goodman John Smith")* I were at Mr Beard's a while in the evning. Mr Scutt sent for his hog per Thomas Muzzall and Jack Howard.

The 6th December 1727 Wednesday. A smart frost.
Will return'd from Horsham yesterday. Kill'd 2 hogs. Win'd 13 bushels head 1½ tail of barly of John Gun's thrashing and as much of D d Bonny's. Mr John Hart spent the evning here. John Snashall sr here.

The 7th December 1727 Thursday. A very fine day, frosty. Carry'd some litter into the fatting close. Weigh'd the hog to Mr Scutt 21 nail 2lb at 2s. Paid Mr Price 3s for a gallon of oyl he sent for for me a pretty while ago at Mr Scutt's. Paid Widdow Gun Mr Litchford's 10s yesterday.

The 8th December 1727 Fryday. A gloomy ~~day~~ morning, wet afternoon.

The 9th December 1727 Saturday. A showry day. Mr John Hart carry'd a letter to Lewis to put in the post house there for Jude Storer and an other for Robert Adams. Receiv'd a case to carry pen and ink, sand etc that Mr Beard brought me from London. Spent the afternoon with Mr Henry Campion, Mrs Catherine Beard from home.

The 10th December 1727 Sunday. A gloomy day. Mr William Martin preacht.
I were with Mr Henry Campion after evning prayr with Stephen Bine. He sent for SB and I to sign a kind of certificate from him to Mr Peter Courthope to enable him to sell something for him in the South Sea. Dr Vicent and Mr Keatin there.

The 11th December 1727 Munday. A stormy day. Mr William Martin went home betimes. Receiv'd a letter from Jude Storer and Mr Picknall. John Norton of Stuckles and I met at the Royall Ok with John Snashall and John Bodle to settle the rent of Randiddle's house between them. At last they agreed that John Snashall was to live there for one year. I think longer if he pleas'd at £7 per annum to keep 4 hogs to have the stable and orchard.

The 12th December 1727 Tuesday. A dry day. I were at the club with Mr Henry Campion, Mr Beard, Mr Scutt, Mr John Hart, Dr Vicent and Mr Richard Whitpaine and Stephen Bine. Paid Mr Beard 2s-3d for a case to carry pen and ink etc in, which he bought for me in London. My Brother Peter here and at John Smith's widdow's. Receiv'd 40s of John Snashall jr in full of all. He likewise gave me a pint of ink. Sold Stephen Bine 6 qarters of barly at 22s per qarter.

The 13th December 1727 Wednesday. A very fine day. My Wife and I at Lewis. I din'd at Mr Wheatly's and she at TF. Paid £3 to Mr Wheatly in full for Molly's board.

Paid 34s to Mr Friend for what goods we had now. Paid 10d to the Smith in the Clock House for 2 new shooes to my wive's double horse.

The 14th December 1727 Thursday. A dry day, frosty. Johnson, a drover at Newhouse set out for London with my 2 last oxen and a steer. My Brother Peter had 2 went with 'em.

The 15th December 1727 Fryday. A gloomy day, frosty. Weigh'd John Snashall cow at John Bodle's yesterday. Weigh'd 70 nail 5lb and comes to £4-8s-2½d at       per nail *(Ed: left blank but works out at 15d)* 5 qarters. Memdum I sold her like a fool she being much better meat than I (for want of care or judgment) took her to be.

The 16th December 1727 Saturday. A fine day. Will and my Brother Peter set out for part of the way to London. Jack Bartlet was at Lewis yesterday with 2 bushels of apples. Brought a waistcoat for Will and some currents etc for my Wife. I had the black horse dockt shorter a Thursday. Jack Herriot the fiddler lay here a Thursday or Fryday night. Mr William Martin came on foot about noon, but Jack Bartlet was gone with a horse for him.

The 17th December 1727 Sunday. A dry day. Mr William Martin preacht. He and I were at Mrs Anne Beard's De School towards night. Mr Mitchell of Stenning there and Mr Beard. Mr Henry Campion went to London a Thursday haveing an account sent him that Mr H Civar goeing to have the smallpox.

The 18th December 1727 Munday. A frosty morning, a pretty deep snow afternoon. Win'd 4 qarters bushel of Bonny's barly reckon'd and clear'd. Paid him at the rate of 10d per qarter for thrashing it.

The 19th December 1727 Tuesday. A gloomy day, some snow. Carry'd 4 qarters of barly to Thomas Elvey per Marrian Edwards and Will. Receiv'd £4 of him towards it, remains 8s.

The 20th December 1727 Wednesday. A gloomy day. Had my horse shoo'd.

The 21st December 1727 Thursday. A gloomy day, very thick mist. Jack Bartlet and I set out for Petworth, carry'd 1½ bushel of beans to       Booker's of

Stenning. Hir'd    Booker to go with us to Stenning at 2s-6d, which I paid him. Came in dark.

The 22nd December 1727 Fryday. A gloomy day, very thick mist. I waited at the Duke of Somerset's all day but could not speak with him. Mr Gaytonby (who is a porter etc to the dock at Portsmouth and showed us all when we were there) was at the Duke's and waited there all the while I did. There came 3 of the Dutchesses brothers and others which was one reason I could not see him. Mr Scutt came to Petworth this evning not a dry, we lay together this night.

The 23rd December 1727 Saturday. A gloomy, frosty, misty day. Mr Scutt and I return'd by Arundell late. Lay there, I at Jack Picknall's and he at the George. There was Mrs Gratwick etc. We supt at the George.

The 24th December 1727 Sunday. A very gloomy day and very thick mist. I return'd from Petworth, the worst journey, I think that ever I rode.

The 25th December 1727 Xas day. Munday.
A very gloomy day. ♃ workmen din'd here as usual. Robert Adams and R Bevis here afternoon. Appointed to come here a Fryday next about our accounts of William Balcomb's matters. Mr John Hart and my Brother Peter supt and spent the evning here but Mr John Hart supt at home. I bought a fine jack in Petworth market a Saturday and brought it home with us. Kill'd 5 roasting pigs this evning and 2 before. Receiv'd the account of my market at Smithfield from Robert Skinner that he had sold my steer for £7 and that he had paid £5-13-8d to Mr Wilkin which was all the mony left.

The 26th December 1727 Tuesday. A dry day.
All kept holy day. Some few of us met at Church, but did not pretend to nominate surveyors because neither constable nor headburrough was there.

The 27th December 1727 Wednesday. A gloomy day.
Harry Wickham's mother buried yesterday.
*(Ed: Hurst Parish Register shows "Mary Wickham, widow")*
Thomas Norton North End, Dr Vicent, Mrs Scutt, Mr John Hart etc din'd here and supt too.

The 28th December 1727 Thursday. A gloomy day.
All kept holy day.

The 29th December 1727 Fryday. A drizling day.
Win'd 3 qarters 1½ bushels of John Gun's oates. Robert Adams, Nick Plaw, Thomas Box here about their accounts.

The 30th December 1727 Saturday. A dry day.
I were at Lewis. Went to Dr Tabor at Mr John Hart's reqest. Din'd at the Starr. Paid Thomas Marten the brickmaker 15s for 750 slats which I had of T Tuppen of Brighton when I turn'd the healing of my house.

The 31st December 1727 Sunday. A showry day.
Mr William Martin preacht. My Wife and I receiv'd the sacrament.

The 1st January 1727 Munday. A gloomy day.
Receiv'd a letter from Jude Storer with one inclosed for Mr John Pimton at the Duke of Somerset's. Mr William Martin and I went to Mr Beaumont's after dinner. Mr Price and Mr John Hart came to us, supt and spent the evning there. I order'd and desir'd Mr Price to send for a new fashend lamp for me.

The 2nd January 1727 Tuesday. A wet day.
My old paceing horse died last night. Thomas Butcher came hither last Saturday night and he buried the horse to day. Dr Vicent here to invite us to dine with him a Thursday.

The 3rd January 1727 Wednesday. A gloomy day.
Jack Bartlet and I went to Arundell, thence to Petworth.

The 4th January 1727 Thursday. A gloomy day.
Lay at the Half Moon last night. Waited at the Duke of Somerset's all day allmost but could not see him.

The 5th January 1727 Fryday. A gloomy day.
Lodg'd the same, waited as yesterday but at last talkt with his Grace and appointed to be there a Tuesday next at farthest. Talkt with Mrs Hugh, William Perring with me. Return'd to Arundell.

The 6th January 1727 Saturday. A very wet afternoon, return'd home. Lay at Mr Picknall's last night.

The 7th January 1727 Sunday. A dry day.
Mr Jeremiah Dodson preacht. We had a vestry and past accounts as usual. I think I was at Mr Beard's in the evning.

The 8th January 1727 Munday. A showry day.
Got ready for my journey to morrow etc. Settled my Land Tax with Stephen Bine jr and gave a note for the mony £12-15s-11d¼ payable at sight to Mr Dee at Petworth on order. Clear'd accounts with John Westover about this time but I have forgot what day. I think Mr John Hart spent the evning with us.

The 9th January 1727 Tuesday. A showry day.
My Wife and I, Nanny, Jack Bartlet and his father and Henry White set out for Petworth, went no further than Stenning.

The 10th January 1727 Wednesday. A very fine day.
We went to Petworth. Mr Booker went with us as far as Stoppham for which I gave him 2s-6d. We came to the Half Moon in Petworth about 2 aclock. Din'd at the inn. Went afterwards to Mr John Hart's a shopkeeper and agreed for Nanny to board there at £12 per annum. We sent for Molly Courtness to the inn to us from Mr Nashe's (with whom she lives) to tell her of her brother Will's death. He died (I think) a Fryday last but my Wife did not tell her of it to night.

The 11th January 1727 Thursday. A gloomy day.
We breakfasted at Mr Hunt's. I din'd at my Lord Duke's and I was sent to look over Rothersbridge Farme where (at present), lives one           Rapley. The farme, but more especially, the repairs much out of order. Return'd and gave his Grace an account of it. Mr Fowler, one of my Lord Duke's baylifs, went with me. Sent my horse to my Lord Duke's stable per Jack Bartlet and the old mare to grass there.

The 12th January 1727 Fryday. A gloomy day.
My Wife went to look on the house I am to have but did not like it. Return'd as far as Stenning with William Bartlet and White. I did not see his Grace to day.

The 13th January 1727 Saturday. A very wet day.
Breakfasted at the Half Moon, went up to the Duke's, din'd and supt there but did not see His Grace. I was informed by Mr Fowler that Mr E....]was playing an underhand game in order to have me sent home again. I staid there till midnight. Nanny lay at Mr Hunt's.

The 14th January 1727 Sunday. A very wet day.
I were at prayrs with the family in the lobbee. Din'd at Mrs Berry's Table. Farmer Martin there too. William Perring shav'd me in the morning.

The 15th January 1727 Munday. A gloomy day.
I were to look on Mr Chessum's rooms and agreed for 2s per week for my lodging there and paid her for a week beforehand. Mr Fowler and I lookt again over Rotherbride and Perryfields farm, of which I gave my Lord Duke an account ~~of which I gave~~ in the evning and took orders for to morrow. *(Ed: Recorded in Hurst Parish Register as "Goodman John Smith)*

The 16th January 1727 Tuesday. A fine day.
Harry White brought a bed etc from home, had home the white mare and left the black horse in her roome. I rode to what they call the Little Park and lookt over severall things.

The 17th January 1727 Wednesday. A showry day.
I talkt with my Lord Duke and pursuant to his orders went and lookt over Gohanne and Joshurst Farmes that is under William Keen's care. Sent in an account but did not see His Grace.

The 18th January 1727 Thursday. A dry morning, very wet after. Paid Jo Litchford 46s in full for all our qarters there. My Lord Duke's smith shood my horse. Thomas Tupper of Bosted not far from Chichester came to treat about takeing my Lord Duke's Rotherbridge Farme. He bad £135 per annum for it and one third of the Land Tax but we were order'd to take no less than £140 and the tennant to enter at Michaelmas last but he would not enter till Michaelmas next. Did not deal. Mr Elder and I treated with Tupper.

The 19th January 1727 Fryday. A very wet day.
Did nothing but eat and drink and set by the fire;and hard work too.

The 20th January 1727 Saturday. A fine day.
I went down in the morning Cowdersall Mill (the miller's name        Warren) to view the repairs but it was so much under water that no account could be taken of it. After I return'd I rode out with his Grace into the Park and lookt over severall matters. His Grace order'd me to take some of the timber there towards repairing Cowdersall Mill.

The 21st January 1727 Sunday. A gloomy day.
I were at prayrs in the chapel in the forenoon and in the lobbee in the evning.

The 22nd January 1727 Munday. A fine day.
Drank tea in Mrs Ann Dodson's chamber in the morning, went afterwards to Little Park with Mr Fowler to let out some ground to be plough'd, mesur'd out something above 21 acres. Took some other instructions.

The 23rd January 1727 Tuesday. A dry day.
My Lord Duke set out about noon for Guildford, in order for London. I receiv'd severall orders and went with His Grace to the farther side of Little Park. Fowler likewise went so far with him and we came back together. I din'd there, spent part of the evning at Mr Hunt's. He receiv'd a letter that his wive's sister was just dead.

The 24th January 1727 Wednesday. A dry day.
Mr Elder set out for London, left some orders with me to view Peter Woods's farme etc besides what my Lord Duke left. I had my head shaved. Receiv'd a letter from my Wife per James Courtness and an other by the post. Mr Hunt went to bury his wife's sister, some where at, or nere Farnham.

The 25th January 1727 Thursday. A very fine day, pretty smart frost. I went to view the repairs of Peter Woods's farme by Gunter's bridge and took an account of it. Pink, my Lord's carpenter went along with me.
We din'd with Peter Woods. I spent the evning and supt at Mr Hunt's. The farme in sad repair.

The 26th January 1727 Fryday. A fine day frosty.
I met William Tester, a millwright at Cowdershall Mill, view'd the repairs there and took a short account of it and appointed Tester to come again to morrow to set out timber in the Park.

The 27th January 1727 Saturday. A fine day, smart frost.
William Tester came and we set out (Sawyer, the keeper being with us) ten pieces of oak timber for repairing the mill 261½ feet. Tester and I were afterwards at the Bull to finish the account of materials etc. Peter Woods came to me there and we went to my lodging and we finisht the account of his repairs, only the house and granery was not view'd but is to be view'd an other time.

Mr Eades came to us at the Bull to ask me why I stopt the teems from fetching wood, which I did because I thought His Grace would be angry, the frost being much thaw'd by the fine sun shiney day and the way very sloppy and Sawyer said he would lock up the gates in Little Park. I were at Mr Rists in the morning with Mr Ede and Mr William Martin.

The 28th January 1727 Sunday. A dry day, frosty.
I were at prayrs with the family in the lobbee.

The 29th January 1727 Munday. A dry day, frosty.
We got 3 teems, vizt Widdow Nilins, Farmer Rapley's and John Lutman's teem fetcht each of 'em 2 loads of wood out of the grubb'd coppice and Farmer Mucher's teem helpt carry ice into the ice house.

The 30th January 1727 Tuesday. A very cold day, frosty.
Farmer Lutman's teem fetcht a load of wood and Farmer Dawtry's teem fetcht 2 loads. I were at Marks's at Widdow Nilin's and at Farmer Bridger's in the forenoon at John Lutman's and at Ancher's. Receiv'd a letter from Mr Elder per post.

The 31st January 1727 Wednesday. A fine day, frosty.
I were with Farmer Ancher in the morning. He, Marks, Lutman and Bayly carry'd each of them 2 loads of wood. I was at Farmer Boxels likewise in the morning. I was also at Farmer Prat's at Upperton. I spent the evning at Mr Hunt's. Paid Mr Chessum 4s in the morning for a load of wood which was brought in afterwards. Receiv'd a letter per post from Mr Williams with directions from my Lord Duke to which I sent an answer by the same post.

The 1st February 1727 Thursday. A gloomy day.
I went to look upon Warr's close with Mr Fowler and William Keen and afterwards went to the Ship and sent for Puttock the tallow chandler and offer'd to let Warr's close to him and he bad us £5-10s per annum for 11 years for it and enter at Michaelmas last. I promis'd to represent it to my Lord Duke. Fowler with me at the Ship. I compar'd my account of wood carryage with Mr Fowler's and there is 37 loads brought home in all. I were a little while at the Half Moon and at Mr Hunt's in the evning.

The 2nd February 1727 Fryday. A fine day.
There were 3 loads of wood brought home by the tennants and 6 by my Lord Duke's teems.

The 3rd February 1727 Saturday. A fine day.
2 loads of wood fetcht by John Lutman and 6 by my Lord Duke's teems. His Grace return'd from London. My Lady Dutchess went to meet him, met just within Little Park. Mr Pointon and I went with her. There was just 54 loads of wood brought home in all. I saw the pipes alter'd and restor'd to their former condition as they were before alter'd by the plumber, according to my orders by yesterday's post.

The 4th February 1727 Sunday. A fine day, frosty.
I were not at the house 'till night, not being very well. I din'd at Mr Hunt's. My Lord Duke's wedding day, two years.

The 5th February 1727 Munday. A fine day, frosty.
Jack Bartlet went to Hurst yesterday, return'd to day. Brought some wildfowl to Mr Hunt and a ribspeare and a chine for Mrs Chessum and some puddings. I rode out with his Grace etc. Receiv'd a letter from Mr John Hart.

The 6th February 1727 Tuesday. A fine day, frosty.
I din'd at Mr Hunt's. Went toward night to view Catchanger Coppice. Mr Fowler with me, found the fence very bad.

The 7th February 1727 Wednesday. A fine day, thawing.
Did nothing. Were sent for into my Lord Duke's rooms and had orders with Mr Eades to go about the Towne to get votes for Mr Butler.

The 8th February 1727 Thursday. A fine day.
Mr Eades and I (by my Lord Duke's order) went to all the free holders about Towne for their votes for Mr Butler and none refus'd that were at home.
We din'd at Mr Goodyers. I did not see my Lord Duke.

The 9th February 1727 Fryday. A fine day.
Mr Eades and I were sent to Sutton to look on several matters of the mannor, took Farmer Neal with us. Went to Parson Thornton's and he promis'd his vote for Mr Butler and to assist in treading the bounds of the mannor. We found some small encroachments.

The 10th February 1727 Saturday. A dry day.
I spent the day in Petworth Market. Went and spent the evning at the House. Din'd there. We had a new gardiner came and bargain'd, his name      Hodges. Paid PL for the crop pieces of bief and J Ransford's wife for a jack. Sent both to Mr Hunt's. Paid 6d yesterday for a pot to fetch water. Paid also 6d for an ink glass.

The 11th February 1727 Sunday. A fine day.
I din'd at Mr Hunt's. Went up to the House and had orders to go to Rotherbridge to morrow morning, with J Martin. Mr Elder came home to day.

The 12th February 1727 Munday. A fine day.
Farmer Martin and I went to see Rotherbridge Farme to find out a pea season etc. The pond in Little Park was fisht, not so good fish in it. Farmer Martin gave my Lord Duke an account of it.

The 13th February 1727 Tuesday. A fine day.
I went to Cathanger coppice with Mr Elder and Mr Eades. The Tennant said it did not belong to him to make the fence. I afterwards rode to Little Park with my Lord Duke and he said I should get a payr of grates to the pond in Stagg park that was fisht lately. I staid very late at the House, saw not the Duke.

The 14th February 1727 Wednesday. A showry day.
I went and took a mesure of the grates in Stagg Park. Talkt with His Grace and Mr Elder, askt leave for me to go to Stenning to morrow.

The 15th February 1727 Thursday. A very fine day.
Nanny and I went to Stenning. Mett my Wife there, din'd and staid 'till night and my Wife and I went to Hurst, Nanny staid there.

The 16th February 1727 Fryday. A very fine day.
Talkt with the school Mistris Anne Beard about my house in Towne, but did not fully agree. Return'd to Petworth, din'd at Mr William Martin's. Call'd at Mr John Hart's in the morning.

The 17th February 1727 Saturday. A fine day.
I were sent to the people spreading gravel etc. Mr Eades and the millwright set out timber for the repair of Cowdershall Mill, as I had done once allready. I talkt with His Grace and he found much fault about the grates that he order'd me to get made, but he was in a cursed humour about the dung-courts etc and sent the teem for hay to William Keen's at 7 aclock at night.

The 18th February 1727 Sunday. A fine day.
I went to Tillington with Mr Hunt and his wife and Nanny.

The 19th February 1727 Munday. A dry day, did but little.

The 20th February 1727 Tuesday. A snowy day.
I went with his Grace to North Chappel in his way for London. I had no orders to do any thing more, nor to forbare. I talkt with Mr Elder at Mr Dee's and he advis'd me to keep on.

The 21st February 1727 Wednesday. A fine day.
I went to William Taylor of Bignall in Carford. I had been told that he was inclin'd to take Rotherbridge Farme and I found it so, but he could not come to see it this week, but he appointed to come to Petworth a Saturday, then to appoint a day to treat of it. Begun board at Mr Hunt's yesterday night. Receiv'd a letter per post from my Wife.

The 22nd February 1727 Thursday. A very wet day.
Peter Woods and I were to talk with Mr Elder in the morning and he advis'd that I should agree with a carpenter that PW proposed to do the repairs of his farme. I were at the Half Moon with Peter Lutman and Mr Nace.

The 23rd February 1727 Fryday. A windy day, some rain.
I din'd with Mr Elder, Mr Moore, Mr Nace, Jo Lickfold and Peter Lutman at the Great House. Staid there 'till night. Receiv'd a letter and more directions for severall things. Sent a letter to his Grace of severall things. There were several men at the Duke's to make affidavit about the highways which my Lord Duke intended indight.

The 24th February 1727 Saturday. A gloomy day.
I were at the house in the morning. Talkt with Mr Elder. I was at the Half Moon with Mr Nash etc. I talkt with Peter Woods and his carpenter T Albury. Saw William Taylor and his mind was chang'd. Talkt with T Gates jr. He desir'd me to write to His Grace or Mr Elder about Glatton Farme (I think) in Sutton parish, the present tennant is        Croucher and will let Mr Gates come in. He will be here again next Saturday.

The 25th February 1727 Sunday. A wet day.
Jack went to Hurst. I was at the house and answer'd my Lord Duke's letter that I receiv'd this day, talkt to Hinton and William Keen. Peter Woods's carpenter came to me at Mr Hunt's and appointed to meet a Wednesday. I were at Peter Lutman's in the evning with Mr Smith and H Sandum.

The 26th February 1727 Munday. A dry day.
My Wife came from Hurst as far as Fiddleworth and staid there at night. I sent one of my Lord Duke's men to Stenning but he mist them.

The 27th February 1727 Tuesday. A fine day.
My Wife came to Petworth this morning early. Goodman Bartlet with her.

The 28th February 1727 Wednesday. A gloomy day.
I met T Albury and an other at Peter Woods but could not agree about any works.

The 29th February 1727 Thursday. A fine day.
I went to Chichester to the election, Mr Butler chosen without any opposition. There were a great many people there. I went and came with Peter Lutman, Mr Witcher and Thomas Rice went with us.

The 1st March 1727 Fryday. A fine day.
John Buckland a carpenter came to talk about the repairs of Gunter's Bridge Farme and appointed to meet there tomorrow morning. I were at Mr Canyon's at Tillington towards night. Supt at Mr Nash's with my Wife and Nanny etc. Lookt on a brown mare of my Lord Duke's farrier's which he offer'd me at 5 guineas. I took her into my keeping on tryal.

The 2nd March 1727 Saturday. A fine day.
Mr Eades and I view'd the repairs. Peter Lutman's farme call'd Tanners Land and met in the evning at the Half Moon to make an estimate of it and I valu'd it at £10 includeing the iron work. Talkt with Mr Gates.

The 3rd March 1727 Sunday. A fine day.
My Wife and I were at Petworth Church. Dr Langwith preacht. Sent a letter to Jacky with a guinea in it. Mr Nashe's man carry'd it to the person that is to carry it, at Fiddleworth.

The 4th March 1727 Munday. A fine day.
Mr Eades and I view'd the repairs of Peter Lutman's farme as above. Mrs Wacklife and her daughters to see my Wife. Paid Jo Lickfold all expences of my Wife's last journey hither being three.

The 5th March 1727 Shrove Tuesday. A fine day.
My Wife return'd to Hurst, Jack Bartlet with her on our Farrier's mare and had home the old grey mare. Mr Mace receiv'd a letter from my Lord Duke wherein my Lord wonder'd I did not send in my bill for my wages.

The 6th March 1727 Wednesday. A fine day.
I were at the stables. Jack return'd from Hurst, brought books, apples etc. Left the old mare at home. I sent a letter per post to John Marchant, Jude Storer and Mr Wilkin. Mr Fowler and I supt at Half Moon. Mr Mace shew'd me a letter wherein (as twas said in that letter) my Lord Duke desir'd an account of what was due to me, because he did not think me fit for his service.

The 7th March 1727 Thursday. A fine day.
I went to Rotherbridge in the morning with Mr Fowler and Martin, I din'd at Mr Hunt's and rode to Little Park. Afterwards call'd at Galloway's as I came back. One of the groomes told me Mr Eades's grey horse was lame in the nere coffin joynt before. Mr Hunt came home allmost fuddled in the evning.

The 8th March 1727 Fryday. A fine day.
His Grace return'd from London. I was at the house but did not see my Lord Duke. Receiv'd a Letter from Mr Wilkin that he had receiv'd the £20 of Mr Hulme in the burrough on Mr Picknall's note and also £15-13s-8d of Robert Skinner for my use.

The 9th March 1727 Saturday. A gloomy day.
I saunter'd about the market, were up at the house, din'd at Half Moon with Farmer J Martin and     Pike, a mason. Deliver'd in a letter in the morning of my demand for wages. Were at the house again in the evning. Staid late. Talkt with Mr Williams. He gave me the letter and John Buckland's account that I sent in it to A Elder pretending that Elder had not time to shew it to His Grace.

The 10th March 1727 Sunday. A fine day.
I were not at Church. My Wife, Harry White and William Edwards came in the evning.

The 11th March 1727 Munday. A fine day.
Mr Elder return'd from London. Receiv'd £15-12s-4d of the Duke of Somerset by the hands of Mr Williams jr in full of my salary, due to last Wednesday *(Ed: pro rata salary for 57 days)*. I din'd with Mr Elder.

The 12th March 1727 Tuesday. dry fine day.
My Wife went home in the morning. I saunter'd about all day. Drank with Farmer J Martin at the Half Moon and he promis'd to speak to my Lord Duke as I desir'd. Mr Hunt return'd from the Fair.

The 13th March 1727 Wednesday. A dry day.
Took my horse out of my Lord Duke's stable and brought him to Mr Hunt's. Had a small bundle of hay of Peter Lutman and half a bushel of oates of Mr Hunt.

The 14th March 1727 Thursday. A gloomy day some rain. I were at Arundell Market. Din'd at the George. Drank with Mr Scutt and Stephen Bine.
Spoke to Mr Picknall of his daughter Nanny and JS

The 15th March 1727 Fryday. A gloomy day.
Mr Hunt set out for Salisbury Fair with some others. Din'd with Mr Hunt. I was at the Half Moon in the evning.

The 16th March 1727 Saturday. A dry day.
I saunter'd about the market. Din'd at Mr Hunt's. Drank with Mr Gates jr and with Mr Milne before at Half Moon.

The 17th March 1727 Sunday. A fine day.
I were not at Church.

The 18th March 1727 Munday. A dry day.
I went Did nothing. Paid Mrs Hunt and Mrs Chessum all that was due to them.

The 19th March 1727 Tuesday. A gloomy day.
I went up to the Duke's to take my leave of the family.

The 20th March 1727 Wednesday. A gloomy forenoon wet after. I came away from Petworth with Nanny and Jack Bartlet and all we could bring. Came to Stenning.

The 21st March 1727 Thursday. A dry forenoon, wet after. Lay at John Box's of Stenning last night, return'd to Hurst to day. Jack Bartlet went to Hurst last night and came for us to Stenning again to day.

The 22nd March 1727 Fryday. A gloomy day some rain. Did nothing.

The 23rd March 1727 Saturday. A dry cold day.
My birthday, 51 years. I went to Lewis. Left a letter at George Dykes for Robert Adams.

The 24th March 1727 Sunday. A dry day.
Mr William Martin preacht. We had a vestry after evning service. I were at Mr Henry Campion's in the evning.

## 1728

The 25th March 1728 Munday. A fine day.
I were at Ditcheling Fair. Din'd at Old Land with Mr P Short and Wood.

The 26th March 1728 Tuesday. A gloomy day some rain. Win'd wheat of Harry White's thrashing. John Gun helpt winnow and skreen'd barly after. Jack Bartlet set out for Petworth with 2 horses for my cloaths, bed etc. Marrian Edwards set out a Sunday for Oxford to fetch John Marchant home, because the smallpox is so much there. Mr William Martin very bad here with an ague. Will went to Poynings yesterday to weigh a hog he sold thither.

The 27th March 1728 Wednesday. A gloomy day.
Did nothing

The 28th March 1728 Thursday. A gloomy day. Some rain. Mr William Martin and I were to see Mr John Hart afternoon. Paid John Stubbs £11-5s for both the Poor Books. Will also paid him for Rickman's. Mr William Osbourne here about the Towne House but did not agree.

The 29th March 1728 Fryday. A gloomy day.
Did little. Marrian Edwards return'd from Oxford, brought word that Jack had the smallpox.

The 30th March 1728 Saturday. A dry cold day.
Mr William Martin came. Thomas Elvey set out for Oxford betimes in the morning. My Cousin Bett
*(Ed: xxx text deleted xxx)*

The 31st March 1728 Sunday. A gloomy day.
Mr William Martin, Mr Healy's man set out in the morning with my Cousin Sarah Norton for Oxford. William Mar........]and John Lindfield went as far as Leatherhead with my Cousin Bett yesterday and return'd to day about noon.

The 1st April 1728 Munday. A cold dry day.
Mr Lamb of Ditcheling went to Stenning to take care of Mr William Martin's school till his returne. I went with him and we din'd at Butcher Hill's together and agreed with them to board him. I went to Mr Norcroft to Wiston and he promis'd me to officiate in the forenoon at Broadwater for Mr William Martin next Sunday. Receiv'd a letter from Oxford per post from Mr Ratcliff to let us know that Jack was very full of the smallpox and a very bad sort. Mrs Anne Beard of the school, Mr John Hart and his wife and Nick Plaw, here in the evning.

The 2nd April 1728 Tuesday. A dry day.
Will went to Shoreham Market, Mr Bridger not at home, wheat £11. Harry White went to Chiltington after a maid for Sarah Norton, 'twas White's daughter there. She promis'd to come to Edgly to morrow.

The 3rd April 1728 Wednesday. A gloomy day.
Mrs Catherine Beard lay with my Wife, no news from Oxford. Win'd the last of John Gun's oats at Tully's. Mr John Hart here towards night. Paid Thomas Smith the 15s per Will, that he paid in London be return'd to Oxford. TS left it with Mr Wilkin.

The 4th April 1728 Thursday. A showry day.
Mr Healy's man return'd from Oxford, brought letters that Jack was not worse. He brought home Sarah Norton's horse and Edward Elvey's. Paid Mr Healy's man 17s that he had expend'd and gave him 5s. Mrs Catherine Beard and Mrs Barbara Campion here and Mr John Hart.

The 5th April 1728 Fryday. A very wet day.
Made sacks etc.

The 6th April 1728 Saturday. A stormy day.
Wrote to Mr William Martin at Oxford per post. I were at Mr Sixsmith's to desire him to preach here for Mr William Martin to morrow senight which he readily promis'd. Call'd at Mr Lamb's as I came home.

The 7th April 1728 Sunday. A dry day.
Mr Jeremiah Dodson preacht. Mr John Hart etc here towards night.

The 8th April 1728 Munday. A fine day. Thomas Elvey and Marrian Edwards return'd from Oxford and brought the dismal news that Jack Marchant died a Fryday night last about eleven aclock. *(Ed: Thomas's son)*

The 9th April 1728 Tuesday. A gloomy day, small rain. Don't know what was done but we kill'd the porkers yesterday and John Bartlet set out for Petworth to day to fetch my bed and things left there. Brought also 3½ yards of hair shag black to make me a payr of breechs with buttens etc with a letter from Mr Fowler and Mr Hunt.

The 10th April 1728 Wednesday. A very fine day. Jack Bartlet went to Petworth yesterday as 'tis mention'd but return'd with the things to day. My Brother James Burt had likewise a quarter of seed barly at 25s and the rest in mony and paid him in full for a years intrest on bond due about Michaelmas last done yesterday too. Reckon'd also with Mr Beard and clear'd accounts. All this was done yesterday. Mrs Scutt, my Aunt Courtness, Mr John Hart and his wife and Mrs Catherine Beard were afternoon here. Mr John Hart and his wife and Mrs Scutt supt here.

The 11th April 1728 Thursday. A dry day. I think they plough'd and sow'd in the field per John Reeve.

The 12th April 1728 Fryday. A dry day.
Plough'd and sow'd I think.

The 13th April 1728 Saturday. A dry day. Plough'd and sow'd I think. I din'd at Mr Price's with Mr John Hart and his wife. Mr John Hart and I went after dinner to Mr Springet's of Plumpton to desire him or his curate to officiate on Easter Sunday for Mr William Martin and Mr Springet very readily granted that his curate should come if he would and his curate, Mr Hampton as readily promis'd to come. We return'd by Mr Price's. I staid late.

The 14th April 1728 Sunday. A fine day.
Mr Sixsmith preacht in the forenoon, no service afternoon. My Cousin Marchant's wife Sarah of Lewis came yesterday, return'd this evning. Paid her 2s-6d being the exectess for Pullbarrow horse _____ which she said she had paid for me. Sent a letter to Mr William Martin by her to post in the post at Lewis and Mrs Catherine Beard's to buy him 2 horses or mares.

The 15th April 1728 Munday. A fine day.
Sent a letter to Mr Hunt with an other to Mr Fowler in it. Ended ploughing the field per John Reeve. I were at the Royall Oak designing to go to the Court Baron but the Court was over before I came. It was the first court since Mr Beard was steward, I drank with the tennants and reckon'd and clear'd accounts with my Cousin Bett for her journey to Oxford.

The 16th April 1728 Tuesday. A dry day. Finisht the field with clover allmost. Will went to Shoreham market after and sold a load of wheat to Mr Bridger at £11-10s.

The 17th April 1728 Wednesday. A dry day. Harrow'd and roll'd and begun the Rookwood, Pross Belchamber here clipping the sheep. Paid him 2s for this and jobb before. My Cousin John Bodle here to buy ten dry sheep. But we did not deal. Nick Plaw here afternoon.

The 18th April 1728 Thursday. A dry day.
Plough'd and sow'd in Rookwood. I spent the afternoon at Wanbarrow. Spent an hour at Isaac Muzzall's shop with Abel Muzzall. I believe they very nere ended ploughing the Rookwood. Mrs Scutt spent the afternoon here. Mrs Hart here at night.

The 19th April 1728 Fryday. A dry day.
Mr John Hart preacht, no service afternoon. I spent good part of the afternoon with Mr Beard, order'd him to write to Robert Adams. Gave Mr Henry Campion an account what mony I paid Mrs Burry for the coppice. Ended sowing the Rookwood barly and allmost finisht him.

The 20th April 1728 Saturday. A very wet day.
Winno'd the last of the barly 79 quarters 1 bushel, and measur'd for the malter. 13 quarters 6 bushels, there being 69 quarters head win'd before. Mr John Hart was here towards night.

The 21st April 1728 Easter Sunday. A fine day.
Mr Hampton preacht in the forenoon. No service afternoon. Jonathan Walls din'd here, I went with him to Mr Scutts. Call'd at Mr Beard's.

The 22nd April 1728 Munday. A dry cold day. Mr Jeremiah Dodson read prayrs. We past the Churchwardens and overseers accounts and Mr Jeremiah Dodson chose Stephen Bine again and the parish me and we nominated six new men for overseers. Mr Henry Campion took in his formentioned note and gave me a new one of £50 on a banker, his name        Fowler to be paid at sight to Sir Robert Fagg. He sent from London for mony. Nick Plaw came from Albourne and left a man there.

The 23rd April 1728 Tuesday. A dry day.
Deliver'd a load of wheat to Mr Bridger of Southweek Green yesterday per Will, Thomas Bignall and Marrian Edwards at £11-10s. Borrow'd 3 of my Brother Peter's horses. James Chapman came from Rusper towards night. I went up to Mr Beard's with him in the evning.

The 24th April 1728 Wednesday. A very fine day.
Mr Ward of West Grinsted was carry'd home in a herse to be buried from Randiddles. James Chapman return'd ~~from~~ to Rusper afternoon.

The 25th April 1728 Thursday. A fine day rain in the evning. I were at Lewis Fair and went to Mr Spence of Malling and he gave me an order under his hand to pay all arrears of rent due from ~~Sir Robert~~ William Balcomb to Sir Robert Fagg, deceas'd, to the present Sir Robert. Mr John Heaves and Mr Fagg the Younger (I think) of Green Lee was there and saw Mr Spence give me the order just without the back door. Receiv'd an angry letter from Sir Robert by the post which my Wife sent to me to the Fair. Will bought a payr of oxen of Thomas Vinall at the Fair at £14. Oxen and other beasts were very dear.

The 26th April 1728 Fryday. A dry day.

The 27th April 1728 Saturday. A dry day. Receiv'd a bill of £20 of Mr Henry Campion on Mr Fowler etc as before and a bill of £40 of Thomas Smith on Robert Skinner with both which bills I sent Thomas Elvey to London to pay the mony to Thomas Tourl for Sir Robert Fagg's use.

The 28th April 1728 Sunday. A gloomy day.
Mr John Hart preacht in the forenoon and gave the sacrament and Mr Bear afternoon. I went to Mr Lamb at Ditcheling after evning prayr and he promis'd to go to Stenning again to morrow. Thomas Penfold brought home the payr of barrens that Will bought at Crawley Fair at _____ .

The 29th April 1728 Munday. A windy day, some rain.
I wrote to Mr William Martin per post directed to his father's. Paid Abraham Muzzall 3s-6d for makeing my black shag breeches and clear'd all accounts.

The 30th April 1728 Tuesday. A stormy day. Sent a bushel of tail barly to mill for the young ducks. Thomas Elvey return'd from London and brought a receit from Thomas Tourl for £60 vizt both the notes for Sir Robert Fagg's use.

The 1st May 1728 Wednesday. A dry day. I were at Lindfield Fair, at my Aunt Mills's, left a letter there for my Cousin Allan Mills. Din'd at my Brother John Courtness's, tryd'd and liked my new hat at 10s-6d.

The 2nd May 1728 Thursday. A wet day. All jobb'd. Receiv'd a new hat from my Brother John Courtness at 10s-6d. Paid Jack Howard 6d to carry a letter to Robert Adams to morrow as he goes to Lewis.

The 3rd May 1728 Fryday. A gloomy forenoon. Very wet after. I went to Stenning, call'd at Mr Newlin's and desir'd him to preach at Broadwater a Sunday next which he readily promis'd to do in the afternoon. Went thence to Stenning. Din'd at Butcher Thomas Hill's. Spent best part of the afternoon at Mr Brown's with Mr Leach and Mr Lamb. Had the saddle mended.

The 4th May 1728 Saturday. A gloomy day.
Mr Lamb call'd here in his way home from Stenning. Mrs Anne Beard De School spent the afternoon here. Sent a letter to Allan Mills per Jack Bartlet. Sold Thomas Smith 10 tags at 10s-6d each to be fetch away next Tuesday. Reckon'd with Old Smither the carrier and he gave me a receit on his bill and gave him a note of my hand for £3-15s on demand.

The 5th May 1728 Sunday. A fine day. Mr Jeremiah Dodson preacht twice. We had a vestry afternoon. Robert Pierce and Richard Lashmer enter'd on the office of overseers. I were at Church afternoon, not in the forenoon. Mr William Martin return'd from his journey. Brought home a new horse for Mr Healy if he like him.

The 6th May 1728 Munday. A dry day. Mr Healy here but did not conclude to have the horse. Receiv'd the 50s and intrest due from my Cousin Allan Mills on bond.

The 7th May 1728 Tuesday. A fine day.
I were at the visitation at Lewis. Paid all the briefs in my hands and receiv'd (I think) 5 new ones. Nick Plaw and I went and return'd together. Paid Norman 3s-8d for 2 large sheets of stampt paper. Paid Thomas Smith the £40 _____ and outsetting the 5 guineas above mention'd due for 10 tags which he drew to day.

The 8th May 1728 Wednesday. A fine day.
Mr Adams came to Towne in the evning and spoak to Mr Scutt (I suppose) about our meeting to morrow because he could not come himself. My Wife and I spent

biggest part of the afternoon at Mr John Hart's, he took with somewhat like an ague. Mr Bear and a young gentleman with him call'd there.

The 9th May 1728 Thursday. A fine day.
Mr Ralph Beard, Mr Scutt, Thomas Box, John Norton of Chestham, Nick Plaw and I met at T Smith's and begun settle Mary Balcomb's accounts. Paid, that is, spent there 2s-9½d. Mr R Richard Barcroft came in the evning. So did Evan Shelby to whome I ow'd £20 for runts. Robert Adams promis'd to pay the mony in London but never did it (I thank him).

The 10th May 1728 Fryday. A very fine day. Mr Richard Barcroft went away. Paid him half a year's rent due at Lady Day last, outset a year's Lord's rent and taxes. Paid Evan Shelby £20 due to him on a note of my hand for runts and he gave me a receit and promis'd to deliver the note of my hand to Mr Wilin in London in a few days.

The 11th May 1728 Saturday. A dry day, 'till near night and then rain, thunder and lightning and a very great storm and tempest. Mr Lamb and his wife and one child din'd here. Mr William Martin paid him for teaching school at Stenning while he was gone. They rode home on Mr John Hart's mare and my horse, the child staid behind and the servant girl. Jack Bartlet went to London.

The 12th May 1728 Sunday. A dry day.
Mr William Martin preacht. Begun at 2 aclock afternoon. Read prayrs and went to Newtimber after. We had a vestry after evning prayr allow'd the Widdow Marshall 16s per month.

The 13th May 1728 Munday. A gloomy day. The storme mention'd a Saturday was very great, especially the hail prodigious, many stones as bigg or bigger than an hen's egg, the windows of some houses allmost all broak, very great damage done to corne etc. Jack Bartlet return'd from London and brought the horse again the jockey refuseing to take him again on any terms. Receiv'd a letter per post from Mr Fowler.

The 14th May 1728 Tuesday. A fine day.
Will went to Shoreham Market, sold a load of wheat to Richard Smith at 11s-10s. Win'd Bony's wheat 5 quarters head, 3 bushel tail. Deliver'd 2½ bushel of barly to my Brother James Burt yesterday at 18s per quarter. Sold him an other parcell at 20s per quarter.

The 15th May 1728 Wednesday. A gloomy day. Thomas Hamper's man T Reeve workt here. Set up a gate post goeing into the hovelfield. Marrian Edwards and his brother plough'd at Rickman's.

The 16th May 1728 Thursday. A fine day.
Sent a letter to Fowler at Petworth per post. Thomas Hamper and his man at the Towne House. Marrian Edwards and his brother plough'd at Rickman's. Thomas Hamper set up my Father and Mother Stone's pictures in the parlour.

The 17th May 1728 Fryday. A dry day.
Mr Beard, Mr Scutt, Thomas Box, John Norton, Nick Plaw and I met again at Thomas Smith's about Mr Balcomb's accounts, expences 3s. Mr William Martin came in the evning. Sold the black colt to Edward Elvey at £8-1s. Receiv'd 1s in hand. Mr Beard said 'twas for him. Paid Mr Beard the rest and order'd him to pay Mr Henry Campion ten guineas.

The 18th May 1728 Saturday. A very fine day.
Plough'd at Rickman's. Carry'd 2 locks to my Lord Treep to alter. My Cousin Sarah Norton here, my Wife paid her 2 guineas. Shut up the calves to weaning.

The 19th May 1728 Sunday. A dry day.
Mr William Martin preacht twice. Moll Terry and her brother Jack din'd here. Mr Henry Campion and Mr Beard and Dr Vincent here after evning service.

The 20th May 1728 Munday. A very fine day.
Will, with Marrian Edwards, etc and some of my Brother Peter's horses carry'd a load of wheat to Richard Smith of Shoreham at £11-16s and I think he paid him for it, brought home a load of seacoal for Mr Scutt. William Savage here, mending ploughs etc. Nick Plaw here, cut our calves. Turn'd the working oxen to pasture in the lower ground. Marrian Edwards's brother here to take work.

The 21st May 1728 Tuesday. A dry day.
Marrian Edwards plough'd at Rickman's. Did some jobbs after. Paid my Lord Treep 5s for altring post locks and making 4 keys to 'em. I were at the club.

The 22nd May 1728 Wednesday. A showry day. Plough'd part of the day with 2 teems in Churchfield. Will sold Robert Ockley of Rigate his ten lambs at          and 25 of mine at £10 to be drawn 2 weeks after Midsummer.

The 23rd May 1728 Thursday. A very fine day. Both teems plough'd. Lent my Brother Peter my Wive's double horse to go to Crawley for the Dr for my Mother. Thomas Smith return'd from London. William Savage here again fitting up ploughs.

The 24th May 1728 Fryday. A dry day. Plough'd etc.

The 25th May 1728 Saturday. A dry day. Plough'd etc.

The 26th May 1728 Sunday. A dry day. Mr William Martin preacht. Three of Sir George Parker's daughters supt and spent the evning here. They came to dwell in my Towne House a Fryday last at £3 per quarter for the kitchin end and the use of the goods. Danny teem brought them 50 faggots and half a cord of wood yesterday.

The 27th May 1728 Munday. A very fine day. Nick Plaw, Thomas Box and I met Mr Adams and Mr Lindfield's son of Horsham at the Royall Oak about William Balcomb's accounts. He, Mr Lindfield, carry'd my accounts away with him, promis'd to give them to me again. Thomas Roberd's man here mending harness. Marrian Edwards's brother here towards night.

The 28th May 1728 Tuesday. A fine day. Marrian Edwards's brother begun mow thistles in Homefield. Thomas Vallence workt on the Towne House. Will went to Shoreham. I were at the club with Mr John Hart, Mr William Martin, Mr Naldrit, Dr Vincent and Mr Harsey of Horsham.

The 29th May 1728 Wednesday. A fine day. Vallence workt on the Towne House. Paid Thomas Elvey 8s-6d for 2 bushels of malt for the Mrs Parkers. Sent a coppy of William Balcomb's sale bills per Cooter the sheppard to Mr Lindfield for Robert Adams.

The 30th May 1728 Thursday. A fine day. Receiv'd a letter from Mr Fowler at the Duke of Somerset's, sent an answer. Vallence workt at Towne.

The 31st May 1728 Fryday. A fine day. Somebody from Stenning brought strawberrys and some beans from Mr William Martin. Hyder's beasts and my own too in the oats yesterday. John Gun mow'd clover to day and 2 days before. Harry White _____ on the pond and 1 day before. Receiv'd 8s-6d of Mrs J Parker for the malt mention'd yesterday.

The 1st June 1728 Saturday. A fine day. Carry'd dung.

The 2nd June 1728 Sunday. A fine day. Mr Jeremiah Dodson preacht. We had a vestry. Settled accounts. I were at Mr Beard's with Lox Mr Richard Whitpaine etc.

The 3rd June 1728 Munday. A gloomy day. Horsham Fair. Jack Bartlet rode Mr William Martin's horse to the Fair. I were at Mr Jeremiah Dodson's in the morning. Settled accounts for all our tithes. I were at Danny in the afternoon.

The 4th June 1728 Tuesday. A gloomy day. Mr William Martin and I went to Mr Hampton's, to Mr Springet's, to Mr Sixsmith's and to Mr Lamb's. The Mrs Parkers supt here. The men carry'd dung to the mixen.

The 5th June 1728 Wednesday. A fine day. Carry'd dung. Thomas Hamper and his son at Towne.

The 6th June 1728 Thursday. A fine day. Receiv'd a letter from Mr Fowler telling me he was out. I wrote him an answer. Thomas Box brought a mare to my young horse.

The 7th June 1728 Fryday. A hot day. I were at Horsham. Talkt with Mr Parham, Mr Wicker and T Wickenden. Receiv'd 45s of Daniel Groombridge for half a year's rent. Allow'd nothing for taxes nor anything else. Din'd at the Starr, talkt with my Brother Will.

The 8th June 1728 Saturday. A fine day. I begun way mending in the afternoon with 2 teems, carry'd 3 loads. Carry'd the last of the stump of hay to Thomas Smith. Paid Tom Edwards 3s and 2s before and half a bushel of tail wheat he had at 2s. Laid 2 loads of chalk in the new way and 1 by William Bond's.

The 9th June 1728 Sunday. A fine day. Mr William Martin preacht. Thomas Elvey went with Mr William Martin's horse for Chichester Fair and for Broadwater, went first to Arundell and was to take Mr Picknall's advice and directions. I wrote to him and Mr Hunt of Petworth.

The 10th June 1728 Munday. A fine forenoon, rain after. Carry'd some clover hay and took up more barly. Mr William Martin and I at Mr Scutt's afternoon. Goodman Soaper of Roffee was here with a petition for mony, I gave him 1s and his dinner.

The 11th June 1728 Tuesday. A showry day. The boys and Marrian Edwards kept holy day. John Gh and Tom Edwards mended gaps part. The Mrs Parkers din'd here. Thomas Elvey came home with the horse late.

The 12th June 1728 Wednesday. A gloomy day, some rain. Fetcht a load of flints into the highways per Will and Marrian Edwards. Thomas Hamper begun set up a falling post goeing into Fifteen Acres. Paid the Weaver Hudson 3s-6d for Moll Kapp and 10s she had of my Wife.

The 13th June 1728 Thursday. A gloomy day, some rain. Will went to Cuckfield Fair.
Receiv'd a letter from Mr Fowler and sent an answer to be put in the post, with a letter to Mr Hunt per Jonathan Walls. He and Becket of Falmer were here with some coppies etc.

The 14th June 1728 Fryday. A fine day.
Carry'd hay and gather'd cherrys.

The 15th June 1728 Saturday. A dry day. Carry'd hay out of Edgley mead and the ponds. Frank the horse rider here. The Mrs Parkers here. My Wife etc took a walk. Paid Roach 8s-8d in full of all. Molly rode to Lewis behind Jack Howard yesterday on my wive's horse.

The 16th June 1728 Sunday. A fine day.
Mr William Martin preacht in the forenoon, begun at 2 in the afternoon, had prayrs only and he went to Newtimber and preacht afterwards. The Mrs Parkers here in the evning. I was at Mrs Catherine Beard's after afternoon service.

The 17th June 1728 Munday. A very hot day.
The mowers begun again. Receiv'd a letter from my Brother William yesterday. Paid the bearer 18d for bringing it. A tempest of thunder and lightning in the evning. Mrs Parker's here.

The 18th June 1728 Tuesday. A gloomy day. some rain. Will went to Rigate, brought home 12lb of turnip seed at 6d per pound. Tom Edwards and Marrian Edwards washt all the sheep. George West gather 11lb of cherrys at d½per lb. Young Bonny too gather'd and young Pointin a while.

The 19th June 1728 Wednesday. A gloomy day, some rain. Plough'd. Frank the horse rider call'd here. My Brother John Courtness at Towne and his sister Molly. I wrote to Mr Fowler and to Mr William Martin by her. She proposes to go home to morrow. Jack Bartlet excessive drunk with brandy, which he did to put away an ague. Coply the painter her, I sent him to Stephen Bine. An other swarme of bees.

The 20th June 1728 Thursday. A gloomy day, some rain towards night. I were at St John's Comon for Pross Belchamber to come to morrow to sheer my sheep. Went over Heath's Farme as I came home.

The 21st June 1728 Fryday. A showry day.
I went to Horsted Kynes. Paid the Widdow Weller a year's intrest. Din'd at my Brother John Courtness's as I came home, bad him 13s a yard for a coat of dark grey cloath. Left a saddle at J Rankorn that I had at Byshop's. It is the little black saddle that we use to the forehorse to the chaese. Harry Chapman of Rusper and Daws of Lockfield here to buy wheat. Sold Nick Plaw half a load at 6 guineas.

The 22nd June 1728 Saturday. A gloomy day.
Sow'd part of the Churchfield with turnips.

The 23rd June 1728 Sunday. A fine day.
Mr William Martin preacht. Went to Church afternoon at 2 aclock and preacht at Newtimber after. I was at Mrs Parker's with Mr Henry Campion etc and at Mrs Beard's afterwards. Receiv'd a letter from Mr Fowler per JC.

The 24th June 1728 Munday. A fine day.
I were at St John's Comon Fair, Mr Beard bought 70 lambs of Nick Friend at 4s-6d per lamb and I bought 10 the worst of them of Mr Beard at 2s-6d each. Din'd at Byshops with Richard Smith of Shoreham.

The 25th June 1728 Tuesday. A fine day.
Pross Belchamber made an end of sheering my sheep and Wills paid him 3s-6d in full of all and 10 dry sheep. Clear'd all accounts with my Aunt Courtness as well on book, as a bond of £50 to me.

The 26th June 1728 Wednesday. A wet day and part of last night so. Paid Mr Henry Campion £30 in part of mony paid for me in London for Sir Robert Fagg's use. I went to Danny. Spent the afternoon there with Mr Henry Campion, Mr Price, Mr Healy, Mr Scutt and Richard Whitpaine. Will Marchant there a while.

The 27th June 1728 Thursday. A gloomy morning fine after. Plough'd etc. Thomas Elvey brought his new mare. Tanner Burtenshaw here. Desir'd me to fetch a load of tann from Bolny at 8s. I promis'd. TE said he would set out for Tunbridge to morrow early and return to Wivelsfield Fair a Saturday and treat with Old Relph.

The 28th June 1728 Fryday. A dry day. Hay'd etc.

The 29th June 1728 Saturday. A dry day.
I went to Horsham. Receiv'd and borrow'd £50 of my Brother Will and the 3s he had of the wooden ware seller that was left there for a cheese fellow[?]. Paid Stephen Carter's son and daughter 6s-10d for 14lb of turnip seed had last year.

The 30th June 1728 Sunday. A fine day.
Mr William Martin preacht. Went to Newtimber again after prayers here.

The 1st July 1728 Munday. A fine day.
Carry'd hay etc. Mr William Martin return'd to Stenning this morning. Mr Fowler came here a little afternoon, _____ to talk with T Smith in the evning, but he made a very uncertain piece of a story of it.

The 2nd July 1728 Tuesday. A fine day.
Carry'd hay. Mr Fowler and J and Thomas Elvey went to Old Rolfs at Wivelsden to see a paceing mare. We went all together to E Carters at Wivelsfield Fair place but we could not agree for the mare. Mr Fagg, Mr Scutt, Thomas Elvey, Mr Fowler and I spent the evning here.

The 3rd July 1728 Wednesday. A fine day. Mr Fowler and I breakfasted at Mr Scutt's. The teem fetch a load of tann from Bolny for Henry Burtenshaw. Mr Fowler and I went afternoon for Mr Price's but call'd at Danny and staid there 'till night. Saker of Rigate, a lamb buyer, was there and bought a load of wheat of Mr Henry Campion or six quarters at £14 per load at Hand Cross.

The 4th July 1728 Thursday. A fine day. Saker took the lambs away and paid for 'em and bought four more at 8s each and a tag and a ewe at 20s. Paid for all. Mr Fowler and Mr Scutt went afternoon to Mr Price's, staid there 'till night. There was Mr Lamb, Allan Mills, William Norton, E Harraden and Mr Miller, Danny gardner. Paid half a guinea for a sack of tares _____ to William Norton which he is to bring home to morrow.

The 5th July 1728 Fryday. A fine day.
Mr Fowler went home. I went to Stenning with him. Stephen Bine din'd here. Paid him my Land Tax and Will paid his. William Norton brought the tares.

The 6th July 1728 Saturday. A fine day.
Carry'd hay. Mr Price and Mr Jeremiah Dodson and Mr Scutt here afternoon. Mr William Martin came towards night talkt with Mr Jeremiah Dodson and return'd late. Mr Price and I appointed to go to Petworth a Tuesday next, to meet at Pycomb at 7.

The 7th July 1728 Sunday. A fine day. Mr Jeremiah Dodson preacht, no service afternoon. I were at Wanbarrow, paid my Mother half a year's thirds to Michaelmas last. My Wife went to Lewis afternoon. Jack Bartlet carry'd her. Will and Thomas Box went to Major Moore's afternoon. Thomas Elvey return'd from Canterbury haveing sold Mr William Martin's horse there at £6 which he paid me for Mr William Martin.

The 8th July 1728 Munday. A fine day.
Carry'd hay out of the field by Hyder's to the lower side of Tully's Mead. My Wife return'd from Lewis. TE went to _____ brought a new pillion girt. Mr Lamb here afternoon.

The 9th July 1728 Tuesday. A dry morning, very wet towards night. Mr Price and I went to Petworth. Call'd at Stenning.

The 10th July 1728 Wednesday. A very wet afternoon. Mr Hunt's daughter Elizabeth was christen'd, Mr Price was godfather. My Wife and Mrs Eliz Lafitte were godmothers, Mrs Mary Wicklitse stood for my Wife.

The 11th July 1728 Thursday. A dry day.
Mr Lafitte came to Petworth. He gave me an account in writeing of an assault that was made on him some time ago. The account was as Mr Eades had (or pretended) to have it from Henry Rook now a tennant to Sir Robert Fagg. Mr Lafitte desir'd to try I could get Sir Robert Fagg to talk to Rook about it.

The 12th July 1728 Fryday. A dry day.
Mr Price and I return'd from Petworth, din'd late at Mr William Martin's and he came with us. Parted with Mr Price at Mr Beard's. We call'd at Mr Pinnels at Fiddleworth as we came home. Paid Mr Hunt 6s yesterday, or t'other day for a payr of stockins.

The 13th July 1728 Saturday. A dry day. Carry'd hay etc.

The 14th July 1728 Sunday. A fine day. Mr William Martin preacht. We had a vestry afternoon. Allow'd Thomas Surgeant's wife 3s per week, he is newly run away.

The 15th July 1728 Munday. A gloomy day. Carry'd some hay etc. Nick Plaw here afternoon, sold him what wheat I have to spare at 6s-6d per bushel. Receiv'd 6s-6d of him for half a load already deliver'd. William Haslegrove came to speak with me at _____ yesterday after evning service.

The 16th July 1728 Tuesday. A very wet day. Win'd 14 bushels head and 3 tail of Tom Edwards's thrashing. Nick Plaw's man brought 2 bushels of oates and carry'd away 3 bushels of wheat and Marrian Edwards etc carry'd 10 bushels more.

The 17th July 1728 Wednesday. A dry day. Plough'd and cut pease. I went to Danny to look on Mr Henry Campion's wheat, Nick Friend there. Richard Lashmer sick, came before I came away.

The 18th July 1728 Thursday. A dry day, afternoon (sic). Plough'd etc. I were at Church with Mr Beard to see the painter, sent for him up to Mr Beard, Stephen Bine there with us, we order'd the painter to rub out all again that is done and begin again larger. Will and I supt at Mr John Hart's. Carry'd Mr Hay's book home to Mr Henry Campion.

The 19th July 1728 Fryday. A showry day. John Gun and Edwards begun reap in the Fifteen Acres at 6s-8d per acre. Dr Vincent here afternoon. I were at Church again to look on the painter.

The 20th July 1728 Saturday. A dry day. Receiv'd a Let Pass for my wool by the post with notice that I must make oath before a Justice of the Peace that I had what wool I mention'd to be workt out last year. My Wife, Mr William Martin and I supt at W Parker's. Thomas Elvey brought home a new horse out of Kent. Paid Ockley and Saker a guinea which they gave Earnest for the lambs and forgot it when they paid for the lambs. Paid them at Mrs Parker's back door.

The 21st July 1728 Sunday. A dry day. Mr William Martin preacht. Mr Henry Campion and Dr Vincent here towards night.

The 22nd July 1728 Munday. A fine day. My Wife and I went to Lewis.

The 23rd July 1728 Tuesday. A fine day. Lay at the Starr. Din'd at Mr Fusler's. Paid Stephen Avery's bill in full of all.

The 24th July 1728 Wednesday. A gloomy day. Carry'd some wheat etc.

The 25th July 1728 Thursday. St James's day. A gloomy day. Will went to Lindfield Fair. Jack Bartlet carry'd my wool to Thomas Friend of Lewis, 3 todd wanting a pound at 16s per todd. Brought 4 bottles of spaw water and 2 bottles of white wine from Mr Ayres's.

The 26th July 1728 Fryday. A wet day. Will came home towards night. John Snashall was here and made 2 Junes in my __ . Mr Beard had 12 ox bows per Richard Banks.

The 27th July 1728 Saturday. A gloomy day. R Cox reapt in Bankfield. Mr William Martin came on Mr Elvey's horse.

The 28th July 1728 Sunday. A fine day. Mr Price preacht. Mr William Martin went to Clayton and Kmer. I was at Mr Beard's with Mr Price etc.

The 29th July 1728 Munday. A fine day. Dick Wood shood with new shooes my horse's fore feet and let him bleed. J Boniface fetcht the old horse from Stenning. Brought 5 pidgeons etc.

The 30th July 1728 Tuesday. A dry day. Carry'd some oates and some wheat. Mr Price here and Mr John Hart the evning. Lent Mrs Scutt the old horse to go to Lewis, Mrs Bett sick.

The 31st July 1728 Wednesday. A dry day. Idger here from Lewis, carry'd some wood, some wheat etc.

The 1st August 1728 Thursday. A dry day. I din'd at Mr Price's. Mr John Hart came thither about 4 aclock and we came home together. Carry'd some wheat and oates.

The 2nd August 1728 Fryday. A dry day.
Carry'd the rest of the wheat at Rickman's, 2 small loads. Talkt with Mr _____ .

The 3rd August 1728 Saturday. A fine day.
I went to Lewis. Paid Thomas Friend all that is due on his book and left £29 with him which he is to pay to Mr Wilkin to be sent to Oxford. Carry'd the rest of the Hovelfield oates and some wheat. Thomas Osbourne brought home the little grey colt whilst I were gone to Lewis and Will paid him. I saw him afterwards at Lewis.

The 4th August 1728 Sunday. A fine day.
Mr Jeremiah Dodson preacht. We had a vestry as usual. Mr Dodson's proposals not alltogether approved.

The 5th August 1728 Munday. A very fine hot day.
Carry'd some wheat. I were at Nick Plaw's in the evning. Receiv'd a letter from Mr Fowler per post.

The 6th August 1728 Tuesday. A fine day.
Carry'd some oates and wheat.

The 7th August 1728 Wednesday. A fine day.
Harry Morley begun thatch the wheat rick. Thomas Roach and a taylor made an end of reaping the Bankfield and reapt with John Gun afternoon. Paid Roach and the taylor 7s-6d each for their 3 days reaping.

The 8th August 1728 Thursday. A very fine day.
Will and Thomas Elvey went to a Plate Race at Lewis. Mr Price, Mr Hunt and Mr Thomas Rice at Petworth were before Nick. I went with them to Mr Price's to dinner. John Gun and Edwards ended their reaping. Receiv'd a letter from Mr Redclife per Oxford.

The 9th August 1728 Fryday. A fine day.
Mr Hunt, Mr Denham and Mr Rice of Petworth din'd here and Mr William Martin with'em. Went to Lewis races, Will Marchant went with them. Receiv'd a pound of tobacco of Mr Hunt. Harry Morley and his boy here.

The 10th August 1728 Saturday. A fine day. Our Fair.
Mr Hunt and Mr Rice call'd here in the forenoon. Paid Mr Hunt 26s in full of all. Mrs Lamb and 2 daughters and Mr Luxford with Mr Jane and Mrs Phill Parker and Mr William Martin din'd here. Paid Harry Morley 13s for thatching the wheat rick.

The 11th August 1728 Sunday. A fine day. Mr William Martin preacht twice. We had a vestry afternoon about Thomas Nye sr, _____ . Our family supt at Mrs Parker's.

The 12th August 1728 Munday. A dry day.
Carry'd oates etc.

The 13th August 1728 Tuesday. A dry day.
Ended carrying oates. I were at Mr John Hart's with Mrs Barbara Campion etc. Paid Mrs Campion 20 guineas in the morning.

The 14th August 1728 Wednesday. A dry day.
Tipt and begun tip and cut some ricks and carry'd some faggots. Will went to Major Moore's yesterday to shoot.

The 15th August 1728 Thursday. A dry day.
Tipt ricks and carry'd faggots.

The 16th August 1728 Fryday. A dry day.
Carry'd faggots and wood. Tipt ricks.

The 17th August 1728 Saturday. A fine day.
Fetcht home wood and carry'd a load of wood to Thomas Hamper's, his man T Reeve workt here to day and Thursday, 2 men this afternoon. Receiv'd a letter from Mr Wilkin and sent an answer with Mr _____ note in it endorsed as desir'd.

The 18th August 1728 Sunday. A dry day.
Mr William Martin preacht. Was at the Royall Oak with Thomas Norton etc.

The 19th August 1728 Munday. A gloomy day.
Fetcht 100 faggots from Rickman's. Carry'd some barly.

The 20th August 1728 Tuesday. A ~~wet~~ showry day.
Reckon'd and clear'd accounts with William Baker for my black breeches etc. ~~Thomas Preese stackt faggots and carry'd to William Roach.~~ Carry'd some barly.

The 21st August 1728 Wednesday. A wet showry day.
Stackt faggots etc.

The 22nd August 1728 Thursday. A gloomy day, some rain. Plough'd. Mr Wilkin here. Reckon'd and paid him 6s in full of all. Receiv'd £3 of Stephen Bine towards the Church painting. Paid Mrs Barbara Campion £10 more in the morning. Receiv'd £8 of John Bodle in the morning. Supt and spent the evning with Mr John Hart at Mr Beard's.

The 23rd August 1728 Fryday. A cloudy day.
Carry'd barly per John Reeve and in Rookwood. Paid Thomas Muzzall and John Kneller for their work and John Reeve. James, John Bodle's man, thrasht Frank the colt rider last night which (I think) was well done. Paid Robert Smith the painter £7 for painting the Church. Stephen Bine here with him, both din'd here. Mr William Martin came towards night.

The 24th August 1728 Saturday. A fine day.
Ended harvest by 1aclock. Henry Ford at the Comon here about apples.

The 25th August 1728 Sunday. A dry day.
Mr William Martin preacht. We had a vestry afternoon about the highways. I was at Mr Henry Campion's afterwards, supt at Mrs Parker's.

The 26th August 1728 Munday. A dry day.
Begun stir the Marldfield oates earsh.

The 27th August 1728 Tuesday. A very fine day.
Mrs Phil Parker, my Wife, Nanny and I with Thomas Elvey, John Kneller and James Banks set out for Rusper. Went to James Chapman's and after dinner went to see Nunnery House.

The 28th August 1728 Wednesday. A very wet day.
Return'd from Rusper. Paid Mrs Pryaulx 17s-8d for the brick and carriage that were laid in Nunnery churchyard and gave James Chapman orders to sell them. Talkt with Goodman Lucas a mason and he would not undertake to set up the tomb stones with stone.

The 29th August 1728 Thursday. A very fine day.
Begun stir the field above Tully's coppice. John Bodle fetcht the [.......er] black runt. H Pockny here to examine the black colt. Sold Let Holden of Brighton a load of turnips at 1s per bushel. Delivr'd there.

The 30th August 1728 Fryday. A dry day. Plough'd etc.

The 31st August 1728 Saturday. A fine day.
Ended ploughing the field by the coppice. Receiv'd a letter from Mr Fowler telling me that he was gone into Lincolnshire. The Mrs Parkers, my Wife, Thomas Elvey and Will went to Shoreham to see the place.

The 1st September 1728 Sunday. A fine day.
Mr Jeremiah Dodson preacht. I were not at Church in the forenoon. We had a vestry afternoon. My Brother Peter here towards night.

The 2nd September 1728 Munday. A fine day.
Pull'd turnips and loaded the waggon with turnips for Shoreham to morrow 40 bushels.

The 3rd September 1728 Tuesday. A fine day.
Carry'd out 40 bushels of turnips. Left     bushels at Poynings Place and the rest at Portslade and Southwick all but ten bushels and the rest with Goody Weymouth at Shoreham to sell. Reckon'd and clear'd accounts with Richard Smith only half a load of coal we had to day at _____. Mr Thomas Middleton brought the major's hounds hither for night. Will and he kill'd a hare about Poynings to day.

The 4th September 1728 Wednesday. A dry day.
The hounds kill'd a hare and ate part of her. Pull'd turnips.

The 5th September 1728 Thursday. A dry day.
The dogs out again, kill'd nothing. Carry'd (I think) 33 bushels of turnips to Let Holden's.

The 6th September 1728 Fryday. A wet day.
Carry'd 13 bushels of turnips to J Byshop at the Comon and 24 bushels to my Brother John Courtness's to be sold for me. Sold 4 bushels as we went. I rode Thomas Elvey's horse. Mr Middleton went home. John Bodle kill'd the white faced cow yesterday, or t'other day.

The 7th September 1728 Saturday. A fine day.
Old William Brand buried here. *(Ed: shown as Goodman William Brand in Hurst Parish Register)* George West carry'd 6 bushels of turnips to Samuel Hart's. Plough'd at Rickman's with 2 teems. I was at Mr John Hart's after the funeral with Mr William Martin.

*(Ed: Thomas died on 14th September and was buried 3 days later in the northern part of the churchyard of St Lawrence's church at Hurst)*

October the 9th 1728 *(Ed: this is in a different hand)* Mrs Parkers paid their rent for ¾ of a year. John Gun made syder. George West carry'd 6 bushels of turnips to Blackstone.

## Glossary to Diary

| | |
|---|---|
| Aberton | Edburton |
| Accadence | Education |
| Agdean | Egdean |
| Ague | Fit of shivering, malaria |
| Allhallantide | All Saints Day |
| Amercement | A fine whose amount is fixed by the court; |
| Anchor | 8 1/3 imperial gallons |
| Apple cracker | A device for crushing apples during the process of making cider |
| Auger | Pointed tool for boring holes |
| Bayard | 1. Magical legendary horse in medieval chivalric romances. |
| | 2. Mock-heroic name for any horse. |
| | 3. Bay horse (archaic) |
| Beans | Probably 'horse' or 'tick' beans grown as animal fodder |
| Betimes | In good time |
| Blew cloth | Blue cloth |
| Bohea | Tea |
| Bonifort wheat | Variety of wheat |
| Bottom | A valley floor, particularly in the Downs |
| Brandled | Brindled - tawny coloured with darker stripes |
| Breaking pease | Possibly beans grown for animal food which would then be ground |
| Brew fat | Brew vat |
| Bridge bat | Part of a cart |
| Brief | A royal mandate for collection towards deserving causes. The brief address to the minister and churchwardens was read from the pulpit. The collection total was endorsed on the brief and the money paid to an authorized agent. See Turner's diary. |
| Broadpiece | A hammer struck gold coin, especially Jacobean and Caroline sovereigns, superseded in 1663 by the guinea, but still legal tender until 1733. |
| Brod | Type of nail |
| Broyler | An oven or part of a stove used for broiling |

| | |
|---|---|
| Bucken tubb | A tub specifically for washing |
| Bucket timber | 10 foot of my bucket timber |
| Bull stag | The male of the common ox castrated. |
| Bullock | Gelded bull, steer-collectively fattening cattle |
| Burrough book | Book of the local headborough |
| Bushel | 8 gallons [dry or liqid] or 36.368 litres |
| Buttery | Small room used for the storage of food, pots and barrels of beer |
| Callimanco | Satin twilled woollen cloth |
| Camlet | Light cloth of various materials for cloaks etc. Originally costly Eastern stuff of silk and camel's hair |
| Candlemas | 2nd February formerly the Feast of Purification of Vgin Mary. In Roman Catholic churches all candles needed during the year are consecrated on that day. |
| Cannel coal | A light bituminous coal which does not soil the fingers. Probably a corruption of 'candle' because it burns without smoke It is very fine-grained, composed in the main of finely comminuted vegetable matter etc. |
| Cast box | Cast iron box, the hardened centre of a wheel on which the arm runs. |
| Caul | Thin membrane covering the lower intestines of various animals, formerly used to make sausage skins. |
| Causey | A causeway or raised, stone paved path |
| Chaese | Light open carriage |
| Chaldron | Any of various old units of measure varying from 32 to 72 imperial bushels |
| Chaldron | See measures |
| Chamber | pper room e.g. parlour chamber was the room over the parlour |
| Chape | The part of a buckle by which it is fastened to a strap. |
| Charl coal | Charcoal |
| Chine | cut of meat across the ribs including backbone e. g. saddle of lamb |
| Chisel pare | Vriety of pear |
| Chucks | Large chips of wood. |
| Chit | Apart from written notes, also the third swarm of bees from a hive |
| Cirb | Kerb or rim |
| Closet | Small private room or recess |
| Clout | Nail |

| | |
|---|---|
| Coaping | Þpermost course of a wall, usually slanted to allow water to drain off. |
| Cock | A small pile (as of hay) |
| Colter | Sharp blade or wheel used to cut ground in advance of the plough share |
| Composition | Settling of a debt by arrangement |
| Coney | Rabbit |
| Copper still | Apparatus for distilling |
| Cord | 128 cubic feet (measure of wood) |
| Coursing | Hunting with dogs trained to chase game by sight instead of scent |
| Court Baron | Assembly of freehold tenants of a manor under the Lord |
| Cramming | Feeding to excess for fattening (*cf foie gras*). |
| Crooper dock | Leather band which fastens around the root of the horse's tail |
| Crying a sale | Announcing a forthcoming sale |
| Cutting calves | Castrating calves |
| Daffy's elexir | A patent tonic medicine |
| Darkin | Dorking (reveals Thomas's Sussex accent) |
| Deal | Plank of soft wood generally 9"x 3"(or less) x 6'. |
| Denshire | Old grass is pared from fields, allowed to dry and then burned and the ashes spread. High potash content. |
| Dill | Part of harness, otherwise known as thill |
| Dine | To take a midday meal |
| Dock | To remove part of a tail |
| Double horse | Horse to be ridden by two people |
| Draw flax | Flax has to be pulled rather than cut |
| Draw lambs | To select lambs for sale, tupping etc |
| Drawing mare | Horse used to pull as opposed to a riding horse |
| Drench | Medicine forced down an animal's throat |
| Dress flax, to | George begun dress flax. |
| Dripping pan | A pan placed under roasting meat to catch the drips |
| Drugget | A woven and felted coarse woollen fabric used for floor and table coverings |
| Dry sheep | Sheep which has weaned its lambs |
| Dune cow | Probably dun cow ie dull or dingy brown. |

| | |
|---|---|
| Dware | Cross bar in the floor of a wagon |
| Earsh | Stubble field, often pronounced "ash" |
| Edder | Flexible wood workt into the top of hedge stakes, to bind them together. |
| Eddered hedge | Layered hedge |
| Electuary | A medicine composed usually of a powder mixed into a paste with syrup or honey |
| Ell | 1.25 yards |
| Factor | Agent |
| Faggot | Bundle of sticks, hedge trimmings tied into bundles for kindling |
| Fallow | Ploughed land left unused for the year |
| Falling post | A type of gate which has the appearance of a fence but with rails which can rise and fall on a pivot thus enabling someone to step easily over one end. |
| Farrow | To give birth |
| Fat | M |
| Fatting rick | Rick positioned near the yards for cattle to be fattened for slaughter |
| Ferret | Narrow tape of cotton or silk used for binding |
| Fish tun | Large cask for moving fish |
| Flea | Flay |
| Fleath | Fleed (Fleche, French.) The inside fat of a hog before it is melted into lard |
| Flitch | Side of meat, salted and cured |
| Founder'd | Lameness in the foot of a horse, occasioned by inflammation |
| Froward | Perverse |
| Fuller | Bleacher or cleanser of cloth |
| Fustian | Coarse, twilled, short-napped cotton fabric, usually dyed dark |
| Gambrel | A stick or iron for suspending slaughtered animals |
| Garret | Loft |
| Gill | A deep, rocky ravine, often wooded forming the course of a stream |
| Gleab | Glebe - land in the village fields kept for the parson to farm |
| Goodman | Term of address for the master of the house |
| Goody | Old title for an elderly widow |
| Gossip | Sponsor at a baptism |

| | |
|---|---|
| Graft | To make or craft |
| Grate | Probably grating |
| Grease sheep | Applying ointment to sheep to combat insects |
| Gripe | Small ditch or furrow |
| Grist | Low qality corn to be ground |
| Grizzled | Grey or mixed with grey |
| Groat | A silver coin worth 4d but which was only issued from 1351 until 1662 -the name perhaps still used in Thomas's time to refer to another coin. |
| Grub | To clear by digging up roots and stumps |
| Grubber | Tool for drawing roots of weeds |
| Gudgons | Pins or hinges; also the bearings of a shaft |
| Guinea | 21 shillings, £1.05 |
| Half a crown | Two shillings and sixpence, 12d½ |
| Hames | Curved pieces of iron or wood forming part of the collar of a draught horse. |
| Hamm | Enclosure |
| Hamwoods | Pieces of wood on the collar of a horse to which the traces are fixed hames. |
| Harrow | Break up soil |
| Hasp | Strap passing under horse's throat to keep bridle in position. |
| Hatch | Door, half-door, opening, trap-door |
| Haulm | Straw of pease, beans or tares |
| Head burrough | Deputy constable |
| Head wheat | The better grain |
| Healing | Roofing |
| Heifer | Yung cow |
| Herriot | Payment made to the Lord of the Manor on the death of his tennant |
| Hitcholl | Flax comb |
| Hitcholling | Combing out flax before spinning |
| Hog | Castrated male pig |
| Holland | bleached linen cloth |
| Horne main combe | Comb made of horn for combing horse's mane. |

| | |
|---|---|
| Hot bed | Bed for forcing vegetables using the heat of rotting dung |
| Houseing | Cloth covering for a horse |
| Hovel | Shed, shelter or small dwelling |
| Intry | Entry |
| Irish cloath | Embroidery in white thread on white ground |
| Kanester | Container |
| Kathern | auldron. |
| Kibe | A chap or crack in the flesh occasioned by cold; an ulcerated chilblain; as in the heels |
| Knees | Curved branches used as brackets in buildings and ships |
| Knock flax, to | Part of retching process when processing flax |
| Lades | Rails around a cart |
| Lady Day | 25 March i. e. new year and quarter day. The day of the annunciation of the holy virgin, March 25th |
| Lag | A long, narrow, marshy meadow |
| Lain | open tract of land at the foot of the Downs |
| Lanthorn | Lantern |
| Lath | Normally a thin strip of wood e.g. lath and plaster, roofing laths (battens) |
| Lath string | 10d for a bunch of large cat gut for a _____y lath string |
| Leash | Leash of hares |
| Let pass | Licence to move wool |
| Lilt | Covering for a hooped wagon |
| Lime kill | This does mean kiln (see Dictionary of Sussex Dialect) |
| Linsy | Thin coarse stuff of linen or cotton and wool mixed |
| Litchford's Charity | Leonard Litchford set up a charity in the 18th century to provide 10s yearly for 10 poor aged people |
| Lug | Harness – the leather loop or ear by which a shaft is held up. |
| Malago | Malago sugar |
| Male pillion | Saddle; and a cushion/saddle for a person to ride behind an other |
| Marking sheep | Marking to identify, often clipping ears |
| Marl | Limy clay often used as manure |

| | |
|---|---|
| Mash | Crushed chalk |
| Mead | Meadow |
| Memdum | Memorandum, note |
| Metrotinto prints | Copper plate engravings in which surface is roughened and then partially scraped away to give tones and half tones |
| Michaelmas | 29 September. A quarter day |
| Mixen | Dunghill |
| Mokair | Mohair |
| Mountebank | Quack doctor |
| Mow burn'd | Fermented in the stack or in the mow |
| Mud caster | Used to spread mud (probably from ponds) as fertiliser |
| Nail | 8lbs or 2.25 inches |
| Neat | Ox, cow or bull |
| Neb | The pole of an ox cart |
| Nest of draws | Small chest of drawers |
| Noble | 8 shillings or gold coin, 1/3 rd of £1 |
| Non-juror | Someone who had refused to swear an oath of allegiance |
| Nonpareil | Type of apple believed to have been introduced by the Jesuits in Tudor times; famous for its flavour |
| Nonsuch | Kind of lucerne, cloverlike plant used for fodder; improved the flavour of butter |
| Oast | Kiln for drying hops |
| Okum tow | Oakum fibre from ropes |
| Outset | Offset, expend |
| Ox | Castrated bull used for farm work or meat |
| Ox bow | The wooden hoop part of a yoke |
| Paceing horse | Horse which sets the pace for the team |
| Pale fence | A fence comprising narrow planks set with a gap between or a series of stakes e.g. chestnut pale fence |
| Paper of nails | A paper containing a definite amount of nails |
| Pattens | Overshoe with leather straps and a wooden sole |
| Paun | Pawn, security |

| | |
|---|---|
| Pease hook | sickle for cutting pease |
| Pease mow | Mown peas |
| Peck | 2 gallons, measure for dry goods |
| Peeking, peaking | peaky ie slightly unwell. |
| Pell | 1. wash away the ground by force of water; 2. broad shallow piece of water larger than a pond. |
| Penstock | Sluice or floodgate for regulating water |
| Perry | Cider made from pears |
| Pitching | Cobbled paving |
| Plate Race | Race usually for a silver plate. The King's Plate worth 100 guineas was run at Lewis over 4 miles |
| Poll | 1. to cut off or cut back the top of (as a tree); |
| | 2. to cut off or cut short the horns of (cattle) |
| | 3. An inflammatory swelling or abscess on a horse's head, confined beneath the great ligament of the neck. |
| Pollard | Tree cut back to trunk in order to produce dense mass of branches |
| Porker | Pig fattened for food |
| Porrige? | Porringer i.e. silver, pewter or earthenware vessel for soup or porridge. |
| Portion | Bride's money |
| Portmantue | Portmanteau; long leather trunk |
| Prab | Common barley. |
| Presentments | Complaint made by the Constable at Court |
| Pug clover, to | Part of seed cleaning process |
| Pumps | Low-heeled shoe without a fastening for dancing.[see stays] |
| Quarter | 8 bushels or 28 lbs |
| Quicksets | Plant cuttings set in the ground to grow especially in a hedgerow |
| quit rent | Yearly money paid to the Lord of the Manor |
| rack | Fodder rack |
| raddle | to interweave |
| radix | Root |
| reeve | Bailiff or steward appointed by the manor court |

| | |
|---|---|
| ribspeare | Spare rib |
| rid | Free from undergrowth. |
| ridder | Oblong, coarse wire sieve used with a blower for winnowing corn |
| Roller | Surely a large iron field-roller. |
| Round frock | Working smock |
| roundle | Washer |
| Rowber | Rubber?as a winnowing fan had to be flexible. |
| Rowel | Circular piece of leather etc with a hole in centre inserted between horse's skin and flesh to discharge humours |
| Run lime | quicklime |
| Runnet | Meat of a steer |
| Runt | Weakest animal in the litter but also a steer |
| Scotch cloth | Fabric resembling lawn but cheaper;said to have been made from nettle fibre. |
| Scotchman | Pedlar, traveler |
| Sea coal | Coal deliver'd by sea - Newcastle coal |
| Sedge | Grasslike marsh plant |
| Senight | A week, the space of seven nights and days |
| Serve | To feed animals |
| Serving rope | Material used to bind a larger rope. |
| Shalloon | Light twilled woollen cloth for coat linings and women's dresses |
| Shammes | Chamois leather |
| Shaw | Small area of woodland |
| Shift | Undergarment |
| Ship | Sheep |
| Sink | Drain |
| Skreen | Winnow or sieve |
| Slip | Narrow strip of land or passage way |
| Slouch | A soft hat with a broad flexibe rim |
| Small beer | Weak beer made in the home and often drunk by children |
| Smith, Henry (Dog) | He set up a charity in the 17th century to provide for the aged poor |
| Snaffell | Slender, jointed bit used on a bridle |

| | |
|---|---|
| Sorrel | Reddish brown |
| Spatterdashes | Long gaiter or legging |
| Spill wood | Kindling |
| Spire tree | A tree allowed to grow to full height |
| Spitter | Spade (to dig a spit deep) |
| Spoon net | Type of landing net used in fishing |
| Spray | small or fine twigs of trees or shrubs for firewood. |
| Stag | Castrated bull |
| Stampt paper | Paper with government revenue stamp for legal documents |
| Stantions | Stanchions, upright bars or posts e.g. in a cattle stall |
| Stays | Laced under-bodice, stiffened with strips of whalebone, wood or metal, to give shape to the body (plural because two halves were laced together). |
| Steddle-stone | Mushroom shaped stone on which granaries and ricks were built. The steddle itself was the framework of timber resting on the stones on which the rick was built. The cap would help prevent rodents entering the rick. |
| Steer | Castrated ox or bull |
| Stew | A pool in which fish are kept for the table |
| Stifle | The joint next above the hock in the hind leg of a qadruped (as a horse or dog) corresponding to the human knee |
| Stilliards | Scales of the beam and balance type |
| Stir a field | cultivate |
| Stoned colt | A castrated colt |
| Store fish | fish for further growing before being sold for eating |
| Stoughton drops | A proprietary medicine |
| Strake | Any one section of the metal tire on a wooden wheel |
| Strod(d) | Fork branch of a tree like the letter Y |
| Stuff | Material, woollen fabric |
| Sup | To take an evening meal |
| Swad | A bushel basket, generally used in selling fish |
| Swath (hay) | Pronounced $warth$ a row of cut grass as it is laid on the ground by mowers |
| Swingled | Threshed; the swingle was the part of the flail that beat the corn |
| Syder | Cider |

| | |
|---|---|
| Tabby | Watered fabric, especially silk or plain weave. |
| Tack | Hanging shelf. |
| Tag | Sheep in its first year |
| Tail wheat | Smaller grains not suitable for milling |
| Tallow chandler | a person who made or sold candles |
| Tan | Soaked bark of trees used in the making of leather |
| Tarras | Or trass - volcanic earth formerly transported as cement material |
| Teary? | Containing tares ie weed-ridden;common vetch used for fodder. |
| Teg | A sheep in its second year |
| Thicksett | Heavy fustian cloth |
| Thirds | The third part of the estate of a deceased husband, which by law the widow is entitled to enjoy during her life. |
| Thrash | Thresh |
| Thwartled | Cross ploughed |
| Tine | Sharp projecting prong on an ox harrow |
| Tire | High qality flax |
| Todd | Weight for wool usually 28lb |
| Tow | Fibre of flax, coarse and broken parts of flax separated from the finer parts in hackling |
| Traises | Traces |
| Trayn oyl | Oil made by boiling down whale blubber or fish |
| Tree nailes | Timber pegs |
| Trencher | Flat wooden platter |
| Trow | Trough |
| Tuggs | iron chains which fit into the hames and shafts |
| Tunn | Barrel |
| Turnrist | Plough which turns up the 2nd furrow on to the first |
| Twelve monthling | One year old animal |
| Tythe | tenth of income or crop ceded to church as tax |
| Tythe feast | Gathering at which the tythe is paid |
| Ailes | Present given to the servant over and above wages |

| | |
|---|---|
| Vestry | A meeting of the parishioners entitled to share in the management of ecclesiastical affairs of the parish |
| Wainhouse | Cart lodge. |
| Wanty | A girth band fitted to a cart and passing under the horse's belly to prevent the cart from tipping up or a rope or band to secure a pack |
| Warp | Piece of ploughed land of 10 or more ridges with a furrow to carry off surface water. |
| Wash balls | Balls of soap. |
| Water furroughs | Ploughing across the field to allow water to drain away |
| Water shoot | Discharge shoot for rainwater |
| Watertable bricks | Waterproof bricks |
| Wattle | Hurdle |
| Weather | Wether, castrated sheep |
| Wift | Bundle of twigs for binding faggots |
| Winnow | to separate grain from chaff |
| Wintermilch | Cow that gives milk in winter |
| Woolstaple | Wool market |
| Woolstapler | A person who sorted the wool into different grades. |
| Worme tub | Tub used for distilling |

Printed in March 2021
by Rotomail Italia S.p.A., Vignate (MI) - Italy